Communication Research Measures II

Expanding and building on the measures included in the original 1994 volume, *Communication Research Measures II: A Sourcebook* provides new measures in mass, interpersonal, instructional, and group/organizational communication areas, and highlights work in newer subdisciplines in communication, including intercultural, family, and health. It also includes measures from outside the communication discipline that have been employed in communication research.

The measures profiled here are "the best of the best" from the early 1990s through today. They are models for future scale development as well as tools for the trade, and they constitute the main tools that researchers can use for self-administered measurement of people's attitudes, conceptions of themselves, and perceptions of others. The focus is on up-to-date measures and the most recent scales and indexes used to assess communication variables.

Providing suggestions for measurement of concepts of interest to researchers; inspiring students to consider research directions not considered previously; and supplying models for scale developers to follow in terms of the work necessary to produce a valid and reliable measurement instrument in the discipline, the authors of this key resource have developed a significant contribution toward improving measurement and providing measures for better science.

Communication Research Measures II

A Sourcebook

Rebecca B. Rubin
Alan M. Rubin
Elizabeth E. Graham
Elizabeth M. Perse
David R. Seibold

 Routledge
Taylor & Francis Group

NEW YORK AND LONDON

This edition published 2011 by Routledge
2 Park Square, Milton Park, Abingdon, Oxon OX14 4RN
711 Third Avenue, New York, NY 10017, USA

Routledge is an imprint of the Taylor & Francis Group, an informa business

Typeset in GillSans and Sabon
by Swales & Willis Ltd, Exeter, Devon

Library of Congress Cataloging-in-Publication Data
   Communication research measures II: a sourcebook.
   by Rebecca B. Rubin . . . [et al.].
   p. cm.
   Includes index.
   1. Communication—Research. 2. Communication—
   Methodology. I. Rubin, Rebecca B.
   P91.3.C623 2009
   302.207'2—dc22
   2009004670

ISBN 10: 0–8058–5132–1 (hbk)
ISBN 10: 0–8058–5133–X (pbk)
ISBN 10: 0–203–87153–7 (ebk)

ISBN 13: 978–0–8058–5132–8 (hbk)
ISBN 13: 978–0–8058–5133–5 (pbk)
ISBN 13: 978–0–203–87153–9 (ebk)

Contents

Part III
IMPORTED MEASURES

Authors and Contributors

Rebecca B. Rubin (Ph.D., University of Illinois at Urbana-Champaign, 1975) is Professor Emerita at Kent State University (Ohio, USA), having served as Director of the KSU Communication Research Center and Graduate Coordinator of the School of Communication Studies. Her areas of expertise include interpersonal relationship development, communication competence assessment, instructional communication, and the interface of personal and mediated communication. Besides having written or edited several books and chapters—including Volume I of *Communication Research Measures: A Sourcebook*—and serving recently as the Educational Communication Area Editor of the *International Encyclopedia of Communication*, Rebecca's research has been published in many communication journals, placing her as one of the most prolific researchers in the discipline.

Alan M. Rubin (Ph.D., University of Illinois at Urbana-Champaign, 1976) is Professor Emeritus and Director Emeritus of the School of Communication Studies at Kent State University (Ohio, USA). He has studied the uses and effects of the media, including news and entertainment, personal and mediated communication, and newer communication technologies. In addition to books and chapters, he has published in such journals as the *Journal of Communication* (JOC), the *Journal of Broadcasting & Electronic Media* (JOBEM), *Human Communication Research*, and *Communication Research*. He is past editor of the JOC and JOBEM, and has served on numerous editorial boards and as a consultant to media, industry, and education. He is a Fellow of the International Communication Association and received the Distinguished Scholar Award from the Broadcast Education Association.

Elizabeth E. Graham (Ph.D., Kent State University, 1987) is a Professor in the School of Communication Studies at Ohio University (USA). She teaches courses in interpersonal communication, research methods, and statistics on the undergraduate and graduate level. Her research interests include communication in families experiencing transition, change, and reconfiguration. In addition to contributing to the first volume of *Communication Research Measures: A Sourcebook,* her research has been published in *Communication Monographs, Communication Education, Communication Quarterly, Western Journal of Communication, Communication Research Reports,* and *Communication Reports.* She also serves on several editorial boards. Until recently, Elizabeth was the University Ombuds at Ohio University.

Elizabeth M. Perse (Ph.D., Kent State University, 1987) is Professor and Chair of the Department of Communication at the University of Delaware, Newark (USA). She is currently researching and teaching mass communication theory and the uses of newer communication technologies. She has been identified as a prolific researcher in Communication, having published one scholarly book, two textbooks, and more than 50 journal articles and book chapters. Her research has been published in such journals as *Journal of Broadcasting & Electronic Media, Communication Research, Journal of Communication, Human Communication Research, Communication Quarterly, Communication Research Reports, Journalism Quarterly,* and *Health Communication.* Elizabeth serves on several editorial boards and is a past Chair of the Mass Communication Division of NCA.

David R. Seibold (Ph.D., Michigan State University, 1975) is Professor of Communication (Division of Social Sciences), and Co-Director of the Graduate Program in Management Practice (College of Engineering), at the University of California, Santa Barbara (USA). Author of more than 100 publications on organizational communication, group processes, and interpersonal influence, his scholarship has appeared in all of the major journals in communication and in venues across nearly a half-dozen disciplines. He has received numerous research and teaching awards, and in 2006 was elected a Distinguished Scholar in the National Communication Association. A former chair of interpersonal, group, and organizational communication divisions in the International Communication Association and the National Communication Association, David is also a past editor of the *Journal of Applied Communication Research* and serves on the boards of many other journals. He has also consulted widely with more than 75 business, government, and health organizations.

Additional Contributors

Nichole Egbert (Ph.D., University of Georgia, 2000) is Associate Professor in the School of Communication Studies at Kent State University (Ohio, USA). Her research interests focus on intersections of relational communication and health behavior (such as social support, patient advocacy, health literacy, and caregiving). Her work has appeared in journals such as *Health Communication, Journal of Health Communication, Communication Studies,* and *Communication Quarterly.* Nichole is currently working on an NIH-funded project aimed at enhancing the emotional support skills of women caring for their husbands who have had a stroke.

Joseph P. Mazer (M.S., Illinois State University, 2006) is a Doctoral Candidate and Graduate Teaching Associate in the School of Communication Studies at Ohio University. His scholarly interests are in instructional communication and new communication technologies. He has published in *Communication Education, Communication Research Reports, The Journal of General Education,* and *The Journal of the California Caucus of College and University Ombuds.* Joe teaches public speaking, small group communication, interpersonal communication, statistics in communication research, and communication pedagogy.

Scott Titsworth (Ph.D., Nebraska, 1999) is an Associate Professor in the School of Communication Studies at Ohio University. His primary research interest is instructional communication, with a particular emphasis in connections between affect, emotion, learning, and classroom communication. Scott teaches a variety of graduate and undergraduate classes including research methods, ANOVA, and regression.

Preface

Since the first volume of *Communication Research Measures: A Source-book* was published in 1994, there has been extraordinary (and positive) feedback about the value of this volume to graduate students and faculty in the discipline. Some of our colleagues have encouraged us to produce a second edition, one that updates the original scales and the psychometric data generated since the early 1990s. Conversely, others have "nominated" additional measures for inclusion in such a volume, many of which were new or promising for future research.

Once we realized how many scales, indexes, or questionnaires might be in such a second edition, we opted instead for a second volume that would include those "promising" measures identified in the first, plus all the newer measures created within the past 15 years. In addition to new measures in Mass, Interpersonal, Instructional, and Group/Organizational areas, we also added some of the newer subdisciplines in communication—Intercultural, Family, and Health—and looked at measures from outside the discipline that have been employed in our research over the years. These measures, then, have truly been helpful in generating research.

Several uses, actually, are forefront. One use of this sourcebook has been to provide suggestions for measurement of concepts of interest to researchers. Rather than "reinvent the wheel" each and every time one develops a research project, researchers can use instruments that have stood the test of time and validity/reliability testing. Another use of the sourcebook has been to inspire graduate students to consider research directions previously not considered. A third use is to provide models for scale developers to follow in terms of the work necessary for producing a valid and reliable measurement instrument in the discipline.

As with the first volume, our goal is to improve measurement and provide measures for better science. We used criteria similar to those employed in the first volume for selecting scales to profile. We wanted measures that not only had face validity, but some sort of track record of reliability as well. We also wanted to include newer measures that reflect the current status of the field. Now that communication has blossomed into a mature discipline, researchers need measurement instruments that are theoretically sound and methodologically refined. Those profiled in this volume are "the best of the best" from the early 1990s on. They're models for future scale development as well as tools for the trade.

Acknowledgments

Rebecca and Alan Rubin extend a warm thank you to Linda Bathgate who stayed with the project through the years, weathering delays and change of publishers. Also, thanks go to Nuchada Dumrongsiri and Vikky Pornskavich, former KSU graduate students in measurement classes, and all scale authors who came through with directions for using their scales or permissions for reprinting the scale in this volume. They also thank their coauthors for bringing the project to completion.

Elizabeth Graham extends special thanks to Joseph Mazer and Yuxia Qian for assisting with the compilation of research materials necessary for this project. Additional appreciation is extended to Lynn Harter, Andrew Ledbetter, Katherine Ziff, and Katherine Gehlfuss for providing thoughtful and valuable insights to this manuscript.

Elizabeth Perse would like to thank three of her former students for contributing to the research on mass communication measurement: Noel Sarah Dietrich (M.A., University of Delaware), Albert A. Sheilds (M.A., University of Delaware), and Rebecca Shirley (B.A., University of Delaware).

Dave Seibold wishes to acknowledge the assistance of the following in choosing and refining his profiles and chapters: Angel Ampas, Dawna Ballard, Shereen Bingham, Mark Cipolla, Phillip Clampitt, Timothy Coombs, Lynn Cooper, Carrie Cropley, Andrew Flanagin, Tyler Frank, Doug Furano, Brandon Ghect, Felipe Gomez, Carla Hensley, Mitchell Hammer, Lovely Hoffman, Laura Jones, Jean Kim, Breanna Larrazolo, Carmen Lee, Michele Maehler, Matt Martin, Karen Matsumoto, Megan Moore, Steven Mortenson, Karen Myers, Kalin Pharis, Heather Phillips, Kristoffer Quan, Ron Rice, Loren Riehl, Nicole Taher, Charnae Wright, and Joanna Zetah.

Introduction

Part I contains a series of chapters about various facets of the communication discipline. Each of the authors was responsible for one or two of these. By examining the current literature, asking colleagues' opinions, and searching the databases, we were able to identify several valid measures in each area. But the chapters presented in Part I present an overview of measurement issues encountered over the past 15 years.

Part II contains the profiles of the selected measures. The format for the profiles is standard. We begin each profile with an overview of the concept being measured and how the original scale began. Then we summarize the validity—content, construct, concurrent, etc.—and reliability data available in the communication field. We then note, in the comments section, any controversy surrounding the instrument or issues users should be aware of when using the measure. Finally, we give the location of the instrument and the scale/measure itself (when possible). We do NOT intend for users to simply photocopy the measure for use, but we provide as much information as was available for replication of the measure so that all can use it in a standardized manner.

As we noted in Volume I, we're relying on standard definitions of validity and reliability in the profiles (Babbie, 2004; Kerlinger & Lee, 2000). *Reliability* is how consistent, stable, dependable, predictable, or precise a measure is. If two or more individuals assign behaviors to nominal-level categories, the stability of the coding system is determined by their *intercoder reliability*—or agreement. *Interrater reliability*, similarly, assesses agreement between two researchers who are using an interval or ratio scale to assign value to such behavior. *Test-retest reliability* is often achieved by correlating scores from two or more administrations of the same measure to the same group of people; high correlations indicate that the measure is stable—that is, those completing the scale are using it in consistent ways. *Split-half reliability* looks at how stable a scale is by randomly choosing half the items and correlating that subscale with those that remain. A more common form of reliability, however, is *internal consistency*; most scale developers report a Cronbach alpha as an index of how each item in the scale relates to all the other items.

Validity is an indication of how closely the scale or index actually measures what it purports to measure. *Face validity* is achieved when the measure is examined by users or researchers and they agree that the items are representative of the construct being measured. *Content validity* refers to the representativeness of the items to the realm of what is being measured: are all items represented and in the right proportions? *Criterion-related validity* is achieved when an independent variable measure accurately predicts a dependent variable. *Concurrent validity* refers to when scores on two measures are statistically related to one another when they should be (e.g., two measures of anxiety should be positively correlated). And *construct validity*, perhaps the best indicator of the validity of a measure, refers directly to the meaning of what is being measured. Researchers often use both convergence (finding significant relationships between measures that SHOULD be related) and divergence/discriminability (no significant relationship between measures that SHOULD NOT be related) procedures, but more recently we see the use of confirmatory factor analysis to confirm the identity of subscale items for elements of the construct being examined. Meta-analysis of results—over time—can provide both reliability and validity information for scales developed in the past.

Part III is devoted to an overview and discussion of measures borrowed from outside the communication discipline. These measures often are used variably as independent, moderating, mediating, or dependent variables, depending on the concept or theory being tested. As you will note, most are from psychology. Because of page restrictions, these were excluded from Volume I, but we felt that the overwhelming use of these instruments in communication research couldn't allow that to happen again. So we identify several—particularly those used in several areas of the discipline—and provide location information for them. Many of these instruments are protected by copyright issues, several different forms, or mandated training programs that we couldn't overcome, so we encourage readers to investigate each further prior to adoption.

We encourage readers to examine the following sources for additional information on measurement issues that impact communication research. In addition, we list some periodicals, series, and collections that contain both old and new measures for consideration in communication research.

Texts

Babbie, E. R. (2007). *The practice of social research* (11th ed.). Belmont, CA: Thomson Wadsworth.

Cliff, N., & Keats, J. A. (2003). *Ordinal measurement in the behavioral sciences.* Mahwah, NJ: Erlbaum.

Drasgow, F., & Olson-Buchanan, J. (1999). *Innovations in computerized assessment.* Mahwah, NJ: Erlbaum.

Guilford, J. P. (1954–). *Psychometric methods*. New York: McGraw-Hill.

Kerlinger, F. N., & Lee, H. B. (2000). *Foundations of behavioral research* (4th ed.). Fort Worth, TX: Harcourt.

Measurement Periodicals

Applied Psychological Measurement (1977–)
Communication Methods and Measures (2007–)
Communication Research Reports (1984–)
Educational and Psychological Measurement (1941–)
Health and Psychosocial Instruments (2985–)
Journal of Educational Measurement (1964–)
Journal of Personality and Social Psychology (1965–)
Journal of Personality Assessment (1971–)
Journal of Psychoeducational Assessment (1983–)
Psychological Reports (1955–)

Collections

American College Personnel Association & Science Research Associates. (1941–). *Educational and psychological measurement*. Durham, NC: Educational and Psychological Measurement.

Anastasi, A. (1988). *Psychological testing*. New York: Macmillan.

Groth-Marnat, G. (2003). *Handbook of psychological assessment*. Hoboken, NJ: John Wiley & Sons.

Chelune, G. J., McReynolds, P., & Rosen, J. C. (1968). *Advances in psychological assessment*. Palo Alto, CA: Science and Behavior Books.

Chun, K-T, Cobb, S., & French, J. R. P., Jr. (1975). *Measures for psychological assessment: A guide to 3,000 original sources and their applications*. Ann Arbor: University of Michigan Survey Research Center, Institute for Social Research.

Emmert, P., & Barker, L. L. (Eds.). (1989). *Measurement of communication behavior*. New York: Longman.

Fredman, N., & Sherman, R. (1987). *Handbook of measurements for marriage and family therapy*. New York: Brunner/Mazel.

Maddox, T. (1997). *Tests: A comprehensive reference for assessments in psychology, education, and business (4th ed.)*. Austin, TX: Pro-Ed.

Mental measurements yearbook. (1940–). Highland Park, NJ: The Mental Measurements Yearbook.

Mitchell, J. V. (1983). *Tests in print III: An index to tests, test reviews, and the literature on specific tests*. Lincoln, NE: Buros Institute of Mental Measurements, University of Nebraska-Lincoln.

Reynolds, R. A., Woods, R. & Baker, J. D. (Eds.) (2006) *Handbook of research on electronic surveys and measurements*. Hershey, PA: Information Science Reference.

Robinson, J. P., Shaver, P. R., & Wrightsman, L. S. (Eds.). (1991). *Measures of personality and social psychological attitudes*. San Diego, CA: Academic Press.

Rosen, J. C., & McReynolds, P. (1992). *Advances in psychological assessment.* New York: Plenum Press.

Rubin, R. B., Palmgreen, P., & Sypher, H. E. (1994/2004). *Communication research measures: A sourcebook.* Mahwah, NJ: Erlbaum.

Spitzberg, B. H., & Cupach, W. R. (1989). *Handbook of interpersonal competence research.* New York: Springer-Verlag.

Sweetland, R. C., & Keyser, D. J. (1983). *Tests: a comprehensive reference for assessments in psychology, education, and business.* Kansas City: Test Corp. of America.

Tardy, C. H. (Ed.). (1988). *A handbook for the study of human communication: Methods and instruments for observing, measuring, and assessing communication processes.* Norwood, NJ: Ablex.

Touliatos, J., Perlmutter, B. F., & Straus, M. A. (1990). *Handbook of family measurement techniques.* Newbury Park, CA: Sage.

Part I

Measurement Trends and Issues

Measurement in Family Communication

Elizabeth E. Graham and Joseph P. Mazer

Family communication has been the subject of academic inquiry for several years, yet, by scholarly standards, family communication is a relative newcomer (Segrin, 2006). Initially organized as an interest group in the National Communication Association (NCA) in 1989 (Whitchurch, 1993) and later a division in 1995 (Whitchurch & Dickson, 1999), at present, NCA is the only communication association that includes a family division.

In Volume 1 of *Communication Research Measures: A Sourcebook* (Rubin, Palmgreen, & Sypher, 1994), family communication measures were not specifically featured but rather were subsumed in the interpersonal section of the book. Since that time, research has blossomed and therefore an independent chapter is devoted to the study and measurement of family communication. The scope of this chapter is limited to a discussion of quantitative issues in the conduct of family communication research focusing specifically on measurement indices and scales.

Criteria Employed for Measure Selection and Subsequent Profiling

Decisions regarding selection of measures for inclusion in this current effort will mirror the criteria employed in the first volume, subject to a few notable changes. In addition to meeting the standards of sufficient reliability and validity, which often results in frequency of use, attention was afforded to measures that offer "promise." It is important to note that instruments developed prior to the publication of the first volume in 1994, but not widely employed, were subject to consideration for inclusion in the second volume. It is quite possible that the time between when a measure was introduced to the discipline and its subsequent use in research is not

Note: Measures that are profiled in this volume (in Part II) are typed in capital letters when cited in the text.

amenable to the timeframe of the publication of Volumes 1 and 2. For example, The REVISED FAMILY COMMUNICATION PATTERNS INSTRUMENT developed in 1990 by Ritchie and Fitzpatrick was not profiled in the interpersonal section of Volume 1 (although it was featured in the Mass Communication section) because it had not enjoyed widespread use. However, since the publication of the first volume this measure has become a mainstay in family communication research and does warrant inclusion in Volume 2. In sum then, the focus in Volume 2 is on newer measures (post 1994) although instruments developed prior to this date were also considered for inclusion in this volume.

Many instruments have been employed in the conduct of family communication research, however only those measures with an explicitly stated family focus and function are highlighted in this chapter. As a consequence of this refined view, the family communication measures featured in this volume include: the CHILD–PARENT COMMUNICATION APPREHENSION SCALE (Lucchetti, Powers, & Love, 2002); INDIVIDUALS' CRITERIA FOR TELLING FAMILY SECRETS (Vangelisti, Caughlin, & Timmerman, 2001); the REVISED FAMILY COMMUNICATION PATTERNS INSTRUMENT (Ritchie & Fitzpatrick, 1990), and the FAMILY COMMUNICATION STANDARDS INSTRUMENT (Caughlin, 2003). Detailed profiles of these instruments are available in Part II of this volume.

Methodological Trends in Family Communication Research

In an effort to contextualize family communication scholarship, researchers have canvassed the communication literature and concluded that the majority of research conducted between 1990 and 2001 is dominated by empirically oriented work, guided by systems theory, attachment theory, symbolic interaction, and social exchange theory (Duck & Crumm, 2004; Stamp, 2004). Our post 2001 analysis of the literature supports these findings and reveals additional topics of interest to family communication scholars.[1] Specifically, Family Communication Patterns, and its attendant measure, the REVISED FAMILY COMMUNICATION PATTERNS INSTRUMENT (Ritchie & Fitzpatrick, 1990), have been used extensively in family research.[2] Marital and family satisfaction, a mainstay in communication scholarship and a key barometer of relationship and communication quality, continue to be salient concerns in family studies.[3] Furthermore, our review of recent literature reveals a "marriage" of sorts between family and health communication which reflects the extent to which issues of wellness have pervaded our collective consciousness.[4]

Method

Experiments continue to be rare in family communication research as most scholarship reflects quasi-experimental or correlational designs (Metts & Lamb, 2006; Noller & Feeney, 2004). Nonetheless, research in family communication is primarily influenced by a social science/logical empirical perspective (Baxter & Braithwaite, 2006) and self-report methods (i.e., survey/questionnaires) are principally the means by which data are gathered (Noller & Feeney, 2004). The shortcomings of self-reports are widely articulated, however the benefits have been afforded much less attention. More important than their efficiency and ease of administration, self-reports permit access to retrospective and prospective affective states and cognitive dispositions not likely to be evidenced in laboratory and observation-oriented research designs (Metts & Lamb, 2006; Metts, Sprecher, & Cupach, 1991; Noller & Feeney, 2004). Furthermore, self-reports are effective in gaining access to *private fields* that characterize close personal relationships (Baxter, 1992). Family settings, characteristically personal, are private, often inaccessible, and not readily amenable to observational study. It is important to note that despite the methodology and design implemented, the introduction of any intrusive and obtrusive device, instrument, or person into the research mix will likely prompt a reactivity effect and consequently antisocial behaviors, if they do exist, will more than likely be temporarily quelled. Regardless of these shortcomings, self-reports remain foundational in communication research in general and family communication study in particular.

In addition to self-report measures, diaries are a useful method of data collection that permit access to private fields and also offer an *in the moment* entrée to emotional and cognitive dispositions (Turner & West, 2006). Furthermore, diaries are well suited to *process-oriented* research, so coveted and rather absent in communication studies. Although not their stated purpose, one means of alleviating the tendency of participants to neglect recording entries in their diary, Huston and his colleagues telephoned couples nine evenings over the course of a few weeks in an effort to assess their marital satisfaction (Huston, McHale, & Crouter, 1986). As Turner and West (2006) pointed out, diaries are well-suited to capture the everyday mundane aspect of family life not amenable to survey research methods.

Numerous coding/rating systems have been developed in family communication that we could not consider in this volume because of space constrictions. For example, Pecchioni and Nussbaum (2001) assessed behaviors for exhibited conflict and control strategies in mother-daughter dyads. Gottman, Levenson, and Woodin (2001) coded married couples' facial expressions from videotape and Heatherington, Escudero, and Friedlander (2005) analyzed relational control behavior during problem

discussions between engaged couples. In an interesting application of narrative theory, Kellas (2005) employed videotaped storytelling to explore
family identity construction. Ideally, insider (self-report) and outsider
(observational studies) are best used in conjunction and offer a degree of
internal and external validity that independently each method cannot
(Noller & Feeney, 2004).

Sample

The reliance on convenient samples remains prevalent in family communication research (see Basil, Brown, & Bocarnea, 2002 for a discussion of
convenience samples). Historically, convenience samples produced equal
representation of men and women. This parity is no longer possible as the
percentage of male undergraduates dropped 24% from 1970 to 2000.
Indeed, the gender balance at many state universities represents a 60–40
split (Ange Peterson, American Association of Collegiate Registrars and
Admissions Officers, 2006). Consequently, if we continue to tap students
as participants in our research, we need to be aware of a female bias. Interestingly, access to non-student populations is often the result of sampling
student populations. In other words, we enlist the assistance of college students in an effort to garner the participation of an adult population. This
practice can generate a duplicative, though older, demographic segment of
society.

Despite Fitzpatrick's (2006) advice to draw representative samples that
feature a diverse sample adequate in size to ferret out similarities and
differences in families, we persist in privileging the voice of middle class,
educated, white, Christian, heterosexual men and women in our research.
However, a few scholars have integrated diverse samples in the study of
family communication. Oetzel, Ting-Toomey, Chew-Sanchez, Harris,
Wilcox, and Stumpf (2003) explored face and facework in conflict with
parents and siblings and their sample included individuals from Germany
and Japan. In a similar vein, Weiner, Silk, and Parrott (2005) examined
African Americans and European Americans' knowledge, attitudes, and
behaviors associated with human genetics and the impact of family communication on such issues. In addition, researchers have explored conflict
styles in Chinese parent-child relationships (Zhang, 2007) and communication patterns, advertising attitudes, and mediation behaviors among
Indian mothers in urban India (Mukherji, 2005).

While a majority of family communication scholarship has favored heterosexual relationships within the traditional husband-wife dyad (Turner
& West, 2003), there has been a subtle shift to "widen the circle of family
communication" (Floyd & Morman, 2006, p. xv). For example, the study
of understudied family forms has featured same-sex families (Haas &
Stafford, 2005; Turner & West, 2003), postmarital families (Afifi &

McManus, 2006; Graham, 2003), stepfamilies (Braithwaite, Schrodt, & Baxter, 2006), racially and ethnically diverse families (Sabourin, 2003), families formed through adoption (Galvin, 2006), and aging in families (Hummert, 2007). Investigating diverse family configurations is part of "expanding the social recipe" (Turner & West, 2006, p. 206) in family life and ongoing empirical efforts will illuminate the nuances of these growing yet historically neglected family forms and issues.

Reliability

When James McCroskey was named editor of *Human Communication Research* in 1977, he required authors to report reliability estimates for measures used in the research (McCroskey, 2006), and consequently most communication journals featuring social scientific scholarship today require reliability disclosures. Our review of family communication measures reveals that Cronbach's (1951) alpha is the most frequently employed measure of internal consistency. Other measures of reliability such as split-half estimates are rarely used as Cronbach's alpha is recognized as a superior measure of internal consistency. Test-retest methods of assessing reliability are also seldom employed (for exceptions see Ritchie & Fitzpatrick, 1990) in family communication research and perhaps this is because stability rather than change is a featured priority. Although problems with reliability are largely a problem of the past (Kerlinger & Lee, 2000), issues of validity have been less easily resolved.

Validity

Our analysis of the literature reveals that instrument development in family communication is characterized by an emphasis on conceptually rich and theoretically sound hypothesis-driven research. In essence, construct validity, the most important form of validity, is well-attended to in the development of family communication measures. For example, John Caughlin's (2003) FAMILY COMMUNICATION STANDARDS INSTRUMENT is the result of three independent studies in which a constellation of central relationship qualities such as satisfaction, family communication schema, conflict, topic avoidance, and maintenance behaviors are tested. In developing the INDIVIDUALS' CRITERIA FOR TELLING FAMILY SECRETS scale, Anita Vangelisti and colleagues examined how the topic of the secret, perception of the secret, and the relationship between the secret sharer and the recipient impacts the revealing of secrets. In both cases, the construct validity of the measures were assessed from a theoretical standpoint and evaluated for its ability to progress from conceptualization to operationalization to generalization.

One of the clearest manifestations of how a measure is conceptualized is evidenced through its content validity. For example, how items for a scale are generated and the degree to which those items reflect the theoretical construct is a crucial first step in scale construction. A perusal of recently developed measures illustrates how previously established instruments have served as the basis for new scales that reflect communication in the family. For example, The CHILD–PARENT COMMUNICATION APPREHENSION (C-PCA) scale (Lucchetti et al., 2002) is reflective of several context specific measures of apprehension. Furthermore, the REVISED FAMILY COMMUNICATION PATTERNS INSTRUMENT (RFCP) (Ritchie & Fitzpatrick, 1990) is a modified version of McLeod and Chaffee's (1972) Family Communication Patterns Scale, primarily used in mass communication research. While the practice of adapting a measure is not necessarily problematic, additional validity work is required to validate the new measure. In the case of both the C-PCA and RFCP, the authors conducted several tests to further assess the validity of the new measures.

Ecological validity (Keyton, 2006) is largely absent in family communication research. For instance, the variables of time and change are rarely incorporated in research designs and are often simply controlled for or tolerated as a form of uncontrollable error. As Segrin (2006) astutely pointed out:

> There are few areas in communication that are more tightly tied to the passage of time than family processes. Adolescents become young adults, husbands and wives become fathers and mothers, married couples divorce, divorced people remarry, spouses become widows, friends become spouses, family members become ill (and hopefully recover), and parents become grandparents. (pp. 13–14)

Longitudinal studies, although the exception in family studies, are necessary for the establishment of ecological validity as they would naturally incorporate a life course perspective which in essence features change and instability (Duck & Crumm, 2004). As noted previously, the rhetoric of *change* is threaded throughout family communication dialogue, but the methodological choices privilege *stability*.

Attitudes reflect emotional predispositions, affective orientations, and cognitive schema which in turn, influence our understanding of family functioning and behavior. Attitudinal and emotional dispositions are best measured with self-report instruments if we want to know how people feel and think. Although memory distortions and bias are always present, self-reports are powerful tools in our arsenal of data gathering techniques. The four measures profiled in this volume each employ Likert formats and participants are requested to indicate the degree to which they agree/disagree with items that assess perceptions, feelings, and tendencies to reveal family secrets, ease of talking with family members, family standards, and conversation or conformity orientated communication in the family. Although perceptions of emotions, attitudes, cognitions, and behaviors are important and valid information to gather, we would benefit from additional indexes that assess the frequency and types of behavioral aspects of family communication as we continue to validate knowledge claims generated from our research.

Methodological Issues of Interest and Concern

There are several issues of concern that detract from the validity of family communication research. First, family communication is often studied at the dyadic level—as in parent/child, husband/wife–and neglect the whole family (Duck & Crumm, 2004). Indeed, *family* is not often studied from the perspective of the *family* as the unit of analysis (Baxter & Braithwaite, 2006) (for exceptions see Koerner & Cvancara, 2002; Sillars, Koerner, & Fitzpatrick, 2005). Similar criticisms have been leveled against interpersonal communication research as well.

Relatedly, we continue to conduct research as though families are comprised of several independent units and as a consequence, we often only assess one family member, generalize to the other members, and consequently, reach potentially invalid conclusions (Metts & Lamb, 2006). This was no truer than in Derek Freeman's (1983) depiction of Margaret Mead's (1928) research detailed in his book titled *Margaret Mead and Samoa: The making and unmaking of an anthropological myth.* According to Freeman, Margaret Mead based her conclusions of Samoan sexual behavior on the playful and jesting comments of two young adolescent women and falsely concluded that Samoan women were quite promiscuous. Freeman, on the other hand, reports Kirk and Miller (1986) reached the opposite conclusion, namely that young Samoan women were quite chaste. Not surprisingly, Freeman's findings were based on questioning Samoan fathers' about their daughters' sexual behavior. In truth, both Mead and Freeman produced a very different and partial rendering of the history of sexual behavior in Samoa.

Recent advances in statistical modeling (see Cook & Kenny, 2005), in particular the actor-partner interdependence model tested through structural equation modeling, permit separation of dyadic effects from individual effects. Indeed, Kashy, Jellison, and Kenny (2004) caution that "most standard statistical techniques assume independence of cases—i.e., data collected from one participant are not influenced by the responses of another participant" (p. 266) and yet when conducting research we ignore the reality of interdependence of family members.

Second, family communication is often examined and measured through the marital relationship filter (Duck & Crumm, 2004) and by virtue of filtering, presents an opaque and potentially distorted view of family functioning. Mounting evidence (Ritchie & Fitzpatrick, 1990; Sillars et al., 2005) suggests that children and parents experience fluctuations in perceptual understanding of family life and therefore caution is warranted when generalizing to the entire family unit when only one member is assessed. Third, family research is typically conceived from a life-course point of view, grounded in the development of children, which in addition to excluding those families without children, privileges linearity and neglects the reality that not all families move from one stage to the next without some unexpected and perhaps unwelcome transitions (e.g., death, divorce, and family reconfiguration) (Duck & Crumm, 2004).

Fourth, an informal assessment of journal articles published in *Communication Monographs* and *Human Communication Research* between 1996 and 2000 revealed that the use of inferential statistics is widespread and ANOVA is the "statistic of choice" (Smith, Levine, Lachlan, & Fediuk, 2002, p. 515). Indeed, conventional statistical analyses are, by their very nature, data reduction techniques (e.g., ANOVA, factor analysis) and, as a consequence, when used in family research, can diminish important differences between and among family members (Kashy et al., 2004). To address this issue, Kashy et al. (2004) suggested that innovative data collection methods need to be analyzed with equally new analytic techniques such as structural equation modeling (for more information see Holbert & Stephenson, 2002; Kashy et al., 2004; Schrodt & Ledbetter, 2007).

Finally, measures are not necessarily portable from culture to culture, although our practices suggest otherwise. McCroskey (2006) cautioned that semantic differential scales, in particular, do not translate well across cultures and advises developing new measures that are culture-specific. Given the complexities associated with communication in relationships, research that employs diverse sample characteristics and spans cultural boundaries is crucial to providing a better understanding of familial relationships.

Measurement Influences from Outside the Discipline

Perhaps more than other sub-disciplines in communication, the study of family has been, and continues to be, eclectic and interdisciplinary (Segrin, 2006). Scholars outside the communication discipline have created reliable and valid measures applicable to family communication research. Two instruments, developed from psychology, are the Lifespan Sibling Relationship Scale (LSRS) (Riggio, 2000) and the Parental Stress Scale

(Berry & Jones, 1995). Grounded in attitude structure, the 48-item LSRS measures three dimensions of the sibling relationship in childhood and adulthood including: frequency and positivity of behavior toward the sibling, affect toward the sibling, and beliefs about the sibling and the sibling relationship. The measure contains six subscales: adult affect, adult behavior, adult cognitions, child affect, child behavior, and child cognitions. The LSRS possesses high internal consistency across the six subscales, a coherent factor structure, and stability of responses over time.

Berry and Jones' (1995) 18-item Parental Stress Scale is highly reliable and related to other measures of stress. Factor analysis reveals that the Parental Stress Scale consists of four factors: parental rewards, parental stressors, lack of control, and parental satisfaction. Results also suggest the validity of the Parental Stress Scale to be supported by predicted correlations with measures of relevant emotions and role satisfaction (Berry & Jones, 1995).

Promising New Measures in Family Communication Research

We would be remiss if we did not recognize new family communication measures that hold much promise for future research. Recently, Schrodt (2006a) developed and validated the Stepfamily Life Index. Grounded in schema theory, the Stepfamily Life Index features 34 items and five factors which include: stepfamily dissension, involvement, avoidance, flexibility, and expressiveness. Schrodt (2006a) reported acceptable subscale reliabilities ranging from .83 for stepfamily expressiveness, to .96 for stepfamily dissension. However, he cautioned readers that the flexibility subscale produced a relatively weak reliability estimate ($\alpha = .59$). Despite this potential concern, the flexibility construct is well documented in the stepfamily literature (Braithwaite, Olson, Golish, Soukup, & Turman, 2001; Golish, 2003; Henry & Lovelace, 1995), and, as a result, future research can increase the number of items to assess this important construct (Schrodt, 2006a).

Schrodt (2006b) also developed and validated the Stepparent Relationship Index. Much like the Stepfamily Life Index, the Stepparent Relationship Index is a multidimensional measure that is grounded in schema theory. The Stepparent Relationship Index contains 18 items and features three factors: Positive regard, (step)parental authority, and affective certainty. Schrodt (2006b) reported that each subscale produced acceptable reliability estimates and initial tests of concurrent validity look promising.

In both studies, Schrodt (2006ab) encouraged readers to interpret the results with caution because the samples consisted of primarily white, college-educated stepchildren and the methods featured exploratory factor analysis techniques that are highly susceptible to fluctuations in the data. Fortunately, the self-correcting nature of replication work will flush out these and other concerns if they surface in future research.

In this chapter, we identified methodological trends and issues of concern and interest to family communication scholars. Since scholarly inquiry in family communication first emerged in the discipline, we have witnessed tremendous growth as evidenced by our attention to conceptual and methodological advances in understanding and measuring family processes and functions (Floyd, 2004). Family communication is consequential and thoughtful evaluation of measurement instruments and practices is integral to a sustained effort to critically examine the scope and quality of family communication scholarship.

Notes

1 Analysis features articles from 2001–2007 in *Journal of Family Communication, Communication Monographs, Human Communication Research, Journal of Applied Communication Research, Communication Research, Communication Education, Western Journal of Communication, Communication Quarterly, Communication Reports,* and *Communication Research Reports.*

2 Respect to college student adjustment (Orrego & Rodriguez, 2001), children's mental well being (Schrodt, Ledbetter, & Ohrt, 2007), interpersonal competence and adolescent risk behaviors (Koeston & Anderson, 2004), and interpersonal communication motives (Barbato, Graham, & Perse, 2003). For additional information see the RFCP profile in Part II of this volume.

3 Satisfaction has been studied in relation to emotional expressiveness (Yelsma & Marrow, 2003), spousal support (Xu & Burleson, 2004), relational maintenance (Weigel & Ballard-Reisch, 2001), patterns of demand/withdraw between parents and adolescents (Caughlin & Malis, 2004), and religious orientation (Hughes & Dickson, 2005). In their analysis of premarital relationships, Fitzpatrick, Feng, and Crawford (2003) found social competence factors such as self-disclosure and conflict resolution to partially mediate the relationship between affective characteristics and satisfaction. Segrin and Flora (2001) explored the association between loneliness and marital satisfaction in a unique analysis of incarcerated spouses.

4 Scholars have explored diverse issues ranging from the effects of maternal and paternal expectations on college student suicidality (Miller & Day, 2002), the relationship between mother-daughter communication and child eating disorders (Prescott & LePoire, 2002), and the association between familial support and skin cancer control in farmers (Parrott & Lemieux, 2003). In addition, researchers have examined how family members communicate about cancer (Beach, 2007), communication in the decision to talk with family about organ donation (Afifi, Morgan, Stephenson, Morse, Harrison, Reichert, & Long, 2006), communication with depressed individuals in romantic relationships (Duggan & LePoire, 2006), and wives' interactions with husbands afflicted with adult dementia (Baxter, Braithwaite, Golish, & Olson, 2002). Family communication scholars have been certain to explore the relationship between family communication and numerous other characteristics and constructs including conflict styles (Dumlao & Botta, 2000; Zhang, 2007), parental mediation styles (Fujioka & Austin, 2002); reticence (Kelly, Keaten, Finch, Duarte, Hoffman, &

Michels, 2002), and personality characteristics such as desire for control, self-esteem, and sociability (Huang, 1999).

References

Afifi, T. D., & McManus, T. (2006). Investigating privacy boundaries: Communication in post-divorce families. In K. Floyd & M. T. Mormon (Eds.), *Widening the family circle: New research on family communication* (pp. 171–187). Thousand Oaks, CA: Sage.

Afifi, W. A., Morgan, S. E., Stephenson, M. T., Morse, C., Harrison, T., Reichert,T., & Long, S. D. (2006). Examining the decision to talk with family about organ donation: Applying the theory of motivated information management. *Communication Monographs, 73,* 188–215.

Barbato, C. A., Graham, E. E., & Perse, E. M. (2003). Communicating in the family: An examination of the relationship of family communication climate and interpersonal communication motives. *Journal of Family Communication, 3,* 123–148.

Basil, M. D., Brown, W. J., & Bocarnea, M. C. (2002). Differences in univariate values versus multivariate relationships: Findings from a study of Diana, Princess of Wales. *Human Communication Research, 28,* 501–514.

Baxter, L. A. (1992). Interpersonal communication as dialogue: A response to the "social approaches" forum. *Communication Theory, 2,* 330–337.

Baxter, L. A., & Braithwaite, D. O. (2006). Introduction: Meta-theory and theory in family communication. In D. O. Braithwaite & L. A. Baxter (Eds.), *Engaging theories in family communication: Multiple perspectives* (pp. 1–15). Thousand Oaks, CA: Sage.

Baxter, L. A., Braithwaite, D. O., Golish, T. D., & Olson, L. N. (2002). Contradictions of interaction for wives of husbands with adult dementia. *Journal of Applied Communication Research, 29,* 221–247.

Beach, W. A. (2007). Conversational interaction: Understanding how family members talk through cancer. In B. B. Whaley & W. Samter (Eds.), *Explaining communication: Contemporary theories and exemplars* (pp. 333–350). Mahwah, NJ: Erlbaum.

Berry, J. O., & Jones, W. H. (1995). The Parental Stress Scale: Initial psychometric evidence. *Journal of Social and Personal Relationships, 12,* 463–472.

Braithwaite, D. O., Olson, L., Golish, T. D., Soukup, C., & Turman, P. (2001). "Becoming a family": Developmental processes represented in blended family discourse. *Journal of Applied Communication Research, 29,* 221–247.

Braithwaite, D. O., Schrodt, P., & Baxter, L. A. (2006). Understudied and misunderstood: Communication in stepfamily relationships. In K. Floyd & M. T. Mormon (Eds.), *Widening the family circle: New research on family communication* (pp. 153–170). Thousand Oaks, CA: Sage.

Caughlin, J. P. (2003). Family communication standards: What counts as excellent family communication and how are such standards associated with family satisfaction? *Human Communication Research, 29,* 5–40.

Caughlin, J. P., & Malis, R. S. (2004). Demand/withdraw communication between parents and adolescents as a correlate of relational satisfaction. *Communication Reports, 17,* 59–71.

Cook, W. L., & Kenny, D. A. (2005). The actor-partner interdependence model: A model of bidirectional effects in developmental studies. *International Journal of Behavioral Development, 29*, 101–109.

Cronbach, L. J. (1951). Coefficient alpha and the internal structure of tests. *Psychometrika, 16*, 297–334.

Duck, S., & Crumm, R. (2004). Proteus in the family castle: Studying the inconstant using the unwieldy in unison. *Journal of Family Communication, 4*, 337–345.

Duggan, A. P., & LePoire, B. A. (2006). One down, two involved: An application and extension of inconsistent nurturing as control theory to couples including one depressed individual. *Communication Monographs, 73*, 379–405.

Dumlao, R., & Botta, R. A. (2000). Family communication patterns and the conflict styles young adults use with their fathers. *Communication Quarterly, 48*, 174–189.

Fitzpatrick, J., Feng, D., & Crawford, D. (2003). A contextual model analysis of women's social competence, affective characteristics, and satisfaction in premarital relationships. *Journal of Family Communication, 3*, 107–122.

Fitzpatrick, M. A. (2006). Epilogue: The future of family communication theory and research. In L. H. Turner & R. West (Eds.), *The family communication sourcebook* (pp. 491–495). Thousand Oaks, CA: Sage.

Floyd, K. (2004). An introduction to the uses and potential uses of physiological measurement in the study of family communication. *Journal of Family Communication, 4*, 295–317.

Floyd, K., & Morman, M. T. (2006). Introduction: On the breath of the family experience. In K. Floyd & M. T. Mormon (Eds.), *Widening the family circle: New research on family communication* (pp. xi–xvi). Thousand Oaks, CA: Sage.

Freeman, D. (1983). *Margaret Mead and Samoa: The making and unmaking of an anthropological myth*. Cambridge, MA: Harvard University Press.

Fujioka, Y., & Austin, E. W. (2002). The relationship of family communication patterns to parental mediation styles. *Communication Research, 29*, 642–665.

Galvin, K. M. (2006). Diversity's impact on defining the family: Discourse-dependence and identity. In L. H. Turner & R. West (Eds.), *The family communication sourcebook* (pp. 3–19). Thousand Oaks, CA: Sage.

Golish, T. D. (2003). Stepfamily communication strengths: Understanding the ties that bind. *Human Communication Research, 29*, 41–80.

Gottman, J., Levenson, R., & Woodin, E. (2001). Facial expressions during marital conflict. *Journal of Family Communication, 1*, 37–57.

Graham, E. E. (2003). Dialectic contradictions in postmarital relationships. *Journal of Family Communication, 3*, 193–214.

Haas, S. M., & Stafford, L. (2005). Maintenance behaviors in same-sex and marital relationships: A matched sample comparison. *Journal of Family Communication, 5*, 43–60.

Heatherington, L., Escudero, V., & Friedlander, M. L. (2005). Couple interaction during problem discussions: Toward an integrative methodology. *Journal of Family Communication, 5*, 191–207.

Henry, C. S., & Lovelace, S. G. (1995). Family resources and adolescent family life satisfaction in remarried family households. *Journal of Family Issues, 16*, 765–786.

Holbert, R. L., & Stephenson, M. T. (2002). Structural equation modeling in the communication sciences, 1995–2000. *Human Communication Research, 28,* 531–551.

Huang, L. N. (1999). Family communication patterns and personality characteristics. *Communication Quarterly, 47,* 230–243.

Hughes, P. C., & Dickson, F. C. (2005). Communication, marital satisfaction, and religious orientation in interfaith marriages. *Journal of Family Communication, 5,* 25–41.

Hummert, M. L. (2007). As family members age: A research agenda for family communication. *Journal of Family Communication, 7,* 3–21.

Huston, T. L., McHale, S. M., & Crouter, A. C. (1986). When the honeymoon's over: Changes in the marriage relationship over the first year. In R. Gilmour & S. Duck (Eds.), *The emerging field of personal relationships* (pp. 109–132). Hillsdale, NJ: Erlbaum.

Kashy, D. A., Jellison, W. A., & Kenny, D. A. (2004). Modeling the interdependence among family members. *Journal of Family Communication, 4,* 265–293.

Kellas, J. K. (2005). Family ties: Communicating identity through jointly told family stories. *Communication Monographs, 72,* 365–389.

Kelly, L., Keaten, J. A., Finch, C., Duarte, I. B, Hoffman, P., & Michels, M. M. (2002). Family communication patterns and the development of reticence. *Communication Education, 51,* 202–209.

Kerlinger, F. N., & Lee, H. B. (2000). *Foundations of behavioral research* (4th ed.). Fort Worth, TX: Harcourt.

Keyton, J. (2006). *Communication research: Asking questions, finding answers* (2nd ed.). Boston: McGraw–Hill.

Kirk, J., & Miller, M. L. (1986). *Reliability and validity in qualitative research.* Newbury Park, CA: Sage.

Koerner, A. F., & Cvancara, K. E. (2002). The influence of conformity orientation on communication patterns in family conversations. *Journal of Family Communication, 2,* 133–152.

Koeston, J., & Anderson, K. (2004). Exploring the influence of family communication patterns, cognitive complexity, and interpersonal communication competence on adolescent risk behaviors. *Journal of Family Communication, 4,* 99–121.

Lucchetti, A. E., Powers, W. G., & Love, D. E. (2002). The empirical development of the child-parent communication apprehension scale for use with young adults. *Journal of Family Communication, 2,* 109–131.

McCroskey, J. C. (2006). Reliability and validity of the Generalized Attitude Measure and Generalized Belief Measure. *Communication Quarterly, 54,* 265–274.

McLeod, J. M., & Chaffee, S. H. (1972). The construction of social reality. In J. Tedeschi (Ed.), *The social influence processes* (pp. 50–99). Chicago, IL: Aldine-Atherton.

Mead, M. (1928). *Coming of age in Samoa.* New York: Morrow.

Metts, S., & Lamb, E. (2006). Methodological approaches to the study of family communication. In L. H. Turner & R. West (Eds.), *The family communication sourcebook* (pp. 83–105). Thousand Oaks, CA: Sage.

Metts, S., Sprecher, S., & Cupach, W. R. (1991). Retrospective self-reports. In

B. M. Montgomery & S. Duck (Eds.), *Studying interpersonal interaction* (pp. 162–178). New York: Guilford.

Miller, M., & Day, L. E. (2002). Family communication, maternal and paternal expectations, and college students' suicidality. *Journal of Family Communication, 2,* 167–184.

Mukherji, J. (2005). Maternal communication patterns, advertising attitudes, and mediation behaviours in urban India. *Journal of Marketing Communications, 11,* 247–262.

Noller, P., & Feeney, J. A. (2004). Studying family communication: Multiple methods and multiple sources. In A. L. Vangelisti (Ed.), *Handbook of family communication* (pp. 31–50). Mahwah, NJ: Erlbaum.

Oetzel, J., Ting-Toomey, S., Chew-Sanchez, M., Harris, R., Wilcox, R., & Stumpf, S. (2003). Face and facework in conflicts with parents and siblings: A cross-cultural comparison of Germans, Japanese, Mexicans, and U.S. Americans. *Journal of Family Communication, 3,* 67–93.

Orrego, V. O., & Rodriguez, J. (2001). Family communication patterns and college adjustment: The effects of communication and conflictual independence on college students. *Journal of Family Communication, 1,* 175–189.

Parrott, R., & Lemieux, R. (2003). When the worlds of work and wellness collide: The role of familial support on skin cancer control. *Journal of Family Communication, 3,* 95–106.

Pecchioni, L. L., & Nussbaum, J. F. (2001). Mother-adult daughter discussions of caregiving prior to dependency: Exploring conflicts among European-American women. *Journal of Family Communication, 1,* 133–150.

Peterson, A. (2006). American Association of Collegiate Registrars and Admissions Officers. *Newsweek.* Accessed April 23, 2007 from http://www.msnbc. msn.com/id/10965522/site/newsweek.

Prescott, M. E., & LePoire, B. A. (2002). Eating disorders and mother-daughter communication: A test of inconsistent nurturing as control theory. *Journal of Family Communication, 2,* 59–78.

Riggio, H. R. (2000). Measuring attitudes toward adult sibling relationships: The Lifespan Sibling Relationship Scale. *Journal of Social and Personal Relationships, 17,* 707–728.

Ritchie, D. L., & Fitzpatrick, M. A. (1990). Family communication patterns: Measuring intrapersonal perceptions of interpersonal relationships. *Communication Research, 17,* 523–544.

Rubin, R. B., Palmgreen, P., & Sypher, H. E. (Eds.) (1994). *Communication research measures: A sourcebook.* New York: Guilford.

Sabourin, T. C. (2003). *The contemporary American family: A dialectical perspective on communication and relationships.* Thousand Oaks, CA: Sage.

Schrodt, P. (2006a). Development and validation of the stepfamily life index. *Journal of Social and Personal Relationships, 23,* 427–444.

Schrodt, P. (2006b). The stepparent relationship index: Development, validation, and associations with stepchildren's perceptions of stepparent communication competence and closeness. *Personal Relationships, 13,* 167–182.

Schrodt, P., & Ledbetter, A. M. (2007). Communication processes that mediate family communication patterns and mental well-being: A mean covariance structures analysis of young adults from divorced and non-divorced families. *Human Communication Research, 33,* 330–356.

Schrodt, P., Ledbetter, A. M., & Ohrt, J. K. (2007). Parental confirmation and affection as mediators of family communication patterns and children's mental well-being. *Journal of Family Communication, 7,* 23–46.

Segrin, C. (2006). Family interactions and well-being: Integrative perspectives. *Journal of Family Communication, 6,* 3–21.

Segrin, C., & Flora, J. (2001). Perceptions of relational histories, marital quality, and loneliness when communication is limited: An examination of married prison inmates. *Journal of Family Communication, 1,* 151–173.

Sillars, A., Koerner, A., & Fitzpatrick, M. A. (2005). Communication and understanding in parent-adolescent relationships. *Human Communication Research, 31,* 102–128.

Smith, R. A., Levine, T. R., Lachlan, K. A., & Fediuk, T. A. (2002). The high cost of complexity in experimental design and data analysis: Type I and Type II error rates in multiway ANOVA. *Human Communication Research, 28,* 515–530.

Stamp, G. H. (2004). Theories of family relationships and a family relationships theoretical model. In A. Vangelisti (Ed.), *Handbook of family communication* (pp. 1–30). Mahwah, NJ: Erlbaum.

Turner, L. H., & West, R. (2003). Breaking through silence: Increasing voice for diverse families in communication research. *Journal of Family Communication, 3,* 181–186.

Turner, L. H., & West, R. (2006). Understanding relationships in family communication research: Expanding the social recipe. In K. Floyd & M. T. Mormon (Eds.), *Widening the family circle: New research on family communication* (pp. 193–206). Thousand Oaks, CA: Sage.

Vangelisti, A., Caughlin, J., & Timmerman, L. (2001). Criteria for revealing family secrets. *Communication Monographs, 68,* 1–27.

Weigel, D. J., & Ballard-Reisch, D. S. (2001). The impact of relational maintenance behaviors on marital satisfaction: A longitudinal analysis. *Journal of Family Communication, 1,* 265–279.

Weiner, J. L., Silk, K. J., & Parrott, R. L. (2005). Family communication and genetic health: A research note. *Journal of Family Communication, 5,* 313–324.

Whitchurch, G. G. (1993). Designing a course in family communication. *Communication Education, 42,* 255–267.

Whitchurch, G. G., & Dickson, F. C. (1999). Family communication. In M. Sussman, S. K. Steinmetz, & G. W. Peterson (Eds.), *Handbook of marriage and the family* (2nd ed.) (pp. 687–704). New York: Plenum Press.

Xu, Y., & Burleson, B. R. (2004). The association of experienced spousal support with marital satisfaction: Evaluating the moderating effects of sex, ethnic culture, and type of support. *Journal of Family Communication, 4,* 123–145.

Yelsma, P., & Marrow, S. (2003). An examination of couples' difficulties with emotional expressiveness and their marital satisfaction. *Journal of Family Communication, 3,* 41–62.

Zhang, Q. (2007). Family communication patterns and conflict styles in Chinese parent-child relationships. *Communication Quarterly, 55,* 113–128.

Measurement in Organizational and Group Communication

David R. Seibold

Downs, DeWine, and Greenbaum (1994), writing in the first volume of *Communication Research Measures: A Sourcebook* (Rubin, Palmgreen, & Sypher, 1994), surveyed more than 50 measures of organizational and team/group communication published between 1957 and 1991. The instruments they discussed were among more than 500 identified by Greenbaum and Gardner (1985) as having been cited in communication journals and dissertations over more than three decades, although only 20% of those had been used as many as three times and many within the originators' own programs of research. Nearly all the measures discussed by Downs et al. (1994) appeared in print before the mid-1980s, the beginning of the "interpretive turn" in organizational communication research that followed from a summer conference at Alta, Utah, in the early 1980s (Putnam & Pacanowsky, 1983). Numerous changes in the areas of organizational and group communication have affected the number and type of measures developed since the Downs et al. (1994) review, the period that is the primary focus of this chapter.

On one hand, and notwithstanding efforts to find common ground (Corman & Poole, 2000), the turn among organizational communication scholars from a post-positivist approach (Corman, 2004; K. I. Miller, 2000) to interpretive (Cheney, 2000) and critical (Mumby, 2000) perspectives correlatively limited the number of researchers and research studies in the area employing measures in quantitative investigations. Furthermore, while Downs et al. (1994) treated group measures as part of organizational communication scholarship, the formation later in the 1990s of the Group Communication Division in the National Communication Association not only created a unique research entity and drew scholars away from the organizational and interpersonal communication units in that scholarly society, but encouraged examination of communication in natural groups (Frey, 1994). This change in focus occasioned a change in methods toward ethnographic practices (Dollar & Merrigan, 2002) and to content analyses of group and organizational members' interactions (Poole, Keyton, & Frey, 1999), the latter thrust associated with the development of numerous coding schemes rather than new measures. Finally, refinement of instruments by scholars who left full-time roles in the academy, where the measures were developed, to form consulting practices led to some prominent measures being proprietary in nature. The requirement that potential users receive "training" by the developers (e.g., Wheelan & Hochberger 1996, p. 166; Wheelan is now president of GDQ Associates — see Wheelan, 2005, p. 581) may have led to less widespread use of some measures in research studies.

On the other hand, several factors sustained the use of existing organizational and group measures and stimulated the development of new ones. For example, the1990s were marked by the emergence of important scholarly venues that published research with new organizational and group communication measures (notably *Management Communication Quarterly* and *Small Group Research*). There also was a continuing trend toward inter-disciplinarity in group and organizational studies (Clegg, Hardy, & Nord, 1996; Poole, 1994; Poole & Hollingshead, 2005) that encouraged sharing of methods and measures in addition to theories and constructs. Furthermore, the increase in large-scale grant-funded research in communication (Seibold, 2000; 2008) included projects in which communication investigators utilized established measures and developed new ones. Additionally, the acceptance of mixed-method research in organizational communication (K. I. Miller, 2001) fostered studies in which instruments were among the multiple methods employed. Finally, the broadening of scholarly interests to new theoretical and topical areas of organizations and groups (Taylor, Flanagin, Cheney, & Seibold, 2000) was associated with the creation of measurement instruments as well. All these forces contributed to the development, utilization, and refinement of organizational and group measures in communication and in other disciplines since the early 1990s measures that closed the Downs et al. (1994) review. A survey of communication and related journals in management and the social sciences identified more than 40 new survey self-report measures of group and organizational communication in print since then, and at least three times that number of organizational and group measures that did not contain major communication components but might be of interest to communication researchers (Carless & De Paola, 2000; Taggar & Brown, 2001; Wanous, Reichers, & Austin, 2000; Wekselberg, Goggin, & Collings, 1997; Welbourne, Johnson, & Erez, 1998).

Criteria for Inclusion of Measures Reviewed and Profiled

Many criteria were utilized in selecting which of those measures to review in this chapter and, especially, which to profile later in this volume. Several criteria were appropriated from Downs et al. (1994) in the first volume: evidence of validity of the measure and acceptable reliability; preference for measures developed by communication scholars; at least one communication component in the measure when developed outside the field; and selection of measures that may be new but are "promising." A criterion that was central to the choices made by Downs et al.—preference for comprehensive measures—was abandoned in this chapter because no new measures have attempted to examine communication comprehensively in organizations and/or groups. Furthermore, not discussed in this chapter are organizational and group measures available in other compendia (e.g., Fields, 2002) and websites (e.g, W. Robert Sampson Measures of Organizational Communication at http://www.uwec.edu/Sampsow/Measures.htm; the Working Climate Survey at organizational communication scholar and consultant Phillip Clampitt's www.imetacom.com; and numerous original measures at http://jamescmccroskey.com/measures/—also see McCroskey, Richmond, Johnson, & Smith, 2004). Finally, for the most part, studies that rely on only one organization for scale development were not chosen for discussion (e.g., Chiles & Zorn, 1995) nor were instruments that had not been used widely and/or were challenging to administer or score (e.g. Jorgensen & Petelle, 1992).

However, this chapter also includes measures based on additional criteria to those shared with Downs et al. (1994). First, three measures not discussed by Downs et al. because they were nascent at that time are treated now. Second, a measure that was profiled by Downs et al. is revisited here, given extensive commentary about it over the past decade. Third, important theoretical advances have occurred during the past fifteen years, and related measurement developments are discussed in this chapter (and three of those measures are profiled). Fourth, given new topical areas that group and organizational communication scholars have entered since the Downs et al. chapter, several measures have been developed in those emerging areas that are discussed below (one of which is profiled later). Fifth, measures created by organizational and group communication researchers that have the potential to create intra-disciplinary bridges to other areas of communication scholarship also served as a criterion for inclusion in this review (and one is profiled). Sixth, in light of the trend toward increased inter-disciplinarity noted earlier, measures developed by communication researchers that are likely to be of interest to organizational and group researchers in other disciplines are surveyed (and two are profiled). Seventh, given the historical roots of organizational and group communication in practice (Seibold, 1995; 2005) and the move toward even deeper modes of engagement (Simpson & Shockley-Zalabak, 2005), measures with the potential for both research and practice are included in this chapter (and two of these are profiled). By these many criteria, approximately 25 measures of group and organizational communication published between 1991 and 2003 are noted in this chapter, nine of which are profiled later in the volume. The trends reflected in the criteria above also serve as bases for the organization of the discussion that follows and for the order of the seven subsections in which the measures are considered.

Addendum to Downs, DeWine, and Greenbaum (1994)

Additional Measures

Three measures that were coming to the fore as Downs et al. (1994) were finishing their review are worth noting here for continuity as much as for utility. Morrill and Thomas (1992) introduced an Organizational Conflict Management Scale as they investigated the problem of social escalation in disputes. The 5-item Openness Toward Change Scale was created by V. D. Miller, Johnson, and Grau (1994) to measure with Likert-type responses individuals' willingness to support organizational change and their positive affect toward it.

Especially noteworthy is V. D. Miller and Jablin's (1991) treatment of information seeking during organizational entry. They offered a model of factors that influence newcomers' information seeking behaviors (uncertainty, social costs, information source and content, individual differences and contextual factors, outcomes), as well as tactics used in gaining information (overt questions, indirect questions, third parties, testing limits, disguising conversations, observing, and surveillance). With a study by V. D. Miller (1996) most exemplary, many investigations have developed items to measure different of the factors and subsets of the information seeking tactics (e.g., Casey, Miller, & Johnson, 1997; Jablin & Kramer, 1998; Kramer, 1993; 1994; Kramer, Callister, & Turban, 1991; S. A. Myers, 1998; Rodrick & Knox, 2002; Sias, Kramer, & Jenkins, 1997; Teboul, 1995; Wolfe Morrison, 1995). Many of the subscales developed in these studies evidence high levels of reliability, but no definitive and unified measure of information-seeking behaviors has been created.

Organizational Identification Questionnaire

The Organizational Identification Questionnaire (Cheney, 1983) is a 25-item measure of an individual's identification with an organization, the result of "an active process by which individuals link themselves" (p. 342) to the organization's values, identity, and image. With modifications and adaptations to specific contexts or samples in several investigations, the OIQ has been used often in organizational studies since the Downs et al. (1994) review, both in other disciplines and especially in communication (J. R. Barker & Tompkins, 1994; Jian & Jeffres 2006; Kuhn & Nelson,

2002; Russo, 1998; Schrodt, 2002; C. R. Scott, 1997; C. R. Scott et al., 1999). W. L. Johnson, Johnson, and Heimberg (1999) refer to it as the most frequently used measure of organizational identification.

However, before (Barge & Schleuter, 1988; Sass & Canary, 1991) and shortly after (V. D. Miller, J. Johnson, & Grau, 1994) inclusion of the OIQ in *Communication Research Measures: A Sourcebook* (Rubin et al., 1994), concerns were evident about the conceptual overlap between organizational identification as construed by Cheney and conceptualizations of organizational commitment; strong empirical relationships between the OIQ and a commonly used measure of organizational commitment; findings from factor analyses of the OIQ that were inconsistent with the theorized unidimensionality; and the general lack of validation studies of the OIQ. Several of these problems were acknowledged in the individual profile of the measure (Downs, 1994) and in the chapter by Downs et al. (1994), together with their caveat that the OIQ appeared both to be highly correlated with measures of, and conceptually a communication measure of, organizational *commitment*.

Recent criticisms of the OIQ support that prescient view. In addition to the critiques just noted, others criticisms have been leveled at the stability of the OIQ over time, the relatively few items in the OIQ that assess communication, the scant contribution that they and some other items make to the measure, and the predictive validity of the OIQ. The most compelling evidence of the need for a reconsideration of the OIQ has been supplied by V. D. Miller, Allen, Casey, and J. Johnson (2000). Factor analytic findings from their longitudinal and cross-sectional data suggest that the OIC is unidimensional, but that fewer than half of the 25 items contribute to measurement of the construct. Especially important, the 12 items that are conceptually coherent constitute an affective measure of organizational *commitment*, "or the degree to which employees have positive, neutral, or negative feelings to the organization" (p. 649). Furthermore, these 12 commitment items are unidemsional, have high internal reliability, high test-retest reliability, and criterion and construct validity. Therefore, V. D. Miller et al. (2000) "call for a moratorium on the use of OIQ as a measure of organizational identification" (p. 648) and, noting that problems are also apparent with other new identification measures, they urge scholars to pursue "a more robust operationalization of the organizational identification construct" (p. 654).

Although some of the studies noted above appear to have been unaware of or unpersuaded by these findings, even the studies with modifications of the OIQ may be perpetuating conceptual, empirical, or interpretational difficulties with the OIQ — especially under- or over-estimation of identification effects and spurious correlations when organizational commitment measures also were utilized in the study. Scott, Corman, and Cheney (1998) helped to shore up the communication bases of organizational identification which has aided later empirical work on the measure (e.g., Fontenot & Scott, 2007), and C. R. Scott (2007) has used social identity theory to clarify the relationship between organizational identification and commitment. From a measurement standpoint, the development that has been most responsive to the indictments of the OIQ by V. D. Miller et al. (2000) and the most promising method of measuring organizational identification is the 9-item Communicative Organizational Identification (C-OI) measure reported by Fontenot and Scott (2007). A measure of solidarity with the values of a collective (e.g., organization) expressed to others inside the collective (one subscale) and external to it (a second subscale), this new self-report survey instrument was validated across three waves with working adults. However, much work remains, not least of which is comparing the C-OI with measures of affective commitment to ensure the new measure does not evidence the same major problem as the OIQ.

After Downs, DeWine, and Greenbaum (1994)

New Theoretical Advances and New Measures

Taylor et al. (2000) identify theoretical advances in organizational and group communication, including several that are pertinent for this chapter because they have been associated with the development of new measures. Kassing's (2000) 18-item ORGANIZATIONAL DISSENT SCALE, which assesses "how employees verbally express their contradictory opinions and disagreements about organizational phenomena" (Kassing, 1998, p. 183), represents part of the theoretical move to refining our understanding of discourse in organizations (Taylor et al., 2000), including power and resistance. In connection with theoretical developments linking material and symbolic dimensions of organizations (Taylor et al., 2000), as well as extending structurational analyses (Taylor et al., 2000), Ballard and Seibold (2000; 2003) explored objective and subjective dimensions of time as they are grounded in, and ground, organizational communication. Based upon those theoretical efforts Ballard and Seibold (2004) developed the 11-dimension (subscales) ORGANIZATIONAL TEMPORALITY SCALE, a promising measure profiled later.

Not profiled, but associated with other theoretical advances noted by Taylor et al. (2000), are several other measures that have appeared since the Downs et al. (1994) chapter. As part of advances in what Taylor et al. (2000) refer to as organizing for and communicating about change, Lewis and Seibold (1996) developed measures of group and organizational members' coping responses to innovations and intra-organizational innovation adoption. Moreover, two new group measures are part of the increased attention to what Taylor et al. (2000) term groups as mediating structures. Henry, Arrow, and Carini (1999) grounded their Group Identification

Scale in a three-dimensional model of group identification. The 12-item GIS utilizes three 4-item subscales to measure, with 7-point responses, the affective, cognitive and behavioral sources of an individual's identification with the group. Hoyle and Crawford (1994) reported on the Perceived Cohesion Scale, a 6-item measure of two underlying dimensions of cohesion (sense of belonging and sense of morale) with responses scored on Likert-type scales from 0 (strongly disagree) to 10 (strongly agree) (also see Chin, Salisbury, Pearson, & Stollack, 1999). Finally, the Trust in Top Management and the Trust in Immediate Supervisor scales developed by Ellis and Shockley-Zalabak (2001; see also Hubbell & Chory-Assad, 2005) are at the nexus of two other new topics of research identified by Taylor et al. (2000), ethics and old/new leadership respectively. The top management scale contains 6 items and the immediate supervisor scale is comprised of 14 items, all responded to on Likert-type scales (1=very little to 5=very much).

New Topics and New Measures

Several new measures have been developed within topical areas of group and organizational research that have emerged since the Downs et al. (1994) review. For example, the emphasis on groups and/in organizations (Poole, 1998; Taylor et al., 2000) — which also incorporates a concern for the "relational side" of groups rather than only the task dimension (V. Barker et al., 2000; Keyton, 1999)—includes work by Anderson, Martin, and Riddle (2001) to measure members' satisfaction with relationships and relational communication in their group. Their 12-item SMALL GROUP RELATIONAL SATISFACTION SCALE, in which relational satisfaction is defined as "the building and maintaining of member relationships during communicative processes and practices throughout the life span of the group" (Anderson et al., 2001; p. 220), is profiled later.

Taylor et al. (2000) note another new topic of organizational communication scholarship: how relationships at work relate to relationships in other domains. One line of research in that area, which has followed from Hochschild's (1983) seminal work, is examination of how employees manage emotion labor (C. W. Scott & Myers, 2005; Tracy, 2005). The Emotion Labor Scale developed by Kruml and Geddes (2000) is part and parcel of that type of research. Measured on 5-point Likert-type response scales (1=never to 5=always), the 7-item Emotion Labor Scale assesses two dimensions of the construct: emotive dissonance (3 items) and emotive effort (4 items).

New Measures Bridging to Other Areas of Communication

The proliferation of divisions and interest groups in professional associations of communication researchers has blurred distinctions among traditional sub-areas of the field, especially since the new units' membership includes scholars also identified with, and still active in, longstanding units in those societies. This increased *intra*-disciplinarity is reflected in new group and organizational communication measures that help bridge to interests and issues in other areas of the field. For example, several new measures draw on theories from both organizational communication and interpersonal communication, such as the Frameworks for Interaction (FINT) Scale (J. D. Johnson, 1997), a 19-item measure of five underlying frameworks for communication in organizations (formal, exchange, sentiments, normative, and negotiated order). There also is the extensive set of Maintenance Communication Behaviors identified by Lee and Jablin (1995), or tactics and strategies that subordinates enact in order to maintain stable relationships with their superiors. They are measured in terms of frequency of use and perceived effectiveness on five-interval scales in Lee's research on superior-subordinate work relationships (Lee, 1998; 2001). Finally, the Troublesome Others Scale (Harden Fritz, 2002) reflects part of interpersonal communication scholars' interest in the "dark side" of personal non-personal relationships (Cupach & Spitzberg, 2007).

The increasing emphasis among organizational communication scholars on discursive fields (Fairhurst & Putnam, 1999; 2004) not merely *in* but *around* organizations (Taylor et al., 2000), and the associated connections between organizational rhetoric (Cheney, 1991; Cheney & Christensen, 2001) and public relations (Cheney & Christensen, 2006; Cheney & Frenette, 1993), help explain the development of measures such as the Coombs and Holladay (1996) ORGANIZATIONAL REPUTATION SCALE. The 10-item scale is part of the research program of Coombs (1998, 1999) and colleagues (Coombs & Holladay, 2002; 2006) on organizational responses to crises. Central to their work is research on strategies for protecting organizational reputation, or how an organization is perceived by its publics.

New Measures Bridging to Other Disciplines

Research in organizational and group communication has not been characterized only by the *intra*-disciplinary theoretical and measurement advances above. Theoretical and measurement developments since Downs et al. (1994) published their review have been *inter*-disciplinary as well, which is consistent with the roots of the area in several disciplines (Redding & Tompkins, 1988). One such area of organizational communication scholarship with close connections to organizational studies in sociology, organizational behavior, and management, and an area that has seen a theoretical, methodological, empirical, and critical resurgence in communication (Allen, 2005; Barge & Schlueter, 2004; Jablin, 2001; V. D. Miller, Hart, Dibble, & Harden Fritz, 2005; K. K. Myers, 2005;

K. K. Myers & McPhee, 2006), is that of research on organizational social-ization and assimilation. These reciprocal constructs concern, respectively, the tactics *organizations* use to facilitate newcomers' and transitioning members' full functional involvement and commitment to the organiza-tion, as well as the communicative processes by which *individuals* acquire knowledge and adopt the attitudes and behaviors necessary to participate as organizational members while simultaneously influencing the organiza-tion. The Feedback Seeking Scale (Callister, Kramer, & Turban, 1999) is a new measure in this area, but based upon previous scales outside the disci-pline on monitoring and inquiring feedback seeking. Although its focus is on proactive communication associated only with career transitions, its potential to bridge back to those disciplines rests in the communication-relevant distinction between source of the feedback: from peer(s) (7 items) and from supervisor (4 items). K. K. Myers and Oetzel (2003) developed a more wide ranging and potentially inter-disciplinary ORGANIZA-TIONAL ASSIMILATION INDEX. The 20-item OAI measures six dimensions of organizational assimilation: familiarity with others, organi-zational acculturation, recognition, involvement, job competency, and adaptation/role negotiation. It is profiled in this volume.

The last measurement development in organizational communication (OAI) has a parallel development in the area of group communication. Riddle, Anderson, and Martin (2000) published the SMALL GROUP SOCIALIZATION SCALE. The 14-item measure assesses "people's per-ceptions of the communication effectiveness of group communication that includes task and relationship dimensions" (p. 555). It follows from theo-retical work by Anderson, Riddle, and Martin (1999) concerning how members and groups affect the group's task and one another, as well as socialization processes within the group.

While not focused on socialization and assimilation processes, the GROUP DEVELOPMENT QUESTIONNAIRE reported by Wheelan and Hochberger (1996) is part of the same trend in inter-disciplinary measures. Group development also has been a central concern among group commu-nication theorists and researchers (Gouran, 1999), and the 60-item GDQ is comprised of four 15-item subscales based on the first four stages in Whee-lan's (1994) five-stage model: dependency and inclusion, counterdepen-dency and fight, trusting and structure, work and productivity, and termination (also see Wheelan & Williams, 2003). The work by Lester, Meglino, and Korsgaard (2002) extending the 8-item Group Potency meas-ure is another among these inter-disciplinary measurement developments.

New Measures for Engagement

Simpson and Shockley-Zalabak (2005) compiled original essays exploring the theory, praxis, and pedagogy of engagement in organizational communication scholarship, the role and impact of organizational communication in practitioner communities. Several of the contributors, and many other group and organizational communication scholars, rely upon communication measures in connection with their organizational engagements. At least two measures that have appeared since Downs et al. (1994) reported the results of their survey of organizational and group measures have the potential to be used in traditional research studies and by practitioner communities. Cooper (1997) and colleagues (Cooper & Buchanan, 1999; 2003) developed a 30-item ORGANIZATIONAL LISTENING SURVEY that focuses on the job-related listening competency of members at any level of organizations (Form C = self-rating and Form D = rating by others). The instrument measures competencies along two dimensions: listening for accuracy (acquiring information through discriminating/ evaluating and recalling listening behaviors) and listening for support (attending, clarifying, responding, affiliating, and accommodating listening behaviors). It is profiled later.

Similarly, the SEXUAL HARASSMENT PROCLIVITY INDEX (Bingham & Burleson, 1996) has utility for both theory-relevant research and for practice. The primary goal of the SHPI is to provide a framework for assessing sexual harassment proclivity in men, and therefore to offer potential redress to a major organizational/workplace problem. The 16-item measure contains 9 items that represent forms of harassing behavior comprising what Bingham and Burleson term intrusive harassment and 7 items represent quid pro quo harassment. The Workforce Diversity Questionnaire created and validated by Larkey (1996) also has research and applied uses for assessing interactions in workplace groups characterized by cultural, gender, or general diversity. The 28-item WDQ assesses the workforce along eight dimensions (each a subscale with three or four items): inclusion, ideation, understanding, treatment, power, cohesiveness, detail, and values.

Conclusion

Developments in the measurement of organizational and group communication since the Downs et al. (1994) review have been enabled and constrained by many factors: ideological turns; new (sub)communities of scholars with new interests and new methods; models for utilizing multiple methods; funded large-scale research projects; theoretical advances; new topical foci and areas of research interest; blurring of distinctions between traditional divisions within communication associations and among their members; inter-disciplinarity in both organizational and group research; and scholars engagement beyond the campus and student research participants in ways that promote use of measures in research *and* practice. Those forces also have shaped which measures were selected for discussion above, how discussion of them was organized, and to a lesser degree which ones are profiled later in this volume.

Trends in quantitative research in organizational and group communication during the past two decades also have had important contextual effects on measurement developments in those areas. Advances associated with multi-level, multi-method, and multi-source research (and implications for validity and common method variance), sampling and data collection, aggregation of data and level-of-analysis issues, statistical techniques (especially factor analysis and confirmatory factor analysis, applications of hierarchical linear modeling and dealing with non-independent data, and advances in structural equation modeling), and appropriate use of difference scores all have brought into sharp relief the measures that have appropriated these techniques (e.g., Ellis & Shockley-Zalabak, 2001; J. D. Johnson, 1997; V. D. Miller et al., 1994). Many of these advances also have been key to the development of new measures introduced above and profiled later (e.g., Cooper & Buchanan, 1999; Ballard & Seibold, 2004; K. K. Myers & Oetzel, 2003).

Finally, prominent debates about existing measures in group, organizational, and other communication areas (e.g., Levine et al., 2003; V. D. Miller et al., 2000) have raised awareness of measurement issues and problems. For example, powerful statistical and data analytical techniques like those just mentioned helped identify problems noted earlier with the Organizational Identification Questionnaire. In turn, the conceptual and measurement advances in the assessment of this prominent but challenging construct have aided scholars in that area. And those advances serve to model, for organizational and group communication researchers and the field as a whole, what V. D. Miller and colleagues (2000) note is the foundational character of social science: evaluating previous findings and developing refined or new measures to extend it.

References

Allen, B. J. (2005). Social constructionism. In S. May & D. K. Mumby (Eds.), *Engaging organizational communication: Theory and research* (pp. 35–54). Thousand Oaks, CA: Sage.

Anderson, C. M., Martin, M. M., & Riddle, B. L. (2001). Small group relational satisfaction scale: Development, reliability, and validity. *Communication Studies, 52,* 220–233.

Anderson, C. M., Riddle, B. L., & Martin, M. M. (1999). Socialization processes in groups. In L. R. Frey, D. S. Gouran, & M. S. Poole (Eds.), *The handbook of group communication theory and research* (pp. 139–166). Thousand Oaks, CA: Sage.

Ballard, D. I., & Seibold, D. R. (2000). Time orientation and temporal variation across work groups: Implications for group and organizational communication. *Western Journal of Communication, 64,* 218–242.

Ballard, D. I., & Seibold, D. R. (2003). Communicating and organizing in time: A meso-level model of organizational temporality. *Management Communication Quarterly, 16,* 380–415.

Ballard, D. I., & Seibold, D. R. (2004). Organizational members' communication and temporal experience: Scale development and validation. *Communication Research, 31*(2), 135–172.

Barge, J. K., & Schlueter, D. W. (1998). A critical evaluation of organizational commitment and identification. *Management Communication Quarterly, 2,* 116–133.

Barge, J. K., & Schlueter, D. W. (2004). Memorable messages and newcomer socialization. *Western Journal of Communication, 68,* 233–256.

Barker, V., Abrams, J. R., Tiyaamornwong, V., Seibold, D. R., Duggan, A., Park, H. S., & Sebastian, M. (2000). New contexts for relational communication in groups. *Small Group Research, 31*(4), 470–503.

Barker, J. R., & Tompkins, P. K. (1994). Identification in the self-managing organization: Characteristics of target and tenure. *Human Communication Research, 21,* 223–240.

Bingham, S. G., & Burleson, B. R. (1996). The development of a sexual harassment proclivity scale: Construct validation and relationship to communication competence. *Communication Quarterly, 44,* 308–325.

Callister, R. R., Kramer M.W., & Turban, D. B. (1999). Feedback seeking following career transitions. *Academy of Management Journal, 42,* 429–438.

Carless, S. A., & De Paola, C. (2000). The measurement of cohesion in work teams. *Small Group Research, 31,* 71–88.

Casey, M. K., Miller, V. D., & Johnson, J. R. (1997). Survivors' information seeking following a reduction in workforce. *Communication Research, 24,* 755–781.

Cheney, G. (1983). On the various and changing meanings of organizational membership: A field study of organizational identification. *Communication Monographs, 50,* 342–362.

Cheney, G. (1991). *Rhetoric in an organizational society: Managing multiple identities.* Columbia: University of South Carolina Press.

Cheney, G. (2000). Integrating interpretive research: Toward perspectivism about relativism. In S. R. Corman & M. S. Poole (Eds.), *Perspectives on organizational communication: Finding common ground* (pp. 17–45). New York: Guilford.

Cheney, G., & Christensen, L. T. (2001). Organizational identity: Linkages between internal and external organizational communication. In F. M. Jablin & L. L. Putnam (Eds.), *The new handbook of organizational communication: Advances in theory, research, and methods* (pp. 231–269). Thousand Oaks, CA: Sage.

Cheney. G., & Christensen, L. T. (2006). What should PR theory do, practically speaking? *Journal of Communication Management, 10,* 100–102.

Cheney, G., & Frenette, G. (1993). Persuasion and organization: Values, logics and accounts in contemporary corporate public discourse. In C. Conrad (Ed.), *The ethical nexus* (pp. 49–74). Thousand Oaks, CA: Sage.

Chiles, A. M., & Zorn, T. E. (1995). Empowerment in organizations: Employees' perceptions of the influences on empowerment. *Journal of Applied Communication Research, 23,* 1–25.

Chin, W. W., Salisbury, W. D., Pearson, A. W., & Stollak, M. J. (1999). Perceived cohesion in small groups: Adapting and testing the perceived cohesion scale in a small-group setting. *Small Group Research, 30,* 751–766.

Clegg, S. R., Hardy, C., & Nord, W. R. (Eds.) (1996). *Handbook of organization studies.* Thousand Oaks, CA: Sage.

Coombs, W. T. (1998). An analytic framework for crisis situations: Better responses from a better understanding of the situation. *Journal of Public Relations Research, 10,* 177–191.

Coombs, W. T. (1999). *Ongoing crisis communication: Planning, managing, and responding.* Thousand Oaks, CA: Sage.

Coombs, W. T., & Holladay, S. J. (1996). Communication and attributions in a crisis: An experimental study of crisis communication. *Journal of Public Relations Research, 8,* 279–295.

Coombs, W. T., & Holladay, S. J. (2002). Helping crisis managers protect reputational assets: Initial tests of the situational crisis communication theory. *Management Communication Quarterly, 16,* 165–186.

Coombs, W. T., & Holladay, S. J. (2006). Unpacking the halo effect: Reputation and crisis management. *Journal of Communication Management, 10,* 123–137.

Cooper, L. O. (1997). Listening competency in the workplace: A model for training. *Business Communication Quarterly, 60,* 75–84.

Cooper, L. O., & Buchanan, T. (1999). Interrater agreement in judgments of listening competency: An item-based analysis of the Organizational Listening Survey. *Communication Research Reports, 16,* 48–54.

Cooper, L. O., & Buchanan, T. (2003). Taking aim at good targets: Inter-rater agreement of listening competency. *International Journal of Listening, 17,* 88–112.

Corman, S. R. (2004). Postpositivism. In S. May & D. K. Mumby (Eds.), *Engaging organizational communication: Theory and research* (pp. 15–34). Thousand Oaks, CA: Sage.

Corman, S. R., & Poole, M. S. (Eds.) (2000). *Perspectives on organizational communication: Finding common ground.* New York: Guilford.

Cupach, W. R., & Spitzberg B. H. (2007). *The dark side of interpersonal communication* (2nd ed.). Mahwah, NJ: Erlbaum.

Dollar, N. J., & Merrigan, G. M. (2002). Ethnographic practices in group communication research. In L. R. Frey (Ed.), *New directions in group communication* (pp. 59–78). Thousand Oaks, CA: Sage.

Downs, C. W. (1994). Organizational identification questionnaire. In R. B. Rubin, P. Palmgreen, & H. E. Sypher (Eds.), *Communication research measures: A sourcebook* (pp. 268–271). New York: Guilford.

Downs, C. W., DeWine, S., & Greenbaum, H. H. (1994). Measures of organizational communication. In R. B. Rubin, P. Palmgreen, & H. E. Sypher (Eds.), *Communication research measures: A sourcebook* (pp. 57–78). New York: Guilford.

Ellis, K. & Shockley-Zalabak, P. (2001). Trust in top management and immediate supervisor: The relationship to satisfaction, perceived organizational effectiveness, and information receiving. *Communication Quarterly, 49,* 382–398.

Fairhurst, G. T., & Putnam, L. L. (1999). Reflections on the organization-communication equivalency question: The contributions of James Taylor and his colleagues. *Communication Review, 31,* 1–19.

Fairhurst, G. T., & Putnam, L. L. (2004). Organizations as discursive constructions. *Communication Theory, 14,* 5–26.

Fields, D. L. (2002). *Taking the measure of work: A guide to validated scales for organizational research and diagnosis.* Thousand Oaks, CA: Sage.

Fontenot, J. C., & Scott, C. R. (2007, May). *Toward a communication-based measure of organizational identification: Development and validation of the C-OI.* Paper presented at the annual meeting of the International Communication Association. San Francisco.

Frey, L. R. (Ed.). (1994). *Group communication in context: Studies of natural groups.* Hillsdale, NJ: Erlbaum.

Gouran, D. S. (1999). Communication in groups: The emergence and evolution of a field of study. In L. R. Frey, D. S. Gouran, & M. S. Poole (Eds.), *The handbook of group communication theory and research* (pp. 3–36). Thousand Oaks, CA: Sage.

Greenbaum, H., & Gardner, D. (1985, August). *Location, evaluation, and selection of questionnaires for organizational communication research.* Paper presented at the annual meeting of the Academy of Management. Boston.

Harden Fritz, J. M. (2002). How do I dislike thee? Let me count the ways: Constructing impressions of troublesome others at work. *Management Communication Quarterly, 15,* 410–438.

Henry, K. B., Arrow, H., & Carini, B. (1999). A tripartite model of group identification: Theory and measurement. *Small Group Research, 30,* 558–581.

Hochschild, A. R. (1983). *The managed heart: Commercialization of human feeling.* Berkeley: University of California Press.

Hoyle, R. H., & Crawford, A. M. (1994). Use of individual-level data to investigate group phenomena: Issues and strategies. *Small Group Research, 25,* 464–485.

Hubbell, A., & Chory-Assad, R. (2005). Motivating factors: Perceptions of justice and their relationship with managerial and organizational trust. *Communication Studies, 56,* 47–70.

Jablin, F. M. (2001). Organizational entry, assimilation, and exit. In F. M. Jablin & L. L. Putnam (Eds.), *The new handbook of organizational communication: Advances in theory, research, and methods* (pp. 732–818). Thousand Oaks, CA: Sage.

Jablin, F. M., & Kramer, M. W. (1998). Communication-related sense-making and adjustment during job transfers. *Management Communication Quarterly, 12,* 155–182.

Jian, G., & Jeffres, L. W. (2006). Understanding employees' willingness to contribute to shared electronic databases: A three-dimensional framework. *Communication Research, 33,* 242–261.

Johnson, J. D. (1997). A framework for interaction (FINT) scale: Extensions and refinement in an industrial setting. *Communication Studies, 48,* 127–141.

Johnson, W. L., Johnson, A. M., & Heimberg, F. (1999). A primary- and secondary-order component analysis of the Organizational Identification Questionnaire. *Educational and Psychological Measurement, 59,* 159–170.

Jorgensen, J. D., & Petelle, J. L. (1992). Measuring uncertainty within organizational relationships: An analysis of the CLUES instrument. *Management Communication Quarterly, 6,* 180–203.

Kassing, J. W. (1998). Development and validation of the organizational dissent scale. *Management Communication Quarterly, 12,* 183–229.

Kassing, J. W. (2000). Investigating the relationship between superior-subordinate relationship quality and employee dissent. *Communication Research Reports, 17,* 58–70.

Keyton, J. (1999). Relational communication in groups. In L. R. Frey, D. S. Gouran & M. S. Poole (Eds.), *The handbook of group communication theory and research* (pp. 192–222). Thousand Oaks, CA: Sage.

Kramer, M. W. (1993). Communication after job transfers: social exchange processes in learning new roles. *Human Communication Research, 20,* 147–174.

Kramer, M. W. (1994). Uncertainty reduction during job transitions: An exploratory study of the communication experiences of newcomers and transferees. *Management Communication Quarterly, 7,* 384–412.

Kramer, M. W., Callister, R. R., & Turban, D. B. (1991). Information-receiving and information-giving during job transitions. *Western Journal of Communication, 59,* 151–170.

Kruml, S. M., & Geddes, D. (2000). Exploring the dimensions of emotional labor: The heart of Hochschild's work. *Management Communication Quarterly, 14,* 8–49.

Kuhn, T., & Nelson, N. (2002). Reengineering identity: A case study of multiplicity and duality in organizational identification. *Management Communication Quarterly, 16,* 5–38.

Larkey, L. K. (1996). The development and validation of the workforce diversity questionnaire: An instrument to assess interactions in diverse workgroups. *Management Communication Quarterly, 9,* 296–337.

Lee, J. (1998). Effective maintenance communication in superior-subordinate relationships. *Western Journal of Communication, 62,* 181–208.

Lee, J. (2001). Leader-member exchange, perceived organizational justice, and cooperative communication. *Management Communication Quarterly, 14,* 574–589.

Lee, J., & Jablin, F. M. (1995). Maintenance communication in superior-subordinate work relationships. *Human Communication Research, 22,* 220–257.

Lester, S. W., Meglino, B. M., & Korsgaard, M. A. (2002). The antecedents and consequences of group potency: A longitudinal investigation of newly formed work groups. *Academy of Management Journal, 45,* 352–368.

Levine, T. R., Bresnahan, M. J., Park, H. S., Lapinski, M. K., Wittenbam, G. W., Shearman, S. M., Lee, S. Y., Chung, D., Ohashi, D. (2003). Self-construal scales lack validity. *Human Communication Research, 29,* 210–252.

Lewis, L. K., & Seibold, D. R. (1996). Communication during intraorganizational innovation adoption: Predicting users' behavioral coping responses to innovations in organizations. *Communication Monographs, 63,* 131–157.

McCroskey, J. C., Richmond, V. P., Johnson, A. D., & Smith, H. T. (2004). Organizational orientations theory and measurement: Development of measures and preliminary investigations. *Communication Quarterly, 52,* 1–14.

Miller, K. I. (2000). Common ground from the post-positivist perspective: From "straw-person" argument to collaborative research. In S. R. Corman & M. S.

Poole (Eds.), *Perspectives on organizational communication: Finding common ground* (pp. 46–67). New York: Guilford.

Miller, K. I. (2001). Quantitative research methods. In F. M. Jablin & L. L. Putnam (Eds.), *The new handbook of organizational communication: Advances in theory, research, and methods* (pp. 137–160). Thousand Oaks, CA: Sage.

Miller, V. D. (1996). An experimental study of newcomers' information seeking behaviors during organizational entry. *Communication Studies, 47,* 1–24.

Miller, V. D., Allen, M., Casey, M. K., & Johnson, J. R. (2000). Reconsidering the organizational identification questionnaire. *Management Communication Quarterly, 13,* 626–658.

Miller, V. D., Hart, Z., Dibble, J., Harden Fritz, J. (2005, October). *Organizational socialization and the measurement of process.* Paper presented at the annual meeting of the National Communication Association. Boston.

Miller, V. D., & Jablin, F. M. (1991). Information seeking during organizational entry: Influences, tactics and a model of the process. *Academy of Management Review, 16,* 92–120.

Miller, V. D., Johnson, J. R., & Grau, J. (1994). Antecedents to willingness to participate in a planned organizational change. *Journal of Applied Communication Research, 22,* 59–80.

Morrill, C., & Thomas, C. K. (1992). Organizational conflict management as disputing process: The problem of social escalation. *Human Communication Research, 18,* 400–428.

Mumby, D. K. (2000). Common ground from the critical perspective: Overcoming binary oppositions. In S. R. Corman & M. S. Poole (Eds.), *Perspectives on organizational communication: Finding common ground* (pp. 68–86). New York: Guilford.

Myers, K. K. (2005). A burning desire: Assimilation into a fire department. *Management Communication Quarterly, 18,* 344–384.

Myers, K. K., & McPhee, R. D. (2006). Influences on member assimilation in workgroups in high-reliability organizations: A multilevel analysis. *Human Communication Research, 32,* 440–468.

Myers, K. K., & Oetzel, J. G. (2003). Exploring the dimensions of organizational assimilation: Creating and validating a measure. *Communication Quarterly, 51*(4), 438–457.

Myers, S. A. (1998). GTAs as organizational newcomers: The association between supportive communication relationships and information seeking. *Western Journal of Communication, 60,* 54–73.

Poole, M. S. (1994). Breaking the isolation of small group communication studies. *Communication Studies, 45,* 20–28.

Poole. M. S. (1998). The small group should be *the* fundamental unit of communication research. In J. S. Trent (Ed.), *Communication: Views from the helm for the twenty-first century* (pp. 94–97). Needham Heights, MA: Allyn & Bacon.

Poole, M. S., & Hollingshead, A. B. (2005). *Theories of small groups: Interdisciplinary perspectives.* Thousand Oaks, CA: Sage.

Poole, M. S., Keyton, J., & Frey, L. R. (1999). Group communication methodology: Issues and considerations. In L. R. Frey, D. S. Gouran, & M. S. Poole (Eds.), *The handbook of group communication theory and research* (pp. 92–112). Thousand Oaks, CA: Sage.

Putnam, L. L., & Pacanowsky, M. (Eds.) (1983). *Communication and organizations: An interpretive approach*. Beverly Hills, CA: Sage.

Redding, W. C., & Tompkins, P. K. (1988). Organizational communication—past and present tenses. In G. M. Goldhaber & G. A. Barnett (Eds.), *Handbook of organizational communication* (pp. 5–33). Norwood, NJ: Ablex.

Riddle, B. L., Anderson, C. M., & Martin, M. M. (2000). Small group socialization scale: Development and validity. *Small Group Research, 31,* 554–572.

Rodrick, R., & Knox, R. L. (2002). Information seeking among organizational members. *Communication Research Reports, 19,* 372–379.

Rubin, R. B., Palmgreen, P., & Sypher, H. E. (1994). *Communication research measures: A sourcebook*. New York: Guilford.

Russo, T. C. (1998). Organizational and professional identification: A case of newspaper journalists. *Management Communication Quarterly, 12,* 72–111.

Sass, J. S., & Canary, D. J. (1991). Organizational commitment and identification: An examination of conceptual and operational convergence. *Western Journal of Speech Communication, 55,* 275–293.

Schrodt, P. (2002). The relationship between organizational identification and organizational culture: Employee perceptions of culture and identification in a retail sales organization. *Communication Studies, 53,* 189–202.

Scott, C. R. (1997). Identification with multiple targets in a geographically dispersed organization. *Management Communication Quarterly, 10,* 491–522.

Scott, C. R. (2007). Communication and social identity theory: Existing and potential connections in organizational identification research. *Communication Studies, 58,* 123–138.

Scott, C. R., Connaughton, S. L., Diaz-Saenz, H. R., Maguire, K., Ramirez, R., Richardson, B., Shaw, S. P., Morgan, D. (1999). The impacts of communication and multiple identifications on intent to leave: A multimethodological exploration. *Management Communication Quarterly, 12,* 400–435.

Scott, C. R., Corman, S. R., & Cheney, G. (1998). Development of a structurational model of identification. *Communication Theory, 8,* 298–336.

Scott, C. W., & Myers, K. K. (2005). The emotions of socialization and assimilation: Learning emotion management at the fire station. *Journal of Applied Communication Research, 33,* 67–92.

Seibold, D. R. (1995). *Theoria* and *praxis*: Means and ends in applied communication research. In K. Cissna (Ed.), *Applied communication in the 21st century* (pp. 23–38). Hillsdale, NJ: Erlbaum.

Seibold, D. R. (2000). Applied communication scholarship: Less a matter of boundaries than of emphases. *Journal of Applied Communication Research, 28,* 183–187.

Seibold, D. R. (2005). Bridging theory and practice in organizational communication. In J. L. Simpson & P. Shockley-Zalabak (Eds.), *Engaging communication, transforming organizations: Scholarship of engagement in action* (pp. 13–44). Cresskill, NJ: Hampton.

Seibold, D. R. (2008). Applied communication research. In W. Donsbach (Ed.), *The international encyclopedia of communication* (Vol. 1, pp. 189–194). Malden, MA: Wiley-Blackwell.

Sias, P. M., Kramer, M. W., & Jenkins, E. (1997). A comparison of the communication behaviors of temporary employees and new hires. *Communication Research, 24,* 731–754.

Simpson, J. L., & Shockley-Zalabak, P. (Eds.) (2005). *Engaging communication, transforming organizations: Scholarship of engagement in action.* Cresskill, NJ: Hampton.

Taggar, S., & Brown, T. C. (2001). Problem-solving team behaviors: Development and validation of BOS and a hierarchical factor structure. *Small Group Research, 32,* 698–726.

Taylor, J. R., Flanagin, A. J., Cheney, G., & Seibold, D. R. (2000). Organizational communication research: Key moments, central concerns, and future challenges. *Communication Yearbook, 24,* 99–137.

Teboul, J. B. (1995). Determinants of new hire information-seeking during organizational encounter. *Western Journal of Communication, 59,* 305–325.

Tracy, S. J. (2005). Locking up emotions: Moving beyond dissonance for understanding emotion labor discomfort. *Communication Monographs, 72,* 261–283.

Wanous, J. P., Reichers, A. E., & Austin, J. T. (2000). Cynicism about organizational change: Measurement, antecedents, and correlates. *Group & Organization Management, 25,* 132–153.

Wekselberg, V., Goggin, W.C., & Collings, T. J. (1997). A multifaceted concept of group maturity and its measurement and relationship to group performance. *Small Group Research, 28,* 3–28.

Welbourne, T. M., Johnson, D. E., & Erez, A. (1998). The role-based performance scale: Validity analysis of a theory-based measure. *Academy of Management Journal, 41,* 540–555.

Wheelan, S. A. (1994). *Group processes: A developmental perspective.* Needham Heights, MA: Allyn & Bacon.

Wheelan, S. A. (Ed.) (2005). *The handbook of group research and practice.* Thousand Oaks, CA: Sage.

Wheelan, S. A., & Hochberger, J. (1996). Validation studies of the group development questionnaire. *Small Group Research, 26,*143–170.

Wheelan, S. A., & Williams, T. (2003). Mapping dynamic interaction patterns in work groups. *Small Group Research, 34,* 443–467.

Wolfe Morrison, E. (1995). Information usefulness and acquisition during organizational encounter. *Management Communication Quarterly, 9,* 131–155.

Measurement in Health Communication

Nichole Egbert and Rebecca B. Rubin

The founding of the field of Health Communication can be traced to two events in the 1970s: the launching of the first collaborative effort joining medical and communication researchers (the Stanford Heart Disease Prevention Program) and the establishment of the International Communication Association's Division of Health Communication in 1975 (Ratzan, Payne, & Bishop, 1996; Rogers, 1996). Many Communication researchers gravitated to this "applied" area, bringing with them theoretical approaches and validated methodologies. Some interpersonal researchers examined individual relationships between and among health providers (e.g., doctors, nurses, aides) and their patients (and family members). Media campaigners focused on persuasion strategies used or useful in increasing healthful living practices (e.g., smoking cessation, driving sober, not taking drugs, safe sex). In the past 30 years, Health Communication has become an important area of study, accumulating a substantial body of research and becoming one of the most promising areas for Communication researchers to secure funding for their projects.

Provider–Patient Communication

Despite the connection to health promotion campaigns such as the Stanford Heart Disease Prevention Program, a majority of early health communication research has investigated provider–patient communication (Thompson, 2003). Initially, most researchers focused on developing tools and interventions to improve the communication skills of health care providers. Studies typically centered on training primary physicians to improve their ability to build rapport, provide information, elicit patient concerns, break bad news, etc. (see Cegala & Lenzmeier Broz [2002], for a summary of recent studies on health care provider training). This line of

Note: Measures that are profiled in this volume (in Part II) are typed in capital letters when cited in the text.

research paralleled studies of communication competence in the interpersonal and instructional communication literature.

Common means of assessing provider skills in training programs include analyzing videotaped interactions with the aid of an interaction analysis system (IAS). In reviewing literature related to doctor–patient communication, Ong, de Haes, Hoos, and Lammes (1995) defined IAS as "the methodic identification, categorization and quantification of salient features of doctor–patient communications" (p. 905). These quantitative coding systems categorize utterances into categories based on content, form, and function (see Ong et al. for a review). Because of the length of instructions for most coding systems, they are beyond the scope of this present volume.

In the provider–patient area, the most common outcome (i.e., dependent) variable linked with doctor–patient communication has been patient satisfaction (e.g., Evans, Stanley, & Burrows, 1992). In addition, patient recall, understanding, and compliance are also outcomes that were—and still are—related to provider communication skill (Ong et al., 1995). These outcomes typically are assessed using self-report measures that are not unique to health communication. Indeed, many have roots in the area of interpersonal communication satisfaction (Hecht, 1978), resulting in instruments designed specifically for physicians and patients (Buller & Buller, 1987; Burgoon, Birk, & Hall, 1991).

Although professional health care providers have been the predominant target for most skills-based interventions, more recently patients' need for better communication skills has also been highlighted. Most notably, the work of Cegala and colleagues has centered on improving patients' abilities to ask questions and provide information. With the MEDICAL COMMUNICATION COMPETENCE SCALE, both physicians and patients rate themselves and each other on information giving, information seeking, information verifying, and socioemotional communication (Cegala, Coleman, & Turner, 1998). Self-assessments help both groups evaluate their strengths and weaknesses in this interpersonal interaction.

Also important in the provider–patient relationship is the ability of patients to communicate assertively. Patients need to seek useful information and help evaluate treatments based on effectiveness. In addition, as consumers and advocates for their health treatment, patients need to be able to ask questions, express opinions, and reject risky or ineffective treatment regimens. The PATIENT SELF-ADVOCACY SCALE provides a valid and reliable measure of patient health involvement (Brashers, Haas, & Neidig, 1999).

Patient compliance (now often referred to as patient adherence) is an outcome of interest to clinicians and researchers alike. Although indices of actual behavior are preferable, it is common for researchers to rely on measures of patients' reported behavior. For example, researchers have measured adherence (reported behaviors) by asking patients how many medication doses they missed (Schillinger, Wang, Rodriguez, Bindman, & Machtinger, 2006), what types of sun-protective behaviors they perform (Buller et al., 2000), or how often they obtained cancer screenings, such as a Pap test (Ramirez et al., 1999) or a mammogram (Derose, Fox, Reigadas, & Hawes-Dawson, 2000). When these reports of behaviors can be substantiated in some way, the validity of the compliance measure is enhanced, such as in the study by Clarke, Evans, Shook, and Johanson (2005), who were able to verify if seniors actually completed an advance directive as they had reported they had.

Another important interpersonal construct has been social support. With the development of measure such as the Inventory of Socially Supportive Behaviors, patients can provide an assessment of how much support they receive (Barrera, Sandler, & Ramsay, 1981; Stokes & Wilson, 1984). This construct is especially important for health care providers and has been found to be related to health/illness outcomes (Kelly, Soderlund, Albert, & McGarrahan, 1999). (See House, Kahn, McLeod & Williams [1985] and Tardy [1985] for reviews of additional social support measures.)

Health Communication Campaigns

Just as research in provider–patient communication has relied heavily on constructs and measures of interpersonal communication (like communication competence in skills training of physicians and communication satisfaction of patients), research focusing on health communication campaigns has borrowed from theories and strategies used by media and persuasion scholars. Salmon and Atkin (2003) noted that the features of effective campaigns are relatively stable despite their contexts. Thus, health communication campaigners make use of strategies and instruments that offer assistance in audience segmentation, message design, and program evaluation.

One of the most promising avenues in this arena has been the development of the RISK BEHAVIOR DIAGNOSIS SCALE, which is based on the Extended Parallel Process Model (a fear appeal theory) (Witte, Cameron, McKeon, & Berkowitz, 1996). This instrument helps researchers determine the type of message most appropriate for a particular individual or audience to promote motivation for healthy behavior. Rather than have messages backfire, practitioners can craft messages that will point out the risk of engaging in or continuing behaviors that can be harmful.

Similarly, some audiences engage in risk-related behaviors because of sensation seeking personality traits. Drug abuse, unprotected sex, and similar risky behaviors can be prevented with messages that are structured to the audience members' predispositions. The PERCEIVED MESSAGE

SENSATION VALUE SCALE was developed to help assess the sensation value of the advertisement or television program designed to curtail such behavior (Palmgreen, Stephenson, Everett, Baseheart, & Francies, 2002). Once again, focus is on the message and how the message might affect the intended audience.

Conclusions and Observations

At first glance, researchers may find it puzzling that the field of health communication lacks a larger body of standardized measures and instruments. Although a review of the instrumentation commonly used in health communication reveals only a handful of well-recognized communication measures, the reasons for this deficiency are related to the nature of the discipline itself. The applied nature of health communication makes it likely that researchers will borrow theories, measures, and concepts from other areas—both from within Communication Studies and from other disciplines.

On the other hand, designing one's own instruments for specific health-related issues in specific target populations is another common practice among Health Communication researchers. Oftentimes, the problem and/or the population require that the measurement be specialized, and standard measurement templates either do not exist or do not suffice. Thus, researchers conduct qualitative, formative research to assess the culture-specific variables of interest. Tailored, quantitative instruments resulting from these efforts are more likely to be successful in affecting the applied problem in question than are those that are adapted from other populations. Thus, what results is an array of diverse types of measures that are rarely subjected to multiple studies of reliability or validity.

Another common practice in Health Communication that contributes to the non-cohesive body of measurement is the practice of utilizing large population-based data sets, such as the Health Information National Trends Survey (HINTS). These data sets typically do not include many items related to communication, much less established measures of Communication constructs. HINTS was an unusual case, for it focused on information seeking practices related to cancer, thus was especially appropriate for Health Communication research (see the special issue of *Journal of Health Communication*, volume 11, supplement 1, 2006). More often, these national surveys include only a smattering of communication or information-related items, but because of the representativeness of the sample, many researchers see value in creating ad hoc or one-item measures that may shed light on communication processes as they relate to important health issues.

Studying communication processes in applied problems becomes additionally problematic when the audience for the subsequent findings is multifocal. For example, when communication researchers study medical issues, the objective is often to demonstrate to clinicians how the processes affect specific health outcomes. Thus, measurement in these projects takes on a clinical nature. In these cases, Health Communication researchers must consider the use of established clinical screening tools (such as screening for depression) and medical and psychological measures that assess health variables (such as body mass index). Health Communication researchers understand that this focus on physical outcomes is necessary if their work is to be recognized by health care organizations and providers who are intent on "bottom-line" outcomes.

In a related vein, funding agencies stress the importance of "bottom-line" outcomes such as disease prevalence, patient adherence, and rates of morbidity or mortality. Thus, for Health Communication researchers to receive grants to explore the role of communication in these important outcomes, interdisciplinary teamwork is essential. Especially in large-scale initiatives, collaborative partnerships include teams of clinicians, public health officers, community organizations, as well as researchers from multiple disciplines (such as psychology, nursing, and health education, to name a few). This collaboration requires that the teams build a common vocabulary and understanding of the nature of the health issue. Often, the measurement that is ultimately used in these projects is either a long-standing instrument that is accepted in many different disciplines (such as the MOS Health Perception Scale), or, as mentioned earlier, an instrument that is customized for the specific project. Measures that are not as well-known or as trusted by the diverse groups of individuals who make funding decisions are used less frequently.

References

Barrera, M., Jr., Sandler, I. N., & Ramsay, T. B. (1981). Preliminary development of a scale of social support: Studies on college students. *American Journal of Community Psychology, 9*, 435–447.

Brashers, D. E., Haas, S. M., & Neidig, J. L. (1999). The Patient Self-Advocacy Scale: Measuring patient involvement in health care decision-making interactions. *Health Communication, 11*, 97–121.

Buller, M. K., & Buller, D. B. (1987). Physicians' communication style and patient satisfaction. *Journal of Health and Social Behavior, 28*, 375–388.

Buller, D. B., Burgoon, M., Hall, J. R., Levine, N., Taylor, A. M., Beach, B., Buller, M. K., & Melcher, C. (2000). Long-term effects of language intensity in preventive messages on planned family solar protection. *Health Communication, 12*, 261–275.

Burgoon, M., Birk, T. S., & Hall, J. R. (1991). Compliance and satisfaction with physician-patient communication: An expectancy theory interpretation of gender differences. *Human Communication Research, 18*, 177–208.

Cegala, D. J., Coleman, M. T., & Turner, J. W. (1998). The development and partial assessment of the Medical Communication Competence Scale. *Health Communication, 10*, 261–288.

Cegala, D. J., & Lenzmeier Broz, S. (2002). Physician communication skills training: A review of theoretical backgrounds, objectives and skills. *Medical Education, 36*, 1004–1016.

Clarke, P., Evans, S. H., Shook, D., & Johanson, W. (2005). Information seeking and compliance in planning for critical care: Community-based health outreach to seniors about advance directives. *Health Communication, 18*, 1–22.

Derose, K. P., Fox, S. A., Reigadas, E., & Hawes-Dawson, J. (2000). Church-based telephone mammography counseling with peer counselors. *Journal of Health Communication, 5*, 175–188.

Evans, B. J., Stanley, R. O., & Burrows, G. D. (1992). Communication skills training and patients' satisfaction. *Health Communication, 4*, 155–170.

Hecht, M. L. (1978). The conceptualization and measurement of interpersonal communication satisfaction. *Human Communication Research, 4*, 253–264.

House, J. S., Kahn, R. L., McLeod, J. D., & Williams, D. (1985). Measures and concepts of social support. In S. Cohen & S. L. Syme (Eds.), *Social support and health* (pp. 83–108). Orlando, FL: Academic Press.

Journal of Health Communication (Volume 11, Supplement 1). (2006). Philadelphia: Taylor & Francis.

Kelly, K. S., Soderlund, K., Albert, C., & McGarrahan, A. G. (1999). Social support and chronic fatigue syndrome. *Health Communication, 11*, 21–34.

Ong, L. M. L., de Haes, J .C. J. M., Hoos, A. M., & Lammes, F. B. (1995). Doctor-patient communication: A review of the literature. *Social Science & Medicine, 40*, 903–918.

Palmgreen, P., Stephenson, M. T., Everett, M. W., Baseheart, J. R., & Francies, R. (2002). Perceived message Sensation Value (PMSV) and the dimensions and validation of a PMSV Scale. *Health Communication, 14*, 403–428.

Ramirez, A. G., Villarreal, R., Mcalister, A., Gallion, K. J., Suarez, L., & Gomez, P. (1999). Advancing the role of participatory communication in the diffusion of cancer screening among Hispanics. *Journal of Health Communication, 4*, 31–36.

Ratzan, S. C., Payne, J. G., & Bishop, C. (1996). The status and scope of health communication. *Journal of Health Communication, 1*, 25–41.

Rogers, E. M. (1996). The field of health communication today: An up-to-date report. *Journal of Health Communication, 1*, 15–23.

Salmon, C. T., & Atkin, C. (2003). Using media campaigns for health promotion. In T. L. Thompson, A. M. Dorsey, K. I. Miller, & R. Parrott (Eds.), *Handbook of Health Communication* (pp. 449–472). Mahwah, NJ: Erlbaum.

Schillinger, D., Wang, F., Rodriguez, M., Bindman, A., & Machtinger, E. L. (2006). The importance of establishing regimen concordance in preventing medication errors in anticoagulant care. *Journal of Health Communication, 11*, 555–567.

Stokes, J. P., & Wilson, D. G. (1984). The Inventory of Socially Supportive Behaviors: Dimensionality, prediction, and gender differences. *American Journal of Community Psychology, 12*, 53–69.

Tardy, C. H. (1985). Social support measurement. *American Journal of Community Psychology, 13*, 187–202.

Thompson, T. L. (2003). Introduction. In T. L. Thompson, A. M. Dorsey, K. I. Miller, & R. Parrott (Eds.), *Handbook of health communication* (pp. 1–5). Mahwah, NJ: Erlbaum.

Witte, K., Cameron, K. A., McKeon, J. K., & Berkowitz, J. M. (1996). Predicting risk behaviors: Development and validation of a diagnostic scale. *Journal of Health Communication*, 1, 317–341.

Measurement in Instructional Communication

Rebecca B. Rubin

In the first volume of *Communication Research Measures: A Sourcebook* (Rubin, Palmgreen, & Sypher, 1994), Pat Kearney and Michael Beatty (1994) reviewed almost 100 instructional measures that had been used in communication research and categorized them into five main themes: Learning outcomes, teacher behaviors and characteristics, student behaviors and characteristics, communication skills assessment, and measures of communication apprehension. In the past 10+ years, we have seen advances in all of these categories. To provide continuity with Volume I, I'll review new and promising instructional measures in each of these categories as well as identify issues that have arisen over the years.

Learning Outcomes

The measurement of learning in communication research has been problematic (Witt, Wheeless, & Allen, 2004). Ever since Bloom's (1956) tripartite conceptualization of learning as affective, cognitive, or psychomotor, researchers have been searching for valid and reliable ways of measuring learning. As Kearney and Beatty discussed in 1994, learning has mainly been measured through the use of Janis Andersen's Affective Learning Scale, developed in 1979 (see Kearney, Plax, & Wendt-Wasco, 1985). Affective learning basically refers to how much students like the teacher and class. Recent studies have continued to use this instrument and versions of it (Banfield et al., 2006; Pogue & Ah Yun, 2006; Witt & Wheeless, 2001; Zhang & Oetzel, 2006).

An underlying assumption of affective learning—that students learn more from teachers that they like—undergirds the research using such instruments. Very likely this is true, but in some cases students might like teachers who do not enforce learning values in the classroom and dislike those who do not, resulting in unreliable and invalid measurement.

Note: Measures that are profiled in this volume (in Part II) are typed in capital letters when cited in the text.

Cognitive and psychomotor learning are options for future measurement development.

Cognitive learning has been conceived as having six levels: knowledge, comprehension, application, analysis, synthesis, and evaluation (Bloom, 1956). Grades are often used as a measure of cognitive learning; however, factors other than knowledge sometimes are computed into grades (e.g., effort, attendance, anxiety, tardiness). Thus, validity becomes questionable. Occasionally, researchers create a "knowledge test" for a particular course (e.g., Mottet & Beebe, 2006) to focus on one specific learning environment. Allen et al. (2004) in their meta-analysis of student learning measures reported that most indicators of learning (in which distance is compared to classroom) have used exam scores and course grades. However, some studies have dealt with satisfaction (Allen et al., 2002), finding lower satisfaction with the distance format of education than with the traditional classroom format; satisfaction clearly is an affective learning measure.

One standard self-report measure of cognitive learning has been the "Learning Loss" measure (Richmond, McCroskey, Kearney, & Plax, 1987). It is based on two questions, with one item subtracted from the other: "How much did you learn in this class? How much do you think you could have learned in the class had you had an ideal instructor?" Even though the reliability and validity of the scale have been hard to assess, it has been useful for tapping students' perceptions of their classroom learning (see Chesebro & McCroskey, 2000, 2001; Titsworth, 2001; Witt & Wheeless, 2001). Some researchers have viewed this measure as more of an affective learning measure because it does not involve actual grades or tests of learning, however Chesebro and McCroskey (2000) (in a larger study involving immediacy) found that a short test of knowledge and learning loss were correlated at .50. Bensur (2001) argued that the 2-item learning loss measure is valid, and that it can't be reduced to one item. Witt et al. (2004) confirmed that correlations between immediacy and "perceived learning" were similar to those for immediacy and affective learning; correlations between immediacy and cognitive learning were significantly lower. This meta-analysis emphasized the need to measure cognitive learning in a more rigorous manner.

Within the last decade, Frymier and Houser (1999) developed a REVISED LEARNING INDICATORS SCALE, which taps the degree to which students like, think about, and talk about their classes with others. It too has an element of affective learning, in that most of the items ask about thoughts about the class rather than assessing how much is actually learned, but the items refer mainly to cognitive processes about the class and how often they occur. The 7th item—"I feel I have learned a lot in this class"—directly assesses perceptions of knowledge gained. Because single-item indicators are inherently unreliable, the aggregate of the seven items is a more stable measure of learning than the 7th item alone.

Psychomotor learning might best be understood as changes in actions producing improved skill. Musicians, dancers, singers, actors, athletes, and others work on refining actions that produce accurate, economic, or reliable behaviors over time. In communication, psychomotor learning might easily translate to behavioral learning, so that we might see improved interpersonal communication skills (see Spitzberg, 2007), better public speaking performances (see Morreale, Moore, Taylor, Surges-Tatus, & Hulbert-Johnson, 2007), or group interactions that lead to better group outcomes (see Beebe, Barge, & McCormick, 1995). However these behaviors are difficult to measure, given the lack of standard observational rating forms and the inherent unreliability of raters (see Rubin, 1994). This sort of learning also needs to be assessed over time, so demands on researchers to make multiple observations are often too great to overcome (Rubin, Graham, & Mignerey, 1990). Single observations produce snapshots of the moment rather than the learning process, better reflected in increases over time (see Rubin, Welch, & Buerkel, 1995). Consequently, most of the research in communication has used survey methods rather than experimental designs, and researchers have developed mainly self-report measures of affective, cognitive, and psychomotor learning.

Teacher Behaviors and Characteristics

As Kearney and Beatty (1994) noted, teacher behaviors and characteristics continue to be a major independent variable in instructional research. Much of learning—the main instructional dependent variable—can be traced to how teachers act in the classroom. Much of the early research focused on interpersonal communicator style characteristics such as friendliness, attentiveness, openness, and argumentativeness. Two style variables—assertiveness and responsiveness—have emerged as main elements of style, due mainly to the prolific use of the teacher SOCIO-COMMUNICATIVE STYLE measure (McCroskey & Richmond, 1996; Richmond & McCroskey, 1990) in recent instructional communication research (Aylor & Oppliger, 2003; Myers, Martin, & Mottet, 2002). Scores on this measure are often used to partition teachers into four style groups (competents, incompetents, submissives, and aggressives), which are then compared on dependent variables such as student motivation or perceptions of credibility (Martin, Mottet, & Chesebro, 1997).

Additional measures focus on teacher actions in the classroom—such as teacher humor, teacher anger, teacher concern, and affinity-seeking—which are seen as prosocial or antisocial behaviors that should influence student learning. Recent prosocial behaviors of interest include (a) teacher affinity-seeking (Dolin, 1995), or what teachers do to try to get students to like them, (b) teacher communication concern (Feezel & Myers, 1997) or how teachers (in this case, graduate teaching assistants) show students that they are interested in and concerned with their welfare, and (c) teacher use of humor, a style variable focused on instructors' use of humor in lectures and classroom interaction. Antisocial behaviors of recent interest have included teacher misbehaviors such as straying from subject, unfair testing, boring lectures, sarcasm/putdowns, and being absent from class (Kearney, Plax, Hays, & Ivey, 1991; McPherson, Kearney, & Plax, 2006), and teacher use of anger in the classroom (McPherson, Kearney, & Plax, 2003). The TEACHER MISBEHAVIORS SCALE concentrates on these antisocial behaviors and how they affect learning.

Other measures include aspects of interaction between teachers and students. For instance, Ellis (2000) developed a measure of PERCEIVED TEACHER CONFIRMATION which has good reliability and validity (Turman & Schrodt, 2006). Students report on various behaviors that teachers can use in the classroom to validate a student's worth, show interest in students and their learning, and use proactive responses to student questions or comments. This measure truly gets at the interactive nature of classroom behavior from a student's point of view.

Roach (1995) developed a PERCEIVED POWER MEASURE which was based on French and Raven's (1959) five main dimensions: Legitimate, Reward, Punishment, Expert, and Referent. Teacher power is another perception that students make about their teachers based on the frequency of various powerful actions in the classroom.

Several studies have directed their attention away from classroom interaction to out-of-class communication between teachers and students. In 1994, Fusani (JACR) discussed a new concept, then termed *extra-class communication*. Jaasma and Koper (1999) limited formal OCC to office visits, and Aylor and Oppliger (2003) extended this definition to include other interaction as well. Nadler and Nadler (2000) defined OCC as student-faculty interactions that take place outside the classroom, including: advising, discussions about class or non-class issues, or faculty participation in student functions. Frymier (2005) used three items based on this definition, dealing with frequency of contact, which ranged from 0 (never) to 4 (6 or more times). Dobransky and Frymier (2004) extended this to 5 questions, ranging from 1 (not at all likely) to 5 (very likely) dealing with likelihood of engaging in OCC. Myers (2004; Myers, Martin, & Knapp, 2005) developed a 9-item, 5-point scale that had an alpha reliability of .80, finding that students indicating more interaction found their instructors to be more credible (competent, caring). Waldeck, Kearney, and Plax (2001) extended this to the use of email outside of class and developed a Teacher E-mail Interaction Proficiency Scale, used to see how student willingness to communicate online relates to teacher proficiency. All in all, out-of-class communication has been of interest to many instructional researchers, but one measure has failed to rise to prominence in the research.

Student Behaviors and Characteristics

Several teacher behavior lines of research are connected to the Student Behaviors and Characteristics area. In particular, several style variables have been examined as student style variables, and measures looking at interaction between teachers and students necessarily involve student behaviors as well. A third area, motives and motivation, seems to be receiving a lot of attention in recent years.

First, several characteristics of students have been hypothesized to affect their learning and performance in the classroom. Mottet and Beebe (2006) recently had teachers rate their students on a version of the SOCIO-COMMUNICATIVE STYLE measure and student verbal responsiveness (Mottet, Martin, & Myers, 2004) to see if these characteristics might affect perceptions of their speech performance (Morreale et al., 2007) or knowledge about public speaking. Other characteristics of interest have been sensitivity to feedback and punishment (see Smith & King, 2004) and student affect for the teacher (Chesebro & McCroskey, 2002; Mottet, Martin & Fleuriet, 2006).

How well students listen in class is also thought to be related to their school performance. Instead of measuring listening ability, the measures seem to be measuring listening styles (Watson, Barker, & Weaver, 1995), conversational listening (Goss, 1991), or listening fidelity (Mulanax & Powers, 2001). The Watson et al. LISTENING STYLES PROFILE-16 produces individual scores on four listening types, which are useful for self-examination or connection to other interpersonal or instructional variables (see profile in Part II for additional detail).

Motivation has been studied in two main ways: motivation to learn and motives for communication. Frymier, Schulman, and Houser (1996) developed a 35-item LEARNER EMPOWERMENT measure in 1996; empowered learners are students who are intrinsically motivated to learn and are "willing and capable to engage in work (learning)" (Frymier et al., 1996, p. 184). Weber, Martin, and Cayanus (2005) shortened it to 18 items. Others have looked at how motivated students are to achieve academically, having teachers rate their students' motivation on Chiu's (1997) School Achievement Motivation. Christophel's (1990) state and trait motivation scales have been useful in communication to examine motivation's impact on learning outcomes.

The second line of motivation research examines why students communicate in class and outside of class. Martin, Myers, and Mottet (1999, 2002) STUDENT MOTIVES TO COMMUNICATE SCALE identifies five main categories of motives: relational, functional, excuse-making, participation, and sycophancy. This measure has been used in several studies examining relationships between apprehension and motives or between motives and learning outcomes. Waldeck et al. (2001)

extended this to student motives for emailing their professors, finding three main categories: to clarify course materials and procedures, as an efficient communication channel, and for personal/social reasons.

Communication Skills Assessment

Examination of listening ability bridges the two areas (student characteristics and communication skills). One measure of listening focuses on four different styles prevalent in everyday situations. The LISTENING STYLES PROFILE-16 (Watson, 1984; Watson & Barker, 1988) has developed into a 16-item measure of action-, content-, people-, and time-oriented listeners (Watson et al., 1995). In general, research has focused on gender, cultural, or personality differences in listening rather than examining the styles in terms of learning outcomes. Other listening measures examine conversational listening (Goss, 1991) and listening fidelity (Mulanax & Powers, 2001). Goss's Conversational Listening Test contains 12 items through which people self-report on their everyday listening behaviors or style. The Listening Fidelity measure attempts to measure the congruence between what a speaker says and what a listener understands through explanation of a geometric pattern and ultimate comparing the outcome of what is heard with what was communicated. Errors could occur in the presentation as well as the reception of the message.

As noted above, not much progress has been made in the area of speaking skills assessment. Speaking skills are often assessed by trained observers (Morreale, 1994; Rubin, 1994) and training is necessary to increase reliability of raters (Mottet & Beebe, 2006). Other methods of rating speaking skills include obtaining attitudes about the speaker's attractiveness and dynamism (Zahn & Hopper, 1985) or the speakers' self-perceptions of their own competence (McCroskey & McCroskey, 1988). The former measures might lack reliability, and the latter might lack validity.

Measures of Communication Apprehension

Over the years, McCroskey's (1982) Personal Report of Communication Apprehension remains the most often used instrument in the communication discipline to measure state and trait apprehension. State apprehension occurs in one particular setting or context or at one particular time, whereas trait apprehension takes place across time and contexts.

Several research studies have included anxiety as a variable that affects learning. Spielberger's (1983; Spielberger, Gorsuch, & Lushene, 1970) State/Trait Anxiety Measures have been used in communication to look at the broader concept of anticipatory speech anxiety and how that might be influenced by the novelty of the speech assignment (see Behnke & Sawyer, 2000; Witt & Behnke, 2006; Behnke & Sawyer, 2004).

The anxiety concept has been broadened to reception processes. State Receiver Apprehension has been examined as an independent variable, influencing communication behavior (Behnke & Sawyer, 2000; Chesebro, 2003; Chesebro & McCroskey, 2004), and also as a dependent variable, influenced by psychological traits such as self-monitoring (Sawyer & Behnke, 1990). Later, Sawyer and Behnke (2002) suggested that systematic desensitization can reduce anxiety caused by public speaking situations. They also investigated how state anxiety can influence public speaking performance, especially at the beginning of the presentation (Behnke, Sawyer, & King, 1987; Sawyer & Behnke, 2002).

Another line of measurement comes from the Penn State reticence perspective. Reticence is seen as a form of social apprehension that occurs when goals are unclear or poorly planned, so skills need to be developed to reduce the anticipated anxiety about a forthcoming communication event. Keaten, Kelly, and Finch (1997) recently developed the RETICENCE SCALE to measure anxiety feelings and comfort with the five canons of rhetoric: feelings of anxiety, knowledge of communication topics, timing skills, organization of thoughts, delivery skills, and memory skills. The scale measures self-perceived inadequacies in these areas for a holistic indication of anticipated anxiety.

All in all, the area of communication apprehension—despite the measure used—continues to be one of the most productive research areas. Whether self-perceived skill deficits, psychological traits, state apprehension, or communication-focused apprehension measures are used, more than likely there is a relationship discovered with communication skill, performance, or other similar psychological self-perceptions.

Measurement Issues and Updates

In addition to the issues identified above, three additional measurement issues have arisen over the years. One deals with psychometric properties of self-report scales, another deals with changes in one instrument over time, and the third deals with the growing body of research results and what they all mean.

Order of Questions

Bline, Lowe, Meixner, Nouri, and Pearce (2001) compared two presentational orders of Daly and Miller's Writing Apprehension Scale. The original question order was compared with one in which the questions were presented randomly and the two factor structures were found to be comparable. Later, however, Bline, Low, Meixner, and Nouri (2003) compared original and randomized orders of this scale and McCroskey's Personal Report of Communication Apprehension scale and concluded that because the factor structures were weaker and the reliabilities were lower with a randomized order than with the original order, users should be concerned that order might influence the reliability and dimensionality of the instruments. It is possible that certain items influence responses on later items.

Nonverbal Immediacy

The measurement of nonverbal immediacy has evolved over the last several decades. In Volume I of this sourcebook (Rubin et al., 1994), we profiled a 14-item scale, which was later revised to 10 items in 1995 (McCroskey, Richmond, et al.) and 1996 (McCroskey, Fayer, Richmond, Sallinen, & Barraclough). This latter study looked at four cultures and reported an alpha of .81 (range of .69 to .85), and identified four items that were considered poor (involved sitting, standing, and touching) and recommended that two items be reworded to change "smiles" to "frown." A 26-item measure was created in 2003 (Richmond, McCroskey, & Johnson) and is available at http://www.jamescmccroskey.com. A short form containing 16 items for either self-report or other-report can be found in Richmond and McCroskey's (1998) book. Roach, Cornett-DeVito, and DeVito (2005) and reported an alpha of .73 with American students and .64 with French students. They found that nonverbal immediacy was significantly correlated with ratings of instruction, perceptions of the Instructor's affinity seeking, cognitive learning, and affect toward Instructor. One interesting result is that Rocca (2004) found expected correlations between two self-reported measures of attendance and NIM, but the correlation between NIM and recorded attendance was not significant. Student perceptions seem to be aligned with perceptions of teacher NI, but not with attendance reality.

McCroskey (http://www.jamescmccroskey.com) has also reported that gender differences exist with this measure and that researchers should code gender as a variable when considering research with this measure. The observer form does not produce significant differences, so it is possible that self-reports are a function of social desirability during completion.

Meta-Analysis

Mike Allen has led the way in using meta-analysis to examine effect sizes of results of large bodies of literature. Early studies examined the effectiveness of apprehension treatment protocols (Allen, Hunter, & Donohue,

1989) and communication apprehension self-report instruments (Allen & Bourhis, 1996). Interestingly, the latter study found a negative relationship between self-reported apprehension and behavior, which questions the ability of such instruments to produce valid results.

A second area of concern has been with the immediacy construct. In 2004, Witt, Wheeless, and Allen found that both nonverbal and verbal immediacy were correlated with perceived learning and affective learning, but only slightly with cognitive learning. Allen, Witt, and Wheeless (2006) later tested a model that found that the effect of teacher immediacy on cognitive learning was mediated by student motivation to learn. The meta-analysis, then, was not only able to combine multiple findings to uncover average effects, but it also was able to discern possible moderator or mediator variables.

Current studies seem concerned with newer instructional models. For example, meta-analysis of the cognitive outcomes associated with service learning (Novak, Markey, & Allen, 2007) and student satisfaction with distance learning (Allen et al., 2002) allow educators to see trends and patterns in correlational studies reported in the research literature. Continued use of valid and reliable instruments (without alteration by the researchers) will allow for additional meta-analyses in the future.

References

Allen, M., & Bourhis, J. (1996). The relationship of communication apprehension to communication behavior: A meta-analysis. *Communication Quarterly, 44,* 214–226.

Allen, M., Bourhis, J., Mabry, E., Emmers-Sommer, T., Titsworth, S., Burrell, N., Mattrey, M., Crowell, T., Bakkar, A., Hamilton, A., Robertson, T., Scholl, J., & Wells, S. (2002). Comparing student satisfaction of distance education to traditional classrooms in higher education: A meta-analysis. *American Journal of Distance Education, 16,* 83–97.

Allen, M., Hunter, J. E., & Donohue, W. A. (1989). Meta-analysis of self-report data on the effectiveness of public speaking anxiety treatment techniques. *Communication Education, 38,* 54–76.

Allen, M., Mabry, E., Mattrey, M., Bourhis, J., Titsworth, S., & Burrell, N. (2004). Evaluating the effectiveness of distance learning: A comparison using meta-analysis. *Journal of Communication, 54,* 402–420.

Allen, M., Witt, P. L., & Wheeless, L. P. (2006). The role of teacher immediacy as a motivational factor in student learning: Using meta-analysis to test a causal model. *Communication Education, 55,* 21–31.

Andersen, J. G. (1979). Teacher immediacy as a predictor of teaching effectiveness. *Communication Yearbook, 3,* 543–559.

Aylor, B., & Oppliger, P. (2003). Out-of-class communication and student perceptions of instructor humor orientation and socio-communicative style. *Communication Education, 52,* 122–135.

Banfield, S. R., Richmond, V. P., & McCroskey, J. C. (2006). The effect of teacher misbehaviors on teacher credibility and affect for the teacher. *Communication Education, 55*, 63–72.

Beebe, S. A., Barge, K. J., & McCormick, C. (1995, November). *The competent group communicator: Assessing essential competencies of small group problem solving.* Paper presented at the annual meeting of the Speech Communication Association, San Antonio, TX. (ERIC Document Reproduction Service No. ED 392 102).

Behnke, R. R., & Sawyer, C. R. (2000). Anticipatory anxiety patterns for male and female public speakers. *Communication Education, 49,* 187–195.

Behnke, R. R., & Sawyer, C. R. (2004). Public speaking anxiety as a function of sensitization and habituation processes. *Communication Education, 53,* 164–173.

Behnke, R. R., Sawyer, C. R., & King, P. E. (1987). The communication of public speaking anxiety. *Communication Education, 36,* 138–141.

Bensur, B. J. (2001). Is one item an adequate measure of cognitive learning? *Perceptual and Motor Skills, 92,* 606.

Bline, D., Lowe, D. R., Meixner, W. F., & Nouri, H. (2003). Measurement data on commonly used scales to measure oral communication and writing apprehensions. *Journal of Business Communication, 40,* 266–288.

Bline, D., Lowe, D. R., Meixner, W. F., Nouri, H., & Pearce, K. (2001). A research note on the dimensionality of Daly and Miller's Writing Apprehension Scale. *Written Communication, 18,* 61–79.

Bloom, B. S. (1956). *A taxonomy of educational objectives.* New York: Longmans, Green.

Chesebro, J. L. (2003). Effects of teacher clarity and nonverbal immediacy on student learning, receiver apprehension, and affect. *Communication Education, 52,* 135–148.

Chesebro, J. L., & McCroskey, J. C. (2000). The relationship between students' reports of learning and their actual recall of lecture material: A validity test. *Communication Education, 49,* 297–301.

Chesebro, J. L., & McCroskey, J. C. (2001). The relationship of teacher clarity and immediacy with student state receiver apprehension, affect and cognitive learning. *Communication Education, 50,* 59–68.

Chesebro, J. L., & McCroskey, J. C. (Eds.) (2002). *Communication for teachers.* Needham Heights, MA: Allyn & Bacon.

Chiu, L. H. (1997). Development and validation of the School Achievement Motivation Rating Scale. *Educational and Psychological Measurement, 57,* 292–305.

Christophel, D. M. (1990). The relationships among teacher immediacy behaviors, student motivation, and learning. *Communication Education, 39,* 323–340.

Dobransky, N. D., & Frymier, A. B. (2004). Developing teacher-student relations through out of class communication. *Communication Quarterly, 52,* 211–223.

Dolin, D. J. (1995). An alternative form of teacher affinity-seeking measurement. *Communication Research Reports, 12,* 220–226.

Ellis, K. (2004). The impact of perceived teacher confirmation on receiver apprehension, motivation, and learning. *Communication Education, 53,* 264–291.

Feezel, J. D., & Myers, S. A. (1997). Assessing graduate assistant teacher communication concerns. *Communication Quarterly, 45,* 110–124.

French, J. R. P., & Raven, B. (1959). The bases for social power. In D. Cartwright (Ed.), *Studies in social power* (pp. 150–167). Ann Arbor, MI: Institute for Social Research.

Frymier, A. B. (2005). Students' classroom communication effectiveness. *Communication Quarterly, 53,* 197–212.

Frymier, A. B., & Houser, M. L. (1999). The Revised Learning Indicators Scale. *Communication Studies, 50,* 1–12.

Frymier, A. B., Shulman, G. M., & Houser, M. (1996). The development of a learner empowerment measure. *Communication Education, 45,* 181–199.

Fusani, D. S. (1994). "Extra-class" communication: Frequency, immediacy, self-disclosure, and satisfaction in student-faculty interaction outside the classroom. *Journal of Applied Communication Research, 22,* 232–255.

Goss, B. (1991). A test of conversational listening. *Communication Research Reports, 8,* 19–22.

Jaasma, M. A., & Koper, R. J. (1999). The relationship of student-faculty out-of-class communication to instructor immediacy and trust and to student motivation. *Communication Education, 48,* 41–47.

Kearney, P., & Beatty, M. J. (1994). Measures of instructional communication. In R. B. Rubin, P. Palmgreen, & H. E. Sypher (Eds.), *Communication research measures: A sourcebook* (pp. 7–20). New York: Guilford.

Kearney, P., Plax, T. G., Hays, E. R., & Ivey, M. J. (1991). College teacher misbehaviors: What students don't like about what teachers say and do. *Communication Quarterly, 39,* 309–324.

Kearney, P., Plax, T. G., & Wendt-Wasco, N. J. (1985). Teacher immediacy for affective learning in divergent college courses. *Communication Quarterly, 33,* 61–74.

Keaten, J. A., Kelly, L., & Finch, C. (1997). Development of an instrument to measure reticence. *Communication Quarterly, 45,* 37–54.

Martin, M. M., Mottet, T. P., & Chesebro, J. L. (1997). Students' perceptions of instructors' socio-communicative style and the influence on instructor credibility and situational motivation. *Communication Research Reports, 14,* 431–440.

Martin, M. M., Myers, S. A., & Mottet, T. P. (1999). Students' motives for communicating with their instructors. *Communication Education, 48,* 155–164.

Martin, M. M., Myers, S. A., & Mottet, T. P. (2002). Student motives for communicating in the college classroom. In J. L. Chesebro & J. C. McCroskey (Eds.), *Communication for teachers* (pp. 35–46). Boston: Allyn & Bacon.

McCroskey, J. C. (1982). *An introduction to rhetorical communication* (4th ed.). Englewood Cliffs, NJ: Prentice Hall.

McCroskey, J. C., Fayer, J. M., Richmond, V. P., Sallinen, A., & Barraclough, R. A. (1996). A multi-cultural examination of the relationship between nonverbal immediacy and affective learning. *Communication Quarterly, 44,* 297–307.

McCroskey, J. C., & McCroskey, L. L. (1988). Self-report as an approach to measuring communication competence. *Communication Research Reports, 5,* 108–113.

McCroskey, J. C., & Richmond, V. P. (1996). *Fundamentals of human communication: An interpersonal perspective.* Prospect Heights, IL: Waveland Press.

McCroskey, J. C., Richmond, V. P., Sallinen, A., Fayer, J. M., & Barraclough, R. A. (1995). A cross-cultural and multi-behavioral analysis of the relationship between nonverbal immediacy and teacher evaluation. *Communication Education, 44,* 281–292.

McPherson, M. B., Kearney, P., & Plax, T. G. (2003). The dark side of instruction: Teacher anger as classroom norm violations. *Journal of Applied Communication Research, 31,* 76–90.

McPherson, M. B., Kearney, P., & Plax, T. G. (2006). College teacher misbehaviors. In T. P. Mottet, V. P. Richmond, & J. C. McCroskey (Eds.), *Handbook of instructional communication: Rhetorical and relational perspectives* (pp. 213–234). Boston: Allyn and Bacon.

Morreale, S. P. (1994). Public speaking. In W. G. Christ (Ed.), *Assessing communication education: A handbook for media, speech and theatre educators* (pp. 219–236). Hillsdale, NJ: Erlbaum.

Morreale, S. P., Moore, M. R., Taylor, K. P., Surges-Tatus, D., & Hulbert-Johnson, R. (Eds.) (2007). *The Competent Speaker Speech Evaluation Form.* Washington, DC: National Communication Association.

Mottet, T. P., & Beebe, S. A. (2006). The relationships between student responsive behaviors, student socio-communicative style, and instructors' subjective and objective assessments of student work. *Communication Education, 55,* 295–312.

Mottet, T. P., Beebe, S. A., & Fleuriet, C. (2006). Students' influence messages. In T. P. Mottet, V. P. Richmond, & J. C. McCroskey (Eds.), *Handbook of instructional communication: Rhetorical and relational perspectives* (pp. 143–166). Boston: Allyn & Bacon.

Mottet, T. P., Martin, M. M., & Myers, S. A. (2004). Relationships among perceived instructor verbal approach and avoidance relational strategies and students' motives for communicating with their instructors. *Communication Education, 53,* 116–122.

Mulanax, A., & Powers, W. G. (2001). Listening fidelity development and relationship to receiver apprehension and locus of control. *International Journal of Listening, 15,* 69–78.

Myers, S. A. (2004). The relationship between perceived instructor credibility and college student in-class and out-of-class communication. *Communication Reports, 17,* 129–137.

Myers, S. A., Martin, M. M., & Knapp, J. L. (2005). Perceived instructor in-class communicative behaviors as a predictor of student participation in and out of class communication. *Communication Quarterly, 53,* 437–450.

Myers, S. A., Martin, M. M., & Mottet, T. P. (2002). Students' motives for communicating with their instructors: Considering instructor socio-communicative style, student socio-communicative orientations, and student gender. *Communication Education, 51,* 121–133.

Nadler, M. K., & Nadler, L. B. (2000). Out of class communication between faculty and students: A faculty perspective. *Communication Studies, 51,* 176–188.

Novak, J. M., Markey, V., & Allen, M. (2007). Evaluating cognitive outcomes of service learning in higher education: a meta-analysis. *Communication Research Reports, 24,* 149–157.

Pogue, L. L., & Ahyun K. (2006). The effect of teacher nonverbal immediacy and credibility on student motivation and affective learning. *Communication Education, 55*, 331–344.

Richmond, V. P., & McCroskey, J. C. (1990). Reliability and separation of factors on the assertiveness-responsiveness scale. *Psychological Reports, 67*, 449–450.

Richmond, V. P., & McCroskey, J. C. (1998). *Nonverbal communication in interpersonal relationships* (3rd ed.). Boston, MA: Allyn and Bacon.

Richmond, V. P., McCroskey, J. C., & Johnson, A. D. (2003). Development of the Nonverbal Immediacy Scale (NIS): Measures of self- and other-perceived nonverbal immediacy. *Communication Quarterly, 51*, 502–515.

Richmond, V. P., McCroskey, J. C., Kearney, P., & Plax, T. G. (1987). Power in the classroom VII: Linking behavior alteration techniques to cognitive learning. *Communication Education, 32*, 167–174.

Roach, K. D. (1995). Teaching assistant argumentativeness: Effects on affective learning and student perceptions of power use. *Communication Education, 44*, 15–29.

Roach, K. D., Cornett-Devito, M. & Devito, R. (2005). A cross-cultural comparison of instructor communication in American and French classrooms. *Communication Quarterly, 53*, 87–107.

Rocca, K. A. (2004). College student attendance: impact of instructor immediacy and verbal aggression. *Communication Education, 53*, 185–195.

Rubin, R. B. (1994). *Communication Competency Assessment Instrument* (rev. ed.). New Orleans, LA: Spectra.

Rubin, R. B., & Graham, E. E., & Mignerey, J. (1990). A longitudinal study of college students' communication competence. *Communication Education, 38*, 1–14.

Rubin, R. B., Palmgreen, P., & Sypher, H. E. (1994). *Communication research measures: A sourcebook*. New York: Guilford.

Rubin, R. B., Welch, S. A., & Buerkel, R. (1995). Performance-based assessment of high school speech instruction. *Communication Education, 44*, 30–39.

Sawyer, C., & Behnke, R. (1990). The role of self-monitoring processes in the communication of public speaking anxiety. *Communication Reports, 3*, 70–74.

Sawyer, C., & Behnke, R. (2002). Reduction in public speaking state anxiety during performance as a function of sensitization processes. *Communication Quarterly, 50*, 110–121.

Smith, C. D., & King, P. E. (2004). Student feedback sensitivity and the efficacy of feedback interventions in public speaking performance improvement. *Communication Education, 53*, 203–216.

Spielberger, G. D. (1983). *State-Trait Anxiety Inventory* (Form Y). Redwood City, GA: Mind Garden.

Spielberger, C. D., Gorsuch, R. L., & Lushene, R. E. (1970). *Manual for the State-Trait Anxiety Inventory*. Palo Alto, CA: Consulting Psychologist Press.

Spitzberg, B. H. (2007). *Conversational Skills Rating Scale: An instructional assessment of interpersonal competence*. Washington, DC: National Communication Association.

Titsworth, B. S. (2001). The effects of teacher immediacy, use of organizational lecture cues, and students' notetaking on cognitive learning. *Communication Education, 50*, 283–297.

Turman, P. D., & Schrodt, P. (2006). Student perceptions of teacher power as a function of perceived teacher confirmation. *Communication Education, 55*, 265–279.

Waldeck, J. H., Kearney, P., & Plax, T. G. (2001). Teacher e-mail message strategies and students' willingness to communicate online. *Journal of Applied Communication Research, 29*, 54–70.

Watson, K. W. (1984). *Listener Preference Profile.* New Orleans, LA: Spectra.

Watson, K. W., & Barker, L. L. (1988). *Listener Preference Profile.* New Orleans, LA: Spectra.

Watson, K. W., Barker, L. L., & Weaver, J. B., III. (1995). The Listening Styles Profile (LSP-16): Development and validation of an instrument to assess four listening styles. *International Journal of Listening, 9*, 1–13.

Weber, K., Martin, M. M., & Cayanus, J. L. (2005). Student interest: A two-study re-examination of the concept. *Communication Quarterly, 53*, 71–86.

Witt, P. L., & Behnke, R. R. (2006). Anticipatory speech anxiety as a function of public speaking assignment type. *Communication Education, 55*, 167–177.

Witt, P. L., & Wheeless, L. R. (2001). An experimental study of teachers' verbal and nonverbal immediacy and students' affective and cognitive learning. *Communication Education, 50*, 327–342.

Witt, P. L., Wheeless, L. R., & Allen, M. (2004). A meta-analytical review of the relationship between teacher immediacy and student learning. *Communication Monographs, 71*, 184–207.

Zahn, C. J., & Hopper, R. (1985). Measuring language attitudes: The Speech Evaluation Instrument. *Journal of Language and Social Psychology, 4*, 113–123.

Zhang, Q., & Oetzel, J. G. (2006). Constructing and validating a teacher immediacy scale: A Chinese perspective. *Communication Education, 55*, 218–241.

Measurement in Cross-Cultural and Intercultural Communication

David R. Seibold, Rebecca B. Rubin, and Alan M. Rubin

This chapter focuses on measures and measurement issues central to research in cross-cultural (CC) and intercultural (IC) communication. Although the terms cross-cultural and intercultural often are used synonymously, Gudykunst (2002) noted the distinction between them: "Cross-cultural research involves comparing behavior in two or more cultures. . . . Intercultural research involves comparing behavior when members of two or more cultures interact. . . . Intercultural behavior often is compared with intracultural behavior. . . . Understanding cross-cultural differences in behavior is a prerequisite for understanding intercultural behavior" (pp. 175–176). The last point is echoed by Rogers and Hart (2002).

These distinctions are evident, and perhaps clearer, in the types of research in which CC and IC measures have been used. First, examples abound of the use of such instruments within *one culture*. Some studies focus on respondents' *own* culture. For example, Oetzel, Ting-Toomey, Yokochi, Masumoto, and Takai (2000) investigated facework with best friends and strangers in the same culture. Naumov and Puffer (2000) examined Russian culture using Hofstede's (1980) dimensions. Yashima, Zenuk-Nishide, and Shimizu (2004) studied willingness to communicate in a second language in Japan. Other studies use CC and IC measures in only one culture, but it is a *different* culture from that of the research participants. For instance, Crano and Crano (1993) reported six dimensions of strain in international students' adjustment to a new culture. Zimmermann (1995) examined international students' perceptions of intercultural communication competence and adaptability to education in the United States, and found that they varied along affective and behavioral dimensions. B. Lee and Chen (2000) looked at communication competence related to the immigrant family's transition from China to Canada. Monthienvichienchai, Bhibulbhanuwat, Kasemsuk, and Speece (2002) studied the communication competence, cultural awareness, and apprehension of United Kingdom teachers in an international school in Thailand. S-K Lee, Sobal, and Frongillo (2003) analyzed acculturation of Korean Americans.

Second, scholarly investigations *comparing* persons from different cultures also rely on CC and IC measures. Hofstede (1980) compared cultures around the world on four main value dimensions. Hammer, Nishida, and Jezek (1988) looked at how important intercultural effectiveness dimensions are to nationals from Japan, Mexico, and the United States. Martin and Hammer (1989) reported on perceptions and behavioral categories of intercultural communication competence. Dean and Popp (1990) studied the intercultural communication effectiveness of U.S. managers in Saudi Arabia and French managers in the United States. Cocroft and Ting-Toomey (1994) examined facework in Japan and the United States, and Hasegawa and Gudykunst (1998) compared silence in those two countries. Gallois, Giles, Jones, Cargile, and Ota (1995) summarized their accommodation theory research on communication between cultures and linguistic groups (also see Gallois, Ogay, & Giles, 2005). M-S Kim, Aune, Hunter, Kim, and Kim (2001) examined effects of culture and self-construal on communication predispositions in Korea, Hawaii, and the United States. Oetzel and Ting-Toomey (2003) studied facework cross culturally with persons from China, Germany, Japan, and the U.S. McCann and Giles (2006) reported on workplace communication with people of different ages in America and Thailand.

Third, and more specific than the point above, CC and IC measures have been used to enable comparison of people in a variety of cultures in terms of *communication predispositions* and behaviors. Regarding *predispositions*, Applbaum, Applbaum, and Trotter (1986) compared the communication apprehension (PRCA) of Hispanic college students with that of U.S. students. Rubin, Fernandez-Collado, and Hernandez-Sampieri (1992) compared Mexican students with U.S. students and adults on interpersonal communication motives. M-S Kim et al. (2001) compared undergraduates in Korea, Hawaii, and the continental United States in terms of self-construal, communication apprehension, and argumentativeness. Cai and Fink (2002) compared the conflict styles of individualists and collectivists. And, Pekerti and Thomas (2003) compared East Asians and Anglo-European New Zealanders on communication style.

Within this third area, studies comparing people in a variety of cultures on communication *behaviors* also are pervasive. For example, Olebe and Koester (1989) studied behavioral assessment of intercultural communication competence. Elsayed-Ekhouly and Buda (1996) compared organizational conflict across cultures. Huang (2001) examined organization-public relationships across cultures. Oetzel, Ting-Toomey, Masumoto, et al. (2001) compared respondents from China, Germany, Japan, and the United States on how they described interpersonal conflict. And, Oetzel, Ting-Toomey, Chew, et al. (2003) examined conflicts with parents and siblings across Germans, Japanese, Mexicans, and Americans.

Overview

Measures used in CC and IC studies like those above were not absent from *Communication Research Measures: A Sourcebook* (Rubin, Palmgreen, & Sypher, 1994). Indeed, some of the measures profiled in Rubin et al. (1994)—for example, the Argumentativeness Scale, Interpersonal Communication Motives Scale, Nonverbal Immediacy Behaviors Instrument, and Relational Communication Scale—had been used in CC and IC studies to that date, and are the bases for other measures developed since then and noted throughout this review. However, the Rubin et al. volume could have been more helpful to CC and IC researchers in at least two respects. First, there was no overview chapter that offered a survey of CC and IC measures and noted challenges for measurement of CC and IC. Moreover, no measures were profiled that were exclusively the province of CC and IC researchers.

Both limitations are redressed in this volume. First, this chapter contains a review of major lines of research in CC and IC research (highlighting measures in each of those lines), together with commentary about major measurement challenges in these areas. Second, three measures are profiled that are heavily utilized by CC and IC researchers, including two of the most prominent measures in those areas (SELF-CONSTRUAL SCALES, INTERCULTURAL DEVELOPMENT INVENTORY) and one that is promising (AUCKLAND INDIVIDUALISM AND COLLECTIVISM SCALE) insofar as it has been developed in response to limitations in its predecessors. Consequently this chapter and the measures profiled in this volume do not simply update the Rubin et al. (1994) volume, but treat ICC and IC measures that date to the 1960s (near the origins of these fields, according to Y. Kim, 2000).

Major Lines of Research in Cross-Cultural and Intercultural Communication Measurement

Individual Differences

A large corpus of research has examined individual characteristics of the communicators in CC and IC contexts. This investigative thrust has involved many CC and IC measures. We highlight individual differences measures in four areas: self-construal, competence/effectiveness, apprehension/anxiety, and communicator styles.

Self-construal. Self-construal is considered to be the constellation of thoughts, feelings, and actions regarding an individual's relationships to others and the self as distinct from other people (Constantine & Yeh, 2001). It is the individual-level, personality equivalent (Kim, 2000) to the culture-level dimension of individualism-collectivism (Hofstede, 1980).

Although disputed by some communication scholars (see Levine et al., 2003a; Levine et al., 2003b), there is empirical evidence for two orthogonal dimensions of self that exist within each individual regardless of his/her cultural identity and that can be measured as such. Interdependent self-construal includes the realization that one's part in a social interaction depends on the other's actions and feelings. Independent self-construal refers to one's self as independent of others, thus focus on saying what one believes to fulfill one's goals. There are several prominent measures of these dimensions: SELF CONSTRUAL SCALES (Gudykunst et al., 1996); SELF-CONSTRUAL SCALE (M-S Kim et al., 2001; T. Leung & Kim, 1997); SELF-CONSTRUAL SCALE (Singelis, 1994; Singelis, Triandis, Bhawuk, & Gelfand, 1995).

Competence/effectiveness. Communicator *competence* in CC and IC contexts refers to the ability to interact interpersonally with people of different cultures. Representative measures include the Behavioral Assessment Scale for Intercultural Communication (Olebe & Koester, 1989), Intercultural Communication Competence (G. Chen, 1989), Japanese Communication Competence (Takai & Ota, 1994), Intercultural Competence and Adaptation (Zimmermann, 1995), Host and Native Communication Competence Scale (Lee & Chen, 2000), Intercultural Communication Competence (Bush, Rose, Gilbert, & Ingram, 2001), and Cross-Cultural Communication Competence (Matveev & Nelson, 2004). Wiseman, Hammer, and Nishida (1989) examined predictors of intercultural communication competence, and Martin and Hammer (1989) reported behavioral categories of intercultural communication competence. Finally, Graf (2004) evaluated the impact of national culture on intercultural competencies when investigating the screening and training of intercultural competencies. (For an alternative theoretical approach to intercultural competence, and measurement implications, see Hajek & Giles, 2003.)

The widely used INTERCULTURAL DEVELOPMENT INVENTORY (IDI) was created by Mitchell Hammer (1998; Hammer & Bennett, 1998; Hammer, Bennett, & Wiseman, 2003; also see Greenholtz, 2000) based upon Milton Bennett's Development Model of Intercultural Sensitivity (DMIS) (Bennett, 1986). The DMIS focuses on processes of intercultural adaptation vis-à-vis six orientations that people appear to move through as they develop intercultural competence. The first three orientations—*Denial, Defense, Minimization*—are ethnocentric (i.e., a perceiver's own culture is central to how reality is constructed), and the latter three orientations—*Acceptance, Adaptation, Integration*—are ethnorelative (i.e., the perceiver's own culture is interpreted in the context of another culture) (Paige, Jacobs-Cassuto, Yershova, & DeJaeghere, 2003). The IDI measures the developmental orientations toward cultural differences described in the DMIS. A comprehensive analysis and revision of the IDI (Hammer et al., 2003, Table 1) produced a measure with more than 50 items loading on five factors corresponding to the orientations of the DMSI: (a) DD (Denial/Defense) scale (14 items), (b) R (Reversal) scale (9 items), (c) M (Minimization) scale (10 items), (d) AA (Acceptance/Adaptation) scale (14 items), and (e) EM (Encapsulated Marginality) scale (5 items). Administered as a self-assessment instrument, participants rate their agreement on a 5-point response scale: 1 = *disagree*, 2 = *disagree somewhat more than agree*, 3= *disagree some and agree some*, 4 = *agree somewhat more than disagree*, and 5 = *agree* (Hammer et al., 2003).

Effectiveness measures assess the ability to accomplish goals in interpersonal communication in CC and IC contexts. Studies measuring intercultural effectiveness are reported by Abe and Wiseman (1983), Hammer, Nishida, and Jezek (1988), Cui and Awa (1992), and Dean and Popp (1990). Redmond and Bunyi (1993) utilized the Effective Intercultural Communication Competence measure, and G. Chen (1993) employed the Intercultural Sensitivity Scales.

Apprehension/anxiety. Several measures have been developed to assess CC and IC communication apprehension (i.e., a feeling of anxiety when engaging in interaction with people of other cultures) and approach/avoidance (the willingness to interact with others and to seek or avoid conversations with people from other cultures). Examples include the Cultural-Transfer Reticence Scale (Anderson & Gray, 1981), General Trait Anxiousness (Endler, 1980), Intercultural Willingness to Communicate (Yang & Rancer, 2003), and Intercultural Communication Apprehension (Yang & Rancer, 2003).

Styles. Measures of intercultural communication styles, or consistent individual differences in interaction with others, have been developed and used in CC and IC research. Noteworthy are measures of Intercultural Conflict Styles (Oetzel & Ting-Toomey, 2003) and Idiocentric-Sociocentric Communication Styles (Pekerti & Thomas, 2003).

Adjustment to New Cultures

Besides the measures employed in studies of individual differences in cross-cultural and intercultural communication such as those noted above, CC and IC researchers have used measures designed to assess participants' abilities to adopt (i.e., internalize) the behavioral norms of a new culture, or adapt to those norms when necessary. Scales for measuring acculturation can be found in the study of acculturation in Mexican American populations by Cuellar, Harris, and Jasso (1980), the treatment by Berry, Trimble, and Olmedo (1986) of the assessment of acculturation, Mendoza's (1989) development of a measure of acculturation type and degree, an analysis of intercultural adaptation by Gao and Gudykunst (1990), and the K-S Lee et al. (2003) investigation of acculturation among Korean Americans.

Cultural Dimensions

Although several communication theories address cross-cultural communication differences at the individual or cultural level (e.g., face-negotiation theory, Ting-Toomey, 1988; conversational constraints theory, Y.
Kim, 1995), to some degree they each appropriate dimensions of cultural
variability identified by Hofstede (1980, 1991, 2001). According to this
view, cultures vary in terms of underlying values concerning low-high
power distance (i.e., the degree to which less powerful members accept
that power is unequally distributed); *masculinity-femininity* (i.e., distinct
vs. overlapping gender roles that value assertiveness, performance, power,
ambition, and possessions as opposed to valuing service, caring for others,
and nurturance); *uncertainty avoidance* (i.e., rules and norms that direct
action vs. less rigidity concerning appropriate conduct); and *individualism-collectivism* (i.e., focus on self and family vs. additional loyalty to col-
lectivities and in-groups). As Gudykunst (2005) noted, "both ends of each
dimension exist in every culture, although one tends to be dominant and
individual members of cultures learn the predominate tendencies of their
cultures to various degrees" (p. 8).

Focal among these dimensions has been the measurement of individualism-collectivism, and Hui (1988) and colleagues (Hui & Triandis, 1986; Hui
& Yee, 1994) developed the widely used INDCOL measure. The original
INDCOL scale is a 63-item instrument using a 6-point Likert scale. Items
measure seven aspects of collectivism: (a) consideration of implications
(costs and benefits) of one's own decisions and/or actions for other people,
(b) sharing of material resources, (c) sharing of nonmaterial resources, (d)
susceptibility to social influence; (e) self-presentation and face-work, (f)
sharing of outcomes, and (g) feeling of involvement in others' lives. Individualism is represented by low scores on these collectivist attitudes, beliefs, and
behaviors. When administered, reference is made to specific target groups in
a specific hypothetical event. Many changes have been made to the scale during the past two decades, including development of a shortened version by
Hui (1994) and modifications by other researchers. For example, Cai, Wilson, and Drake (2000) further shortened the INDCOL when studying the
relationship between intercultural negotiation and individualism-collectivism. After removing items that lacked face validity and internal consistency through factor analysis, 3 subscales and 11 items remained.

The AUCKLAND INDIVIDUALISM AND COLLECTIVISM SCALE
(AICS; Shulruf, Hattie, & Dixon, 2007) is a promising, brief, easy to use,
and reliable measure of individualism and collectivism. The 30-item
scale assesses three dimensions of *individualism*—(a) responsibility
(acknowledging one's responsibility for one's actions), (b) uniqueness
(distinction of the self from the other), (c) competitiveness (one's
primary interest is striving for personal goals), and two dimensions of

collectivism—(a) advice (seeking advice from persons close to one before making decisions) and (b) harmony (seeking to avoid conflict). The scale attempts to minimize problems associated with previously developed and frequently used scales that are wholly or partly focused on individualism and collectivism (Levine et al., 2003a; Li & Aksoy, 2007). In particular, the AICS is based on frequency of behavior and, therefore, is less influenced by context factors. The AICS also integrates theoretical refinements of individualism-collectivism dimension components (Oyserman, Coon, & Kemmelmeir, 2002), and related empirical findings, that have occurred since Hui (1988) introduced the INDCOL scales.

Situational Behaviors

Researchers also have developed instruments to assess communication-related behaviors in specific CC and IC situations. In the CC area, for instance, Oetzel et al. (2001) measured facework in a cross-cultural comparison of communication in conflict situations involving participants from China, Germany, Japan, and the U.S. Within IC research, L. Chen (2002) developed a perceptual measure of intercultural interaction behaviors in initial encounters of persons from different cultures.

Marketing/Advertising/Public Relations

Whereas intercultural (IC) research focuses on heterophilous *interpersonal* communication between members of different cultures (Rogers & Hartt, 2002; emphasis added), cross-cultural (CC) communication studies cast a broader net. The measures developed by CC researchers are more representative of the interests of scholars and students in the communication discipline in general. For example, Lorimor and Dunn (1967) reported on four measures of cross-cultural advertising effectiveness. More recently, Huang (2001) developed the OPRA measure, a cross-cultural, multiple-item scale for measuring organization-public relationships.

Issues in Cross-Cultural and Intercultural Measurement

Gudykunst (2002) identified numerous methodological issues in conducting theory-based research in cross-cultural communication: conducting *etic* versus *emic* research; making theoretical predictions; designing theory-testing research; isolating cultural effects; establishing equivalence in the cross-cultural comparisons made; developing derived etic measures; and establishing reliability and validity of measures. He treated these issues in light of cross-cutting problems in cross-cultural research: conducting Western and Asian studies in lieu of, for example, African, Arab, and Latin studies; using only one dimension of cultural variability in explaining communication across cultures; restricting most comparisons to only two cultures; ignoring individual-level factors that mediate cultural-level phenomena; using samples of respondents that are not representative of the cultures studied; failing to analyze data with the appropriate statistical technique(s); and using only one method to study behavior across cultures instead of multiple methods. In this section we extend Gudykunst's fine analysis of *methods* matters by focusing on *measurement* issues. Specifically, we address five issues surrounding measurement in CC and IC communication research: (a) culture-level vs. individual level effects, (b) individual and cultural differences, (c) equivalency, (d) language, and (e) technology. We begin with two examples that bring these issues to the fore.

When Merkin (2000) applied Hofstede's (1980) cultural dimensions to examine facework in different cultures, she developed English, Spanish, and Japanese language versions of her questionnaire and asked participants in six cultures (Japan, Sweden, Israel, Hong Kong, Chile, and the U.S.) to complete the instrument. The questionnaires were translated into a language by one person fluent in that language and then back-translated by another person fluent in that language. She found that masculinity and individualism influenced facework strategies. Similar to some intercultural studies, the measures did not all behave as expected. She also noted that the Chilean responses were linked to higher social desirability scores. Merkin suggested that such self-report studies would be better if they were triangulated with other methods, and asked, "What method of studying culture is most valid?" (p. 139).

When Chikombero (2004) collected the quantitative and qualitative data to study televised public service announcements and AIDS in Zimbabwe, she found the study would have been improved if she was on site during the surveys and the focus groups to clarify the actual differences between self-efficacy and response-efficacy measures, which seemed to meld into a single construct. She noted that being on site would have permitted including PSAs transmitted by the other government-controlled media besides television in the content analysis (for which the coding categories needed to be sensitive to the study's cultural context). In addition, measures (e.g., multidimensional health locus of control) created in other cultures did not behave in the same manner, and produced less than desirable reliabilities. Social desirability and culturally bound gender differences were also factors in focus group discussions of safe sex, AIDS, and exposure to public service announcements.

Parsing Culture-Level Effects

As these examples—together with numerous other investigations and theories—make clear, *culture matters* in the effective conduct of CC and IC research. Gudykunst (2002) elaborated: culture-level and individual-level effects (e.g., self-construal) must be disambiguated and the former (e.g., individualism-collectivism) "must be derived from the norms and rules of the culture" (p. 166). Researchers in the CC and IC areas note important implications for measurement.

Nwosu, Taylor, and Onwumechili (1995) observed that we need to consider altering our measures or creating measures that are sensitive to the culture where the research is being conducted. For example, Nwosu et al. noted that responses in survey research are influenced by *demographic factors* (e.g., age, gender, status), *group norms*, for instance, "resistance to self-disclosure in collectivist, high context cultures" and the country's *political situation*, "whether or not the questioner is from within or outside of the group being interviewed and willingness of other members of the household to permit one member to be interviewed separately" (p. 411). Harkness (1999) argued for the importance of quality *monitoring* and evaluation or assessment at all stages of conducting cross-national survey research. Matveev (2002) stressed the importance of *triangulating* quantitative and qualitative research methods for more flexible, holistic, and reliable intercultural communication research.

K. Leung and Bond (1989) provided an insightful discussion of culture-level effects on measurement data, and proposed a method for *parsing both culture-level and individual-level effects*. First, a *patterning* effect may occur in which culture affects the relationship among items (e.g., negatively correlated in one culture, positively correlated in another, and uncorrelated in a third). Second, a *positioning* effect may occur in which culture affects mean responses within different cultures (e.g., although the correlation between two items may be the same in two cultures, mean responses to those items within each culture—indicative of the average member—may differ). Although well established pancultural and statistical techniques enable CC and IC researchers to isolate both patterning and positioning culture level effects (see Gudykunst, 2002), K. Leung and Bond discuss an *isoregion* analysis, which enables isolation of the individual-level effects that are of theoretical interest to CC and IC researchers. An isoregion analysis is a statistical analysis of data that has first been standardized within individuals and then standardized within cultures.

Individual and Cultural Differences

By extension, the relationship between *individual traits* or characteristics and cultural differences also matters for measurement in CC and IC research. For example, those in *collective* and *high context* cultures might provide more socially desirable responses than those in *individual* and *low context* cultures (Hall, 1976). The same would apply to those who are more *interdependent* (as identified on self-construal scales), suggesting that actions are influenced by how we perceive others would like us to act, as compared with those in a culture emphasizing more *independent* traits. In fact, Levine et al. (2003a, 2003b) found weak and inconsistent evidence for expected cultural differences based on *self-construal*, and that self-construal scales were multidimensional and unstable across cultures, did not reliably reflect the intended cultural differences, and lacked validity. The data presented by Levine et al. suggest the results obtained from self-construal scales are incompatible with the constructs the scales were designed to measure. This is also problematic in studies in which self-construal has been linked to communication behaviors: uncertainty, anxiety, and perceived communication effectiveness (Gudykunst & Nishida, 2001), conflict style and facework (Gao & Ting-Toomey, 1998), silence (Hasegawa & Gudykunst, 1998), and cooperative and competitive behaviors (Oetzel, 1998), among others.

Equivalency

This discussion points to serious concerns about the stable and consistent applicability and the *equivalency* of *research measurement* in different cultures. How do we know if measures are valid and reliable across cultures? How do we know if measures act in an equivalent fashion across cultures? How do we know if the differences we find (or fail to find) are the result of the appropriate conceptualization and prediction of relationships, or of faulty measurement and related concerns?

For instance, Varona (1996) compared links between communication satisfaction and organizational commitment in three organizations in Guatemala. He used standard organizational commitment and satisfaction measures developed in the U.S., and found a positive relationship between satisfaction and employees' commitment. The measures, though, behaved differently with Guatemalan organizations. Factor structures differed and reliabilities were less stable, raising validity and reliability issues about using research instruments in cross-cultural studies.

Byrne and Watkins (2003) found "measurement and structural noninvariance" in cross-cultural research across two culturally diverse samples of adolescents from Australia and Nigeria. This adds to the literature questioning whether measuring instruments should ever be considered "totally equivalent" in such comparisons.

Gudykunst (2002) illuminated the equivalence problem in reviewing five types of equivalence: "lack of equivalence in any of these areas can lead to rival hypotheses to explain results on cross-cultural studies" (p. 169). *Functional* equivalence must be established at the cultural level between observations and inferences made from the observations. *Conceptual* equivalence requires establishing that concepts studied mean the same thing to members of the cultures studied. *Sample* equivalence occurs when comparable samples are used to make cross-cultural comparisons. *Linguistic* equivalence, which we take up later, entails ensuring that the language used in methods (e.g., interviews and instructions) and measures (e.g., questionnaires and instruments) with participants in one culture are equivalent to the language employed with the same methods and measures employed with participants in other cultures. *Metric* equivalence involves scale response scores secured in one culture being equal to score levels from responses obtained in other cultures.

Metric equivalence is of special concern for CC and IC *measures*. As Gudykunst (2002) noted, because research (e.g., C. Chen, Lee, & Stevenson, 1995; Peng, Nisbett, & Wong, 1997) indicates that Asians do not use extreme scores (scale end points such as *strongly disagree* or *strongly agree*) to the extent that Americans and Asian Americans do, lower scores on measures may be an artifact of measurement technique rather than actual cultural differences.

Language

As is evident from the notion of linguistic equivalence noted above, *language* is an issue in intercultural research in general and for CC and IC measures in particular. The concern is similar to that voiced by Solano-Flores and Trumbull (2003) when they examined the *context of language* for "the valid and equitable assessment of English language learners." Ensuring the accuracy and equivalence in meaning of wording (i.e., "proper syntactic structures") is essential for effective intercultural research involving different populations, whether the method uses questionnaires, interviews, focus groups, or the like. As Solano-Flores and Trumbull pointed out, this needs to reflect "culturally determined discourse patterns" and visual presentation as well.

For example, in the realm of industrial and organizational psychology, Leslie and Penny (2002) discovered differences in performance assessment owing to *language and culture*. They examined the equivalence in measurement of 98 items from a managerial checklist, SKILLSCOPE®, which they translated into Japanese for use in Japanese leadership training. They found 40% of the items functioned differently due to "translation error, cultural differences in Japanese and U.S. managerial style, or poorly constructed items," and 15% of the items functioned differently due to the cultural perspective of the rater. They suggested differences may be due to greater power distances in Japanese culture.

Furthermore, in the area of educational testing, Robin, Sireci, and Hambleton (2003) observed the complexity of adapting a credentialing exam to multiple languages. They noted that many factors need to be considered—content specifications, directions, and the context of administering the exam—when addressing the equivalence of different language versions of the exams. The implications for constructing valid and reliable measures and questionnaires in cross-cultural and intercultural research are clear.

Technology

Changes in *technology* have the potential to alter how we communicate, and this is equally true for the study of cross-cultural and intercultural communication. Newer electronic media pose special challenges and opportunities for CC and IC research.

As Rogers (2002) observed, the *Internet* has altered the nature of international communication, providing inexpensive and quick access to participants from other countries in our research, and raising new issues for conducting research. So has *electronic* mail. G. Chen and Kim (1998) suggested that because thinking patterns and expression styles differ among high-context and low-context cultures, email communications should be designed differently for those participants in high- versus low-context cultures. This affects a researcher's ability to increase participation rates in research using the newer media, and the design of questionnaires and the like distributed electronically.

According to Daniels, Cronje, and Sokolowski (1998), intercultural communication researchers need to be aware that *ideologies* of participating cultures "saturate" the communication context and workplace technologies. They examined medical information dissemination via the Internet between healthcare agencies and professionals in the U.S. and Russia. They contended that without addressing challenges presented by the Internet of overcoming "cultural biases and infrastructural limits," the gap between the "wired world" and "marginalized countries" will widen.

Finally, Rivenburgh and Manusov (2002) proposed that online dialog allows intercultural researchers to examine questions about *cultural identity* and to engage in research and theory development that is culture-general and cost effective. This approach must address several challenges: (a) the ethics of "permissions, confidentiality, and disclosure" (so that people are not just lurking on others' conversations); (b) the use of translations; and (c) the fact that international research is not culture free in its "formation, execution, interpretation, or presentation."

Conclusion

Differences between intercultural and cross-cultural research are evident in the measurement of relevant constructs. Some researchers use measures in one culture, while others compare people from different cultures or compare communication predispositions and behaviors of people in a variety of cultures. Volume I of *Communication Research Measures: A Sourcebook* (Rubin et al., 1994) profiled measures that have been applied in IC and CC research, but not measures that were exclusive to this subdivision of the field. Volume II redresses that omission.

Several major lines of IC and CC research are apparent in the literature. Individual differences research has examined self-construal, competence/effectiveness, apprehension/anxiety, and communication styles. A second line of research is adjustment to new cultures, by both sojourners and immigrants. Third, researchers have examined basic cultural dimensions to describe how people from different countries differ in their interactions with others. Fourth, some have identified situational behaviors (e.g., facework) that differ from culture to culture. And fifth, a line of research in marketing, advertising, and PR makes cross-cultural comparisons.

IC and CC researchers face several measurement challenges. Most important of these are (a) whether to examine culture-level or individual-level effects, (b) how individual and cultural differences affect completion of various measures, (c) how equivalent research measures are in different cultures, (d) language differences and translation issues in using various measures, and (e) the use of new technology in conducting research.

References

Abe, H., & Wiseman, R. (1983). A cross-cultural confirmation of the dimensions of intercultural effectiveness. *International Journal of Intercultural Relations, 7,* 53–67.

Anderson, R. D., & Gray, G. (1981). The cultural-transfer reticence scale: A means of measuring minority reticence. *Communication, 10,* 157–176.

Applbaum, R., Applbaum, S., & Trotter, R. (1986). Communication apprehension and Hispanics: An exploration of communication apprehension among Mexican Americans. *World Communication, 15,* 11–30.

Bennett, M. J. (1986). Towards ethnorelativism: A developmental model of intercultural sensitivity. In R. M. Paige (Ed.), *Cross-cultural orientation: New conceptualizations and applications* (pp. 27–70). New York: University Press of America.

Berry, J. W., Trimble, J. E., & Olmedo, E. L. (1986). Assessment of acculturation. In W. J. Lonner & J. W. Berry (Eds.), *Field methods in cross-cultural research* (pp. 291–324). Beverly Hills, CA: Sage.

Bush, V. D., Rose, G. M., Gilbert, F., & Ingram, T. N. (2001). Managing culturally diverse buyer-seller relationships: The role of intercultural disposition and adaptive selling in developing intercultural communication competence. *Journal of the Academy of Marketing Science, 29,* 391–404.

Byrne, B. M., & Watkins, D. (2003). The issue of measurement invariance revisited. *Journal of Cross-Cultural Psychology, 34,* 155–175.

Cai, D. A., & Fink, E. L. (2002). Conflict style differences between individualists and collectivists. *Communication Monographs, 69,* 67–87.

Cai, D. A., Wilson, S. R., & Drake, L. E. (2000). Culture in the context of intercultural negotiation: Individualism-collectivism and paths to integrative agreements. *Human Communication Research, 26,* 591–617.

Chen, C. S., Lee, S. Y., & Stevenson, H. (1995). Response style and cross-cultural comparisons of rating scales among East Asians and North American students. *Psychological Science, 6*, 170–175.

Chen, G. M. (1989). Relationship of the dimensions of intercultural communication competence. *Communication Quarterly, 37*, 118–133.

Chen, G. M. (1993). Intercultural communication education: A classroom case. *Speech Communication Annual, 7*, 33–46.

Chen, G. M., & Kim, C. (1998). *Intercultural communication via e-mail debate.* Retrieved 11/24/04 from: http://www.interculturalrelations.com/v1i4Fall1998/f98chen.htm.

Chen, L. (2002). Perceptions of intercultural interaction and communication satisfaction: A study on initial encounters. *Communication Reports, 15*, 133–147.

Chikombero, P. M. (2004). *An analysis and interpretation of televised anti-HIV/AIDS public service announcements in Zimbabwe.* Unpublished doctoral dissertation, Kent State University, Kent, OH.

Cocroft, B. K., & Ting-Toomey, S. (1994). Facework in Japan and the United States. *International Journal of Intercultural Relations, 18*, 469–506.

Constantine, M. G., & Yeh, C. J. (2001). Multicultural training, self-construals, and multicultural competence of school counselors. *Professional School Counseling, 4*, 202–207.

Crano, S. L., & Crano, W. D. (1993). A measure of adjustment strain in international students. *Journal of Cross-Cultural Psychology, 24*, 267–283.

Cuellar, I., Harris, L. C., & Jasso, R. (1980). An acculturation scale for Mexican American normal and clinical populations. *Hispanic Journal of Behavioral Sciences, 2*, 199–217.

Cui, G., & Awa, N. E. (1992). Measuring intercultural effectiveness: An integrative approach. *International Journal of Intercultural Relations, 16*, 311–328.

Daniels, J. K., Cronje, R. J., & Sokolowski, B. C. (1998, Summer). Exchanging medical information with Eastern Europe through the Internet. *Technical Communication Quarterly, 7*(3), 301–317.

Dean, O., & Popp, G. E. (1990). Intercultural communication effectiveness as perceived by American managers in Saudi Arabia and French managers in the U.S. *International Journal of Intercultural Relations, 14*, 405–424.

Elsayed-Ekhouly, S. M., & Buda, R. (1996). Organizational conflict: A comparative analysis of conflict style across cultures. *International Journal of Conflict Management, 7*, 71–81.

Endler, N. S. (1980). Person-situation interaction and anxiety. In I. L. Kutash & L. B. Schlesinger (Eds.), *Handbook on stress and anxiety: Contemporary knowledge, theory, and treatment* (pp. 249–266). San Francisco: Jossey-Bass.

Gallois, C., Giles, H., Jones, E., Cargile, A. C., & Ota, H. (1995). Accommodating intercultural encounters: Elaborations and extensions. In R. L. Wiseman (Ed.), *Intercultural communication theory* (pp. 115–147). Thousand Oaks, CA: Sage.

Gallois, C., Ogay, T., & Giles, H. (2005). Communication accommodation theory: A look back and a look ahead. In W. B. Gudykunst (Ed.), *Theorizing about intercultural communication* (pp. 121–148). Thousand Oaks, CA: Sage.

Gao, G., & Gudykunst, W. B. (1990). Uncertainty, anxiety, and adaptation. *International Journal of Intercultural Relations, 4*, 301–317.

Gao, G., & Ting-Toomey, S. (1998). *Communicating effectively with the Chinese.* Thousand Oaks, CA: Sage.

Graf, A. (2004). Screening and training inter-cultural competencies: Evaluating the impact of national culture on inter-cultural competencies. *International Journal of Human Resource Management, 15,* 1124–1148.

Greenholtz, J. (2000). Assessing cross-cultural competence in transnational education: The Intercultural Development Inventory. *Higher Education in Europe, 25,* 411–416.

Gudykunst, W. B. (2002). Issues in cross-cultural communication research. In W. B. Gudykunst & Bella Moody (Eds.), *Handbook of international and intercultural communication* (2nd ed.) (pp. 165–177). Thousand Oaks, CA: Sage.

Gudykunst, W. B., Lee, C., Nishida, T., & Ogawa, N. (2005). Theorizing about intercultural communication: An introduction. In W. B. Gudykunst (Ed.), *Theorizing about intercultural communication* (pp. 3–32). Thousand Oaks, CA: Sage.

Gudykunst, W. B., Matsumoto, Y., Ting-Toomey, S., Nishida, T., Kim, K., & Hayman, S. (1996). The influence of cultural individualism-collectivism, self-construal, and individual values on communication styles across cultures. *Human Communication Research, 22,* 510–543.

Gudykunst, W. B., & Nishida, T. (2001). Anxiety, uncertainty, and perceived effectiveness of communication across relationships and cultures. *International Journal of Intercultural Relations, 25,* 55–72.

Hajek, C., & Giles, H. (2003). Intercultural communication competence: A critique and alternative model. In B. Burleson & J. Greene (Eds.), *Handbook of communicative and social skills* (pp. 933–957). Mahwah, NJ: Lawrence Erlbaum.

Hall, E. T. (1976). *Beyond culture.* Garden City, NY: Anchor.

Hammer, M. R. (1998). A measure of intercultural sensitivity: The Intercultural Development Inventory. In S. Fowler & M. Fowler (Eds.), *The intercultural sourcebook: Volume 2.* Yarmouth, ME: Intercultural Press.

Hammer, M. R., & Bennett, M. J. (1998). *The Intercultural Development Inventory (IDI) manual.* Portland, OR: The Intercultural Communication Institute.

Hammer, M. R., Bennett, M. J., & Wiseman, R. (2003). Measuring intercultural sensitivity: The Intercultural Development Inventory. *International Journal of Intercultural Relations, 27,* 421–443.

Hammer, M. R., Nishida, H., & Jezek, L. (1988). A cross-cultural comparison of intercultural effectiveness: Japan, Mexico and the United States. *World Communication, 17*(1), 119–144.

Harkness, J. (1999). In pursuit of quality: Issues for cross-national survey research. *International Journal of Social Research Methodology, 2*(2), 125–140.

Hasegawa, T., & Gudykunst, W. B. (1998). Silence in Japan and the United States. *Journal of Cross-Cultural Psychology, 29,* 668–684.

Hofstede, G. (1980). *Culture's consequences: International differences in work-related values.* Beverly Hills, CA: Sage.

Hofstede, G. (1991). *Cultures and organizations: Software of the mind.* London: McGraw-Hill.

Hofstede, G. (2001). *Culture's consequences* (2nd ed.). Thousand Oaks, CA: Sage.

Huang, Y. H. (2001). OPRA: A cross-cultural, multiple-item scale for measuring organization-public relationships. *Journal of Public Relations Research*, *13*, 61–90.

Hui, C. H. (1988). Measurement of individualism-collectivism. *Journal of Research in Personality*, *22*, 17–36.

Hui, C. H., & Triandis, H. C. (1986). Individualism-collectivism: A study of cross-cultural researchers. *Journal of Cross-Cultural Psychology*, *17*, 225–248.

Hui, C. H., & Yee, C. (1994). The shortened individualism-collectivism scale: Its relationship to demographic and work-related variables. *Journal of Research in Personality*, *28*, 409–424.

Kim, M-S, Aune, K. S., Hunter, J. E., Kim, H-J, & Kim, J-S. (2001). The effect of culture and self-construals on predispositions toward verbal communication. *Human Communication Research*, *27*, 382–408.

Kim, Y. Y. (1995). Toward an interactive theory of communication acculturation. In R. L. Wiseman (Ed.), *Intercultural communication theory* (pp. 170–194). Thousand Oaks, CA: Sage.

Kim, Y. Y. (2000). Mapping the domain of intercultural communication: An overview. *Communication Yearbook*, *24*, 139–157.

Lee, B. K., & Chen, L. (2000). Cultural communication competence and psychological adjustment: A study of Chinese immigrant children's cross-cultural adaptation in Canada. *Communication Research*, *27*, 764–792.

Lee, S-K, Sobal, J., & Frongillo, E. A. (2003). Comparison of models of acculturation: The case of Korean Americans. *Journal of Cross-Cultural Psychology*, *34*, 282–296.

Leslie, J. B., & Penny, J. (2002, April). *Assessing individual managerial skill across cultures: The influence of language and rating source on 360-degree feedback*. Paper presented at the annual meeting of the Society for Industrial and Organizational Psychology, Toronto, Canada.

Leung, K., & Bond, M. H. (1989). On the empirical identification of dimensions for cross-cultural comparisons. *Journal of Cross-Cultural Psychology*, *20*, 133–151.

Leung, T., & Kim, M. S. (1997). *A revised version of self-construal scale*. Honolulu: University of Hawaii at Manoa.

Levine, T. R., Bresnahan, M. J., Park, H. S., Lapinski, M. K., Wittenbam, G. W., Shearman, S. M., Lee, S. Y., Chung, D., & Ohashi, D. (2003a). Self-construal scales lack validity. *Human Communication Research*, *29*, 210–252.

Levine, T. R., Bresnahan, M. J., Park, H. S., Lapinski, M. K., Lee, T. S., & Lee, D. W. (2003b). The (in)validity of self-construal scales revisited. *Human Communication Research*, *29*, 291–308.

Li, F., & Aksoy, L. (2007). Dimensionality of individualism and collectivism and measurement equivalence of Triandis and Gelfand's scale. *Journal of Business and Psychology*, *21(3)*, 313–329.

Lorimor, E. S., & Dunn, S. W. (1967). Four measures of cross-cultural advertising effectiveness. *Journal of Advertising Research*, *7(4)*, 11–13.

Martin, J. N., & Hammer, M. R. (1989). Behavioral categories of intercultural communication competence: Everyday communicator's perceptions. *International Journal of Intercultural Relations*, *13*, 303–332.

Matveev, A. V. (2002). The advantages of employing quantitative and qualitative methods in intercultural research: Practical implications from the study of the perceptions of intercultural communication competence by American and Russian managers. In I. N. Rozina (Ed.), *Collected research articles: Bulletin of Russian Communication Association. Issue 1. Theory of communication and applied communication* (pp. 59–67). Rostov-on-Don, Russia: Institute of Management, Business and Law Publishing.

Matveev, A. V., & Nelson, P. E. (2004). Cross cultural communication competence and multicultural team performance: Perceptions of American and Russian managers. *International Journal of Cross Cultural Management, 4,* 253–270.

McCann, R. M., & Giles, H. (2006). Communication with people of different ages in the workplace: Thai and American data. *Human Communication Research, 32,* 74–108.

Mendoza, R. H. (1989). An empirical scale to measure type and degree of acculturation in Mexican-American adolescents and adults. *Journal of Cross-Cultural Psychology, 20,* 372–385.

Merkin, R. (2000). *A cross-cultural examination of facework communication: An application of Hofstede's cultural dimensions.* Unpublished doctoral dissertation, Kent State University, Kent, OH.

Monthienvichienchai, C., Bhibulbhanuwat, S., Kasemsuk, C., & Speece, M. (2002). Cultural awareness, communication apprehension, and communication competence: A case study of Saint John's International School. *International Journal of Educational Management, 16,* 288–296.

Naumov, A. I., & Puffer, S. M. (2000). Measuring Russian culture using Hofstede's dimensions. *Applied Psychology: An International Review, 49,* 709–718.

Nwosu, P., Taylor, D., & Onwumechili, C. (1995). Search for appropriate research methods in the African context. In P. Nwosu, C. Onwumechili, & R. M'Bayo (Eds.), *Communication and the transformation of society: A developing region's perspectives* (pp. 397–426). Lanham, MD: University Press of America.

Oetzel, J. G. (1998). Culturally homogeneous and heterogeneous groups: Explaining communication processes through individualism-collectivism and self-construal. *International Journal of Intercultural Relations, 22*(2), 135–161.

Oetzel, J. G., & Ting-Toomey, S. (2003). Face concerns in interpersonal conflict: A cross-cultural empirical test of the face negotiation theory. *Communication Research, 30,* 599–624.

Oetzel, J. G., Ting-Toomey, S., Chew, M., Harris, R., Wilcox, R., & Stumpf, S. (2003). Face and facework in conflicts with parents and siblings: A crosscultural comparison of Germans, Japanese, Mexicans, and U.S. Americans. *Journal of Family Communication, 3,* 67–93.

Oetzel, J., Ting-Toomey, S., Masumoto, T., Yokochi, Y., Xiaohui, P., Takai, J., & Wilcox, R. (2001). Face and facework in conflict: A cross-cultural comparison of China, Germany, Japan, and the United States. *Communication Monographs, 68,* 235–258.

Oetzel, J. G., Ting-Toomey, S., Yokochi, Y., Masumoto, T., & Takai, J. (2000). A typology of facework behaviors in conflicts with best friends and relative strangers. *Communication Quarterly, 48, 397–419.*

Olebe, M., & Koester, J. (1989). Exploring the cross-cultural equivalence of the Behavioral Assessment Scale for Intercultural Communication. *International Journal of Intercultural Relations, 13*, 333–347.

Oyserman, D., Coon, H. M., & Kemmelmeir, M. (2002). Rethinking individualism and collectivism: Evaluation of theoretical and meta-analyses. *Psychological Bulletin, 128*(1), 3–72.

Paige, R. M., Jacobs-Cassuto, M., Yershova, Y. A., & DeJaeghere, J. (2003). Assessing intercultural sensitivity: An empirical analysis of the Hammer and Bennett Intercultural Development Inventory. *International Journal of Intercultural Relations, 27*, 467–486.

Pekerti, A. A., & Thomas, D. C. (2003). Communication in intercultural interaction: An empirical investigation of idiocentric and sociocentric communication styles. *Journal of Cross-Cultural Psychology, 34*, 139–154.

Peng, K., Nisbett, R. E., & Wong, N. (1997). Validity problems of cross-cultural value comparison and possible solutions. *Psychological Methods, 2*, 329–341.

Redmond, M. V., & Bunyi, J. M. (1993). The relationship of intercultural communication competence with stress and the handling of stress as reported by international students. *International Journal of Intercultural Relations, 17*, 235–254.

Rivenburgh, N. K., & Manusov, V. (2002, July). *Intercultural on-line forums for grounded theory development: An analysis of Barcelona 2004's virtual dialogue on cultural identity.* Paper presented at the annual meeting of the International Association for Mass Communication Research. Barcelona, Spain.

Robin, F., Sireci, S. G., & Hambleton, R. K. (2003). Evaluating the equivalence of different language versions of a credentialing exam. *International Journal of Testing, 3*(1), 1–20.

Rogers, E. M. (2002). Funding international communication research. *Journal of Applied Communication Research, 30*(4), 341–349.

Rogers, E. M., & Hart, W. B. (2002). The histories of intercultural, international, and development communication. In W. B. Gudykunst & Bella Moody (Eds.), *Handbook of international and intercultural communication* (2nd ed.) (pp. 1–18). Thousand Oaks, CA: Sage.

Rubin, R. B., Fernandez-Collado, C., & Hernandez-Sampieri, R. (1992). A cross-cultural examination of interpersonal communication motives in Mexico and the United States. *International Journal of Intercultural Relations, 16*, 145–157.

Rubin, R. B., Palmgreen, P., & Sypher, H. E. (Eds.) (1994). *Communication research measures: A sourcebook.* New York: Guilford.

Shulruf, B., Hattie, J., & Dixon, R. (2007). Development of a new measurement tool for individualism and collectivism. *Journal of Psychoeducational Assessment, 25*(4), 385–401.

Singelis, T. M. (1994). The measurement of independent and interdependent self-construals. *Personality & Social Psychology Bulletin, 20*, 580–590.

Singelis, T. M., Triandis, H. C., Bhawuk, D. S., & Gelfand, M. (1995). Horizontal and vertical dimensions of individualism and collectivism: A theoretical and measurement refinement. *Cross-Cultural Research, 29*, 240–275.

Solano-Flores, G., & Trumbull, E. (2003). Examining language in context: The need for new research and practice paradigms in the testing of English-language learners. *Educational Researcher, 32*(2), 3–13.

Takai, J., & Ota, H. (1994). Assessing Japanese interpersonal communication competence. *Japanese Journal of Experimental Social Psychology, 33*, 224–236.

Ting-Toomey, S. (1988). Intercultural conflict styles: A face-negotiation theory. In Y. Y. Kim & W. B. Gudykunst (Eds.), *Theories in intercultural communication* (pp. 213–238). Newbury Park, CA: Sage.

Varona, F. (1996). Relationship between communication satisfaction and organizational commitment in three Guatemalan organizations. *Journal of Business Communication, 33*(2), 111–140.

Wiseman, R. L., Hammer, M. R., & Nishida, H. (1989). Predictors of intercultural communication competence. *International Journal of Intercultural Relations, 13*, 349–370.

Yang, L., & Rancer, A. S. (2003). Ethnocentrism, intercultural communication apprehension, intercultural willingness-to-communicate, and intentions to participate in an intercultural dialogue program: Testing a proposed model. *Communication Research Reports, 20*, 189–191.

Yashima, T., Zenuk-Nishide, L., & Shimizu, K. (2004). The influence of attitudes and affect on willingness to communicate and second language communication. *Journal of Learning Language, 54*(1), 119–152.

Zimmermann, S. (1995). Perceptions of intercultural communication competence and international student adaptation to an American campus. *Communication Education, 44*, 321–335.

Measurement in Interpersonal Communication

Elizabeth E. Graham and Scott Titsworth

Since the first interpersonal communication course was introduced at Antioch College in the mid-20th century, society has changed markedly. Historical shifts in attitudes and values have resulted in a focus on human rights, women's rights, sexual freedoms, no-fault divorce, family first initiatives, and a host of other social transitions and changes. Moreover, revolutionary technologies have emerged that facilitate communication to anyone, anywhere, at anytime.

Amidst these wholesale and monumental changes, the human condition remains intact, as does the essence of communication. Then, as now, people to seek affection, cherish virtue, keep secrets, engage in patterned communication, avoid topics, value interpersonal competence, practice dominance, celebrate civility, experience jealousy, enjoy humor, tolerate uncertainty, and participate in relationships with disliked others. Moreover, these qualities remain endemic to human communication and continue to be the focus of interpersonal communication research. Emblematic of this dialectic, a remarkable degree of instability *and* consistency remains as we seek to answer many of the same fundamental questions that have guided scholars for decades.

In an effort to understand these forces, we examine measurement practices in interpersonal communication research spanning the past 15 years. We focus on measurement indices and scale development. We seek to illustrate that, although our ways of studying interpersonal communication are evolving to keep pace with changes in theory, if not the social world that we theorize about, many of the fundamental questions about how communication creates, sustains, or disrupts social relationships continue to underpin the field. We begin with a brief overview describing how measures were selected for inclusion in this volume and then proceed to discussing important methodological advances and changes in the study of interpersonal communication.

Selection of Measures

Measures were subjected to two primary criteria before they were selected for inclusion in this volume and include: (1) Does the measure display sufficient validity and reliability and (2) Does the measure enjoy frequent and substantial application in communication research. Several measures profiled in Volume 1 of *Communication Research Measures* (Rubin, Palmgreen, & Sypher, 1994) afforded the benefit of almost 25 years of use from which to draw on and render decisions about. With newer measures, the benefit of longevity is not a commodity provided; rather we cautiously relied on *promise* as a third criterion as we arrived at decisions for inclusion of measures in this volume.

Importantly, measures developed prior to the publication of the first volume, but not widely employed at that time, were considered for inclusion in this series. For example, the RELATIONAL MAINTENANCE STRATEGY MEASURE developed in 1992 by Canary and Stafford was not featured in Volume 1 because, at the time, it did not have a sufficient record of use. However, since then, this scale has enjoyed widespread application and therefore is included in this current volume. In total, 17 interpersonal communication measures are profiled in this volume (see Table 1, p. 89).

The Interrelated Nature of Research in Interpersonal Communication

In concert with the development of interpersonal communication measurement are advances in theory, enhanced conceptualization of variables, and refinement in procedures used to analyze quantitative data. Importantly, these aspects of the research process are interrelated, and therefore, iterative in nature (Tracey & Glidden-Tracey, 1999). Suppose a researcher wanted to test a hypothesized causal connection between two or more variables—a particular type of reasoned argument. A well-developed theory implying causal connections would require a certain type of research design (e.g., an experiment) and a certain way of operationalizing variables (e.g., controlled manipulations). Likewise, a researcher wanting to establish that a particular theory is generalizable across realistic but varied situations would need to confront entirely different measurement and design decisions—for instance, obtaining valid and reliable scales and selecting a representative sample of participants in a way that promotes ecological validity.

Recognizing the interrelated and interdependent nature of research, we assume that trends stemming from the litany of methodological and theoretical decisions made by scholars over the past several years would be evident. Indeed, the absence of such substantiation would be unlikely. At the same time, the ability to document, describe, characterize, and explain those trends are another matter. After all, because the research process is interconnected, a change in one level (e.g., the natural progression of theory) would influence many other aspects of research (e.g., the development of new measures, new design options, etc.). Thus, rather than noting "trends" it might be more likely to see a collection of scholars making decisions in ways that resemble a herd of kindergartners released into a puppy kennel—there might be a coherent underlying motivation but the outward observable behaviors would appear chaotic.

After reviewing more than 40 measurement indexes (see Table 1, p. 89, for a list of measures) developed over the past several decades, and profiling 17 measures employed in the conduct of interpersonal communication study, we devised a method to describe the status as well as the characteristics of interpersonal communication research. In our review, we identified seven trends that fall along three general dimensions that organize and clarify the iterative process of research in interpersonal communication. The next section defines these general dimensions and analyzes current measurement topics with respect to the seven trends.

Dimensions and Trends in Interpersonal Communication Research

In an effort to articulate the methodological trends characteristic of the field, this discussion is organized around the following three dimensions: conceptual expansion, increased precision, and claim sophistication. Dimensions refer to the broad class of decisions and issues that encompass the major parts of the research process (i.e., specifying theory, selecting measures, designing studies). Trends relate to specific trajectories of research and decision-making observed within those dimensions. Trends are characterized as conceptual moves back and forth from one position (or decision) to another, taking in effect, fluid dialectical turns. As such, the trends are characterized more by movement in practice (which is nonlinear) than by movement in time (which is linear), as the term typically suggests.

Dimension 1: Conceptual Expansion

Conceptual expansion is the extent to which researchers broaden the scope and nature of theory in interpersonal processes. Paradoxically, conceptual expansion can produce differentiation, and in effect, prompt the need for integration. Fincham (1995) applied Heinz Werner's orthogenic principle to the study of personal relationships and offered the cautionary note that differentiation without benefit of integration can produce "complete splintering to the point where it [the field] will cease to exist as an entity" (p. 526). In effect, growth (i.e., conceptual expansion) without benefit of definition is inadequate at best and dangerous at worst. Attention to both ends of the expansion–integration continuum is necessary to the health and well-being of personal relationship research. Emblematic of conceptual expansion and integration are two trends: (a) valence and (b) agency.

Trend 1: Tacking Between the Light and the Dark (Valence)

Perhaps due to the early influence of the Human Relations Movement, interpersonal communication research reflects a desire to improve the human condition and enhance social relations. Recently developed measures continue to reflect the tendency to affect positive outcomes and values. For example, instruments have been introduced that feature goodwill, humor, interpersonal competence, affectionate communication, love and sex, empathy, marital virtues, and friendship.

While much energy has been expended in the pursuit of understanding the positive features of interpersonal relationships, an examination of the full continuum of communication practices and behaviors is only recently in evidence. Indeed, Steve Duck (1994) argued several years ago "personal relationship researchers . . . focus on the positive aspects of relationships and the full range of difficulties experienced in everyday life . . . have been given almost no attention" (p. 3). Contemporary scholars have begun to address and measure the communication challenges, or what we might call deficits or low points, individuals deal with in the course of everyday life. New measures featuring interpersonal dominance, communication conflict, sexual harassment, intimate coping, jealousy, telephone apprehension, children's apprehension, and sadness have been the subject of recent scale development. Privileging the full spectrum of relationship life (i.e., the light and the dark side) presents a realistic and enhanced portrayal of relationships.

Trend 2: Moving Between Reactive and Strategic Behaviors (Agency)

Another facet of conceptual expansion is the trend to conceptualize communication and communicators as more than reactors to stimuli, but rather as social actors who have agency and are strategic in their communication choices. Previous research tended to explore communication from a psychological, retrospective, and reactive point of view. Nevertheless, a fundamental, though perhaps unspoken assumption of strategic processes is that people are mindful, and goal directed in their communication. Social actors have agency, and in effect, are the architects of their social world who are motivated to control and influence their environment. Interpersonal communication measures that assess RELATIONAL DISTANCE (Hess, 2003) and AFFECTIONATE COMMUNICATION (Floyd & Morman, 1998) require a degree of cognitive processing and interactional awareness that is central to their success. As a consequence of conceptual and methodological expansion, increasingly sophisticated knowledge claims regarding communication in relationships have been articulated.

Dimension 2: Increased Precision

Conceptual expansion without benefit of increased precision would not do justice to the complexity of personal relationship research. The adage that to capture the true essence of a phenomenon requires both a telescope and a microscope is best captured by the twin goals of conceptual expansion (dimension 1) and increased precision (dimension 2). Precision is the degree of confidence assigned to a measurement technique. Measurement precision allows variance to be identified more readily, even when such variance is relatively small. Precision is therefore a manifestation of the integrity of an instrument and a critical component of the reliability and validity of a measurement tool. In an effort to refine the notion of precision, Emmert and Barker (1989) coined the term *measurability index* to articulate the variability and the difficulty in capturing and measuring elusive concepts. For example, measuring shoe size, a low measurability index item, is much less challenging than operationalizing a high measurability construct such as faith or hope. In concert with a constellation of other measurement concerns, the measurability index of a construct is necessary to consider when evaluating the precision of a measurement tool as expectations will likely vary from construct to construct. Claims of increased precision in interpersonal communication measurement practices are evidenced by two trends: (a) specificity and (b) realism.

Trend 3: Moving Between High-Inference and Low-Inference (Specificity)

Interpersonal communication research relies on high-inference and low-inference assessments. Low inference refers to easily observable behaviors that require less subjective judgment on the part of respondents (for discussion, see Civikly, 1992). High inference variables, contrasted with low and intermediate inference variables, are more likely global, affective judgments about people, behaviors, and/or concepts and are not necessarily subject to ready observation.

Traditionally, interpersonal communication research has been conducted from a social science perspective (Allen & Walker, 2000) that privileges perception and cognitively based assessments (high inference) more so than interaction-based data (low inference). The reliance on perceptual and cognitively based research measures is perhaps an artifact of what Baxter (1992) refers to as "*the private fields*" that characterize personal relationships. Indeed, as much as we encourage the gathering of interaction-based data, the reality is that the interpersonal setting is not amenable to third party observation. Hence, we resort to asking individuals and couples to retrospectively or prospectively report how they would, or did, behave and what they would, or did, say in particular interactions. In effect, high-inference assessments are an artifact of perception-based measures and remain integral to the study of personal relationships. It is prudent to be mindful that high-inference observations, while necessary, vary in the degree to which they can, and do, reflect how people process and attend to social behavior.

One means of minimizing the negative consequences of high-inference measures is to enhance the precision and definition of the construct and augment its content validity. Item generation and the degree to which those items reflect the theoretical construct is a crucial first step in scale construction. Tracey and Glidden-Tracey (1999) in an essay articulating the importance of the relationship between theory and measurement, refer to this issue as concreteness. They suggest, "Ideally, the discrepancy between manifest indicators and the latent construct should be as low as possible. The relationship is guided by the degree of specificity of the construct—how abstract is the construct and how specific is the guiding theory" (p. 311).

An excellent example of thoughtful attention to content validity is the COMMUNICATION RESPONSES TO JEALOUSY MEASURE developed by Guerrero, Andersen, Jorgensen, Spitzberg, and Eloy in 1995. In an exhaustive effort to identify responses to jealousy, the researchers initially generated 962 articulations of behaviors or types of communication used to cope with feelings of jealousy. After this qualitative procedure, they then subjected the responses to coding and data reduction techniques to arrive at a 51-item measure of jealousy. Through such robust and grounded approaches, the validity and precision of scales is increased.

Validity is not a commodity ever fully achieved but rather a goal that researchers strongly endorse and enthusiastically seek. To accomplish this requires that measurement remain fluid and as such, open to adaptation and change. One means of contributing to a measure's validity is to continually refine, modify, and achieve additional specificity of the construct of interest. For example, measures of TOPIC AVOIDANCE (Guerrero & Afifi, 1995) and RELATIONAL UNCERTAINTY (Knobloch & Solomon, 1999) are regularly refined as new information is revealed about these topics. Other measures have been tested and improved as well. For instance, Dillard, Solomon, and Palmer (1999) refined Burgoon and Hale's (1987) Relational Communication Scale by conducting additional study and factor analysis. Further examination and refinement (conducted by L. L. McCroskey, J. C. McCroskey, & Richmond, 2006) resulted in second-generation measures of McCroskey, Richmond, and Daly's (1975) measure of homophily and McCroskey and McCain's (1974) Interpersonal Attraction Instrument. And, recent analysis of the Infante and Wigley's (1986) one-dimensional Verbal Aggressiveness Scale suggests multidimensionality (Levine, Beatty, Limon, Hamilton, Buck, & Chory-Assad, 2004). These refinements coupled with newly developed measures illustrate continued growth and specificity in the study of interpersonal communication.

Trend 4: Moving Between Control and Contextualization (Realism)

Striking a balance between internal validity directives that feature control and external validity mandates that encourage generalizability is a singular concern for social scientists. To privilege one can jeopardize the other. The host of social and environmental influences is real and cannot simply be controlled, held constant, or considered "statistical noise." To capture, through measurement, the *"true"* essence of a variable requires retaining a degree of control through standardization of research protocols while incorporating the host of variables embedded in the social context. The practicality of exercising experimental control while incorporating the nuances and contextual forces in the research environment necessitates nimbleness and creativity on the part of researchers. While there is ample evidence to suggest that attention to *control is thriving,* less consideration is afforded to *contextualizing* the focus of study.

Interpersonal communication research continues to rely on college student samples and, to some extent, this population is ideal for study. At no other point do individuals develop, maintain, and dissolve as many relationships as college students do. The mere access and opportunity for social development and interaction is so rich in the college environment that it is reasonable to tap into this domain to study relationships. However, the heavy reliance on convenience samples is problematic because it limits the ability to offer generalizable claims. Furthermore, dependence on college student samples no longer produces equal gender representation as the percentage of male undergraduates has dropped 24% from 1970 to 2000. Indeed, the gender balance at many state universities represents a 60–40 split (Ange Peterson, American Association of Collegiate Registrars and Admissions Officers, 2006). Consequently, if we continue to tap students as participants in our research, we need to be cognoscenti of a female participant bias simply due to their over-representation in research studies.

To introduce a bit of balance to the demonization associated with the reliance on college-student sampling practice, Basil, Brown, and Bocarnea (2002) offered that validity is not singularly dependent on the characteristics of the sampling distribution and concluded: "Sampling methodology is only one factor in determining the validity of research. Other factors, such as logic behind the study, the way variables were conceptualized and operationalized, the inclusion or exclusion of third variables, the form of the evidence, the validity and reliability of manipulations and measurement, the strength of observed relationships, and replications all determine the validity of the study. Faulting a study that is strong in regard to these dimensions but relies on a nonrepresentative sample may be penny-wise and pound foolish" (p. 513). As a consequence of increased precision, manifested in specificity and realism, increasingly sophisticated knowledge claims regarding communication in relationships can be drawn.

Dimension 3: Claim Sophistication

The aforementioned enhancements in conceptual expansion and increased precision of interpersonal communication measures, coupled with advances in theory, point to changes in the types of conclusions that inter-personal scholars can reach. The final dimension characterizing develop-ments in interpersonal communication research suggests that the claims advanced by scholars are increasingly more sophisticated. We highlight three specific trends: (a) focus, (b) influence, and (c) parsimony.

Trend 5: Moving Between Monadic and Dyadic (Focus)

Although many measures continue to emphasize individual rather than rela-tional behaviors, there is a subtle shift occurring. For example, Kashy and Levesque (2000) speak of the many ways our questions are starting to incor-porate mutual influence rather than individual perception. In their words, "interdependence between related individuals should not simply be consid-ered statistical annoyance. Rather, it should be embraced as an opportunity to ask old questions in new ways, to ask new questions, and to test theoret-ical propositions that are explicitly about interdependence" (p. 4).

Consistent with the movement to feature interactional data in research design is the focus on process rather than outcomes. For example, the ten-dency to identify a specific outcome such as satisfaction as the ultimate indicator of the value of the relationship quality has emphasized individu-als' perceptions of relational communication rather than the process of communication within relationships. Although we observed evidence of interpersonal theory moving away from the monadic model, much work, particularly in terms of measurement and research design options remains. To fully incorporate contemporary communication theory, researchers should continue to explore how to best examine relational aspects of the communication process. This refocusing will undoubtedly contribute to sophisticated knowledge claims.

Trend 6: Moving Between Independence and Interdependence (Influence)

The consequent tendency to assess interpersonal interactions at the monadic rather than the dyadic level, despite theoretical orientations to the contrary, has been referred to as "ignoring interdependence." Indeed Kashy and Levesque (2000) suggest the mere essence of interpersonal communication is all about interdependence except when it comes to measurement. Thus, the drive for greater specificity, while advantageous in some respects, can prevent interpersonal researchers from fully considering communication as a relational and transactional accomplishment.

An informal assessment of journal articles published in *Communication Monographs* and *Human Communication Research* between 1996 and 2000 revealed that the use of inferential statistics is widespread and ANOVA is the "statistic of choice" (Smith, Levine, Lachlan, & Fediuk, 2002, p. 515). Indeed, conventional statistical analyses are, by their very nature, data reduction techniques (e.g., ANOVA and factor analysis) and consequently diminish the importance of interdependent communication behaviors in interpersonal research (Kashy et al., 2004). As Aron and Aron (1995) aptly observed, "the extreme moments in life *do not reveal themselves easily in averages and correlations*" (p. 560).

New analytic techniques such as structural equation modeling (for more information see Holbert & Stephenson, 2002; Kashy, Jellison, & Kenny, 2004; Schrodt & Ledbetter, 2007) can be used to preserve some of the nuances that are lost with traditional data reduction statistical procedures. Whereas more commonly employed statistical techniques (e.g., correlation and ANOVA) emphasize a focus on the individual, structural equation modeling and hierarchical linear modeling allow process-oriented relational dimensions to be taken into account. Recent advances in statistical modeling (see Cook & Kenny, 2005), in particular the actor-partner interdependence model, permits separation of dyadic effects from individual effects. Indeed, Kashy et al. (2004) caution that "most standard statistical techniques assume independence of cases—i.e., data collected from one participant are not influenced by the responses of another participant" (p. 266). The application of this reasoning has not been fully realized in interpersonal communication research.

Trend 7: Moving Between Reduction and Representation (Parsimony)

Several authors (Boster, 2002; Smith et al., 2002) caution that complexity need not be the prime objective of research. Indeed, the very essence of *simple elegance* (a measurement standard) rests with achieving the twin goals of retaining the integrity (i.e., representation) while simultaneously operationalizing (i.e., reduction) the construct of interest. Accomplishing both is perhaps at the core of validity and central to the charge of researchers.

Typologies are one means of striking a balance between reduction and representation. Over the last several decades we have witnessed the development of several classification schemes, taxonomies, and typologies that have been central to the study of marital types (Fitzpatrick, 1988), family communication patterns (McCloud & Chaffee, 1972; Ritchie & Fitzpatrick, 1990), compliance-gaining strategies (Marwell & Schmitt, 1967), and stepfamily types (Schrodt, 2006). Typologies are very functional in interpersonal communication research, especially at the conceptual level of idea generation, because they crystallize and systematize concepts of interest (see Aron & Aron, 1995; Shrodt, 2006).

The practice of merging measures is an indication of theoretical and methodological pluralism and a healthy indicator that we are better positioned to measure the constellations of related communication constructs. For example, the Relational Dimensions Instrument (Fitzpatrick, 1988) and the Revised Family Communication Scale (Ritchie & Fitzpatrick, 1990) have been modified/merged to form the Family Communication Environment Measure (Fitzpatrick & Ritchie, 1994). Moreover, through such integration the reductive nature of the separate scales is minimized as researchers consider more holistic constellations of variables. In so doing, the nature of family communication, for example, is represented more broadly and is more commensurate with contemporary perspectives on communication (e.g., communication is interactive and contextual).

It is evident that through synthesis and continued refinement, measures of interpersonal communication have simultaneously increased the sophistication of conclusions that can be drawn while also improving parsimony. At the same time, it is also apparent that many of the questions that characterized early interpersonal communication research remain a part of contemporary scholarly dialogue.

Additional Considerations

In this last section we discuss additional issues related to methodological sophistication including: Use/misuse of factor analysis (i.e., PCA/EFA/CFA), conventions and adjustments of alpha, the need for replication, sample bias, faulty comparisons, application of single-use measures, and the identification of guiding assumptions. The topics discussed here were observed in our review of scales and represent important method-related decisions that should be more transparent in subsequent interpersonal research. Thus, our analysis in this final section should be read as topics to consider when planning studies, regardless of specific measures employed.

One indication of the health and vibrancy of a field is the extent to which lively discussion and debate of issues of importance is encouraged. Although Hewes (2003) laments the relative absence of attention paid to methodological matters, there is nonetheless evidence that this condition is changing. Indeed, a special issue of *Human Communication Research* (2002, vol. 28, no. 4), which is a continuation of the disciplinary dialogue that began in 1979 (see *Human Communication Research*, vol. 5, no. 4), is devoted solely to statistical and methodological concerns. Curiously, some of the same issues that warranted attention in 1979 continue to be of considerable interest in 2002. Featured topics include generalizability (Shapiro, 2002), error rates (Smith et al., 2002), standardized scores (Hunter & Hamilton, 2002), exploratory and principal components factor analysis (Park, Dailey, & Lemus, 2002), the halo effect (Feeley, 2002), and measures of association (Beatty, 2002). Although the purpose of this review is not to enter the ongoing debate, several issues warrant pointed attention and subsequent discussion.

(1) *Use of appropriate data reduction techniques.* Several researchers (Fabrigar, Wegener, MacCallum, & Strahan, 1999; Park et al., 2002; Ragsdale & Brandau-Brown, 2004; Smith et al., 2002) have noted that our journals contain a number of instances of the inappropriate use of PCA (principal components factor analysis) instead of EFA (exploratory factor analysis). Smith et al. reviewed articles in *Human Communication Research, Communication Monographs, and Communication Research* between the years 1990 and 2000 and concluded that 53% employed PCA even when the goal was to identify underlying concepts and structures. Levine (2005) raised similar concerns in regard to confirmatory factor analysis pointing out that even when researchers harbor expectations about how items will factor, they resort to using exploratory factor analysis. McCroskey and Young proffered very much the same arguments and cautions in 1979 suggesting that at least in this domain, our field is not reaping the twin benefits associated with age, that of maturity and wisdom (Park et al., 2002). The rise in popularity of confirmatory factor analysis has the potential to diminish reliance on exploratory procedures in favor of theoretically driven tests of hypothesized measurement models.

(2) *Thoughtful consideration of acceptable type 1 error rates.* O'Keefe (2003) insisted that the use of family-wise alpha adjustment is misguided and at best, unjustified. Tutzauer (2003) and Hewes (2003) responded that thoughtful use of alpha-adjustment procedures are both useful in certain circumstances and necessary to the practice of offering relatively error-free claims. Relatedly, the standard alpha used for significance testing and error rates is by convention set at $p < .05$. However, several researchers (Smith et al., 2002) caution that this is an arbitrary standard and Sauley and Bedeian (1989), in their article entitled *.05: A case of the tail wagging the distribution*, echo this concern and claim that .05 is not the gold standard by which measures are deemed reliable or valid. Instead, they call for a more encompassing set of criteria to consider such as sample size, effect size, measurement error, practical consequences of the null hypothesis, underlying theory, degree of experimental control, and robustness as a means of setting a significance level. These admonitions are

consistent with the arguments proffered in defense of the use of convenience sampling, which in effect warn that adherence to any rigid investigative protocol, without benefit of consideration of the constellation of interdependent research contingencies, is shortsighted at best and problematic at worst. Evidence and rationale for the occasional use of a liberal alpha (i.e., $p < .10$) can be found in interpersonal communication research (see Caughlin, 2002). Such thoughtful consideration of research conventions should be more transparent in manuscripts.

One-tailed and two-tailed tests have direct implications on alpha level and significance levels. In particular, Levine and Banas (2002) recommend that authors restrict their use of one-tailed F-tests in particular and caution against the use of one-tailed tests in general. While the growing popularity of SEM may start to replace experiments as the quantitative design of choice, Levine and Banas' admonition should be carefully considered within the context of specific designs.

(3) *Consider the value of replication efforts.* One of the benefits of social science is that it is self-correcting; however, without replication work the self-correcting function of science is delayed and often impossible to achieve. Limited journal space contributes to less than full disclosure of statistical procedures employed which restricts meta-analysis and replication efforts (for additional discussion see Boster, 2002). In addition, Shapiro (2002) encourages journal authors and reviewers to be more mindful of how multiple studies contribute to generalizability.

(4) *Enact steps to reduce sampling bias.* We introduce sample bias when we privilege the voice of the middle class, educated, white, Christian, physically and mentally fit, heterosexual men and women in our research. Neglected from examination and study are the vast numbers of people who do not fit this demographic (for further discussion see Wood, 1995). Furthermore, the ambiguous terminology used to describe research participants continues to be problematic. To truly recognize and describe our diverse society will require a more inclusive lexicon to identify gender, living arrangements, sexual orientations, political affiliations, and marital status. For example, an exit survey from a large group event featured the following response options for marital status: single, married, polyamorous, domestic partner—shacking up, etc. Humor aside, the point is clear: terminology has not kept pace with relational status and living-arrangements. Moreover, even gender, often measured as a binary category, is not determined solely by biological sex. Furthermore, income and social class continue to be conflated without regard for education level and occupational status (Wood, 1995). The increasingly fluid nature of social life is not so amenable to simple fixed categorization.

(5) *Be careful of comparing apples to oranges.* Comparing results across studies can be problematic when little detail is offered that describes the factors that distinguish one study from another. As a result, claims of

measurement instability can oftentimes be the consequence of studies not being amenable to comparison, yet comparisons are drawn nonetheless. According to Ragsdale and Brandau-Brown (2004) there are four possible causes of measurement instability that include the composition of the population (i.e., undergraduate students, married couples, married persons, and workers), the relationship type (i.e., friendship, marriage, co-workers), the response elicitation (i.e., Likert scale versus diary method), and factor analytic method employed (i.e., exploratory versus confirmatory factor analysis). Full disclosure detailing the sample, relationship type, response options, and methods utilized is necessary for valid comparisons between and across studies.

(6) *Avoid the application of single-use measures.* There is a tendency to craft single item measures and deploy them as though they have been developed, tested, and undergone scrutiny and critical evaluation to the same extent as a fully vetted measure. Results obtained from this practice are consequently suspect but rarely treated as such. Essentially this is a validity concern and a trend that if continued, requires informed discussion and attention. A variation on this theme is the practice of modifying measures without conducting a factor analysis and subsequently employing the modified measure as though it will perform similar to the original measure. Furthermore, if factor analyses are conducted, the procedures and criteria employed are often not detailed in print.

(7) *Identify guiding assumptions.* Tracey and Glidden-Tracey (1999) offer a series of suggestions for analyzing measures. Of central significance to the validity of research is the articulation of assumptions. More specifically Tracey and Glidden-Tracey suggested, "Quality of the study is proportional to the extent to which assumptions are made explicit" (p. 302). This sentiment has been expressed in the communication literature as well. Indeed, Wilson (1994) suggested commencing research studies with the introduction of "Hello, my name is . . . and I'm a social scientist and these are my deeply held assumptions about the nature of communication . . ." (p. 25). Articulating our theoretical orientations, decision-making processes, and even our discarded ideas, would not only inform the reader but also would prompt discussion and debate which inevitably enhances any scholarly endeavor. Unfortunately, only modest journal space is devoted to the justification of measurement tools employed (see Tracey & Glidden-Tracey, 1999), let alone any thoughtful statements about the researcher's motivations and/or background.

Concluding Remarks

The 15 years since the publication of the first volume of *Communication Research Measures* saw rapid growth in both the quantity and quality of interpersonal communication research measures. Clearly, there is a good amount of research activity within the interpersonal communication context that reflects growth and maturity and evidence of efforts to find new ways to measure the dynamics of interpersonal relationships. Advances in measurement, research design, analytical techniques, and theory are providing increasingly robust explanations of interpersonal processes. While the significant work by scholars over the past several decades has done much to refine the study of interpersonal communication, we see this momentum as ongoing, fluid, and ripe for creative engagement by new generations of scholars.

Table 1 Interpersonal Communication Measures

Intimate Friendship Scale (1994)	Sharabany, R.	*Journal of Social and Personal Relationships, 11, 449–469*
Investment Model Scale (1998)	Rusbult, C. E., Martz, J. M., & Agnew, C. R.	*Personal Relationships, 5, 357–391*
The Lifespan Sibling Relationship Scale (2000)	Riggio, H. R.	*Journal of Social and Personal Relationships, 17, 707–728*
The Love Attitudes Scale: Short Form (1998)	Hendrick, C., Hendrick, S. S., & Dicke, A.	*Journal of Social and Personal Relationships, 15, 147–159*
*Marital Opinion Questionnaire (1976)	Campbell, A., Converse, P. E., & Rodgers, W. L.	In R. Gilmour & S. Duck (Eds.), *The emerging field of personal relationships* (pp. 109–132).
*Measure of Source Credibility (1999)	McCroskey, J. C., & Teven, J. J.	*Communication Monographs, 66, 90–103*
Message Elaboration Measure (1997)	Reynolds, R. A. 1997	*Communication Research Reports, 14, 269–278*
Multidimensional Intimate Coping Questionnaire (1999)	Pollina, L. K., & Snell, W. E.	*Journal of Social and Personal Relationships, 16, 133–144*
*The Need for Cognition Measure (1984); (1982)	Cacioppo, J. T., Petty, R. E., & Kao, C. F.; Cacioppo, J. T., & Petty, R. E.	*Journal of Personality Assessment, 48, 306–307; Journal of Personality and Social Psychology, 42, 116–131*
*Normative Message Processing Scale (1994)	Aune, R. K., & Reynolds, R. A.	*Communication Monographs, 61, 135–160*
The Parental Stress Scale (1995)	Berry, J. O., & Jones, W. H.	*Journal of Social and Personal Relationships, 12, 463–472*
Perceived Acceptance Scale (1998)	Brock, D. M., Sarason, I. G., Sanghvi, H., & Gurung, R. A. R.	*Journal of Social and Personal Relationships, 15, 5–21*

Perceived Masculinity Questionnaire (2001)	Chesbro, J. W. & Fuse, K. 2001	*Communication Quarterly, 49,* 203–278
Perceptions of Love and Sex Scale (2002)	Hendrick, S. S., & Hendrick, C.	*Journal of Social and Personal Relationships, 19,* 361–378
*Personal Report of Marital Virtues Scale (2003)	Strom, B.	*Journal of Family Communication, 3,* 21–40
*Reactance Restoration Scale (2007)	Quick, B. L., & Stephenson, M. T.	*Communication Research Reports, 24,* 131–138
*Relational Distance Index (2003)	Hess, J. A.	*Personal Relationships, 10,* 197–215
*Relational Maintenance Strategy Measure (1992)	Canary, D. J., & Stafford, L.	*Communication Monographs, 59,* 243–267
*Relational Uncertainty Measure (1999)	Knobloch, L. K., & Solomon, D. H.	*Communication Studies, 50,* 261–278
Relationship Assessment Scale (1988)	Hendrick, S. S.	*Journal of Marriage and the Family, 50,* 93–98
Relationship Stage Measure (2002)	Welch, S-A., & Rubin, R. B.	*Communication Quarterly, 50,* 24–40
Revised Taking Conflict Personally Scale (1995)	Hample, D., & Dallinger, J. M.	*Communication Quarterly, 43,* 297–319
Schema of Partner Empathic Responses to Anger (1998)	Sanford, K.	*Journal of Social and Personal Relationships, 15,* 490–501
*Sexual Harassment Proclivity Index (1996)	Bingham, S. G., & Burleson, B. R.	*Communication Quarterly, 44,* 308–325
Social Skills Inventory (1986)	Riggio, R. E.	*Journal of Personality and Social Psychology, 51,* 649–660
Survey of Imagined Interactions (2005)	Honeycutt, J.	*Imagined Interaction: Daydreaming about Communication.* Thousand Oaks, CA: Sage
*Topic Avoidance (1995)	Guerrero, L. K., & Afifi, W. A.	*Parents, children, and communication: Frontiers of theory and research* (pp. 219–245).
Trait Affection Given (2002)	Floyd, K.	*Communication Quarterly, 50,* 135–151
Trait Affection Received (2002)	Floyd, K.	*Communication Quarterly, 50,* 135–151

* Indicates that this measure is profiled in another section of the book.

References

Allen, K. R., & Walker, A. J. (2000). Qualitative research. In C. Hendrick & S. S. Hendrick (Eds.), *Close relationships: A sourcebook* (pp. 19–30). Thousand Oaks, CA: Sage.

Aron, A., & Aron, E. N. (1995). Three suggestions for increased emphasis in the study of personal relationships. *Journal of Social and Personal Relationships, 12,* 559–562.

Basil, M. D., Brown, W. J., & Bocarnea, M. C. (2002). Differences in univariate values versus multivariate relationships. Findings from a study of Diana, Princess of Wales. *Human Communication Research, 28,* 501–514.

Baxter, L. A. (1992). Interpersonal communication as dialogue: A response to the "social approaches" forum. *Communication Theory, 2,* 330–337.

Beatty, M. J. (2002). Do we know a vector from a scalar? Why measures of association (not their squares) are appropriate indices of effect. *Human Communication Research, 28,* 605–611.

Boster, F. J. (2002). On making progress in communication science. *Human Communication Research, 28,* 473–490.

Burgoon, J. K., & Hale, J. L. (1987). Validation and measurement of the fundamental themes of relational communication. *Communication Monographs, 54,* 19–41.

Canary, D. J., & Stafford, L. (1992). Relational maintenance strategies and equity in marriage. *Communication Monographs, 59,* 243–267.

Caughlin, J. P. (2002). The demand/withdraw pattern of communication as a predictor of marital satisfaction over time. Unresolved issues and future directions. *Human Communication Research, 28,* 49–85.

Civikly, J. (1992). Clarity: Teachers and students making sense of instruction. *Communication Education, 41,* 138–152.

Cook, W. L., & Kenny, D. A. (2005). The actor-partner interdependence model: A model of bidirectional effects in developmental studies. *International Journal of Behavioral Development, 29,* 101–109.

Dillard, J. P., Solomon, D. H., & Palmer, M. T. (1999). Structuring the concept of relational communication. *Communication Monographs, 66,* 49–65.

Duck, S. (1994). Stratagems, spoils, and a serpent's tooth: On the delights and dilemmas of personal relationships. In W. R. Cupach & B. H. Spitzberg (Eds.), *The dark side of interpersonal communication* (pp. 3–24). Hillsdale, NJ: Erlbaum.

Emmert, P., & Barker, L. L. (1989). *Measurement of communication behavior.* New York: Longman.

Fabrigar, L. R., Wegener, D. T., MacCallum, R. C., & Strahan E. J. (1999). Evaluating the use of exploratory factor analysis in psychological research. *Psychological Methods, 4,* 272–299.

Feeley, T. H. (2002). Comment on halo effects in rating and evaluation research. *Human Communication Research, 28,* 578–586.

Fincham, F. D. (1995). From the orthogenic principle to the fish-scale model of omniscience: Advancing understanding of personal relationships. *Journal of Social and Personal Relationships, 12,* 523–527.

Fitzpatrick, M. A. (1988). *Between husbands and wives.* Beverly Hills, CA: Sage.

Fitzpatrick, M. A., & Ritchie, L. D. (1994). Communication schemata within the family: Multiple perspectives on family interaction. *Human Communication Research, 20,* 275–301.

Floyd, K., & Morman, M. T. (1998). The measurement of affectionate communication. *Communication Quarterly, 46,* 144–162.

Guerrero, L. K., & Afifi, W. A. (1995). What parents don't know: Topic avoidance in parent-child relationships. In T. Socha & G. H. Stamp (Eds.), *Parents, children, and communication: Frontiers of theory and research* (pp. 219–245). Mahwah, NJ: Erlbaum.

Guerrero, L. K., Andersen, P. A., Jorgensen, P. F., Spitzberg, B. H., & Elroy, S. V. (1995). Coping with the green-eyed monster: Conceptualizing and measuring communicative responses to romantic jealousy. *Western Journal of Communication, 59,* 270–304.

Hess, J. (2003). Measuring distance in personal relationships: The Relational Distance Index. *Personal Relationships, 10,* 197–215.

Hewes, D. E. (2003). Methods as tools. A response to O'Keefe. *Human Communication Research, 29,* 448–454.

Holbert, R. L., & Stephenson, M. T. (2002). Structural equation modeling in the communication sciences, 1995–2000. *Human Communication Research, 28,* 531–551.

Hunter, J. E., & Hamilton, M. A. (2002). The advantages of using standardized scores in causal analysis. *Human Communication Research, 28,* 552–561.

Infante, D. A., & Wigley, C. J., III. (1986). Verbal aggressiveness: An interpersonal model and measure. *Communication Monographs, 53,* 61–69.

Kashy, D. A., Jellison, W. A., & Kenny, D. A. (2004). Modeling the interdependence among family members. *Journal of Family Communication, 4,* 265–293.

Kashy, D. A., & Levesque, M. J. (2000). Quantitative methods in close relationship research, In C. Hendrick & S. S. Hendrick (Eds.), *Close relationships: A sourcebook* (pp. 3–17). Thousand Oaks, CA: Sage.

Knobloch, L. K., & Solomon, D. H. (1999). Measuring the sources and content of relational uncertainty. *Communication Studies, 50,* 261–278.

Levine, T. R. (2005). Confirmatory factor-analysis and scale validation in communication research. *Communication Research Reports, 22,* 335–338.

Levine, T. R., & Banas, J. (2002). One-tailed F-tests in communication research, *Communication Monographs, 69,* 132–143.

Levine, T. R., Beatty, M. J., Limon, S., Hamilton, M. A., Buck, R., & Chory-Assad, R. M. (2004). The dimensionality of the verbal aggressiveness scale. *Communication Monographs, 71,* 245–268.

Marwell, G., & Schmitt, D. R. (1967). Dimensions of compliance-gaining behavior: An empirical analysis. *Sociometry, 30,* 350–364.

McCroskey, J. C., & McCain, T. A. (1975). The measurement of interpersonal attraction. *Speech Monographs, 41,* 261–266.

McCroskey, L. L., McCroskey, J. C., & Richmond, V. P. (2006). Analysis and improvement of the measurement of interpersonal attraction and homophily. *Communication Quarterly, 54,* 1–31.

McCroskey, J. C., Richmond, V. P., & Daly, J. A. (1975). The development of a measure of perceived homophily in interpersonal communication. *Human Communication Research, 1,* 323–331.

McCroskey, J. C., & Young, T. J. (1979). The use and abuse of factor analysis in communication research. *Human Communication Research, 5,* 375–382.

McLeod, J. M., & Chaffee, S. H. (1972). The construction of social reality. In J. Tedeschi (Ed.), *The social influence processes* (pp. 50–99). Chicago, IL: Aldine-Atherton.

O'Keefe, D. J. (2003). Against familywise alpha adjustment. *Human Communication Research, 29,* 431–447.

Park, H. S., Dailey, R., & Lemus, D. (2002). The use of exploratory factor analysis and principle components analysis in communication research. *Human Communication Research, 28,* 562–577.

Peterson, A. (2006). American Association of Collegiate Registrars and Admissions Officers. *Newsweek.* Accessed April 23, 2007 from http://www.msnbc.msn.com/id/10965522/site/newsweek.

Ragsdale, J. D., & Brandau-Brown, F. E. (2004). Measuring relational maintenance in marriage: Theoretical and methodological issues. *Southern Communication Journal, 69,*121–135.

Ritchie, D. L., & Fitzpatrick, M. A. (1990). Family communication patterns: Measuring intrapersonal perceptions of interpersonal relationships. *Communication Research, 17,* 523–544.

Rubin, R. B., Palmgreen, P., & Sypher, H. E. (1994). *Communication Research Measures: A Sourcebook.* New York: Guilford.

Sauley, K. S., & Bedeian, A. G. (1989). .05: A case of the tail wagging the distribution. *Journal of Management, 15,* 335–344.

Schrodt, P. (2006). A typological examination of communication competence and mental health in stepchildren. *Communication Monographs, 73,* 309–333.

Schrodt, P., & Ledbetter, A. M. (2007). Communication processes that mediate family communication patterns and mental well-being: A mean and covariance structures analysis of young adults from divorced and non-divorced families. *Human Communication Research, 33,* 330–356.

Shapiro, M. A. (2002). Generalizability in communication research. *Human Communication Research, 28,* 491–500.

Smith, R. A., Levine, T. R., Lachlan, K. A., & Fediuk, T. A. (2002). The high cost of complexity in experimental design and data analysis. Type I and Type II error rates in multiway ANOVA. *Human Communication Research, 28,* 515–530.

Tracey, T. G., & Glidden-Tracey, C. E. (1999). Integration of theory, research, design, measurement, and analysis: Toward a reasoned argument. *The Counseling Psychologist, 27,* 299–324.

Tutzauer, F. (2003). On the sensible application of familywise alpha adjustment. *Human Communication Research, 29,* 455–463.

Wilson, B. J. (1994). A challenge to communication empiricists: Let's be more forthcoming about what we do. *Western Journal of Communication, 58,* 25–31.

Wood, J. T. (1995).The part is not the whole: Weaving diversity into the study of relationships. *Journal of Social and Personal Relationships, 12,* 563–567.

Measurement in Mass Communication

Elizabeth M. Perse

Traditional mass communication research continues to thrive. Scholars continue to explore questions about children and the mass media, the effects of antisocial media content, and ways to improve the social contributions of the mass media (see Preiss, Gale, Burrell, Allen, & Bryant, 2007, for a compilation of that research). The years since the publication of the first volume of this set, however, have marked a stimulating time for mass communication researchers. The development of Web as a medium for news and entertainment, the refinement of interactive entertainment (e.g., video games), and the adoption of the digital video recorder (DVR) and digital music players has stimulated research about the uses of these technologies and their subsequent effects—on the audience and on the traditional mass media. The past decade has also seen the emergence of growing areas of research into the melding of entertainment and politics, the third-person effect, and selective exposure to the increased range of programming.

Scholars have adapted traditional measures to aid their research, especially those that have been shown to be reliable and valid. In some cases, new measures have been developed in some notable areas. This chapter reports on the state of mass communication measurement in this shifting media environment.

Criteria for Selecting Measures to be Included in this Volume

There were two steps taken to identify the measures included in this volume. First, an examination of the list of interesting measures compiled for the first volume (see Rubin & Perse, 1994, Table 9) revealed four older measures that have seen consistent and growing utility. So, the SOCIAL PRESENCE SCALE (Short, Williams, & Christie, 1976), the PERCEIVED

Note: Measures that are profiled in this volume (in Part II) are typed in capital letters when cited in the text.

REALISM SCALE (Potter, 1986), the COGNITIVE ELABORATION SCALE (1990), and the SELF-ASSESSMENT MANIKIN (Bradley & Lang, 1994) were all included in this volume.

Second, similar to the procedures of the first volume, we examined the scholarly literature of mass communication, with a focus on new measures developed since the publication of that volume. The criteria for a measure to be included were (a) substantial application in the mass communication literature, (b) self-report measures, (c) broad utility, (d) promise, and (e) evidence of reliability and validity. Based on these criteria, the newer mass communication measures profiled in this work are the SAD FILMS SCALE (Oliver, 1993), THIRD-PERSON EFFECT (McLeod, Eveland, & Nathanson, 1997), the TELEVISION MEDIATION SCALE (Valkenburg, Krcmar, Peeter, & Marseille, 1999), the ORGANIZATION-PUBLIC RELATIONSHIP SCALE (Kim, 2001), the WILLINGNESS TO CENSOR SURVEY (Lambe, 2002), the TELEVISION ADDICTION SCALE (Horvath, 2004), and the PRESENCE QUESTIONNAIRE (Witmer & Singer, 2005). These latter scales can be best characterized as promising, as they have not had as wide a use as older, more established measures.

Methodological Trends in Empirical Mass Communication Research

Adaptation of Measures to New Technology

The significant changes to the mass communication environment have led to research on new content, new channels, and new technologies. One major trend in mass communication research is the adaptation of traditional measures to that new environment. This adaptation has been most notable in studies of uses and gratifications and media credibility.

Uses and Gratifications. Uses and gratifications studies typically accompany the adoption of new types of media technologies and content. Since the publication of the first volume in this set, scholars have been interested in why people adopt and are attracted to Internet-based channels, new mass communication technology, and newer types of media content.

Some initial research about the audience's use of the Internet and Web used motivation scales developed for earlier technology. Ferguson and Perse (2000), for example, used Rubin's Television Viewing Motives Scale (profiled in the first volume) to explore how similar Web use was to television use. Ferguson, Greer, and Reardon (2007) also used Rubin's scale to explore motives for using MP3 players. Because of their focus on several uses of the Internet, mass and interpersonal, other scholars (Flaherty, Pearce, & Rubin, 1998; Papacharissi & Rubin, 2000) combined Rubin's Television Viewing Motives Scale and the Interpersonal Communication

Motives Scale (profiled in the first volume) to explore how people use the Internet. Holbert, Lambe, Dudo, and Carlton (2007) used a reduced version of the Political Media Gratifications Scale (profiled in the first volume) to assess college students' gratifications sought for watching *The Daily Show*.

More recent research has recognized that new technologies and content are marked by unique uses. So, researchers have created new scales to measure motives for playing video games (Sherry, Lucas, Greenberg, & Lachlan, 2006), watching reality television programs (Nabi, Stitt, Halford, & Finnerty, 2006), Fantasy Sports (Farquhar & Meeds, 2007), listening to MP3s, podcasts, and Internet and satellite radio (Albarran et al., 2007), and using the Internet as a commercial medium (Stafford, Stafford, & Schkade, 2004). Several of these scales appear to have strong face validity because they were developed from focus group interviews. Future research should explore their reliability and validity across studies as they are used and adapted.

Credibility. Mass communication scholars and practitioners recognize that information cannot be useful unless it is credible. Research on source credibility has a long history in communication research dealing with persuasion and message effects. The first volume of this set profiled several credibility measures, including Gaziano and McGrath's (1986) News Credibility Scale. The development of the Web and its delivery of online information have created a new information environment that can affect perceptions of the credibility of that information. Online information can be created by nonprofessional sources (e.g., blogs and citizen journalism) posted on personal sites or on news websites (e.g., comments on news stories, CNN's iReport). The need for "instant" news to feed the online audience can lead to inaccuracies and premature conclusions. Online "polls" created to allow the audience to express opinions and feedback are rarely based on random or representative samples. Metzger, Flannagin, Eyal, Lemus, and McCann (2003) suggested that lack of gatekeeping and convergence of information genres (blending news, marketing, and entertainment) affect editorial review and trustworthiness.

Scholars have used scales adapted from traditional media credibility research to compare traditional and online news and political information (e.g., Johnson & Kaye, 1998, 2000, 2002; Kiousis, 2001), traditional and online information sources (Flannagin & Metzger, 2000), and to assess the credibility of blogs (Johnson & Kaye, 2004). This research has not used the full scales of prior research, but instead four to five items, typically drawn from Gaziano and McGrath's (1986) News Credibility Scale. Although these shortened scales limit multidimensional assessment of credibility and sometimes have reduced reliability, shortened scales are necessary when respondents are assessing credibility of several different channels in the same study.

Measures Developed for Growing Areas of Mass Communication Research

Significant trends in mass communication grow from three growing areas of mass communication research: third-person effects research, an interest in explaining the processes behind media selection and effects, and the exploration of new concepts important to new technologies.

Third-Person Effects Research. The exploration of the third-person effect has generated substantial research in recent years. The third-person effect is the examination of how people believe others are affected by media content and the consequences of those perceptions. Research has explored the two parts of the effect: the perceptual hypothesis, or how and why people assume others are more affected, and the behavioral hypothesis, or the actions that people take or endorse, based on that perceptual effect (see Perloff, 2002). This survey- and self-report based area of political communication research has produced a substantial amount of research, generating measures to assess relevant constructs such as third- and first-person perceptions, social distance, message desirability, and censorship. This volume profiles the measure of perceptual effects used by McLeod and his colleagues (1997) primarily because it is one of the few that does not employ a single-item measure. Future research in third-person effects should be aware of reliability and validity issues in measurement.

Processes. Several self-report measures have been created specifically to explore cognitive processes underlying media selection and effects. These measures have been used to test hypotheses about selective exposure to sad films, about the mental processing of news and political messages, and cognitive/physiological responses to media stimuli.

Oliver (1993) developed her SAD FILM SCALE to explore the contradictory evidence that some people enjoy watching movies that make them feel sad, a negative emotion. The scale, profiled in this volume, measures respondents' emotional responses to sad films and their pleasure in feeling sad. This scale can be used to test hypotheses about the influence of meta-emotions on selective exposure.

Perse's (1990) COGNITIVE ELABORATION SCALE was developed as a measure of audience cognitive activity that reflected greater mental activity while watching television. Eveland and his colleagues (Eveland, 2001; Eveland, Shah, & Kwak, 2003) expanded that notion of elaboration to develop the cognitive elaboration model of learning from the news to test hypotheses connecting instrumental gratifications sought from news, news attention, news elaboration, and public affairs knowledge. The scale and Eveland's versions represent a way to measure the mental process that leads to knowledge: cognitive processing of news content.

Emotional reactions to media content are understood to mediate several responses. Feeling angry or frightened increase attention to and learning of news stories (e.g., Newhagen & Reeves, 1992; Perse, 1998; Pouliot & Cowen, 2007). Children's emotional reactions to television programs, news, and movies can have long-term negative impacts on psychological health (Buijzen, Walma van der Molen, & Sondij, 2007; Cantor, 2002). Over the years, scholars have used self-report questionnaire formats and Likert and semantic differential scale items to assess emotional reactions. The SELF-ASSESSMENT MANIKIN (SAM; Bradley & Lang, 1994) expands self-report methods. Because it is a visual measure, it can be used to test hypotheses with children and other samples that might not be able to use Likert and semantic differential scales reliably.

Measures for New Technologies

New mass communication technologies often require new measures. Scholars have adapted existing measures to new domains, but measures do not exist for all new areas of research. A review of literature reveals that research on "presence" has stimulated a large of amount of research, and a large number of new ways to measure the concept. Short, Williams, and Christie (1976) were the first to identify the notion of "presence" as the degree to which participants perceive that a medium communicates the actual presence of the communicating participants. Their scale, the SOCIAL PRESENCE SCALE, has been widely used in research to assess the suitability of different media for different tasks.

The concept of presence, however, has become richer with the development of more interactive media. Presence research now considers how media can evoke actual sensations of people and environments and mediate media effects (e.g., Persky & Blascovich, 2007). Heeter (1992) suggested that presence can be environmental (a characteristic of media or environment), social (similar to Short and his colleagues' concept), and personal (perceptions of the participant). Most conceptualizations of presence now consider it be either subjective (perceptions of users) or objective (characteristics of technology or environment). These different conceptualizations have led to the development of several measures of the concept. The scale developed by Witmer and Singer (2005) to assess subjective presence—PRESENCE QUESTIONNAIRE—was selected to be profiled in this volume because of its wide use and adoption by communication scholars. Other measures do exist, however. See van Baren and Ijsselsteijn (2005) and Lessiter, Freeman, Keogh, and Davidoff (2001) for a summary of some of those measures. Some of these measures are copyrighted, however, and their use requires registration or payment (e.g., Lessiter et al., 2001).

Emphasis on External Validity

Measurement in mass communication has not developed as quickly this past decade as in prior eras because of a desire to increase external validity. Several of the measures in Volume 1 were used with purposive samples (e.g., quota, convenience). Although these samples allow theory testing and development (Courtright, 1996), the nature of mass communication also demands that results be generalizable beyond specific samples. There has been an increase in published research in mass communication that uses random samples. Research on political communication (e.g., Feldman & Price, 2008), public affairs knowledge (e.g., Eveland, 2001), third-person effects (e.g., Hoffner & Buchanan, 2002), and adoption of new technology (e.g., Linn, 2006), for example, have all been conducted with national and regional probability samples. This important methodological emphasis allows greater knowledge about media selection, consumption, and effects. The use of telephone surveys, though, requires shorter and simpler measures. As a result, measurement has not grown in areas that depend on probability sampling. Eveland's cognitive mediation model (Eveland, 2001), for example, is a well-developed theoretical approach to understanding the processes underlying learning from the media. It has wide support from a range of studies. Its central construct, elaboration, however, has not been consistently measured. A review of the cognitive mediation literature makes it apparent that, at this time, no elaboration scale has been adopted for consistent use by communication scholars, though the majority derive their items from Perse (1990, profiled in this volume) or Eveland (2001). It is notable that elaboration scales with even few items, such as Perse's (1990) have proven to be very reliable. Other elaboration scales with lower reliability have been useful in research (e.g., Eveland, 2001; Beaudoin & Thorson, 2004). Consistent measurement is desirable to allow comparison across studies. But, clearly, this area of research gives evidence that some constructs are robust even when shorted measures are used.

Promising Areas for Measurement Development

After examining the mass communication literature to identify new and promising areas in measurement, three areas of research appear ripe for measurement development.

Censorship

Lambe's (2002) WILLINGNESS TO CENSOR SURVEY is included in this volume. It represents the most comprehensive scale developed for application to mass communication research. But, as Lambe (2002) notes, there are four distinct areas of censorship research: representing political tolerance, reactions to specific controversies, opinions about free expression, and censorship as individual attribute. Lambe's scale assesses the fourth type of censorship. This promising scale is certainly useful in exploring the consistency and development of people's attitudes about free speech. But, there has been little effort to develop consistent measures dealing with the other three types of censorship.

Research on the third-person effect has grown over the past decade. An important aspect of the topic is the behavioral hypothesis, or how third-person perceptions contribute to actions—most typically endorsing censorship of media content that is seen as harmful to others. This type of censorship falls under Lambe's (2002) second category, reactions to specific controversies. Scholars have developed reliable censorship scales specifically to these third-person research hypotheses (e.g., McLeod, Eveland, & Nathanson, 1997; Rojas, Shah, & Faber, 1996). This lag in development of consistent scales for this body of research might limit replication and advancement. This is an area ripe for work.

Identification

Identification is a concept that has a long history in audience research (Cohen, 2001). In the past 10 years, however, there has been an increase in studies that have begun to explore the concept. Identification is a concept that offers increased knowledge about the appeal of different types of media personalities (e.g., Hoffner & Buchanan, 2005) and emotional responses to media content (e.g., Chory-Assad & Cicchirillo, 2005). It is also hypothesized to be a theoretically relevant mediator of modeling effects in video game play (e.g., Schneider, Lang, Shin, & Bradley, 2004) and in modeling attitudes and opinions (e.g., Brown, Basil, & Borcarnea, 2003).

Cohen (2001) distinguished identification from three related concepts, parasocial interaction, imitation, and liking. He proposed a 10-item scale. Because it is conceptually derived and includes items drawn from a range of prior research, it has a good deal of face validity. Although some research has adapted some of his proposed items, the scale has yet to be used in published research. As this is a relevant and potentially useful concept, future research should explore the utility, reliability, and validity of Cohen's (2001) measure.

Interactivity

As Kiousis (2002) noted, "the use of interactivity as a variable in empirical investigations has dramatically increased with the emergence of new communication channels" (p. 355). Interactivity is certainly an attribute of certain new mass media, but it is also a concept that is multidimensional. Liu and Shrum (2002) pointed out that the concept has structural (media and environment) and experiential (based on user perceptions) dimensions. Interactivity, like presence, is a potentially rich concept to represent how new media technologies can change the audience's perceptions about and responses to media content. Interactivity has also been hypothesized to be linked to traditional concepts such as cognitive involvement and thus affect cognitive effects of the mass media (Liu & Shrum).

Kiousis (2002) and others (e.g., Liu & Shrum, 2002; Steuer, 1992) have presented explications of the concept and summarized related areas of research. The development of a scale to assess the experiential aspect of interactivity is a potentially fruitful area for future measurement.

Conclusion

Mass communication continues to be a vibrant area for research. Traditional measures are useful to continue to explore enduring theoretical and practical questions. They are also adaptable to new types of content and channels. Questions dealing with reliability and validity of mass communication measures, though, have taken a bit of a back stage in the years between the two volumes of this set. Scholars have become more interested in external validity, and have turn more to regional and national probability samples to describe media practices and answer theoretical questions. Scholars are also grappling with conceptualizing new concepts to explore emerging areas of research. The next volume of this series will no doubt include new measures that have grown from theoretical questions about interactive media.

References

Albarran, A. B., Anderson, T., Bejar, L. G., Bussart, A. L., Daggett, E., Gibson, S., et al. (2007). "What happened to our audiences?" Radio and new technology uses and gratifications among young adult users. *Journal of Radio Studies, 14,* 92–101.

Beaudoin, C. E., & Thorson, E. (2004). Testing the cognitive mediation model: The role of news reliance and three gratifications sought. *Communication Research, 31,* 446–471.

Bradley, M. M., & Lang, P. J. (1994). Measuring emotion: The self-assessment manikin and the semantic differential. *Journal of Behavior Therapy and Experimental Psychology, 25,* 49–59.

Brown, W. J., Basil, M. D., & Bocarnea, M. C. (2003). The influence of famous athletes on health beliefs and practices: Mark McGwire, child abuse prevention, and androstenedione. *Journal of Health Communication, 8,* 41–57.

Buijzen, M., Walma van der Molen, J. H., & Sondij, P. (2007). Parental mediation of children's emotional responses to a violent news event. *Communication Research, 34,* 212–230.

Cantor, J. (2002). Fright reactions to mass media. In J. Bryant & D. Zillmann (Eds.), *Media effects: Advances in theory and research* (pp. 287–306). Mahwah, NJ: Erlbaum.

Chory-Assad, R. M., & Cicchirillo, V. (2005). Empathy and affective orientation as predictors of identification with television characters. *Communication Research Reports, 22,* 153–158.

Cohen, J. (2001). Defining identification: A theoretical look at identification of audiences with media characters. *Mass Communication & Society, 4,* 245–264.

Courtright, J. A. (1996). Rationally thinking about nonprobability. *Journal of Broadcasting & Electronic Media 40,* 414–421.

Eveland, W. P., Jr. (2001). The cognitive mediation mode of learning from the news: Evidence from nonelection, off-year election, and presidential election contexts. *Communication Research, 28,* 571–601.

Eveland, W. P., Jr., Shah, D. V., & Kwak, N. (2003). Assessing causality and learning in the cognitive mediation model: A panel study of motivations, information processing and learning during campaign 2000. *Communication Research, 30,* 359–386.

Farquhar, L. K., & Meeds, R. (2007). Types of fantasy sports users and their motivations. *Journal of Computer-Mediated Communication, 12,* 1208–1228.

Feldman, L., & Price, V. (2008). Confusion or enlightenment? How exposure to disagreement moderates the effects of political discussion and media use on candidate knowledge. *Communication Research, 35,* 61–87.

Ferguson, D. A., Greer, C. F., & Reardon, M. E. (2007). Uses and gratifications of MP3 players by college students: Are iPods more popular than radio? *Journal of Radio Studies, 14,* 102–121.

Ferguson, D. A., & Perse, E. M. (2000). The World Wide Web as a functional alternative to television. *Journal of Broadcasting & Electronic Media, 44,* 155–174.

Flaherty, L. M., Pearce, K. J., & Rubin, R. B. (1998). Internet and face-to-face communication: Not functional alternatives. *Communication Quarterly, 46,* 250–268.

Flanagin, A. J., & Metzger, M. J. (2000). Perceptions of Internet information credibility. *Journalism & Mass Communication Quarterly, 77,* 515–540.

Gaziano, C., & McGrath, K. (1986). Measuring the concept of credibility. *Journalism Quarterly, 63,* 451–462.

Heeter, C. (1992). Being there: The subjective experience of presence. *Presence: Teleoperators and Virtual Environments, 1,* 262–271.

Hoffner, C., & Buchanan, M. (2002). Parents' responses to television violence: The third-person perception, parental mediation, and support for censorship. *Media Psychology, 4,* 231–252.

Hoffner, C., & Buchanan, M. (2005). Young adults' wishful identification with television characters: The role of perceived similarity and character attributes. *Media Psychology, 7,* 325–351.

Holbert, R. L., Lambe, J. L., Dudo, A. D., & Carlton, K. A. (2007). Primacy effects of *The Daily Show* and national TV news viewing: Young viewers, political gratifications, and internal political self-efficacy. *Journal of Broadcasting & Electronic Media, 51,* 20–38.

Horvath, C. W. (2004). Measuring television addiction. *Journal of Broadcasting & Electronic Media, 48,* 378–398.

Johnson, T. J., & Kaye, B. K. (1998). Cruising is believing? Comparing Internet and traditional sources on media credibility measures. *Journalism & Mass Communication Quarterly, 75,* 325–340.

Johnson, T. J., & Kaye, B. K. (2000). Using is believing: The influence of reliance on the credibility of online political information among politically interested Internet users. *Journalism & Mass Communication Quarterly, 77,* 865–879.

Johnson, T. J., & Kaye, B. K. (2002). Webelievability: A path model examining how convenience and reliance predict online credibility. *Journalism & Mass Communication Quarterly, 79,* 619–642.

Johnson, T. J., & Kaye, B. K. (2004). Wag the blog: How reliance on traditional media and the Internet influence perceptions of credibility of web logs among blog users. *Journalism & Mass Communication Quarterly, 81,* 622–642.

Kim, Y. (2001). Searching for the organization-public relationship: A valid and reliable instrument. *Journalism & Mass Communication Quarterly, 4,* 799–815.

Kiousis, S. (2001). Public trust or mistrust? Perceptions of media credibility in the information age. *Mass Communication & Society, 4,* 381–403.

Kiousis, S. (2002). Interactivity: A concept explication. *New Media & Society, 4,* 355–383.

Lambe, J. L. (2002). Dimensions of censorship: Reconceptualizing public willingness to censor. *Communication Law & Policy, 7,* 187–235.

Lessiter, J., Freeman, J., Keogh, E., & Davidoff, J. (2001). A cross-media presence questionnaire: The ITC-Sense of Presence Inventory. *Presence: Teleoperators and Virtual Environments, 10,* 282–297.

Lin, C. A. (2006). Predicting satellite radio adoption via listening motives, activity, and format preferences. *Journal of Broadcasting & Electronic Media, 50,* 140–159.

Liu, Y., & Shrum, L. J. (2002). What is interactivity and is it always such a good thing? Implications of definition, person, and situation for the influence of interactivity on advertising effectiveness. *Journal of Advertising, 31,* 53–64.

McLeod, D. M., Eveland, W. P., Jr., & Nathanson, A. I. (1997). Support for censorship of misogynic rap lyrics: An analysis of the third-person effect. *Communication Research, 24,* 153–174.

Metzger, M. J., Flanagin, A. J., Eyal, K., Lemus, D. R., & McCann, R. M. (2003). Credibility for the 21st century: Integrating perspectives on source, message, and media credibility in the contemporary media environment. *Communication Yearbook, 27,* 293–335.

Nabi, R. L., Stitt, C. R., Halford, J., & Finnerty, K. L. (2006). Emotional and cognitive predictors of enjoyment of reality-based and fictional television programming: An elaboration of the uses and gratifications perspective. *Media Psychology, 8,* 421–447.

Newhagen, J., & Reeves, B. (1992). The evening's bad news: Effects of compelling negative television news images on memory. *Journal of Communication, 42*(2), 25–41.

Oliver, M. J. (1993). Exploring the paradox of the enjoyment of sad films. *Human Communication Research, 19,* 315–342.

Papachiarissi, Z., & Rubin, A. M. (2000). Predictors of Internet use. *Journal of Broadcasting & Electronic Media, 44,* 175–196.

Perloff, R. M. (2002). The third-person effect. In J. Bryant & D. Zillmann (Eds.), *Media effects: Advances in theory and research* (pp. 489–506). Mahwah, NJ: Erlbaum.

Perse, E. M. (1990). Involvement with local television news: Cognitive and emotional dimensions. *Human Communication Research, 16*, 556–581.

Perse, E. M. (1998). Implications of cognitive and affective involvement for channel changing. *Journal of Communication, 48*(3), 49–68.

Persky, S., & Blascovich, J. (2007). Immersive virtual environments versus traditional platforms: Effects of violent and nonviolent video game play. *Media Psychology, 10*, 135–156.

Potter, W. J. (1986). Perceived reality and the cultivation hypothesis. *Journal of Broadcasting & Electronic Media, 30*, 159–174.

Pouliot, L., & Cowen, P. S. (2007). Does perceived realism really matter in media effects? *Media Psychology, 9*, 241–259.

Preiss, R. W., Gayle, B. M., Burrell, N., Allen, M., & Bryant, J. (Eds.). (2007). *Mass media effects research: Advances through meta-analysis.* Mahwah, NJ: Erlbaum.

Rojas, H., Shah, D. V., & Faber, R. J. (1996). For the good of others: Censorship and the third person effect. *International Journal of Public Opinion Research, 4*, 163–186.

Rubin, A. M., & Perse, E. M. (1994). Measures of mass communication. In R. B. Rubin, P. Palmgreen, & H. E. Sypher (Eds.), *Communication research measures: A sourcebook* (pp. 37–56). New York: Guilford.

Schneider, E. F., Lang, A., Shin, M., & Bradley, S. D. (2004). Death with a story: How story impacts emotional, motivational, and physiological responses to first-person shooter video games. *Human Communication Research, 30*, 361–375.

Sherry, J. L., Lucas, K., Greenberg, B. S., & Lachlan, K. (2006). Video game uses and gratifications as predictors of use and game preference. In P. Vordere & J. Bryant (Eds.), *Playing video games: Motives, responses, and consequences* (pp. 213–224). Mahwah, NJ: Erlbaum.

Short, J., Williams, E., and Christie, B. (1976). *The social psychology of telecommunications.* New York: Wiley.

Stafford, T. F., Stafford, M. R., & Schkade, L. L. (2004). Determining uses and gratifications for the Internet. *Decision Sciences, 35*, 259–288.

Steuer, J. (1992). Defining virtual reality: Dimensions determining telepresence. *Journal of Communication, 42*(4), 73–93.

Witmer, B. G., & Singer, M. J. (2005). The factor structure of the Presence Questionnaire. *Presence: Teleoperators and Virtual Environments, 14*, 298–312.

Valkenburg, P. M., Krcmar, M., Peeters, A., & Marseille, N. M. (1999). Developing a scale to assess three styles of television mediation: "restrictive mediation," "instructive mediation," and "social coviewing." *Journal of Broadcasting and Electronic Media, 43*, 52–66.

Van Baren, J., & Ijsselsteijn, W. (2005). Compendium of presence measures. Retrieved February 4, 2008, from Presence-Research.org, http://www.presence-research.org/Overview.html

Part II

Measure Profiles

Affectionate Communication Index (ACI)

Profile by Elizabeth E. Graham

Recognizing the critical importance of affectionate communication in relationship development, Kory Floyd and Mark Morman (1998) developed a means of measuring this concept. This scale, termed the Affectionate Communication Index (ACI), is a 19-item self-report multidimensional measure that indexes the degree to which a specific relationship is distinguished by verbal, nonverbal, and supportive indicators of affectionate communication. In concert with the development of the Affectionate Communication Index, Floyd (2006) also conceptualized a theory of affection termed the Affection Exchange Theory. The motivation to engage in affectionate communication rests on the desire to share relational resources and thus contribute to others' (particularly children's) viability and suitability as relational partners and parents. The ACI is an improvement over previous efforts that were limited in their operationalization of affectionate behaviors, relied solely on direct observation, and were quite labor intensive. The authors conducted a series of preliminary studies to validate both the conceptualization and measurement of affectionate communication.

In the first study, which was concerned primarily with content validity, items were generated from a large pool of participants who responded to the request to describe how they communicate affection to others (Floyd & Morman, 1998). This process resulted in 67 items, and upon further refinement, was reduced to a 34-item scale. The second study sought to verify the factor structure, reliability, and construct validity of the 34 items. After a series of factor analyses, a three-factor, 19-item solution was determined to be most suitable. The first factor, nonverbal affection, refers to hugging, kissing, and other nonverbal displays of affection. Verbal expressions of affection, the second factor, reference the articulation of affection in words spoken. The third factor, termed social supportiveness, includes helping, sharing, and acknowledging affection.

Reliability

The internal consistency of each factor was deemed acceptable with reliabilities as follows: nonverbal affection α = .91; verbal affection α = .80; and social supportiveness α = .77 (Floyd & Morman, 1998, 2005). Test-retest results also support the stability of the measure over time (see Floyd & Morman, 1998). Related research supports a single-factor structure of the ACI as well, suggesting that the one-or three-factor instrument can be useful (Floyd & Morman, 1998). Recent research has supported the internal consistency of the measure as well (see Rittenour, Myers, & Brann, 2007).

Validity

The authors conducted a series of studies to provide evidence of the measure's convergent, construct, and discriminant validity. Consistent with expectations, correlation analysis revealed that the three affection subscales were positively related to relational closeness and communication satisfaction and negatively associated with psychological distance (Floyd & Morman, 2000, 2001; Floyd & Morr, 2003) and Floyd, Sargent, and DiCorcia (2004) reached similar conclusions. In addition to the host of positive social consequences associated with affectionate communication, Floyd and associates illustrated the health benefits of affectionate communication (i.e., verbal and supportive) (Floyd et al., 2007). Importantly, social desirability was not related to any of the variables tested. Further analysis revealed that the Affectionate Communication Index could discriminate between affectionate and nonaffectionate relationships, and Floyd and Morman (1998) concluded that affectionate communication is positively predicated on nonverbal immediacy and expressiveness of adult platonic friends. These latter finding are particularly compelling and provide evidence of the ecological validity of the ACI because nonverbal immediacy and expressiveness scores were derived from actual behavior.

Further research efforts featuring the father-son relationship were conducted in an effort to extend the measure's known associations and outcomes. For example, it was reasoned that affectionate communication would be positively predicted by the level of femininity and negatively associated with masculinity exhibited by fathers and sons. This prediction was supported for sons but not fathers (Floyd & Morman, 1998; Morman & Floyd, 1999). It seems that fathers were not as likely to engage in affectionate communication because of a feminine orientation but, rather, it was an affective orientation (i.e., extent to which feelings guide behaviors) that was most responsible for fathers' affectionate communication. These findings provide partial support for the long-held belief that affectionate behavior and femininity are closely tied. Interestingly, heterosexual men report receiving more affection from their fathers than homosexual or bisexual men (Floyd et al., 2004). Furthermore, fathers' knowledge of sons' sexual orientation is an influential factor in the amount of affection communicated to those sons.

Floyd and Morman (2005), operating from the naïve theory of affection (i.e., the belief that parents' love and affection is a finite resource) concluded that sons' believe that they receive less affection from their father if there are siblings (specifically brothers) vying for the same scarce resource. Fathers however, report no difference in sharing affection with sons, regardless of the presence of other children. This study supports the construct and external validity of the ACI because it tests a prevailing theory concerning implicit beliefs about affection and extends the applicability of the measure by sampling adult children.

The construct validity of the ACI and support for the gendered closeness perspective was provided by Morman and Floyd (1999) and Floyd et al. (2004) as they concluded that fathers and sons are more likely to communicate affection through shared activities rather than verbal and nonverbal communications. They also revealed that the social supportiveness subscale (i.e., shared activities) was positively correlated with closeness, self-disclosure, and communication satisfaction. Although the verbal and nonverbal dimensions were related to these variables, they accounted for much less variance than the supportiveness subscale. Additional research (Floyd & Morman, 2001, 2003) produced conflicting findings concerning whether affectionate communication is influenced by the type of relationship (biological and nonbiological).

Floyd and Morman (2000) noted that there are two leading schools of thought that explain the level of affection shared between fathers and sons. The first, the modeling hypothesis, suggests that men simply model for their own sons the same level of affection they received from their fathers. Conversely, the compensation hypothesis predicts that men who received very little attention and affection from their father will do precisely the opposite with their own sons. The authors proposed and supported a hybrid perspective that marries the modeling and compensation hypothesis and revealed that those men who received very little or very much affection from their fathers will exhibit more affection with their own sons than those men who received moderate affection from their fathers. Perhaps due to age, fathers reported sharing more affection with sons than sons did with their fathers (Morman & Floyd, 1999). Furthermore, Floyd and colleagues (Floyd & Morman, 2005; Morman & Floyd, 2002) determined that men felt closer, were more satisfied, and exhibited more affection (verbal, nonverbal, supportiveness) to their own sons as opposed to their fathers, suggesting that "fatherhood" in America is changing.

Comments

The Affectionate Communication Index is a relatively new measure that shows great promise. Current efforts (Floyd, 2006) have continued to refine our understanding of the communication of affection by articulating Affectionate Exchange Theory. Continued testing of the theory and measure is underway and will undoubtedly yield further understanding of how affection is communicated. Evidence suggests that the measure is reliable and valid. Recent research (Floyd & Morman, 2007) illustrates the utility of affectionate communication. Future research, in varied contexts and relationships, would contribute to the utility and subsequently, the validity, of this measure.

Location*

Floyd, K., & Morman, M. T. (1998). The measurement of affectionate communication. *Communication Quarterly, 46*, 144–162.

References

Floyd, K. (2001). Human affection exchange: I. Reproductive probability as a predictor of men's affection with their sons. *Journal of Men's Studies, 10*, 39–50.

Floyd, K. (2006). *Communicating affection: Interpersonal behavior and social context*. Cambridge: Cambridge University Press.

Floyd, K., Mikkelson, A. C., Tafoya, M. A., Farinelli, L., La Valley, A. G., Judd, J., Davis, K. L., Haynes, M. T., & Wilson, J. (2007). Human affection exchange: XIV. Relational affection predicts resting heart rate and free cortisol secretions during acute stress. *Behavioral Medicine, 32*, 151–156.

Floyd, K., & Morman, M. T. (2000). Affection received from fathers as a predictor of men's affection with their own sons: Tests of the modeling and compensation hypotheses. *Communication Monographs, 67*, 347–361.

Floyd, K., & Morman, M. T. (2001). Human affection exchange: III. Discriminative parental solicitude and men's affectionate communication with their biological and nonbiological sons. *Communication Quarterly, 49*, 310–327.

Floyd, K., & Morman, M. T. (2003). Human affection exchange: II. Affectionate communication in father-son relationships. *The Journal of Social Psychology, 143*, 599–612.

Floyd, F., & Morman, M. T. (2005). Fathers' and sons' reports of fathers' affectionate communication: Implications of a naïve theory of affection. *Journal of Social and Personal Relationships, 22*, 99–109.

Floyd, K., & Morr, M. C. (2003). Human affection exchange: VII. Affectionate communication in the sibling/spouse/sibling-in-law triad. *Communication Quarterly, 51*, 247–261.

Floyd, K., Sargent, J.E., & DiCorcia, M. (2004). Human affection exchange: VI. Further tests of reproductive probability as a predictor of men's affection with their adult sons. *The Journal of Social Psychology, 144*, 191–206.

Morman, M. T., & Floyd, K. (1999). Affectionate communication between fathers and young adult sons: Individual-and relational-level level correlates. *Communication Studies, 50,* 294–309.

Morman, M. T., & Floyd, K. (2002). A "changing culture of fatherhood": Effects on affectionate communication, closeness, and satisfaction in men's relationships with their fathers and their sons. *Western Journal of Communication, 66,* 395–411.

Rittenour, C. E., Myers, S. A., & Brann, M. (2007). Commitment and emotional closeness in the sibling relationship. *Southern Communication Journal, 72,* 169–183.

Scale

Affectionate Communication Index*

Instructions: Please identify how often you engage in the following behaviors when communicating affection using the 7-point Likert-type response options. "1" indicates that you **never** engage in this behavior to communicate affection and "7" indicates that you **always** use this behavior to communicate affection. Be sure to complete the measure with one target person in mind.

Nonverbal Affection

1 Hold Hands
2 Kiss on lips
3 Kiss on cheeks
4 Give massages to each other
5 Put arm around shoulder
6 Hug each other
7 Sit close to each other
8 Look into each other's eyes
9 Wink at each other

Verbal Affection

10 Say "You're a good friend"
11 Say "I like you"
12 Say "I love you"
13 Say "You're my best friend"
14 Say how important relationship is

Supportiveness

15 Help each other with problems
16 Acknowledge each other's birthday
17 Share private information
18 Give each other compliments
19 Praise each other's accomplishments

Attachment Style Measure

Profile by Joseph P. Mazer

An individual's attachment style, manifest through communication in social interaction, refers to the way he or she processes, interprets, and reacts to others' behavior (Bartholomew, 1990; Scher & Mayseless, 1994). A primary element underlying attachment styles is intimacy/avoidance. That is, individuals who have positive models of others display communication styles that reflect intimacy, whereas individuals having negative models of others exhibit communication styles that reflect avoidance and detachment.

In the corpus of attachment style research, researchers frequently ask participants to read attachment style descriptions and indicate which description best characterizes them (Bartholomew & Horowitz, 1991). For instance, a description of a fearful avoidant might read: "I am somewhat uncomfortable getting close to others. I want emotionally close relationships, but I find it difficult to trust others completely, or to depend on them. I sometimes worry that I will be hurt if I allow myself to become too close to others." Descriptions of this nature often serve as the primary operationalization of attachment in research studies. However, scholars have argued that these categorical descriptions are too simplistic to fully capture the differences in attachment styles (Collins & Read, 1990; Feeney, Noller, & Hanrahan, 1994; Fuller & Fincham, 1995; Griffin & Bartholomew, 1994; Guerrero, 1994). In fact, Bippus and Rollin (2003) attributed minimally significant findings to the use of a categorical measure of attachment style and, in a similar vein, 15% of the participants in Guerrero and Burgoon's (1996) sample endorsed two attachment styles strongly and equally. Findings of this nature resulted in a call for continuous measures (as opposed to categorical measures) to further explore the dimensions that underlie attachment, reveal more fine-grained distinctions among attachment styles, and obtain a more precise assessment of the construct (Collins & Read, 1990; Feeney et al., 1994).

Laura Guerrero developed the Attachment Style Measure in 1996 to address these concerns. Portions of Guerrero's continuous measure are typically utilized in conjunction with categorical measures in attachment style research. Participants are instructed to complete Guerrero's Attachment Style Measure before reading and responding to the categorical measures. In a study exploring attachment style differences in the experience and expression of romantic jealousy, Guerrero (1998) emphasized the need to examine both attachment categories and attachment dimensions. Comparisons between attachment categories, she argued, can clarify how mental models of self and other function and provide parsimonious representations of the combined influence of mental models of self and others. In addition, she noted that attachment style dimensional analyses can reveal more precise information through interval measures and uncover associations that are not typically found through categorical (nominal) measures.

With items adopted from prior research (Collins & Read, 1990; Feeney et al., 1994; Griffin & Bartholomew, 1994) and largely consistent with dimensions found by Feeney et al. (1994), Guerrero's Attachment Style Measure is a 30-item Likert-type scale that assesses five attachment style dimensions: General Avoidance (avoid intimacy), Lack of Confidence (anxiety), Preoccupation (craving excessive intimacy), Fearful Avoidance (fear intimacy), and Relationships as Secondary (relationships are not the primary focus of an individual's life).

Reliability

The initial study revealed a consistent and reliable measure of attachment style (Guerrero, 1996). Reliabilities for each factor were: $\alpha = .79$, General Avoidance; $\alpha = .83$, Lack of Confidence; $\alpha = .81$, Preoccupation; $\alpha = .78$, Fearful Avoidance; $\alpha = .84$, Relationships as Secondary. More recently, reliabilities were $\alpha = .87$ for Preoccupation and ranged from $\alpha = .77$ to .82 for General Avoidance and $\alpha = .81$ to .84 for Lack of Confidence (Bachman & Bippus, 2005; Guerrero & Bachman, 2006; Guerrero & Jones, 2003).

Validity

Although detailed scale development procedures were not described in the original article, Guerrero reported that the five factors accounted for 57.2 % of the total variance. Since the measure was first published in 1996, portions of the complete measure have been chiefly used in attachment style studies as a supplement to categorical measures, which typically serve as the primary method of operationalizing attachment style. In her original report that offered initial evidence of construct validity, Guerrero found that intimacy avoidance, a defining feature of *dismissives* and *fearful avoidants*, was negatively associated with nonverbal cues (e.g., gaze) related to immediacy, altercentrism, and positive affect.

Guerrero and Burgoon (1996) explored attachment styles and reactions to nonverbal involvement change in romantic dyads and asked participants to complete the Attachment Style Measure before responding to the categorical measure. Analyses confirmed their predictions—*dismissives* and *fearful avoidants* scored higher on general avoidance than *preoccupieds* and *secures, fearful avoidants* and *preoccupieds* scored higher on lack of confidence than *dismissives* and *secures,* and the highest scores on preoccupation, fearful avoidance, and relationships as secondary were found for *preoccupieds, fearful avoidants,* and *dismissives,* respectively.

In their study of attachment style and social skills, Guerrero and Jones (2003) utilized Bartholomew's commonly reported categorical measure of attachment style to validate Guerrero's instrument. In particular, they used the subscales of avoidance and lack of confidence, and through analysis of variance, they found results consistent with attachment theory. That is, *fearful avoidants* and *preoccupieds* reported more anxiety than *secures* and *dismissives.* In a follow-up study, Guerrero and Jones (2005) explored differences in conversational skills as a function of attachment style. They again utilized a version of Guerrero's Attachment Style Measure (anxiety and avoidance subscales) and found findings consistent with attachment theory, which resulted in additional validity evidence. *Secures* and *dismissives* were less anxious than *fearful avoidants* and *preoccupieds.*

Unlike other studies that utilized the Attachment Style Measure to supplement categorical measures, Bachman and Bippus' (2005) operationalization rested exclusively with Guerrero's continuous measure to evaluate supportive messages from friends and romantic partners. They found that attachment styles indeed play a role in how individuals perceive and interpret support provided by close friends and romantic partners. In particular, people who were more secure and comfortable with close relationships tended to evaluate comfort from friends and partners more positively. Conversely, individuals who were more preoccupied and fearful of intimacy were more negative in their evaluation of comfort providers.

Since Guerrero's continuous measure of attachment style first emerged in the literature, research reports continued to successfully illustrate the collection of variables related to attachment style, which have ultimately contributed to the construct validity of the measure. In this spirit, Guerrero and Bachman (2006) utilized anxiety and avoidance items modeled after the original attachment style measure and found men and women with high anxiety scores tended to report using less social networking, task sharing, and support/comfort. Furthermore, anxious men indicated using less romantic affection and positivity. Men and women high in avoidance reported using less assurances, romantic affection, openness, and social networking. Additionally, avoidant men reported using less comfort/support.

Comments

Over the years, scholars have jointly utilized Guerrero's instrument and categorical measures to operationalize attachment style. At times, portions of the Attachment Style Measure have been used (rather than the full instrument) as a supplement to commonly reported categorical measures, which often serve as the primary operationalization of attachment style. Although little scale development work was reported in the original article and in subsequent studies, from its recent use in the literature, Guerrero's measure appears to be a reasonably reliable and valid continuous measure of attachment style. Future research that employs the entire instrument can offer scholars a detailed continuous measure of attachment style that explores detailed distinctions among attachment styles and ultimately contributes to the reliability and validity of the overall scale.

Location*

Guerrero, L. K. (1996). Attachment-style differences in intimacy and involvement: A test of the four-category model. *Communication Monographs, 63*, 269–292.

References

Bachman, G. F., & Bippus, A. M. (2005). Evaluations of supportive messages provided by friends and romantic partners: An attachment theory approach. *Communication Reports, 18*, 85–94.

Bartholomew, K. (1990). Avoidance of intimacy: An attachment perspective. *Journal of Social and Personal Relationships, 7*, 147–178.

Bartholomew, K. (1993). From childhood to adult relationships: Attachment theory and research. In S. Duck (Ed.), *Understanding relationship processes: Vol. 2 Learning about relationships* (pp. 30–62). Newbury Park, CA: Sage.

Bartholomew, K., & Horowitz, L. M. (1991). Attachment styles among young adults: A test of a four category model. *Journal of Personality and Social Psychology, 61*, 226–244.

Bippus, A. M., & Rollin, E. (2003). Attachment style differences in relational maintenance and conflict behaviors: Friends' perceptions. *Communication Reports, 16*, 113–123.

Bowlby, J. (1973). *Attachment and loss: Vol. 2 Separation*. New York: Basic Books.

Bretherton, I. (1990). Open communication and internal working models: Their role in the development of attachment relationships. In R. A. Thompson (Ed.), *Nebraska Symposium on Motivation: Vol. 36. Socioemotional development* (pp. 57–113). Lincoln: University of Nebraska Press.

Collins, N. L., & Read, S. J. (1990). Adult attachment, working models, and relationship quality in dating couples. *Journal of Personality and Social Psychology, 58*, 644–663.

Collins, N. L., & Read, S. J. (1994). Cognitive representations of attachment: The structure and function of working models. In K. Bartholomew & D. Perlman

(Eds.), *Advances in personal relationships: Vol. 5 Attachment processes in adult-hood* (pp. 53–90). Bristol, PA: Kingsley.

Feeney, J. A., Noller, P., & Hanrahan, M. (1994). Assessing adult attachment: developments in the conceptualization of security and insecurity. In M. B. Sperling & W. H. Berman (Eds.), *Attachment in adults: Clinical and developmental perspectives* (pp. 128–152). New York: Guilford.

Fuller, T. L., & Fincham, F. D. (1995). Attachment style in married couples: Relation to current marital functioning, stability over time, and method of assessment. *Personal Relationships, 2,* 17–34.

Griffin, D. W., & Bartholomew, K. (1994). The metaphysics of measurement: The case of adult attachment. In K. Bartholomew & D. Perlman (Eds.), *Advances in personal relationships: Vol. 5 Attachment processes in adulthood* (pp. 17–52). Bristol, PA: Kingsley.

Guerrero, L. K. (1994). *An application of attachment theory to relational messages and nonverbal involvement behaviors in romantic dyads.* Unpublished doctoral dissertation, University of Arizona, Tucson.

Guerrero, L. K. (1998). Attachment-style differences in the experience and expression of romantic jealousy. *Personal Relationships, 5,* 273–291.

Guerrero, L. K., & Bachman, G. F. (2006). Associations among relational maintenance behaviors, attachment-style categories, and attachment dimensions. *Communication Studies, 57,* 341–361.

Guerrero, L. K., & Burgoon, J. K. (1996). Attachment styles and reactions to nonverbal involvement change in romantic dyads: Patterns of reciprocity and compensation. *Human Communication Research, 22,* 335–370.

Guerrero, L. K., & Jones, S. M. (2003). Differences in one's own and one's partner's perception of social skills as a function of attachment style. *Communication Quarterly, 51,* 277–295.

Guerrero, L. K., & Jones, S. M. (2005). Differences in conversational skills as a function of attachment style: A follow-up study. *Communication Quarterly, 53,* 305–321.

Scher, A., & Mayseless, O. (1994). Mothers' attachment with spouse and parenting in the first year. *Journal of Social and Personal Relationships, 11,* 601–609.

Scale*

Attachment Style Measure
Instructions: [Instructions were not provided in the article and the author failed to provide them. Respondents are asked to reflect on each item and respond using a Likert response format employing ranges of strongly disagree to strongly agree.]

General Avoidance

 1   I find it easy to trust others. (R)
 2   I feel uncomfortable when people get close to me.
 3   I feel uneasy getting close to others.
 4   I prefer to keep to myself.

5   I worry about people getting close to me.
6   I tend to avoid getting close to others.
7   I find it relatively easy to get close to others. (R)

Lack of Confidence

8   I sometimes worry that I do not really fit in with other people.
9   I sometimes worry that I do not measure up to other people.
10 I am confident that other people will like and respect me. (R)
11 I worry that others will reject me.
12 I am confident that others will accept me. (R)

Preoccupation

13 Intimate relationships are the most central part of my life.
14 I feel a very strong need to have close relationships.
15 Sometimes others seem reluctant to get as close to me as I would like.
16 I worry a lot about the well-being of my relationships.
17 I worry that others do not care about me as much as I care about them.
18 I wonder how I would cope without someone to love me.
19 I rarely worry about what relational partners think of me. (R)
20 I sometimes worry that relational partners will leave me.

Fearful Avoidance

21 I would like to trust others, but I have a hard time doing so.
22 I worry about getting hurt if I allow myself to get too close to others.
23 I would like to depend on others, but it makes me nervous to do so.
24 I would like to have closer relationships, but getting close makes me uneasy.
25 I worry that I might get hurt if I get too close to others.
26 Achieving things is more important to me than building relationships.
27 If something needs to be done, I prefer to rely on myself rather than others.
28 I put more time and energy into my relationships than I put into other activities. (R)
29 Maintaining good relationships is always my top priority. (R)
30 Pleasing myself is more important to me than getting along with others.

Note: (R) Indicates reverse-coded item. Scale items should be presented randomly.
* © 1996 by Taylor & Francis.

Auckland Individualism and Collectivism Scale (AICS)

Profile by David R. Seibold

Drawing upon the Oyserman, Coon, and Kemmelmeir (2002) meta-analysis of 83 individualism-collectivism studies, Shulruf, Hattie, and Dixon (2007) conceptualized *individualism* as involving the distinction of self from others, emphasis on self-reliance, pursuing personal goals, and self-reliance over those of society, liking for a style of communication that is direct, and especially the valuing of personal independence. They conceived of *collectivism* as including "a sense of belonging and duty to in-groups, interdependence with group members, maintenance of one's social status, seeking harmony and avoiding conflicts, and a preference for an indirect communication style" (p. 386).

Shulruf et al. (2007) then sought to develop a brief, easy to use, and reliable measure of individualism and collectivism. Their resultant 30-item Auckland Individualism and Collectivism Scale (AICS) is based on the principal dimensions of the Osyerman et al. (2002) meta-analysis. Furthermore, the AICS is intended to redress major problems with other prominent measures of individualism-collectivism, notably INDCOL (Hui, 1988), SCS (Singelis, 1994), and the measurement refinement of the horizontal and vertical dimensions of individualism and collectivism by Singelis, Triandis, Bhawuk, and Gelfand (1995), each of which has had reported problems with reliability and/or validity. In particular, Shulruf and colleagues sought to reduce measurement bias associated with the reference-group effect (Heine, Lehman, Peng, & Greenholtz, 2002), caused when respondents' frame of reference for any scale item is the people they know and their responses to the item are a function of comparisons to others within their own subculture. Shulruf et al. (2007) also aimed to prevent the confounding effect of familialism (Oysterman et al., 2002) in which responses are sensitive to differences in contexts rather than reported in a generalized manner. Shulruf and colleagues attributed both of these problems to the fact that prominent measures of individualism and collectivism, such as the three above, rely on an intensity of agreement set of responses: "they ask respondents to report on their attitudes, values, and beliefs as part of their daily life . . . (but) one can be intense about a belief in some situations and not in others" (2007, p. 387).

The remedy according to Shulruf et al., and foundational to the AICS, is to rely upon frequency rather than agreement scales: "frequency scales relate the prevalence of behavior or thought, unlike agreement scales, which relate to comparisons of values and beliefs to those dominant in the sociocultural environment" (2007, p. 387).

In order to develop a measurement tool for assessing individualism and collectivism, Shulruf et al. (2007) engaged in a multi-step process of selecting "the best set of indicators of each of these dimensions" (p. 388). First, all items from existing tests were combined and supplemented with others developed by Shulruf and colleagues. Following deletion of overlaps, 113 unique items were created. Second, three scholars familiar with the literature were asked to independently assign these to dimensions of individualism and collectivism identified in the Oyserman et al. (2002) meta-analysis. This reduced the list to 79 items. Third, following conceptual critique of several of the Oyserman et al. dimensions and an argument for higher order dimensions, Shulruf further reduced the list of potential scale items to 66. Fourth, in addition to other linguistic modifications, each item was then rephrased to be answered more appropriately with a 6-anchor frequency scale ranging from *Never or Almost Never* to *Always*. Responses to the 66 items from 199 students enrolled in a university in Auckland, New Zealand were submitted to maximum-likelihood factor analysis. Six factors emerged, and 21 items that were neither related to these factors nor any additional factors were dropped from subsequent analyses. Fifth, the remaining 45 items were subject to additional factor analytic and structural modeling procedures that yielded five first-order factors with a subset of 30 items.

The 30-item Auckland Individual and Collectivism Scale measures three dimensions of *individualism*—(a) Responsibility (acknowledging one's responsibility for one's actions), (b) Uniqueness (distinction of the self from the other), (c) Competitiveness (one's primary interest is striving for personal goals), and two dimensions of *collectivism*—(a) Advice (seeking advice from persons close to one before making decisions), and (b) Harmony (seeking to avoid conflict).

Reliability

Shulruf et al. (2007) report that the estimates of reliability (alpha) from the sample of 199 Auckland, New Zealand university students for each scale in the AICS were: .77 for Advice, .71 for Harmony on the collectivism dimensions, and .73 for Responsibility, .76 for Uniqueness, and .78 for Competitiveness on the individualism dimensions.

Validity

Consistent with theoretical expectations, factor analytic and structural modeling procedures with the AICS revealed higher-order factors reflective of individualism and collectivism. Furthermore, the ACIS was able to distinguish between different ethnic groups (Pakeha and Maori) within the New Zealand culture known from previous research to vary in terms of individualism and collectivism.

Comment

The Auckland Individual Collectivism Scale (Shulruf et al., 2007) attempts to minimize problems associated with previously developed and frequently used scales that are wholly or partly focused on individualism and collectivism (Levine, Bresnahan, Park, Lapinski, Wittenbaum, Shearman, Lee, Chung, & Ohashi, 2003). In particular, the AICS is based on frequency of behavior that therefore is less influenced by context factors. The AICS also integrates theoretical refinements of individualism-collectivism dimension components, and related empirical findings, that have occurred during nearly 20 years since Hui (1988) introduced the INDCOL scales. Finally, the ACIS is shorter and easier to use than other measures of individual and collectivism, and it is reliable. However, AICS development is based upon only one sample of 199 participants from New Zealand and concurrent validity is limited to ethnic groups in that sample. While promising, additional research on the AICS is needed.

Location*

Shulruf, B., Hattie, J., & Dixon, R. (2007). Development of a new measurement tool for individualism and collectivism. *Journal of Psychoeducational Assessment, 25*(4), 385–401.

References

Heine, S. J., Lehman, D. R., Peng, K., & Greenholtz, J. (2002). What's wrong with cross-cultural comparisons of subjective Likert scales? The reference group effect. *Journal of Personality and Social Psychology, 82*(6), 903–918.

Hui, C.H. (1988). Measurement of individualism-collectivism. *Journal of Research in Personality, 22*, 17–36.

Levine, T. R., Bresnahan, M. J., Park, H. S., Lapinski, M. K., Wittenbam, G. W., Shearman, S. M., Lee, S. Y., Chung, D., Ohashi, D. (2003). Self-construal scales lack validity. *Human Communication Research, 29*(2), 210–252.

Oyserman, D., Coon, H. M., & Kemmelmeir, M. (2002). Rethinking individualism and collectivism: Evaluation of theoretical and meta-analyses. *Psychological Bulletin, 128*(1), 3–72.

Singelis, T. M. (1994). The measurement of independent and interdependent self-construals. *Personality and Social Psychological Bulletin, 20*(5), 580–591.

Singelis, T. M., Triandis, H., Bhawuk, D., & Gelfand, M. J. (1995). Horizontal and vertical dimensions of individualism and collectivism: A theoretical and measurement refinement. *Cross-Cultural Research: The Journal of Comparative Social Science, 29*(3), 240–275.

Scale

Auckland Individualism and Collectivism Scale (AICS)*
[Note: According to Shulruf et al. (2007, p. 389), all items are answered "using six anchors as part of a frequency scale ranging from *never or almost never* to *always*."]

1 I discuss job or study-related problems with my parents.
2 I consult my family before making an important decision.
3 Before taking a major trip, I consult with most members of my family and many friends.
4 It is important to consult close friends and get their ideas before making a decision.
5 Even when I strongly disagree with my group members, I avoid an argument.
6 I hate to disagree with others in my group.
7 It is important to make a good impression on one's manager.
8 In interacting with superiors, I am always polite.
9 It is important to consider the needs of those who work above me.
10 I sacrifice my self-interest for the benefit of my group.
11 I reveal personal things about myself.
12 I have the feeling that my relationships with others are more important than my own accomplishments.
13 I like to live close to my good friends.
14 To me, pleasure is spending time with my superiors.
15 To me, pleasure is spending time with others.
16 I help acquaintances, even if it is inconvenient.
17 I define myself as a competitive person.
18 I enjoy working in situations involving competition with others.
19 Without competition, it is not possible to have a good society.
20 Competition is the law of nature.
21 I consider my self as a unique person separate from others.
22 I enjoy being unique and different from others.
23 I see my self as "my own person."
24 I take responsibility for my own actions.
25 It is important for me to act as an independent person.
26 Being able to take care of myself is a primary concern for me.
27 I consult with my supervisor on work-related matters.
28 I prefer to be self-reliant rather than depend on others.
29 It is my duty to take care of my family, even when I have to sacrifice what I want.

30   When faced with a difficult personal problem, it is better to decide for myself, than follow the advice of others.

Child–Parent Communication Apprehension (C-PCA)

Profile by Elizabeth E. Graham

Rooted in the belief that quality, anxiety-free communication is central to healthy and satisfying family relationships, Lucchetti, Powers, and Love (2002) developed a measure that focused on context-specific apprehension experienced by young adults when communicating with their parents. Although much is known about the perils of communication apprehension for adults and children, little is known about the communication apprehension of young adults. In developing their measure of child–parent communication apprehension, the authors distinguished between general communication apprehension (i.e., dyadic communication apprehension) and specific person-centered communication apprehension experienced in parent-child relationships.

Lucchetti et al. (2002) drew and modified scale items from related measures of communication apprehension that feature specific contexts such as dating, spousal, and student–teacher relationships (e.g., Spouse Communication Apprehension, Powers & Hutchinson, 1979) and additional items were generated by undergraduate students. Subsequent data reduction efforts, including factor analysis, resulted in a 12-item unidimensional measure of child–parent communication apprehension.

Reliability

The internal reliability of the Child–Parent Communication Apprehension Measure resulted in the following Cronbach alphas: $\alpha = .92$ for mothers and $\alpha = .92$ for fathers.

Validity

Support for the construct validity of the Child–Parent Communication Apprehension Scale was assessed by a series of hypotheses that tested and confirmed the relationship between child–parent communication apprehension and dyadic communication apprehension, frequency of contact with parents, level of problematic child–parent communication, and level of openness. Essentially, these results revealed that the apprehension that young adults experience with their parents is related to: their level of communication apprehension in dyads, time spent talking with their parents, degree to which they encounter problematic communication with their parents, and their level of openness with their parents.

Based on a wealth of apprehension research, Lucchetti et al. (2002) hypothesized that child–parent communication apprehension would be negatively correlated with relationship satisfaction. This hypothesis was confirmed, providing evidence of the predictive validity of the Child–Parent Communication Apprehension Measure. In addition, the study results supported the claim that their measure of young adult apprehension does predict relationship satisfaction in addition to general measures of child-parent communication.

Comments

Lucchetti et al. (2002) successfully distinguished group level measures from person-centered measures of communication apprehension. We are now better positioned to focus more clearly on factors relevant to child-parent communication, specifically as they relate to apprehension and anxiety. Preliminary evidence suggests that the Child–Parent Communication Apprehension Scale offers a respectable level of reliability, and a small, but solid, series of studies support several forms of validity. Although this measure is rather new, it does show promise, particularly for family communication research.

Location*

Lucchetti, A. E., Powers, W. G., & Love, D. E. (2002). The empirical development of the child–parent communication apprehension scale for use with young adults. *Journal of Family Communication, 2,* 109–131.

References

Powers, W. G., & Hutchinson, K. (1979). The measurement of communication apprehension in the marriage relationship. *Journal of Marriage and the Family, 41,* 89–95.

Scale

Child–Parent Communication Apprehension Scale (C-PCA)*
Instructions: Please respond to each of the following items using 5-point Likert response options (1 = strongly disagree to 5 = strongly agree).

1 I feel relaxed when talking with my father/mother about things that happened during the day.
2 I have no fear in discussing problems with my father/mother.
3 I am comfortable in developing intimate conversations with my father/mother.
4 I look forward to talks with my father/mother.
5 When in casual conversations with my father/mother I don't feel I have to guard what I say.
6 I am afraid to come right out and tell my father/mother exactly what I mean.
7 I am so relaxed with my father/mother that I can really be an open communicator with him/her.
8 I am tense when developing in-depth conversations with my father/mother.
9 I feel strained when anticipating talks with my father/mother.
10 Even in casual conversations with my father/mother, I feel anxious and must guard what I say.
11 I have no fear telling my father/mother exactly how I feel.
12 I have no anxiety about telling my father/mother my needs.

Cognitive Elaboration Scale

Profile by Elizabeth M. Perse

Mass communication research has moved to considering the mental processes that underlie media effects. Research has integrated various approaches drawn from cognitive psychology, such as accessibility models, cognitive heuristic models, and depth of processing models to explore how people think about messages to explain the effects of those messages (Lang, Bradley, Chung, & Lee, 2003). Perse (1990b) merged cognitive theory and the uses and gratifications concept of audience activity to propose that cognitive elaboration was an important variable to explain people's mental involvement and processing of media messages.

Elaboration is a cognitive process that occurs within the active audience member. It reflects mental involvement with the message and signals active participation in information processing. According to Perse (1990b), elaboration is a motivated cognitive response to media messages that involves relating new information to prior knowledge and attaching meaning to that new information. Elaboration is an aspect of depth of processing mental models because greater elaboration leads to greater memory and recall.

Elaboration has emerged as a central variable in uses and gratifications research (e.g., Perse, 1990a, 1998), media effects research (e.g., Kim & Rubin, 1997), and political communication (e.g., Eveland, Shah, & Kwak, 2003), and processing of Web content (e.g., Eveland, Cortese, Park, & Dunwoody, 2004).

Perse's (1990b) five-item scale is profiled here. It operationalizes a situational cognitive response to particular media messages. Scale items are usually randomly presented within survey instruments and take less than 2 minutes to complete. Responses to the 5-point Likert items are typically averaged.

Reliability

The cognitive elaboration scale has been used reliably. Researchers using five-item versions of the scale report Cronbach alpha reliabilities that range from .81 to .85 (Haridakis, 2006; Kim & Rubin, 1997; Perse, 1990b, 1990c). The four-item version of the scale is also quite reliable. Perse (1990a, 1998) and Schroeder (2005) reported Cronbach alphas that range from .79 to .89. The scale has been use reliably referencing elaboration on local news government reports, local news crime reports, television content, and soap opera stories.

Validity

Perse (1990b) offered some criterion-related validity for the scale. Consistent with expectations that thinking about news would be related to greater cognitive skills (e.g., Tichenor, Donohue, & Olien, 1970), cognitive elaboration with local news government and crime reports is positively correlated with educational level. Perse (1998) also found that more cognitive elaboration while watching a television program was linked to lower levels of channel changing while watching. The cognitive elaboration scale has also been positively associated with information-oriented viewing motives (Perse, 1990b) and greater attention to local news stories (Perse, 1990b) and to television (Perse, 1998). Audiences are also more likely to elaborate on content that they believe is more realistic (Perse, 1998).

There is also evidence for the scale's construct validity. The cognitive elaboration scale was part of multivariate instrumental and ritualistic television viewing patterns (Perse, 1998). That is, elaboration was a significant positive aspect of instrumental television viewing, which is a more active approach to television viewing that focuses on television content. The scale was a significant negative aspect of ritualistic viewing, which is a more passive use of television that focuses more on watching television as an activity than watching particular content. Perse (1990c) also found that cognitive elaboration predicted information holding, a content-oriented effect of watching local news. And, consistent with recent views that cultivation is an effect of automatic, more heuristic processing, Schroeder (2005) found that elaboration was a negative predictor of cultivation.

Comments

The concept of elaboration has been explored in a range of studies that consider how cognitive processes mediate media effects. Eveland (2001) proposed the cognitive mediation model to explain how elaboration is a central concept to understanding such processes as learning from the media (Eveland et al., 2003, 2004) as well as differences in the mental processing of different types of media (e.g., Eveland & Dunwoody, 2002). Scholars have built on Eveland's model using data drawn from large, representative regional and national samples. Because of the reliance on secondary analysis of large data sets, this program of research has not been able to use a single consistent measure of elaboration. The consistent and predictable findings using different measures of elaboration, however, suggest that it is a robust and central concept.

Location*

Perse, E. M. (1990b). Involvement with local television news: Cognitive and emotional dimensions. *Human Communication Research, 16,* 556–581.

References

Eveland, W. P., Jr. (2001). The cognitive mediation mode of learning from the news: Evidence from nonelection, off-year election, and presidential election contexts. *Communication Research, 28,* 571–601.

Eveland, W. P., Jr., Cortese, J., Park, H. S., & Dunwoody, S. (2004). How Web site organization influences free recall, factual knowledge, and knowledge structure. *Human Communication Research, 30,* 208–233.

Eveland, W. P., Jr., & Dunwoody, S. (2002). An investigation of elaboration and selective scanning as mediators of learning from the Web versus print. *Journal of Broadcasting & Electronic Media, 46,* 2002.

Eveland, W. P., Jr., Shah, D. V., & Kwak, N. (2003). Assessing causality and learning in the cognitive mediation model: A panel study of motivations, information processing and learning during campaign 2000. *Communication Research, 30,* 359–386.

Haridakis, P. M. (2006). Men, women, and televised violence: Predicting viewer aggression in male and female television viewers. *Communication Quarterly, 54,* 227–255.

Kim J., & Rubin, A. M. (1997). The variable influence of audience activity on media effects. *Communication Research, 24,* 107–135.

Lang, A., Bradley, S. D., Chung, Y., & Lee, S. (2003). *Journal of Broadcasting & Electronic Media, 47,* 650–655.

Perse, E. M. (1990a). Audience selectivity and involvement in the newer media environment. *Communication Research, 17,* 675–697.

Perse, E. M. (1990b). Involvement with local television news: Cognitive and emotional dimensions. *Human Communication Research, 16,* 556–581.

Perse, E. M. (1990c). Media involvement and local news effects. *Journal of Broadcasting & Electronic Media, 34,* 17–36.

Perse, E. M. (1998). Implications of cognitive and affective involvement for channel changing. *Journal of Communication, 48*(3), 49–68.

Schroeder, L. M. (2005). Cultivation and the Elaboration Likelihood Model: A test of the learning and construction and availability heuristic models. *Communication Studies, 56,* 227–242.

Tichenor, P. J., Donohue, G. A., & Olien, C. N. (1970). Mass media flow and the differential growth in knowledge. *Public Opinion Quarterly, 34,* 159–170.

Scale

Cognitive Elaboration Scale*

Instructions: Read each statement and indicate if you *strongly agree, agree, agree some and disagree some, disagree,* or *strongly disagree* with each.

1   When I watched, I thought about what the program meant to me and my family.
2   When I watched, I thought about how the program relates to other things that I know.
3   When I watched, I thought about what the program meant to other people.
4   When I watched, I thought about the program over and over again.
5   When I watched, I thought about what should be done.

Note: A four-item reliable version of the scale eliminates item no. 5.

* ©1990 by Blackwell Publishing.

Communication Functions Questionnaire (CFQ)

Profile by Elizabeth E. Graham

Burleson and Samter (1990) developed a measure to assess the value people place on communication skills, particularly same-sex friends. The Communication Functions Questionnaire (CFQ) assesses the value placed on ten skills relevant in communication with others and features the management of feelings and the management of behavior. Skills that focus on the management of affect and emotion (i.e., feelings) include: *comforting skills* (assisting others when they are in need) and *ego supportive skills* (boosting another's feelings about him- or herself). The skills that reflect managing activity and behaviors are: *referential skills* (sharing information in a clear and understandable fashion); *conversational skills* (talking with ease in casual settings); *narrative skills* (entertaining by telling jokes and stories); and *persuasion* (influencing others to change or alter their behavior). Two other skills, *conflict management* (solving problems effectively) and *regulation* (helping someone recover from a mistake and remedy the problem), are an indication of both the management of feelings and behaviors and reflect the need to protect the relationship and feelings and thoughts of others. Recent versions of the CFQ include two additional affectively oriented dimensions: expressiveness (the ability to express feelings in a manner accessible to others), and listening (the ability to comprehend the messages of others) (see Jones, 2005).

The original eight skills, identified by Burleson and Samter (1990), were subjected to confirmatory factor analysis and resulted in a 31-item eight-factor model. Secondary factor analysis (exploratory) revealed two secondary factors termed *affectively oriented skills* that encompass ego support, comforting, conflict management, expressivity, and listening skills and *instrumentally oriented skills* (initially termed nonaffectively oriented skills) that include persuasive, narrative, referential, regulative, and conversational skills. Scores for the two factors are the result of averaging the scores on each set of the five variables. Ensuing factor analyses have also supported the initial conceptualization of the CFQ (Burleson,

Kunkel, & Birch, 1994; Burleson, Samter, & Lucchetti, 1992; Samter & Burleson, 1990). The CFQ has been refined and modified over the years and the most recent iteration is a 30-item, 10 factor measure anchored by a 5-point Likert-type response option format. Respondents are requested to indicate the relative importance of a series of communication behaviors relative to a particular relationship (see Burleson et al., 1992; Kunkel & Burleson, 2003; Samter & Burleson, 1990).

Reliability

Burleson and Samter (1990) reported Cronbach alphas of $\alpha = .83$ for the affectively oriented skills and $\alpha = .74$ for the instrumental skills (i.e., non-affectively oriented skills). Reliability information for the eight original factors include: comforting skills $\alpha = .77$; ego supportive skills $\alpha = .82$; conflict management skills $\alpha = .69$; regulative skills $\alpha = .74$; referential skills $\alpha = .81$; conversational skills $\alpha = .72$; narrative skills $\alpha = .84$; and persuasion skills $\alpha = .81$. Jones (2005) reported reliability estimates for the two new subscales and are as follows: expressivity skills $\alpha = .71$ and listening skills $\alpha = .75$. Subsequent research has produced equally, and in some cases higher, reliability estimates (see Burleson et al., 1994). Individual subscales (i.e., comforting skill) have been successfully employed as well, yielding acceptable reliability estimates (see Burleson & Mortenson, 2003; Samter, Whaley, Mortenson, & Burleson, 1997).

Validity

To illustrate the construct validity of the Communication Functions Questionnaire, Burleson and Samter (1990) proposed that cognitively complex people place a higher value on friends' communication skills such that they are more capable of managing conflict and engaging in comforting behaviors. For this reason they tested the relationship between cognitive complexity and communication skill evaluations and found that perceptions of the value of ego support and comforting skills increase as a result of cognitive complexity and perceptions of the importance of narrative and persuasive skills decrease as a consequence of cognitive complexity. Simply put, cognitively complex individuals valued ego support and comforting skills more than those less cognitively complex and low cognitively complex individuals rated referential, persuasive, and narrative skills as more valuable than highly cognitively complex communicators. The second order factors were also examined and it was determined that cognitive complexity was linked to an increase in perceptions of the value of affectively oriented skills and a decrease in the value of instrumental skills. Subsequent research by Aylor (2003) proffered similar conclusions. These results, according to Burleson and Samter (1990), are consistent with prior research which suggests that cognitively complex people "place greater value on communication skills related to the expression, management, and negotiation of affect" (p. 176). The consistency of these findings supports the conceptualization of the Communication Functions Questionnaire.

The CFQ has been linked to various communication dispositions and outcomes that are indicative of the validity of the CFQ. For example, Jones (2005) reported that affective skills including comforting, ego support, expressivity, and listening were dismissed as unimportant by those termed attachment avoidant. These findings are consistent with prior research which suggests that attachment avoidant individuals do not value inter-personal relationships. Furthermore, the endorsement of affectively oriented skills (i.e., comforting and ego support) results in liking and acceptance whereas the endorsement of instrumental skills was strongly associated with being fun. Also, Samter (1992) reported that loneliness levels were lower for those persons who valued affectively oriented communication skills. Furthermore, there is a good deal of research that supports the contention that affectively oriented skills are more valued than instrumental skills in friendship and romance (see Burleson et al., 1996; Burleson & Samter, 1990).

Differences, although tepid, revealed that (a) women view affective skills as more important than men; (b) men view instrumentally oriented skills as more important than women; and (c) both men and women rate affective skills higher than instrumental skills (Burleson, Kunkel, Samter, & Werking, 1996; Burleson et al., 1992; Finn & Powers, 2002; Kunkel & Burleson, 2003; Samter & Burleson, 2005). These findings prompted the conclusion that men and women are more alike than different (Burleson et al., 1996).

Although the CFQ produced little variance with regard to gender, ethnicity was found to produce some distinct differences. More specifically, Samter and Burleson (2005) concluded that European Americans valued the communication skills (affective and instrumental) of same-sex friends as more important that Asian American who likewise valued the same skills more than African American (especially African American women). These findings are consistent with the tendency of Asian Americans to rely on nonverbal contextual forms of communication to converse and share meanings and therefore, it is not surprising that they would endorse affec-tively oriented skills as less important than European Americans. With the recognition that friendship and communication appear to be culture spe-cific qualities, the CFQ has utility beyond the confines of the European American culture.

The CFQ is also sensitive to relationship type and intimacy level. Ini-tially the CFQ was developed to assess the value that friends have for com-munication skills; however Burleson and colleagues (Burleson et al.,

(1994) extended the CFQ into the realm of dating partners and concluded that similarity in evaluation of communication skills results in more satisfaction and attraction. Although as they point out "... similarities in communication values do not influence who people choose to date, such similarities do influence how happy people will be with those whom they do date" (p. 271). Furthermore, friends tend to mirror each other in their regard for communication skills, particularly conflict management, comforting, persuasive skill, and ego support skills (Burleson et al., 1992). Kunkel and Burleson (2003) concluded that love styles are also sensitive to communication skill evaluations, particularly those for affectively oriented communication skills.

Interestingly, research indicates that friends do not similarly regard the importance of communication skills as dating partners do. Indeed, a good deal of research supports the claim that although affectively oriented skills are very important to both friends *and* romantic partners, romantic partners value these communication skills even more so than friends (Burleson et al., 1996; Burleson & Samter, 1990; Burleson et al., 1992). Consistent with these findings, Finn and Powers (2002) also noted that three affectively oriented skills (comforting, conflict management, and ego support) were more appreciated in developed same-sex relationships as compared to less developed relationships. Furthermore, they concluded that affective and instrumental skills are valued in young adult same-sex friendships and affectively oriented skills are more valued in intimate relationships than less intimate relationships. In effect, there is a positive linear relationship between the importance of communication skills and relationship intimacy. This association is especially true for affectively oriented skills.

Comments

Affective and instrumental skills are highly valued by men, women, in romance and friendship. However, as Samter and Burleson's (2005) research revealed, the values embedded in the CFQ are largely reflective of white middle class ideals. Quantifying the variance in the way ethnic groups enact friendship and value communication is a very important and largely under-researched issue in communication scholarship.

The CFQ has enjoyed widespread use in interpersonal domains but has also been applied in organizational settings (see Myers, Knox, Pawlowski, & Ropog, 1999) and instructional contexts (see Aylor, 2003; Frymier & Houser, 2000; Myers, Martin, & Knapp, 2005). The reliability of the CFQ is satisfactory and the many studies employing the measure illustrate its construct validity. The CFQ provides useful insights of the value of communication qualities and behaviors so important in personal relationships.

Location*

Burleson, B. R., & Samter, W. (1990). Effects of cognitive complexity on the perceived importance of communication skills in friends. *Communication Research, 17*,165–182.

References

Aylor, B. (2003). The impact of sex, gender, and cognitive complexity on the perceived importance of teacher communication skills. *Communication Studies, 54*, 496–509.

Burleson, B. R., Kunkel, A. W., & Birch, J. D. (1994). Thoughts about talk in romantic relationships: Similarity makes for attraction (and happiness, too). *Communication Quarterly, 42*, 259–273.

Burleson, B. R., Kunkel, A. W., Samter, W., & Werking, K. J. (1996). Men's and women's evaluations of communication skills in personal relationships: When sex differences make a difference—and when they don't. *Journal of Social and Personal Relationships, 13*, 201–224.

Burleson, B., & Mortenson, S. (2003). Explaining cultural differences in evaluations of emotional support behaviors: Exploring the mediating influences of value systems and interaction goals. *Communication Research, 30*, 113–146.

Burleson, B. R., Samter, W., & Lucchetti, A. E. (1992). Similarity in communication values as a predictor of friendship choices: Studies of friends and best friends. *Southern Communication Journal, 57*, 260–276.

Finn, A., & Powers, W. G. (2002). The value of instrumental and affective communication skills in different relational stages. *Communication Quarterly, 50*, 192–203.

Frymier, A. B., & Houser, M. L. (2000). The teacher-student relationship as an interpersonal relationship. *Communication Education, 49*, 207–219.

Jones, S, M. (2005). Attachment style differences and similarities in evaluations of affective communication skills and person-centered comforting messages. *Western Journal of Communication, 69*, 233–249.

Kunkel, A. W., & Burleson, B. R. (2003). Relational implications of communication skill evaluations and love styles. *Southern Communication Journal, 68*, 181–197.

Myers, S. A., Knox, R. L., Pawlowski, D. R., & Ropog, B. L. (1999). Perceived communication openness and functional communication skills among organizational peers. *Communication Reports, 12*, 71–83.

Myers, S. A., Martin, M. M., & Knapp, J. L. (2005). Perceived instructor in-class communicative behaviors as a predictor of student participation in and out of class *communication*. *Communication Education, 53*, 437–450.

Samter, W. (1992). Communication characteristics of the lonely person's friendship circle. *Communication Research, 19*, 212–239.

Samter, W., & Burleson, B. R. (1990). Evaluations of communication skills as predictors of peer acceptance in a group living situation. *Communication Studies, 41*, 311–326.

Samter, W., & Burleson, B. R. (2005). The role of communication in same-sex friendships: A comparison among African Americans, Asian Americans, and European Americans. *Communication Quarterly, 53*, 265–283.

Samter, W., Whaley, B., Mortenson, S., & Burleson, B. (1998). Ethnicity and emotional support in same-sex friendship: A comparison of Asian Americans, African Americans, and Euro-Americans. *Personal Relationships, 23*, 2, 121–146.

Scale

Communication Functions Questionnaire (CFQ-30)*
Instructions: Below are descriptions of several different kinds of communication skills. Please read through the description carefully. Then, fill in the circle on your answer sheet for the response which best represents your feelings regarding *how important it would be for a very close friend to possess the communication skill.* The items refer to how important you *generally* think these communication behaviors and outcomes are in very close friendships. For each item please use the following scale:

Somewhat Important ____ ____ ____ ____ ____ **Extremely Important**
             A   B   C   D   E

For example, consider the following item:
   "Has the ability to make me believe I have the qualities people will like."
   If you think this would be an important or extremely important skill for a very close friend to possess, you would fill in the circle for option "D" or "E." If you think this would be a moderately important skill for a very close friend to possess, you would fill in the circle for option "C." Finally, if you think this would be only a somewhat important skill for a very close friend to possess, you would fill in the circle option "A" or "B." Please make certain that you read and rate each item.

Comforting

1 Can help me work through my emotions when I'm feeling upset or depressed.
2 Comforts me when I am feeling sad or depressed.
3 Helps make me feel better when I'm hurt or depressed about something.

Conflict Management

4 Shows me it's possible to resolve our disagreements in a way that won't hurt or embarrass each other.
5 Makes me realize that it is better to deal with conflicts we have than to keep things bottled up inside.
6 Can work through our relational problems by addressing the issues rather than engaging in personal attacks.

Conversation

7   Is a good conversationalist.
8   Is able to start up a conversation easily.
9   Can make conversation easy and fun.

Ego Support

10   Makes me feel like I'm a good person.
11   Encourages me to believe in myself.
12   Helps me feel proud of my accomplishments.

Expressiveness

13   Is open in expressing her/his thoughts and feelings to me.
14   Lets me know what's going on in his/her world.
15   Shares his/her joys, as well as sorrows, with me.

Informative

16   Explains things clearly.
17   Makes me understand exactly what he/she is referring to.
18   Can express complicated ideas in a direct, clear way.

Listening

19   Listens carefully when I am speaking.
20   Is an attentive listener when I need to talk to someone.
21   Gives me her/his full attention when I need to talk.

Narrative

22   Can get me laughing because he/she is so good at telling a joke or story.
23   Is able to tell a story in a way that captures my attention.
24   Can make even everyday events seem funny or exciting when telling a story.

Persuasion

25   Makes me feel like I've made my own decision even though I do mostly what he/she wants.
26   Persuades me that doing things his/her way is the best.
27   Can convince me to do just about anything.

Regulative

28   Shows me that I have the ability to fix my own mistakes.

29 Encourages me to feel like I can learn from my mistakes by working through things with me.

30 Helps me see how I can improve myself by learning from my mistakes.

Communicative Responses to Romantic Jealousy Scale (CRJ)

Profile by Elizabeth E. Graham

Recognizing the universal salience of jealousy, Laura Guerrero and associates (Guerrero, Andersen, Jorgensen, Spitzberg, & Eloy, 1995) developed a measure titled the Communicative Responses to Romantic Jealousy (CRJ) Scale. Unlike existing measures of jealousy that are cognitively based, the CRJ is rooted in observable outward responses to jealousy, specifically romantic jealousy. Research suggests that responses to jealousy can reduce uncertainty, maintain and repair relationships, and mend self-esteem (Guerrero & Afifi, 1999). How romantic partners cope with and express feelings of jealousy has direct implications for the management and quality of relationships. Guerrero et al. (1995) defined a communicative response to jealousy as "a behavioral reaction to jealousy that carries communicative value and has the potential to fulfill individual and/or relational goals" (p. 272).

To further conceptualize jealousy, Guerrero and Andersen (1998) developed the componential model of jealousy, which includes concepts related to both the experience (cognitive and emotion) and expression (communication and behavior) of jealousy. The basic premise of the model rests on the claim that different goals (e.g., uncertainty reduction, relational maintenance) and antecedent conditions (e.g., culture, biology, sex, and relationship characteristics) prompt varied reactions to jealousy at the cognitive, affective, and behavioral level. The model also specifies that communicative responses to jealousy affect relational outcomes such as satisfaction, trust, and commitment.

At the onset, a distinction was drawn between interactive and general behavioral responses to jealousy. Interactive responses include face-to-face communication between relationship parties that often prompts a response from the partner whereas general behavioral responses are not necessarily interactive and do not necessarily involve partner response. For example, looking through a partner's belongings would qualify as a general reaction and confronting a partner in an accusatory manner is representative of an interactive reaction to jealousy. With this framework in mind, the authors identified six interactive measures (integrative communication, distributive communication, active distancing, general avoidance/denial, expression of negative affect, and violent communication/threats) and five general responses to jealousy measures (surveillance/restriction, compensatory restoration, manipulation attempts, rival contact, and violent behavior). Over time, the CRJ has been modified and the current 70-item measure consists of fourteen subscales, containing nine interactive and five general responses to jealousy (see Guerrero & Andersen, 1998).

The authors conducted a series of preliminary studies to validate both the conceptualization and measurement of CRJ (see Guerrero et al., 1995).The first interactive measure, integrative communication, refers to direct nonconfrontational communication. The second scale, distributive communication, includes confrontational, threatening, and aggressive communication. Active distancing, the third factor, references passive aggressive behaviors such as giving the partner the silent treatment, and the fourth factor, general avoidance/denial, refers to withdrawal from the partner and denying jealous feelings. Expression of negative affect, the fifth factor, reflects the dark side of jealousy-related feelings such as depression, anger, and frustration. The sixth factor, violent communication/threats, includes behaviors that are aggressive and violent. The three additional measures subsequently developed for inclusion in the CRJ (see Guerrero & Andersen, 1998) include signs of possession (behaviors that indicate that one's partner is taken), derogating competitors (verbally downgrading the rival), and relationship threats (threatening to leave the relationship or have an affair). These nine interactive responses to jealousy vary in terms of how constructive (or prosocial) versus destructive (or antisocial) they are within the context of romantic relationships.

The first general response measure, surveillance/restriction, includes responses that entail investigating the rival relationship. Compensatory restoration, the second factor, refers to endeavors to improve and enhance the relationship. The third factor, manipulation attempts, is composed of behaviors that induce guilt and threaten revenge. The fourth factor, labeled rival contact, involves confronting the rival and the last factor, violent behavior, refers to activities, often conducted in private, such as throwing things and punching pillows. These five general responses to jealousy are distinguished by whether they are directed at the partner or the rival, function to discover or repair the relationship, and are positively or negatively valenced.

Reliability

A series of analyses conducted by Guerrero et al. (1995) on the interactive measures of the CRJ Scale produced acceptable reliability estimates: integrative communication $\alpha = .83$ across two studies; distributive communication

$\alpha = .83$ and .85; active distancing $\alpha = .83$ across two studies; general avoidance/denial $\alpha = .75$ and .77; expression of negative affect $\alpha = .82$ and .81; and violent communication/threats $\alpha = .58$ and .89 (with additional measures added in the second study to boost reliability). The three jealousy responses that were subsequently added to the overall measure (Guerrero & Andersen, 1998) have also produced acceptable reliabilities: signs of possession $\alpha = .85$; derogation of competitors $\alpha = .86$; and relationship threats $\alpha = .79$ (Carson & Cupach, 2000).

The five general response measures of the CRJ produced the following reliability estimates (Guerrero et al., 1995): surveillance/restriction $\alpha = .81$ .89; compensatory restoration $\alpha = .80, .76$; manipulation attempts $\alpha = .73,$ .69; rival contact $\alpha = .78, .84$; and violent behavior $\alpha = .67, .78$. Additional studies (Aylor & Dainton, 2001; Bevan, 2004; Guerrero, Trost, & Yoshimura, 2005) have also produced satisfactory reliability estimates.

Validity

Through correlation and regression analysis, the authors (Guerrero et al., 1995) established preliminary evidence of convergent validity by illustrating the association between the CRJ and other established measures of jealousy (i.e., jealousy expression and jealousy experience). Central to the study of jealousy is Bryson's (1991) dual motivation model that suggests that communicative responses to jealousy are influenced by relationship maintenance and self-esteem concerns.

To examine the construct validity of the CRJ, Guerrero and Afifi (1998) proposed a set of research questions and hypotheses that tested the relationship among types of responses to jealousy, relationship preservation, and self-esteem maintenance. Consistent with expectations, the desire to enhance the relationship and maintain self-esteem was related to an integrative response to jealousy (i.e., talking in a non-threatening manner). Those individuals most desirous of maintaining their relationships (regardless of self-esteem needs) reported using more compensatory restoration communication (being very nice) and negative affect expression (i.e., showing their negative feelings to their partners) than those unmotivated to preserve their relationship. Furthermore, individuals who were motivated to maintain their relationship and less interested in enhancing their self-esteem, were more likely to resort to surveillance techniques (spying on the partner) when dealing with jealousy. Conversely, those individuals motivated to preserve their self-esteem resorted to manipulation strategies (inflicting revenge and making the partner feel jealous and guilty) and more avoidance/denial behaviors as a means of coping with their jealous feelings. Finally, a curvilinear rather than a linear relationship best explains the relationship among some responses to jealousy (i.e., active distancing and distributive reactions to jealousy) and goals, such that the desire to maintain the relationship and enhance self-esteem is simultaneously accompanied by an increase in the use of distributive communication and active distancing—but only up to a point.

Perhaps the most extensive test of the construct validity of the CRJ and Guerrero and Andersen's (1998) componential model of jealousy, experience (cognitive and affective) and expression (communication and behavior) was conducted by Guerrero and Afifi (1999). Specifically, the authors identified six jealousy-related goals that capture the cognitive aspects of jealousy: (1) maintaining the primary relationship, (2) maintaining one's self-esteem, (3) reducing uncertainty about the primary relationship, (4) reducing uncertainty about the rival relationship, and (5) determining and evaluating one's own feelings about the relationship, and (6) restoring equity through retaliation. These six goals were studied in conjunction with the nine (of the fourteen) communicative responses to jealousy (the behavioral components of the model). Based on a series of regression analyses the following hypotheses concerning relationship goals and jealousy responses were supported: (1) relationship maintenance was likely to elicit more compensatory restoration communication and negative affective expression responses, (2) the desire to preserve self-esteem was related to avoidance/denial and negatively associated with negative affect expression, partner surveillance, and rival contact, (3) reducing uncertainty about the primary relationship predicted the use of integrative communication responses to jealousy and the expression of negative affect, (4) reducing uncertainty about the rival relationship predicted the use of surveillance, rival contacts, and active distancing responses to jealousy, (5) the goal of re-assessing the relationship prompted three indirect jealousy responses: manipulation, avoidance/denial, and active distancing, (6) equity restoration through retaliation predicted distributive communication, active distancing, surveillance, manipulation, and rival contacts.

The third component of the model, the emotional or affective level, was operationalized as the intensity and frequency of communicative responses to jealousy. The results support the contention that emotional intensity prompts distributive communication responses to jealousy and frequency of jealousy experiences is predictive of distributive communication, avoidance/denial, and surveillance responses. A later study (Guerrero et al., 2005) demonstrated that specific types of jealousy-related emotions associated with different communicative responses. For example, compensatory restoration was associated with feeling fearful and envious but not hostile. Violent communication associated with high levels of hostility and low levels of guilt. Rival contacts were best predicted by passion and hostility, and integrative communication was reported most often by those who felt irritation (a mild form of anger) rather than hostility (a severe form of anger).

Aylor and Dainton (2001) further refined Guerrero and Andersen's (1998) model by investigating psychological gender *and* biological sex as antecedents to the expression of jealousy. Sex differences were evident for women as they were more likely than men to engage in the following anti-social responses to jealousy: negative affect, distributive communication, active distancing, violent communication, and manipulation. At first these findings might appear counterintuitive as women are rarely more antiso-cial in their communication than men. Perhaps a more salient motivation for women is the expression of feelings—even if the feelings are negative. Conversely, gender, operationalized as femininity/expressiveness and masculinity/instrumentality, produced very different responses to jeal-ousy. Femininity/expressiveness was positively correlated with integrative communication and negatively associated with distributive communica-tion, relationship threats, and manipulation. Furthermore, masculinity/ instrumentality was positively correlated with distributive communica-tion, signs of possession, manipulation, contacting rivals, and violent behavior. These findings support sex role stereotypes as masculinity/ instrumentality is associated with antisocial responses to jealousy and femininity/expressiveness is related to prosocial expressions. Results sug-gest that gender is a better predictor of certain responses to jealousy and sex is a better predictor of others. In many ways these findings are incon-sistent with prior research concerning sex differences and expressions of jealousy (see Carson & Cupach, 1999; Guerrero & Reiter, 1998).

The third antecedent to the expression of jealousy articulated by Aylor and Dainton (2001) concerned the role of relationship type as a factor likely to influence jealousy responses. Not surprisingly they concluded that married people experienced less jealousy and those in new relation-ships reported experiencing the most. In addition, their results support the contention that as we age, expressions of jealousy become less frequent. Furthermore, married individuals were less likely to resort to negative affect, avoidance, signs of possession, and manipulation responses to jeal-ousy. In direct contrast, those in dating relationships reported using active distancing, avoidance, signs of possession, derogating the rival, and manipulation reactions to jealousy. Casual daters, compared to serious daters, resorted to active distancing and avoidance expressions of jeal-ousy, and were not likely to derogate rivals.

Interested in the cognitive elements of jealousy, Carson and Cupach (2000) proposed that rumination (excessive worry) is an influencing factor responsible for differing reactions to jealousy. They determined that rela-tionship rumination was positively related to the following communica-tive responses to jealousy: surveillance, manipulation, relationship threat, rival contact, compensatory restoration, negative affect expression, signs of possession, derogation of competitors, distributive communication, violent behaviors, active distancing, and avoidance/denial. Clearly rumination is an important cognitive predictor of many antisocial counterproductive responses to jealousy.

In an effort to extend the applicability of the CRJ, Bevan and Samter (2004) suggested that jealousy is not limited to romantic concerns or relationships. Rather, they proposed that there are six potential types of jealousy that can be expressed in non-romantic (i.e., cross-sex friendship) relationships and they include: friend jealousy, family jealousy, activity jealousy, power jealousy, intimacy jealousy, and romantic jealousy. They found that cross-sex friends experiencing intimacy concerns are likely to report negative affect expression, distributive communication, and integrative communication more so than other jealousy types.

Revisiting the relationship between jealousy and uncertainty, and taking note of the reflexive nature of communication, Bevan (2004) concluded that uncertainty can result from one's reaction to a partner's expression of jealousy. Furthermore, Bevan found that cross-sex friends were more prone to uncertainty than siblings or daters subsequent to another's expression of jealousy. Use of negative affect as a means of expressing jealous feelings led to more uncertainty (general and relational) than did the use of integrative or distributive communication responses.

In sum, the construct validity of the Communicative Response to Jealousy can easily be surmised from the wealth of research supporting the following claims: Communicative responses to jealousy are associated with psychological gender *and* biological sex (Aylor & Dainton, 2001), relational satisfaction (Guerrero et al., 1995), uncertainty (Afifi & Reichert), attachment style (Guerrero, 1998), rumination (Carson & Cupach, 2000), relationship goals (Guerrero & Afifi, 1999), relationship type (Aylor & Dainton, 2001) emotional intensity and frequency of jealousy experiences (Guerrero & Afifi, 1999), specific types of jealousy-related emotion (Guerrero et al., 2005) and type of jealousy (Bevan & Samter, 2004).

Comments

Evidence suggests that the CRJ offers an acceptable level of reliability and an impressive series of studies are supportive of its validity. An important contribution of Guerrero et al.'s (1995) conceptualization of jealousy is the opportunity to view the expression of jealousy as resulting in positive relational outcomes. Although many of the responses to jealousy are associated with relational dissatisfaction, jealousy can indeed enhance the quality of a relationship through increased communication and understanding between relational partners. Thus far, expressing negative feelings while using integrative communication appears to be the most effective way of coping with jealousy.

As is true of other measures that focus on the dark side of communication, it seems respondents are not as forthcoming about reporting instances of violence and other antisocial reactions to jealousy (i.e, surveillance activities). Indeed the authors (Guerrero et al., 1995) point out that the CRJ is susceptible to a social desirability bias. While the likelihood of this bias occurring can be minimized by ensuring anonymity and letting participants know that people express jealousy in a wide variety of ways, it is, nevertheless, an issue that warrants further attention. An additional issue of concerns rests with the predominant sampling of an undergraduate student population.

Location*

Guerrero, L. K., Andersen, P. A., Jorgensen, P. F., Spitzberg, B. H., & Eloy, S. V. (1995). Coping with the green-eyed monster: Conceptualizing and measuring communicative responses to romantic jealousy. *Western Journal of Communication, 59,* 270–304.

References

Aylor, B., & Dainton, M. (2001). Antecedents in romantic jealousy experience, expression, and goals. *Western Journal of Communication, 65,* 370–391.

Bevan, J. L. (2004). General partner and relational uncertainty as consequences of another person's jealousy expression. *Western Journal of Communication, 68,* 195–218.

Bevan, J. L., & Samter, W. (2004). Toward a broader conceptualization of jealousy in close relationships: Two exploratory studies. *Communication Studies, 55,* 14–28.

Carson, C. L., & Cupach, W. R. (2000). Fueling the green-eyed monster: The role of ruminative thought in reaction to romantic jealousy. *Western Journal of Communication, 64,* 308–329.

Guerrero, L. K. (1998). Attachment-style differences in the experience and expression of romantic jealousy. *Personal Relationships, 5,* 273–291.

Guerrero, L. K., & Andersen, P. A. (1998). Jealousy experience and expression in romantic relationships. In P. A. Andersen & L. K. Guerrero (Eds.), *Handbook of communication and emotion: Research, theory, applications, and contexts* (pp. 155–188). San Diego, CA: Academic Press.

Guerrero, L. K., & Afifi, W. A. (1998). Communicative responses to jealousy as a function of self-esteem and relationship maintenance goals: A test of Bryson's dual motivation model. *Communication Reports, 11,* 111–122.

Guerrero, L. K., & Afifi, W. A. (1999). Toward a goal-oriented approach for understanding communicative responses to jealousy. *Western Journal of Communication, 63,* 216–248.

Guerrero, L. K., Trost, M. R., & Yoshimura, S. M. (2005). Romantic jealousy: Emotions and communicative responses. *Personal Relationships, 12,* 233–252.

Guerrero, L. K., & Reiter, R. L. (1998). Expressing emotion: Sex differences in social skills and communicative responses to anger, sadness, and jealousy. In D. J. Canary & K. Dindia (Eds.), *Sex differences and similarities in communication* (pp. 321–350). Mahwah, NJ: Erlbaum.

Scale

Communicative Responses to Romantic Jealousy Scale (CRJ)*
Instructions: Most people experience jealousy at some point in their romantic relationships. Jealousy occurs when people believe that their relationship is threatened by a third party (sometimes called a "rival"). Please think about the times you have felt jealous in your current romantic during the past six months. Keep these memories in mind while completing this questionnaire.

Please circle the following codes to indicate how frequently you used each of the following behaviors when experiencing jealousy in your relationship over the past 6 months. 1 = strong disagreement (you never use this behavior when jealous), 7 = strong agreement (you tend to use this behavior a lot when you are jealous). Please react to the following question when filling out the scale:

When I Feel Jealous I Tend To:

	SD	SA

Interactive Responses to Jealousy

Active Distancing

1	Physically pull away from my partner	1 2 3 4 5 6 7
2	Give my partner cold or dirty looks	1 2 3 4 5 6 7
3	Decrease affection toward my partner	1 2 3 4 5 6 7
4	Ignore my partner	1 2 3 4 5 6 7
5	Give my partner the "silent treatment"	1 2 3 4 5 6 7

Negative Affect Expression

6	Appear sad and depressed	1 2 3 4 5 6 7
7	Cry or sulk in front of my partner	1 2 3 4 5 6 7
8	Let my partner see how upset I am	1 2 3 4 5 6 7
9	Vent my frustration when with my partner	1 2 3 4 5 6 7
10	Appear hurt in front of my partner	1 2 3 4 5 6 7
11	Wear displeasure on my face for my partner to see	1 2 3 4 5 6 7

Integrative Communication

12	Explain my feelings to my partner	1 2 3 4 5 6 7
13	Share my jealous feelings with my partner	1 2 3 4 5 6 7
14	Discuss bothersome issues with my partner	1 2 3 4 5 6 7
15	Try to talk to my partner and reach an understanding	1 2 3 4 5 6 7
16	Calmly question my partner	1 2 3 4 5 6 7

Distributive Communication

17	Quarrel or argue with my partner	1 2 3 4 5 6 7

18 Make hurtful or mean comments to my partner   1 2 3 4 5 6 7
19 Yell or curse at my partner   1 2 3 4 5 6 7
20 Act rude toward my partner   1 2 3 4 5 6 7
21 Confront my partner in accusatory manner   1 2 3 4 5 6 7

Avoidance/Denial

22 Stop calling or initiating communication
    with my partner   1 2 3 4 5 6 7
23 Get quiet and don't say much   1 2 3 4 5 6 7
24 Become silent   1 2 3 4 5 6 7
25 Act like I don't care   1 2 3 4 5 6 7
26 Deny feeling jealous   1 2 3 4 5 6 7
27 Pretend nothing is wrong   1 2 3 4 5 6 7

Violent Communication/Threats

28 Push, shove, or hit my partner   1 2 3 4 5 6 7
29 Use physical force with my partner   1 2 3 4 5 6 7
30 Threaten to harm my partner   1 2 3 4 5 6 7
31 Become physically violent   1 2 3 4 5 6 7

Signs of Possession

32 Make sure rivals know my partner is "taken"   1 2 3 4 5 6 7
33 Let rivals know that my partner and I
    have a relationship   1 2 3 4 5 6 7
34 Show my partner extra affection when rivals
    are around   1 2 3 4 5 6 7

Derogating Competitors

35 Call the rival names in front of others   1 2 3 4 5 6 7
36 Say mean things about the rival   1 2 3 4 5 6 7
37 Make negative comments about the rival in front   1 2 3 4 5 6 7
    of my partner
38 Try to convince my partner that the rival is   1 2 3 4 5 6 7
    not a nice person

Relationship Threats

39 Tell my partner that I want to break-up   1 2 3 4 5 6 7
40 Tell my partner that I will start dating
    other people too   1 2 3 4 5 6 7
41 Threaten to terminate the relationship if s/he sees
    the rival anymore   1 2 3 4 5 6 7

42 Tell my partner to choose between me and the rival 1 2 3 4 5 6 7
43 Threaten to have an affair of my own   1 2 3 4 5 6 7

General Responses to Jealousy

Surveillance/Restriction

44 Look through my partner's belongings
    for evidence of a rival relationship   1 2 3 4 5 6 7
45 Keep closer tabs on my partner   1 2 3 4 5 6 7
46 Spy on or follow my partner   1 2 3 4 5 6 7
47 Restrict my partner's access to the rival   1 2 3 4 5 6 7
48 Try to determine my partner's whereabouts   1 2 3 4 5 6 7
49 Constantly call my partner   1 2 3 4 5 6 7
50 Try to prevent my partner from seeing the rival   1 2 3 4 5 6 7
51 "Check up" on my partner more than usual   1 2 3 4 5 6 7

Compensatory Restoration

52 Try to prove to my partner that I love her/him   1 2 3 4 5 6 7
53 Tell my partner how much I need her/him   1 2 3 4 5 6 7
54 Increase affection toward my partner   1 2 3 4 5 6 7
55 Buy gifts or do special things for my partner   1 2 3 4 5 6 7
56 Try to be the "best" partner possible   1 2 3 4 5 6 7
57 Spend more time with my partner than usual   1 2 3 4 5 6 7
58 Try to be more attractive and appealing than
    the rival   1 2 3 4 5 6 7
59 Tell my partner how much I care for her/him   1 2 3 4 5 6 7

Manipulation Attempts

60 Try to make my partner feel guilty   1 2 3 4 5 6 7
61 Flirt with others in front of my partner   1 2 3 4 5 6 7
62 Bring up the rival's name to see how my
    partner reacts   1 2 3 4 5 6 7
63 Try to get revenge on my partner   1 2 3 4 5 6 7
64 Try to make my partner feel jealous too   1 2 3 4 5 6 7

Rival Contacts

66 Tell the rival not to see my partner anymore   1 2 3 4 5 6 7
67 Confront the rival   1 2 3 4 5 6 7
68 Discuss the situation with the rival   1 2 3 4 5 6 7

Violence Toward Objects

69 Slam doors   1 2 3 4 5 6 7

70   Hit or throw objects   1 2 3 4 5 6 7

Note: The items are presented by response type for ease of interpretation, but when using the CRJ instrument, items should be randomized.

Family Communication Standards Instrument

Profile by Elizabeth E. Graham

Although the term *family values* has been a staple in the American lexicon particularly since *Murphy Brown* and Vice President Dan Quayle offered oppositional views on the subject, little empirical research has investigated the communication behaviors associated with family standards. John Caughlin (2003) noted that most studies of family standards do not focus solely on communication nor do they feature specific behaviors. To remedy this shortcoming, Caughlin conceptualized family communication standards as specific ideal behaviors practiced in a family environment. To gather information, participants reported on their ideal family communication standards and Caughlin augmented the measure by contributing additional items. Subsequent to a series of classification and categorization procedures as well as several factor analyses, 41-items—representing 10 dimensions—were identified, resulting in the Family Communication Standards Instrument.

The first standard, *openness,* refers to sharing openly and freely with family members about feelings and thoughts. *Maintaining structural stability* involves an agreed-upon hierarchy and a consistent family communication structure. The third standard, *expression of affection,* reflects verbal and nonverbal displays of affection. *Emotional/instrumental support*, the fourth standard, speaks to being there and offering social and emotional support to one another. The ability to know and understand what is going on with a family member without being told is the essence of the fifth standard, *mindreading. Politeness,* the sixth standard, involves refraining from rudeness and insensitivity with family members. Rules and consequences reflect the standard termed *discipline.* Family standard number eight, *humor/sarcasm,* relates to having fun and teasing one another. The ninth standard, *regular routine interaction* captures the regularity of spending time together. And last, *avoidance,* the tenth standard, refers to avoiding hurtful and painful discussions.

Caughlin (2003) tested the utility of three competing hypotheses in an attempt to understand the relationship between family standards and family satisfaction. The distressful ideals hypothesis claims that certain beliefs about family can lead to (dis)satisfaction and, in effect, those beliefs are the motivation for the development of certain relationship standards. The unmet ideals hypothesis suggests dissatisfaction is the result of the any discrepancy between real and anticipated (i.e., ideal) evaluation of relationships. And, finally, the discrepancy evaluation hypothesis asserts that positive differences between real and anticipated evaluation of relationships would result in satisfaction, whereas differences resulting in a negative valence would detract from perceptions of family satisfaction. Results revealed that the unmet ideals hypothesis best accounted for the association between family satisfaction and family standards. However, the distressful ideals hypothesis did provide additional information related to satisfaction that the unmet ideals hypothesis did not account for. The discrepancy evaluation hypothesis failed to provide any meaningful information with regard to the relationship between family standards and satisfaction. Examination of the correlations between distressful ideals and family standards revealed positive associations for openness, expression of affection, emotional/instrumental support, politeness, discipline, and regular routine interaction. All ten family communication standards correlated with the unmet ideals hypothesis. Thus both the unmet ideals and the distressful ideals hypotheses are useful explanations of family satisfaction and central to the conceptualization of family communication standards.

Reliability

Caughlin (2003) conducted two studies that assessed the internal reliability of the Family Communication Standards Instrument. The findings revealed the following Cronbach alphas: openness α = .88 and .90; maintaining structural stability α = .74 and .82; expression of affection α = .95 and .94; emotional/instrumental support α = .93 and .94; mindreading α = .87 and .87; politeness α = .79 and .83; discipline α = .83 and .80; humor/sarcasm α = .82 and .82; regular routine interaction α = .78 and .72; and avoidance α = .80 and .88.

Validity

Caughlin (2003) established the convergent validity of the Family Communication Standards Instrument by examining the relationship between the theoretically consistent yet distinct constructs of family communication schemata and family standards. The premise for this conception is rooted in the belief that cognitions about family (i.e., schemata) influence perceptions of family standards such that certain schemata facilitate the endorsement of particular family standards. As hypothesized, openness (i.e., family standard) was positively correlated with expressiveness (i.e., family communication schemata); and maintaining structural stability (i.e., family communication standard) was positively related to structural traditionalism (i.e., family communication schemata), and avoidance standard (family communication standard) was positively associated with the avoidance family communication schemata.

Family communication standards also serve to moderate the relationship between family communication behaviors and family satisfaction. More specifically, Caughlin (2003) reported partial support for the hypothesis that family communication standards moderate the relationship among topic avoidance, family conflict, and family maintenance behaviors and family satisfaction. Consistent with expectations, satisfaction was positively related to the trio of constructs in the anticipated direction. Further analysis revealed topic avoidance was inversely related to family satisfaction more so when accompanied by a standard of expressing affection and less when humor/sarcasm was endorsed. In addition, several family standards (openness, expression of affection, emotional/instrumental support, politeness, and regular routine interaction) moderated the relationship between maintenance behaviors and satisfaction suggesting that the presence of certain family standards plays a pivotal role in moderating the relationship between relational maintenance behaviors and family satisfaction. Family standards did not moderate the association between conflict/negativity and satisfaction. Collectively these results provide initial support for the construct validity of the Family Communication Standards Instrument.

Comments

Caughlin's research served to marry the study of family standards and communication by illustrating the centrality of communication in family relationships. Though unspoken, a central assumption of Caughlin's conception of family standards is that the endorsement of certain standards is crucial to good family communication, whereas the endorsement of other standards is more idiosyncratic (i.e., there are multiple viable stances with respect to them).

Preliminary evidence suggests that the Family Communication Standards Instrument offers a respectable level of reliability and a small, but solid, series of studies supportive of several forms of validity. Although this scale is quite new, all indications suggest that it is a promising and viable measure of family communication standards.

Location*

Caughlin, J. P. (2003). Family communication standards. What counts as excellent family communication and how are such standards associated with family satisfaction? *Human Communication Research, 29,* 5–40.

Scale

Family Communication Standards Instrument*
Instructions: Different people have different beliefs about how family members should communicate with each other. Family members may live up to those standards sometimes but not other times. For this questionnaire, think about what you think counts as good family communication. Then, respond to each of the following items in terms of the extent to which it reflects good family communication. Remember, these are your beliefs about what things should be, it doesn't necessarily mean your own family always lived up to these expectations. Each item starts off with "People in families with good communication . . ." Please respond to the 41-item instrument using 7-point Likert response options (1 = strongly disagree to 7 = strongly agree).

People in good families with good communication . . .

Openness

1   ... Can talk openly to one another about any topic.
2   ... Share their feelings (both good and bad).
3   ... Openly discuss topics like sex and drugs.
4   ... Freely deal with issues that may be upsetting.
5   ... Share their problems with one another.
6   ... Tell other family members when something bothers them.
7   ... Talk about it when something is wrong.

Maintaining Structural Stability

8   ... Let one person control most conversations.
9   ... Have one person who dominates family decisions.
10   ... Have one person in the family who everyone else always listens to and obeys.
11   ... Do not worry about showing that they like some family members more than others.
12   ... Know that there are certain people in the family who will always take their side and certain people who don't.
13   ... Only deal with conflict when everyone can do it without getting emotional about it.

Expression of Affection

14   ... Hug one another a lot.
15   ... Often say things like "I love you" to other family members.
16   ... Are very affectionate with one another.
17   ... Show love through physical means like hugging.

Emotional/instrumental support

18   ... Are able to count on one another no matter what.

19 ... Know other family members would help them get through hard times.
20 ... Support one another whatever the situation.
21 ... Help one another when they need it.

Mindreading

22 ... Know what is going on in other family member's lives without asking.
23 ... Know one another so well that they don't have to be told when another family member needs something.
24 ... Are able to understand what other family members are feeling without having to discuss it.
25 ... Just know what other family members think or feel, even when they don't really talk about it.

Politeness

26 ... Are never rude to one another.
27 ... Never talk back to their parents.
28 ... Are not rude to one another.
29 ... Don't call other family members bad names or swear to their face.

Discipline

30 ... Have clear rules for family members.
31 ... Know that there are serious consequences for breaking family rules.
32 ... Have many family rules.
33 ... Understand that there will be swift punishment for violating family rules.

Humor/sarcasm

34 ... Tease other family members.
35 ... Are sarcastic or "cut up" with one another.

Regular routine interaction

36 ... Do things as a group even when it might be more efficient to split up and work separately.
37 ... Set aside certain times for everyone to talk together.
38 ... Meet regularly to discuss things.

Avoidance

39 ... Avoid topics that are too personal.
40 ... Avoid topics that are too hurtful.

Note: Subscale labels should be removed and items randomly ordered prior to administration.

Group Development Questionnaire (GDQ)

Profile by David R. Seibold

After a comprehensive review of the literature dealing with group development, Wheelan (1994) proposed an integrated group development model. The model identifies five stages of group development. Stage 1, labeled *dependency and inclusion*, is characterized by "the significant amount of member dependency on the designated leader" (Wheelan & Hochberger, 1996, p. 148). The second stage, titled *counterdependency and fight*, is defined "by conflict among members and between members and leaders" (Wheelan & Hochberger, 1996, p. 148). Stage 3, *trust and structure*, is marked by more trusting relationships and "a more mature negotiation process about group goals, organizational structure, procedures, roles, and division of labor" (Wheelan & Hochberger, 1996, p. 150). Next, the group performs the stage called *work and productivity* where they are able to effectively complete their task(s). The last stage is *termination*, and it applies only to temporary groups, for it marks their end.

The Group Development Questionnaire (GDQ) was formulated from an extensive list of characteristics for each stage, leaving out stage 5. Specifically, the GDQ is composed of "four scales that correspond to the first four stages of group development:

Scale I: Dependency and Inclusion, Stage 1
Scale II: Counterdependency and Fight, Stage 2
Scale III: Trust and Structure, Stage 3
Scale IV: Work and Productivity, Stage 4" (Wheelan & Hochberger, 1996, p. 153)

According to Wheelan, Murphy, Tsumara, and Kline (1998, p. 377), items on Scale 1 assess the amount of energy group members are expending in coping with dependency and inclusion issues. Items on Scale 2 focus on dynamics surrounding conflict and counterdependency, among others. Scale 3 questions help assess the degree of structure and trust in the group. Scale 4 items concern the group's level of effectiveness and the amount of work group members are accomplishing.

The GDQ is comprised of 60 items, 15 per scale, with responses ranging from 1 (*never true of this group*) to 5 (*always true of this group*) (Wheelan, 1996, p. 672). The minimum score for any of the four scales is 15 and the maximum is 75. "On each scale, the higher the scores, the more involved a group is with the issues measured by that scale. Thus low scores on Scales 1 and 2 and high scores on Scales 3 and 4 would indicate a more effective group than the reverse" (Wheelan et al. 1998, p. 379). An Effectiveness Ratio (ER) also can be calculated by dividing the actual mean score on Scale IV with the maximum potential score of 75. The ER then ranges from 20% to 100%. Wheelan also proposed use of a criterion measure of group productivity by averaging group members' responses to the question "In your opinion, how productive is this group?" with responses ranging from 1 (*not productive at all*) to 4 (*very productive*) (Wheelan, 1996, pp. 672–673).

Reliability

According to Wheelan and Hochberger (1996) test-retest reliability for the GDQ ranged from .69 to .89 across the scales; "all correlations were highly significant and supported the reliability of GDQ scales across time" (p. 158). Internal consistency was measured with Cronbach's alpha and all coefficients were statistically significant: Scale I = .66, Scale II = .88, Scale III = .74, and Scale IV = .88.

Validity

To assess concurrent validity, the GDQ was compared to a similar scale, the Group Attitude Scale (GAS; Evans & Jarvis, 1986). The "results indicate that the concurrent validity of the GDQ and GAS is in the moderate range, with a significant positive correlation between the two measures overall and on all scales except Scale I" (Wheelan & Hochberger, 1996, p. 160).

In terms of criterion-related validity, the GDQ has been found effective. "Work groups that ranked high on organizational measures of productivity had significantly higher scores on GDQ Scales III and IV, the effectiveness ratio, and the productivity mean than groups that ranked low on these external productivity measures"(Wheelan, Davidson, & Tilin, 2003, p. 233). Conversely, high ranked groups scored lower on GDQ Scale I and II (Wheelan et al., 1998; Wheelan & Lisk, 2000; Wheelan & Tilin, 1999).

Comments

The GDQ has been found effective across a wide array of organizational types and work groups, from team work effectiveness (Buzaglo & Wheelan, 1999) to complex interaction patterns (Wheelan & Williams, 2003).

The GDQ also has been used to measure group development internationally. The GDQ has also been found valid and reliable in its translated versions of Spanish, El Cuestionario de Desarrollo de Grupos (CDG), and Japanese, the Group Development Questionnaire-Japanese (GDQ-J; Wheelan, Buzaglo, & Tsumura, 1998). Although no specific criticisms of the GDQ have appeared in the research literature, it may be worth noting that linear, unitary sequence "stage models" of *decision* development have been challenged theoretically, methodologically, and empirically (Poole & Roth, 1989).

Location*

Wheelan, S. A., & Hochberger, J. (1996). Validation studies of the group development questionnaire. *Small Group Research, 26*(4), 143–170.

References

Buzaglo, G., & Wheelan, S. A. (1999). Facilitating work team effectiveness: Case studies from Central America. *Small Group Research, 30*, 108–129.

Evans, N., & Jarvis, D. (1986). The group attitude scale: A measure of attraction to group. *Small Group Behavior, 17*, 203–216.

Poole, M. S., & Roth, J. (1989). Decision development in small groups IV: A typology of group decision paths. *Human Communication Research, 15*(3), 323–356.

Wheelan, S. A. (1994). *Group processes: A developmental perspective.* Needham Heights, MA: Allyn & Bacon (The Simon & Schuster Education Group).

Wheelan, S. A. (1996). Effects of gender composition and group status differences on member perceptions of group developmental patterns, effectiveness, and productivity. *Sex Roles: A Journal of Research, 34*(9/10), 665–686.

Wheelan, S. A., Buzaglo, G., & Tsumura, E. (1998). Developing assessment tools for cross-cultural group research. *Small Group Research, 29*, 359–370.

Wheelan, S. A., Davidson, B., & Tilin, F. (2003). Group development across time: Reality or illusion? *Small Group Research, 34*, 223–245.

Wheelan, S. A., & Hochberger, J. (1996). Validation studies of the group development questionnaire. *Small Group Research, 26*, 143–170.

Wheelan, S. A., & Lisk, A. R. (2000). Cohort group effectiveness and the educational achievement of adult undergraduate students. *Small Group Research, 31*, 724–738.

Wheelan, S. A., Murphy, D., Tsumura, E., & Fried Kline, S. (1998). Member perceptions of internal group dynamics and productivity. *Small Group Research, 29*, 371–393.

Wheelan, S. A., & Tilin, F. (1999). The relationship between faculty group development and school productivity. *Small Group Research, 30*, 59–81.

Wheelan, S. A., & Williams, T. (2003). Mapping dynamic interaction patterns in work groups. *Small Group Research, 34*, 443–467.

Scale

Group Development Questionnaire*
[Sample Items (3 from 15 per scale)]

Scale   Sample Questions

GDQ I   Members tend to go along with whatever the leader suggests.
             There is very little conflict expressed in the group.
             We haven't discussed our goals very much.

GDQ II   People seem to have very different views about how things
             should be done in this group.
             Members challenge the leader's ideas.
             There is quite a bit of tension in the group at this time.

GDQ III   The group is spending its time planning how it will get its work
             done.
             We can rely on each other. We work as a team.
             The group is able to form subgroups, or subcommittees, to
             work on specific tasks.

GDQ IV   The group gets, gives, and uses feedback about its effectiveness
             and productivity.
             The group acts on its decisions.
             This group encourages high performance and quality work.

Note: As explained by Wheelen and Hochberger (1996, p. 166): "The reader will note that the GDQ instrument itself is not included in this report. This is so because, like many assessment instruments, training is required to ensure its proper and ethical use in both research and applied settings . . . . To avoid such misuse as much as possible, a GDQ training program has been established" (Wheelan & Hochberger, 1996, p. 166). Dr. Susan A. Wheelan, past professor of psychological studies in education at Temple University, is president of GDQ Associates. Information about the GDQ and about the training program for its use can be obtained at gdq@gdqassoc.com, via phone call to Dr. Wheelan (508-487-3750), or via mail:

Dr. Susan A. Wheelan, President
GDQ Associates
16 Aunt Sukey Way
Provincetown, MA 02657

Humor Orientation Scale (HOS)

Profile by Elizabeth E. Graham

The Humor Orientation Scale (HOS) was developed in 1991 by Steven and Melanie Booth-Butterfield to assess individual differences in humor production. Rooted in the cognitive science perspective and consistent with symbolic processing models (Anderson, 1983; Booth-Butterfield, 1987; Greene, 1988), the Booth-Butterfields concluded that the use of humor is the result of mindful, intentional, and strategic communication that is strongly influenced by information processing skills. Consistent with other communication predispositions, "individuals appear to develop differing levels of expertise in choosing, producing, and timing humor" (S. Booth-Butterfield & M. Booth-Butterfield, p. 206). Simply put, some people are funnier than others are and it is this variation that the Humor Orientation Scale measures.

The Booth-Butterfields conducted four studies in the course of developing and refining the Humor Orientation Scale. Scale development commenced with the authors canvassing the literature and crafting items to reflect the use of humor in interpersonal settings. The first study explored the factor structure of the humor orientation items, and after a series of statistical analyses, the authors determined that one factor best captured the essence of humor orientation. The resulting measure focuses on the frequency, intentionality, and effective use of humor and is comprised of a 17-item, unidimensional, self/other-report scale, anchored by a 5-point Likert response format. The central question that the Humor Orientation Scale assesses is: Do you use humor regularly and effectively in your communication?

Reliability

A series of studies conducted by the authors revealed a consistent and reliable measure of humor orientation. The single factor generated Cronbach alphas ranging from .89 to 91. Split-half reliabilities were equally robust (α = .88 to .93). Test-retest correlations, with an eight-week interval between administrations, were also highly significant suggesting that the measure is consistent and stable over time (S. Booth-Butterfield & M. Booth-Butterfield, 1991). Bippus (2000) provided evidence that even a shortened version (7 items) of the HOS produced very acceptable reliabilities (α = .92 for self ratings and α = .91 for other ratings). Additional studies, employing both self and other report versions of the scale, support the internal reliability of the measure as well (see M. Booth-Butterfield, S. Booth-Butterfield, & Wanzer, 2007; Wanzer, M., Booth-Butterfield, S. Booth-Butterfield, 1995, 1996; Wanzer & Frymier, 1999; Wrench & Booth-Butterfield, 2003).

Validity

The Booth-Butterfield's individual differences conceptualization of humor orientation is confirmed by results that suggest that people do differ in the contexts perceived as appropriate for humorous communication, as well as the complexity, specificity, frequency, and spontaneity of humor usage. In addition, humorous individuals reported possessing, and deploying, a larger repertoire of humorous behaviors. The third study conducted by the authors (S. Booth-Butterfield & M. Booth-Butterfield, 1991) requested participants to respond, in writing, using humorous communication, to a situation in which "you have met a new person and you want them to like you." The authors used the materials generated from this study and determined that those high in humor orientation were able to craft more detailed and lively communications with others in a more spontaneous fashion than those low in humor orientation.

The last study that the authors relied on to validate the Humor Orientation Scale successfully ruled out *mood* as a factor that might have influenced self-perceived humor orientation scores. They based this conclusion on the significant high correlation between scores attained on the Humor Orientation Scale administered twice, to the same sample, with an eight-week interval between administrations. The series of studies conducted in the course of developing this measure provide support for the author's conceptualization of humor orientation and in effect the content validity of the Humor Orientation Scale.

Conceptual coherence between select personality traits and humor orientation was offered by Wanzer et al. (1995, 1996), concluding that self and other reported humor orientation are related to communicator adaptability, concern for creating positive impressions and affective responses in others, sense of humor, social attractiveness, and less loneliness. Additionally, Merolla (2006) confirmed that decoding ability (i.e., conversational sensitivity, nonverbal sensitivity, receiver apprehension), an important conversational quality, is related to humor orientation. These findings elevate the production of humor on par with valuable communication skills that undoubtedly facilitate positive interactions with others. These studies have successfully mapped out the constellation of variables hypothetically related to humor orientation and subsequently have contributed to the construct validity of the Humor Orientation Scale.

Whether self-reported humor producers were really funnier was the focus of the research of Wanzer et al. (1995) research. The results of a discriminant analysis revealed that indeed those with a high humor orientation were perceived by others as funnier joke tellers, contributing to the criterion validity for the Humor Orientation Scale. In addition, Wanzer et al. (1996) reported a positive correlation between one's self-reported humor orientation and others' reports of that person's humor orientation, again, lending credence to the conclusion that those high in humor orientation are perceived by others as funnier.

Wrench and McCroskey (2001) generated data to measure the consistency between the Humor Orientation Scale and related qualities of humor (i.e., sense of humor, extraversion, and cheerfulness). The positive correlation among the three humor measures provides promising evidence for the convergent validity of the Humor Orientation Scale. Likewise, the authors offered support for the discriminant validity of the HOS by reporting negative correlations among humor orientation, seriousness, and bad mood. Bippus (2003) offered a further refinement of the utility of the HOS as she investigated the viability of humor use in conflict situations. Contrary to conventional wisdom, not all enactments of humor are welcome as "comic relief" in conflict situations. For humor to be successful in de-escalating conflict, the humor must be externally motivated, funny, and appropriate, otherwise negative outcomes could ensue.

The Humor Orientation Scale has been successfully employed in a variety of contexts including classrooms, health care, and work settings, and marital settings, lending additional validation to the measure. For example, Wanzer and Frymier's (1999) research supports an association between students' perception of teacher humor orientation and student learning, teacher responsiveness, assertiveness and immediacy. Bippus (2000) suggested that humor is effective in comforting those in distress. Furthermore, Wrench and Booth-Butterfield (2003) found that physicians perceived to be high in humor orientation were also thought to be responsible for encouraging patient compliance, more likely to be perceived as credible, which resulted in enhanced patient satisfaction. In addition to patient benefits, a high humor orientation is useful for health care providers too because humor use is associated with coping efficacy and emotional expressivity which ultimately contributes to job satisfaction (Wanzer, Booth-Butterfield, & Booth-Butterfield, S., 2005). M. Booth-Butterfield, S. Booth-Butterfield, and Wanzer (2007) found much the same result for employed students.

Honeycutt and Brown (1998) extended the utility of the HOS by predicting differences in marital types and humor orientation. Using

Fitzpatrick's (1988) marital typology, the authors concluded that traditional couple types were more likely to use humor in conversation that either individual or separate couple types. In addition, they determined husbands were more predisposed to humor use than their wives. These two findings are best understood in conjunction with each other. Traditional couples adhere to conventional sex-role behaviors and expectations, including the use of humor. From this perspective, it would be consistent for husbands to be the joke tellers, in essence the producers of humor, and wives to be the receivers of the jokes, in effect, the appreciators of humor. These conclusions contribute to the construct validity of the Humor Orientation Scale.

Comments

The Humor Orientation Scale is a useful addition to the individual differences arsenal of communication traits that have influenced the measurability of many predispositions so valuable in communication research. Although some research has been conducted with non-student populations, the majority of conclusions are based on student responses to the Humor Orientation Scale. Results normed on an adult population might enhance the generalizability and ecological validity of this measure.

Recent research (Wrench & McCroskey, 2001; Wrench & Richmond, 2004) has questioned the content validity of the HOS suggesting that it is solely a measure of *tendency to tell jokes and stories* and is not a holistic measure of humor production. This conceptual ambiguity, according to the authors, is the result of the HOS only minimally assessing whether respondents actually use humor when communicating. Additional research regarding the actual deployment of humor, in naturalistic, conversational settings, is necessary to determine the validity of this claim.

Location*

Booth-Butterfield, S., & Booth-Butterfield, M. (1991). Individual differences in the communication of humorous messages. *Southern Communication Journal, 56,* 205–218.

References

Anderson, J. (1983). *The architecture of cognition.* Cambridge, MA: Harvard University Press.

Bippus, A. M. (2000). Humor usage in comforting episodes: Factors predicting outcomes. *Western Journal of Communication, 64,* 359–384.

Bippus, A. M. (2003). Humor motives, qualities, and reactions in recalled conflict episodes. *Western Journal of Communication, 67,* 413–426.

Booth-Butterfield, S. (1987). Action assembly theory and communication apprehension: A psychophysiological study. *Human Communication Research, 13,* 386–398.

Booth-Butterfield, M., Booth-Butterfield, S., & Wanzer, M. (2007). Funny students cope better: Patterns of humor enactment and coping effectiveness. *Communication Quarterly, 55,* 299–315.

Greene, J. (1988). A cognitive approach to human communication: An action assembly theory. *Communication Monographs, 51,* 289–306.

Honeycutt, J. M., Brown, R. (1998). Did you hear the one about?: Typological and spousal differences in the planning of jokes and sense of humor in marriage. *Communication Quarterly, 46,* 342–352.

Merolla, A. J. (2006). Decoding ability and humor production. *Communication Quarterly, 54,* 175–189.

Wanzer, M., Booth-Butterfield, M., & Booth-Butterfield, S. (1995). The funny people: A source-orientation to the communication of humor. *Communication Quarterly, 43,* 142–154.

Wanzer, M., Booth-Butterfield, M., & Booth-Butterfield, S. (1996). Are funny people popular? An examination of humor orientation, loneliness, and social attraction. *Communication Quarterly, 44,* 42–52.

Wanzer, M., Booth-Butterfield, M., & Booth-Butterfield, S. (2005). "If we didn't use humor, we'd cry": Humorous coping communication in health care settings. *Journal of Health Communication, 10,* 105–125.

Wanzer, M. B., & Frymier, A. B. (1999). The relationship between student perceptions of instructor humor and students' reports of learning. *Communication Education, 48,* 48–62.

Wrench, J. S., & Booth-Butterfield, M. (2003). Increasing patient satisfaction and compliance: An examination of physician humor orientation, compliance-gaining strategies, and perceived credibility. *Communication Quarterly, 51,* 482–503.

Wrench, J. S., & McCroskey, J. C. (2001). A temperamental understanding of humor communication and exhilartability. *Communication Quarterly, 49,* 142–159.

Wrench, J. S., & Richmond, V. P. (2004). Understanding the psychometric properties of the Humor Assessment Instrument through an analysis of the relationship between teacher humor assessment and instructional communication variables in the college classroom. *Communication Research Reports, 21,* 92–103.

Scale

The Humor Orientation Scale*

Instructions: [Instructions were not provided, but one can conclude that participants are asked to reflect on their own or someone else's humor orientation and respond to the following statement using a 5-point Likert response format employing ranges of strongly agree to strongly disagree.]

1   I regularly tell jokes and funny stories when I am with a group.

2 People usually laugh when I tell a joke or story.
3 I have no memory for jokes or funny stories.
4 I can be funny without having to rehearse a joke.
5 Being funny is a natural communication style with me.
6 I cannot tell a joke well.
7 People seldom ask me to tell stories.
8 People don't seem to pay close attention when I tell a joke.
9 Even funny jokes seem flat when I tell them.
10 I can easily remember jokes and stories.
11 People often ask me to tell jokes or stories.
12 My friends would not say that I am a funny person.
13 I don't tell jokes or stories even when asked to.
14 I tell stories and jokes very well.
15 Of all the people I know, I'm one of the funniest.
16 I use humor to communicate in a variety of situations.

Individuals' Criteria for Telling Family Secrets

Profile by Elizabeth E. Graham

Continuing in the great tradition of self-disclosure research, Anita Vangelisti pioneered the study of secrets, particularly family secrets. Since the early 1990s, she has investigated the forms, functions, and topics of family secrets and has devised instruments to measure these variables as well. Although Vangelisti initially focused on the functions served by *concealing* family secrets (e.g., Vangelisti, 1994), more recently, *revealing* family secrets has been the focus of her research efforts. Realizing that sharing family secrets can have an enormous impact on, and consequences for, personal as well as relational outcomes, Anita Vangelisti, John Caughlin, and Lindsay Timmerman (2001) sought to uncover the criteria people use to determine whether or not to reveal a secret. Specifically, they were interested in what factors contribute to the revelation of secrets held by all family members and kept private from outsiders.

In the first phase of their research, they asked participants to provide criteria they would use to determine if they would reveal a secret. After a series of data analyses, Vangelisti et al. (2001) concluded that there are 10 criteria people employ when deciding to reveal a secret: intimate exchange (revealing a secret to enhance comfort and closeness), exposure (revealing a secret because it might be exposed anyway), urgency (revealing a secret due to a critical immediate need), never (revealing a secret would never occur), acceptance (revealing a secret if not judged too harshly), conversational appropriateness (revealing a secret if it seemed appropriate to the conversation), relational security (revealing a secret if the recipient was closer and could be trusted), important reason (revealing a secret for a pressing need), permission (revealing a secret if permission from family was granted), and family membership (revealing a secret to a new member of the family). These 10 criteria were cast into 50 items assessing individuals' criteria for telling family secrets. In an effort to identify influencing constructs that account for the decision to reveal a secret, the authors conducted additional studies.

Reliability

Vangelisti et al. (2001) reported the following reliabilities for the newly developed measure: intimate exchange α = .93; exposure α = .95; urgency α = .90; never α = .96; acceptance α = .77; conversational appropriateness α = .97; relational security α = .89; important reason α = .86; permission α = .83; and family membership α = .94. Satisfactory reliabilities also emerged when Afifi and colleagues (Afifi & Olson, 2005; Afifi, Olson, & Armstrong, 2005) employed the "never" subscale and reported reliability estimates of .90.

Validity

Vangelisti et al. (2001) tested the construct validity of the criteria for secret disclosure by investigating the topic of the secret, perception of the secret, and the relationship between the secret sharer and the recipient. Prior research (Vangelisti, 1994; Vangelisti & Caughlin, 1997) revealed that the topics of family secrets fall into three categories: taboo topics, rule violations, and conventional secrets. This current study employed the same three categories and the findings suggest very little interaction between criteria employed to decide whether to reveal the secret and the topic of the secret.

However, there was a strong association between all the criteria (except permission) used to decide to reveal a secret and perceptions of the secret (i.e., identification—whether it is an extremely significant—insignificant secret, valence—extremely good—extremely bad secret, and intimacy—extremely intimate secret—not at all intimate). Specifically, respondents' identification with the secret was positively associated with relational security and family membership and negatively related to conversational appropriateness. Furthermore, Vangelisti et al. (2001) reported that perceiving a secret as negatively valenced resulted in a positive association with intimate exchange, urgency, acceptance, relational security, and important reason. Interestingly, as Vangelisti et al. pointed out, "seeing a secret as negative invoked even more criteria than did identifying with the secret" (p. 23). Not surprisingly, respondents reported that they were less likely to conceal a positively valenced secret. Consistent with prior research (Vangelisti & Caughlin, 1997), viewing a secret as highly intimate was positively related to never revealing the secret and negatively associated with intimate exchange, exposure, urgency, acceptance, conversational appropriateness, important reason, and family membership.

Results revealed that the psychological closeness of the person to whom a secret is revealed is a positive predictor of many (eight out of ten) of the criteria used to determine whether to reveal the secret (i.e., intimate exchange, exposure, urgency, acceptance, conversational appropriateness, and permission) and a negative predictor of relational security and never criteria. This finding is consistent with previous self-disclosure research that indicates that personal closeness is a precursor to revelation. While controlling for psychological closeness, everyday contact was negatively associated with the intimate exchange criteria, suggesting that the norm of reciprocity is less salient in relationships characterized by frequent contact. And finally, similarity was positively related to the important reason criteria. Perhaps the perceived tie to oneself (e.g., similarity) prompted a felt saliency from the secret bearer such that the need to reveal a secret for an important reason seemed more probable.

Vangelisti et al. (2001) supported the hypothesis that the criteria people report using when considering whether to reveal a secret are significantly related to the tendency to reveal that secret to an outsider. Furthermore, participants reported that they would not tell a secret to a "least likely" target and, conversely, readily prone to reveal a secret to a "most likely" target. As expected, respondents reported revealing a secret to a "moderately likely" target less so that a "likely target" but more so than a "least likely" target. However, two criteria, relational security and important reason, cut across the least, most, and moderately likely target groups and suggest that having an important reason to reveal a secret or requiring a minimum level of relational security may override other considerations when one is deciding to reveal a secret.

Recent research by Afifi and Olson (2005) supported the findings reached by Vangelisti et al. (2001) by concluding that secrets are concealed when they are perceived as intimate and personal. In addition, Afifi and Olson reported that secrets are concealed when families are high in conformity and low on conversation orientation (as measured by Revised Family Communication Patterns measure, Ritchie & Fitzpatrick, 1990) and when there was the presence of coercive power in the family. In a related manner, families high in conversation and low on conformity orientation also reported concealing secrets, but for different reasons. It seems that the presence of coercive power in the family contributes to a decrease in closeness and it is this factor that accounts for concealing family secrets. Additional construct validity can be culled from the findings provided by Afifi et al. (2005) that suggest that people conceal secrets to protect themselves and others. Although both studies (Afifi & Olson, 2005; Afifi et al., 2005) only employed a single subscale (i.e., never), their results replicate prior research and extend our thinking about the constellation of constructs related to the concealment of secrets.

Comments

Individuals' Criteria for Telling Family Secrets is a relatively new measure that shows great promise. Research to date suggests that the scale offers excellent reliability estimates and acceptable validity indicators as well. Although secrets have been traditionally associated with negative relational consequences, Vangelisti's work illustrates that secrets can indeed enhance the quality of relationships. The simple act of concealing information from others can result in positive relational outcomes such as family bonding and identification (for extended discussion of secrets and privacy see Caughlin & Petronio, 2004).

As is true of many communication measures, the predominant sampling of an undergraduate student population continues to be a concern (for exceptions see Afifi & Olson, 2005; Afifi, Olson, & Armstrong, 2005). Future research, with non-student populations, in varied contexts, would contribute to the utility and subsequently, the validity, of this measure.

Location*

Vangelisti, A., Caughlin, J., & Timmerman, L. (2001). Criteria for revealing family secrets. *Communication Monographs, 68,* 1–27.

References

Afifi, T. D., & Olson, L. (2005). The chilling effect in families and the pressure to conceal secrets. *Communication Monographs, 72,* 192–216.

Afifi, T. D., & Olson, L., Armstrong, C. (2005). The chilling effect and family secrets. Examining the role of self-protection, other protection, and communication efficacy. *Human Communication Research, 31,* 564–598.

Caughlin, J. P., & Petronio, S. (2004). Privacy in families. In A. L. Vangelisti (Ed.), *Handbook of family communication* (pp. 379–412). Mahwah, NJ: Erlbaum.

Ritchie, L. D. & Fitzpatrick, M. A. (1990). Family communication patterns: Measuring interpersonal perceptions of interpersonal relationships. *Communication Research, 17,* 523–544.

Vangelisti, A. L. (1994). Family secrets: Forms, functions, and correlates. *Journal of Social and Personal Relationships, 11,* 113–135.

Vangelisti, A. L., & Caughlin, J. P. (1997). Revealing family secrets: The influence of topic, function, and relationships. *Journal of Social and Personal Relationships, 14,* 679–705.

Scale

Individuals' Criteria for Telling Family Secrets Scale*

Instructions: Please respond to the 50-item instrument using 7-point Likert response options (1 = strongly disagree to 7 = strongly agree). Complete the measure with one target person in mind.

Intimate Exchange

1 If my [relation] had a similar problem, I would reveal the secret.

2 I would reveal the secret if I thought my [relation] needed to know he/she wasn't "alone."

3 I would reveal the secret if [relation] first told me a similar story about his/her family.

4 If I thought knowing the secret would comfort my [relation], I would tell.

5 If my [relation] first disclosed something along the same lines, I would reveal the secret.

6 I would tell if I thought knowing the secret would help [relation].

7 I would tell if my [relation] and I were having a "heart to heart" discussion.

8 If my [relation] and I were having a really intimate conversation, I would tell.

Exposure

9 I would tell my [relation] if it was inevitable that the secret would be revealed to him/her anyway.

10 I would tell my [relation] about the secret if he/she questioned me directly.

11 I would tell my [relation] if I knew he/she was likely to find out the secret.

12 I would tell my [relation] if he/she confronted me about the secret.

13 If my [relation] found out about the secret from someone else, I would tell.

14 If my [relation] started quizzing me about the secret, I would reveal it.

15 If my [relation] was going to discover the secret without me telling it, I would go ahead and reveal the secret.

16 If my [relation] asked me about the secret, I would tell him/her.

Urgency

17 I would reveal the secret to my [relation] if the secret became a more critical concern than it is right now.

18 If the secret involved a problem, and that problem got worse, I would tell my [relation].

19 If the secret involved a problem that was resolved, and the problem began again, I would tell my [relation].

20 I would tell my [relation] if I really needed to talk about the secret.

21 If I couldn't hold in the secret any longer, I would reveal it to my [relation].

22 I would tell my [relation] if I really needed someone to confide in.

23 If I thought my [relation] was the only one I could talk to, I would tell him/her the secret.

24 If the secret started causing more difficulties than it currently does, I would tell my [relation].

Never

25 There is no chance I would ever reveal the secret to my [relation].
26 I would never tell my [relation].
27 No matter what, I will keep the secret from my [relation].
28 There is nothing that would make me reveal the secret to my [relation].

Acceptance

29 I would reveal the secret to my [relation] if he/she wouldn't disapprove of me after hearing it.
30 If I knew my [relation] would still accept me after hearing the secret I would tell.
31 If my [relation] wouldn't attack me about the secret, I would tell.
32 I would tell my [relation] if I knew he/she wouldn't judge me.

Conversational Appropriateness

33 I would reveal the secret to my [relation] if it seemed to fit into the conversation.
34 If the secret was an appropriate conversational topic, I would tell my [relation].
35 I would tell the secret to my [relation] if we were discussing a subject related to the secret.
36 If the topic came up in conversation, I would tell the secret to my [relation].

Relational Security

37 If I trusted my [relation] more than I do now, I would reveal the secret.
38 I would tell my [relation] if I had a more intimate relationship with him/her.
39 If I felt much closer to my [relation] I would tell the secret.
40 If I knew my [relation] wouldn't tell the secret to others, I would tell him/her.

Important Reason

41 If a crisis arose that necessitated my revealing the secret to my [relation], I would tell.
42 If there was a pressing need for my [relation] to know the secret, I would tell.
43 I would reveal the secret to my [relation] if I thought it was essential for him/her to know.
44 I would tell my [relation] if I thought there was a really good reason for him/her to know the secret.

Permission

45 I would tell my [relation] if my family members thought it was okay to tell.
46 I would tell my [relation] if someone in my family gave me permission to tell the secret.
47 If the person who is the focus of the secret died, I would reveal the secret to my [relation].
48 I would feel okay telling my [relation] once a certain person in my family died.

Family Membership

49 I would reveal the secret to my [relation] if he/she was going to marry into my family.
50 I would tell the secret to my [relation] if he/she somehow became a relative or family member.

Note: Subscale labels should be removed and a target individual inserted in the items prior to administration.

* © 2001 by Taylor & Francis.

Intercultural Development Inventory (IDI)

Profile by David R. Seibold

The Intercultural Development Inventory (IDI) was created by Mitchell Hammer (1998; Hammer & Bennett, 1998; Hammer, Bennett, & Wiseman, 2003) based upon Milton Bennett's Development Model of Intercultural Sensitivity (DMIS) (Bennett, 1986). The DMIS focuses on processes of intercultural adaptation viz. six orientations that people appear to move through as they develop intercultural competence. The first three orientations—*Denial, Defense, Minimization*—are ethnocentric (i.e., perceiver's own culture is central to how reality is constructed), and the latter three orientations—*Acceptance, Adaptation, Integration*—are ethnorelative (i.e., perceiver's own culture is interpreted in the context of other culture) (Paige, Jacobs-Cassuto, Yershova, & DeJaeghere, 2003). As summarized by Hammer, Bennett, and Wiseman (2003) concerning these six DMSI stages: "*Denial* of cultural difference is the state in which one's own culture is experienced as the only real one. . . . *Defense* against cultural difference is the state in which one's own culture is experienced as the only viable one. A variation on Defense is *Reversal*, where an adopted culture is experienced as superior to the culture of one's primary socialization ("going native" or "passing"). . . . Minimization of cultural difference is the state in which elements of one's own cultural worldview are experienced as universal. . . . *Acceptance* of cultural difference is the state in which one's own culture is experienced as just one of a number of equally complex worldviews. . . . *Adaptation* to cultural difference is the state in which the experience of another culture yields perception and behavior appropriate to that culture. . . . *Integration* of cultural difference is the state in which one's experience of self is expanded to include the movement in and out of different cultural worldviews" (pp. 424–425).

The IDI was constructed to measure the developmental orientations toward cultural differences described in the DMIS. The most recent and comprehensive analysis and revision of the IDI (see Hammer et al., 2003, Table 1) produced a 50-item measure with items loading on five factors corresponding to the orientations of the DMSI: 1) DD (Denial/Defense) scale (14 items), 2) R (Reversal) scale (9 items), 3) M (Minimization) scale (10 items), 4) AA (Acceptance/Adaptation) scale (14 items), and 5) EM (Encapsulated Marginality) scale (5 items). Three sample items for each of the five IDI subscales are reprinted at the end of this profile. Administered as a paper-and-pencil self-assessment instrument, partici-pants rate their agreement on a 5-point response scale: 1 = *disagree*, 2 = *dis-agree somewhat more than agree*, 3 = *disagree some and agree some*, 4 = *agree somewhat more than disagree*, and 5 = *agree* (Hammer et al., 2003).

Reliability

According to Hammer et al. (2003), reliabilities (coefficient alphas) for the final items on each scale were as follows: DD scale (.85), R scale (.80), M scale (.85), AA scale (.84), and the EM scale (.80).

Validity

Both content and construct validity have been investigated to establish the validity of the IDI. The content validity was addressed during an initial stage of development of the measure in which participants from different cultures were interviewed. Because these interviews were transcribed, Hammer and colleagues were able to identify a wide range of statements and to relate them to the different cultural orientations of the participants and the factors identified within the DMIS (Hammer et al., 2003). Content validity also was established through raters and experts who categorized the statements included within the instrument. Hammer and Bennett (1998) reported that four expert raters categorized all statements about orientations to cultural differences from initial interviews with an inter-rater reliability of .85 – .95 (Spearman's *rho*).

Construct validity was established by relating the participants' scores for the DD, R, M, AA, and EM scales to two theoretically related vari-ables: Worldmindedness and Intercultural Anxiety (Hammer et al., 2003). Results supported the theoretically predicted relationships among the IDI scales and the two validation measures: "the DD scale, the AA, and the EM scales were significantly correlated in the direction hypothesized with both the Worldmindedness and Intercultural Anxiety measures" (p. 438). Additionally the confirmatory factor analysis revealed "that a five-factor solution (DD, R, M, AA, and EM scales) provides a good fit to the data. Further, in a direct comparison of the five-factor solution with both the original, seven-dimensional model of interpersonal sensitivity proposed by Bennett . . . and a two-dimensional, more global model (of ethnocen-trism and ethnorelativism), the five-factor solution was found to be superior" (p. 439).

Comments

Hammer and colleagues have sought to create reliable and valid measures of DMSI-guided intercultural sensitivity and competence. The IDI has been utilized widely by researchers (Altshuler, Sussman, & Kachur, 2003; Endicott, Bock, & Narvaez, 2003; Paige et al., 2003; Straffon, 2003). Hammer et al (2003) concluded their most recent effort: "we feel that the final, 50-item IDI can be used with confidence as a measurement of the five dimensions of the DMIS identified in this research" (p. 441). In addition to numerous scholarly investigations of DMSI and intercultural dynamics that these five IDI dimensions enable, Hammer et al. proposed that the IDI measures should be helpful for "assessing training needs, guiding interventions for individual and group development of intercultural competence, contributing to personnel selection, and evaluating programs" (p. 441).

Location

Hammer, M. R. (1998). A measure of intercultural sensitivity: The Intercultural Development Inventory. In S. Fowler & M. Fowler (Eds.), *The intercultural sourcebook: Volume 2*. Yarmouth, ME: Intercultural Press.

Hammer, M. R., & Bennett, M. J. (1998). *The Intercultural Development Inventory (IDI) manual*. Portland, OR: The Intercultural Communication Institute.

Hammer, M. R., Bennett, M. J., & Wiseman, R. (2003). Measuring intercultural sensitivity: The Intercultural Development Inventory. *International Journal of Intercultural Relations*, 27, 421–443. *

References

Altshuler, L., Sussman, N. M., & Kachur, E. (2003). Assessing the changes in intercultural sensitivity among physician trainees using the Intercultural Development Inventory. *International Journal of Intercultural Relations*, 27, 387–401.

Bennett, M. J. (1986). Towards ethnorelativism: A developmental model of intercultural sensitivity. In R. M. Paige (Ed.), *Cross-cultural orientation: New conceptualizations and applications* (pp. 27–70). New York: University Press of America.

Endicott, L., Bock, T., & Narvaez, D. (2003). Moral reasoning, intercultural development, and multicultural experiences: Relations and cognitive underpinnings. *International Journal of Intercultural Relations, 27*, 403–419.

Hammer, M. R. (1998). A measure of intercultural sensitivity: The Intercultural Development Inventory. In S. Fowler & M. Fowler (Eds.), *The intercultural sourcebook: Volume 2*. Yarmouth, ME: Intercultural Press.

Hammer, M. R., & Bennett, M. J. (1998). *The Intercultural Development Inventory (IDI) manual*. Portland, OR: The Intercultural Communication Institute.

Hammer, M. R., Bennett, M. J., & Wiseman, R. (2003). Measuring intercultural sensitivity: The Intercultural Development Inventory. *International Journal of Intercultural Relations, 27*, 421–443.

Paige, R. M., Jacobs-Cassuto, M., Yershova, Y. A., & Dejaeghere, J. (2003). Assessing intercultural sensitivity: An empirical analysis of the Hammer and Bennett Intercultural Development Inventory. *International Journal of Intercultural Relations, 27*, 467–486.

Straffon, D. A. (2003). Assessing the intercultural sensitivity of high school students attending an international school. *International Journal of Intercultural Relations, 27*, 487–501.

Scale

Intercultural Development Inventory
(Sample items from 50-item IDI, adapted from Hammer et al., 2003, p. 433)

DD scale:

1   It is appropriate that people do not care what happens outside their country.
2   People should avoid individuals from other cultures who behave differently.
3   Our culture's way of life should be a model for the rest of the world.

R scale:

1   People from our culture are less tolerant compared to people from other cultures.
2   People from our culture are lazier than people from other cultures.
3   Family values are stronger in other cultures than in our culture.

M scale:

1   Our common humanity deserves more attention than culture difference.
2   Cultural differences are less important than the fact that people have the same needs, interests and goals in life.
3   Human behavior worldwide should be governed by natural and universal ideas of right and wrong.

AA scale:

1   I have observed many instances of misunderstanding due to cultural differences in gesturing or eye contact.
2   I evaluate situations in my own culture based on my experiences and knowledge of other cultures.
3   When I come in contact with people from a different culture, I find I change my behavior to adapt to theirs.

EM scale:

1   I feel rootless because I do not think I have a cultural identification.
2   I do not identify with any culture, but with what I have inside.
3   I do not feel I am a member of any one culture or combination of
     cultures.

Note: Attendance at an IDI Qualifying Seminar is required for permission to use
the instrument. More information can be obtained from:

The Intercultural Communication Institute
8835 SW Canyon Lane
Suite 238
Portland, OR 97235

Interpersonal Communication Competence Scale (ICCS)

Profile by Elizabeth E. Graham

In an effort to develop a comprehensive measure inclusive of all dimensions of interpersonal competence, Rubin and Martin (1994) created the Interpersonal Communication Competence Scale (ICCS). They defined competence as "an impression or judgment formed about a person's ability to manage interpersonal relationships in communication settings" (Rubin & Martin, 1994, p. 33). The ICCS is reflective of Spitzberg and Cupach's (1984) relational approach to competence which claims that judgments of effectiveness and appropriateness are at the heart of goal-directed prosocial behavior.

After an extensive review of the communication literature, Rubin and Martin (1994) identified 10 dimensions of competence: self-disclosure (sharing information with others that otherwise would not be known), empathy (feeling with another person), social relaxation (comfort and ease with self and others), assertiveness (asserting one's own rights while respecting the rights of others), interaction management (navigating conversations effectively and appropriately), altercentrism (willingness to be responsive to others), expressiveness (expressing thoughts and feelings), supportiveness (confirming communication), immediacy (emotional and physical availability), and environmental control (managing communication effectively).

After a series of data reduction techniques, the resulting measure is a 30-item self-report Likert-type scale that can be used to assess global communication skills. The authors note that the ICCS can be used as an other-report of interpersonal competence as well. Rubin and Martin also developed a 10-item short-form version of the ICCS-SF that is comprised of one item (the items with the highest inter-item correlation) from each dimension of the measure.

Reliability

Rubin and Martin (1994) reported the following reliability estimates for the ICCS: self-disclosure, $\alpha = 63$; empathy $\alpha = .49$; social relaxation α = .63; assertiveness α = .72; interaction management α = .41; alter-centrism α = .49; expressiveness α = .46; supportiveness α = .43; immediacy α = .45; and environmental control α = .60. Reliability estimates for the entire measure were α = .86. Additional research (Anders & Tucker, 2000; Haselwood, Joyner, Burke, Geyerman, Czech, Munkasy, & Zwald, 2005) produced comparable reliability estimates.

The low alpha levels for some of the ICC subscales are an artifact of the small number of items associated with each dimension as well as the number of dimensions (Rubin & Martin, 1994). Principal component factor analysis revealed that the majority of the items had primary loadings on one factor, suggesting that the ICCS is a unidimensional measure. The 10-item short-form version of the ICCS also produced acceptable internal consistency estimates α = .63. Subsequent research by Rubin and Martin (1994) produced slightly higher reliability estimates (α = 71). The correlation between the 10 and 30-item versions of the ICCS was .86.

Validity

Content validity for the ICCS was established in two ways. First, scale items were developed for each subscale that were reflective of existing measures of competence, and second, items were crafted that operationalized the conceptualization of the subscales. This process resulted in 60-items (6 for each of the 10 dimensions). Items that produced the lowest inter-item total correlations were dropped from the scale which resulted in the final 30-item measure.

Consistent with prior theory and research, Rubin and Martin (1994) found an association between interpersonal competence and communication satisfaction. Furthermore, interpersonal communication competence, as measured by the ICCS, was also related to motives for initiating conversation with others. Rubin, Martin, Bruning, and Powers (1993) tested a self-efficacy model of interpersonal communication and concluded that self-efficacy is an influencing agent on interpersonal competence which is directly responsible for satisfying and rewarding communication. Collectively, these findings contribute to the construct validity of the ICCS.

In a second study, Rubin and Martin (1994) provided evidence of the concurrent validity of the ICCS by revealing the positive relationship among cognitive and communication flexibility (both considered central elements of interpersonal competence) and interpersonal competence. These results suggest that interpersonally competent individuals also report being cognitively and communicatively flexible. Further concurrent validity for the ICCS was provided by Rubin et al. (1993) when they reported strong positive correlations between each of the 10 dimensions of the ICCS and 10 parallel and established measures of each interpersonal communication skill. In both of these studies, the 10-item version of the Interpersonal Communication Competence Scale was employed.

Haselwood et al. (2005) extended the use of the Interpersonal Communication Competence Scale into the realm of sports and coaching. They concluded that female head coaches were more likely to practice self-disclosure than male head coaches with both male and female athletes. When rank ordering the ten competence dimensions, male and female coaches rated themselves highest in immediacy and lowest in interaction management. Interesting research investigating the link among social support, attachment styles, and interpersonal communication competence was conducted by Anders and Tucker (2000). They concluded that anxious and avoidant attachment styles were related to deficits in interpersonal competence. Furthermore, they found that interpersonal competence mediated the association between social support and attachment such that competence plays a central role in explaining why "less secure individuals (both anxious and avoidant) have difficulty in developing broad and satisfying social support networks" (p. 385). Indeed the social consequences of incompetence have implications for one's social and emotional well-being.

Comments

Rubin and Martin's goal of developing a measure of competence inclusive of its many dimensions has been accomplished and is evidenced in the content validity of the Interpersonal Communication Competence Scale. The authors suggested that due to the molar nature of this measure, *self* and *other* assessment is more readily accessible and that these contribute to the accuracy of the evaluations. Furthermore, the ICCS is adaptable for use in various contexts. In instructional settings, the ICCS can be a valuable tool for assessing student skill development.

Rubin et al. (1993) responded to the lack of a theoretical base in the study of competence when they introduced the self-efficacy model of interpersonal competence. Although their efforts contributed to the construct validity of the ICCS, future theorizing will undoubtedly influence this measure as well as other measures aimed at measuring interpersonal competence.

Location**

Rubin, R. B., & Martin, M. M. (1994). Development of a measure of interpersonal communication competence. *Communication Research Reports, 11,* 33–44.

References

Anders, S. L., & Tucker, J. S. (2000). Adult attachment style, interpersonal communication competence, and social support. *Personal Relationships, 7,* 379–389.

Haselwood, D. M., Joyner, A. B., Burke, K. L., Geyerman, C. B., Czech, D. R., Munkasy, B. A., & Zwald, A. D. (2005). Female athletes' perceptions of head coaches' communication competence. *Journal of Sport Behavior, 28,* 216–230.

Rubin, R. B., Martin, M. M., Bruning, S. S., & Powers, D. E. (1993). Test of a self-efficacy model of interpersonal competence. *Communication Quarterly, 41,* 210–220.

Spitzberg, B. H., & Cupach, W. R. (1984). *Interpersonal communication competence.* Beverly Hills, CA: Sage.

Scale

Interpersonal Communication Competence Scale (ICCS)**

Instructions: Here are some statements about how people interact with other people. For each statement, circle the response that best reflects YOUR communication with others. Be honest in your responses and reflect on your communication behavior very carefully.

> If you ALMOST ALWAYS interact in this way, circle the 5.
> If you communicate this way OFTEN, circle the 4.
> If you behave in this way SOMETIMES, circle the 3.
> If you act this way only SELDOM, circle the 2.
> If you ALMOST NEVER behave in this way, circle 1.

Self Disclosure

1 I allow friends to see who I really am.* 5 4 3 2 1
2 Other people know what I am thinking.
3 I reveal how I feel to others.

Empathy

4 I can put myself in others' shoes.*
5 I don't know exactly what others are feeling. (R)
6 Other people think that I understand them.

Social Relaxation

7 I am comfortable in social situations.*
8 I feel relaxed in small group gatherings.
9 I feel insecure in groups of strangers. (R)

Assertiveness

10 When I've been wronged, I confront the person who wronged me.*
11 I have trouble standing up for myself. (R)
12 I stand up for my rights.

Altercentrism

13   My conversations are pretty one-sided.* (R)
14   I let others know that I understand what they say.
15   My mind wanders during conversations.

Interaction Management

16   My conversations are characterized by smooth shifts from one topic to the next.*
17   I take charge of conversations I'm in by negotiating what topics we talk about.
18   In conversations with friends, I perceive not only what they say but what they don't say.

Expressiveness

19   My friends can tell when I am happy or sad.*
20   It's difficult to find the right words to express myself. (R)
21   I express myself well verbally.

Supportiveness

22   My communication is usually descriptive, not evaluative.*
23   I communicate with others as though they're equals.
24   Others would describe me as warm.

Immediacy

25   My friends truly believe that I care about them.*
26   I try to look others in the eye when I speak with them.
27   I tell people when I feel close to them.

Environmental Control

28   I accomplish my communication goals.*
29   I can persuade others to my position.
30   I have trouble convincing others to do what I want them to do. (R)

Note 1: Items with asterisks are included in the short-form (ICCS-SF) version of the ICCS.

Note 2: (R) indicates reverse coding. All items should be arranged randomly and subscale labels removed when administered.

** © 1994 by Taylor & Francis.

Interpersonal Dominance Instrument

Profile by Elizabeth E. Graham

Noting that the construct of dominance, and its counterpart, submission, are at the center of relational life, Burgoon and colleagues (Burgoon, Johnson, & Koch, 1998) developed a measure to reflect the interactional nature of this concept. Mindful of the psychological, sociological, and biological influences, as well as restrictions that these perspectives place on the current understanding of dominance, the authors suggested an alternative view. Dominance, when viewed through a communication lens, is a commodity of a relationship, not an individual, and therefore, is socially constructed. In kind, the social construction of dominance is created and shared through verbal and nonverbal communication behaviors. In sum, this view, termed the interactionist perspective, asserts that dominance behaviors are responsive to the situation, influenced by the relationship participants, and transformed by these mediating factors (Burgoon & Dunbar, 2000).

Historically, dominance has been synonymous with power, aggression, and force and stereotypically identified as *male* behavior, prompting a characteristically negative and masculine view of dominance. The dominance construct also suffers from conceptual ambiguity, as it has been characterized in so many ways. To remedy these limitations, the authors offered a broader conceptualization that recognizes the centrality of communication and highlights the positive social competence attributes of dominance. This reconceptualization served to de-gender and reframe interpersonal dominance, concluding that dominance displays are indeed the purview of the socially skilled communicator and are not solely the domain of masculine communication styles (Burgoon & Dunbar, 2000). The results of their efforts are two measures that honor the interactional and relational nature of interpersonal dominance.

The first instrument is impressionistic and designed to characterize qualities reflective of dominance (and submission). Items for the instrument were culled from prior personality research as well as generated by students, and the authors. These endeavors resulted in a 120-item adjective list. After a series of reductionistic analyses, the final measure (termed the attribution-based instrument) is comprised of 41 items (31 dominant items and 10 submissive items) organized as a checklist. The resulting index provides global and subjective judgments that assess the qualities and characteristics associated with dominance and submissiveness (Burgoon et al., 1998; Dunbar & Burgoon, 2005a).

The behavior-based measure is a 31-item instrument of which 16 items were culled from the Gough, McClosky, and Meehl's (1951) personality dominance scale and the remaining items were generated by the authors to reflect the multidimensional nature of dominance (i.e., social skills, assertiveness, panache, and dynamism). The resulting instrument, anchored by a 7-point Likert response format, is comprised of five subscales: influence, conversational control and impulsivity, focus and poise, panache, and self-assurance. Influence refers to persuasiveness, while focus and poise are evidence of social skills. Conversational control refers to having more and longer turns at talk, and panache references a dramatic and strong social presence. The last factor, self-assurance, taps a degree of brashness, arrogance and confidence. Dunbar and Burgoon (2005b) note that the first three subscales (i.e., influence, conversational control and impulsivity, focus and poise) are consistent with a relationally based view of dominance and the last two subscales (i.e., panache and self-assurance) reflect individual communicator style qualities. This measure, according to Burgoon et al. (1998) "allows for a more precise assessment of what dominant and nondominant individuals actually do" (p. 329). Due to the high inter-item correlations among the five subscales, the measure can be used as a unidimensional assessment thereby collapsing all the subscales into one overall measure of dominance or conversely, to measure specific behavioral qualities of dominance, the individual subscales may be employed (Dunbar & Burgoon, 2005b).

Reliability

A series of studies conducted by Burgoon et al. (1998) employing the behavior-based measure produced acceptable reliability estimates: influence, α = .88, .82; conversational control and impulsivity, α = .79, .71; focus and poise, α = .78, .77; panache, α = .88, .80; and self-assurance, α = .73, .65. Reliability estimates for the unidimensional measure of the behavior-based instrument were robust and ranged from .90 to .93. Individual items from the behavior-based instrument have been used in related studies and have continued to produce acceptable alpha levels (Burgoon & Dunbar, 2000). Satisfactory reliabilities also emerged when Burgoon and associates (Burgoon, Bonito, Bengtsson, Ramirez, Dunbar, & Miczo, 1999; Burgoon, Bonito, Ramirez, Dunbar, Kam & Fischer, 2002) employed a single dominance subscale, featuring a 7-interval semantic differential response format (α = .66 and .73 respectively). The attribution-based index is a checklist and therefore no reliability estimates are available.

Validity

The content validity of the interpersonal dominance construct has been the focus of research since Burgoon and Hale (1987) introduced their fundamental topoi of relational communication. Relying on these earlier efforts, and drawing upon the rich traditions of psychology, sociology, biology and communication, Burgoon et al. (1998) articulated the extent to which their conception of dominance, and the resultant measure, corresponded to the theoretical and collective understanding of interpersonal dominance. Of particular importance is the finding that there are positive aspects to dominant behavior. Indeed, as Burgoon et al. concluded "it may be that the most skillful performance of dominance interlaces elements of submissiveness . . ." (p. 331). Further support for the reconceptualization of dominance was offered by Burgoon and Dunbar (2000) as they proposed a series of hypotheses testing the interactionist view of dominance. Indeed, dominance is sensitive to situation and relationships and those with greater social skills do engage in displays of dominance more so than those less skilled. These results provide an empirical foundation on which the content validity of the measure might rest.

A series of studies were conducted by Burgoon et al. (1998) to test the validity of the attribution and behavior-based measures of dominance. The results of a discriminant analysis suggest that the attribution-based instrument is capable of discriminating between those more and less dominant. As expected, correlation tests revealed a significant negative correlation between the dominance and submissive items. Further analyses revealed that the dominance and submissive items were significantly correlated (in the expected direction) with the behavior-based measure of dominance, thus confirming the correspondence between impression (attribute) and interaction (behavior) based methods of measuring dominance. These results contribute to the criterion validity of the attribution- and behavior-based measure of dominance. Further support for the validity of the Interpersonal Dominance Instrument was offered by Dunbar and Burgoon (2005a) when they reported a significant positive correlation between perception of dominance for participants and third party observers (coders).

The behavior-based instrument is also capable of successfully discriminating between the most and least dominant target individuals. A series of exploratory and confirmatory factor analyses support a five factor structure of the behavior-based dominance measure which include: influence, conversational control and impulsivity, focus and poise, panache, and self-assurance. The results of the factor analysis provide support for the construct validity of the behavior-based instrument.

Comments

The theme of dominance, and its manifestation in communication, has been said to be a significant quality and of "elemental significance" in the definition of interpersonal relationships (Burgoon et al., 1998, p. 314). Consistent with this theme, the correspondence between the conceptualization and measurement of interpersonal dominance is very evident. This instrument articulates and focuses on communication qualities and characteristics of dominance displays. In addition, the broadening of the conceptualization of dominance to include positive social skills enhances the representational validity and utility of this measure. Furthermore, The Interpersonal Dominance Instruments are adaptable as they can be used to measure more global and subjective assessments of dominance as well as precise indications of what behaviors dominant people engage in.

Location*

Burgoon, J. K., Johnson, M. L., & Koch, P. T. (1998). The nature and measurement of interpersonal dominance. *Communication Monographs, 65,* 308–335.

References

Burgoon, J. K., Bonito, J. A., Bengtsson, B., Ramirez, A., Dunbar, N. E., & Miczo, N. (1999). Testing the interactivity model: Communication processes, partner assessments, and the quality of collaborative work. *Journal of Management Information Systems, 16,* 33–56.

Burgoon, J. K., Bonito, J. A., Ramirez, A, Dunbar, N. E., Kam, K., & Fischer, J. (2002). Testing the interactivity principle: Effects of mediation, propinquity, and verbal and nonverbal modalities in interpersonal interaction. *Journal of Communication, 52,* 657–677.

Burgoon, J. K., & Dunbar, N. E. (2000). An interactionist perspective on dominance-submission: Interpersonal dominance as a dynamic, situationally contingent social skill. *Communication Monographs, 67,* 96–121.

Burgoon, J. K., & Hale, J. L. (1987). Validation and measurement of the fundamental themes of relational communication. *Communication Monographs, 54,* 19–41.

Dunbar, N. E., & Burgoon, J. K. (2005a). Perceptions of power and interactional dominance in interpersonal relationships. *Journal of Social and Personal Relationships, 22,* 231–257.

Dunbar, N. E., & Burgoon, J. K. (2005b). The measurement of nonverbal dominance. In V. Manusov (Ed.), The *sourcebook of nonverbal measures: Going beyond words* (pp. 361–374). Mahwah, NJ: Erlbaum.

Gough, H. G., McCloskey, H., & Meehl, P. E. (1951). A personality scale for dominance. *Journal of Abnormal and Social Psychology, 46,* 360–366.

Scale

Interpersonal Dominance Instrument*
Instructions: Please respond to the 31-item instrument using 7-point Likert response options (1 = strongly disagree to 7 = strongly agree). Be sure to complete the measure with one target person in mind.

Influence

1 People often turn to this person when decisions have to be made.
2 This person rarely influences others. (R)
3 This person has very little skill in managing conversations. (R)
4 I am often influenced by this person.
5 This person has a natural talent for winning over others.
6 This person is usually successful in persuading others to act.
7 It seems as if this person finds it hard to keep his/her mind on the conversation. (R)

Conversational Control

8 The person usually takes charge of conversations.
9 This person usually does more talking than listening.
10 This person often wins any arguments that occur in our conversations.
11 This person is often responsible for keeping the conversation going when we talk.
12 This person often insists on discussing something even when others don't want to.
13 This person often stops to think about what to say in conversations. (R)

Focus and Poise

14 This person shows a lot of poise during interactions.
15 This person is usually relaxed and at ease in conversations.
16 This person is not very smooth verbally. (R)
17 This person has a way of interacting that draws others to him/her.
18 This person is completely self-confident when interacting with others.
19 This person often acts impatient during conversations. (R)
20 This person remains task oriented during conversations.

Panache

21 This person is very expressive during conversations.
22 This person is often the center of attention.
23 This person has a dramatic way of interacting.
24 This person often makes his/her presence felt.
25 This person has a memorable way of interacting.

Self-Assurance

26 This person often acts nervous in conversations. (R)
27 This person is often concerned with other's impressions of him/her. (R)
28 This person seems to have trouble concentrating on the topic of conversation. (R)
29 This person often avoids saying things in conversation because he/she might regret it later. (R)
30 This person is more of a follower than a leader. (R)
31 This person often has trouble thinking of things to talk about. (R)

Note: Items 2, 3, 7, 13, 16, 19, 26, 27, 28, 29, 30, and 31 require reverse-scoring (R), i.e., 7 = 1, 6 = 2, 5 = 3, 3 = 5, 2 = 6, 1 = 7. Higher scores on all dimensions should be associated with greater dominance.

Learner Empowerment

Profile by Rebecca B. Rubin

Empowered learners are students who are intrinsically motivated to learn and are "willing and capable to engage in work (learning)" (Frymier, Schulman, & Houser, 1996, p. 184). The concept is adapted from Block's (1987) initial work on manager-employee relationships in which communication is viewed as the means through which employees are motivated to engage in tasks beneficial to the organization. Thomas and Velthouse (1990) conceptualized empowerment in corporations as consisting of meaningfulness, competence, impact, and choice. Meaningful work consists of tasks that are seen to be beneficial presently or in the future. Competence means that the individual believes that he or she is able to perform the tasks necessary to achieve personal goals. Impact refers to a feeling that the tasks accomplished will make a difference in the long run. And choice refers to a sense that the individual, rather than someone else, can determine the means or methods of task accomplishment. Frymier et al.'s (1996) study served as a framework for the development of the Learner Empowerment measure for use in educational contexts.

In 1993, Schultz and Shulman were the first to adapt this concept for educational settings (cited in Frymier et al., 1996). Their 30-item scale (see Frymier et al., 1996, p. 187) contained items from each of the four predetermined dimensions: meaningfulness, competence, impact, and choice. They tested the construct validity of this measure in a series of studies. In the first, the factor structure of the scale was examined and a three-factor solution emerged. Choice was not a distinct factor. The overall reliability of the measure was .90. All in all, Frymier et al. found that learner empowerment was positively and significantly correlated, as hypothesized, with state motivation, teachers' use of relevance strategies, teacher immediacy, and self-esteem.

In the second study (Frymier et al., 1996), items were added and revised to reflect greater perceived empowerment. This 38-item measure was again tested with college students and, again, three distinct factors emerged. Impact consisted of both impact and choice items, whereas meaningfulness and competence were comprised of a priori items. The impact dimension had an alpha reliability of .95 (M = 30.43, SD = 6.40), the meaningfulness dimension had an alpha of .94 (M = 20.99, SD = 8.08), and the competence dimension had an alpha of .92 (M = 26.83, SD = 6.40). As hypothesized, significant positive correlations were found with state motivation, relevance, and learning.

The Learner Empowerment scale contains 35 items, and students are asked to think of a particular class (typically the class they went to prior to the data collection) when completing it; thus the scale deals with empowerment within a particular classroom environment. Students use a 5-point scale, ranging from Never (0) to Very Often (4) to indicate how often they feel this way in the class. The time required is less than 5 minutes for completion.

Reliability

Weber (2004) found that the subscales—impact, competence, and meaningfulness—had coefficient alphas of .88, .92, and .91. Impact and overall LES scores were positively correlated with prosocial behavioral alteration techniques (BATs) of teachers, but correlations with meaningfulness and competence weren't significant. The anti-social BATS weren't related, as hypothesized, but the author performed lots of correlations and ultimately regression, but should have used discriminant analysis instead.

Weber and Patterson (2000) previously found the Learner Empowerment measure to be highly reliable (.93 alpha for the total scale, and .88 for impact, .92 for competence, and .91 for meaningfulness), but suggested that the concept is ambiguous because it so similar to interest (consisting of meaningfulness of material, learner involvement, and learner prior knowledge). Indeed, the three dimensions were highly correlated with a measure of student interest. Weber, Martin, and Patterson (2001) also found high alpha reliabilities for the subscale and overall measure.

Validity

Several studies have looked at empowerment concurrently with other variables. Dobransky and Frymier (2004) selected 10 items from the impact dimension (coefficient alpha of .86) and used these to measure shared control. They had predicted that shared control would be correlated with affective and cognitive learning and this hypothesis was supported. Weber (Weber & Patterson, 2000; Weber et al., 2001) found correlations between the LES and motivation. Weber, Fornash, Corrigan, and Neupauer (2003) manipulated interest level of a class lesson and student in the high interest group scored higher on the LES and confirmed that interest was necessary for cognitive learning to take place.

Weber, Martin, and Cayanus (2005) attempted to shorten the LES and, through confirmatory factor analysis, produced an 18-item version that closely resembles the original scale. In addition, they added to the construct validity of the measure by looking at motives for communication. For the 18-item version, the means, standard deviations, and alphas in Study 1 were: impact (M=3.91, SD=1.22, $alpha$ = .88), competence (M=5.93, SD = .85, $alpha$ =.92); meaningfulness (M= 4.88, SD=1.40, $alpha$ = .91). In study 2, they were: impact (M=3.53, SD = 1.16, $alpha$ = .81), meaningfulness (M=4.48, SD = 1.36, $alpha$ = .88); competence (M = 5.84, SD = 0.97, $alpha$ = .85). As hypothesized, interest was related to motives for communicating with one's instructor. In addition, a canonical correlation found that interest had different relationships with motives and the authors explain how this contributes to the construct validity of the scale.

Comments

One concern with this scale has been face validity. Just what is being measured? Weber and Patterson (2000) wondered if the scale wasn't simply measuring interest in the class, and Weber has used it in this manner in several studies (Weber et al., 2005). The scale seems to provide students affective reactions to instruction, a form of self-efficacy and involvement in the class. A student who thinks "I can do it" seems to feel more in control and is more likely to succeed. Thus, the scale is useful for measuring such a construct.

Location

Frymier, A. B., Shulman, G. M., & Houser, M. (1996). The development of a learner empowerment measure. *Communication Education, 45*, 181–199.**
Weber, K., Martin, M. M., & Cayanus, J. L. (2005). Student interest: A two-study re-examination of the concept. *Communication Quarterly, 53*, 71–86.***

References

Block, P. (1987) *The empowered manager: Positive political skills at work.* San Francisco: Jossey-Bass.
Dobransky, N. D., & Frymier, A. B. (2004). Developing teacher-student relationships through out of class communication. *Communication Quarterly, 52*, 211–223.
Schultz, S., & Schulman, G. (1993, April). *The development and assessment of the job empowerment instrument (JEI).* Paper presented at the joint annual meetings of the Central States Communication Association and Southern States Communication Association, Lexington, KY.
Thomas, K., & Velthouse, B. (1990). Cognitive elements of empowerment: And "interpretive" model of intrinsic task motivation. *Academy of Management Review, 15*, 666–681.

Weber, K. (2004). The relationship between student interest and teacher's use of behavior alteration techniques. *Communication Research Reports, 21,* 428–436.

Weber, K., Fornash, B., Corrigan, M., & Neupauer, N. (2003). The effect of interest on recall: An experiment. *Communication Research Reports, 20*(2), 116–123.

Weber, K., Martin, M. M., & Patterson, B. R. (2001). Teacher behavior, student interest, and affective learning: Putting theory to practice. *Journal of Applied Communication Research, 29,* 71–90.

Weber, K., & Patterson, B. R. (2000). Student interest, empowerment, and motivation. *Communication Research Reports, 17,* 22–29.

Scale

Learner Empowerment (Frymier, Schulman, & Houser) * *
Instructions: Please respond to the statements in terms of the class you take *(prior to this one, after this one).* Visualize the class situation or atmosphere. Please use the following scale to respond to each of the following statements.

Never = 0   Rarely = 1   Occasionally = 2   Often = 3   Very Often = 4

Impact

1 I have the power to make a difference in how things are done in this class.
*2 I have a choice in the methods I can use to perform my work.
3 My participation is important to the success of this class.
*4 I have freedom to choose among options in this class.
5 I can make an impact on the way things are run in this class.
*6 Alternative approaches to learning are encouraged in this class.
7 I have the opportunity to contribute to the learning of others in this class.
*8 I have the opportunity to make important decisions in this class.
9 I cannot influence what happens in this class. (R)
10 I have the power to create a supportive learning environment in this class.
11 My contribution to this class makes no difference. (R)
*12 I can determine how tasks can be performed.
13 I make a difference in the learning that goes on in this class.
*14 I have no freedom to choose in this class. (R)
15 I can influence the instructor.
16 I feel appreciated in this class.

Meaningfulness

1 The tasks required of me in this class are personally meaningful.

2   I look forward to going to this class.
3   This class is exciting.
4   This class is boring. (R)
5   This class is interesting.
6   The tasks required of me in this class are valuable to me.
7   The information in this class is useful.
8   This course will help me achieve my future goals.
9   The tasks required in this course are a waste of my time. (R)
10 This class is not important to me. (R)

Competence

1   I feel confident that I can adequately perform my duties.
2   I feel intimidated by what is required of me in this class. (R)
3   I possess the necessary skills to perform successfully in class.
4   I feel unable to do the work in this class. (R)
5   I believe that I am capable of achieving my goals in this class.
6   I have faith in my ability to do well in this class.
7   I have the qualifications to succeed in this class.
8   I lack confidence in my ability to perform the tasks in this class. (R)
9   I feel very competent in this class.

Note 1: Items should be randomly mixed to avoid response bias. (R) Item should be reverse-coded prior to scoring

Note 2: The Weber, Martin, & Cayanus*** 18-item measure contains Impact items 1, 3, 9, 15, Meaningfulness item 10, and Competence item 9 plus the following:

1   I can help others lean in this class.
2   My participation in this class makes no difference.
3   The work that I do in this class is meaningful to me.
4   The work that I do for this class is valuable to me.
5   The things I learn in this class are useful.
6   This class will help me achieve my goals in life.
7   The work I do in this class is a waste of my time.
8   I can do well in this class.
9   I don't think that I can do the work in this class.
10 I believe in my ability to do well in this class.
11 I have what it takes to do well in this class.
12 I don't have the confidence in my ability to do well in this class.

*– indicates an a priori choice dimension item

**© 1996 by Taylor & Francis.

***© 2005 Taylor & Francis.

Listening Styles Profile—16

Profile by Rebecca B. Rubin

Measurement in the area of listening has mainly focused on listening skills, comprehension, and ability issues. Typically, a test of listening is developed to assess hearing, perceiving, attending, comprehending, remembering, and responding (see Rubin & Roberts, 1994), although no one test assesses all of these components. And skills tests cannot incorporate a self-report format because there are correct answers to questions based on the stimulus materials that are heard (see Watson & Barker, 1983). However, people can self-report their typical listening style.

The Listening Styles Profile measure was originally published by Watson in 1984 and by Watson and Barker in 1988 as a 30-item measure of individual approaches to listening, but Watson, Barker, and Weaver (1995) report research designed to reduce the instrument to 16 items, measuring four distinct styles. *People-oriented listeners* are concerned with others and their feelings. *Action-oriented listeners* have a need for clear, organized presentations. *Content-oriented listeners* need facts and details for later decisions. And *time-oriented listeners* focus on how little time they have for listening. These styles were based on advice from listening experts and research literature.

Watson et al. (1995) tested the 16-item version (with items derived from initial pilot tests of the original 30 items) with about 1,800 undergraduate students. Four items represent each of the four styles, and response categories include: always (4), frequently (3), sometimes (2), infrequently (1), and never (0). It takes respondents only a few minutes to complete.

Validity and Reliability

Factor analysis with oblique rotation produced the four factors, accounting for 50% of the variance, indicating construct validity (Watson et al., 1995). Men were found to be more action- and time-oriented listeners, whereas women were more people- and content-oriented listeners. Coefficient alphas for the factors ranged from .58 (content) to .65 (time).

Test-retest reliability correlations, after a two-week wait, ranged from .68 (people) to .75 (action).

The scale has been used to compare college students in Germany, Israel, and the United States (Kiewitz, Weaver, Brosius, & Weimann, 1997). The four dimensions were again found, but cultures differed in terms of preferences. Germans preferred the action style, Americans favored people and time, and Israelis favored the content style. In addition, Weaver, Watson, and Barker (1996) found listening styles associated with personality dimensions; extraversion was linked to people-oriented listening, neuroticism was linked to time-oriented listening, and psychoticism was linked to action and content listening.

Additional research has uncovered gender differences in listening style. Johnson, examined both biological gender and gender role type for 769 female and 1,003 male students and found males scoring higher on action and time styles, and females scoring higher for people-orientation style. In terms of gender role, communal gender role participants had higher people listening styles than undifferentiated gender roles. Agentic roles had higher content, time, and action styles than the other roles, as expected.

Comments

This instrument is useful as a quick self-report measure of typical listening behavior, not as a measure of listening skill or comprehension. This is often useful for educational or organizational training sessions where instruction will be given post-test scores compared with pre-test scores. It is also good for self-analysis and introspection and for comparison of intercultural differences.

However, Kiewitz et al. (1997) indicated cultural differences in terms of listening style. It is not clear whether cultures naturally have different styles (as might subcultures, which have not been examined) or if the respondents interpret the items differently based on translation of the statements or inherent cultural values. In addition, all studies have been conducted with college students; thus, age differences in terms of style should be examined as well.

The LSP-16 has modest (but somewhat low) coefficient alphas, thus indicating internal consistency. Test-retest reliability research should be considered to assess reliability over time. Also, research has not yet provided data on predictive, concurrent, or content validity. Additional research on construct validity is necessary, as well.

Location*

Watson, K. W., Barker, L. L., & Weaver, J. B., III. (1995). The Listening Styles Profile (LSP-16): Development and validation of an instrument to assess four listening styles. *International Journal of Listening, 9,* 1–13.

References

Johnston, M. K., Weaver, J. B., Watson, K. W., & Barker, L. B. (2000). Listening styles: Biological or psychological differences? *International Journal of Listening, 14*, 32–46.

Kiewitz, C., Weaver, J. B., Brosius, H. B., & Weimann, G. (1997). Cultural differences in listening style preferences: A comparison of young adults in Germany, Israel, and the United States. *International Journal of Public Opinion Research, 9*, 233–247.

Rubin, R. B., & Roberts, C. V. (1987). A comparative examination and analysis of three listening tests. *Communication Education, 36*, 142–153.

Watson, K. W. (1984). *Listener preference profile.* New Orleans, LA: SPECTRA Communication Associates.

Watson, K. W., & Barker, L. L. (1983). *Watson-Barker listening test.* Auburn, AL: SPECTRA, Inc.

Watson, K. W., & Barker, L. L. (1988). *Listener preference profile.* New Orleans, LA: SPECTRA Communication Associates.

Weaver, J. B., Watson, K. W., & Barker, L. L. (1996). Individual differences in listening styles: Do you hear what I hear? *Personality and Individual Differences, 20*, 381–387.

Scale

Listening Styles Profile—16*
Instructions: For each of the following statements, please indicate how well each applies to you. If the statement applies to you Always, mark a 4, if Frequently, a 3, Sometimes, a 2, Infrequently, a 1, or Never, a 0.

Always (4) Frequently (3) Sometimes (2) Infrequently (1) Never (0)

People

1 I focus my attention on the other person's feelings when listening to them.
2 When listening to others, I quickly notice if they are pleased or disappointed.
3 I become involved when listening to the problems of others.
4 I nod my head and/or use eye contact to show interest in what others are saying.

Action

5 I am frustrated when others don't present their ideas in an orderly, efficient way.
6 When listening to others, I focus on any inconsistencies and/or errors in what's being said.
7 I jump ahead and/or finish thoughts of speakers.
8 I am impatient with people who ramble on during conversations.

Time

9 I prefer to listen to technical information.
10 I prefer to hear facts and evidence so I can personally evaluate them.
11 I like the challenge of listening to complex information.
12 I ask questions to probe for additional information.

Content

13 When hurried, I let the other person(s) know that I have a limited amount of time to listen.
14 I begin a discussion by telling others how long I have to meet.
15 I interrupt others when I feel time pressure.
16 I look at my watch or clocks in the room when I have limited time to listen to others.

Note: Items should be mixed randomly to avoid response bias.

Marital Opinion Questionnaire (MOQ)

Profile by Elizabeth E. Graham

Ted Huston, Susan McHale, and Ann Crouter (1986) were interested in changes in marital relationships during the early years of marriage. Their efforts spearheaded the PAIR Project (Process of Adaptation in Intimate Relationships) which resulted in a 13-year longitudinal study of courtship, marriage, and adaptation of 168 married couples and included four phases of data collection. To assess partners' marital satisfaction, the authors developed the Marital Opinion Questionnaire (MOQ). This measure was adopted from Campbell, Converse, and Rogers' (1976) measure of life satisfaction. The MOQ is a 10-item seven point semantic differential scale that is anchored in evaluative subjective qualities of marriage that include: (1) miserable-enjoyable, (2) rewarding-disappointing, (3) full-empty, (4) discouraging-hopeful, (5) interesting-boring, (6) doesn't give me much chance-brings out the best in me, (7) lonely-friendly, (8) worthwhile-useless, (9) hard-easy, and (10) tied down-free. In addition, a single 7-point semantic differential question captures a holistic assessment of overall marital satisfaction and is bounded by two bipolar adjectives: completely satisfied to completely dissatisfied. Factor analysis revealed that the *hard-easy and free-tied-down* dimensions did not cluster with the other eight items and were therefore eliminated (Campbell et al., 1976). However, recent research has employed the two items without consequence (see Schrodt & Afifi, 2007; Vangelisti, Maguire, Alexander, & Clark, 2007).

Reliability

Caughlin (2002) reported Cronbach's coefficient alphas that ranged from .83 to .90 for husbands and wives respectively. Vangelisti and Crumley (1998) employed a modified version of the scale and reported an alpha level of $\alpha = .97$. Several researchers (Afifi & Schrodt, 2003; Schrodt & Afifi, 2007; Vangelisti et al., 2007; Young, Kubicka, Tucker, Chavez-Appel, & Rex, 2005) have extended the MOQ for use in families and have reported robust reliability estimates. Strong correlations ($r = .72$) between the 10 marital satisfaction items and the single global rating of satisfaction were reported by Huston et al. (1986). Huston and Vangelist (1991) reported similar correlations between the single-item and the cluster of satisfaction items for several phases of study ($r = .63$ to $.80$).

Validity

The individual items that comprise the MOQ have not been tested to determine their ability to capture the full essence of marital satisfaction. However, the content validity of the MOQ is enhanced by the efforts the authors made to adhere to the suggestion to avoid assessing both behavioral and affective oriented items in the same measure (see Norton, 1983, for more details). The MOQ is a pure evaluative measure of feelings about marital quality (Caughlin & Huston, 2002; Huston et al., 1986) and as a result, offers a truer (less inflated) measure of marital satisfaction (Vangelisti & Crumley, 1998; Vangelisti et al., 2007). Support for the convergent validity of the MOQ has been provided by Huston and Vangeslisti (1991) and Aida and Falbo (1991) through their research linking the Marital Opinion Questionnaire with Spanier's (1976) Dyadic Adjustment Scale.

The construct validity of the Marital Opinion Questionnaire can be assessed through reviewing the conclusions derived from the PAIR project (Huston, Caughlin, Houts, Smith, & George, 2001; Huston et al., 1986; Vangelisti & Huston, 1994). Analysis of the initial data that was collected via face-to-face and phone interviews three months post wedding and then a year later, provided support for the contention drawn by Waller (1938) that the antidote for love is marriage (Huston et al., 1986). In essence, Huston and colleagues determined that marital satisfaction declines subsequent to marriage and the first anniversary and this decline is not related to prior cohabitation or the result of becoming parents. Rather, couples reported dissatisfaction with the quantity of their interaction, the initiation of pleasurable activities, the display of negativity, and the frequency of physical intimacy. Although these changes are real, the authors caution that these are an indication of adjustment not dysfunction.

Subsequently, Vangelisti and Huston (1994) examined the data for three phases of the PAIR Project and, consistent with prior results, surmised that over time, both spouses report less satisfaction with their communication quality, ability to have influence in their marriage, and sexual relationship. More specifically, Vangelisti and Huston reported that newly married wives are more satisfied with their marriage if they are afforded time to spend with their spouse, family, and friends. In the second year of marriage, wives' communication and their sexual relationship were strong predictors of their marital satisfaction. In the third year of marriage, for wives, the sexual relationship was no longer a predictor of marital satisfaction but was replaced by the amount of influence they exerted in their marriage and the equitable division of household tasks.

Vangelisti and Huston (1994) reported that after the first year of marriage, the amount of influence experienced was responsible for husbands' satisfaction. An analysis of the longitudinal findings suggest that wives' satisfaction is very much rooted in socioemotional interaction concerns and husbands' marital satisfaction hinges on instrumental aspects of the relationship such as the division of labor in the household. In a thirteen year follow-up study, identified as phase four, Huston et al. (2001) determined that patterns of behavior evidenced in the newlywed years were a good predictor of subsequent marital satisfaction providing further support for the criterion validity of the MOQ.

Additional studies have illustrated the construct validity of the MOQ. Consistent with a social learning perspective, spouses' marital satisfaction is influenced by affectional expression, negativity, anxiety, moodiness, and nervousness (Caughlin & Huston, 2002; Caughlin Huston, & Houts, 2000; Huston & Vangelisti, 1991). In effect, unpleasant behaviors are met with dissatisfaction and pleasant behaviors result in marital satisfaction. These results also support the emotional contagion perspective that suggests that spouses *catch* each others' bad moods and negativity thus affecting their marital satisfaction (Caughlin et al., 2000). Furthermore, Caughlin (2002) and Caughlin and Huston (2002) reported that demand/withdraw communication patterns between husbands and wives is related to marital satisfaction although the relationship is complex in that affectional expression and negativity moderates the effect that demand/withdraw pattern sometimes has on marital satisfaction.

Relatedly, Aida and Falbo (1991) concluded that marital satisfaction is more likely to occur in marriages characterized as equal rather than traditional and dissatisfaction more prevalent in couples that resort to indirect power strategies. The Marital Opinion Questionnaire is also sensitive to how family members process and respond to hurtful messages (Vangelisti et al., 2007; Vangelisti & Crumley, 1998; Vangelisti & Young, 2000; Young et al., 2005), conflict (Schrodt & Afifi, 2007), uncertainty (Afifi & Schrodt, 2003), and topic avoidance (Dailey & Palomares, 2004).

Comments

The MOQ is relatively short measure (compared to more laborious marital satisfaction measures) and is very easy to complete. The internal reliability of the MOQ is satisfactory and there is a substantial amount of research supportive of its construct validity. The PAIR Project and subsequent research (e.g., Caughlin, 2002; Huston & Vangelisti, 1991) that has employed the MOQ, is noteworthy because conclusions are based on longitudinal data, a design so very valuable but so absent in marital research.

To compute the marital satisfaction tallies the average score of the eight semantic differential items are added to the score on the single question assessing the overall assessment of marital satisfaction and then divided by two to create an index of marital satisfaction with possible scoring ranges from low (1) to high (7) marital satisfaction (Huston & Vangeslisti, 1991, p. 724). Couple scores were defined as measuring "happy" if both spouses' satisfaction scores were greater than 4 and if either member of the couple scored 4 or below, they were termed "not happy" (see Huston et al., 2001 for more details).

Location**

Campbell, A., Converse, P. E., & Rodgers, W. L. (1976). *The quality of American life. Perceptions, evaluations, and satisfactions.* New York: Russell Sage Foundation.

References

Afifi, T. D., & Schrodt, P. (2003). Uncertainty and the avoidance of the state of one's family in stepfamilies, postdivorce single-parent families, and first-marriage families. *Human Communication Research, 29,* 516–532.

Aida, Y., & Falbo, T. (1991). Relationships between marital satisfaction, resources, and power strategies. *Sex Roles, 24,* 43–56.

Caughlin, J. P. (2002). The demand/withdraw pattern of communication as a predictor of marital satisfaction over time. Unresolved issues and future directions. *Human Communication Research, 28,* 49–85.

Caughlin, J. P., & Huston, T. L. (2002). A contextual analysis of the association between demand/withdraw and marital satisfaction. *Personal Relationships, 9,* 95–119.

Caughlin, J. P., Huston, T. L., & Houts, R. M. (2000). How does personality matter in marriage? An examination of trait anxiety, interpersonal negativity, and marital satisfaction. *Journal of Personality and Social Psychology, 78,* 326–336.

Dailey, R. M. & Palomares, N. A. (2004). Strategic topic avoidance: An investigation of topic avoidance frequency, strategies used, and relational correlates. *Communication Monographs, 71,* 471–496.

Huston, T. L., Caughlin, J. P., Houts, R. M., Smith, S. E., & George, L. J. (2001). The connubial crucible: Newlywed years, as predictors of marital delight, distress, and divorce. (2001). *Journal of Personality and Social Psychology, 80,* 237–252.

Huston, T. L., McHale, S. M., & Crouter, A. C. (1986). When the honeymoon's over: Changes in the marriage relationship over the first year. In R. Gilmour & S. Duck (Eds.), *The emerging field of personal relationships* (pp. 109–132). Hillsdale, NJ: Erlbaum.

Huston, T. L., & Vangelisti, A. L. (1991). Socioemotional behavior and satisfaction in marital relationships: A longitudinal study. *Journal of Personality and Social Psychology, 61,* 721–733.

Norton, R. (1983). Measuring marital quality: A critical look at the dependent variable. *Journal of Marriage and the Family, 45,* 141–151.

Schrodt, P., & Afifi, T. D. (2007). Communication processes that predict young adults' feelings of being caught and their associations with mental health and family satisfaction. *Communication Monographs, 74*, 200–228.

Spanier, G. B. (1976). Measuring dyadic adjustment: New scales for assessing the quality of marriage and similar dyads. *Journal of Marriage and the Family, 38*, 15–28.

Vangelisti, A. L., & Crumley, L. P. (1998). Reactions to messages that hurt: The influence of relational contexts. *Communication Monographs, 65*, 173–196.

Vangelisti, A. L., & Huston, T. L. (1994). Maintaining marital satisfaction and love. In D. J. Canary & L. Stafford (Eds.), *Communication and relational maintenance* (pp. 165–186). San Diego, CA: Academic Press.

Vangelisti, A. L., Maguire, K. C., Alexander, A. L., & Clark, G. (2007). Hurtful family environments: Links with individual, relationship, and perceptual variables. *Communication Monographs, 74*, 357–385.

Vangelisti, A. L., & Young, S. L. (2000). When words hurt: The perceived intentionality on interpersonal relationships. *Journal of Social and Personal Relationships, 17*, 393–425.

Waller, W. (1938). *The family: A dynamic interpretation.* New York: Cordon.

Young, S. L., Kubicka, T. L., Tucker, C. E., Chavez-Appel, D., & Rex, J. S. (2005). Communicative responses to hurtful messages in families. *The Journal of Family Communication, 5*, 123–140.

Scale

Marital Opinion Questionnaire (MOQ)**

Instructions: Below are some words and phrases which we would like you to use to describe how you feel about your marital satisfaction. Please indicate your impressions of your marriage by circling the appropriate number between the pairs of adjectives below. The closer the number is to an adjective, the more certain you are of your evaluation.

1	Boring	1 2 3 4 5 6 7	Interesting
2	Miserable	1 2 3 4 5 6 7	Enjoyable
3	Hard*	1 2 3 4 5 6 7	Easy
4	Useless	1 2 3 4 5 6 7	Worthwhile
5	Lonely	1 2 3 4 5 6 7	Friendly
6	Empty	1 2 3 4 5 6 7	Full
7	Discouraging	1 2 3 4 5 6 7	Hopeful
8	Tied-down*	1 2 3 4 5 6 7	Free
9	Disappointing	1 2 3 4 5 6 7	Rewarding
10	Doesn't give me much chance	1 2 3 4 5 6 7	Brings out the best in me
11	Low marital satisfaction	1 2 3 4 5 6 7	High marital satisfaction

Note: Items should be reverse ordered randomly to avoid a response effect.

*Items eliminated due to weak factor loadings

** © 1986 by the Russell Sage Foundation.

Measure of Source Credibility

Profile by Elizabeth E. Graham

From Aristotle to McCroskey, credibility has been conceptualized as comprised of three components: competence, trustworthiness, and goodwill. The last dimension, goodwill, according to McCroskey and Teven (1999), has been neglected because . . . of misanalysis and/or misinterpretation of data in a wide variety of empirical studies. To remedy this omission, James McCroskey and Jason Teven developed a measure of ethos/credibility in an attempt to recapture the "lost dimensions" of the goodwill construct. Goodwill has been conceptualized as intent-toward-receiver (McCroskey & Young, 1981) and perceived caring (McCroskey, 1992; Teven & McCroskey, 1997). Competence has been defined as expertise and intelligence, while trustworthiness references qualities such as honesty and character. Scale items for the three dimensions were generated from prior studies (McCroskey, 1966; McCroskey & Young, 1981; Teven & McCroskey, 1997). The resulting measure is comprised of 18 items representing the three subscales mentioned above and employs a 7-point semantic differential response option format.

To explore the factor structure of the credibility construct, and replicate prior research conducted by Teven and McCroskey (1997), data were subjected to a series of factor analyses employing unrotated and rotated iterations. Results support the utility of both a unidimensional (unrotated) and a three dimensional (rotated) version of the Measure of Source Credibility. Furthermore, this research employed a considerably large sample (N = 783) and utilized three different stimulus communication sources (i.e., political figures, public figures, interpersonal contacts).

Building on prior research (Teven & McCroskey, 1997), McCroskey and Teven (1999) sought to provide additional validity for their conceptualization of credibility by testing its association with the twin notions of believability and likeability. Resting on the premise that we like and believe people we deem credible, results of multiple correlation analysis revealed that each of the three components of source credibility are independently related to believability and likeability. However, the strongest relationships were revealed when the three dimensions were collapsed into a unidimensional measure.

Reliability

McCroskey and Teven (1999) assessed the internal reliability of the Measure of Source Credibility and reported the following Cronbach alphas: competence $\alpha = .85$; trustworthiness $\alpha = .92$; and goodwill $\alpha = .92$. An alpha of .94 was reported for the overall scale. Subsequent research efforts have produced equally, and in some cases higher, reliability estimates (Cole & McCroskey, 2003; McCroskey & Richmond, 2000; Meyers, 2001; Paulsel, Richmond, McCroskey, & Cayanus, 2005; Teven, 2007).

Validity

The Measure of Source Credibility has been successfully employed to investigate communication phenomenon in work environments, interpersonal relations, the classroom, and health care settings. Testing the applicability of reciprocity and accommodation theories to superior subordinate relationships, McCroskey and Richmond (2000) concluded that assertiveness and responsiveness contribute to subordinates' perception of supervisors' credibility. Conversely, Teven, McCroskey, and Richmond (2006) revealed that supervisors' credibility, as assessed by subordinates, is inversely related to supervisor Machiavellianism. Cole and McCroskey (2003) provided additional support for the construct validity of the scale by replicating prior research that suggests that supervisors and roommates are perceived to lack credibility if they are verbally abusive and/or apprehensive in their communications with others. Meyers (2001) reached similar conclusions and found that students rated verbally aggressive instructors low in credibility. Recent research is consistent with these findings revealing that teacher misbehaviors negatively impact perceptions of teacher credibility (Banfield, Richmond, & McCroskey, 2006) and caring (Teven, 2007).

Paulsel et al. (2005) illustrated that the credibility measure has utility in health care contexts and concluded that when patients perceive nurses, physicians, and support staff as credible (i.e., competent and caring/goodwill) they are confident that their medical records will be treated confidentially. Furthermore, physicians' responsive communication style contributes significantly to patients' perceptions of satisfaction with, and credibility of, the physician, and further enhances patient satisfaction with their care (Richmond, Smith, Heisel, & McCroskey, 2002). Relatedly, physician humor was positively associated with patients' views of physician credibility and patient satisfaction (Wrench & Booth-Butterfield,

2003). In sum, these research efforts are indicative of the versatility and in effect, validity, of the Measure of Source Credibility.

Comments

McCroskey (2006) suggests that "these scores should not be summed to create a single score. To do so would be adding the proverbial apples and oranges (and watermelons). They should not be employed in stepwise regression analyses because their colinearity will violate the assumptions of this statistical procedure. However, they can be used in regular multiple regression and in canonical correlational analyses, as well as for computing individual simple correlations" (McCroskey, J.C. 2007, http://www.jamescmccroskey.com/measures/source_credibility.htm).

Although this particular version of the ethos/credibility concept is quite new, the study of source credibility has been a consistent concern and of critical importance in the communication discipline in general and persuasion research in particular. The benefits of this long history is manifest in our familiarity with, and confidence in, the current effort to reestablish the "lost dimension" of goodwill in the re-conceptualization of source credibility.

Location*

McCroskey, J. C., & Teven, J. J. (1999). Goodwill: A reexamination of the construct and its measurement. *Communication Monographs, 66,* 90–103.

References

Banfield, S. R., Richmond, V. P., & McCroskey, J. C. (2006). The effect of teacher misbehaviors on teacher credibility and affect for the teacher. *Communication Education, 55,* 63–72.

Cole, J. G., & McCroskey, J. C. (2003). The association of perceived communication apprehension, shyness, and verbal aggression with perceptions of source credibility and affect in organizational and interpersonal contexts. *Communication Quarterly, 51,* 101–110.

McCroskey, J. C. (1966). Scales for the measurement of ethos. *Speech Monographs, 33,* 65–72.

McCroskey, J. C. (1992). *An introduction to communication in the classroom.* Edina, MN: Burgess International Group.

McCroskey, J. C. (2007). Source credibility measures. Retrieved March 12, 2008 from http://www.jamescmccroskey.com/measures/source_credibility.htm).

McCroskey, J. C., & Richmond, V. P. (2000). Applying reciprocity and accommodation theories to supervisor/subordinate communication. *Journal of Applied Communication Research, 28,* 278–289.

McCroskey, J. C., & Young, T. J. (1981). Ethos and credibility: The construct and its measurement after three decades. *Central States Speech Journal, 32,* 24–34.

Meyers, S. A. (2001). Perceived instructor credibility and verbal aggressiveness in the college classroom. *Communication Research Reports, 18*, 354–364.

Paulsel, M. L., Richmond, V. P., McCroskey, J. C., & Cayanus, J. L. (2005). The relationships of perceived health professionals' communication traits and credibility with perceived patient confidentiality. *Communication Research Reports, 22*, 129–142.

Richmond, V. P., Smith, R. S., Heisel, A. D., & McCroskey, J. C. (2002). The association of physician socio-communicative style with physician credibility and patient satisfaction. *Communication Research Reports, 19*, 207–215.

Teven, J. J. (2007). Teacher caring and classroom behavior: Relationships with student affect and perceptions of teacher competence and trustworthiness. *Communication Quarterly, 55*, 433–450.

Teven, J. J., & McCroskey, J. C. (1997). The relationship of perceived teacher caring with student learning and teacher evaluation. *Communication Education, 46*, 1–9.

Teven, J. J., McCroskey, J. C., & Richmond, V. P. (2006). Communication correlates of perceived Machiavellianism of supervisors: Communication orientations and outcomes. *Communication Quarterly, 54*, 127–142.

Wrench, J. S., & Booth-Butterfield, M. (2003). Increasing patient satisfaction and compliance: An examination of physician humor orientation, compliance-gaining strategies, and perceived credibility. *Communication Quarterly, 51*, 482–503.

Scale

Measure of Source Credibility*

Instructions: Please indicate your impressions of the person (identified by the researcher) by circling the appropriate number between the pairs of adjectives below. The closer the number is to an adjective, the more certain you are of your evaluation.

Competence

1 Intelligent	1 2 3 4 5 6 7	Unintelligent (R)
2 Untrained	1 2 3 4 5 6 7	Trained
3 Inexpert	1 2 3 4 5 6 7	Expert
4 Informed	1 2 3 4 5 6 7	Uninformed (R)
5 Incompetent	1 2 3 4 5 6 7	Competent
6 Bright	1 2 3 4 5 6 7	Stupid (R)

Goodwill

7 Cares about me	1 2 3 4 5 6 7	Doesn't care about me (R)
8 Has my interests at heart	1 2 3 4 5 6 7	Doesn't have my interests at heart (R)
9 Self-centered	1 2 3 4 5 6 7	Not self-centered
10 Concerned with me	1 2 3 4 5 6 7	Not concerned with me (R)

| 11 | Insensitive | 1 2 3 4 5 6 7 | Sensitive |
| 12 | Not understanding | 1 2 3 4 5 6 7 | Understanding |

Trustworthiness

13	Honest	1 2 3 4 5 6 7	Dishonest (R)
14	Untrustworthy	1 2 3 4 5 6 7	Trustworthy
15	Honorable	1 2 3 4 5 6 7	Dishonorable (R)
16	Moral		
17	Moral	1 2 3 4 5 6 7	Immoral (R)
18	Unethical	1 2 3 4 5 6 7	Ethical
19	Phoney	1 2 3 4 5 6 7	Genuine

Note: Items should be randomly ordered, without subscale labels.

(R) Reverse code items: 1, 4, 6, 7, 8, 10, 13, 15, 16

* © 1998 by Taylor & Francis.

Medical Communication Competence Scale

Profile by Rebecca B. Rubin

Patient satisfaction is consistently linked to good communication between patients and doctors. Good communication has been defined as having two goals: socioemotional communication and information exchange (Cegala, Coleman, & Turner, 1998, p. 263). A variety of doctor–patient scales exist, but most lack an information-exchange (i.e., seeking, giving, and verifying information) component. Cegala et al. (1998) reported on their scale, which contains both components.

Validity and Reliability

The first stage of scale development occurred in 1996 (Cegala, McGee, & McNeilis). Doctors and patients completed the initial instrument and then described behaviors that influenced their ratings. The content analysis confirmed the two dimensions and provided additional items for the second study, in which 56 items were tested for *importance* with 65 physicians and 52 patients (Cegala et al., 1998). Those items deemed "important" were retained in the final instrument. Two data files were created containing 117 doctor/patient responses (one for doctor self-competence and patient's evaluation of the physician, and one for patient's self- and doctor's view of the patient) were cluster analyzed and results confirmed the original dimensions: information giving, information seeking, information verifying, and socioemotional communication. Alpha reliabilities ranged from .83 to .92 for physician version and from .83 to .87 for the patient version. Two items that loaded onto the information-verifying cluster for patients were kept with the information-giving cluster to maintain conceptual clarity.

In the Cegala et al. study (1998), hypotheses comparing self-ratings and other-ratings were confirmed as well: both doctors and patients thought they had higher socioemotional skills than information skills, and this was confirmed by the dyad partner (i.e., their doctor or patient). Patients also rated doctors higher in both dimensions than doctors rated themselves, while doctors rated patients lower in information exchange than patients rated themselves. A variety of other analyses supported the construct validity of the scale.

A couple of items were later added to the scale and a couple removed. Today, the physician version contains 36 items (23 self-competence and 13 patient-competence items) and the patient version contains 39 items (16 self-competence and 23 physician-competence items). Data from both physicians and patients are necessary in order to compute information and socioemotional cluster scores (see below). Respondents are asked to use a 7-point Likert scale, ranging from Strongly Agree to Strongly Disagree and cluster scores can be computed from these.

Location*

Cegala, D. J., Coleman, M. T., & Turner, J. W. (1998). The development and partial assessment of the medical communication competence scale. *Health Communication, 10*, 261–288.

References

Cegala, D. J., McGee, D. S., & McNeilis, K. S. (1996). Components of patients' and doctors' perceptions of communication competence during a primary care medical interview. *Health Communication, 8*, 1–27.

Scale

Medical Communication Competence Scale*

Directions for Doctors:

The purpose of this questionnaire is to obtain your views about communication during the interview you just had. There are two parts to the questionnaire. In the first part, you are asked to make judgments of your own communication. In the second part, you are asked to make judgments of the patient's communication.

For each item, please circle the most appropriate alternative. If you do not believe an item is relevant to this particular interview, please write NA next to the item.

Directions for Patients:

The purpose of this questionnaire is to obtain your views about communication during the interview you just had. There are two parts to the questionnaire. In the first part, you are asked to make judgments of your own communication. In the second part, you are asked to make judgments of the doctor's communication.

For each item, please circle the alternative that best describes how you feel. If you do not believe an item applies to this particular interview, please write NA next to the item.

Table 1

Strongly Agree 7	Slightly Agree 6	Agree 5	Not Sure 4	Slightly Disagree 3	Strongly Disagree 2	Disagree 1

Doctor's Self-Competence Items

I provided good explanations of the following to the patient:

1 The diagnosis of his/her medical problem.
2 The causes of his/her medical problem.
3 The treatment for his/her medical problem.
4 The advantages and disadvantages of treatment options.
5 The purpose of any tests that were needed.
6 How prescribed medication will help his/her problem.
7. How to take prescribed medication.
8 The possible side effects of the medication.
9 The long-term consequences of his/her medical problem.

I did a good job of:

10 Reviewing or repeating important information for the patient.
11 Making sure the patient understood my explanations.
12 Making sure the patient understood my directions.
13 Checking my understanding of information the patient provided.
14 Using language the patient could understand.
15 Asking the patient the right questions.
16 Asking questions in a clear, understandable manner.
17 Using open-ended questions.
18 Being warm and friendly.
19 Contributing to a trusting relationship.
20 Showing the patient I cared about him/her.

21 Making the patient feel relaxed or comfortable.
22 Showing compassion.
23 Being open and honest.

Doctor's Other-Competence Items

The Patient did a good job of:

24 Providing relevant history associated with his/her medical problem.
25 Explaining symptoms associated with his/her medical problem.
26 Identifying what medications he/she is taking.
27 Answering my questions thoroughly.
28 Answering my questions honestly.
29 Letting me know when he/she didn't understand something.
30 Asking me to explain terms he/she didn't understand.
31 Letting me know when I needed to repeat something.
32 Asking questions about his/her medical problem.
33 Pursuing answers to his/her questions.
34 Asking appropriate questions.
35 Contributing to a trusting relationship.
36 Being open and honest.

Clusters:
Information Giving: Doctor 1–9 & Patient 25–29
Information Receiving: Doctor 15–17 & Patient 32–34
Information Verifying: Doctor 10–14 & Patient 29–31
Socioemotional: Doctor 18–23 & Patient 35–36

Patients' Self-Competence Items

I did a good job of:

1. Presenting important history associated with my medical problem.
2. Describing the symptoms of my medical problem.
3. Explaining my medical problem.
4. Identifying what medicines I am taking.
5. Answering the doctor's questions thoroughly.
6. Answering the doctor's questions honestly.
7. Letting the doctor know when I didn't understand something.
8. Letting the doctor know when I needed him/her to repeat something.
9. Making sure I understood the doctor's directions.
10. Repeating important information to make sure I understood correctly.
11. Asking the doctor to explain terms I didn't understand.
12. Asking the doctor all the questions that I had.
13. Getting the answers to my questions.
14. Getting all the information I needed.
15. Contributing to a trusting relationship.
16. Being open and honest.

Patients' Other-Competence Items

The doctor explained the following to my satisfaction:

17. What my medical problem was.
18. The causes of my medical problem.
19. What I could do to get better.
20. The benefits and disadvantages of treatment choices (that is, choices about what I could do to get better).
21. The purpose of any tests that were needed.
22. How prescribed medicine would help my problem.
23. How to take prescribed medicine.
24. The possible side effects from the medicine.
25. The long-term consequences of my medical problem.

The doctor did a good job of:

26. Reviewing or repeating important information.
27. Making sure I understood his/her explanations.
28. Making sure I understood his/her directions.
29. Using language I could understand.
30. Checking his/her understanding of what I said.
31. Asking me questions related to my medical problem.
32. Asking me questions in a clear, understandable manner.
33. Asking questions that allowed me to elaborate on details.
34. Being warm and friendly.
35. Contributing to a trusting relationship.
36. Showing he/she cared about me.
37. Making me feel relaxed or comfortable.
38. Showing compassion.
39. Being open and honest.

Clusters:
Information Giving: Doctor 17–25 & Patient 1–6
Information Receiving: Doctor 31–33 & Patient 12–14
Information Verifying: Doctor 26–30 & Patient 7–11
Socioemotional: Doctor 34–39 & Patient 15–16

Note: Doctor version is on p. 208 and Patient version is on p. 209.

Normative Message Processing Scale (NMPS)

Profile by Joseph P. Mazer

Human information processing employs multiple modes of processing (Berry & Broadbent, 1987, 1988; Hayes & Broadbent, 1988). In certain cases, individuals are deliberate and effortful, able to make distinctions among message qualities, and carefully evaluate message content. In other cases, individuals exert less effort, are guided by already established distinctions among message qualities, and can poorly evaluate message content. Despite these potential differences, a primary consensus exists in the message processing literature: Individuals have dominant processing responses. However, these dominant processing responses must be superseded by contingencies that prompt an adaptation to another processing mode or to multiple processing modes.

To address these issues, R. Kelly Aune and Rodney Reynolds (1994) developed the Normative Message Processing Scale (NMPS). They argued for a need to develop a measure that distinguishes between the inclination to engage in message processing that is selective, deliberate, and characterized by high effort and message processing that is unselective, nondeliberate, and characterized by low effort. Their research spanned three phases across five studies. Phase one consisted of item generation and initial factor analysis. Phase two involved confirmatory factor analysis and tests of construct validity. Phase three provided tests of predictive validity. The resulting scale is a 24-item two-dimensional (analytical and intuition factors) measure of normative message processing with Likert response options.

Reliability

The series of studies (Aune & Reynolds, 1994) revealed acceptable Cronbach alphas. Reliabilities ranged from $\alpha = .79$ to .87 for the analytical factor and $\alpha = .77$ to .83 for the intuition factor.

Validity

Pool items were generated from the literature and from individuals with an interest in the research project. During the item generation process, research assistants critiqued items, discussed the essence of cognitive processing, and identified aspects of cognitive processing that were not represented in the item pool. The resulting pool of 40 items reflected an individual's tendency to rely on hunches and intuitions, utilize analysis and evaluation, preference for a specific message form and structure, recollection of memory structure and retrieval processes, and tendency to simultaneously process multiple message codes. The 40 items were subjected to exploratory factor analysis that revealed three factors. The first factor appeared to indicate a tendency to carefully and deliberately analyze messages, while the third factor assessed the tendency for an individual to rely on hunches, intuition, and first impressions when assessing message quality. The second factor was problematic and subsequently excluded from further analysis. Before beginning the second phase, poorly loaded items were dropped from the scale and new items that reflected an emphasis on the noteworthy characteristics of the two remaining factors were written.

Phase two involved confirmatory factor analysis—including tests for content homogeneity, internal consistency, parallelism, and reliability—and resulted in 15 analysis items and 9 intuition items. The second version of the NMPS consisted of 17 items that were indicative of the selective, analytical processing dimension and 13 items indicating unselective, intuitive processing experiences. Confirmatory factor analysis led to the elimination of five items that resulted in acceptable homogeneity and satisfied a test for unidimensionality. Internal consistency was established after eliminating one item from the analytical processing factor. Both factors satisfactorily met the test of parallelism. Alpha reliability for the two factors was acceptable: analytical factor $\alpha = .87$; intuition factor $\alpha = .79$. Phase two continued with construct validity tests utilizing convergent-discriminant analysis.

The constructs of need for cognition (NCS; Cacioppo & Petty, 1982), information processing, which represents an individual's preferences for information processing (HIPS; Taggart & Torrance, 1984), and unwillingness to communicate (Burgoon, 1976) were utilized to test convergent and discriminant validity of the NMPS. Crowne and Marlowe's (1964) Social Desirability Scale was used to test for possible effects. Aune and Reynolds reported that construct validity was well supported, as most correlations were reflective of their predictions; however, an unexpected social desirability effect emerged. That is, greater analytical and effortful processing was positively correlated with social desirability, while intuitive and hunch-based processing was negatively correlated with social desirability. Aune and Reynolds cited sample demographic issues (i.e., ethnic and cultural differences) as an explanation for evidence of social desirability. In the end, they argued that the results of phase two strongly support the structural and construct validity of the NMPS. Confirmatory factor analysis supported a slightly reduced version of the two-factor solution. Convergent-discriminant validity tests revealed that the two subscales are tapping expected differences in message processing characteristics, and the NMPS is free of potential confounds as evidenced by comparisons among similar instruments.

Phase three involved three studies that provided tests of predictive validity through correlation and regression analyses. Study one predicted a positive relationship between preferences for analytical processing, need for cognition, and reports of expended cognitive effort and message recall. In addition, the study explored a possible negative relationship between intuitive processing preferences and effort and recall. To explore these relationships, participants were asked to read a narrative advocating tuition raises and then list as many of the message arguments they could recall. Undergraduate research assistants, blind to the purpose of the project, assessed the amount of information recalled. Small correlations supported the predictive validity of the NMPS. Scores on the analytical factor of the NMPS were positively related with reported expended effort ($r = .18$) and amount of message content recalled ($r = .25$). Scores on the intuition factor were negatively related with amount of message content recalled ($r = -.27$). Expended effort was not significantly related to intuition scores. Need for cognition was positively related to recall ($r = .15$) and expended effort ($r = .17$). Regression analysis was used to explore the recall and expended effort variance that could be attributed to the NMPS beyond that due to need for cognition. Analyses revealed that the intuition dimension of the NMPS still accounted for a significant amount of the variance in recall. With need for cognition and intuition removed, the analysis dimension of the NMPS also accounted for significant variance in recall.

Studies two and three tested the predictive validity of the NMPS by exploring expected differences in the nonverbal processing abilities predicted by scores on the NMPS, HIPS, and NCS. With the inherent demands of nonverbal coding in mind, Aune and Reynolds predicted a positive correlation between intuition factor scores and nonverbal decoding skill. On the other hand, because the more analytical processors will focus on individual cues, they predicted a negative correlation between scores on the analytical factor and nonverbal decoding skills. Aune and Reynolds attributed similar arguments to the HIP scale—people who score high in right hemispheric processing might be more skilled at processing information that is communicated nonverbally, while the more left hemispheric processors who focus on analytical information processing should be less accurate when processing nonverbal information. Finally, citing high and low need for cognition individuals and processing mode, Aune and Reynolds expected a negative relationship between need for cognition and the accuracy of nonverbal decoding.

To explore these predicted relationships, the authors utilized the Facial Meaning Sensitivity Test (FMST; Leathers, 1992). The FMST consisted of 30 pictures of a woman's face expressing one of 10 different affective states. Participants were asked to select three photographs that they thought best depicted each of the 10 affective states. Results revealed a positive relationship between intuition scores and the number of accurate responses on the FMST ($r = .28$) and a negative relationship between analytical factor scores and decoding accuracy ($r = -.38$). Additionally, the left hemispheric portion of the HIPS yielded a negative correlation with decoding accuracy ($r = -.32$). Regression analysis was used to examine whether the NMPS accounted for a significant portion of the variance after the variance accounted for by the HIPS had been removed. Entering the left and right HIPS dimensions first, the analytical factor still accounted for significance variance in decoding accuracy; however, the intuition factor fell short of significance.

The results of the studies in phase three support the predictive validity of the NMPS. Scores on the NMPS were significantly related to participants' expenditures of cognitive effort and their ability to recall message content and decode nonverbal information. Furthermore, findings indicate that the NMPS can account for additional variance beyond simply that attributed to differences between need for cognition and hemispheric processing.

Comments

The NMPS was rigorously developed across three phases and five studies that established the conceptual and predictive validity of the measure. As the authors note, the NMPS offers an advantage over other message and information processing scales—it conceptualizes and assesses message processing along two dimensions (analytical and intuition), rather than a single dimension.

One can argue that, in terms of nonverbal decoding ability, the results were limited to a test employing only a single nonverbal code and channel. Additional research in this area can explore the degree to which similar effects can be found with messages employing multiple codes and channels. Unfortunately, a search of the literature reveals a considerable lack of published studies that utilize the NMPS. Undoubtedly, future research can further enhance the reliability and validity of this carefully crafted measure.

Finally, although college student populations provide important evidence of how a specific age group processes messages, results normed on diverse populations (age, occupation, socioeconomic status, culture) can enhance the generalizability and ecological validity of the NMPS.

Location*

Aune, R. K., & Reynolds, R. A. (1994). The empirical development of the normative message processing scale. *Communication Monographs, 61*, 135–160.

References

Berry, D. C., & Broadbent, D. E. (1987). The combination of implicit and explicit learning processes. *Psychological Research, 49*, 7–15.

Berry, D. C., & Broadbent, D. E. (1988). Interactive tasks and the implicit-explicit distinction. *British Journal of Psychology, 79*, 251–272.

Burgoon, J. K. (1976). The Unwillingness to Communicate Scale: Development and validation. *Communication Monographs, 43*, 60–69.

Cacioppo, J. T., & Petty, R. E. (1982). The need for cognition. *Journal of Personality and Social Psychology, 42*, 116–131.

Crowne, D., & Marlowe, D. (1964). *The approval motive.* New York: Wiley.

Hayes, N. A., & Broadbent, D. E. (1988). Two modes of learning for interactive tasks. *Cognition, 28*, 249–276.

Leathers, D. G. (1992). *Successful nonverbal interaction.* New York: Macmillan.

Taggart, W., & Torrance, E. P. (1984). *Human information processing survey: Administrator's manual.* Bensenville, IL: Scholastic Testing Service.

Scale

Normative Message Processing Scale (NMPS)*

Instructions: [Instructions were not provided in the article; however, the authors reported that responses were scored using a – 4 to + 4 Likert-type scale. One can conclude that anchors of "strongly agree" and "strongly disagree" were employed.]

1 I know when a message makes sense because it just seems to feel right.
2 After making a decision about someone's argument, I usually know the thought processes that led to my decision.
3 Objectivity and analysis are *not* my primary tools for assessing persuasive messages. (R)
4 The best way for me to assess a person's argument is through careful analysis.
5 I analyze each point of a message one at a time and very carefully.
6 My intuition plays only a weak role in my analysis of a person's message. (R)
7 When developing a message, I don't think much about the order of the specific points of the message. (R)
8 I don't need to completely understand a message to know if it makes sense. (R)
9 When I read or listen to a message I pay close attention to each point that is made and decide whether it is a good point or not.

10 Hunches and intuitions are *not* my primary tools for assessing persuasive messages. (R)
11 When I'm listening to an explanation about something, I stop everything else so that I can pay close attention to what is being said.
12 My best decisions about a message come from careful analysis and reflection about the content of the message.
13 It takes me a while to understand an argument because I carefully think about each point presented.
14 When assessing the validity of an argument, I rank each point in order of importance and then consider whether it makes sense.
15 I don't like to rely on my hunches about the validity of people's arguments. (R)
16 When assessing the validity of a person's argument I rely a lot on my feelings and intuitions.
17 When assessing a persuasive argument I try to remain objective and analyze the content of the message.
18 I don't usually have hunches or intuitions about messages. (R)
19 When I listen to a speaker I concentrate on the content of the message and don't let myself get distracted by anything else.
20 I don't usually go with my first impressions when making an important decision; I prefer to take my time. (R)
21 Having a good hunch is often as useful as developing a good understanding.
22 I'm not very careful or deliberate when I'm listening to a message. (R)
23 I don't always know what leads me to believe or reject an argument; it just happens.
24 I assess a person's argument by evaluating each point, one at a time.

(R) Indicates reverse-coded item

Organizational Assimilation Index (OAI)

Profile by David R. Seibold

Myers and Oetzel (2003) created and validated a measure of organizational assimilation. Organizational assimilation processes have received considerable theoretical, practical, and critical attention in organizational studies, especially in management, organizational behavior, and communication. Myers and Oetzel defined organizational assimilation as the interactive mutual acceptance of newcomers into organizational settings.

Organizational members from six industries participated in two phases of their research to create and validate the OAI (Myers & Oetzel, 2003). In the first phase, participants' responses to depth interviews suggested six dimensions of organizational assimilation that were consistent with previous research: familiarity with others, organizational acculturation, recognition, involvement, job competency, and adaptation/role negotiation.

In the second phase, Myers and Oetzel (2003) developed 61 items to represent these six dimensions of organizational assimilation. Three hundred and forty-two employees in different industries (lodging, banking, advertising, publishing, hospitality, and a nonprofit service agency) utilized the 61 items to assess their own assimilation experiences. Organizations sampled included four hotels from one company located in Arizona, California, and Washington. The bank (two branches), advertising agency, and nonprofit agency were located in a large city in the southwestern United States. The 61-item initial questionnaire had nine to eleven items reflecting the specific content of the six themes of organizational assimilation identified in the first phase. Responses to all items were recorded on a 5-point scale in a Likert format (1 = *strongly agree*, 5 = *strongly disagree*).

Confirmatory factor analysis of the OAI provided empirical support for the six dimensions identified in the first phase (see Validity section below) (Myers & Oetzel, 2003). The first factor involved *Familiarity with Supervisors*. Getting to know supervisors was seen as the first step of fitting into organizations, and results indicated that respondents' feelings toward their organizations changed as a result of becoming acquainted with superiors. The second factor was *Organizational Acculturation*, including accepting the organization's culture, willingness to make personal changes in order to integrate into it, development of a shared understanding by organizational members, and becoming familiar with organizational goals and values. The third factor, *Recognition*, involved perceiving one's value to the organization and feeling recognized by superiors. *Involvement*, the fourth factor, encompassed many aspects of being a part of organizations (volunteering for extra organizational duties, figuring out ways to accomplish work more efficiently, and feeling involved in the organization). The fifth factor, *Job Competency*, related to members' beliefs that they were able to adequately perform their designated duties. Finally, although the results from the first phase suggested that the processes of adaptation and role negotiation would cluster to form the sixth factor, confirmatory factor analysis produced evidence for *Role Negotiation* only. Role negotiation entailed ways newcomers interact with others in the organization in an attempt to compromise on ways a role should be enacted. Results of the factor analyses and reliability assessments yielded a final 20-item Organizational Assimilation Index, with two to four items for each of the six dimensions of organizational assimilation (see OAI instrument reprinted below).

Reliability

The six dimensions of the Organizational Assimilation Index demonstrated homogeneous item content, and estimated reliability (Cronbach's alpha) ranged from good to adequate: Recognition $\alpha = .86$, Familiarity $\alpha = .73$, Acculturation $\alpha = .73$, Involvement $\alpha = .72$, Role Negotiation $\alpha = .64$, Job Knowledge $\alpha = .62$ (Myers & Oetzel, 2003). Estimates of retest reliability were, similarly, good to adequate: Recognition $r = .85$, Familiarity $r = .77$, Acculturation $r = .71$, Involvement $r = .70$, Role Negotiation $r = .57$, Job Knowledge $r = .66$. Myers and Oetzel also examined each factor's reliability for consistency across the sample. Reliability coefficients did not vary significantly across organizations or organizational level, nor did they vary as a function of the language of the questionnaire or sex of the respondents. Their results suggest a reliable set of measures for assessing members' perceptions of their organizational assimilation experiences.

Validity

Myers and Oetzel (2003) subjected the data from Phase Two to confirmatory factor analysis to establish content validity of the a priori six dimensions. Several criteria were used to determine the inclusion of the items and model fit. First, items had to have a primary factor loading of .40. Second, items had to be unidimensional as demonstrated by the tests of internal consistency and parallelism (Hunter & Gerbing, 1982). Third, the items had to have homogeneous content. Fourth, the items needed to show an acceptable level of reliability (Cronbach's alpha).

After removing items from the model in line with the first two criteria, Myers and Oetzel (2003) concluded that the empirically-derived model corresponded to the six dimensions of the conceptual model. The chi-square to degrees of freedom ratio suggested an adequate fit. Further, the model fit indices were at or above the recommended .90 (Hoyle & Panter, 1995). Additionally, there were no deviations in internal consistency or parallelism for the items. The six dimensions of the Organizational Assimilation Index also demonstrated homogeneous item content.

To provide evidence for the discriminant validity of the six dimensions of organizational assimilation, Myers and Oetzel (2003) specified a single factor solution that alternatively assumed that the items represent a single construct. This model provided a poor fit to the data. A comparison of the fit between the two models indicated that the six-factor model exhibited a significantly better fit to the data, Myers and Oetzel therefore rejected the assumption that a single factor underlies these measures.

Finally, the OAI's construct validity was tested through the use of three other scales: Brayfield and Rothe's (1951) Job Satisfaction Scale, Lyons's Propensity to Leave Scale (1971), and six randomly selected items from Cheney's (1983) Organizational Identification Questionnaire. Myers and Oetzel (2003) used correlation analysis to examine the relationships of the OAI factors to participants' reported job satisfaction, propensity to leave, and organizational identification. As expected, OAI responses for each of the dimensions were positively associated with job satisfaction and organizational identification and negatively associated with propensity to leave. All correlations were statistically significant.

Comments

Myers and Oetzel's (2003) final 20-item Organizational Assimilation Index measures six distinct and empirically verified aspects of organizational assimilation: Familiarity with Supervisors, Organizational Acculturation, Recognition, Involvement, Job Competency, and Role Negotiation. Across a two-phase research process, they demonstrated face, content, and construct validity for the OAI. Myers and Oetzel note that while each dimension provides valuable information in its own right, the index as a whole yields a full measure of organizational assimilation.

Location*

Myers, K. K., & Oetzel, J. G. (2003). Exploring the dimensions of organizational assimilation: Creating and validating a measure. *Communication Quarterly, 51* (4), 438–457.

References

Brayfield, A. H., & Rothe, H. F. (1951). An index of job satisfaction. *Journal of Applied Psychology, 35*, 307–311.

Cheney, G. (1983). On the various and changing meanings of organizational membership: Field study of organizational identification. *Communication Monographs, 50*, 342–362.

Hoyle, R. H., & Panter, A. T. (1995). Writing about structural equation models. In R. H. Hoyle (Ed.), *Structural equation modeling: Concepts, issues, and applications* (pp. 158–176). Thousand Oaks, CA: Sage.

Hunter, J. E., & Gerbing, D. W. (1982). Unidimensional measurement, second order factor analysis, and causal models. *Research in Organizational Behavior, 4*, 267–320.

Lyons, T. F. (1971). Role clarity, need for clarity, satisfaction, tension, and withdrawal. *Organizational Behavior and Human Performance, 6*, 99–110.

Scale

Organizational Assimilation Index*

Instructions: Please respond to a series of questions about feeling a part of this organization. For this research, organization refers to your place of work. There are no right or wrong answers in this survey; I simply want to know what you think about and feel about your organization. REMEMBER, YOUR ANSWERS WILL REMAIN CONFIDENTIAL. YOUR EMPLOYER WILL NOT SEE YOUR RESPONSES TO THE QUESTIONS. For each question, please circle your response according to the following scale:

Strongly Disagree	Disagree	Neutral	Agree	Strongly Agree
1	2	3	4	5

Supervisor Familiarity

1 I feel like I know my supervisor pretty well.   1 2 3 4 5
2 My supervisor sometimes discusses problems with me.   1 2 3 4 5
3 My supervisor and I talk together often.   1 2 3 4 5

Acculturation

4 I understand the standards of the company.   1 2 3 4 5
5 I think I have a good idea about how this organization
   operates.   1 2 3 4 5
6 I know the values of my organization.   1 2 3 4 5

Recognition

7 My supervisor recognizes when I do a good job.   1 2 3 4 5
8 My boss listens to my ideas.   1 2 3 4 5

 9 I think my supervisor values my opinions.   1 2 3 4 5

10 I think my superior recognizes my value to the
organization.   1 2 3 4 5

Involvement

11 I talk to my coworkers about how much I like it here.   1 2 3 4 5
12 I volunteer for duties that benefit the organization.   1 2 3 4 5
13 I talk about how much I enjoy my work.   1 2 3 4 5
14 I feel involved in the organization.   1 2 3 4 5

Job Competency

15 I often show others how to perform our work.   1 2 3 4 5
16 I think I'm an expert at what I do.   1 2 3 4 5
17 I have figured out efficient ways to do my work.   1 2 3 4 5
18 I can do others' jobs, if I am needed.   1 2 3 4 5

Role Negotiation

19 I have offered suggestions for how to improve
productivity.   1 2 3 4 5
20 I have helped to change the duties of my position.   1 2 3 4 5

Note: Items should be randomly ordered and subscale titles removed prior to administration.

Organizational Dissent Scale (ODS)

Profile by David R. Seibold

Focused on assessing "how employees verbally express their contradictory opinions and disagreements about organizational phenomena" (Kassing, 1998, p. 183), the Organizational Dissent Scale (ODS) measures the ways in which employees communicate opinions of their organization along different dimensions, to different audiences, and in multiple directions (upward, horizontal, external). Developed by Jeffrey Kassing, the ODS examines the expression of dissent "which entails expressing disagreement or contradictory opinions about organizational practices, policies, and operations (1998, p. 183).

Based upon extant dissent literature and an earlier theoretical model of employee dissent (Kassing, 1997), the ODS originally measured dissent along three dimensions: *Articulated, Antagonistic (Latent)*, and *Displaced* (Kassing, 1998). Articulated dissent is expressed "when employees believe they will be perceived as constructive and that their dissent will not lead to retaliation" (Kassing, 1997, p. 326). Expressing dissent to members of organizations (supervisors, managers, officers) who have the ability to make change undergirds the Articulated dimension of the ODS. Kassing (1997) described the Antagonistic dimension as a form of dissent in which those who express believe they will be perceived as adversarial—yet feel that they are relatively safe from retaliation because they posses organizational leverage of some kind. Familial relationships, minority status, and expertise are forms of organizational leverage that afford employees a safeguard against retaliation. Antagonistic dissent is often about personal-advantage issues, may be characterized by aggression, and typically is expressed to audiences that are captive and or influential (Kassing, 1997; 1998). The Antagonistic subscale of the ODS was renamed Latent dissent by Kassing (1998) because the final items comprising this dimension suggest that "dissent readily exists but is not always observable and that dissent becomes observable . . . when frustration mounts" (p. 211). Displaced dissent "entails disagreeing without confronting or challenging" (Kassing, 1998; p. 192). It occurs when employees perceive that their dissent will be viewed as confrontational and could lead to retaliation, and hence is expressed to external audiences (non-work friends, spouses/partners, strangers, and family members) and/or to ineffectual internal audiences (coworkers without the power to redress the problem). The absence of confrontation, combined with the desire to avoid retaliation, are at the heart of the Displaced dimension of the Organizational Dissent Scale (Kassing, 1997, 1998).

The final 18-item version of the Organizational Dissent Scale (Kassing, 2000a) measures employees' dissent along just two of these dimensions: Articulated and Latent. The measure is comprised of positive and negative declarative statements reflecting employees' degree of agreement—assessed with 5-point Likert-type scales (1 = *strongly disagree* to 5 = *strongly agree*)—with how they express their concerns about their organization. Preliminary studies (especially three studies reported in Kassing, 1998) used more items, measured them on scales with more response options, and relied on items representing all three dimensions in the Kassing (1997) model. Because problems with the ODS revealed in Kassing's early studies (Kassing, 1998; Kassing & Avtgis, 1999) led to revisions that comprise the 18-item final version (Kassing, 2000a), these investigations will be reviewed before turning in the Comments section to the final version of the ODS reprinted here.

In Study 1 of Kassing (1998), 347 questionnaires were administered in seven organizations located throughout the United States that varied in size and type. One hundred and ninety-one questionnaires were returned, a response rate of 55%. Utilizing 45 items measured on 7-point Likert-type scales, a three-factor solution accounted for 35.9% of the total variance. The factor reflecting Articulated dissent accounted for 16.1% of the variance, the factor reflecting Antagonistic (Latent) dissent accounted for 10.6% of the variance, and the factor reflecting Displaced dissent accounted for 9.2% of the variance. In Study 2, 776 questionnaires were distributed in two large organizations located on the east and west coasts of the United States as well as in Ohio. One hundred and ninety-five questionnaires were returned, a response rate of 25%. Utilizing 27 items measured on 5-point Likert-type scales (1= *strongly agree* to 5 = *strongly disagree*) that asked respondents to report their dissent levels, a three-factor solution accounted for 50.9% of the total variance. The 9-item factor reflecting Articulated dissent accounted for 22.2% of the variance. The 5-item factor reflecting Displaced dissent accounted for 15.5% of the variance. The 6-item factor reflecting Antagonistic (Latent) dissent accounted for 13.2% of the variance.

Reliability

Internal reliability estimates (Cronbach's alpha) for the 20 retained items comprising the three Organizational Dissent Scale subscales in Study 2 (Kassing, 1998) were .88 (Articulated), .87 (Displaced), and .76 (Latent).

Using responses to the 20-item version from 192 employees of organiza- tions throughout Ohio, Kassing and Avtgis (1999) reported reliabilities of .81 (Articulated), .80 (Displaced), and .64 (Latent) for the three subscales.

Kassing (1998), in Study 3, also sought to establish the temporal stability of the ODS by administering the measure to two groups of 61 students in graduate business classes at two large universities with a two-week interval between administrations. Test-retest Pearson's Product-Moment correlations were .84 for the Articulated dimension, .77 for the Displaced dimension, and .71 for the Latent Dimension. Cronbach alphas for the three subscale dimensions were also computed at both Time 1 and Time 2, and they ranged from .66 (Latent) to .86 (Articulated).

Hence, and irrespective of method used to assess reliability, the Articulated and Displaced subscales of the original 20-item ODS yielded acceptable levels of reliability, while the Latent dimension of the earliest formulation did not.

Validity

Kassing (1998), Study 2, reported evidence for the construct validity of the ODS and its three dimensions based upon responses from 195 respondents from non-management members of two other organizations with multiple sites in the United States. Support for the Articulated dimension was found in its positive correlation with employee satisfaction, strength of relationship with one's supervisor, and one's perception of their ability to personally influence an organization. The Latent dimension correlated negatively with employees' perceptions of workplace freedom of speech, employee commitment, strength of relationship with superior, perceptions of management's openness to employee input, and employees' perception of their ability to personally influence the organization. The Displaced dimension correlated negatively with organizational commitment and with employees' perceptions of their ability to personally influence an organization. However, the items comprising this dimension were not significantly associated with perceptions of management, supervisory relationship, and employee satisfaction. Furthermore, research by Kassing and Avtgis (1999) revealed that none of the independent variables examined (argumentativeness, verbal aggressiveness, organizational position, and present job tenure) were significant predictors of displaced dissent. Therefore there was limited evidence for the validity of the Displaced dimension of the original 20-item ODS.

Comments

Kassing (1997, 1998, 1999, 2000a, 2000b, 2001) and his colleagues (Kassing & Armstrong, 2001, 2002; Kassing & Avtgis, 1999, 2001;

Kassing & DiCoccio, 2004) have studied organizational dissent quite programmatically, often utilizing the ODS and its subscales to explore empirical relationships between organizational dissent and other communication constructs and processes. Several of these studies shed additional light on the ODS, both underscoring the two problems noted above (reliability of the Latent dimension and validity of the Displaced dimension) and leading to revisions to the ODS reported below. For example, in their study of the relationship between organizational dissent and aggressive communication Kassing and Avtgis (2001) reported reliabilities of .81 for the Articulated dimension, .64 for the Latent dimension, and .80 for the Displaced dimension. Kassing and Armstrong (2001) selected portions of the ODS to test relationships between dissent-triggering events and dissent expression. Items of the ODS used in their study were modified by the authors to better reflect the focus of their study on situations that brought about organizational dissent and their impact on the expression of dissent. Reliabilities were .94 for Displaced dissent, .86 for Upward dissent, and .93 for Other-Focused (Latent) dissent. Additional factor analysis specific to the modified dimensions of the ODS used in Kassing and Armstrong (2001) was performed and Upward, Displaced, and Other-Focused (Lateral) accounted for 59.52%, 61.04%, 68.78% of the variance respectively.

The most important and enduring changes to the original 20-item Organizational Dissent Scale (Kassing, 1998) were reported by Kassing (2000a). The resultant revised and final 18-item ODS measures how employees verbally express their disagreement and contradictory opinions about work-related matters in their organization. The measure continues to utilize a 5-point Likert-type scale but now ranges from *strongly disagree* (1) to *strongly agree* (5). Furthermore, while the original 20-item ODS (Kassing 1998) measured employees' dissent along the three dimensions discussed above (Articulated, Latent, Displaced), the revised 18-item version of the ODS (Kassing, 2000) measures only Articulated and Latent dissent. Kassing (2000) reported that the Displaced dimension was dropped because it failed to produce hypothesized relationships in previous studies (Kassing, 1998; Kassing & Avtgis, 1999). Too, Kassing noted that the revised 18-item measure "includes five additional items that Kassing (1998) wrote and suggested for use in future studies to boost consistently poor reliabilities for the Latent dimension" (p. 63). The Displaced items from the 2-item version that have been omitted from 18-item final measure can be identified by comparing the 20-item version of ODS in Appendix A of Kassing (1998)—which includes 4 "Potential Additional Latent Items—with the 18-item ODS reprinted below from Appendix A of Kassing (2000a). The new items on the Latent dimension in the final 18-item ODS reprinted below also are readily identifiable: they were suggested and listed in Appendix B of Kassing (1998).

Kassing considered the two-dimensional 18-item measure to be the best and final version of the Organizational Dissent Scale, and in his recent work (Kassing, 2000a, 2000b; Kassing & Armstrong, 2001) he has utilized it rather than the earlier 20-item and 24-item three-dimensional versions. Kassing (2000a) reported that a two-factor solution accounted for 46.8% of the total variance in 232 Arizona employees' responses to the 18-item ODS. The Articulated dissent factor accounted for 25.8% of the variance, and the Latent dissent factor accounted for 21% of the variance. According to Kassing (2000a, 2000b) internal reliability coefficients for the 18-item ODS ranged from .83 (9-item Articulated dissent dimension) to .87 (9-item Latent dissent dimension). As predicted both forms of dissent also have been found to be associated with employees' perceptions of workplace freedom of speech and with employees' levels of organizational identification (Kassing, 2000b). Also as predicted, articulated dissent was associated with management status, and latent dissent with management status, increases in present job tenure, and decreases in number of full-time employers and total years of work experience (Kassing & Armstrong, 2001).

However, recent studies have utilized the original ODS (Kassing, 1998) that Kassing (2000a, 200b) disavowed. For example, Avtgis, Thomas-Maddox, Taylor, and Patterson (2007) utilized the 20-item version of the ODs *and* the 4 "additional potential latent items," all items noted in Appendix A of Kassing (1998), to create a 24-item measure of organizational dissent. Cronbach alpha reliabilities for the articulated, displaced, and latent dissent dimensions were .86, .85, and .84 respectively. Although findings from the 209 employees of organizations in two midsized metropolitan areas of the Midwest revealed that persons experiencing three burnout symptoms express low levels of articulated dissent and avoid latent dissent strategies, displaced dissent was not a consequence of reported burnout.

Similarly, Payne (2007) used the 20-item version of the ODS from Kassing (1998) and found reliabilities of .83, .72., and .71 for the articulated, latent, and displaced dimensions of dissent respectively. However, while specific levels of both articulated and latent dissent expression were related to 179 employees' reports of organization-based self-esteem, expressions of displaced dissent was not a factor. This finding may be additional evidence for Kassing's (2000a) eschewal of the Displaced dimension and encouragement for researchers to utilize only the 18-item, 2-dimesion (Articulated dissent [9 items], and Latent dissent [9 items]) Organizational Dissent Scale found in Kassing (2000a) and noted below.

Location*

Kassing, J. W. (2000a). Investigating the relationship between superior-subordinate relationship quality and employee dissent. *Communication Research Reports, 17,* 58–70.

References

Avtgis, T. A., Thomas-Maddox, C., Taylor, E., & Patterson, B. R. (2007). The influence of employee burnout syndrome on the expression of organizational dissent. *Communication Research Reports, 24,* 97–102.

Kassing, J. W. (1997). Articulating, agonizing, and displacing: A model of employee dissent. *Communication Studies, 48,* 311–331.

Kassing, J. W. (1998). Development and validation of the organizational dissent scale. *Management Communication Quarterly, 12,* 183–229.

Kassing, J. W. (2000a). Investigating the relationship between superior-subordinate relationship quality and employee dissent. *Communication Research Reports, 17,* 58–70.

Kassing, J. W. (2000b). Exploring the relationship between workplace freedom of speech, organizational identification, and employee dissent. *Communication Research Reports, 17,* 387–396.

Kassing, J. W. (2001). From the looks of things: Assessing perceptions of organizational dissenters. *Management Communication Quarterly, 14,* 442–470.

Kassing, J. W. (2002). Speaking up: Identifying employees' upward dissent strategies. *Management Communication Quarterly, 16,* 187–209.

Kassing, J. W., & Armstrong, T. A. (2001). Examining the association of job tenure, employment history, and organizational status with employee dissent. *Communication Research Reports, 18,* 264–273.

Kassing, J. W., & Armstrong, T. A. (2002). Someone's going to hear about this: Examining the association between dissent-triggering events and employees' dissent expression. *Management Communication Quarterly, 16,* 39–65.

Kassing, J. W., & Avtgis, T. A. (1999). Examining the relationship between organizational dissent and aggressive communication. *Management Communication Quarterly, 13,* 100–115.

Kassing, J. W., & Avtgis, T. A. (2001). Dissension in the organization as it relates to control expectancies. *Communication Research Reports, 18,* 118–127.

Kassing, J. W., & DiCoccio, R. L. (2004). Testing a workplace experience explanation of displaced dissent. *Communication Reports, 17,* 113–120.

Payne, H. J. (2007). The role of organization-based self-esteem in employee dissent expression. *Communication Research Reports, 24,* 235–240.

Scale

Organizational Dissent Scale*
(18-Item Version, Kassing, 2000a)
Instructions: This is a series of statements about how people express their concerns about work. There are no right or wrong answers. Some of the items may sound similar, but they pertain to slightly different issues. Please respond to all items. Considering how you express your concerns at work, indicate your degree of agreement with each statement by placing the appropriate number in the blank to the left of each item.

1 = strongly disagree
2 = disagree
3 = agree some and disagree some
4 = agree
5 = strongly agree

1 _____ I am hesitant to raise questions or contradictory opinions in my organization.

2 _____ I complain about things in my organization with other employees.

3 _____ I criticize inefficiency in this organization in front of everyone.

4 _____ I do not question management.

5 _____ I'm hesitant to question workplace policies.

6 _____ I join in when other employees complain about organizational changes.

7 _____ I share my criticism of this organization openly.

8 _____ I make certain everyone knows when I'm unhappy with work policies.

9 _____ I don't tell my supervisor when I disagree with workplace decisions.

10 _____ I bring my criticism about organizational changes that aren't working to my supervisor or someone in management.

11 _____ I let other employees know how I feel about the way things are done around here.

12 _____ I speak with my supervisor or someone in management when I question workplace decisions.

13 _____ I do not criticize my organization in front of other employees.

14 _____ I make suggestions to management or my supervisor about correcting inefficiency in my organization.

15 _____ I do not express my disagreement to management.

16 _____ I hardly ever complain to my coworkers about workplace problems.

17 _____ I tell management when I believe employees are being treated unfairly.

18 _____ I speak freely with my coworkers about troubling workplace issues.

Note: Items, 1, 4, 5, 9, 10, 12, 14, 15, and 17 comprise the Articulated dimension. Items 2, 3, 6, 7, 8, 11, 13, 16, and 18 comprise the Latent dimension. Items 1, 4, 5, 9, 13, 15, and 16 are reverse-coded for data analysis.

* © 2000 by Taylor & Francis.

Organizational Listening Survey (OLS)

Profile by David R. Seibold

Over the past fifteen years Lynn Cooper, Robert Husband, and colleagues have developed the Managerial Listening Survey (MLS) and modified it into the more general Organizational Listening Survey (OLS) (see Cooper & Buchanan, 2003; Cooper & Husband, 1993; Husband, Cooper, & Monsour, 1988). Their goal has been to develop a valid and reliable measure of individuals' job-related listening competency in organizations. Cooper and Husband (1993) defined listening competency as the "knowledge and ability to effectively use behaviors which show an *accurate* understanding of the message as well as demonstrate *support* for the relationship between the communication participants, within the appropriate boundaries of the organizational situation" (pp. 13–14).

Cooper and colleagues' initial efforts were focused on assessing *supervisors'* listening. Following a review of the theoretical and training literature, 60 survey items were formulated. Evaluation by a panel of communication scholars, professionals, and managers led to the creation a more restricted 40-item questionnaire called the *Managerial Listening Survey* (MLS). The self-report measure was first completed by 122 managers and lead supervisors from a utility company in the midwestern United States. Participants indicated the extent to which they displayed each of the listening behaviors in the MLS, and their responses were recorded on 7-point Likert-type scales (anchored by 1 = *Always* and 7 = *Never*). *Listening for accuracy* (acquiring information through discriminating/evaluating and recalling listening behaviors) and *listening for support* (attending, clarifying, responding, affiliating, and accommodating listening behaviors) emerged from analysis of the seven factors accounting for 81.3% of common variance (Husband, Cooper, & Monsour, 1988).

Husband, Schenck, and Cooper (1988) modified the MLS to a 35-item measure, dropping items that were more dispositional than behavioral. The researchers also revised the MLS to incorporate an "other-report form" (Form B). This "subordinate" form was identical to the "supervisor" form (Form A), save that questions were posed as "My supervisor . . . ." This enabled ratings by a sample of subordinates of each supervisor who completed Form A of the MLS. Two hundred and seventy-two managers and supervisors from the same utility company completed the revised MLS, as did a random sample of two or three subordinates for each supervisor. Subordinates' responses indicated that they perceived their supervisors' listening as less frequent and less effective than did the supervisors' self-ratings.

Cooper and Husband (1993) made additional changes to the MLS, including changing its name to the *Organizational Listening Survey* (OLS). They reduced the measure to 30 items due to redundancy in items and to ensure relevance across organizational contexts. Five molar, criterion variables were included in the revised MLS: frequency of communication, medium of communication, satisfaction with position, satisfaction with coworker relationship, and perceived effectiveness as a listener. Twelve items were reverse coded to prevent response bias. Importantly, the MLS also was modified to obtain responses from a manager's peers and supervisors as well as subordinates. By changing the wording to "coworkers" in Forms A and B, organizational members who did not supervise others could still provide self-ratings (Form C) of their listening behaviors and any of their coworkers could complete the companion other-rating of them (Form D). Indeed, this change in wording in the instrument, and the resultant ability to utilize it to assess the listening competency of *all organizational members in any position*, led to a correlative change in the name of the instrument: Forms C and D became known as the Organizational Listening Survey (OLS). One hundred and eighty-two employees of a petrochemical company and 398 of their coworkers completed the respective forms, enabling the former to compare self-perceptions of their listening behaviors (Form C) with their coworkers' ratings of their listening (Form D). Results of factor analytic procedures with the self-report data supported the two-factor model of listening accuracy (14 items) and listening support (11 items).

Subsequent studies examined the other-rating OLS data and inter-rater agreement between self- and other-ratings. Cooper, Seibold, and Suchner (1997) studied OLS data from 593 employees of the petrochemical company and non-faculty college employees. They found that a 19-item subset of the 30-item OLS best measured ratings of *others'* listening competency (Form D), accuracy and support. Using those 19 items and the same data set, Cooper and Buchanan (1999) reported a strong overall level of agreement among multiple raters of listening competency skills measured by the OLS. That is, "co-workers tend to be highly consistent judges of a supervisor's listening competency . . . [and] co-workers are more likely to agree in their judgments of a listeners' [sic] supportive behaviors than whether or not they are accurate" (p. 52). Cooper and Buchanan (2003) found several factors underlying others' rating of listening competency. The 19-item subset of OLS ratings of others' general listening competency contained not only accuracy (5 items) and support (4 item) dimensions, but openness (3 items), verbal cues (3 items), and nonverbal cues (3 items). These are now treated as subscales of the OLS other-ratings.

Reliability

The listening competency measure has proved to be internally consistent and reliable. Husband et al. (1988) reported a Cronbach alpha of .82 for the 40-item MLS. A slightly modified version of the 35-item MLS (Form B) yielded alphas of .82 overall, .88 listening for accuracy, and .77 listening for support (Stine, Thompson, & Cusella, 1995). Cooper and Husband (1993) obtained reliability coefficients of .93 for the 30-item OLS self-ratings and .91 for other-reports. All of the 30 items on the OLS have been shown to have high agreement rates (James, Demaree, & Wolf, 1993); they ranged from .85 to .92, with an average agreement rate across the 30-item OLS of .88 (Cooper & Buchanan, 1999).

Validity

Cooper and Husband (1993) provided evidence for the convergent validity of the OLS. More than 57% of the variance in perceived listening effectiveness was explained by the two-factor (listening for accuracy, listening for support) OLS items. The accuracy dimension was more strongly linked to perceived listening effectiveness (beta = .60) than support (beta = .30). Relatedly, 26% of coworkers' satisfaction with their workplace relationship with ratees was accounted for by those ratees' listening competency as measured by the OLS (support dimension beta = .40). Cooper and Buchanan (1999) reported findings supporting the divergent validity and discriminant validity of the OLS.

Comments

Cooper and Buchanan (1999) summarily noted that the Organizational Listening Survey "has demonstrated solid psychometric qualities associated with classical measurement theory (i.e., internal consistency and both convergent and divergent validity)" (p. 49). The OLS (Form C) offers a useful self-report measure of listening behaviors, a measure that can be meaningfully distinguished along dimensions of listening for accuracy and listening for support. The ratee can be a supervisor, but the form can be used by "any and all organizational members: managers/supervisors, professionals, front line employees, and support staff" (Cooper et al., 1997, p. 318). Its companion (Form D) yields multiple others' assessments of the (Form C) ratee's listening behaviors. The Form D data can be interpreted in terms of general listening competency and subscales of accuracy, support, openness, verbal cues and nonverbal cues. The molecular 30 items, 5 subscales, 2 dimensions, and general listening competence (19 items) can be related to several molar variables that are collected on both forms (e.g., perceived effectiveness as a listener, satisfaction with relationship). As Cooper and Buchanan (1999) concluded, "this instrument appears to provide consistent and helpful information about listeners' communication skills" (p. 55).

Location*

Husband, R. L., Cooper, L. O., & Monsour, W. M. (1988). Factors underlying supervisors' perceptions of their own listening behavior. *Journal of International Listening, 2*, 97–112. (40-item Managerial Listening Survey)

Cooper, L. O., & Buchanan, T. (1999). Interrater agreement in judgments of listening competency: An item-based analysis of the "Organizational Listening Survey." *Communication Research Reports, 16*(1), 48–54. (30-item Organizational Listening Survey used but not published; 19 items are summarized in Table 1.)

References

Cooper, L. O. (1997). Listening competency in the workplace: A model for training. *Business Communication Quarterly, 60* (4), 75–84.

Cooper, L. O., & Buchanan, T. (1999). Interrater agreement in judgments of listening competency: An item-based analysis of the "Organizational Listening Survey". *Communication Research Reports, 16*, 48–54.

Cooper, L. O., & Buchanan, T. (2003). Taking aim at good targets: Inter-rater agreement of listening competency. *International Journal of Listening, 17*, 88–112.

Cooper, L. O., & Husband, R. L. (1993). Developing a model of organizational listening competency. *Journal of the International Listening Association, 7*, 6–34.

Cooper, L. O., Seibold, D. R., & Suchner, R. (1997). Listening in organizations: An analysis of error structures in models of listening competency. *Communication Research Reports, 14*, 312–320.

Husband, R. L., Cooper, L. O., & Monsour, W. M. (1988). Factors underlying supervisors' perceptions of their own listening behavior. *Journal of International Listening, 2*, 97–112.

Husband, R. L., Schenck, T., & Cooper, L. O. (1988, March). *A further look at managerial listening.* Paper presented at the annual meeting of the International Listening Association. Scottsdale, AZ.

James, L. R., Demaree, R. G., & Wolf, G. (1993). r_{wg}: An assessment of within-group interrater agreement. *Journal of Applied Psychology, 78*, 306–309.

Stine, M., Thompson, T., & Cusella, L. (1995). The impact of organizational structure and supervisory listening indicators on subordinate support, trust, intrinsic motivation and performance. *International Journal of Listening, 9*, 84–105.

Scale

Managerial Listening Survey*
(Husband et al., 1988)

FORM A
Purpose of the Questionnaire
   Listening has been identified by many researchers as an important tool of effective management. The reasons why listening is important, and exactly what is communicated between manager and staff is not well understood. The purpose of this survey is to gather more information on this subject by having you describe, as accurately as you can, your listening behavior.
   Please read each of the following statements. Each item describes a specific kind of behavior but doesn't ask you to judge whether the behavior is desirable or undesirable. Although some items may appear similar, they represent subtle differences that are important. If you are uncertain of any response, please leave that statement blank.

Note: The terms "staff" and "staff members" in the following items, refer to all of the people in the department, division, or other unit of organization that you supervise.

Directions: Indicate how you feel each statement relates to our listening habits on the job by placing an "X" in the blank space which best indicates what you do as a listener. For example:
   I think about how my staff might react to what is said.

$$\text{Always} \underline{\quad} : \underline{\quad} : \underline{\ X\ } : \underline{\quad} : \underline{\quad} : \underline{\quad} : \underline{\quad} \text{ Never}$$

1 I separate personal problems from professional difficulties when listening to my staff.
2 I know what the staff member will say before it is said.
3 I say something when listening to staff members to show I understand.
4 I ask my staff what words mean when they are used in unfamiliar ways.
5 I watch for tones and gestures to help me understand what staff members are trying to tell me.
6 I make eye contact when I am listening.
7 I view listening to my staff as important as getting the job done.
8 I am friendly and approachable.
9 I listen to every word in order to get the main ideas my staff are trying to communicate.
10 I take the time to listen to staff members.
11 I try to describe the feelings staff members are showing when they talk with me.

12   It is easier for me to listen to staff members who have similar views.
13   I am willing to listen to staff concerns even when they don't require my action.
14   I ask simple questions when listening to clarify what staff members are saying.
15   I recall significant details of conversation with my staff.
16   I give staff members straight-forward information in response to their questions.
17   I am non-judgmental and non-critical.
18   I listen with a great deal of concentration and thoughtfulness.
19   I try to think of points to contribute while staff members are speaking.
20   I hide any disapproval I feel when listening to staff members.
21   I tell staff when I don't have time to listen.
22   I pretend to listen to staff members even when not concentrating on their concerns.
23   I find it difficult to keep my personal reactions in line when listening.
24   I restate what I hear a staff member say when he or she is finished speaking.
25   My listening effects staff members' behavior.
26   I remember relevant details of past conversations when staff members bring their particular concerns to me.
27   I discriminate fact from opinion.
28   I express my ideas or opinions during conversations with staff members.
29   I use positive nonverbal expressions when listening to my staff.
30   I evaluate a staff member's credibility when listening.
31   I try to make staff members feel at ease when talking with me.
32   I eliminate outside interruptions or distractions when listening to my staff.
33   I analyze what is said to determine the facts.
34   I take note of how a staff member is using words.
35   I sit where I can easily listen to a staff member.
36   I make positive verbal statements when listening to my staff.
37   I try to anticipate what a staff member will say next.
38   I ask clarifying questions during conversations with staff members.
39   I listen for consistency, in facts and logic, when staff members talk.
40   I take notes when listening.

Please indicate your name: Company:
My position title is:
How many people report directly to you?   Years at this position:
Sex: Age: Last year of formal education completed:

Note: Only Form A of the original MLS has been printed in the research literature (see Appendix A of Husband et al., 1988). However, that was the earliest version of the measure—before the 40-item instrument was reduced, and before the focus of the MLS on *supervisory* listening (Form A = self-rating by manager, and Form B = rating of manager by others) was shifted to a focus on listening competency of *organizational members at any level* in the 30-item OLS (Form C = self-rating and Form D = rating by others). The revised Organizational Listening Survey (Forms C and D) repeatedly has been referred to in the literature—and selected items noted in tables and figures (e.g., Cooper & Husband, 1993, Figure 1; Cooper et al., 1997, Table 1; Cooper & Buchanan, 1999, Table 1; Buchanan & Cooper, 2003, Table 1)—but the full OLS instrument has not been published in those articles. The complete and most current versions of the Organizational Listening Survey (Forms C and D) may be obtained from Dr. Lynn Cooper via e-mail (Lynn.L.Cooper@wheaton.edu), via phone request (630-752-5095), or via post:

Dr. Lynn Cooper
Department of Communication
Wheaton College
501 College Avenue
Wheaton, IL 60187

Organizational Reputation Scale

Profile by David R. Seibold

Working within the crisis communication, management communication, and public relations literatures, Coombs (1995, 1998, 1999a, 1999b) and colleagues (Coombs & Holladay, 1996, 2001, 2002, 2004; Coombs & Schmidt, 2000; Laufer & Coombs, 2007) have explicated a broad-based, prescriptive, and situational approach to organizational responses to crises. Central to their work is research on strategies for protecting organizational reputation, namely how an organization is perceived by its publics.

Coombs and Holladay (1996) developed the 10-item Organizational Reputation Scale, adapted from the Character subscale of McCroskey's (1966) scale for measuring ethos. "Character is conceptualized as the trustworthiness and good will of the source, that is, an assessment of the degree to which the source is concerned with the interests of others" (Coombs & Hollladay, 2002, p. 174). Coombs and Holladay (1996) altered the Character items by substituting the term *organization* (or *company*) for *speaker* in McCroskey's subscsale. Examples of Organizational Reputation Scale items include: "The company is basically honest," "The company is not concerned with the well-being of its publics," "I do not trust the organization to tell the truth about the incident" (Coombs & Holladay, 1996, p. 288). Responses are measured on a 5-point Likert-type scale ranging from 1 (*Strongly Disagree*) to 5 (*Strongly Agree*). The Organizational Reputation Scale typically is administered and completed after respondents have read a packet containing a cover page with directions and stimulus crisis case(s).

Reliability

When all 10 items of the Organizational Reputation Scale have been utilized in studies, Cronbach's alpha coefficients of .82 (Coombs & Holladay, 1996) and .92 (Coombs, 1998) have been obtained. Coombs and Holladay (2002) used 5 items from the ORS and reported Cronbach's alpha reliability of .87, and in another report (Coombs & Holladay, 2006) they observed .85 reliability in Study One and .82 reliability in Study Two for the 5-item version of Organizational Reputation Scale. Only 3 ORS items were employed in a different investigation (Coombs, 1999a), and Cronbach's alpha of .81 was found.

Validity

While the validity of the Organizational Reputation Scale has not yet been fully investigated, concurrent validity appears to be strong. Organizational Reputation Scale responses consistently correlate negatively with crisis responsibility as predicted in the Coombs and Holladay (2002) theoretical perspective. ORS responses also are positively correlated with behavioral intentions—as Coombs and Holladay (2002) predict. However, the connection with (organizations') behavioral intentions was only examined in two studies (Coombs & Holladay, 2004; Coombs & Schmidt, 2000) while the negative relationship to crisis responsibility has been more widely documented (e.g., Coombs, 1998, 1999a; Coombs & Holladay, 1996, 2002; Coombs & Schmidt, 2000). Coombs and Holladay (2006) found that a halo effect (shielding organizations from reputational damage following a crisis) operated in a limited range for organizations with very favorable prior reputations, as predicted.

Comments

Organizational reputation is treated as a proxy for organizational image. The roots of the Organizational Reputation Scale in McCroskey's Character subscale make the links among character, reputation and image somewhat problematic. As Coombs and Holladay (2004) acknowledged, although character is vital to public relations because credibility is key to public relations practice, "character may not be perfect measure for reputation" (p. 103). And as Coombs and Holladay (1996) noted, character is an imperfect measure for image. They indicated that it would be preferable to identify key image dimensions for evaluation by relevant publics. Finally, the factor structure of the ORS has not been reported, and additional studies validating the measure are needed.

Location*

Coombs, W. T., & Holladay, S. J. (1996). Communication and attributions in a crisis: An experimental study of crisis communication. *Journal of Public Relations Research, 8*, 279–295.

References

Coombs, W. T. (1995). Choosing the right words: The development of guidelines for the selection of the "appropriate" crisis response strategies. *Management Communication Quarterly, 8*, 447–476.

Coombs, W. T. (1998). An analytic framework for crisis situations: Better responses from a better understanding of the situation. *Journal of Public Relations Research, 10,* 177–191.

Coombs, W. T. (1999a). Information and compassion in crisis responses: A test of their effects. *Journal of Public Relations Research, 11,* 125–142.

Coombs, W. T. (1999b). *Ongoing crisis communication: Planning, managing, and responding.* Thousand Oaks, CA: Sage.

Coombs, W. T., & Holladay, S. J. (1996). Communication and attributions in a crisis: An experimental study of crisis communication. *Journal of Public Relations Research, 8,* 279–295.

Coombs, W. T., & Holladay, S. J. (2001). An extended examination of the crisis situation: A fusion of the relational management and symbolic approaches. *Journal of Public Relations Research, 13,* 321–340.

Coombs, W. T., & Holladay, S. J. (2002). Helping crisis managers protect reputational assets: Initial tests of the situational crisis communication theory. *Management Communication Quarterly, 16,* 165–186.

Coombs, W. T., & Holladay, S. J. (2004). Reasoned action in crisis communication: An attribution theory-based approach to crisis management. In D. P. Millar & R. L. Heath (Eds.), *Responding to crisis: A rhetorical approach to crisis communication* (pp. 95–115). Mahwah, NJ: Lawrence Erlbaum Associates.

Coombs, W. T., & Holladay, S. J. (2006). Unpacking the halo effect: Reputation and crisis management. *Journal of Communication Management, 10,* 123–137.

Coombs, W. T., & Schmidt, L. (2000). An empirical analysis of image restoration: Texaco's racism crisis. *Journal of Public Relations Research, 12,* 163–178.

Laufer, D., & Coombs, W. T. (2007). How should a company respond to a product harm crisis? The role of consumer reputation and consumer-based cues. *Business Horizons, 49,* 379–385.

McCroskey, J. C. (1966). *An introduction to rhetorical communication.* Englewood Cliffs, NJ: Prentice Hall.

Scale

Organizational Reputation Scale*

Instructions: Think about the case you have just read. The items below concern your impression of the organization and the crisis. Circle one number for each of the questions. The responses range from 1 = STRONGLY DISAGREE to 5 = STRONGLY AGREE.

STRONGLY DISAGREE 1 2 3 4 5 STRONGLY AGREE

1 The organization is basically honest.
2 The organization is concerned with the well-being of its publics.
3 I do trust the organization to tell the truth about the incident.
4 I would prefer to have NOTHING to do with this organization.
5 Under most circumstances, I WOULD NOT be likely to believe what the organization says.

6 The organization is basically DISHONEST.
7 I do NOT trust the organization to tell the truth about the incident.
8 Under most circumstances, I would be likely to believe what the organization says.
9 I would buy a product or service from this organization.
10 The organization is NOT concerned with the well-being of its publics.

*© 1996 by Taylor & Francis. Measure supplied by:
Dr. W. Timothy Coombs
Department of Communication Studies
CH 1814
Eastern Illinois University
600 Lincoln Avenue
Charleston, IL 61920
cfwtc@eiu.edu

Organizational Temporality (Temporal Experience) Scale

Profile by David R. Seibold

Within a longstanding tradition of theoretical and empirical interest in "time" in the social sciences, yet limited attention to it in communication, Ballard and Seibold (2000, 2003, 2004a, 2004b, 2006) have conceptualized time as a social construction rooted in communication, proposed a model of members' temporality in organizational workgroups, developed the Organizational Temporality Scale, and reported empirical associations between dimension of members' experiences of time and more than a half-dozen variables of interest to organizational communication scholars. Their work integrates time as shared experiences (intersubjective sense), personal conceptions of time (subjective sense), as well as institutionally driven, formal temporal parameters on members' work processes measured in clock time (objective sense).

The Organizational Temporality Scale also is referred to as the Temporal Experience Scale when utilized in non-traditional organizations and in non-formal collectives. The "group/unit" and "organization" referent was developed (and should be used) as part of the Organizational Temporality Scale to direct respondents' attention to shared temporal experiences among those with whom they work. However, for the large number of employed persons who do not have a work unit or group in which they are embedded (e.g., independent contractors, freelancers, and the like), eliminating group/unit/organization and simply referring to the measure as the *Temporal Experience Scale* has proven theoretically sound and empirically necessary.

To assess members' senses of time associated with their interactions in work environments, 393 respondents rated a series of 57 words and phrases in terms of how strongly they agreed or disagreed with them (Ballard & Seibold, 2004a). The stimuli were derived from descriptions of time, views of time, and time use found in a variety of popular and scholarly literatures. Consistent with a theoretical model reported by Ballard and Seibold (2003), confirmatory factor analytic procedures employing maximum likelihood estimation revealed eleven temporal dimensions reflecting two conceptual categories: *enactments of time (scheduling,*

linearity, pace, delay, flexibility, separation, and *punctuality*) and construals of time (*urgency, scarcity,* as well as *present* and *future time perspective*) (Ballard & Seibold, 2004a).

Temporal *enactments* are the ways in which work group and organizational members "perform" objective, subjective, and intersubjective time
(Ballard & Seibold, 2006). The tendency of members to multi-task, how
punctual they are in completing tasks, how flexible they are concerning
work plans and timing, how tightly scheduled their time is, how fast or
slow they work, and whether they separate themselves from distractions in
order to do their work are dimensions of the way time is enacted by organizational and workgroup members. Organizational units and their members create temporal norms for behavior through regularized patterns of
interaction. Their interactions and behaviors are both mediums and outcomes of their enactments of temporality along the following dimensions:
scheduling—the extent to which the sequencing and duration of plans,
activities, and events are formalized (Ballard & Seibold, 2000; Hall, 1983;
McGrath & Kelly, 1986; Yakura, 2002; Zerubavel, 1981); *linearity*—the
extent to which tasks are completed one at a time (Bluedorn, 2002; Graham, 1981); *pace*—tempo or rate of activity per unit period of time
(Levine, 1988; Okhuysen & Waller; 2002); *delay*—being behind in completing task (orthogonal with punctuality); *flexibility*—the degree of non-
rigidity in time structuring and task completion plans (Starkey, 1989);
separation—the extent to which extraneous factors are eliminated or
engaged in the completion of work (Perlow, 1997); and *punctuality*—the
exacting nature of timing and deadlines (Schriber & Gutek, 1987).

Temporal *construals* represent the way organizational and group members "interpret" or orient to time. Whether members see time as fleeting or
limited, and whether they are more focused on long-term plans or immediate concerns, characterize their experience of time. Specifically, construals include *urgency*—preoccupation with deadlines and task completion
(Perlow, Okhuysen, & Repenning, 2002; Waller, Conte, Gibson, &
Carpenter, 2001); *scarcity*—a focus on time as a limited and exhaustible
resource (Karau & Kelly, 1992; Perlow, 1999); and *present* as well as
future time perspective—orthogonal dimensions characterized by intentions oriented, respectively, toward immediate action or long-term planning (Jones, 1988; Lauer, 1981).

As Gomez (in press) noted, although there are other scales that measure
temporal perceptions, the Ballard and Seibold (2004) measure captures
temporal experience as inter-subjective—emerging from communication
among organizational members by focusing on how organizational members "talk about time" or how members "discuss events that happen at
work." Framing questions in this manner ensures that the items reflect
what organizational members talk about rather than what individual
organizational members perceive.

Reliability

In the development of the Organizational Temporality Scale (also called the Temporal Experience Scale), Ballard and Seibold (2004a) reported reliability coefficients in the .70 to .80 range for seven of the eleven subscales—considered strong for early research in an area (Nunnally, 1978). Reliabilities for two other subscales were .65 and .68, acceptable for a nascent measure. Two subscales (*separation* and *scheduling*) had coefficients just above .50—considered marginal but permissible when theoretically promising (Nunnally, 1978). Specifically, Cronbach alpha reliabilities for the individual subscales were as follows: *urgency* = .85, *scarcity* = .85, *flexibility* = .70, *separation* = .52, *pace* = .85, *punctuality* = .68, *delay* = .75, *scheduling* = .53, *linearity* = .65, *present time perspective* = .76, *future time perspective* = .87. In a subsequent investigation, Nunes, Seibold, and Metzger (2006) found that reliability for subscales in that study were as follows: *urgency* = .83, *flexibility* = .84, *pace* = .84, *scheduling* = .51, and *present time perspective* = .79. Items in the *scheduling* subscale thus continued to yield low levels of internal consistency, but other subscales yielded acceptable levels of reliability. However, the *scheduling* subscale proved to be reliable in other studies. In Ramgolam's (2007) study of virtual work practices and the experience of time with 477 members of a world-wide software corporation, (alpha) reliabilities for the dimensions were *urgency* = .79, *scarcity* = .78, *future time perspective* = .80, *present time perspective* = .82, *flexibility* = .79, *pace* = .82, *linearity* = .74, *delay* = .80, *punctuality* = .88, *separation* = .70, and–to the point here—*scheduling* = .74. While scheduling was not included, reliability analyses of responses to on-line survey responses to several of the subscales by 626 users of a social site on the Internet (Hyder, 2008) yielded alphas for *pace* = .88, *urgency* = .82, *present time perspective* = .78, *delay* = .89, and *punctuality* = .89. Finally, Gomez (in press) obtained the following levels of reliability for some of the subscales of the Organizational Temporality Scale in his study of temporality and socialization among 244 educational institution administrators: *scarcity* = .91, *pace* = .73, *flexibility* = .68, *scheduling* = .78, *present time focus* = .69; *future time focus* = .89. However, some of those reliabilities were achieved with changes to the Ballard and Seibold (2004a) measure, primarily by dropping items from the *pace*, *flexibility*, and *present time* subscales. These abridgements can be examined in Gomez (in press) and may prove useful in future research.

Validity

Ballard and Seibold (2004a) utilized confirmatory factor analysis to establish construct validity for the Organizational Temporality Scale. They first sought evidence of the convergent validity of the eleven dimensions of the

Organizational Temporality Scale by assessing whether the 49 items in the measurement model resulted from 11 distinct factors or if there was sufficient similarity across dimensions such that all 49 items measure the same thing. Results indicated that the 49 items result from 11 unique dimensions. Ramgolam's (2007) factor analysis of responses by 477 associates of a world-wide software corporation also found evidence for all eleven dimensions of the Organizational Temporality Scale (administered as the Temporal Experience Scale, given the freelance nature of the employment relationships many had as well as their virtual work arrangements).

Ballard and Seibold (2004a) also addressed the issue of divergent validity of the Organizational Temporality Scale. Divergent validity is established through differentiating between two theoretically distinct (though perhaps related) constructs. The researchers compared a scale that measures organizational members' satisfaction regarding the communication among departments (Interdepartmental Communication Satisfaction, ICS) with the 11 temporality subscales. ICS was chosen because of the focus in the literature on communication challenges among organizational members from departments with contrasting temporal experiences (Dubinskas, 1988; Zerubavel, 1981). The ICS measure was found to be related to, but distinct from, members' experience of time.

Comments

Even at this relatively early stage in the development of the Organizational Temporality Scale, the measure has been central to a number of reported findings. Analyses of data from five residential services departments in a West Coast University revealed that differences in coordination method, technology type, and feedback cycle characteristics helped to shape members' experience of nine dimensions of time—*flexibility, linearity, pace, punctuality, delay, scheduling, urgency,* and *future* and *present time perspectives* (Ballard & Seibold, 2004b). Members of work groups whose feedback cycles included an extended task completion interval and high task variability exhibited a greater *future time perspective* than group members whose feedback cycles were characterized by brief intervals and low task variability. Based on the same dataset, Ballard and Seibold (2006) found that organizational members who experienced their time as more *delayed,* more *flexible,* and more oriented toward the *future* tended to report higher levels of communication load. Additionally, members who characterized their work as more *punctual* and oriented toward the *future* were more satisfied with their jobs, while those who experienced work as faster *paced* were less satisfied. Finally, the organizational members most satisfied with communication among departments reported their work patterns as more *linear* and more strongly oriented toward the *future,* while members who reported their work as more *delayed* were least satisfied with such interdepartmental interactions. In a study by Nunes et al. (2006) involving 137 members of 13 California organizations and focused primarily on one dimension of workgroup members' temporality, as predicted temporal *pace* in the workplace was negatively related to communication satisfaction, work quality, and perceived organizational innovativeness. Part-time employees' construals of temporal pace were more varied than those of full-time employees (who reported higher levels of commitment to the organization), and part-time employees reported a more present temporal focus. Ramgolam (2007) found that a high degree of virtuality was highly correlated with the temporal dimension of *punctuality* among members of a large software corporation. Gomez (in press) reported a negative relationship between time *scarcity* and the structures that allow newcomers to predict their career path. Too, a *future temporal focus* was a significant predictor of formal structures that promote socialization of newcomers, structures that help newcomers predict their career path, and social support structures.

Nonetheless, much work remains. Recommendations for scale development and validation proposed by Judd, Jessor, and Donovan (1986) imply establishing additional types of validity for the Organizational Temporality Scale (Temporal Experience Scale), especially predictive and differential predictive validity, including through the use of longitudinal models.

Location*

Ballard, D. I., & Seibold, D. R. (2004a). Organizational members' communication and temporal experience: Scale development and validation. *Communication Research, 31*, 135–172.

References

Ballard, D. I. & Seibold, D. R. (2000). Time orientation and temporal variation across work groups: Implications for group and organizational communication. *Western Journal of Communication, 64*, 218–242.

Ballard, D. I., & Seibold, D. R. (2003). Communicating and organizing in time: A meso-level model of organizational temporality. *Management Communication Quarterly, 16*, 380–415.

Ballard, D. I., & Seibold, D. R. (2004a). Organizational members' communication and temporal experience: Scale development and validation. *Communication Research, 31*, 135–172.

Ballard, D. I., & Seibold, D. R. (2004b). Communication-related organizational structures and work group temporal experiences: The effects of coordination method, technology type, and feedback cycle on members' construals and enactments of time. *Communication Monographs, 71*, 1–27.

Ballard, D. I., & Seibold, D. R. (2006). The experience of time at work: Relationship to communication load, job satisfaction, and interdepartmental communication. *Communication Studies, 57*, 317–340.

Bluedorn, A. C. (2002). *The human organization of time: Temporal realities and experience.* Stanford, CA: Stanford Business Books.

Dubinskas, F. (1988). Janus organizations: Scientists and managers in genetic engineering firms. In F. Dubinskas (Ed.), *Making time: Ethnographies of high-technology organizations* (pp. 170–232). Philadelphia: Temple University Press.

Gómez, L. F. (in press). Time to socialize: Organizational socialization structures and temporality. *Journal of Business Communication.*

Graham, R. J. (1981). The role of perception of time in consumer research. *Journal of Consumer Research, 7,* 335–342.

Hall, E. T. (1983). *The dance of life.* New York: Doubleday.

Hyder, S. (2008). *Twitter and the experience of time.* Unpublished Masters Thesis, Department of Communication, University of Texas, Austin.

Jones, J. M. (1988). Cultural difference in temporal perspectives: Instrumental and expressive behaviors in time. In J. E. McGrath (Ed.), *The social psychology of time: New perspectives* (pp. 21–38). Newbury Park, CA: Sage.

Judd, C. M., Jessor, R., & Donovan, J. E. (1986). Structural equation models and personality research. *Journal of Personality, 54,* 149–198.

Karau, S. J., & Kelly, J. R. (1992). The effects of time scarcity and time abundance on group performance quality and interaction processes. *Journal of Experimental Social Psychology, 28,* 542–571.

Lauer, R. H. (1981). *Temporal man: The meaning and uses of social time.* New York: Praeger.

Levine, R. V. (1988). The pace of life across cultures. In J. E. McGrath (Ed.), *The social psychology of time: New perspectives* (pp. 39–60). Newbury Park, CA: Sage.

McGrath, J. E., & Kelly, J. R. (1986). *Time and human interaction: Toward a social psychology of time.* New York: Guilford.

Nunes, K., Seibold, D. R., & Metzger, M. J. (2006). *Racing against time: Communication and correlates of temporal pace in the workplace.* Unpublished manuscript. Department of Communication, University of California, Santa Barbara.

Nunnally, J. C. (1978). *Psychometric theory.* (2nd ed.) New York: McGraw-Hill.

Okhuysen, G. A., & Waller, M. J. (2002). Focusing on midpoint transitions: An analysis of boundary conditions. *Academy of Management Journal, 45,* 1056–1065.

Perlow, L. A. (1997). *Finding time: How corporations, individuals, and families can benefit from new work practices.* Ithaca, NY: Cornell University Press.

Perlow, L. A. (1999). The time famine: Toward a sociology of work time. *Administrative Science Quarterly, 44,* 57–81.

Perlow, L. A., Okhuysen, G. A., & Repenning, N. P. (2002). The speed trap: Exploring the relationship between decision making and temporal context. *Academy of Management Journal, 45,* 931–955.

Ramgolam, D. I. (2007). *Virtual work practices and the experience of time.* Unpublished Masters Thesis, Department of Communication, University of Texas, Austin.

Schriber, J. B., & Gutek, B. A. (1987). Some time dimensions of work: The measurement of an underlying dimension of organizational culture. *Journal of Applied Psychology, 72,* 642–650.

Starkey, K. (1989). Time and work: A psychological perspective. In P. Blyton, J. Hassard, S. Hill, & K. Starkey (Eds.), *Time, work, and organization* (pp. 57–78). New York: Routledge.

Waller, M. J, Conte, J. M, Gibson, C. B., & Carpenter, M. A. (2001). The effect of individual perceptions of deadlines on team performance. *Academy of Management Review, 26,* 586–600.

Yakura, E. K. (2002). Charting time: Timelines as temporal boundary objects. *Academy of Management Journal, 45,* 956–970.

Zerubavel, E. (1981). *Hidden rhythms: Schedules and calendars in social life.* Chicago: University of Chicago Press.

Scale

Organizational Temporality Scale*
(Temporal Experience Scale)
Instructions: Please think about the ways you typically refer to time in the course of carrying out your daily tasks at work. Read the statements below and then rate each of the words or phrases that follow based upon how well they describe the way you talk about time with others in your immediate work group or work unit on most days. The words/phrases are NOT meant to reflect your EXACT language, but the kinds of issues that come up in your communication. Please **circle the number** to the right of each word or phrase that best represents your answer.

I talk about *time* as…

		Strongly Disagree					Strongly Agree

URGENCY

1	pressing	1	2	3	4	5	6
2	an emergency	1	2	3	4	5	6
3	urgent	1	2	3	4	5	6
4	running out	1	2	3	4	5	6
5	"down to the wire"	1	2	3	4	5	6

SCARCITY

6	inadequate	1	2	3	4	5	6
7	scarce	1	2	3	4	5	6
8	not enough	1	2	3	4	5	6
9	*plentiful*	1	2	3	4	5	6
10	*abundant*	1	2	3	4	5	6
11	limited	1	2	3	4	5	6

I talk about *events that happen* in terms of ...

FUTURE TIME PERSPECTIVE

12	future developments	1	2	3	4	5	6
13	long-term plans	1	2	3	4	5	6
14	anticipated events	1	2	3	4	5	6
15	projected dates	1	2	3	4	5	6
16	long-term expectations	1	2	3	4	5	6
17	upcoming activities	1	2	3	4	5	6

PRESENT TIME PERSPECTIVE

18	what is 'pressing'	1	2	3	4	5	6
19	unfolding developments	1	2	3	4	5	6
20	immediate consequences	1	2	3	4	5	6
21	the here-and-now	1	2	3	4	5	6
22	presently developing issues	1	2	3	4	5	6
23	what is urgent today	1	2	3	4	5	6

I talk about *my actions or activities* as ...

		Strongly Disagree				Strongly Agree	

FLEXIBILITY

24	*set in stone*	1	2	3	4	5	6
25	*inflexible*	1	2	3	4	5	6
26	*fixed*	1	2	3	4	5	6
27	*rigid*	1	2	3	4	5	6

PACE

28	fast-paced	1	2	3	4	5	6
29	hurried	1	2	3	4	5	6
30	rapid	1	2	3	4	5	6
31	quick	1	2	3	4	5	6
32	racing	1	2	3	4	5	6

LINEARITY

33	carried out 'one thing at a time'	1	2	3	4	5	6
34	structured	1	2	3	4	5	6
35	having a specific order	1	2	3	4	5	6
36	carried out 'step-by-step'	1	2	3	4	5	6

DELAY

37	behind schedule	1	2	3	4	5	6
38	running late	1	2	3	4	5	6
39	delayed	1	2	3	4	5	6

PUNCTUALITY

40	punctual	1	2	3	4	5	6
41	prompt	1	2	3	4	5	6

SCHEDULING

42	*unplanned*	1	2	3	4	5	6
43	*unscheduled*	1	2	3	4	5	6
44	tightly scheduled	1	2	3	4	5	6

SEPARATION

45	divided up	1	2	3	4	5	6
46	in 'compartments'	1	2	3	4	5	6
47	interrupted	1	2	3	4	5	6
48	screening out distractions	1	2	3	4	5	6
49	separated from each other	1	2	3	4	5	6

Note: Italicized items should be reverse-coded. Subscale titles should be removed prior to administration.

* © by Sage Publications.

Organization-Public Relationship Scale

Profile by Elizabeth M. Perse

Kim (2001) joins others in arguing that the organization-public relationship is "a new paradigm of public relations" (p. 799). Jo and Kim (2003) explained that the relationship between an organization and its public is based on economic and humanistic factors. Economic factors include the ability of the organization to provide goods and services that satisfy the public. Humanistic factors deal with feelings that the public has for the organization, such as comfort and loyalty. Hon and Grunig (1999) explained that "a growing number of public relations practitioners and scholars have come to believe that the fundamental goal of public relations is to build and then enhance on-going or long-term relationship in an organization's key constituencies" (p. 2).

Researchers have begun to develop measures of that "humanistic" factor in organizational-public relationships. Kim (2001) built on earlier work by Grunig and Hon (1999) to develop a concise measure of the organizational-public relationship. Although some scholars argued that public relations is based on a coordination model, in which the perceptions of both the organization and the public are important to assess, Kim focused on assessing the perceptions of the public about their perceived relationship with the organization.

Kim's (2001) organization-public relationship scale contains 16 seven-point Likert-type items. It includes four subscales: trust, commitment, community involvement, and reputation. The subscales have been used independently in research. The scale has not been widely used. Kim (2001) reports scale development. Murdock (2003) used Kim's scale to look at the organization-public relationship for the National Tropical Botanical Garden. Jo and Kim (2003) used portions of the scale to assess the impact of web site interactivity on the organization-public relationship. The scale has been used reliably with college students, visitors to a botanical garden, community members recruited at shopping malls, and customers of an online company.

In developing the scale, Kim (2001) used literature from the fields of interpersonal communication, public relations, and relationship marketing to compile a list of 113 possible items to measure the organization-public relationship. Undergraduate students indicated how relevant each question was as they assessed a potential relationship with an insurance company in their community. Through this process, 57 items were dropped that participants considered irrelevant. At this point, seven more questions that focused upon the public's perceptions toward the organization were then added from the reputation measures in *Fortune*'s annual corporate reputation survey. These 63 items were tested then examined by three judges. Five items were rated irrelevant by at least one of the three judges and were subsequently dropped, leaving 58 items after two pilot tests.

Using data gathered from a student sample, an exploratory factor analysis was conducted to examine the scale's dimensionality. The initial principal component solution was rotated using varimax rotation. After factor analysis, Kim identified five distinct dimensions—commitment, reputation, community involvement, trust, and communal relationship—made of up 21 items that explained 66% of the variance. Items not loading on these five factors were eliminated from further analysis.

Next, a confirmatory factor analysis was used to verify the scale structure. This analysis resulted in the dropping of five variables with low squared multiple correlations (less than .40) and weak regression coefficients (critical value less than 2.99). The resulting 16 item scale was made up of four dimensions: trust (four items), commitment (five items), community involvement (three items), and reputation (four items).

Reliability

The internal consistency of each of the four dimensions of the organizational-public relationship was acceptable in the first administration (using a student sample) of the finalized scale, with Cronbach alphas of .78 for trust, .84 for commitment/satisfaction, .85 for local or community involvement, and .83 for reputation. When Kim (2001) administered the survey to a community sample, reliabilities were even higher, ranging from .82 to .98, and when administered to an online group, reliabilities ranged from .72 to .88. In Murdock's (2003) study, internal consistency ranged from .83 to .97. Jo and Kim (2003) reported Cronbach alphas in that same range.

No studies have looked at test-retest reliability for this measure to date. But, a public's perception of an organization could fluctuate over time as a result of public relations strategies and relevant events.

Validity

The scale has strong content validity because of its theoretical basis in interpersonal and public relations theory. The use of two stages of item analysis reinforces the content validity. Other evidence of validity is limited. Jo and Kim (2003) found that the scale was affected by prior relationships with companies, offering some evidence for concurrent validity.

Jo and Kim (2003) also found that website interactivity results in higher scale scores. Although future research should explore the explanations for that effect, communication research suggests that responsiveness is linked to communication involvement (e.g., Cegala, 1981). The finding offers some evidence of construct validity for the scale.

Comments

Though the measure at hand is in need of more testing, it is a promising scale. It is clear that Kim's (2001) instrument can be applied in a number of ways. Kim (2001) reported that the correlation coefficients between different subscales ranged from .47 to .62. Future research should explore the distinctiveness of the construct's dimensions. One practical application could involve the gathering of "consistent data measuring the bottom line impact of public relations," which could, in turn, be related to financial performance (Kim, 2001, p. 810). With the goal of developing more substantial theory of the organization-public relationship, Kim suggested that future research should also investigate potential causal relationships, such as the one that exists between the organization-public relationship and conflict resolution (p. 810). Additionally, Kim suggested that future studies should go beyond construct validity to look at criterion-related validity for this instrument, in terms of "image variables, conflict resolutions, and other predictive and outcome variables" (p. 810).

Location*

Kim, Y. (2001). Searching for the organization-public relationship: A valid and reliable instrument. *Journalism & Mass Communication Quarterly, 4*, 799–815.

References

Cegala, D. J. (1981). Interaction involvement: A cognitive dimension of communicative competence. *Communication Education, 30*, 109–121.

Hon, L., & Grunig, J. E. (1999). *Guidelines for measuring relationships in public relations.* Retrieved February 15, 2008 from http://www.instituteforpr.org/ipr_info/guidelines_measuring_relationships/

Jo, S., & Kim, Y. (2003). The effect of web characteristics on relationship building. *Journal of Public Relations Research, 15*, 199–223.

Murdock, J. M. P. (2003). An external communication audit of the national tropical botanical garden. Unpublished master's thesis, Brigham Young University.

Scale

Organization-Public Relationship Scale*
Questionnaire Instructions: This questionnaire asks your relationships with and perceptions of (the organization name). Remember that you do

not have to have a direct contact with (the organization) to answer these questions. Your perceptions of (the organization)'s relationship with the general public can be your answers, too. Thank you very much.

Trust

1 (The organization) treats people like me fairly and justly.
2 Whenever (the organization) makes an important decision, I know it will be concerned about people like me.
3 I believe that (the organization) takes the opinions of people like me into account when making decision.
4 Sound principles seem to guide (the organization)'s behavior.

Commitment

5 I can see that (the organization) wants to maintain a relationship with people like me.
6 There is a long-lasting bond between (the organization) and people like me.
7 Both (the organization) and people like me benefit from their relationship.
8 Generally speaking, I am pleased with the relationship (the organization) has established with people like me.
9 I feel people like me are important to (the organization).

Local or Community Involvement

10 (The organization) seems to be the kind of company that invests in the community.
11 I am aware that (the organization) is involved in my community.
12 I think (the organization) is very dynamic in maintaining good relationship *with the community.*

Reputation

13 (The organization) has the ability to attract, develop, and keep talented people.
14 (The organization) uses corporate visible and invisible assets very effectively.
15 (The organization) is financially sound enough to help others.
16 (The organization) is innovative in its corporate culture.

Note: Scale items should be randomly ordered and subscale titles removed prior to administration.

Patient Self-Advocacy Scale (PSAS)

Profile by Rebecca B. Rubin

Health communication literature stresses that patients should be more involved in their treatment and medical decisions by communicating with their physicians assertively, seeking useful information, and evaluating treatments based on their effectiveness. Brashers, Haas, and Neidig (1999) created a scale to measure three dimensions of patient self-advocacy—"(a) increased illness and treatment education, (b) increased assertiveness in health care interactions, and (c) increased potential for nonadherence" (p. 97)—that were originally identified by Brashers, Haas, Klingle, and Neidig (2000). This study was a participant observation, interview, and textual analysis study of AIDS activists in which the three themes emerged; scale items were piloted with 30 HIV patients.

The current scale is based on a participative model of physician-patient interaction in which patients are seen as consumers and advocates for their health treatment. Patients who know more about their illness, know how to ask questions and express their opinions, and reject treatments that don't work or are too risky are considered more involved and more likely to be "activists" for their state of health. This involvement increases a patient's power so as to balance the previously imbalanced or asymmetric patient-physician relationship. The 12-item scale contains four items for each of the three dimensions. A 5-point Likert format is used, ranging from *Strongly Agree* (1) to *Strongly Disagree* (5). Most respondents can complete the scale in one or two minutes.

Reliability

Two samples participated in the first test of the scale: (a) 174 HIV/AIDS patients, and (b) 218 college students, faculty, and their family and friends. Brashers et al. (1999) used principal components factor analysis with oblique rotation and uncovered two factors: Nonadherence and Education-Assertiveness. The original Nonadherence factor had a Cronbach alpha reliability of .82 for sample 1 and .70 for sample 2 (.79 overall), whereas the original Education and Assertiveness reliabilities ranged from .60 to .70. When combined, the Education-Assertiveness reliability was .76 and .78 for the two samples, respectively, and .79 when combined. The 12-item scale reliability was .78. The authors advocate use of the measure as a unidimensional scale, although the subscales might be useful in some research.

Validity

Brashers et al. (1999) also examined criterion, concurrent, and construct validity of the measure. The scale seemed to: (a) discriminate clearly between activist, nonactivist, and general population groups (criterion); and (b) correlate with Desire for Autonomy, external Locus of Control, and information seeking (concurrent). Correlations with Desire for Control and internal and chance Locus of Control were minimal. In addition, Brashers, Haas, Neidig, and Rintamaki (2002) used the PSAS as a back-up measure of activism. An overall scale alpha of .79 was reported. A known-groups technique was used and study participants who attended support groups, AIDS service organization volunteers, and those who had received services at AIDS organizations all had higher PSAS scores than those who did not; in addition, group attendance frequency was positively correlated with PSAS scores (construct).

Comments

Because of the close relationship between the subscales, this measure seems most useful as a one-dimensional scale. Future research with larger populations might help to clarify the dimension issue. Although age was not related to PSAS scores, education level and time since diagnosis were. No other demographic differences were reported. Because of the reference to the United States, the scale would have to be adapted for people of other nations.

Location*

Brashers, D. E., Haas, S. M., & Neidig, J. L. (1999). The Patient Self-Advocacy Scale: Measuring patient involvement in health care decision-making interactions. *Health Communication, 11*, 97–121.

References

Brashers, D. E., Haas, S. M., Neidig, J. L., & Rintamaki, L. S. (2002). Social activism, self-advocacy, and coping with HIV illness. *Journal of Social and Personal Relationships, 19*, 113–133.
Brashers, D. E., & Haas, S. M., Klingle, R. S., & Neidig, J. L. (2000). Collective

AIDS activism and individuals' perceived self-advocacy in physician-patient communication. *Human Communication Research, 26,* 372–402.

Scale

Patient Self-Advocacy Scale (PSAS)*
Instructions: The following questions ask about your feelings about your health care. For each of the following questions, please indicate your level of agreement with the statement by circling SA for Strongly Agree, A for Agree, N for Neutral, D for Disagree, and SD for Strongly Disagree.

Strongly Agree SA	Agree A	Neutral N	Disagree D	Strongly Disagree SD

 1 I believe it is important for persons with my illness to learn as much as they can about the disease and treatments.   SA A N D SD

 2 I actively seek out information on my illness.   SA A N D SD

 3 I am more educated about my illness than most US citizens.   SA A N D SD

 4 I have full knowledge of the problems with people with my illness.   SA A N D SD

 5 I keep notes about my illness and treatment.   SA A N D SD

 6 I research the latest treatments for my illness.   SA A N D SD

 7 I don't get what I need from my physician because I am not assertive enough. (R)   SA A N D SD

 8 I frequently make suggestions to my physician about my health care needs.   SA A N D SD

 9 I am more assertive about my health care needs than most US citizens.   SA A N D SD

10 If my physician prescribes something I don't understand, I ask questions about it.   SA A N D SD

11 I ask a lot of questions of my physician.   SA A N D SD

12 I frequently offer my physician suggestions about my care and treatment.   SA A N D SD

13 Sometimes there are good reasons not to follow the advice of a physician.   SA A N D SD

14 If I am given a treatment by my physician that I don't agree with, I am likely to not take it.   SA A N D SD

15 I don't always do what my physician or heath care worker has asked me to do.   SA A N D SD

16 Sometimes I think I have a better grasp of
    what I need medically than my
    physician does.   SA   A   N   D   SD
17 My physician works for me. I would find
    another physician if I was dissatisfied
    with my health care.   SA   A   N   D   SD
18 I make my own decisions about what
    treatments I will or will not take, even if
    my physician prescribes it.   SA   A   N   D   SD

Note: Items 1–6 are Information Seeking, 7–12 are Assertiveness, and 13–18 are Mindful Noncompliance. Item 7 is reverse scored (R).

*© 1999 by Taylor & Francis.

Perceived Message Sensation Value (PMSV) Scale

Profile by Rebecca B. Rubin

Research has found that people who prefer risky messages (i.e., unconventional, novel, intense, arousing, dramatic) also engage in risky behavior. Donohew, Palmgreen, and Duncan's (1980) activation model, based on Zuckerman's (1969) sensation-seeking theory, suggests that high sensation seekers remember and respond to messages with high sensation value; a measure of message sensation value, therefore, is useful for research involving drug abuse or other risky behavior. The PMSV extended Everett and Palmgreen's (1995) and Stephenson and Palmgreen's (2001) scale work, which helped establish construct validity.

This scale was created in two studies (Palmgreen, Stephenson, Everett, Baseheart, & Francies, 2002). In the first, 368 high school students rated televised anti-marijuana PSAs (Stephenson, 1999; Stephenson & Palmgreen, 2001), and in the second, 444 college students rated televised anti-cocaine PSAs. The high school students rated the PSAs using 17 bi-polar adjective items with Likert-type responses. Reliability was .87 across the six PSAs viewed. Scores averaged below the midpoint of the scale. In the second study, the college students viewed four PSAs and the coefficient alpha was .93. The second study explored similar research questions, but the main goal was to examine the dimensions of the scale. Using exploratory factor analysis separately for each group, a three-factor solution (Emotional Arousal, Dramatic Impact, Novelty) emerged, and the factors were moderately correlated. Confirmatory factor analysis of the data indicated a good fit of the data with a three-factor model. Coefficient alphas ranged from .85 to .89. Pearson correlations were examined between the PMSV factors and dimensions of affect, and these provided evidence of construct validity.

The scale contains 17 bi-polar adjectives with a 7-point semantic differential style response format. Subscales are calculated for three main factors: emotional arousal, dramatic impact, and novelty. Items are summed and averaged. It takes only a few minutes for completion.

Reliability

Stephenson (2003) reported coefficient alphas across several PSA of .84. In addition, he found that subscales were intercorrelated. For high sensation seekers, the correlations ranged from .42 to .79, and for low sensation seekers, the subscales correlated at .36 to .74.

Validity

Several studies have examined qualities of the individuals viewing the PSAs. Lang et al. (2005) suggested that age and sensation-seeking make a difference for those producing PSA in that younger and higher sensation seekers need more arousing content and faster pacing. Stephenson (2003) also found that the PMSV influenced high and low sensation seekers differently. Also, Niederdeppe (2005) found that older teens reacted to more frequent cuts and suspenseful features.

Comments

The scale can be used to measure either the dimensions of message sensation or summed to measure overall sensation. Research has shown that it can be used for high school students and older. However people of other cultures may have different meanings for the adjectives used. Translation would require additional testing. In addition, because of some inconclusive evidence with the confirmatory factor analysis, users of the scale might want to replicate this work when using scale dimensions.

Location*

Palmgreen, P., Stephenson, M. T., Everett, M. W., Baseheart, J. R., & Francies, R. (2002). Perceived message sensation value (PMSV) and the dimensions and validation of a PMSV scale. *Health Communication, 14,* 403–428.

References

Donohew, L., Palmgreen, P., & Duncan, J. (1980). An activation model of information exposure. *Communication Monographs, 47,* 295–303.

Everett, M. W., & Palmgreen, P. (1995). Influences of sensation seeking, message sensation value, and program context on effectiveness of anticocaine public service announcements. *Health Communication, 7,* 225–248.

Lang, A., Chung, Y., Lee, S., Schwartz, N., & Shin, M. (2005). It's an arousing, fast-paced kind of world: The effects of age and sensation seeking on the information processing substance-abuse PSAs. *Media Psychology, 7,* 421–454.

Niederdeppe, J. D. (2005). Syntactic indeterminacy, perceived message sensation value-enhancing features, and message processing in the context of anti-tobacco advertisements. *Communication Monographs, 72,* 324–344.

Stephenson, M. T. (1999). *Message sensation value and sensation seeking as determinants of message processing.* Unpublished doctoral dissertation, University of Kentucky, Lexington.

Stephenson, M. T. (2003). Examining adolescents' responses to anti-marijuana PSAs. *Human Communication Research, 29,* 343–369.

Stephenson, M. T., & Palmgreen, P. (2001). Sensation seeking, perceived message value, personal involvement, and processing of anti-marijuana PSAs. *Communication Monographs, 68,* 49–71.

Zuckerman, M. (1969). Theoretical formulations. In J. P. Zubeck (Ed.), *Sensory deprivation: Fifteen years of research* (pp. 407–432). New York: Appleton-Century-Crofts.

Scale

Perceived Message Sensation Value (PMSV) Scale*

Instructions: We would like you to rate the PSA (ad, message) you just saw on the following scales. For example, on the first pair of adjectives if you thought the ad was very *unique* give a "1." If you thought it was very *common*, give it a "7." If you thought it was somewhere in between, give it a 2, 3, 4, 5, or 6.

1	Unique	1	2	3	4	5	6	7	Common (R)
2	Powerful impact	1	2	3	4	5	6	7	Weak impact (R)
3	Didn't give me goose bumps	1	2	3	4	5	6	7	Gave me goose bumps
4	Novel	1	2	3	4	5	6	7	Ordinary (R)
5	Emotional	1	2	3	4	5	6	7	Unemotional (R)
6	Boring	1	2	3	4	5	6	7	Exciting
7	Strong visuals	1	2	3	4	5	6	7	Weak visuals (R)
8	Not creative	1	2	3	4	5	6	7	Creative
9	Not graphic	1	2	3	4	5	6	7	Graphic
10	Arousing	1	2	3	4	5	6	7	Not arousing (R)
11	Unusual	1	2	3	4	5	6	7	Usual (R)
12	Involving	1	2	3	4	5	6	7	Uninvolving (R)
13	Not intense	1	2	3	4	5	6	7	Intense
14	Weak sound track	1	2	3	4	5	6	7	Strong sound track
15	Undramatic	1	2	3	4	5	6	7	Dramatic
16	Stimulating	1	2	3	4	5	6	7	Not Stimulating (R)
17	Strong sound effects	1	2	3	4	5	6	7	Weak sound effects (R)

Note: (R) Reverse coding. Emotional Arousal Items: 2, 5, 6, 7, 10, 12, 16, 17; Dramatic Impact items: 3, 8, 9, 13, 14, 15; Novelty items: 1, 4, 11.

Perceived Power Measure (PPM)

Profile by Rebecca B. Rubin

K. David Roach developed a measure of how frequently instructors use power strategies in the classroom to motivate or encourage students to learn or behave in other positive ways in the classroom. The theoretical foundation for the measure was originally developed by French and Raven (1959) who identified five power base dimensions: expert, referential, reward, coercive, and legitimate. Expert power is a perception that the other person has expertise or knowledge that would justify compliance. Referential power seeks compliance through identification with the other or a desire to please the other. Reward power is based on a perception that the other can provide a reward or incentive to reinforce the behavioral compliance. Coercive power refers to perceptions that punishment will result if they do not comply with power figure's request. And legitimate power is based on a perception that the other has justifiable or rightful power in this situation. Roach (1995) created four items to tap each of these five dimensions and gathered data from almost 1,000 college students about their perceptions of their teaching assistant's (TA) use of power in the college classroom.

The "power in the classroom" line of research focused mainly on how students' perception of their instructor's power and compliance gaining were related to student learning, motivation, and liking. Certain behavior alteration techniques and messages have been connected to student affect towards the instructor and affective learning (Kearney, Plax, Richmond, & McCroskey, 1985; McCroskey & Richmond, 1983). For a summary of this research, see Golish and Olson (2000, pp. 295–296).

Roach (1995) examined similar constructs, using this new measure. Coercive power, with a mean of 3.70 (SD = –3.44), was perceived as the least used. Next was Referent Power with a mean of 5.01 (SD = 3.80), Reward power (M = 7.37, SD = 4.06), Legitimate Power (M = 7.64, SD = 4.15), and Expert power (M= 8.62, SD = 3.94). As hypothesized, levels of reward, legitimate, referent, and expert power differed for TAs perceived as high and low argumentative, but perceptions of high/low argumentatives didn't differ significantly for coercive power. Golish and

Olson (2000) found similar results for the overall use of power in the classroom.

Reliability

Roach (1995) reported an overall alpha of .90 for the PPM. Later, Roach, Cornett-DeVito, and DeVito (2005) explored cultural differences between French and American instructors. The coefficient alpha for the scale was .92 for American students and .70 for French students.

Golish (1999) examined the reliability of four versions of the PPM and found acceptable alpha levels for students' perceptions of (a) their own power with their TA (.89), (b) their own power with their professor (.76), (c) their TA's power (.85), and (d) their professor's power (.90). The subscale dimensions ranged from .66 to .90. In another study, subscale reliabilities for students (identifying their own power in the classroom) ranged from .71 to .75 and perceptions of instructor power subscale alphas ranged from .70 to .76 (Golish & Olson, 2000). In this latter study, alphas for the overall scales were .81 for students and .83 for instructors.

Validity

In the Roach et al. (2005) American sample, use of coercive power was inversely related to student affective learning, affect towards instructor, and ratings of instruction, as expected. Reward and Referent power were positively related to affective learning, as was Expert power, which was also related to cognitive learning, affect towards the Instructor and ratings of instruction. In the French sample, coercive and expert power were positively related to cognitive learning, while referent power was positively related to affective learning. Reward power was positively related to greater affect toward the instructor, and referent and expert power were related to higher student ratings of instruction. Golish and Olson (2000) found that students' perceptions of their own power were modestly (.43) and significantly related to perceptions of their instructors' power. In addition, students have reported greater feelings of self-power with their TAs than with their professors (Golish, 1999) and that their professors had greater coercive, legitimate, and expert power than do their TAs.

Schrodt, Witt, and Turman (2007; see also Turman & Schrodt, 2006) conducted three studies designed to examine the construct validity of the PBM. Confirmatory factory analysis supported item loadings for the original measure, however aggregate scores didn't represent the construct of teacher power when the model was tested. They advocate using their new scale—Teacher Power Use Scale—instead.

Comment

This measure provides an alternative to behavior alternation techniques and behavior alteration message scales developed by Kearney et al. (1994). It was developed with and for college students, but could be adapted for teachers of all levels with some simplification of language.

Location*

Roach, K. D. (1995). Teaching assistant argumentativeness: Effects on affective learning and student perceptions of power use. *Communication Education, 44,* 15–29.

References

French, J. R. P., & Raven, B. (1959). The bases for social power. In D. Cartwright (Ed.), *Studies in social power* (pp. 150–167). Ann Arbor, MI: Institute for Social Research.

Golish, T. D. (1999). Students' use of compliance gaining strategies with graduate teaching assistants: Examining the other end of the power spectrum. *Communication Quarterly, 47,* 12–32.

Golish, T. D., & Olson, L. N. (2000). Students' use of power in the classroom: An investigation of student power, teacher power, and teacher immediacy. *Communication Quarterly, 48,* 293–310.

Kearney, P., Plax, T. G., Richmond, V. P., & McCroskey, J. C. (1985). Power in the classroom III: Teacher communication techniques and messages. *Communication Education, 34,* 19–28.

McCroskey, J. C., & Richmond, V. P. (1983). Power in the classroom I: Teacher and student perceptions. *Communication Education, 32,* 175–184.

Roach, K. D., Cornett-DeVito, M., & DeVito, R. (2005). A cross-cultural comparison of instructor communication in American and French classrooms. *Communication Quarterly, 53,* 87–107.

Schrodt, P., Witt, P. L., & Turman, P. D. (2007). Reconsidering the measurement of teacher power use in the college classroom. *Communication Education, 56,* 308–332.

Turman, P. D., & Schrodt, P. (2006). Student perceptions of teacher power as a function of perceived teacher confirmation. *Communication Education, 55,* 265–279.

Scale

Perceived Power Measure*

Instructions: At times, your instructor will communicate to try to influence you to do something (e.g., giving directions, assignments, stopping inappropriate classroom behaviors, etc.). Indicate on the following scale the frequency with which this instructor uses the following communication strategies/impressions to get you to do something:

0 = Never   1 = Rarely   2 = Occasionally   3 = Often   4 = Very Often

1 The student will be punished if he/she does not comply with instructor requests.
2 The student should comply out of his/her friendship relationship with the instructor.
3 The student must comply because it is required by the instructor.
4 The student should comply because the instructor has great wisdom/knowledge behind the request.
5 The student will receive some kind of tangible or intangible reward for complying with instructor requests.
6 The instructor will ensure that something bad will happen to the student if he/she does not comply.
7 The student should comply so he/she can imitate beneficial instructor characteristics.
8 The student must comply because it is required by the department.
9 The instructor is only seeking compliance because he/she knows it is in the student's best interest.
10 The instructor will see to it that the student acquires some desirable benefit if he/she does what is suggested.
11 The student will experience negative consequences for noncompliance with instructor requests.
12 The student should comply to please the instructor.
13 The student must comply because it is a university rule or expectation.
14 The instructor is seeking compliance from the student based on the instructor's experience in this area.
15 The student will gain, short-term or long-term, from compliance with instructor requests.
16 There will be a corrective discipline for noncompliance with instructor requests.
17 The student should comply so he/she can model or be like the instructor.
18 The student must comply because the instructor has the authority/right to direct students in this context.
19 The student should comply because the instructor has much training/skill/mastery in this area.
20 If the student complies with instructor requests, he/she will receive some type of compensation or prize.

Note: Coercive items are 1, 6, 11, and 16. Referent items are 2, 7, 12, and 17; Legitimate items are 3, 8, 13, and 18; Expert items are 4, 9, 14, and 19; Reward items are 5, 10, 15, and 20.

Perceived Teacher Confirmation Scale

Profile by Rebecca B. Rubin

Teacher confirmation is "the process by which teachers communicate to students that they are valuable, significant individuals" (Ellis, 2000, p. 265). Research that examines confirmation is based on the tenet that students need to perceive that they are accepted by teachers and need to have their ideas and behaviors reinforced.

Kathleen Ellis (2000) developed the items for the scale by conducting two studies. In the first, she conducted telephone interviews and focus groups with undergraduate students. In these, students identified behaviors that indicated confirmation, and the 40 most-often mentioned behaviors were included in the initial scale. A group of 446 undergraduate students then thought of the professor of the class they had just prior to the research session and completed the scale using Likert-type responses. Confirmatory factor analysis, redundancy analysis, and factor loadings helped reduce the 40 items to 27. A four-factor solution was confirmed. The factors and coefficient alpha reliabilities were: Teachers' response to students' questions/comments (.86), demonstrated interest in the student (.85), teaching style (.85), and absence of disconfirmation (.92). The alpha for the entire 27-item scale was .95.

In a second study (Ellis, 2000), the fourth factor failed to emerge and it was dropped from the scale. This resulted in a 3-factor, 16-item scale with an overall alpha of .93 and .84 alpha for Teacher's response, .85 alpha for interest, and .83 for teaching style. Concurrent validity was established with a reported correlation of .71 with nonverbal teacher immediacy and a .80 correlation with the Teacher Caring Scale. Ellis also found that between 50% and 64% of the variance was shared with these two scales, indicating discriminant validity as well. Ellis also reported significant correlations with affective and cognitive learning.

In a later series of studies, Ellis (2004) secured responses from 295 undergraduates, using similar procedures (i.e., thinking of a professor of a class prior to the session), and again found high reliability (.95) for the scale and a one-factor solution (using exploratory factor analysis). Results indicated that over 60% of the variance between perceived teacher confirmation and perceived confirmation was shared. Study 2 examined 358 undergraduates and the relationship between teacher confirmation and receiver apprehension, state motivation, and affective and cognitive learning. As hypothesized, over 50% of the variance in receiver apprehension was accounted for by perceived teacher confirmation. In addition, test of a path model indicated indirect effects of confirmation on motivation and learning was mediated by receiver apprehension.

As a result of these two studies, it appears that the scale—although containing three to four aspects of teacher confirmation—could and should be considered unidimensional. Students can respond to the 27 items in about 5 minutes. A Likert-type format makes it relatively easy to administer.

Reliability

Coefficient alphas from the initial development studies are promising. Alphas for the 27-item scale have been consistently at .95 (Ellis, 2000, 2004). The 16-item version alpha was .93. Turman and Schrodt (2006) reported subscale alphas of .86 to .87 for the 16-item scale. Test-retest reliability research is needed to assess stability.

Validity

The reports on the development of this scale, outlined above, indicate good face, content, and concurrent validity. Predictive validity studies are limited to perceived learning (rather than actual learning) and construct validity evidence is growing. The fact that the effects are mediated by receiver apprehension might indicate other factors affecting students' perceptions. In addition, Ellis (2004) found that the PTC scale was strongly related to students' feelings of being confirmed or disconfirmed, evidence that the perceptions evoke similar feelings in students.

Comments

In addition to test-retest reliability, construct validity research is needed for this measure. Perhaps coding actual teacher behaviors and comparing with this other-perception scale would provide strong confirmation for the scale (Daly, 2000). The unstable factor structure indicates that some items might be related for some populations, but not for all. The instrument, however, has good content validity and seems to encompass all facets of the construct. Additional considerations and directions for future research might examine factors such as age, time, culture, and need for approval as factors that might influence students' perceptions. Because some students need continuous or extra approval from teachers, they may be tougher in their appraisals than others. Demographic (Daly, 2000) and psychological features always influence appraisals of self and others and, in this case, need for approval might mediate perceptions of how attentive and confirming the teacher appears to be. Averaging multiple perceptions (e.g., an entire class) should provide a good profile of a specific teacher.

Location*

Ellis, K. (2000). Perceived teacher confirmation: The development and validation of an instrument and two studies of the relationship to cognitive and affective learning. *Human Communication Research, 26,* 264–291.

References

Daly, J. A. (2000). Colloquy: Getting older and getting better. Challenges for communication research. *Human Communication Research, 26,* 331–338.

Ellis, K. (2004). The impact of perceived teacher confirmation on receiver apprehension, motivation, and learning. *Communication Education, 53,* 1–20.

Turman, P. D., & Schrodt, P. (2006). Student perceptions of teacher power as a function of perceived teacher confirmation. *Communication Education, 55,* 265–279.

Scale

Teacher Confirmation Scale (TCS)*

Instructions: Below are statements that describe behaviors that teachers may or may not exhibit. Please respond to the questions in terms of *the teacher of the class you attend immediately before the class in which you are answering these questions.*

Please indicate your level of agreement with the following statements:

STRONGLY DISAGREE	DISAGREE	UNDECIDED	AGREE	STRONGLY AGREE
0	1	2	3	4

1 Communicates that he or she is interested in whether students are learning.
2 Indicates that he or she appreciates students' questions or comments.
3 Makes an effort to get to know students.
4 Belittles or puts students down when they participate during class. (R)
5 Checks on students' understanding before going on to the next point.
6 Gives oral or written praise on students' work.
7 Establishes eye contact during class lectures.
8 Talks down to students. (R)
9 Is rude in responding to some students' comments or questions during class. (R)

10 Uses an interactive teaching style.
11 Listens attentively when students ask questions or make comments during class.
12 Displays arrogant behavior (e.g., tries to look "smart" in front of the students or communicates a "big me, little you" attitude. (R)
13 Takes time to answer students' questions fully.
14 Embarrasses students in front of the class. (R)
15 Communicates that he or she doesn't have time to meet with students. (R)
16 Intimidates students. (R)
17 Shows favoritism to certain students. (R)
18 Puts students down when they go to the teacher for help outside of class.
19 Smiles at the class.
20 Communicates that he or she believes that students can do well in the class.
21 Is available for questions before and after class.
22 Is unwilling to listen to students who disagree (closed-minded). (R)
23 Uses a variety of teaching techniques to help students understand course material.
24 Asks students how they think the class is going and/or how assignments are coming along.
25 Incorporates exercises into lectures when appropriate.
26 Is willing to deviate slightly from the lecture when students ask questions.
27 Focuses on only a few students during class while ignoring others. (R)

   (R) Item reversed for scoring.

Note: The TCS measures four dimensions of teacher confirmation:

a   Teacher's responses to students' questions or comments: Items 2, 11, 13, 21, 26
b   Demonstrated interest in students and in their learning: Items 1, 3, 7, 19, 20, 24
c   Teaching style: Items 5, 6, 10, 23, 25
d   Absence of disconfirmation: Items 4, 8, 9, 12, 14, 15, 16, 17, 18, 22, 27

Perceptions of Television Reality

Profile by Elizabeth M. Perse

Perceived realism has played an important role in media effects studies and in designing television literacy curricula. In these approaches, perceived realism is not an attribute of media content, but a perception about content that varies across people (Potter, 1988a). Perceived realism is important because it reflects how critical people are when they watch television and thus is a moderator of media effects. Perceived realism, however, has not been treated identically by researchers (Busselle & Greenberg, 2000). Some studies use measures that assume that realism is unidimensional (e.g., Greenberg, 1974; Rubin, 1981, see the measure profiled in Volume 1 of this series). Hawkins (1977) and Potter (1986), however, developed scales to measure perceived realism as a multidimensional construct.

Hawkins (1977) hypothesized that perceived realism had two dimensions. Magic Window assesses whether television accurately represents real life. Social Expectations marks how well television fits the way people expect the world to be. Hawkins also expected television realism to vary according to level of specificity: television in general, program type, or specific program. He developed 30 scale items, one statement to represent perceived realism of people and events for each dimension at each level of specificity. Pretests revealed that 30 items were too many for younger children. Thus, 20 5-point Likert-type scales were administered to a range of children from 6th grade to nursery school age.

Factor analysis with varimax rotation identified four factors accounting for 52% of the variance that partially supported the hypothesized dimensions. The two most substantial factors were Magic Window about people and a Social Expectations factor. The other two factors, accounting for only 17% of the total variance, were extensions of Magic Window and Social Expectations, at different levels of specificity (families vs. police). Hawkins concluded that perceived realism could be measured along two dimensions by collapsing levels of specificity.

Potter (1986) extended Hawkins' work on perceived realism and identified three dimensions of the concept. Magic Window, as in Hawkins' conceptualization, is "the degree to which a viewer believes television content is an unaltered, accurate representation of actual life" (p. 162). Identity, an elaboration of Hawkins' social expectations dimension, is "the degree of similarity the viewer perceives between television characters and situations and the people and situations experienced in real life" (p. 163). Instruction is "beliefs about television as an instructional aid" (p. 162). Potter (1986) developed a 20-item Likert scale to assess these three dimensions.

Potter's (1986) 20-item scale is reported here. Like Hawkins', it conceptualizes perceived realism specifically—at the program and character level. Although the scale items here reference specific television programs and characters, it can be modified to reference other programs and characters, or to reference programming and characters in general (Potter, 1992).

Potter (1986) used 5-point Likert responses from *strongly agree* (1) to *strongly disagree* (5). In his research on perceived realism, Hawkins (1977) suggested that younger children have the items read to them. For younger children, Hawkins trained respondents to use pictorial response categories. Children marked circles that ranged in size, representing how true they thought statements were.

Reliability

Potter (1986, 1988b, 1992) indicates that all three dimensions of his scale are reliable: Magic Window (alphas range from .68 to .77), Instruction (alphas range from .75 to .82), and Identity (alphas range from .77 to .83). His 1986 factor analysis accounted for 70.4% of the variance and replicated the three-dimensional structure. Potter's scale has been used reliably with public school high school students, students enrolled in a developmental research school (grades 8 through 12), and college students.

Writers have noted the perceived realism is responsive to age and media literacy instruction (Busselle & Greenberg, 2000). Test-retest measures support the notion that perceived realism is not stable. Potter (1992) found that respondents' scores on the three dimensions were related only weakly over 2 year time periods for his sample of high school students (r ranges from .04 to .51).

Validity

Content validity from Potter's three-dimensional scale is shown in the conceptual similarity between his Magic Window dimension and that of Hawkins (1977). There is evidence of construct validity for the three subscales. Potter (1992) found that, in general, perceived realism on all dimensions decreased as adolescents grew older. Magic Window scores were negatively linked to parents' educational level; Identity scores were negatively related to child's IQ scores. These relationships reflect adolescents' growing media literacy skills.

Potter's (1986) research provides additional evidence of construct valid-ity. Beliefs in the realism of television content should be linked to greater effects of that content. He found that his dimensions of perceived realism were related to cultivation effects: "people who exhibit stronger beliefs of a mean and violent world are those people who are more likely to say that television is a magic window, that they seek instruction from television, and that the identify with the characters" (Potter, 1986, p. 168). Busselle (2001) offered the theoretical explanation for the relationship between perceived realism and cultivation: Television content that is perceived as real is processed differently from fictional content; it is encoded more eas-ily into cognitive knowledge structures and more easily accessed.

Comments

There appears to be conceptual similarity between the Magic Window dimension and Greenberg's (1974) unidimensional scale. There is, how-ever, evidence for the multidimensional structure of the concept. Although Potter used oblique rotation in developing his scale, the three dimensions are not highly correlated.

The specificity of the perceived realism items reported in Potter's (1986) scale require that items be updated and modified to make them relevant to the sample. The several scale items that access specific program knowledge should be reappraised or reworded in future research. Busselle and Greenberg (2000), however, pointed out that research has found that lev-els of perceived realism differ by levels of specificity; more specific scales generating more realism than general scale. They suggested that these dif-ferences and their causes be explored in future research. For those researchers interested in a more general scale, Rubin (1981, profiled in Volume 1 of the series) created a unidimensional scale and Potter (1992) has created a more generally worded version of his multidimensional scale.

Location

Potter, W. J. (1986). Perceived reality and the cultivation hypothesis. *Journal of Broadcasting & Electronic Media, 30*, 159–174.

References

Brusselle, R. W. (2001). Television exposure, perceived realism, and exemplar accessibility in the social judgment process. *Media Psychology, 3*, 43–67.

Busselle, R. W., & Greenberg, B. S. (2000). The nature of television realism judg-ments: A reevaluation of their conceptualization and measurement. *Mass Communication & Society, 3*, 249–268.

Greenberg, B. S. (1974). Gratifications of television viewing and their correlates for British children. In J. G. Blumler, & E., Katz (Eds.), *The uses of mass communications: Current perspectives on gratifications research* (pp. 71–92). Beverly Hills: Sage.

Hawkins, R. P. (1977). The dimensional structure of children's perceptions of television reality. *Communication Research, 4,* 299–320.

Potter, W. J. (1988a). Perceived reality in television effects research. *Journal of Broadcasting & Electronic Media, 32,* 23–41.

Potter, W. J. (1988b). Three strategies for elaborating the cultivation hypothesis. *Journalism Quarterly, 65,* 930–939.

Potter, W. J. (1992). How do adolescents' perceptions of television reality change over time? *Journalism Quarterly, 69,* 392–405.

Rubin, A. M. (1981). An examination of television viewing motives. *Communication Research, 8,* 141–165.

Scale

Perceptions of Television Reality Scale*

Instructions: Please read each statement about TV use and indicate whether you strongly agree (5), agree (4), agree some and disagree some (3), disagree (2), or strongly disagree (1) with each.

Magic Window

1   The people I see playing parts on TV are just like their characters when they are off camera in real life.

2   The people who act in TV shows about families probably behave the same way in their real lives.

3   The people who are funny as characters on comedy shows are probably very funny in their real lives.

4   John Ritter who plays Jack on *Three's Company* probably acts in real life the way Jack does on the TV show.

5   The things that happen to John Ritter in real life are probably the same as the things that happen to his character (Jack) on TV.

6   The things that happen to Alan Alda in real life are probably the same as the things that happen to his character (Hawkeye) on $M*A*S*H$.

7   Alan Alda who plays Hawkeye on $M*A*S*H$ probably acts in real life the same as Hawkeye does on the TV show.

Instruction

1   I feel I can learn a lot about people from watching TV.

2   I get useful ideas about how I should act around my friends and family by watching characters on situation comedies.

3   By watching TV I feel I can learn about life's problems and situations.

4   The characters I see on situation comedies help give me ideas about how to solve my own problems.

5   I feel I can learn a lot about people by watching the father on *Eight Is Enough*.

6   I feel I can learn a lot about people by watching Jack on *Three's Company*.

Identity

1   There are certain characters on TV shows that I admire.

2   There are a few characters in TV shows that I would like to be more like.

3   I know someone in real life like J. R. Ewing on *Dallas*.

4   I know someone in real life like the father on *Eight Is Enough*.

5   On *Little House on the Prairie* the father is like someone I know in my life.

6   On the TV show *Three's Company*, Jack acts like someone I know in my life.

Note: Scale items need to be updated to include references to characters and shows that are currently the most popular and identifiable among respondents. The structure of the question should remain the same, with only updated program titles and character names substituted.

Personal Report of Marital Virtues Scale (PV)

Profile by Elizabeth E. Graham

In an effort to understand marital quality better, Bill Strom (2003) developed a measure of personal virtues. *Virtue* is defined as "being and doing good" whereas *vice* represents the opposite, the act of "being and doing ill." Virtue (and vice) are evidenced in behaviors, emotions, willful acts, and intentional rational decisions. From a review of the marital communication literature, Strom identified five personal virtues that have been identified as contributing to quality marriages: self-control (in control of one's impulses), wisdom (ability to know and do the right thing), humility (ability to self-assess), industry (mature work ethic), and faithfulness (committed and true).

Strom (2003) generated scale items from the conceptualization of virtue and vice proffered by Holmes (1991). After a series of analyses, the resulting measure is comprised of 21 items representing the five subscales mentioned above and uses a 7-point semantic differential response option. There are two versions of the scale: a personal virtue (PV) version and a perceived spousal virtue (PSV) version. The author suggests that marital partners complete both versions of the measure (i.e., PV and PSV) to be consistent with current relationship research that is encouraging study of self and other.

Reliability

Cronbach alphas for the subscales are as follows: self-control = .71; humility = .69; wisdom = .76; faithfulness = .80; and industry = .79. No data were provided for the reliability of the total measure.

Validity

Strom (2003) established initial support for the convergent validity of the Personal Report of Marital Virtues Scale by positively correlating it with McCroskey and Teven's (1999) measure of source credibility (a construct thought to be conceptually similar to virtue). In addition, evidence of concurrent validity was suggested by the strong positive correlation between the marital virtues scale and believability (a subscale of McCroskey and Teven's source credibility measure). Construct validity was assessed by posing theoretically sound hypotheses between personal virtues and other related constructs. For example, Strom reported a positive correlation between spouses' perceptions of one another's virtue and marriage quality (i.e., satisfaction) for both husbands and wives, reasoning that "gracious perceptions of each other appear to beget positive assessments of their shared marriage relationship" (Strom, 2003, p. 35). Furthermore, women, more often than men, rated their marriage quality as high when their husband would self-assess as virtuous, particularly in regard to his self-reported faithfulness. And the more faithful husbands reported to be, the more wives reported that their husbands shared emotionally.

Comments

Although the Personal Report of Marital Virtues Scale (PV) is quite new, preliminary evidence suggests that it is a promising and viable measure. However, there is an underlying assumption in this measure that that good people produce good marriages. As with many measures that assess intangible outcomes such as quality and satisfaction, there are bound to be discrepant views concerning the conceptual definitions of these concepts. In view of the current interest in the study of spirituality, issues of virtue and vice will more than likely receive more scholarly attention.

Location*

Strom, B. (2003). Communicator virtue and its relation to marriage quality. *Journal of Family Communication, 3*, 21–40.

References

Holmes, A. (1991). *Shaping character.* Grand Rapids, MI: William B. Eerdmans.
McCroskey, J., & Teven, J. (1999). Goodwill: A reexamination of the construct and its measurement. *Communication Monographs, 66,* 90–103.

Scale

Personal Report of Marital Virtues Scale (PV)*
Perceived Spousal Virtue Scale (PSV)*
Instructions: Please indicate your impressions of yourself (or spouse/mate) below by circling the appropriate number between the pairs of descriptors. The closer the number is to the descriptor, the more certain you are of your evaluation.

Self-Control

		1	2	3	4	5	6	7	
1	Shows self-control	1	2	3	4	5	6	7	Lacks self-control
2	Is unpredictable	1	2	3	4	5	6	7	Is predictable
3	Acts impulsively and regrets it later	1	2	3	4	5	6	7	Acts deliberately and sees good come of it
4	"Flies off the handle" emotionally	1	2	3	4	5	6	7	Doesn't "fly off the handle emotionally

Humility

		1	2	3	4	5	6	7	
5	Often acts proudly (in a bad way)	1	2	3	4	5	6	7	Doesn't act proudly
6	Shows humility	1	2	3	4	5	6	7	Doesn't show humility
7	Often brags of accomplishments	1	2	3	4	5	6	7	Never brags of accomplishments

Wisdom

		1	2	3	4	5	6	7	
8	Often makes dumb decisions	1	2	3	4	5	6	7	Usually makes wise decisions
9	Speaks and acts appropriately	1	2	3	4	5	6	7	Does not speak and act appropriately
10	Knows what to do in new or challenging situations	1	2	3	4	5	6	7	Doesn't know what to do in new or challenging situations
11	Is a wise person	1	2	3	4	5	6	7	Is not a wise person

Faithfulness

		1	2	3	4	5	6	7	
12	Is committed to me	1	2	3	4	5	6	7	Is not committed to me
13	Follows through on Promises	1	2	3	4	5	6	7	Fails to deliver on promises
14	Is disloyal	1	2	3	4	5	6	7	Is loyal
15	Fumbles on obligations	1	2	3	4	5	6	7	Fulfills obligations
16	Is unreliable	1	2	3	4	5	6	7	Is reliable

Industry

		1	2	3	4	5	6	7	
17	Works hard	1	2	3	4	5	6	7	Avoids work
18	Enjoys working	1	2	3	4	5	6	7	Hates working
19	Has an immature work ethic	1	2	3	4	5	6	7	Has a mature work ethic
20	Sees work as a burden	1	2	3	4	5	6	7	Views work as a gift
21	Often fails to meet work deadlines	1	2	3	4	5	6	7	Usually completes work on time

Note: Items should be randomly ordered and subscale labels removed prior to administration.

Presence Questionnaire

Profile by Elizabeth M. Perse

Mass communication scholars have always faced questions regarding the impact of media on audience members. New, increasingly interactive media can simulate reality or create the experience of presence in a media or virtual environment. Presence can serve as a dependent variable when researchers ask which characteristics of a medium predict feelings of presence. Presence can also serve as an independent variable leading to various media effects. Scholars, however, have not agreed on a single definition for "presence." Several writers propose that there are two main types of presence: personal, or the extent to which one senses being actually located in a physical environment, and social, or the sense of feeling *with* others (see Lee, 2004, for a review).

There are many measures of presence in the literature, reflecting different conceptualizations and research needs. Witmer and Singer's (1998, 2005) scale is profiled here. It is a widely used scale that has been adapted for use in a wide range of research contexts, such as video games (Eastin, 2006), virtual reality (Witmer & Singer, 1998), virtual navigation (Witmer & Singer, 2005), and sexual preference (Renaud, Rouleau, Granger, Barsetti, & Bouchard, 2002). Witmer and Singer's measure assesses personal presence. They define presence as "a psychological state of 'being there' mediated by an environment that engages our senses, captures our attention, and fosters our active involvement" (2005, p. 298). The Presence Questionnaire (PQ) measures the degree to which people experience presence in an environment.

The PQ was developed after reviewing the literature related to four factors that influence presence: control factors, or feelings of personal control over an environment; sensory factors, or sensory richness; distraction factors, or selective attention to the environment; and realism factors, or perceived realism of the environment. Three versions of the PQ have been used in research: the original 32-item form (Witmer & Signer, 1998), a shorted 19-item version (Witmer & Singer, 1998), and Version 3.0, a 29-item version (Witmer & Singer, 2005). The 29-item version is comprised of the 19-item scale and additional items to assess sensory experiences and feeling at ease in the environment. Responses are measured on a seven-point semantic-differential scale with a midpoint anchor. The scale is designed to be administered immediately following exposure to an "immersive experience." Presence scores are created by averaging or summing item responses. The scale has been used with a variety of different samples: college students, infantry soldiers, and adult volunteers.

Reliability

Witmer and Singer (1998) reported that the initial 32-item scale and the 19-item version of that scale were both reliable: 32-item α = .81; 19-item α = .88. Eastin (2006) used the 32-item scale reliably in his study of female video game players: α = .93. The 29-item scale is also reliable: α = .91 (Witmer & Singer, 2005). Witmer and Singer (1998) reported results of a cluster analysis of their scale, but research has not used PQ subscale scores. Most recently, however, Witmer and Singer's (2005) factor analysis identified four correlated factors: involvement (12 items, α = .89), sensory fidelity (6 items, α = .84), adaptation/immersion (8 items, α = .84), and interface quality (3 items, α = .57). Test-retest reliability has not been reported. As the PQ assesses immediate responses to an environment, stability over time might not be a relevant measure.

Validity

Because items that speak to the aspects of involvement and immersion were based on factors derived from a review of the presence literature, this measure has content validity.

Although Witmer and Singer (1998, 2005) did not seek to create a multidimensional presence measure, their cluster and factor analyses identified theoretically meaningful aspects of presence. Subsequent studies have used related measures to replicate these dimensions of presence, offering content validity for the PQ (Lessiter, Freeman, Keogh, & Davidoff, 2001; Schubert, Friedmann, & Regenbrecht, 1999, 2001).

Usoh, Catena, Arman, and Slater (2000) argued that all questionnaires looking at presence should undergo a "reality test," in which data collected in a virtual environment is compared to data obtained in the real world. The reality test assesses how well a presence measure discriminates between reality and the virtual realm. In a between-subjects design, Usoh et al. (2000) found that PQ scores measured for virtual environments were not significantly lower than those measured after performing a task in a real environment. Although this finding calls into the question the criterion validity of the PQ, it should be noted that these results were based on a small sample size (N = 20) and could be attributed to Type II error. Scholars might also consider the assumption undergirding the "reality test," that is, that virtual environments can be discriminated from real experiences.

There is limited evidence of criterion validity. Eastin (2006) found that same-sex character/avatar representation is associated with higher PQ scores. Witmer and Singer (1998) report a significant correlation between the PQ and the Immersive Tendency Questionnaire, which looks at an individual's capability or tendency to become involved or immersed in a virtual environment ($r = .24$, $p < .01$). The correlation between the two scales, however, was not universal across all types of virtual environments.

The construct validity of the PQ is demonstrated by the correlation of scores with other constructs associated with presence. Witmer and Singer (1998) reported that PQ scores were significantly and negatively correlated with the Simulator Sickness Questionnaire. That is, presence was negatively related to reports of simulation sickness. PQ scores are positively linked to task performance (Riley, Kaber, & Draper, 2004; Stanney, Kingdon, Greaber, & Kennedy, 2002; Witmer & Singer, 1998) and mental workload (Riley et al., 2004). That is, presence appears to increase performance and ease in the environment.

Comments

The PQ has been criticized. Strongest criticisms are based on the conceptualization of presence underlying the scale (Slater, 1999; Schubert et al., 2001). The PQ is a measure of subjective presence, from the standpoint of the human experiencing the environment. Writers have argued that the PQ makes it impossible to separate individual differences from presence experiences that occur due to characteristics of the virtual environment. By controlling for some individual difference traits (see Sas & O'Hare, 2003, for a discussion of individual difference variables that may impact the experience of presence) when using the PQ, future research might be able to better determine whether this concern, typically associated with self-reports, is justified.

Another shortcoming of this questionnaire involves its focus on only one aspect of presence, personal presence. It does address social presence, or the degree to which the experience of interacting in a mediated environment feels similar to face-to-face interaction to the participants (Lombard & Ditton, 1997; Short, Williams, & Christie, 1976).

Location*

Witmer, B. G., & Singer, M. J. (2005). The factor structure of the Presence Questionnaire. *Presence: Teleoperators and Virtual Environments*, *14*, 298–312.

References

Eastin, M. S. (2006). Video game violence and the female game player: Self- and opponent gender effects on presence and aggressive thoughts. *Human Communication Research, 32,* 352–372.

Lee, K. M. (2004). Presence, explicated. *Communication Theory, 14,* 27–50.

Lessiter, J., Freeman, J., Keogh, E., & Davidoff, J. (2001). A cross-media presence questionnaire: The ITC-sense of presence inventory. *Presence: Teleoperators and virtual environments, 10,* 282–298.

Lombard, M., & Ditton, T. (1997). At the heart of it all: The concept of presence. *Journal of Computer-Mediated Communication, 3*(2), Retrieved November 28, 2004 from http://www.ascusc.org/jcmc/vol3/issue2/lombard.html

Renaud, P., Rouleau, J. L., Granger, L., Barsetti, I., & Bouchard, S. (2002). Measuring sexual presences in virtual reality: A pilot study. *CyberPsychology & Behavior, 5,* 1–9.

Riley, J. M., Kaber, D. B., & Draper, J. V. (2004). Situation awareness and attention allocation measures for quantifying telepresence experiences in teleoperation. *Human Factors and Ergonomics in Manufacturing, 14,* 51–67.

Sas, C., & O'Hare, G. (2003). The presence equation: An investigation into cognitive factors underlying presence. *Presence: Teleoperators and Virtual Environments, 12,* 523–537.

Schubert, T., Friedmann, F., & Regenbrecht, H. (1999). Embodied presence in virtual environments. In Ray Paton & Irene Neilson (Eds.), *Visual representations and interpretations* (pp. 268–278). London: Springer-Verlag.

Schubert, T., Friedmann, F., & Regenbrecht, H. (2001). The experience of presence: Factor analytic insights. *Presence: Teleoperators and Virtual Environments, 10,* 266–281.

Short, J., & Williams, E., and Christie, B. (1976). *The social psychology of telecommunications.* London: Wiley.

Slater, M. (1999). Measuring presence: A response to the Witmer and Singer presence questionnaire. *Presence: Teleoperators and Virtual Environments, 8,* 560–565.

Stanney, K. M., Kingdon, K., Graeber, D., & Kennedy, R. S. (2002). Human performance in immersive virtual environments: Effects of duration, user control, and scene complexity. *Human Performance, 15*(4), 339–366.

Usoh, M., Catena, E., Arman, S., & Slater, M. (2000). Using presence questionnaires in reality. *Presence: Teleoperators and Virtual Environments, 9,* 497–503.

Witmer, B. G., & Singer, M. J. (1998). Measuring presence in virtual environments: A presence questionnaire. *Presence: Teleoperators and Virtual Environments, 7,* 225–240.

Scale

Presence Questionnaire*

Instructions: Characterize your experience in the environment, by marking an "X" in the appropriate box of the 7-point scale, in accordance with the question content and descriptive labels. Please consider the entire scale when making your responses, as the intermediate levels may apply. Answer the questions independently in the order that they appear. Do not skip questions or return to a previous question to change your answer.

WITH REGARD TO THE EXPERIENCED ENVIRONMENT

1 How much were you able to control events?

|___| |____| |____| |____| |____| |____| |____| |____|

NOT AT ALL   SOMEWHAT   COMPLETELY

2 How responsive was the environment to actions that you initiated (or performed)?

|___| |____| |____| |____| |____| |____| |____| |____|

NOT   MODERATELY   COMPLETELY
RESPONSIVE   RESPONSIVE   RESPONSIVE

3 How natural did your interactions with the environment seem?

|___| |____| |____| |____| |____| |____| |____| |____|

EXTREMELY   BORDERLINE   COMPLETELY
ARTIFICIAL   NATURAL

4 How much did the visual aspects of the environment involve you?

|___| |____| |____| |____| |____| |____| |____| |____|

NOT AT ALL   SOMEWHAT   COMPLETELY

5 How much did the auditory aspects of the environment involve you?

|___| |____| |____| |____| |____| |____| |____| |____|

NOT AT ALL   SOMEWHAT   COMPLETELY

6 How natural was the mechanism which controlled movement through the environment?

|___| |____| |____| |____| |____| |____| |____| |____|

EXTREMELY   BORDERLINE   COMPLETELY
ARTIFICIAL   NATURAL

7 How compelling was your sense of objects moving through space?

|___| |____| |____| |____| |____| |____| |____| |____|

NOT AT ALL   MODERATELY   VERY
                          COMPELLING   COMPELLING

8 How much did your experiences in the virtual environment seem consistent with your real world experiences?

|___| |____| |____| |____| |____| |____| |____| |____|

NOT   MODERATELY   VERY
CONSISTENT   CONSISTENT   CONSISTENT

9 Were you able to anticipate what would happen next in response to the actions that you performed?

|___| |____| |____| |____| |____| |____| |____| |____|

NOT AT ALL   SOMEWHAT   COMPLETELY

10 How completely were you able to actively survey or search the environment using vision?

|___| |____| |____| |____| |____| |____| |____| |____|

NOT AT ALL   SOMEWHAT   COMPLETELY

11 How well could you identify sounds?

|___|___|___|___|___|___|___|___|___|___|
NOT AT ALL   SOMEWHAT   COMPLETELY

12 How well could you localize sounds?

|___|___|___|___|___|___|___|___|___|___|
NOT AT ALL   SOMEWHAT   COMPLETELY

13 How well could you actively survey or search the virtual environment using touch?

|___|___|___|___|___|___|___|___|___|___|
NOT AT ALL   SOMEWHAT   COMPLETELY

14 How compelling was your sense of moving around inside the virtual environment?

|___|___|___|___|___|___|___|___|___|___|
NOT   MODERATELY   VERY
COMPELLING   COMPELLING   COMPELLING

15 How closely were you able to examine objects?

|___|___|___|___|___|___|___|___|___|___|
NOT AT ALL   PRETTY   VERY
                              CLOSELY   CLOSELY

16 How well could you examine objects from multiple viewpoints?

|___|___|___|___|___|___|___|___|___|___|
NOT AT ALL   SOMEWHAT   EXTENSIVELY

17 How well could you move or manipulate objects in the virtual environment?

|___|___|___|___|___|___|___|___|___|___|
NOT AT ALL   SOMEWHAT   EXTENSIVELY

18 How involved were you in the virtual environment experience?

|___|___|___|___|___|___|___|___|___|___|
NOT   MILDLY   COMPLETELY
INVOLVED   INVOLVED   ENGROSSED

19 How much delay did you experience between your actions and expected outcomes?

|___|___|___|___|___|___|___|___|___|___|
NO DELAYS   MODERATE   LONG
                              DELAYS   DELAYS

20 How quickly did you adjust to the virtual environment experience?

|___|___|___|___|___|___|___|___|___|___|
NOT AT ALL   SLOWLY   LESS THAN
                                                          ONE MINUTE

21 How proficient in moving and interacting with the virtual environment did you feel at the end of the experience?

|___|___|___|___|___|___|___|___|___|___|
NOT   REASONABLY   VERY
PROFICIENT   PROFICIENT   PROFICIENT

22 How much did the visual display quality interfere or distract you from performing assigned tasks or required activities?

|_____| |_____| |_____| |_____| |_____| |_____| |_____|

NOT AT ALL   INTERFERED   PREVENTED
                              SOMEWHAT   TASK PERFORMANCE

23 How much did the control devices interfere with the performance of assigned
tasks or with other activities?

|_____| |_____| |_____| |_____| |_____| |_____| |_____|

NOT AT ALL   INTERFERED   INTERFERED
                              SOMEWHAT   GREATLY

24 How well could you concentrate on the assigned tasks or required activities
rather than on the mechanisms used to perform those tasks or activities?

|_____| |_____| |_____| |_____| |_____| |_____| |_____|

NOT AT ALL   SOMEWHAT   COMPLETELY

25 How completely were your senses engaged in this experience?

|_____| |_____| |_____| |_____| |_____| |_____| |_____|

NOT   MILDLY   COMPLETELY
ENGAGED   ENGAGED   ENGAGED

26 How easy was it to identify objects through physical interaction; like touching
an object, walking over a surface, or bumping into a wall or object?

|_____| |_____| |_____| |_____| |_____| |_____| |_____|

IMPOSSIBLE   MODERATELY   VERY EASY
                             DIFFICULT

27 Were there moments during the virtual environment experience when you felt
completely focused on the task or environment?

|_____| |_____| |_____| |_____| |_____| |_____| |_____|

NONE   OCCASIONALLY   FREQUENTLY

28 How easily did you adjust to the control devices used to interact with the virtual environment?

|_____| |_____| |_____| |_____| |_____| |_____| |_____|

DIFFICULT   MODERATE   EASILY

29 Was the information provided through different senses in the virtual environment (e.g., vision, hearing, touch) consistent?

|_____| |_____| |_____| |_____| |_____| |_____| |_____|

NOT   SOMEWHAT   VERY
CONSISTENT   CONSISTENT   CONSISTENT

Scoring Instructions

Simply score the boxes for each question from left to right beginning
with one and increasing in value to the box the subject has marked, and the
number of that box becomes the score. Some of the questions have
reversed response anchors, and are scored so the left-most box receives a
seven and the rest decrease in value. The subscale scores are the sum of the
scores for each item in the subscale. There is no weighting of items or subscales. The questionnaire total and subscales are comprised as follows:

PRESENCE QUESTIONNAIRE

Involvement: Items 1, 2, 3, 4, 6, 7, 8, 10, 14, 17, 18, & 26.
Sensory Fidelity: Items 5, 11, 12, 13, 15, & 16.
Adaptation/Immersion: Items 9, 20, 21, 24, 25, 27, 28, & 29.
Interface Quality: Items 19, 22, & 23.

Note: Items 19, 22, and 23 have to be reverse scored in order to contribute to the subscales.

Reactance Restoration Scale (RRS)

Profile by Joseph P. Mazer

Communication scholars recently began to utilize psychological reactance theory (PRT) as a theoretical framework to explore why certain health messages are ineffective (Burgoon, Alvaro, Grandpre, & Voulodakis, 2002). PRT explains how individuals respond to the threat or elimination of a freedom and assumes that people cherish their ability to choose among alternatives in a particular situation (Brehm, 1966). In essence, a persuasive message that threatens or eliminates an individual's freedom to choose among a given behavior or alternatives to a behavior will trigger reactance. Comprised of anger and negative cognitions, reactance essentially motivates people to reassert their threatened or eliminated freedom (Dillard & Shen, 2005). Further defined, scholars have distinguished state and trait reactance and have developed reliable and valid measures to assess each construct (Dillard & Shen, 2005; Shen & Dillard, 2005).

In an effort to advance the utility of PRT, Brian Quick and Michael Stephenson developed the Reactance Restoration Scale (RRS) to assess how individuals restore their threatened or eliminated freedoms following a persuasive message. Historically, reactance restoration has been considered an outcome of state reactance (Brehm, 1966). Most recently, however, relevant research has revealed that reactant individuals expressed negative attitudes (Dillard & Shen, 2005; Rains & Turner, 2007), exhibited behavioral intentions opposing a message (Buller, Borland, & Burgoon, 1998), reported poor message evaluations (Grandpre, Alvaro, Burgoon, Miller, & Hall, 2003; Quick & Considine, 2008; Quick & Stephenson, 2007), and derogated the freedom-threatening source (Miller, Lane, Deatrick, Young, & Potts, 2007). Although this line of research has utilized conventional reactance measures, Quick and Stephenson (2008) argue that they are not entirely consistent with Brehm's (1966) original claim that state reactance includes energizing or motivational qualities. That is, measuring attitudes, intentions, and message and source derogation are plausible outcomes of reactance; however, assessing motivations seems to be more consistent with Brehm's original work.

Brehm and Brehm (1981) asserted that individuals can restore their threatened or eliminated freedom in a number of ways. Building upon Brehm and Brehm's (1981) assertions, Quick and Stephenson classified three reactance restoration processes: (1) *boomerang effect*—individuals express their behavior in ways opposite the threat; (2) *related boomerang effect*—individuals perform a behavior that is related to the threat; (3) *vicarious boomerang effect*—individuals vicariously perform the threat by observing others behave in a freedom-restoring manner (often described as indirect restoration, Brehm & Brehm, 1981).

Citing the presence of conceptual clarity but the unfortunate absence of a reliable and valid scale to measure reactance restoration, Quick and Stephenson utilized persuasive health messages related to exercise and sunscreen usage to test the psychometric properties of the RRS. In addition, they located the measure in a nomological network containing trait and state reactance to explore the construct validity of the RRS. The scale is a 12-item measure of three, four-item subscales (boomerang effects, vicarious-boomerang effects, related-boomerang effects), anchored by a 7-point semantic differential response format.

Reliability

All three subscales—boomerang effects, vicarious-boomerang effects, and related-boomerang effects—achieved good overall reliability. Cronbach alphas ranged from .93 to .97 in the initial scale development study and in a recent study by Quick and Stephenson (2008). Both studies utilized the RRS to explore reactance restoration with persuasive messages related to exercise and sunscreen usage.

Validity

As an initial test of construct validity, Quick and Stephenson explored reactance restoration in the context of print messages that advocated participation in a weekly exercise routine and sunscreen usage when directly exposed to the sun. To assess the construct validity of the RRS, Quick and Stephenson located the RRS in a nomological network of theoretically valid constructs, including state and trait reactance. Developed by Cronbach and Meehl (1955) as a view of construct validity, the nomological network includes a theoretical framework for the construct that a researcher is attempting to measure, an empirical framework for how the researcher is going to measure it, and an explanation of the linkages between and among those two frameworks. Quick and Stephenson then employed confirmatory factor analysis to measure the association between scale items and found good model fit for both the exercise and sunscreen measurement models. They found that both state and trait reactance was positively associated with boomerang, related-, and vicarious-boomerang effects for the exercise and sunscreen messages.

In a recent study, Quick and Stephenson (2008) explored the impact of trait reactance and sensation seeking on a perceived threat to freedom, state reactance, and reactance restoration. Again utilizing structural equation modeling as a data analytic technique, they predicted a positive association between state reactance and reactance restoration within the context of exercise and sunscreen messages.

Within the context of an exercise message, analysis revealed a significant positive association between state reactance and boomerang effects for low trait reactant (LTR) individuals and high sensation seekers (HSS). For sunscreen messages, a significant positive association between state reactance and boomerang effects emerged for high trait reactant (HTR) individuals and HSS. For LTR individuals in the context of exercise messages, a significant positive association was found for vicarious-boomerang effects and state reactance.

For sunscreen messages, state reactance was positively associated with boomerang effects for HTR individuals although this association emerged for LTR individuals following exposure to exercise messages. Quick and Stephenson (2008) were uncertain as to why state reactance and a boomerang effect was positively associated for HTR individuals within the context of sunscreen messages and not exercise messages. In a similar vein, they reported an additional surprising finding in that a positive association between state reactance and a boomerang effect for LTR individuals emerged within the context of exercise messages. Calling for future research in this area, they conclude that issue involvement might moderate the association between state reactance and boomerang effects for LTR and HTR individuals.

For HSS, a positive association with state reactance and boomerang effects emerged within both sunscreen and exercise message contexts. However, no relationship was found between state reactance and boomerang, related-boomerang, or vicarious-boomerang effects for low sensation seekers (LSS). In short, Quick and Stephenson (2008) concluded that HSS were likely to restore their threatened freedom by not expressing motivation to perform the specific behavior.

Both studies discussed herein provide initial validity evidence for the RRS. However, Quick and Stephenson have aptly called for additional research in this area to further validate the RRS as a reliable and valid measure.

Comments

Although the RRS is new to the literature, preliminary evidence suggests that it is a promising and viable measure. Quick and Stephenson report that the RRS displays stable psychometric properties across two message contexts (exercise and sunscreen usage) and is associated with related constructs, which provides initial evidence of construct validity. In both studies, their use of structural equation modeling serves as a rigorous method of data analysis.

Although the nomological network scheme utilized in the initial scale development study provides a philosophical foundation for construct validity, the multi-trait-multi-method matrix might serve as the next phase in the evolution of construct validity. Additionally, future research might move beyond exercise and sunscreen messages and explore reactance restoration in varied message contexts among diverse populations. Although college student populations provide important evidence of how a specific age group consumes and reacts to persuasive messages, results normed on diverse populations (age, occupation, socioeconomic status, culture) can enhance the generalizability and ecological validity of this measure.

Location*

Quick, B. L., & Stephenson, M. T. (2007). The reactance restoration scale (RRS): A measure of direct and indirect restoration. *Communication Research Reports, 24*, 131–138.

References

Brehm, J. W. (1966). *A theory of psychological reactance.* New York: Academic Press.

Brehm, J. W., & Brehm, S. S. (1981). *Psychological reactance: A theory of freedom and control.* San Diego, CA: Academic Press.

Buller, D. B., Borland, R., & Burgoon, M. (1998). Impact of behavioral intention on effectiveness of message features: Evidence from the family sun safety project. *Human Communication Research, 24*, 433–453.

Burgoon, M., Alvaro, E., Grandpre, J., & Voulodakis, M. (2002). Revisiting the theory of psychological reactance: Communicating threats to attitudinal freedom. In J. P. Dillard & M. Pfau (Eds.), *The persuasion handbook: Developments in theory and practice* (pp. 213–232). Thousand Oaks, CA: Sage.

Cronbach, L., & Meehl, P. (1955). Construct validity in psychological tests. *Psychological Bulletin, 52*, 281–302.

Dillard, J. P., & Shen, L. (2005). On the nature of reactance and its role in persuasive health communication. *Communication Monographs, 72*, 144–168.

Grandpre, J. R., Alvaro, E. M., Burgoon, M., Miller, C. H., & Hall, J. R. (2003). Adolescent reactance and anti-smoking campaigns: A theoretical approach. *Health Communication, 15*, 349–366.

Miller, C. H., Lane, L. T., Deatrick, L. M., Young, A. M., & Potts, K. A. (2007). Psychological reactance and promotional health messages: The effects of controlling language, lexical concreteness, and the restoration of freedom. *Human Communication Research, 33*, 219–240.

Quick, B. L., & Considine, J. R. (2008). Examining the use of forceful language when designing exercise advertisements for adults: A test of conceptualizing reactance arousal as a two-step process. *Health Communication, 23*, 483–491.

Quick, B. L., & Stephenson, M. T. (2008). Examining the role of trait reactance and sensation seeking on perceived threat, state reactance, and reactance restoration. *Human Communication Research, 34*, 448–476.

Quick, B. L., & Stephenson, M. T. (2007). Further evidence that psychological reactance can be modeled as a combination of anger and negative cognitions. *Communication Research, 34*, 255–276.

Rains, S. A., & Turner, M. (2007). Psychological reactance and persuasive health communication: A test and extension of the intertwined model. *Human Communication Research, 33*, 241–269.

Shen, L., & Dillard, J. P. (2005). Psychometric properties of the Hong Psychological Reactance Scale. *Journal of Personality Assessment, 85*, 74–81.

Scale

Reactance Restoration Scale (RRS)*
Instructions: [Instructions were not clearly stated in the article, but one can conclude that participants are asked to insert each of the anchored response options into the blank as they read the item. Then participants should respond to the item using a 7-point semantic differential response format.]

Boomerang effects

1   Right now, I am_____to (exercise/use sunscreen the next time I am exposed to direct sunlight for an extended period of time [greater than 15 minutes])

Motivated	1 2 3 4 5 6 7	Unmotivated
Determined	1 2 3 4 5 6 7	Not determined
Encouraged	1 2 3 4 5 6 7	Not encouraged
Inspired	1 2 3 4 5 6 7	Not inspired

Vicarious boomerang effects

2   Right now, I am_____to be around others who (exercise/use sunscreen the next time I am exposed to direct sunlight for an extended period of time [greater than 15 minutes])

Motivated	1 2 3 4 5 6 7	Unmotivated
Determined	1 2 3 4 5 6 7	Not determined
Encouraged	1 2 3 4 5 6 7	Not encouraged
Inspired	1 2 3 4 5 6 7	Not inspired

Related boomerang effects

3	Right now, I am_____to do something totally unhealthy.								
	Motivated	1	2	3	4	5	6	7	Unmotivated
	Determined	1	2	3	4	5	6	7	Not determined
	Encouraged	1	2	3	4	5	6	7	Not encouraged
	Inspired	1	2	3	4	5	6	7	Not inspired

Relational Distance Index (RDI)

Profile by Elizabeth E. Graham

Countering the prevailing claim that individuals voluntarily develop relationships with *liked* partners, Jon Hess (2000) suggested that people often engage in nonvoluntary relationships with liked *and* disliked partners. Hess posited that *liking* is only one of many reasons that account for relational development and maintenance. Nonvoluntary relationships can be found in families (e.g., in-laws, siblings, step siblings, parents, step parents), the workplace (e.g., co-workers, bosses, colleagues), and in many other social situations. These relationships might be difficult to terminate, and are, therefore, deemed *nonvoluntary*. However, they are not necessarily unsatisfying.

Rooted in a social exchange framework, nonvoluntary relationships are considered viable to the extent that other alternatives are not, regardless of the level of satisfaction. Hess hypothesized that people maintain involuntary relationships with disliked partners by creating social distance. Hess (2003) echoed Kantor and Lehr's (1975) sentiments by suggesting that distance, like closeness, is of vital importance to the functioning and study of relationships. Furthermore, although closeness and distance are two binary opposites on the same continuum, Hess (2003) made explicit that distance is not merely the absence of closeness. Over the course of several studies, Hess developed a measure of relational distance entitled the Relational Distance Index (RDI).

Hess (2000) generated a comprehensive list of 36 distancing behaviors culled from the literature as well as from contributions from research participants. Next, participants responded to the distance tactics with either a liked or disliked partner in mind about their maintenance of a voluntary or a nonvoluntary relationship. With the assistance of cluster analysis, Hess categorized the 36 distancing behaviors into three clusters: expressing detachment, avoiding involvement, and showing antagonism. These clusters were conceptualized and categorized by how often each tactic was used in conjunction with the other tactics and, therefore, were inadequate as a classification scheme of how people create distance in social interaction.

To remedy this shortcoming, Hess (2002) asked participants to offer narrative accounts concerning how they maintain relationships with liked and disliked partners. From these accounts, the 36 distance tactics were reduced to 15 and a classification scheme was produced that revealed three overarching distancing strategies (i.e., general plans to accomplishing goals): avoidance (tactics that reduce amount of interaction), disengagement (tactics such as concealing information about the self or treating the other impersonally), and cognitive dissociation (tactics that are characterized by a mental detachment and disregard for the other).

In a subsequent effort by Hess (2003), the three conceptual strategies were subjected to a series of exploratory and confirmatory factor analyses, which resulted in a 17-item, two-factor index that drew from all three conceptual strategies. They were labeled *unfriendly* (items that are negative in nature, n = 9) and *withdrawal* (items that reflect avoidance and nonimmediacy, n = 8). In addition to the 17-item RDI, Hess developed a shortened 8-item version, as well (4 unfriendly items and 4 withdrawal items).

Reliability

Data from several studies conducted by Hess (2003) revealed satisfactory reliability estimates for the 17-item index (overall α = .88 and .95, unfriendly α = .86 and withdrawal α = .74). Application of the shortened 8-item version also produced acceptable reliability coefficients (overall α = .80 and .92, unfriendly α = .78 and .85 and withdrawal α = .73 and .92).

Hess (2003) assessed and supported the stability of the RDI by conducting test-retest reliability trials over short time intervals. Reliability estimates for Time 1 and 2 for the17-item index were α = .87 and .86, and for the 8-item measure, reliability was α = .70 and .72, respectively. Hess conducted additional studies with nonstudent populations that also produced equally acceptable reliability results.

Validity

In an effort to test the utility of the distance measure, Hess (2003) conducted several validity tests of the RDI. The convergent validity of the RDI was assessed by examining the relationship between distance and subjective (gestalt) perceptions of distance and conflict avoidance. Hess hypothesized that one common means of enacting distance is to avoid conflict resolution. This contention was upheld as was the association between the RDI and subjective perceptions of distance. In addition, the discriminant validity of the RDI was supported by the negative relationship between distance and closeness, affectionate communication, and liking. To evaluate the external validity of the RDI, these same hypotheses were tested and supported with a nonstudent population. In both populations, and as predicted, the desire for distance was positively associated with avoidance and negatively related to affection, closeness, and liking. As expected, people in nonvoluntary relationships with disliked partners reported an increased use of distancing tactics than those in relationships with liked partners (this test employed the 8-item RDI). Hess (2003) also gauged the stability of the RDI by illustrating the consistency of participant responses to the RDI over short time intervals. And last, Hess (2003) provided evidence that the RDI is not vulnerable to a social desirability bias.

Comments

Although the RDI is a relatively new instrument, it promises to be a useful tool in the assessment of understudied relationships, i.e. nonvoluntary personal relationship with disliked others. Although the 17-item RDI offers slightly higher reliability estimates and conceptual breadth, Hess suggests that researchers use the 8-item version because the factor loadings provide more clarity. In addition, Hess warns researchers to treat the 17-item version of the RDI as a unidimensional measure due to the redundancy in factor loadings.

Hess's ambitions not only produced a viable measure of relational distance but, perhaps more importantly, represent a paradigmatic shift, one that challenges the *ideology of choice*. This reconceptualization suggests that not all relationships are chosen but can be nonetheless viable and enduring. Distance is a feasible alternative to closeness and is useful in relationship maintenance. People do indeed engage in relationships involuntarily with those they do not necessarily like. These views will undoubtedly contribute to a more balanced perspective of relationship maintenance. The conceptual development of the measure, coupled with the painstaking efforts to evaluate its reliability and validity, serve as an exemplar of instrument development.

Location**

Hess, J. A. (2003). Measuring distance in personal relationships: The Relational Distance Index. *Personal Relationships, 10*, 197–215.

References

Hess, J. A. (2000). Maintaining nonvoluntary relationships with disliked partners: An investigation into the use of distancing behaviors. *Human Communication Research, 26*, 458–488.

Hess, J. A. (2002). Distance regulation in personal relationships: The development of a conceptual model and a test of representational validity. *Journal of Social and Personal Relationships, 19*, 663–683.

Kantor, D., & Lehr, W. (1975). *Inside the family.* San Francisco: Jossey-Bass.

Scale

The Relational Distance Index (RDI)**
Instructions: With a disliked person in mind, please rate how frequently you did these things, from never (1) to every time you saw the person (7).

1 = I never did this
2 = I rarely did this
3 = I did this periodically, but it wasn't the norm
4 = I did this a moderate number of times
5 = I did this often
6 = I did this almost every time possible
7 = I did this every time possible

Avoidance

1 *I changed my behavior to avoid encountering this person whenever possible. W
2 *When this person was around me, I did not acknowledge her/his presence. U
3 *When I was talking to this person, I would do things to make the interaction as short as possible, such as pretending to agree or not asking questions. W
4 I tried to interact with this person in the company of other people, rather than interacting one-on-one. W
5 *When in this person's presence, I kept to myself and spoke less than I would have if I liked her/him. W

Disengagement

6 *When talking to this person, I kept the conversation away from topics that were intimate or personal. W
7 I intentionally misled or lied to this person on information about myself. U
8 When interacting with this person, I focused my attention away from her/him, such as by paying attention to something else or just simply "zoning out." U
9 When interacting with this person, I avoided nonverbal cues that would show closeness (e.g., I reduced the amount of smiling, touching, eye contact, etc.). W
10 I avoided doing things that I would normally do (joking with someone) because they might have made this person and myself closer. W
11 I treated this person impersonally; that is, I treated her/him as I would treat a stranger. W

12   *When this person was speaking, I humored her/him and treated her/him as being less capable of acting responsibly than other people. U

Cognitive Dissociation

13   When listening to this person, I disregarded her/his message or interpreted it in a way to minimize its importance. U
14   *I mentally degraded this person, such as by seeing her/him as less than human, less capable, or having fewer rights than others. U
15   *I ignored this person's thoughts, feelings, and intentions. U
16   I tried to prevent myself from developing feelings about this person, or tried to avoid acting on the negative feelings I already had. U
17   I felt that this person belonged to a different social group than I did. U

Note 1: Items marked with an asterisk (*) are included in the 8-item version of the RDI. Items should be presented randomly and subscale labels removed prior to administration.

Note 2: U = Unfriendly factor loading and W = Withdrawal factor loading

Note 3: On item 5, you may substitute "than I would normally" for "than I would have if I liked her/him" if using the scale for assessing distance in a neutral or affectively positive relationship.

Relational Maintenance Strategy Measure (RMSM)

Profile by Elizabeth E. Graham

Prior to the 1990s, romantic relationship research was primarily concerned with initial interaction and dissolution processes. Responding to Duck's (1988) edict that we spend more time maintaining rather than developing or dissolving relationships, Laura Stafford and Daniel Canary initiated a program of study on relational maintenance. Their work identified various relational maintenance strategies that people employ to sustain their ongoing relationships (Canary & Stafford, 1992; Stafford & Canary, 1991). Rooted in the claim that communication serves a central role in how people relate to one another, a belief that equity theory influences relational choices, and the underlying assumption that people are motivated to maintain equitable relationships, Stafford and Canary (1991) developed the Relational Maintenance Strategies Measure (RMSM). They defined relational maintenance as "communication . . . people use to sustain desired relational definitions" (Canary & Stafford, 1992, p. 243). Operating from a dyadic level perspective, they highlight the value of investigating relational maintenance from the perspective of both the communicator and his/her partner.

Stafford and Canary (1991) created a maintenance strategy typology through surveying the literature and generating responses from couples (married and dating) reporting on their maintenance behaviors. The RMSM includes five maintenance strategies: positivity, openness, assurances, networks, and sharing tasks. *Positivity* refers to interacting with one's partner in an optimistic, cheerful, and supportive manner and avoiding criticism. *Openness* involves discussing the relationship, negotiating rules, and disclosing hopes about the relationship. *Assurances* involves stressing one's desire for the relationship to continue, stressing one's commitment, and supporting the partner. Interacting with or relying upon affiliations with others is the use of *social networks*. In addition, individuals may *share tasks* to maintain the relationship; that is, they may perform their share of duties or obligations, such as household chores (Stafford & Canary, 1991). Participants are asked to report on their own and/or their partner's use of these strategies either currently or the recent past (e.g., the previous two weeks). In ensuing research (Canary & Stafford, 1992) additional items were generated resulting in a five factor 29-item self and other report Likert scale.

A series of studies, in varied contexts, employing different populations, have resulted in several modified versions of the relational maintenance measure. For example, Stafford and colleagues (Stafford, Dainton, & Hass, 2000) reconceptualized maintenance to include strategic as well as routine (i.e., nonstrategic) maintenance behaviors (see Stafford et al., 2000, for scale items). Their belief is that routine behaviors "are those that people perform that foster relational maintenance more in the manner of a 'by-product'" (p. 307). Hass and Stafford (2005) adapted the routine maintenance measure as a coding scheme employed to categorize open–ended participant responses salient in homosexual populations. Messman, Canary, and Hause (2000) detailed maintenance behaviors relevant to platonic opposite-sex friendships while others (Morr Serewicz, Dickson, Huynh Thi Anh Morrison, & Poole, 2007; Vogl-Bauer, Kalbfleisch, & Beatty, 1999) extended the utility of the RMSM for use in families.

Reliability

Research by Canary and Stafford (1992) using the RMSM has revealed a consistent and reliable (measured by Cronbach's alpha) self-report measure of relational maintenance strategies that include positivity α = .89; openness α = .86; assurances α = .76; networks α = .82; and sharing tasks α = .87. Other–report reliabilities were equally robust: positivity α = .90; openness α = .86; assurances α = .79; networks α = .85; and sharing tasks α = .91. The two additional routine maintenance behaviors introduced by Stafford et al. (2000) also produced acceptable reliability estimates and include conflict management (α = .81) and advice (α = .70). Additional studies, employing both self and other report versions of the scale, support the internal reliability of the measure as well (Rabby 2007; Stafford & Canary, 2006). The assurance subscale consistently produces the lowest reliability estimate.

Validity

Several studies attest to the validity of the Relational Maintenance Strategy Measure. More precisely, the predictive validity of the RMSM is illustrated by the links between maintenance and relational characteristics, such as commitment and stability (Canary & Stafford, 1992, 1993; Canary, Stafford, & Semic, 2002; Guerrero, Eloy, & Wabnik, 1993; Stafford & Canary, 1991; Weigel & Ballard–Resich, 1999). Moreover, the variation in use of maintenance strategies among types of romantic couples (Guerrero & Bachman, 2006; Stafford & Canary, 1991; Weigel & Ballard-Reisch, 1999), cultural groups (Yum, 2003), and loneliness groups (Henson, Dybvig-Pawelko, & Canary, 2004) is indicative of the discriminant validity of the RMSM. Furthermore, maintenance behaviors are associated with a host of psychological correlates and communication behaviors including attachment styles (Dainton, 2007; Guerrero & Bachman, 2006), uncertainty (Guerrero & Chavez, 2005), and commitment in online and offline relationships (Rabby, 2007).

Support for the construct validity of the maintenance measure is found in equity theory as an explanatory framework for maintenance research. There is a curvilinear relationship between maintenance strategies use and equity. For example, Canary and colleagues (Canary & Stafford, 1992; Stafford & Canary, 2006) concluded that when wives are in underbenefited relationships they report engaging in fewer maintenance behaviors than when they perceive their relationship as equitable. Not surprisingly, underbenefited husbands report receiving fewer offers of maintenance strategies from wives. In sum, underbenefited spouses engage in, and perceive to be the recipient of, fewer maintenance behaviors than equitably treated spouses. Furthermore, both husbands and wives in overbenefited relationships, as opposed to equitable relationships, also reported participating in fewer maintenance activities. In addition, when wives perceived the marriage as equitable, they claimed a greater presence (given and received) of all five maintenance behaviors when compared to overbenefited couples.

A consistent finding across several research studies (i.e., Canary & Stafford, 1992; Dainton & Stafford, 1993; Ragsdale, 1996) supports the claim that women (wives) use more maintenance behaviors than men (husbands). However, Stafford et al. (2000) concluded that gender role, rather than biological sex was responsible for maintenance behavior use and reported that femininity, rather than biological sex or masculinity, was the best predictor of maintenance behaviors. These results are consistent with what we would expect of the association between femininity and attention to relationship concerns.

Further, Canary and Stafford (1992) proposed that three relational outcomes are central to relational maintenance and include control mutuality, liking and commitment. Control mutuality references the extent to which partners concur on the power balance in the relationship. Liking is considered a necessary element integral to relationship success and well-being. Finally, commitment corresponds to one's wish to maintain involvement in a relationship. Results revealed that self and other reports of maintenance strategies are positively related to each relational outcome (control mutuality, liking, and commitment). More specifically, for both husbands and wives, self-reported positivity was the best predictor of control mutuality. In addition, husbands' perception of their wives social networks use contributed to control mutuality predictions. Furthermore, wives' self-reported assurances and openness as well as husbands' use of social networks was responsible for predictions of control mutuality. Both husbands and wives' perception of their partners' positivity and social network use predicted the second relational outcome, liking. Finally, husbands' commitment, the third relational quality, was predicted by perceptions of wives' assurances. In a related study, Stafford et al. (2000) found that the use of assurances was a strong predictor of four relational characteristics (control mutuality, liking, commitment, and satisfaction). Finally, Canary and Stafford (2001) and Stafford and Canary (2006) found that maintenance strategies use (positivity, openness, assurances, network, and task sharing) was positively correlated with satisfaction. Collectively these findings contribute to the construct validity of the Relational Maintenance Strategy Measure.

Comments

Although ample research supports the theoretical and methodological coherence of the Relational Maintenance Strategy Measure, a series of studies have questioned the stability of the factor structure and the theoretical underpinnings of the maintenance construct (Ragsdale, 1996; Ragsdale & Brandau-Brown, 2004, 2005, 2007a, 2007b). Ragsdale and colleagues failed to replicate the initial factor structure or the item assignment offered by Canary and Stafford as their data revealed both a three (the assurance and network factor did not load) and four-factor structure (the assurance factor did not load). They attribute the factor variation to the influence of sample and population differences (i.e., gender, relationship type). Entertaining the possibility that the variation in their factor structure was the result of the data gathering method (diary log versus Likert scale) Ragsdale and Brandau-Brown (2004) determined that there were discrepancies in the factor structure between studies employing the same method.

Stafford and Canary (2006) concurred with the likelihood that different factor structures might emerge across relationship types. They did, however, counter the instability claim by suggesting that divergent methodology that Ragsdale and colleagues employed might explain the conflicting factor structures. Canary and Stafford (2007) asserted that their use of the daily tally of diary data is suspect because the RMSM does not translate into the diary format. More specifically, they explained that their measure was designed for use with a Likert (i.e., agree–disagree) response format not a frequency count. Furthermore, Stafford and Canary (2006) cautioned that multiple daily performances of several of the maintenance items would likely reflect a dysfunctional relationship. For instance, asking "how my partners' day has gone" ceases to be a maintenance behavior and starts to resemble dysfunctional communication if asked repeatedly.

The second countervailing conclusion offered by Ragsdale and Brandau-Brown (2005, 2007a, 2007b) suggests that equity theory is an incomplete explanation of maintenance behaviors. They proposed that individual communicator variables (i.e., self-monitoring, Machiavellianism), relationship length, and other perspectives (i.e., communal concerns, interdependence interpretation) might serve as a complimentary lens in which to study relational maintenance. Stafford and Canary (2006) tested the viability of equity theory and, consistent with prior research, found that two social exchange constructs (i.e., equity and satisfaction) function to predict maintenance behaviors. Ragsdale (1996) did not find support for satisfaction and the relational maintenance strategies.

The third countervailing claim converges on design implementation (i.e., length of marriage, relationship type, gender of participants), data interpretation (construal of significance tests and variance accounted for), and claim derivation (i.e., conclusions derived from correlational data) (see Canary & Stafford, 2007; Ragsdale & Brandau-Brown, 2007a, 2007b; Stafford & Canary, 2006 for detailed discussion of these issues).

Perhaps continued dialogue will determine the validity of these conflicting claims. As Stafford (2003) astutely noted, "researchers are often their own best critics and as such continue to refine their theories that may in turn contribute to application" (p. 74). In the meantime, The Relational Maintenance Strategies Measure provides ample evidence that it is a useful addition to the arsenal of relational communication measurement tools.

Location*

Canary, D. J., & Stafford, L. (1992). Relational maintenance strategies and equity in marriage. *Communication Monographs, 59,* 243–267.

References

Canary, D. J., & Stafford, L. (1993). Preservation of relational characteristics: Maintenance strategies, equity, and locus of control. In P. J. Kalbfleisch (Ed.), *Interpersonal communication: Evolving interpersonal relationships* (pp. 237–259). Hillsdale, NJ: Erlbaum.

Canary, D. J., & Stafford, L. (2001). Equity in the preservation of personal relationships. In J. H. Harvey & A. Wenzel (Eds.), *Close romantic relationships Maintenance and enhancement* (pp. 133–152). Mahwah, NJ: Erlbaum.

Canary, D. J., & Stafford, L. (2007). People want—and maintain—fair marriages: Reply to Ragsdale and Brandau-Brown. *Journal of Family Communication, 7,* 61–68.

Canary, D. J., & Stafford, L., & Semic, B. A. (2002). A panel study of the associations between maintenance strategies and relational characteristics. *Journal of Marriage and the Family, 64*, 395–406.

Dainton, M. (2007). Attachment and marital maintenance. *Communication Quarterly, 55*, 283–298.

Dainton, M., & Aylor, B. (2001). A relational uncertainty analysis of jealousy, trust, and maintenance in long-distance versus geographically close relationships. *Communication Quarterly, 49*, 172–188.

Dainton, M., & Stafford, L. (1993). Routine maintenance behaviors: A comparison of relationship type, partner similarity and sex differences. *Journal of Social and Personal Relationships, 10*, 255–271.

Duck, S. W. (1988). *Relating to others*. Chicago, IL: Dorsey.

Guerrero, L. K., & Bachman, G. F. (2006). Associations among relational maintenance behaviors, attachment-style categories, and attachment dimensions. *Communication Studies, 57*, 341–361.

Guerrero, L. K., & Chavez, A. M. (2005). Relational maintenance in cross-sex friendships characterized by different types of romantic intent: An exploratory study. *Western Journal of Communication, 69*, 339–358.

Guerrero, L. K., Eloy, S. V., & Wabnik, A. I. (1993). Linking maintenance strategies to relationship development and disengagement: A reconceptualization. *Journal of Social & Personal Relationships, 10*, 273–283.

Haas, S. M., & Stafford, L. (2005). Maintenance behaviors in same-sex and marital relationships: A matched sample comparison. *Journal of Family Communication, 5*, 43–61.

Henson, D. F., Dybvig-Pawelko, K. C., & Canary, D. J. (2004). The effects of loneliness on relational maintenance behaviors: An attributional perspective. *Communication Research Reports, 21*, 411–419.

Messman, S. J., Canary, D. J., Hause, K. S. (2000). Motives to remain platonic, equity, and the use of maintenance strategies in opposite-sex friendships. *Journal of Social and Personal Relationships, 17*, 67–94.

Morr Serewicz, M. C., Dickson, F. C., Huynh Thi Anh Morrison, J., & Poole, L. L. (2007). Family privacy orientation, relational maintenance, and family satisfaction in young adults' family relationships. *Journal of Family Communication, 7*, 123–142.

Rabby, M. K. (2007). Relational maintenance and the influence of commitment in online and offline relationships. *Communication Studies, 58*, 315–337.

Ragsdale, J. D. (1996). Gender, satisfaction level, and the use of relational maintenance. *Communication Monographs, 63*, 354–369.

Ragsdale, J. D., & Brandau-Brown, F. E. (2004). Measuring relational maintenance in marriage: Theoretical and methodological issues. *Southern Communication Journal, 69*, 121–135.

Ragsdale, J. D., & Brandau-Brown, F. E. (2005). Individual differences in the use of relational maintenance strategies in marriage. *Journal of Family Communication, 5*, 61–75.

Ragsdale, J. D., & Brandau-Brown, F. E. (2007a). Could relational maintenance in marriage really be like grocery shopping? A reply to Stafford and Canary. *Journal of Family Communication, 7*, 47–60.

Ragsdale, J. D., & Brandau-Brown, F. E. (2007b). Asked, but not answered: A second reply to Stafford and Canary. *Journal of Family Communication, 7,* 69–73.

Stafford, L. (2003). Maintaining romantic relationships: Summary and analysis of one research program. In D. J. Canary & M. Dainton (Eds.), *Maintaining relationships through communication* (pp. 51–77). Mahwah, NJ: Erlbaum.

Stafford, L., & Canary, D. J. (1991). Maintenance strategies and romantic relationship type, gender, and relational characteristics. *Journal of Social and Personal Relationships, 8,* 217–242.

Stafford, L., & Canary, D. J. (2006). Equity and interdependence as predictors of relational maintenance strategies. *Journal of Family Communication, 6,* 227–254.

Stafford, L., Dainton, M., & Haas, S. (2000). Measuring routine and strategic relational maintenance: Scale revision, sex versus gender roles, and the prediction of relational characteristics. *Communication Monographs, 67,* 306–323.

Vogl-Bauer, S., Kalbfleisch, P. J., & Beatty, M. J. (1999). Perceived equity, satisfaction, and relational maintenance strategies in parent–adolescent dyads. *Journal of Youth and Adolescence, 28,* 27–49.

Weigel, D. J., & Ballard-Reisch, D. S. (1999). All marriages are not maintained equally: Marital type, marital quality, and the use of maintenance behaviors. *Personal Relationships, 6,* 291–303.

Yum, Y.-O. (2003). The relationships among loneliness, self/partner constructive maintenance behavior, and relational satisfaction in two cultures. *Communication Studies, 54,* 451–467.

Scale

Relational Maintenance Strategies Measure*
Instructions (Self-Report): The following items concern things people might do to maintain their relationships. Please indicate the extent to which you perceive each of the following statements describes your current (over the past two weeks, for example) methods of maintaining your relationship. Respond to the following statement using a 7-point Likert response format employing ranges of 1 = strongly disagree and 7 = strongly agree.

Instructions (Other/Partner Report): Please indicate the extent to which you perceive each of the following describes your partners' current (over the past two weeks, for example) methods of maintaining your relationship. Respond to the following statement using a 7-point Likert response format employing ranges of 1 = strongly disagree and 7 = strongly agree.

Positivity

1 Attempt to make our interactions very enjoyable.
2 Am cooperative in the ways I handle disagreements between us.
3 Try to build up his/her self-esteem, including giving him/her compliments, etc.

4   Ask how his/her day has gone.
5   Am very nice, courteous, and polite when we talk.
6   Act cheerful and positive when with him/her.
7   Do not criticize him/her.
8   Try to be romantic, fun, and interesting with him/her.
9   Am patient and forgiving of him/her.
10 Present myself as cheerful and optimistic.

Openness

11 Encourage him/her to disclose thoughts and feelings to me.
12 Simply tell him/her how I feel about our relationship.
13 Seek to discuss the quality of our relationship.
14 Disclose what I need or want from our relationship.
15 Remind him/her about relationship decisions we made in the past (for example, to maintain the same level of intimacy).
16 Like to have periodic talks about our relationship.

Assurances

17 Stress my commitment to him/her.
18 Imply that our relationship has a future.
19 Show my love for him/her.
20 Show myself to be faithful to him/her.

Network

21 Like to spend time with our same friends.
22 Focus on common friends and affiliations.
23 Show that I am willing to do things with his/her friends or family.
24 Include our friends or family in our activities.

Tasks

25 Help equally with tasks that need to be done.
26 Share in the joint responsibilities that face us.
27 Do my fair share of the work we have to do.
28 Do not shirk my duties.
29 Perform my household responsibilities.

Note: Items should be ordered randomly and subscale labels removed prior to administration.

Relational Uncertainty Measure

Profile by Elizabeth E. Graham

In an effort to tailor the uncertainty construct to the context of close relationships, Knobloch and Solomon (1999) created a means of assessing the
content and the sources of relational uncertainty. While being true to
Berger and Calabrese's (1975) early rendering of Uncertainty Reduction
Theory (URT), Knobloch and colleagues depart from URT's conceptualization of uncertainty in two significant ways. First, they focus on established relationships, limiting their measure to the doubts people
experience in intimate associations rather than the ambiguity that may
arise in other relationship phases. Second, although Berger and Calabrese
conceptualized uncertainty as stemming from self, partner, and relationship sources, measurement efforts have focused chiefly on predicting a
partner's behavior (see for example Clatterbuck, 1979; Parks & Adelman,
1983). For these reasons, Knobloch and Solomon (1999) developed three
measures that assess with whom the relational uncertainty lies (i.e., source
[self, partner, relationship]) and what the nature of that relational uncertainty concerns (i.e., content [desire, evaluation, goals, norms, mutuality,
definition, and future]).

The first source, uncertainty about self, concerns the questions people
have about their own involvement in a relationship. The second source,
partner uncertainty, refers to the inability to predict a partner's involvement in the relationship. Finally, relationship uncertainty occurs when
people are unsure about the nature and status of the relationship itself. In
addition to relying on the literature for item construction, Knobloch and
Solomon (1999) also solicited input from several participants and asked
them to discuss relational uncertainty experiences within several phases of
relationship development (i.e., relational uncertainty in casual dating to
relational uncertainty in pre-marriage relationships).

In addition to identifying the source of relational uncertainty, Knobloch
and Solomon (1999) focused next on the content of the relational uncertainty measure. The authors concluded that self and partner uncertainty
revolve around questions about people's desire for the relationship, their
evaluation of its worth, and their goals for its development. Relationship

uncertainty stems from questions about the norms for behavior, mutuality of feelings between partners, the definition of the relationship, and the future of the relationship.

After a series of statistical analyses including item clarification and confirmatory factor analyses, three separate scales were developed to measure self, partner, and relationship uncertainty. The self-uncertainty measure is comprised of 19 items reflected in three factors representing ambiguity about the respondent's desire for the relationship, evaluation of its worth, and goals for its progression. The desire subscale references ambiguity about commitment to the relationship. The second subscale, evaluation, refers to doubts about the value and worth of the relationship. The last subscale, goals, speaks to questions about the future of the relationship.

The partner uncertainty scale is also 19 items and identical to the self-uncertainty measure (questions about desire, evaluation, and goals). Please note that the self and partner relational uncertainty measures were initially comprised of 16 and 15 items, respectively. Subsequent research (Knobloch & Solomon, 2005) enhanced each measure to arrive at the current 19-item composition.

The third scale developed, the relationship uncertainty measure, is a 16-item four factor instrument designed to assess questions about the relationship itself. The four subscales are comprised of 4 items each. The first subscale, *behavioral norms*, refers to questions about appropriate and inappropriate conduct in the relationship. The *mutuality* subscale stresses uncertainty about the degree of reciprocity in the relationship. *Definition*, the third subscale, assesses doubts about the state of the relationship. And last, the *future* subscale refers to questions about the possible prospects and opportunities for the relationship. A series of confirmatory factor analyses supported the structure and consistency of the three relational uncertainty measures. Although the three components of relational uncertainty are positively correlated, repeated confirmatory factor analyses have consistently supported the conceptual independence of the three relational uncertainty measures (Knobloch, 2006, 2007; Knobloch & Solomon, 2005).

Reliability

The responses to the items are averaged to compute the subscales, and the subscales are averaged to compute the composite measures. The three relational uncertainty measures are highly reliable producing Cronbach alphas of .95 for self-uncertainty, .96 for partner uncertainty, and .94 for relationship uncertainty. Subsequent research (Knobloch & Solomon, 2002) employing a slightly modified version of the measures has also been found to be internally consistent (α = .97 for self-uncertainty, α = .98 for partner uncertainty, and α = .94 for relationship uncertainty). Subsequent research has continued to produce results indicating that the three measures are internally consistent (see Bevan, 2004; Knobloch, 2006, 2007).

Validity

To understand how relational uncertainty is shaped and shapes related variables, Knobloch and associates (Bevan, 2004; Knobloch, 2007; Knobloch & Carpenter-Theune, 2004; Knobloch & Solomon, 2002, 2003; Solomon & Knobloch, 2001; Theiss & Solomon, 2006) conducted a series of studies incorporating a constellation of relationship qualities including intimacy, topic avoidance, power, jealousy, information seeking, and emotion. Consistent with Berger and Calabrese's (1975) early renderings of URT, the successful resolution of relational uncertainty can serve to bolster intimacy in initial encounters *and* developed relationships (Knobloch & Solomon, 2002). Furthermore, we can conclude that people generally do not talk about sensitive topics until relational uncertainty is reduced and indeed, relational uncertainty mediates the relationship between topic avoidance and intimacy (Knobloch & Carpenter-Theune, 2004). Collectively, these results suggest that both relational certainty and relational uncertainty have value in relationships. These recent findings contribute to the criterion and construct validity of the relational uncertainty measures.

Consistent with the belief that the transition from casual dating to serious involvement may result in relational uncertainty, Solomon and Knobloch (2004) developed the relational turbulence model. In the model, relational uncertainty (self, partner, and relationship) is prominently positioned to directly and/or indirectly mediate the association between communication behaviors and predispositions and relationship turmoil. A series of sophisticated studies unveils several rather complex associations between relational uncertainty and intimacy (Knobloch, Miller, & Carpenter, 2007), directness (Theiss & Solomon, 2006), sadness and jealousy (Bevan, 2004; Knobloch, Miller, & Carpenter, 2007; Knobloch, Solomon, & Cruz, 2001), narrative instability and relationship thinking (Knobloch, 2007), message production and processing (Knobloch, 2006; Knobloch, Miller, Bond, & Mannone, 2007), message features (i.e., verbal fluency, affiliativeness, relationship focus, explicitness, perceived effectiveness) in relation to date requests (Knobloch, 2006), and perceived helpfulness and hindrance (criticism, questioning, avoidance) from others (Knobloch & Donovan-Kicken, 2006). Collectively these studies serve the twin goals of supporting the consequential role that relational uncertainty plays in relationship transitions and the enhancement of the construct validity of the Relational Uncertainty Measure.

Comments

When Knobloch and Solomon (1999) first introduced the Relational Uncertainty Measure they cautioned users that further research was needed to determine if the factors were truly distinct and independent of each other. Subsequent and repeated confirmatory factor analyses provide ample evidence of both the conceptual and statistical uniqueness and independence of the three measures of relational uncertainty (see Knobloch, 2006, 2007; Knobloch & Solomon, 2005).

The three relational uncertainty scales (self, partner, and relationship) have been continuously verified through confirmatory factor analyses which have resulted in slightly different versions of each measure. This variability should not be interpreted as instability of the measure but rather as a true artifact of how most measures would perform if subjected to repeated factor analysis. Regardless of item variability, The Relational Uncertainty Measure is a comprehensive, multidimensional, extensively tested, and valid measure that is a useful addition to the battery of interpersonal communication tools.

Location*

Knobloch, L. K. & Solomon, D. H. (1999). Measuring the sources and content of relational uncertainty. *Communication Studies, 50,* 261–278.

References

Berger, C. R., & Calabrese, R. J. (1975). Some explorations in initial interactions and beyond: Toward a developmental theory of interpersonal communication. *Human Communication Research, 1,* 99–112.

Bevan, J. L. (2004). General partner and relational uncertainty as consequences of another person's jealousy expression. *Western Journal of Communication, 68,* 195–218.

Clatterbuck, G. W. (1979). Attributional confidence and uncertainty in initial interactions. *Human Communication Research, 5,* 147–157.

Knobloch, L. K. (2006). Relational uncertainty and message production within courtship: Features of date request messages. *Human Communication Research, 32,* 244–273.

Knobloch, L. K. (2007). Perceptions of turmoil within courtship: Associations with intimacy, relational uncertainty, and interference from partners. *Journal of Social and Personal Relationships, 24,* 363–384.

Knobloch, L. K., & Carpenter-Theune, K. E. (2004). Topic avoidance in developing romantic relationships: Associations with intimacy and relational uncertainty. *Communication Research, 31,* 173–205.

Knobloch, L. K., & Donovan-Kicken, E. (2006). Perceived involvement of network members in courtships: A test of the relational turbulence model. *Personal Relationships, 13,* 281–302.

Knobloch, L. K., Miller, L. E., Bond, B. J., & Mannone, S. E. (2007). Relational uncertainty and message processing in marriage. *Communication Monographs, 74*, 154–180.

Knobloch, L. K., Miller, L. E., & Carpenter, K. E. (2007). Using the relational turbulence model to understand negative emotion within courtship. *Personal Relationships, 14*, 91–112.

Knobloch, L. K., & Solomon, D. H. (2002). Information seeking beyond initial interaction: Negotiating relational uncertainty within close relationships. *Human Communication Research, 28*, 243–257.

Knobloch, L. K., & Solomon, D. H. (2003). Responses to changes in relational uncertainty within dating relationships: Emotions and communication strategies. *Communication Studies, 54*, 282–305.

Knobloch, L. K., & Solomon, D. H. (2005). Relational uncertainty and relational information processing: Questions without answers? *Communication Research, 32*, 349–388.

Knobloch, L. K., Solomon, D. H., & Cruz, M. G. (2001). The role of relationship development and attachment in the experience of romantic jealousy. *Personal Relationships, 8*, 205–224.

Parks, M. R., & Adelman, M. B. (1983). Communication networks and the development of romantic relationships: An expansion of uncertainty reduction theory. *Human Communication Research, 10*, 55–79.

Solomon, D. H., & Knobloch, L. K. (2001). Relationship uncertainty, partner interference, and intimacy within dating relationships. *Journal of Social and Personal Relationships, 18*, 804–820.

Solomon, D. H., & Knobloch, L. K. (2004). A model of relational turbulence: The role of intimacy, relational uncertainty, and interference from partners in appraisals of irritations. *Journal of Social and Personal Relationships, 21*, 795–816.

Theiss, J. A., & Solomon, D. H. (2006). A relational turbulence model of communication about irritations in romantic relationships. *Communication Research, 33*, 391–418.

Scale

Relational Uncertainty Measure*
Self-Uncertainty Scale

Instructions: We have listed a number of statements addressing different facets of involvement in dating relationships. We would like you to rate how *CERTAIN* you are about the degree of involvement that you have in your relationship at this time. *PLEASE NOTE:* We are not asking you to rate how much involvement there is in your relationship, but rather how certain you are about whatever degree of involvement you perceive. It might help if you first consider how much of each form of involvement is present in your relationship, and then evaluate how *certain* you are about that perception. For these judgments, you should use the following scale:

The response options include (1) completely or almost completely uncertain; (2) mostly uncertain; (3) slightly more uncertain than certain; (4) slightly more certain than uncertain; (5) mostly certain; and (6) completely or almost completely certain.

How certain are you about . . .

Desire

1 How committed you are to the relationship?
2 Your feelings for your partner?
3 How much you like your partner?
4 How you feel about the relationship?
5 How much you want to pursue this relationship?
6 Whether or not you are ready to commit to your partner?
7 Whether you want a romantic relationship with your partner or to be just friends?
8 How much you want this relationship right now?

Evaluation

9 How important this relationship is to you?
10 How much you are romantically interested in your partner?
11 How ready you are to get involved with your partner?
12 Your view of this relationship?
13 Whether or not you want to maintain your relationship?

Goals

14 Whether or not you want this relationship to last?
15 Whether or not you will want to be with your partner in the long run?
16 Your goals for the future of the relationship?
17 Whether or not you want to stay in a relationship with your partner?
18 Where you want this relationship to go?
19 Whether or not you want this relationship to work out in the long run?

Note: Items have to be reverse-scored to compute a measure of self uncertainty.

Partner Uncertainty Scale
Instructions: We would like to know how certain you are about YOUR PARTNER'S INVOLVEMENT in this relationship. Please use the following scale:

The response options include (1) completely or almost completely uncertain; (2) mostly uncertain; (3) slightly more uncertain than certain; (4) slightly more certain than uncertain; (5) mostly certain; and (6) completely or almost completely certain.

How certain are you about . . .

Desire

1. How committed your partner is to the relationship?
2. How much your partner likes you?
3. How your partner feels about the relationship?
4. How much your partner wants this relationship right now?
5. How much your partner wants to pursue this relationship?
6. Whether your partner wants a romantic relationship with you or to be just friends?
7. Your partner's feelings for you?
8. Whether or not your partner is ready to commit to you?

Evaluation

9. How much your partner is romantically interested in you?
10. How ready your partner is to get involved with you?
11. Whether or not your partner wants to maintain your relationship?
12. Your partner's view of this relationship?
13. How important this relationship is to your partner?

Goals

14. Whether or not your partner wants this relationship to work out in the long run?
15. Whether or not your partner wants this relationship to last?
16. Whether or not your partner will want to be with you in the long run?
17. Your partner's goals for the future of the relationship?
18. Where your partner wants this relationship to go?
19. Whether or not your partner wants to stay in a relationship with you?

Note: Items have to be reverse-scored to compute a measure of partner uncertainty.

Relationship Uncertainty Scale
Instructions: We would like to know how certain you are about aspects of YOUR RELATIONSHIP, in general. Please use the following scale:

The response options include (1) completely or almost completely uncertain; (2) mostly uncertain; (3) slightly more uncertain than certain; (4) slightly more certain than uncertain; (5) mostly certain; and (6) completely or almost completely certain.

How certain are you about . . .

Behavioral Norms

1. What you can or cannot say to each other in this relationship?
2. The boundaries for appropriate and/or inappropriate behavior in this relationship?

3 The norms for this relationship?
4 How you can or cannot behave around your partner?

Mutuality

5 Whether or not you and your partner feel the same way about each other?
6 How you and your partner view this relationship?
7 Whether or not your partner likes you as much as you like him or her?
8 The current status of this relationship?

Definition

9 The definition of this relationship?
10 How you and your partner would describe this relationship?
11 The state of the relationship at this time?
12 Whether or not this is a romantic or platonic relationship?

Future

13 Whether or not you and your partner will stay together?
14 The future of the relationship?
15 Whether or not this relationship will end soon?
16 Where this relationship is going?

Note: Items have to be reverse-scored to compute a measure of relationship uncertainty. For all scales, items should be randomly ordered and subscale labels removed for presentation.

Reticence Scale

Profile by Rebecca B. Rubin

"The reticent person avoids and is inept at social interaction and public performance" (Keaten, Kelly, & Finch, 1997, p. 39). Although the conceptual definition of reticence has evolved over the years (see Keaten & Kelly, 2000), the current definition focuses on skills needed during social interaction. Reticent people feel they don't have the skills necessary to cope with encounters, so tend to avoid those situations.

Keaten et al. (1997) developed 24 statements intended to reflect six dimensions (based on the five canons of rhetoric): feelings of anxiety, knowledge of communication topics, timing skills, organization of thoughts, delivery skills, and memory skills. Respondents use a 6-point Likert-type response scale to indicate their degree of agreement with each statement. Respondents require just a few minutes to complete the scale.

Reliability and Validity

Reliability and validity information is sparse. A coefficient alpha of .95 was reported for an earlier version, with reliabilities of the dimensions ranging from .80 to .92 (cited in Keaten et al., 1997). Face and content validity information has been provided in the original description, as has some concurrent validity data.

Keaten and colleagues have used the instrument in subsequent validity research. In the first study, Keaten et al. (1997) looked at correlations between this measure and three scales thought comparable. Significant correlations with the *Personal Report of Communication Apprehension, Conversational Skills Rating Scale*, and the *Willingness to Communicate Scale* provided evidence of concurrent validity. Later, Kelly, Keaten, and Finch (2004) compared reticent and non-reticent students' media choices for communicating with their instructors. Reticent students preferred indirect contact, such as e-mail, rather than face-to-face meetings with instructors, and all six dimensions of the Reticence Scale were negatively correlated with comfort communicating with instructors in person or on the telephone. This provides some construct validity for the scale.

Kelly et al. (2002) sought the origins of reticence in another study. Although they didn't use the Reticence Scale to place students into reticent and non-reticent groups, they did find that self-reported reticent students came from families where parents were low on conversation orientation: they talked less to their children about thoughts, daily events, and plans for the future, and were less open about emotions. In effect, the parents didn't have effective interpersonal communication skills, nor did their children. However, reticents did not differ from non-reticents on family conformity orientation. High conformity parents are more autocratic and use negative reinforcement parenting techniques.

Comments

The scale is easy to administer and score. Individuals indicate their level of agreement with the items, and then the 6 subscales are computed by addition of the relevant items. Scores for each dimension range from 1 to 21. A low score indicates less anxiety, fewer problems with knowledge, timing, delivery, etc. Test-retest reliability information would be welcome.

Future research might examine potential age and culture influences. Kelly et al. (2002) found some gender differences for family communication patterns, which might be a mediating variable in research focused on conversation skill. Predictive and construct validity research should also be provided in the near future.

Location*

Keaten, J. A., Kelly, L., & Finch, C. (1997). Development of an instrument to measure reticence. *Communication Quarterly, 45*, 37-54.

References

Keaten, J. A., & Kelly L. (2000). Reticence: An affirmation and revision. *Communication Education, 49*, 165–177.

Kelly, L., Keaten, J. A., & Finch, C. (2004). Reticent and non-reticent college students' preferred communication channels for interacting with faculty. *Communication Research Reports, 21*, 197–209.

Kelly, L., Keaten, J. A., Finch, C., Duarte, I. B., Hoffman, P., & Michels, M. M. (2002). Family communication patterns and the development of reticence. *Communication Education, 51*, 202–209.

Scale

Reticence Scale*
Instructions: This assessment instrument is composed of 24 statements concerning your skills as a communicator. Please indicate in the space

provided the degree to which each statement applies to you by marking whether you (1) strongly disagree, (2) disagree, (3) mildly disagree, (4) mildly agree, (5) agree, or (6) strongly agree. These statements refer to your communication skills when meeting a stranger at a social gathering. Please work quickly; just record your first impression.

1 I am nervous when talking.
2 I know what to say.
3 I wait too long to say what I want to say.
4 I organize my thoughts when talking.
5 I stumble over my words.
6 I remember what I want to say when talking.
7 I am relaxed when talking.
8 I am unaware of what to say.
9 I say things at the time I want to say them.
10 My thoughts are disorganized.
11 I clearly say what I want to say.
12 I forget what I want to say when talking.
13 I feel tense when talking.
14 I know what to discuss.
15 I hesitate too long to say what I want to say.
16 I arrange my thoughts when talking.
17 I muddle my words.
18 I recall what I want to say when talking.
19 I am comfortable when talking.
20 I am unfamiliar with what to say.
21 I say things when I want to say them.
22 My thoughts are jumbled.
23 I fluently say what I want to say.
24 I lose sight of what I want to say when talking.

Scoring Instructions:

Anxiety = 11 + Q1 + Q13 − Q7 − Q19
Knowledge = 11 + Q8 + Q20 − Q2 − Q14
Timing = 11 + Q3 + Q15 − Q9 − Q21
Organization = 11 + Q10 + Q22 − Q4 − Q16
Delivery = 11 + Q5 + Q17 − Q11 − Q23
Memory = 11 + Q12 + Q24 − Q6 − Q18

Revised Family Communication Patterns Instrument (RFCP)

Profile by Elizabeth E. Graham

The Revised Family Communication Patterns Instrument (RFCP), developed by Ritchie and Fitzpatrick (1990), is a modified and reconceptualized version of McLeod and Chaffee's (1972) Family Communication Patterns Measure (FCP). In contrast to the original measure, the revised instrument assesses family communication behaviors and patterns rather than children's information processing and decision making. Although the authors believe that family patterns are primarily determined by parents, they do note that children can indeed inspire changes in parental communication as well. Consistent with this premise, the RFCP includes a separate version of the instrument for both parents and children. Unlike many family patterns instruments, the intent of the RFCP is not to distinguish between healthy and unhealthy families but rather to describe the many ways families can and do function.

The RFCP, like its predecessor, the FCP, is premised on the belief that for relatively enduring family communication patterns to develop, a shared social reality among participants is essential. The degree to which members share that reality is the result of coorientation (i.e., accuracy, agreement, and congruence of meanings) and a consequence of family environments that privilege ideas (concept-orientation) or relationships (socio-orientation) (Koerner & Fitzpatrick, 2004; McLeod & Chaffee, 1972; Newcomb, 1953; Ritchie, 1991). The more cooriented a family is, the more its members will cultivate a shared social reality. The process of coorientation, and the resultant shared social reality, are accomplished through communication and ultimately comprise family communication patterns (Koerner & Fitzpatrick, 2004).

Ritchie and colleagues (Fitzpatrick & Ritchie, 1994; Ritchie, 1991; Ritchie & Fitzpatrick, 1990) recast McLeod and Chaffee's concept-orientation as conformity orientation, and socio-orientation was relabeled conversation orientation. The result of these efforts is a 26-item self-report questionnaire anchored by a 7-point Likert response format (however, some studies have employed a 5-point Likert response format). The first dimension, conversation orientation, includes 15 items and emphasizes unrestricted, unrestrained, and frequent communication. Childrens' spontaneous thoughts are welcomed and encouraged. The second dimension, conformity orientation, is comprised of 11 items and is characterized by homogeneous beliefs among family members, a privileging of harmonious interpersonal relations, conflict avoidance, and parental power. Koerner and Fitzpatrick (2002) noted that most studies report a low to moderate negative correlation between the two dimensions, indicating that they are distinct but not independent of each other.

The two dimensions are not binary but continuous in nature; this suggests that one could be higher or lower on either or both of the conformity or conversation dimension. To account for this probability, McLeod and Chaffee (1972) intersected the two dimensions to yield four family types. The first family type, *consensual*, reflects families high on conversation and conformity orientation. Children's thoughts and ideas are valued and conversation is encouraged; however, parents still make most of the family decisions although they go to great efforts to explain those decisions to their children. *Pluralistic*, the second family type, is also high on conversation but low on conformity, indicating that family members are autonomous, open, and uninhibited in their communication with the family. Families low on conversation and high on conformity are termed *protective* and are characterized by a diminished regard for communication and a privileging of parental authority and control. The last family type, *laissez-faire*, is low on conversation and conformity. As the name suggests, there is little communication between parents and children as well as limited guidance in cultivating children's thoughts or ideas.

Reliability

Across numerous studies (Barbato, Graham, & Perse, 2003; Baxter & Clark, 1996; Fitzpatrick & Ritchie, 1994; Koerner & Cvancara, 2002; Koerner & Fitzpatrick, 2002; Ritchie, 1991; Schrodt & Ledbetter, 2007) reliability estimates for the conformity and conversation orientation subscales have consistently produced respectable, and in some cases outstanding, alpha levels. The conversation orientation subscale has produced Cronbach alphas ranging from .84 to .92. Although the conformity orientation subscales produce slightly lowered reliabilities, their range (α = .72 to .87) is quite acceptable. Furthermore, Ritchie and Fitzpatrick (1994) assessed the test-retest reliability of the RFCP Instrument across three different age groups employing a three week interval between administrations and reported alphas of close to 1.00 for the conversation orientation subscale and somewhat lower scores for the conformity orientation subscale (α = .73 – .93). A 13-item version of the scale has also produced satisfactory reliability estimates (Fitzpatrick, Marshall,

Leutwiler, & Krcmar, 1996). It is evident that the RFCP Instrument is a reliable measure of family communication patterns.

Validity

The content validity of the RFCP Instrument was largely established when Ritchie (1991) and others (Ritchie & Fitzpatrick, 1990) reconceptualized the Family Communication Patterns scale by operationalizing the conformity and conversation dimensions to reflect communication behaviors. In addition, the measure was lengthened substantially to encompass a communication rather than an information-processing focus. This revision served to simultaneously broaden the scope of the measure's utility and capture the specificity of family interaction. Moreover, the content validity of the RFCP Instrument rests on the strong conceptual and operational correspondence between the conversation and conformity dimensions and their theoretical counterparts (Koerner & Fitzpatrick, 2002).

There is a wealth of evidence to support the criterion validity of the RFCP Instrument. Koerner and Cvancara (2002) were able to establish a correspondence between scores on the RFCP Instrument and observable speech acts, concluding that family norms and beliefs are evidenced in communication behavior. Indeed, a host of behavioral outcomes and psychological correlates has been associated with the dimensions of the RFCP Instrument. For example, family communication patterns contribute to the development of relational schemata and cognitive processes (Dumlao & Botta, 2000) and demand/withdraw behaviors (Schrodt & Ledbetter, 2007). Furthermore, families high in conversation orientation seek and provide social (and ego) support and comfort and express a desire and ability to resolve conflict (Koerner & Fitzpatrick, 1997; Zhang, 2007) and engage in person-centered communication (Burleson, Delia, & Applegate, 1995). Also, conversation orientation is significantly related to self-esteem, and mental health and well being (Schrodt, Ledbetter, & Ohrt, 2007) and an ability to develop effective communication skills and interpersonal relationships with others (Koerner & Fitzpatrick, 2002; Koesten, 2004; Koesten & Andersen, 2004). Furthermore, conversation-oriented families appreciate and are influenced by sound reasoning as opposed to only the status of the messenger (Fitzpatrick & Ritchie, 1994) and not as likely to suffer from communication apprehension (Elwood & Schrader 1998). In addition, low conformity scores have been linked to the tendency to confirm and acknowledge others and reflect on issues (Koerner & Cvancara, 2002).

Conversely, a conformity orientation is associated with less education, empathy, and perspective taking and more self-disclosure and self-orientation, questioning and advice-giving (Koerner, 1995; Koerner &

Cvancara, 2002). In addition, a conformity orientation is strongly related to position centered communication (Burleson, Delia, & Applegate, 1995) and the expression of negative affect (Fitzpatrick & Koerner, 1997; Koerner & Fitzpatrick, 1997). Families high in conformity have also been found to adhere to rules and norms in regard to family rituals (Baxter & Clark, 1996). A recent set of findings (Schrodt & Ledbetter, 2007; Schrodt et al., 2007) reveal that the negative consequences associated with parental conforming communication are mediated by confirming parental behavior and communication such that children develop a positive sense of self in spite of the conforming orientation in the family. Indeed families high in both conversation and conforming orientations (i.e., consensual families) in families characterized by parental confirming communication may yield the same benefits as those children from high conversation low conforming families (i.e., pluralistic). This research is particularly important, as it is evidence of the importance of examining mediating and moderating effects on family communication patterns (see Schrodt & Ledbetter, 2007; Schrodt et al., 2007).

Studies employing the RFCP Instrument have also been conducted in the workplace and have concluded that conformity is negatively correlated with open and autonomous communication (Ritchie, 1997) (For further information concerning the relationships among the four family types and communication behaviors and outcomes see Fitzpatrick & Koerner, 1997; Koerner & Fitzpatrick, 2004.)

Koerner and Fitzpatrick (2002) suggested that "the evidence of the construct validity of the RFCP is cumulatively provided by the sum total of the research conducted using the RFCP rather than one specific finding" (p. 62). While this may be true, one series of studies has particular bearing on the theoretical and heuristic value of family communication patterns because the interrelated communication network of *all family* members are studied. Specifically, Fitzpatrick and Ritchie (1994) proposed a series of hypotheses suggesting that how a couple defines their marriage (using the Relational Dimensions Instrument [RDI], Fitzpatrick, 1988) and how parents and children define their family (using the RFCP Instrument) are interdependent. Indeed, strong relationships were found among conversation oriented families and parents' scores on sharing and conflict acceptance. Likewise, their research supported a positive correlation between parents' traditionalism scores and conformity orientation in the family. Furthermore, families headed by traditional and independent parents report a commitment to a conversation oriented family communication patterns. Finally, there was support for the hypothesis that families headed by traditional, separate, and separate/traditional parents were more likely to engage in conformity oriented communication. The confirmation of the proposed hypotheses provides theoretical support for the underlying conceptual framework upon which the RFCP Instrument rests.

Family Typing Instructions and Considerations

McLeod and Chaffee (1972) derived the four family types by employing the median split method (i.e., splitting the sample at the median of both subscales) whereby classifications are based on high or low scores on the conversation and conformity dimensions. Although this method is simple and direct, the consistent negative correlation between the conformity and the conversation dimensions can be problematic and cause inflation or a deflation in scores (for more discussion of this matter see Koerner & Fitzpatrick, 2002). To avoid these biases, and, if necessary, to account for the absence of a large, representative, and/or random sample, Koerner and Fitzpatrick (2002) suggested researchers employ Fitzpatrick and Ritchie's (1994) population means rather than relying on one's own data when deriving median scores for classification purposes.

An additional problem with the median split technique concerns the possibility that there might be differences in perception of each family member's communication pattern (i.e., bias). If the unit of analysis is the family and the data do reveal differing views of family members, Koerner and Fitzpatrick (2002) suggested that the data be converted to z-scores for each family member (father, mother, son, daughter) and that then averages within families (i.e., family z score) be used for classification purposes using the median split method. For detailed instructions for these procedures see the reference noted above.

Cluster analysis is an additional option available for the study of differences in family perceptions regarding family communication patterns. However, a very large sample is required, and the difficulty of this technique does not warrant its use for the researcher simply interested in family types (for more information on this technique see Koerner & Fitzpatrick, 2002; Ritchie & Fitzpatrick, 1990).

Comments

The RFCP has been modified for use with children by casting family conversations into a "talking picture book." Participants respond to representations of the four family types by indicating whether the dialogue in the picture book resembled their family communication. Children report their assessments by choosing among various sized boxes that reflect if the family depicted in the picture book is "a lot," "a little bit," or "not at all like my family" (for more information see Fitzpatrick et al., 1996).

The Revised Family Communication Patterns Instrument is theoretically and methodologically sound and has generated considerable research. The RFCP measure is perhaps the most widely used instrument in family communication research. For this reason, it is particularly well poised for observation-based work, which would enhance the construct validity of the measure. Communication in general, and family communication patterns in particular, are "culture-loaded" as Zhang (2007, p. 114) so aptly notes and are ripe for intercultural application.

The RFCP is consistent with the call to study and measure family communication at the family level. Furthermore, the measure is quite adaptive as the four family types are easily derived, though most research focuses on the two dimensions of conversation and conformity orientation (Baxter & Clark, 1996). The reliability and validity information gathered to date suggests that The Revised Family Communication Patterns measure is internally consistent and capable of generating valid conclusions concerning family communication.

Location*

Ritchie, D. L., & Fitzpatrick, M. A. (1990). Family communication patterns: Measuring intrapersonal perceptions of interpersonal relationships. *Communication Research, 17*, 523–544.

References

Barbato, C. A., Graham, E. E., & Perse, E. M. (2003). Communicating in the family: An examination of the relationship of family communication climate and interpersonal communication motives. *Journal of Family Communication, 3*, 123–148.

Baxter, L. A., & Clark, C. L. (1996). Perceptions of family communication patterns and the enactment of family rituals. *Western Journal of Communication, 60*, 254–268.

Burleson, B. R., Delia, J. G., & Applegate, J. L. (1995). The socialization of person-centered communication: Parents' contributions to their children's social-cognitive and communication skills. In M. A. Fitzpatrick & A. Vangelisti (Eds.), *Explaining family interactions* (pp. 34–76). Thousand Oaks, CA: Sage.

Dumlao, R., & Botta, R. A. (2000). Family communication patterns and the conflict styles young adults use with their fathers. *Communication Quarterly, 48*, 174–189.

Elwood, T. D., & Schrader, D. C. (1998). Family communication patterns and communication apprehension. *Journal of Social Behavior and Personality, 13*, 493–502.

Fitzpatrick, M. A. (1988). *Between husbands and wives*. Newbury Park, CA: Sage.

Fitzpatrick, M. A., & Koerner, A. (1997). Family communication schemata: Effects on children's resiliency. In H. McCubbin (Ed.), *Promoting resiliency in families and children at risk: Interdisciplinary perspectives* (pp. 1–24). Thousand Oaks, CA: Sage.

Fitzpatrick, M. A., Marshall, L. J., Leutwiler, T. J., & Krcmar, M. (1996). The effect of family communication environments on children's social behavior during middle childhood. *Communication Research, 23*, 379–406.

Fitzpatrick, M. A., & Ritchie, L. D. (1994).Communication schemata within the family: Multiple perspectives on family interaction. *Human Communication Research, 20,* 275–301.

Koerner, A. F., & Cvancara, K. E. (2002). The influence of conformity orientation on communication patterns in family conversations. *Journal of Family Communication, 3,* 133–152.

Koerner, A. F., & Fitzpatrick, M. A. (2004). Communication in intact families. In A. L. Vangelisti (Ed.), *Handbook of family communication* (pp. 177–195). Mahwah, NJ: Erlbaum.

Koerner, A. F., & Fitzpatrick, M. A. (2002). Understanding family communication patterns and family functioning: The roles of conversation orientation and conformity orientation. *Communication Yearbook, 26,* 37–69.

Koerner, A. F., & Fitzpatrick, M. A. (1997). Family type and conflict: The impact of conversation orientation and conformity orientation on conflict in the family. *Communication Studies, 48,* 59–75.

Koesten, J. (2004). Family communication patterns, sex of subject, and communication competence. *Communication Monographs, 71,* 226–244.

Koesten, J., & Anderson, K. (2004). Exploring the influence of family communication patterns, cognitive complexity, and interpersonal competence on adolescent risk behaviors. *Journal of Family Communication, 4,* 99–121.

McCleod, J. M., & Chaffee, S. H. (1972). The construction of social reality: In J. Tedeschi (Ed.), *The social influence processes* (pp. 50–99). Chicago, IL: Aldine-Atherton.

Newcomb, T. M. (1953). An approach to the study of communicative acts. *Psychological Review, 60,* 393–404.

Ritchie, L. D. (1997). Parents' workplace experiences and family communication patterns. *Communication Research, 24,* 175–187.

Ritchie, L. D. (1991). Family communication patterns: An epistemic analysis and conceptual reinterpretation. *Communication Research, 18,* 548–565.

Ritchie, L. D., & Fitzpatrick, M. A. (1990). Family communication patterns: Measuring intrapersonal perceptions of interpersonal relationships. *Communication Research, 17,* 523–544.

Schrodt, P., & Ledbetter, A. M. (2007). Communication processes that mediate family communication patterns and mental well-being: A mean and covariance structures analysis of young adults from divorced and nondivorced families. *Human Communication Research, 33,* 330–356.

Schrodt, P., Ledbetter, A. M., & Ohrt, J. K. (2007). Parental confirmation and affection as mediators of family communication patterns and children's mental well-being. *Journal of Family Communication, 7,* 23–46.

Zhang, Q. (2007). Family communication patterns and conflict styles in Chinese parent-child relationships. *Communication Quarterly, 55,* 113–128.

Scale

Revised Family Communication Patterns (RFCP) Instrument*
Instructions: [Instructions were not provided, but one can conclude that participants are asked to reflect on their parent or child and respond to the

following statements using a 5 or 7 Likert response format employing ranges of strongly agree to strongly disagree.]

Conversation Orientation (Parent's Version)

1 In our family we often talk about topics like politics and religion where some persons disagree with others.
2 I often say things like "Every member of the family should have some say in family decisions."
3 I often ask my child's opinion when the family is talking about something.
4 I encourage my child to challenge my ideas and beliefs.
5 I often say things like "You should always look at both sides of an issue."
6 My child usually tells me what s/he is thinking about things.
7 My child can tell me most anything.
8 In our family we often talk about feelings and emotions.
9 My child and I often have long, relaxed conversations about nothing in particular.
10 I think my child really enjoys talking with me, even when we disagree.
11 I encourage my child to express his/her feelings.
12 I tend to be very open about my emotions.
13 We often talk as a family about things we have done during the day.
14 In our family, we often talk about our plans and hopes for the future.
15 I like to hear my child's opinion, even when s/he doesn't agree with me.

Conformity Orientation

16 When anything really important is involved, I expect my child to obey me without question.
17 In our home, the parents usually have the last word.
18 I feel that it is important for the parents to be the boss.
19 I sometimes become irritated with my child's views if they are different from mine.
20 If I don't approve of it, I don't want to know about it.
21 When my child is at home s/he is expected to obey the parents' rules.
22 I often say things like "You'll know better when you grow up."
23 I often say things like "My ideas are right and you should not question them."
24 I often say things like "A child should not argue with adults."
25 I often say things like "There are some things that just shouldn't be talked about."
26 I often say things like "You should give in on arguments rather than risk making people mad."

Conversation Orientation (Child's Version)

27 In our family we often talk about topics like politics and religion where some persons disagree with others.

28 My parents often say things like "Every member of the family should have some say in family decisions."

29 My parents often ask my opinion when the family is talking about something.

30 My parents encourage me to challenge their ideas and beliefs.

31 My parents often say things like "You should always look at both sides of an issue."

32 I usually tell my parents what I am thinking about things.

33 I can tell my parents almost anything.

34 In our family we often talk about feelings and emotions.

35 My parents and I often have long, relaxed conversations about nothing in particular.

36 I really enjoy talking with my parents, even when we disagree.

37 My parents encourage me to express my feelings.

38 My parents tend to be very open about their emotions.

39 We often talk as a family about things we have done during the day.

40 In our family, we often talk about our plans and hopes for the future.

41 My parents like to hear my opinion, even when I don't agree with them.

Conformity Orientation

42 When anything really important is involved, my parents expect me to obey without question.

43 In our home, my parents usually have the last word.

44 My parents feel that it is important to be the boss.

45 My parents sometimes become irritated with my views if they are different from theirs.

46 If my parents don't approve of it, they don't want to know about it.

47 When I am at home, I am expected to obey my parents' rules.

48 My parents often say things like "You'll know better when you grow up."

49 My parents often say things like "My ideas are right and you should not question them."

50 My parents often say things like "There are some things that just shouldn't be talked about."

51 My parents often say things like "A child should not argue with adults."

52 My parents often say things like "You should give in on arguments rather than risk making people mad."

Note: Scale items should be ordered randomly and subscale labels removed when preparing the scale for completion.

Revised Learning Indicators Scale (RLIS)

Profile by Rebecca B. Rubin

Spirited by prior problems in measuring cognitive learning, Frymier, Schulman, and Houser (1996) developed a Learning Indicators scale. It has since been revised to eliminate communication items to avoid bias against those with communication apprehension (Frymier & Houser, 1999). The revised scale was found to be positively correlated with teacher nonverbal immediacy, affective learning, grades, and learner empowerment.

Frymier et al. (1996) developed the 9-item learning indicators scale by asking 60 colleagues to describe what students do when they're learning. An original list of 13 items was reduced to 9 by omitting 4 items that did not correlate with "I learned a lot in this class." The scale uses 5-point interval scale anchored by never (0) and very often (4). Modest evidence of validity was reported in that it was positively correlated with affective learning and state motivation, learner empowerment, and relevance. An alpha reliability of .84 was reported. Because (a) several items contained in-class participation and communication items, (b) such participation is linked to higher grades, and (c) communication apprehension might confound learning indicators, Frymier et al. revised the scale and tested relationships with other factors previously associated with the construct for enhanced construct and concurrent validity.

In the second study (Frymier & Houser, 1999), 182 undergraduates identified a class they had just prior to their communication class to achieve a varied perspective. The original learning indicators scale was used; the alpha was .84. Four new items were added that did not involve communication, but were based on research involving learning in the past. PC oblique FA used to examine the structure. Two factors emerged with eigenvalues exceeding 1.00. Four items were deleted because of low loadings. The first factor had 7 items descriptive of learning activities, but the second factor dealt with oral participation in class. So the first factor only was used; an alpha of .85 was reported. As hypothesized, the original scale was negatively correlated with CA. The revised scale was positively correlated with nonverbal immediacy of the teacher, with students' affective learning and reported grade. The revised scale was not correlated with CA but was highly and positively correlated with affective learning, reported grades, and learner empowerment.

The scale contains 7 (and in some cases 8 items) statements about learning and students are asked how frequently they perform these behaviors in a particular class. Response options range from 0 (never) to 4 (very often). Scale means ranged from 2.32 (SD = 0.79, Frymier and Houser, 2000) for an average score, to 21.75 (SD = 5.12) for a summed score (Frymier, 2005) (M = 15.19, SD = 5.47).

Reliability

Dobransky and Frymier (2004) reported an alpha of .82 (M = 21.75, SD = 5.12) for the RLIS. Learning indicators was significantly correlated with shared control (empowerment), trust, and intimacy. Students who engaged in higher OCC with teachers indicated greater learning. In addition, learning indicators and affective learning were correlated at .58. Frymier (2005) reported an alpha of .83 (M=15.19, SD = 5.47).

Validity

Ellis (2004) tested a learning model for several teacher confirmation variables. She predicted that teacher confirmation would affect learning and found an indirect influence that was mediated by receiver apprehension. This confirms Frymier's initial concern that communication apprehension might influence scores on the scale. Frymier (2005) also found that four predicted variables—interaction involvement, assertiveness, responsiveness, and out of class learning indicators—provided some construct validity.

Comments

One concern about this scale is its face validity; the items are not really geared to how much knowledge students achieve, but more towards affective and behavioral aspects of learning. For instance, it focuses on how important the class communication is and how much it is talked about. Items 1 and 7, for example, are affect-related, whereas items 2 through 6 are behavioral in nature. This scale may be a mix of affective and behavioral learning, rather than cognitive learning. As Frymier and Houser (2000) found, both affective learning and learning indicators were significantly predicted by verbal immediacy and referential skills, so there wasn't much of a difference between them (in fact they were correlated at .53).

Location*

Frymier, A. B., & Houser, M. L. (1999). The Revised Learning Indicators Scale. *Communication Studies, 50,* 1–12.

Frymier, A. B., & Houser, M. L. (2000). The teacher–student relationship as an interpersonal relationship. *Communication Education, 49,* 207–219.

References

Dobransky, N. D., & Frymier, A. B. (2004). Developing teacher-student relations through out of class communication. *Communication Quarterly. 52,* 211–223.

Ellis, K. (2004). The impact of perceived teacher confirmation on receiver apprehension, motivation, and learning. *Communication Education, 53,* 264–291.

Frymier, A. B. (2005). Students' classroom communication effectiveness. *Communication Quarterly, 53,* 197–212.

Frymier, A. B., & Houser, M. L. (2000). The teacher–student relationship as an interpersonal relationship. *Communication Education, 49,* 207–219.

Frymier, A. B., Shulman, G. M., & Houser, M. (1996). The development of a learning empowerment measure. *Communication Education, 45,* 181–199.

McCroskey, J. C., Richmond, V. P., Plax, T. G., & Kearney, P. (1985). Power in the classroom V: Behavior alternation techniques, communication training and learning. *Communication Education, 34,* 214–226.

Witt, P. L., Wheeless, L. R., & Allen, M. (2004). A meta-analytical review of the relationship between teacher immediacy and student learning. *Communication Monographs, 71,* 184–207.

Scale

Revised Learning Indicators Scale (RLIS)*

Directions: Indicate how frequently you perform each of these behaviors in your class that immediately precedes _____. Use the following scale.

Never = 0   Rarely = 1   Occasionally = 2   Often = 3   Very Often = 4

1   I like to talk about what I'm doing in this class with friends and family.
2   I explain course content to other students
3   I think about the course content outside the class.
4   I see connections between the course content and my career goals.
5   I review the course content.
6   I compare the information from this class with other things I have learned.
7   I feel I have learned a lot in this class.

Note: Frymier and Houser (2000) included an additional item: "I discuss course content with other students."

Risk Behavior Diagnosis (RBD) Scale

Profile by Rebecca B. Rubin

The Risk Behavior Diagnosis Scale was developed by Kim Witte in 1995; an article detailing its development and reliability and validity information, however, was published in 1996 by Witte, Cameron, McKeon, and Berkowitz. The scale follows the tenets of the Extended Parallel Processing Model, which explains that when people experience a health threat, they must handle the potential danger by controlling either the threat or their fear of it; this is done by weighing the perceived chance of risking the threat (perceived threat) against behavior that would have to be taken to protect themselves against it (perceived efficacy). When both threat and efficacy are high, people are more likely to follow doctors' orders, but when threat is high and efficacy is low, they then reject doctors' orders through avoidance or denial. When either threat or efficacy is low, health professionals must target messages to those areas. The scale provides health professionals with a quick and easy way to identify low threat and low efficacy.

Content validity was assessed by asking 10 raters to classify each item into the four construct categories—perceived response efficacy, perceived self-efficacy, perceived severity, perceived susceptibility—that were developed previously, and in 94% of the cases they were correctly classified (Witte et al., 1996). Tests of construct validity examined correlations within and between the four dimensions; these results and the factor analysis confirmed the four main components contained in the scale. And tests of predictive validity showed that the scale correctly predicted danger and fear control.

The scale contains 12 items, 6 each for threat and efficacy, and takes only a few minutes to complete. Threat can be broken further into 3-item severity and susceptibility subscales and efficacy into response and self-efficacy subscales. Overall scores are determined by subtracting the population mean from the efficacy score and dividing by the standard deviation of the population. Likewise, the threat score is computed by dividing the population mean from the individual's score and dividing this by the standard deviation of the population. Then the computed threat score is subtracted from the computed efficacy score. If this number is positive, the patient is in danger, and if equal to or less than zero, the patient is in fear control. A detailed manual with sample messages and elaboration on the model is available from Kim Witte.

Reliability

Because of the computations performed, coefficient alphas are not reported. However some have used the subscales without dealing with population means and have reported acceptable alphas (Dassow, 2005; Yun, Govender, & Mody, 2001). Gore and Bracken (2005) reported pre-test and post-test alphas for the subscales ranging from .85 to .97, indicating relative internal consistency. Umphrey (2004) used a 7-item adaptation for breast cancer and self exam research and reported a .90 alpha for self-efficacy and .70 for response efficacy.

Validity

Witte et al. (1996) provided extensive data about content and construct validity. In addition, the RBDS has been used to identify efficacy and threat groups for studies dealing with meningitis (Gore & Bracken, 2005), breast cancer (Umphrey, 2004), HIV/AIDS (Yun et al., 2001), and colon, breast, and osteoporosis screening (Dassow, 2005). In addition, the measure appears to provide data useful in testing the Extended Parallel Processing Model (Gore & Bracken, 2005).

Comments

One possible difficulty of using this scale is the need for normative means and standard deviations. Health professionals would need to test a sample of 50 or more to determine norms. If normative information is not possible, the author suggests merely subtracting the threat score from the efficacy score. This latter method is less precise but provides a general guide for administering health messages. Use of the four subscales, as evidenced in Gore and Bracken (2005) poses potential validity issues when attempting to be consistent with the theoretical foundation.

Location

Witte, K. (2001). The Risk Behavior Diagnosis Scale. In K. Witte, G. Meyer, & D. Martell, *Effective health risk messages: A step-by-step guide* (pp. 67–76). Thousand Oaks, CA: Sage.*

Witte, K., Cameron, K. A., McKeon, J. K., & Berkowitz, J. M. (1996). Predicting risk behaviors: Development and validation of a diagnostic scale. *Journal of Health Communication, 1,* 317–341.**

References

Dassow, P. (2005). Setting educational priorities for women's preventative health: Measuring beliefs about screening across disease states. *Journal of Women's Health, 14*, 324–330.

Gore, T. D., & Bracken, C. C. (2005). Testing the theoretical design of a health risk message: Reexamining the major tenets of the extended parallel process model. *Health Education & Behavior, 32*, 27–41.

Umphrey, L. R. (2004). Message defensiveness, efficacy, and health-related behavioral intentions. *Communication Research Reports, 21*, 329–337.

Witte, K. (1995). Fishing for success: Using the persuasive health message framework to generate effective campaign messages. In E. Maibach, & R. Parrott (Eds.), *Designing health messages: Approaches from communication theory and public health practice* (pp. 145–166). Newbury Park, CA: Sage.

Yun, H., Govender, K., & Mody, B. (2001). Factoring poverty and culture into HIV/AIDS campaigns: Empirical support for audience segmentation. *International Communication Gazette, 63*, 73–95.

Scale

Risk Behavior Diagnosis Scale**

Define Threat:_____

Define Recommended Response:_____

Strongly Disagree	1	2	3	4	5	Strongly Agree

1 [*Recommended response*] is effective in preventing [*health threat*]:

2 [*Recommended response*] work in preventing [*health threat*]:

3 If I [*do recommended response*], I am less likely to get [*health threat*]:

4 I am able to [*do recommended response*] to prevent getting [*health threat*]:

5 I have the [*skills/time/money*] to [*do recommended response*] to prevent [*health threat*]:

6 I can easily [*do recommended response*] to prevent [*health threat*]:

7 I believe that [*health threat*] is severe:

8 I believe that [*health threat*] has serious negative consequences:

9 I believe that [*health threat*] is extremely harmful:

10 It is likely that I will get [*health threat*]:

11 I am at risk for getting [*health threat*]:

12 It is possible that I will get [*health threat*]:

Note: Items 1–3 are Response Efficacy; Items 4–6 are Self-Efficacy, Items 7–9 are Severity, and 10–12 are Susceptability. Efficacy is determined by adding items 1–6 and Threat is computed by adding items 7–12.

* © 2001 by Sage Publications.

** © 1996 by Taylor & Francis.

Sad Film Scale

Profile by Elizabeth M. Perse

Mary Beth Oliver (1993) created the Sad Film Scale in order to understand individuals' seemingly unlikely enjoyment of sad films. Although some tear-jerkers end on an optimistic note, Oliver notes that many "conspicuously lack optimistic or cheerful conclusions" (p. 318). Given the hedonistic assumptions of mood management approaches (Zillmann & Bryant, 1985), these types of movies should be inversely related to enjoyment. This is not, in fact, the case, and Oliver set out to "untangle the paradox of the enjoyment of sad films or tear-jerkers" by looking at the distinction between direct responses (emotional reactions) to the films and meta-emotions. A meta-emotion is a response to an emotional reaction (Feagin, 1983). In other words, a person might experience positive affect following a sad movie if the sadness he or she experiences is perceived as gratifying. In contrast, if the meta-emotions associated with sadness are favorable, a tear-jerker that evokes no feelings of sadness should be perceived as less gratifying than those that arouse sad feelings.

Oliver (1993) developed the Sad Film Scale (SFS) in order to operationalize the pleasurable meta-emotions associated with watching sad films. To develop the SFS, Oliver asked a group of college students why they did or did not like "sad films or tear-jerkers." From their responses, Oliver generated 40 statements pertaining to enjoyment of sad films (Oliver, 1993, p. 325). After pretests and statistical analyses, the scale was reduced to 15 items that reflected either the tendency to experience emotional responses to sad films or the enjoyment of such responses.

The Sad Film Scale has been used to Oliver (1993) and her colleagues (Oliver, Weaver, & Sargent, 2000) to explore the viewer characteristics associated with higher SFS scores. Research using the SFS has tested hypotheses involving gender differences (e.g., Oliver, 1993; Oliver et al., 2000) and dimensions of empathy (Oliver, 1993), defined in this context as generalized concern for the well-being of fictional characters.

The 15-item Sad Film Scale developed by Oliver (1993) is reported here. Respondents report their agreement with each statement on a 7-point scale

(1 = strongly disagree, 7 = strongly agree). Item responses are averaged to yield a SFS score. The scale takes about 2 minutes to complete.

Reliability

The Sad Film Scale has demonstrated reliability. To consider the SFS's temporal stability, Oliver asked 40 participants from her first study to complete the scale a second time approximately 45 days after the initial testing. Test-retest reliabilities were .88 for males and .75 for females. Internal consistency (Cronbach's alpha), also calculated by Oliver (1993), was equal to .94 for males and .95 for females. In their 2000 study, Oliver and her colleagues found a Cronbach alpha of .94.

Validity

There is good evidence of the validity of the Sad Film Scale. Because Oliver's (1993) SFS was intended to reflect both the tendency to experience sadness during tear-jerkers and the tendency to find this emotional experience enjoyable, its construct validity is demonstrated by associations between SFS scores and reported enjoyment, exposure, and sad responses to sad films. To examine these relationships, Oliver (1993) used median splits (calculated separately for each gender) to form low- and high-SFS groups. She then conducted a 2 (SFS Group) $\times$ 2 (Gender) MANOVA using with the following exposure and response measures used as dependent variables: Enjoyment of sad films, frequency of exposure to sad films, number of films viewed from the list of sad films provided in the study, average enjoyment of these films, and average sad responses to films seen (Oliver, 1993, p. 330). A strong main effect was found for SFS Group: Oliver found that the SFS groups differed significantly on all of these measures in the predicted direction. Subsequent analyses that controlled for gender, enjoyment of other film genres, and frequency of viewing other film genres revealed greater enjoyment and frequency of viewing sad films for High SFS respondents, as expected.

Oliver (1993) assessed predictive validity by comparing respondents' scores on the SFS with their reactions to viewing *Cinema Paradiso*, a feature-length sad film. High SFS participants reported significantly more enjoyment of the film, reported experiencing more meta-emotions, and reported marginally more feelings of sadness than the low SFS participants.

To demonstrate the discriminant validity of the instrument, Oliver conducted analyses to ensure that the SFS measures enjoyment of sad films did not reflect enjoyment of films in general. After controlling for gender, high SFS groups reported more enjoyment of romance and drama film genres, those likely to include sad themes. There was no difference in reported enjoyment of seven other film genres, including comedy, suspense, action-adventure, science fiction, horror, documentaries, and adult entertainment.

Two tests provide evidence of construct validity for the measure. The theoretical reasoning underlying the development of the scale holds that enjoyment of sad films is linked to pleasurable meta-emotions. That is, enjoyment results because viewers enjoy feeling sad. Oliver (1993) correlated scores on the SFS with responses to an item that reflected enjoying sad films when they had a happy ending. Consistent with the theoretical reasoning behind the development of the scale, scores on this item were negatively linked to SFS scores ($r = -.14$, $p < .05$). In a later study, Oliver and her associates (2000) created two different descriptions of the same sad film. As part of their experimental manipulation, one description highlighted an agentic theme, focusing on male-oriented concepts of independence and self-assertion. The other description marked a communal theme, which focused on female-oriented concepts such as nurturance, empathy, and emotionality. Although there were predictable gender differences in reactions to the two descriptions, there were no differences between the high and low SFS groups. Enjoyment of the film descriptions did not appear to be linked to agentic or communal themes.

Comments

Although Oliver made an admirable effort to look at both the reliability and validity of this measure, as a new scale, SFS would benefit from further investigation by other researchers. Oliver acknowledges that the films presented to respondents for evaluation could also decrease the validity of uses of this measure. Until a broader sampling of films is used in a variety of studies, it is difficult to determine whether differences reflect characteristics of or individual differences between the few films selected for the study at hand. Likewise, Oliver suggests that an over-representation of films directed toward female audiences from this genre could prove problematic.

Another shortcoming of research completed thus far using SFS lies in the fact that Oliver's (1993) original study, and those that have followed using this scale, have relied exclusively on self-report measures. As Oliver points out, emotion-based measures may be particularly likely to reflect biases due to gender stereotypes regarding socially desirable "male" and "female" emotional reactions (p. 337). Therefore, future research in this area would benefit from less obtrusive physiological or facial expression measures (e.g., Oliver & Green, 2001).

It is also noteworthy that sampling procedures for studies done using this scale thus far have been lacking and have included only college students (Oliver, 1993; Oliver et al., 2000). Although there is no reason to suspect that college students would differ from the rest of the population in terms of this concept, such a sample decreases the external validity of the studies at hand.

Finally, though this scale's recognition of meta-emotions, as distinguished from first-hand emotional reactions, has proven valid and reliable, it is important to recognize other possible gratifications derived from sad entertainment. Neuendorf (1998) studied some of these other gratifications, referring to them as types of "wallowing." She investigated the hypothesis that wallowers are more likely to respond to feelings of sadness and depression with greater functional use of sad content. Respondents were identified as Cathartic Criers if they felt better after crying during a sad show. Out of the three types of wallowers found in Neuendorf's study, this was the only factor index related to a preference for sad films. Neuendorf points out that Cathartic Criers closely fit Oliver's (1993) model of the female fan of sad movies. Neuendorf (1998) argues that sad films can fill other functions for audiences beyond enjoyment. The SFS is, however, a promising instrument that should be used to tap into deeper theoretical questions in the future, and could also be altered to look at other types of media, such as television and sad music.

Location*

Oliver, M. B. (1993). Exploring the paradox of the enjoyment of sad films. *Human Communication Research, 19*, 315–342.

References

Feagin, S. L. (1983). The pleasures of tragedy. *American Philosophical Quarterly, 20*, 95–104.

Neuendorf, K. A. (1998, August). *Mood congruence and the utility of sad media content.* Paper presented to the Communication Theory and Methodology Division of the Association for Education in Journalism and Mass Communication, Baltimore, MD.

Oliver, M. B., & Green, S. (2001). Development of gender differences in children's responses to animated entertainment. *Sex Roles, 45*, 67–88.

Oliver, M. B., Sargent, S. L., & Weaver, J. B., III. (1998). The impact of sex and gender role self-perception on affective reactions to different types of films. *Sex Roles, 38*, 45–62.

Oliver, M. B., Weaver, J. B., III, & Sargent, S. L. (2000). An examination of factors related to sex differences in enjoyment of sad films. *Journal of Broadcasting & Electronic Media, 44*, 282–300.

Zillmann, D., & Bryant, J. (1985). Affect, mood, and emotion as determinants of selective exposure. In D. Zillmann, & J. Bryant (Eds.), *Selective exposure to communication* (pp. 157–190). Hillsdale, NJ: Erlbaum.

Scale

Sad Film Scale *
Directions: Please indicate how much you agree or disagree with the following statements concerning your perceptions of sad films.

| 1 | 2 | 3 | 4 | 5 | 6 | 7 |

Strongly Disagree   Neither Agree   Strongly Agree
                                     Nor Disagree

1 I don't enjoy getting involved in other people's worries or troubles shown in sad movies.
2 I like sad movies because they allow me to become part of another world.
3 Sad movies are too simplistic or unrealistic for me to enjoy.
4 I enjoy feeling strong emotions in response to sad movies.
5 I don't like sad movies because I would rather feel happy than sad when watching a film.
6 One reason I like sad movies is because they help me release my own sadness.
7 I enjoy getting wrapped up in the lives of the characters in sad movies.
8 Sad movies are too depressing for me to enjoy.
9 I find sad movies entertaining because they make me think about life.
10 Sad movies are too dramatic for me to enjoy.
11 I usually find sad movies too boring to be enjoyable.
12 I like watching sad movies because I can relate to the feelings and emotions of the characters.
13 I don't enjoy sad movies because I like to be entertained or stimulated when I watch a film.
14 It feels good to cry when watching a sad movie.
15 I find sad movies silly rather than sad.

Note: Items 1, 3, 5, 8, 10, 11, 13, and 15 are reverse-coded for data analysis.

Self-Assessment Manikin

Profile by Elizabeth M. Perse

The Self-Assessment Manikin (SAM) measures emotional responses to various stimuli by serving as a visual representation of pleasure, arousal, and dominance (PAD). Scholars hold that these three dimensions are the core of human emotion (Merhrabian & Russel, 1974). Created to take advantage of the graphics capabilities of the computer, SAM was initially presented to subjects as an oscilloscope display under the control of a joystick (P. Lang, 1980). The SAM instrument portrays each of the three PAD dimensions with drawings of a character. Respondents are asked to select the figure that is most consistent with their reaction to the stimulus, rating all three dimensions for each message being investigated. Depiction of pleasure ranges from a smiling character to a frowning one, while the arousal dimension progresses from a sleeping avatar to one who is apparently excited. Dominance is portrayed using figures ranging from a small character to a large and imposing one. In its original computerized form, the joystick altered SAM's expression for each of the polar adjective sets on scales that varied continuously from 0 to 64 while increased motion using the computer's animation capability emphasized the character's arousal (P. Lang, 1980).

Subsequent uses of SAM as a pen-and-paper measure have been mainly (but not exclusively) limited to scales comprised of five images for each of the three dimensions (e.g., Lombard, Reich, Grabe, Braken, & Ditton, 2000). After a short orientation to the method, subjects are asked to mark their selection in a circle below a particular image or between two adjacent images, creating nine-point scales for each dimension (Fujioka, 2005; A. Lang, Potter, & Bolls, 1999; Morris, 1995). In another computerized version of SAM, Bradley, Codispoti, Cuthbert, and Lang (2001) used 20-point scales for each of their dimensions.

Though it was conceived in the field of psychology, SAM has proven useful to mass communication scholars, particularly in the study of reactions to television (e.g., A. Lang et al., 1999), radio (Bolls, Lang, & Potter, 2001), news (e.g., Grabe, Zhou, Lang, & Bolls, 2000), music (Morris & Boone, 1998), and in advertising (Morris, 1995). Continuing research has also investigated gender differences and the relative stability of emotional responses to commercials and public-service announcements across subjects through varying presentation order (Morris & Karrh, 1995). More generalized media effects research has used SAM to study the impact of various types of imagery—for example, violence and erotica (Bradley, Codispoti, Sabatinelli, & Lang, 2001)—on viewers' emotional states. A. Lang, Schwartz, Chung, and Lee (2004) also used the instrument to look at adolescents' and college-students' responses to various characteristics of substance abuse public service announcements. A. Lang, Potter, and Grabe (2003) used the arousal dimension of SAM as a predictor of viewer recall of local television news.

The instrument has been used successfully with a variety of different samples. For example, researchers have used SAM to compare responses from general and Hispanic markets in the United States (Fujioka, 2005; Morris, Strausbaugh, & Nthangeni, 1996). It has been used with college student samples (Bradley & Lang, 1994; A. Lang et al., 1999), manual laborers with no more than high school education (Grabe et al., 2000), children (Greenbaum, Turner, Cook, & Melamed, 1990), and adults (Grabe et al., 2003). SAM can be presented via computer screen or paper and pencil.

Reliability

It is difficult to assess the reliability of this measure for two reasons. First, there can be no measure of internal consistency, due to the fact that a single semantic differential scale measures each of the dimensions. Second, assessment of this measure's reliability is also limited by the dynamic nature of human emotion. Arousal, in particular, is an ever-changing state, thus rendering any investigation of stability over time or test-retest reliability basically irrelevant. Bradley and P. Lang (1994), however, offer evidence of measurement stability. SAM scores collected via computer and paper and pencil are strongly related: pleasure ($r = .99$), arousal ($r = .94$) and dominance ($r = .79$). Lombard and his colleagues (2000) treated film scenes (not participants) as the units of analysis in their study of the impact of screen size on perception of presence. As such, valence, arousal, and dominance rating by 65 viewers were averaged to create reliable scales: pleasure $\alpha = .74$, arousal $\alpha = .84$, dominance $\alpha = .85$.

Validity

Content validity establishes that a measure covers the full range of a concept's meaning. SAM improves upon the content validity of verbal measures of PAD (e.g., Mehrabian & Russell, 1974) by eliminating problems typically associated with verbal measures (Morris, 1995). Because verbal measures are cognitively based, participants must think about the emotion and how it relates to the available adjectives. In other words, the meaning of emotional adjectives may vary from person to person (Morris & Boone, 1998). When using open-ended questions, these difficulties become even more apparent, as questions may be interpreted in a variety of ways, and respondents may not possess a sufficient vocabulary to express their feelings precisely. Thus, nonverbal measures like SAM remain closer to the unarticulated nature of emotions.

Research provides strong evidence for the concurrent validity of the pleasure and arousal dimensions of SAM. The correlations between scores obtained using SAM and those obtained from Mehrabian and Russell's (1974) PAD instrument were impressive for both pleasure ($r = .96$) and arousal ($r = .95$), but smaller for dominance ($r = .23$) (Bradley & P. Lang, 1994). Other researchers have demonstrated that the pleasure and dominance measures are consistent with other measures assessing the same emotions. Bradley, Greenwald, Petry, and P. Lang (1992) found that SAM arousal measures covaried with skin conductance, a physiological measure of arousal (Hopkins & Fletcher, 1994). Ravaja, Saari, Kallinen, and Laarni (2006) reported that arousal ratings using computer screen administered SAM paralleled, for the most part, physiological ratings from electrocardiogram and facial EMG activity.

Construct validity is strongly linked to concurrent validity. Fujioka (2005), for example, reports that, consistent with his hypothesis, Mexican Americans reported more arousal than whites while watching news stories about Mexican Americans.

Comments

There is only weak evidence for the concurrent validity of the dominance dimension. For this reason, researchers often look exclusively at the dimensions of arousal and valence. The inconsistent results with the dominance dimensions might indicate a lack of clarity as to whether the subjects are rating their own, as opposed to the stimuli's feelings of control, and may also be due to the strong correlation between the dominance and valence dimensions (Bradley et al., 1992).

The realm of uses for this instrument is vast, as is evident from its widespread application in psychology, communication, and marketing. Other benefits include a rapid response time of less than 15 seconds, allowing more stimuli to be examined, and a smaller degree of participant attrition due to the interesting nature of the images. Children, with or without reading skills, can successfully use this scale (P. Lang, 1980), and cross-cultural studies have also proven successful (e.g., Fujioka, 2005; Morris et al., 1996). The strong evidence of the concurrent validity of the scale suggests that researchers can use it to assess experimental manipulations (e.g., Fujioka, 2005; A. Lang, Dhillon, & Dong, 1995).

Location

Bradley, M. M., & Lang, P. J. (1994). Measuring emotion: The self-assessment manikin and the semantic differential. *Journal of Behavior Therapy and Experimental Psychology, 25*, 49–59.

References

Bolls, P. D., Lang, A., & Potter, R. F. (2001). The effects of message valence and listener arousal on attention, memory, and facial muscular responses to radio advertisements. *Communication Research, 28*, 627–651.

Bradley, M. M., Codispoti, M., Cuthbert, B. N., & Lang, P. J. (2001). Emotion and motivation, I: Defensive and appetitive reactions in picture processing. *Emotion, 1*, 276–299.

Bradley, M. M., Codispoti, M., Sabatinelli, D., & Lang, P. J. (2001). Emotion and motivation, II: Sex differences in picture processing. *Emotion, 1*, 300–319.

Bradley, M. M., Greenwald, M. K., Petry, M. C., & Lang, P. J. (1992). Remembering pictures: Pleasure and arousal in memory. *Journal of Experimental Psychology: Learning, Memory, and Cognition, 18*, 379–390.

Fujioka, Y. (2005). Emotional TV viewing and minority audience: How Mexican Americans process and evaluate TV news about in-group members. *Communication Research, 32*, 566–593.

Grabe, M. E., Zhou, S., Lang, A., & Bolls, P. D. (2000). Packaging television news: The effects of tabloid on information processing and evaluative responses. *Journal of Broadcasting & Electronic Media, 44*, 581–598.

Greenbaum, P. E., Turner, C., Cook, E. W., & Melamed, B. G. (1990). Dentists' voice control: Effects on children's disruptive and affective behavior. *Health Psychology, 9*, 546–558.

Hopkins, R., & Fletcher, J. E. (1994). Electrodermal measurement: Particularly effective for forecasting message influence on sales appeal. In A. Lang (Ed.), *Measuring psychological responses to media* (pp. 113–132). Mahwah, NJ: Erlbaum.

Lang, A., Dhillon, K., & Dong, Q. (1995). The effects of emotional arousal and valence on television viewers' cognitive capacity and memory. *Journal of Broadcasting & Electronic Media, 39*, 313–327.

Lang, A., Potter, D., & Bolls, P. D. (1999). Something for nothing: Is visual encoding automatic? *Media Psychology, 1*, 145–163.

Lang, A., Potter, R. F., & Grabe, M. E. (2003). Making news memorable: Applying theory to the production of local television news. *Journal of Broadcasting & Electronic Media, 47*, 113–123.

Lang, A., Schwartz, N., Chung, Y., & Lee, S. (2004). Processing substance abuse messages: Production pacing, arousing content, and age. *Journal of Broadcasting & Electronic Media, 48*, 61–88.

Lang, P. J. (1980). Behavioral treatment and bio-behavioral treatment: Computer applications. In J. B. Sidowski, J. H. Johnson, & T. A. Williams (Eds.), *Technology in mental health care delivery systems* (pp. 119–137). Norwood, NJ: Ablex.

Lang, P. J., Bradley, M. M., & Cuthbart, B. N. (1997). *International Affective*

Picture System (IAPS). Technical Manual and Affective Ratings. Retrieved, February 15, 2008, from: http://209.85.173.104/search?q=cache: QaBSGEeZrScJ:www.unifesp.br/dpsicobio/adap/instructions.pdf+%22inter-national+affective+picture+system%22&hl=en&ct=clnk&cd=3&gl=us

Lombard, M., Reich, R. D., Grabe, M. E., Bracken, C. C., & Ditton, T. B. (2000). Presence and television: The role of screen size. *Human Communication Research, 26,* 75–98.

Mehrabian, A., & Russell, J. A. (1974). *An approach to environmental psychology,* Cambridge MA: MIT Press.

Morris, J. D. (1995). Observations: SAM: The self-assessment manikin—An efficient cross-cultural measurement of emotional response. *Journal of Advertising Research, 35*(6), 63–68.

Morris, J. D., & Boone, M. A. (1998). The effects of music on emotional response, brand attitude, and purchase intent in an emotional advertising condition. *Advances in Consumer Research, 25,* 518–526.

Morris, J. D., & Karrh, J. A. (1995). Assessing affective response to television advertising using the self-assessment manikin. In C. Madden (Ed.), *Proceedings of the 1995 Conference of the American Academy of Advertising* (pp. 43–50) Waco, TX: Baylor University.

Morris, J. D., Strausbaugh, K. L., & Nthangeni, N. (1996). A design for measuring and interpreting emotional response to advertisements across cultures. In G. Wilcox (Ed.), *Proceedings of the 1996 Conference of the American Academy of Advertising* (pp. 47–54). Austin: University of Texas.

Ravaja, N., Saari, T., Kallinen, K., & Laarni, J. (2006). The role of mood in the processing of media messages from a small screen: Effects on subjective and physiological responses. *Media Psychology, 8,* 239–265.

Scale

Self-Assessment Manikin*
See manual instructions by Lang, Bradley, and Cuthbart (1997).

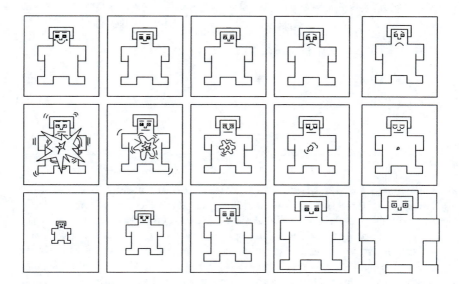

*Reprinted from *Journal of Behavior Therapy and Experimental Psychology*, Vol. 25, by M. M. Bradley & P. J. Lang, Measuring emotion: The self-assessment manikin and the semantic differential, pp. 49–59, 1994, with permission from Elsevier.

Self-Construal Scales

Profile by David R. Seibold

Self-construal is described as the constellation of thoughts, feelings, and actions regarding an individual's relationships to other people and the self as distinct from other people (Constantine & Yeh, 2001). Some research provides empirical evidence that there are two orthogonal dimensions of self that exist within each individual regardless of his/her cultural identity and can be measured as such (Gudykunst et al., 1996; Kim et al., 2001; Singelis, 1994), although recently this has been intensely contested by some communication scholars (Levine et al., 2003a; Levine et al., 2003b), as reviewed in the Comments section below. However, many communication scholars have conducted self-construal research in many and varied venues in communication (see Ellis & Wittenbaum, 2000; Grace & Cramer, 2003; Gudykunst & Lee, 2003; Gudykunst et al., 1994; Kim et al., 2000; Kim & Sharkey, 1995; Oetzel & Oetzel, 1997; Oguri & Gudykunst, 2002; Park, 2001; Sharkey & Singelis, 1995; Singelis et al., 1999).

Independent and interdependent self-construals refer to the degree to which people conceive of themselves as separate or connected to others (Kim & Sharkey, 1995). Independent self-construal is comprised of internal abilities, feelings, and thoughts; being unique and expressing the self; and realizing internal attributes and promoting one's goals (Markus & Kitayama, 1991; Singelis 1994). People who have an interdependent self-construal want to fit in with others, act appropriately, promote others' goals, and value conformity and cooperation (Markus & Kitayama, 1991). Gudykunst et al. (1996) contended that independent self-construal is associated mainly with people of individualistic cultures, whereas interdependent self-construal is associated mainly with people of collectivistic cultures. The self-construal construct is argued to provide individual-level explanation for cultural differences (Park, Levine, & Sharkey, 1998).

There are three distinct scales that are commonly used to measure self-construals (Gudykunst et al., 1996; Leung & Kim, 1997; Singelis, 1994). Each chronologically successive scale appears to be a refinement of earlier measure(s). For example, Gudykunst et al. (1996) included items from Singelis (1994) along with new items, and Leung (1997), in the original version of Leung & Kim (1997), included both Singelis and Gudykunst items. Gudykunst and Lee (2003, p. 268) detail the sources from which items in the Gydykunst et al. (1996) and the Leung and Kim (1997) scales were drawn. Neither Gudykunst et al. nor Leung provide an explanation for why scale revisions were necessary, but the evolution of the scales suggests that subsequent authors were dissatisfied with previous measures (Levine et al., 2003a).

Singelis (1994) Self-Construal Scale

Items were developed to measure the constellation of thoughts, feelings, and actions composing independent and interdependent self-construals (Singelis, 1994). Initially, items were gathered from various instruments including items used by Cross and Markus (1991), Yamaguchi (1994), and Bhawuk and Brislin (1992) among others. The items were then rewritten to focus on the individual's self-construal. All together, 45 items were included in the initial SCS. A principal components factor analysis was then used to determine which of the 45 items were most useful in measuring the two dimensions of self. Items not loading highly (greater than .35) on either factor or loading approximately equally on the two factors were dropped.

The resultant 24-item Self-Construal Scale (SCS) created by Singelis (1994) has two 12-item subscales assessing independent and interdependent self-construal respectively. The measure uses a 7-point Likert scale (1 = *strongly disagree* and 7 = *strongly agree*) (also see Singelis & Brown, 1995; Singelis & Sharkey, 1995).

Gudykunst et al. (1994, 1996) Self Construal Scales

The Self Construal Scales created by Gudykunst et al. (1994, 1996) (who do not use a hyphen with the scale name) consist of 29 items using a 7-point Likert-type response scale (1 = *strongly disagree*, 7 = *strongly agree*). The 14 items used to measure independent self-construals reflect individuals' tendencies to view themselves as autonomous, unique, and bounded entities in relation to others. The 15 items used to measure interdependent self-construals represent individuals "being embedded in group relationships that affect their behaviors" (Gudykunst et al., 1996, p. 527) and their needs to be included and connected to others in social relationships and in their in-groups. All 29 items appear in the Appendix of the response essay by Gudykunst and Lee (2003).

Leung and Kim (1997) Self-Construal Scale

The Leung and Kim (1997) Self-Construal Scale consolidates the most salient elements from prior SCS and incorporates items reflecting concepts related to self-construals not included in previous scales. The instrument uses most items from Singelis's (1994) self-construal scale, the Gudykunst et al. (1996) self construal scales, and instruments employed by Cross (1995) and by Kim, Sharkey, and Singelis (1994). Some items were combined to minimize redundancy, but most items were retained except for grammatical rephrasing. The scale created by Leung and Kim (1997) is a 29-item revised SCS. The independence subscale includes 15 scale items that assess (1) a sense of uniqueness, (2) a sense of self-reliance, and (3) valuing one's personal opinions. The interdependence subscale includes 14 items that assess (1) a sense of uniqueness, (2) a sense of self-reliance, and (3) valuing one's personal opinions (Mortenson, 2005). The measure utilizes a 7-point Likert scale (1 = *strongly disagree* to 7 = *strongly agree*).

Items from each scale are summarized at the conclusion of this profile. All non-redundant items are listed. In order to facilitate comparison across two or three scales, wording of scale items are not exact.

Reliability

Singelis (1994) Self-Construal Scale

Singelis (1994) reported internal consistency coefficients (Cronbach alpha) of .69 and .70 for independent items in Sample 1 and Sample 2 respectively, and .73 and .74 for the interdependent items in the two samples.

Gudykunst et al. (1994, 1996) Self Construal Scales

Gudykunst et al. found the 14 items measuring interdependent self construal to yield internal reliabilities between .80 and .85 across the four cultures sampled, while the 15 items that tap independent self construal yielded alpha coefficients between .77 and .83.

Leung and Kim (1997) Self-Construal Scale

The reliabilities of the independent and interdependent subscales ranged between .89 and .91, and .81 and .89, respectively (Kim et al., 1996).

Validity

Singelis (1994) Self-Construal Scale

Construct validity was demonstrated by comparing an Asian American with a Caucasian American sample. Differences that are consistent with Markus and Kitayama's (1991) characterizations of Asians as interdependent and North Americans as independent would indicate validity. The items on each subscale were averaged to give individuals an independent and interdependent score, higher scores indicating a stronger self-construal. The Asian American group was more interdependent and the Caucasian American group was more independent (Singelis, 1994).

Gudykunst et al. (1994, 1996) Self Construal Scales

A two factor solution (independent versus interdependent self construal) consistent with the Markus and Kitayama's (1991) original construct explication was considered evidence for the construct validity of the Self Construal Scales created by Gudykunst et al. (1994, 1996). The convergent validity of the Gudykunst et al. scales is based on findings that the independence items correlated with individualistic values, whereas the interdependence items correlated with collectivistic values (Oetzel, 2001).

Leung and Kim (1997) Self-Construal Scale

The revised version of self-construal scale by Leung and Kim (1997) produced the expected cross-cultural differences in self-construals that have eluded several previous researchers. However, the scale raised another problem. Respondents scored higher on independent self-construal. A cross-cultural study by Park (1997), which used the same scale, found similar results. However, this finding may not be scale specific. The authors' informal review of 13 studies (involving the use of several different versions of SCS) indicated that persons from collectivistic cultures usually score higher on independent self-construal than on interdependent self-construal. If independent self-construal is emphasized over interdependent self-construal regardless of culture, it is questioned how the theoretical claim that the interdependent self-construal predominates in collectivist cultures can be justified (Park & Levine, 1999). Levine et al. (2003b) found that self-construals appear to lack construct validity because the scales used to measure self-construals may be problematic.

Comments

Self-construal scales by Singelis (1994), Gudykunst et al. (1994, 1996), and Leung and Kim (1997) have appeared in numerous cross-cultural studies. Given the quantity of research using those scales, relatively little validation work has been published. Of the three principal scales, only the original validation of Singelis (1994) and an independent validation of the Gudykunst scale (Hackman, Ellis, Johnson, & Staley, 1999) have been published. Both argued for the validity of the respective scales, but their conclusions are inconsistent with their data (Levine et al., 2003b). For example, Hackman et al. reported a confirmatory factor analysis (CFA) of the Gudykunst scale and found that, in order to make the model fit, they had to disregard tests of parallelism completely, discard six items, and correlate several error terms in internal consistency.

According to Levine and colleagues (2003a), self-construal scales lack validity for three primary reasons. First, their meta-analysis showed massive heterogeneity of effects, suggesting powerful artifacts. Second, priming experiments revealed that self-construal scales are insensitive to priming, whereas previous research consistently demonstrates that alternative measures of the same construct should behave similarly. Third, not only did the examined interdependent and independent self-construal scales lack stability and unidimensionality, but they were invariant as well. Levine et al. (2003b) offered other reasons why the validity of self-construals may be problematic, including sensitivity to situational priming; the existence of a Western, independence bias; faulty scale construction and validation; and an overly simplistic conceptualization of self-construal.

In particular, data presented by Levine et al. (2003b) suggested serious flaws in the three major self-construal scales above. Their data showed that self-construal scales do not reliably reflect the intended cultural differences. The interdependent self-construal scale functions as a stable trait that fails to reflect situationally variable aspects of self-concept. Results obtained using SCS fail to match with the results obtained using alternative measures of the same construct. Too, the intended two-factor measurement fails to fit the data. The data presented by Levine et al. (2003b) demonstrate that the results obtained from self-construal scales are incompatible with the constructs the scales were designed to measure. Additional studies (Matsumoto, 1999; Kanagawa et al., 2001; Kitayama, 2002; Markus & Kitayama, 1998) also indicate that self-report scales may be unsuitable to study interdependent self-construals. Levine et al. (2003b) concluded that future cross-cultural research should avoid using existing self-construal scales, and researchers may wish to rethink if closed-format self-report scales are the best way to assess self-concept in non-Western countries.

However, there is no dearth of alternate views, both about the validity of claims by Levine et al. (2003b) about the invalidity of the self-construal scales and about the validity of the scales themselves. On the first count, Kim and Raja (2003) felt the claims made by Levine et al. (2003b) are over-exaggerated. They noted that "the validity test, which Levine et al. claim to be 'central to the validity' of self-construal scales, consists solely of the authors' preconceived stereotypes of how Westerners ought to be versus how Asians ought to be" (Kim & Raja, p. 277). They further contended, "Crude ethnic stereotypes should not serve as criteria to judge the scales' scientific validity" (Kim & Raja, 2003, p. 277). Gudykunst and Lee (2003) also felt that Levine et al.'s measurement studies did not provide definitive evidence that the two dimensional self construal scales lack validity, asserting the possibility that the data from their measurement studies would yield multiple factors that combine into two self-construals in second-order factor analyses.

For self-construal research to progress, clearer conceptualization and better measurement options are needed (Levine et al., 2003a). For example, using the Singelis self-construal scale, Hardin (2006) supported earlier findings concerning the multidimensionality of both independence (autonomy/assertiveness, individualism, behavioral consistency, and primacy of self) and interdependence (esteem for the group and relational interdependence), and extended the generalizabilty of this structure (compared to the two-factor structure) to samples of Latino/a, African American, Asian, Asian American, and European American samples of college students. Other conceptual developments (Campos, Keltner, Beck, Gonzaga, & John, 2007; Hardie, Critchley, & Morris, 2006; Li, Zhang, Bhatt, & Yum, 2006; Locke & Christensen, 2007; Mortenson, 2005; Pohlmann, Carranza, Hannover, & Iyengar, 2007; White, Lehman, & Cohen, 2006; Zhang & Mittal, 2007), advances surrounding the measurement (Li et al., 2006; Lu & Gilmour, 2007; Singelis et al., 2006) of self-construal, and the reliability of the Singelis self-construal scale (Singelis et al., 2006) and validity of Leung and Kim's self-construal scale (Mortenson, 2005) have been reported since the debate between Levine and colleagues and proponents of the original self-construal scales.

Location

Leung and Kim Self-Construal Scale

*Leung, T., & Kim, M. S. (1997). *A revised self-construal scale*. Honolulu: University of Hawaii at Manoa. Honolulu, HI, USA.

Singelis Self-Construal Scale

Singelis, T.M. (1994). The measurement of independent and interdependent self-construals. *Personality and Social Psychological Bulletin, 20,* 580–591. (24 items printed in Table 1, p. 585)

**Singelis, T. M., & Brown, W. J. (1995). Culture, self, and collectivist communication: Linking culture to individual behavior. *Human Communication Research, 21,* 354–389. (24 items printed for first time in a communication journal; see Appendix B, p. 384)

Gudykunst et al. Self Construal Scales

Gudykunst, W. B., Matsumoto, Y., Ting-Toomey, S., Nishida, T., Kim, K., & Heyman, S. (1994, July). *Measuring self construals across cultures*. Paper presented at the annual meeting of the International Communication Association, Sydney, Australia.

Gudykunst, W.B., Matsumoto, Y., Ting-Toomey, S., Nishida, T., Kim, K., & Heyman, S. (1996). The influence of cultural individualism-collectivism, self-construals, and individual values on communication styles across cultures. *Human Communication Research, 22,* 510–543. (Items first analyzed, but scale not printed.)

***Gudykunst, W. B., & Lee, C. M. (2003). Assessing the validity of self construal scales: A response to Levine et al. *Human Communication Research, 29,* 253–274. (29 items printed in Appendix, p. 267)

References

Bhawuk, D. P. S., & Brislin, R. W. (1992). The measurement of intercultural sensitivity using the concepts of individualism and collectivism. *International Journal of Intercultural Relations, 16,* 413–436.

Campos, B., Keltner, D., Beck, J. M., Gonzaga, G. C., & John, O. P. (2007). Culture and teasing: The relational benefits of reduced desire for positive self-differentiation. *Personality and Social Psychology Bulletin, 33,* 3–16.

Constantine, M. G., & Yeh, C. .J. (2001). Multicultural training, self-construals, and multicultural competence of school counselors. *Professional School Counseling, 4,* 202–207.

Cross, S. E. (1995). Self-construals, coping, and stress in cross-cultural adaptation. *Journal of Cross-Cultural Psychology, 26,* 673–697.

Cross, S. E., & Markus, H. R. (1991, August). *Cultural adaptation and the self: Self-construal, coping, and stress.* Paper presented at the annual meeting of the American Psychological Association, San Francisco.

Ellis, J. B., & Wittenbaum, G. M. (2000). Relationships between self-construal and verbal promotion. *Communication Research, 27,* 704–722.

Grace, S. L., & Cramer, K. L. (2003). The elusive nature of self-measurement: The self-construal scale versus the twenty statements test. *Journal of Social Psychology, 143,* 649–668.

Gudykunst, W. B., & Lee, C. M. (2003). Assessing the validity of self construal scales: A response to Levine et al. *Human Communication Research, 29,* 253–274.

Gudykunst, W. B., Matsumoto, Y., Ting-Toomey, S., Nishida, T., Kim, K., & Heyman, S. (1996). The influence of cultural individualism-collectivism, self-construals, and individual values on communication styles across cultures. *Human Communication Research, 22,* 510–543.

Hackman, M. Z., Ellis, K., Johnson, C. E., & Staley, C. (1999). Self-construal orientation: Validation of an instrument and a study of the relationship to leadership communication style. *Communication Quarterly, 47,* 183–195.

Hardie, E. A., & Critchley, C., & Morris, Z. (2006). Self-coping complexity: Role of self-construal in relational, individual and collective coping styles and health outcomes. *Asian Journal of Social Psychology, 9,* 224–235.

Hardin, E. E. (2006). Convergent evidence for the multidimensionality of self-construal. *Journal of Cross-Cultural Psychology, 37,* 516–521.

Kanagawa, C., Cross, S. E., & Markus, H. R. (2001). "Who am I?" The cultural psychology of the conceptual self. *Personality and Social Psychology Bulletin, 27*, 90–103.

Kim, M. S., Aune, K. S., Hunter, J. E., Kim, H. J., & Kim, J. S. (2001). The effect of culture and self-construals on predispositions toward verbal communication. *Human Communication Research, 27*, 382–408.

Kim, M. S., Hunter, J. E., Miyahara, A., Horvath, A. M., Bresnahan, M., & Yoon, H. J. (1996) Individual- vs. culture-level dimensions of individualism and collectivism: Effects on preferred conversational styles. *Communication Monographs, 63*, 29–49.

Kim, M. S., Klingle, R. S., Sharkey, W. F., Park, H. S., Smith, D. H., & Cai, D. (2000). A test of a cultural model of patients' motivation for verbal communication in patient-doctor interactions. *Communication Monographs, 67*, 262–283.

Kim, M. S., & Raja, N. S. (2003). When validity testing lacks validity: Comment on Levine et al. *Human Communication Research, 29*, 275–290.

Kim, M. S., & Sharkey, W. F. (1995). Independent and interdependent construals of self: Explaining cultural patterns of interpersonal communication in multicultural organizational settings. *Communication Quarterly, 43*, 20–38.

Kim, M. S., Sharkey, W. F., & Singelis, T. M. (1994). The relationship between individuals' self-construals and perceived importance of interactive constraints. *International Journal of Intercultural Relations, 18*, 117–140.

Kityama, S. (2002). Culture and basic psychological processes—Toward a system view of culture: Comment on Oyserman et al. (2002). *Psychological Bulletin, 128,* 89–96.

Leung, T. (1997). Self-construals and situational dependency in conflict style preference. Unpublished master's thesis. University of Hawaii at Manoa, Honolulu.

Leung, T., & Kim, M. S. (1997). *A revised self-construal scale.* Unpublished manuscript. Department of Speech, University of Hawaii at Manoa. Honolulu.

Levine, T. R., Bresnahan, M. J., Park, H. S., Lapinski, M. K., Lee, T. S., & Lee, D. W. (2003a). The (in)validity of self-construal scales revisited. *Human Communication Research, 29*, 291–308.

Levine, T. R., Bresnahan, M. J., Park, H. S., Lapinski, M. K., Wittenbam, G. W., Shearman, S. M., Lee, S. Y., Chung, D., Ohashi, D. (2003b). Self-construal scales lack validity. *Human Communication Research, 29*, 210–252.

Li, H. Z., Zhang, Z., Bhatt, G., & Yum, Y.-O. (2006). Rethinking culture and self-construal: China as a middle land. *Journal of Social Psychology, 146*, 591–610.

Locke, K. D., & Christensen, L. (2007). Re-construing the relational-interdependent self-construal and its relationship with self-consistency star, open. *Journal of Research in Personality, 41*, 389–402.

Lu, L., & Gilmour, R. (2007). Developing a new measure of independent and interdependent views of the self. *Journal of Research in Personality, 41*, 249–257.

Markus, H. R., & Kitayama, S. (1991). Culture and the self: Implications for cognition, emotion, and motivation. *Psychological Review, 98*, 224–253.

Markus, H. R., & Kitayama, S. (1998). The cultural psychology of personality. *Journal of Cross-Cultural Psychology, 29*, 63–87.

Matsumoto, D. (1999). Cultural and self: An empirical assessment of Markus and Kitayama's theory of independent and interdependent self-construals. *Asian Journal of Social Psychology, 2*, 289–310.

Mortenson, S. T. (2005). Examining the link between culture and self-construal through structural equation models. *Journal of Intercultural Communication Research, 34,* 20–46.

Oetzel, J. G. (2001). Self-construals, communication processes, and group outcomes in homogeneous and heterogeneous groups. *Small Group Research, 32,* 19–54.

Oetzel, J. G., & Oetzel, K. B. (1997). Exploring the relationship between self-construals and dimensions of group effectiveness. *Management Communication Quarterly, 10,* 289–315.

Oguri, M., & Gudykunst, W. B. (2002). The influence of self construals and communication styles on sojourners' psychological and sociocultural adjustment. *International Journal or Intercultural Relations, 26,* 577–593.

Park, H. S. (1997). *A cross-cultural test of embarassability.* Unpublished manuscript. University of Hawaii at Manoa, Honolulu.

Park, H. S. (2001). Self-construals as motivating factors in opinion shifts resulting from exposure to majority opinions. *Communication Reports, 14,* 105–116.

Park, H. S., & Levine, T. R. (1999). The theory of reasoned action and self-construal: Evidence from three cultures. *Communication Monographs, 66,* 199–218.

Park, H. S, Levine, T. R., & Sharkey, W. F. (1998). The theory of reasoned action and self-construals: Understanding recycling in Hawaii. *Communication Studies, 49,* 197–208.

Pohlmann, C., Carranza, E., Hannover, B., & Iyengar, S. S. (2007). Repercussions of self-construal for self-relevant and other-relevant choice. *Social Cognition, 25,* 284–305.

Sharkey, W. F., & Singelis, T. M. (1995). Embarrassability and self-construal: A theoretical integration. *Personality and Individual Differences, 19,* 622–644.

Singelis, T. M. (1994). The measurement of independent and interdependent self-construals. *Personality and Social Psychological Bulletin, 20,* 580–591.

Singelis, T. M., Bond, M. H., Sharkey, W. F., & Yiu Lai, C. S. (1999). Unpackaging culture's influence on self-esteem and embarrassability: The role of self-construals. *Journal of Cross-Cultural Psychology, 30,* 315–341.

Singelis, T. M., & Brown, W. J. (1995). Culture, self, and collectivist communication: Linking culture to individual behavior. *Human Communication Research, 21,* 354–389.

Singelis, T. M., & Sharkey, W. F. (1995). Culture, self-construal, and embarrassability. *Journal of Cross-Cultural Psychology, 26,* 622–644.

Singelis, T. M., Yamada, A. M., Barrio, C., Laney, J. H., Ruiz-Anaya, A. & Lennertz, S. T. (2006). Metric equivalence of the bidimensional acculturation scale, the satisfaction with life scale, and the self-construal scale across Spanish and English language versions. *Hispanic Journal of Behavioral Sciences, 28*(2), 231–244.

White, K., Lehman, D. R., & Cohen, D. (2006). Culture, self-construal, and affective reactions to successful and unsuccessful others. *Journal of Experimental Social Psychology, 42,* 582–592.

Yamaguchi, S. (1994). Collectivism among the Japanese: A perspective from the self. In U. Kim, H. C. Triandis, C. Kagitcibasi, & G. Yoon (Eds.), *Individualism and collectivism: Theoretical and methodological issues* (pp. 175–188). Thousand Oaks, CA: Sage.

Zhang, Y., & Mittal, V. (2007). The attractiveness of enriched and impoverished options: Culture, self-construal, and regulatory focus. *Personality and Social Psychology Bulletin, 33*, 588–598.

Self-Construal Scales

Leung & Kim (1997)*
Instructions: Using the scale below, indicate to what degree you disagree/agree with each statement provided. It may be helpful to think of "groups" as your peer group. Please use the following:

Strongly
disagree   1   2   3   4   5   6   7   Strongly agree

1   I should be judged on my own merit. *
2   I voice my opinions in group discussions. *
3   I feel uncomfortable disagreeing with my group.
4   I conceal my negative emotions so I won't cause unhappiness among the members of my group.
5   My personal identity, independent of others, is very important to me. *
6   I prefer to be self-reliant rather than dependent on others. *
7   I act as a unique person, separate from others. *
8   I don't like depending on others. *
9   My relationships with those in my group are more important than my personal accomplishments.
10   My happiness depends on the happiness of those in my group.
11   I often consider how I can be helpful to specific others in my group.
12   I take responsibility for my own actions. *
13   It is important for me to act as an independent person. *
14   I have an opinion about most things: I know what I like and I know what I don't like. *
15   I enjoy being unique and different from others. *
16   I don't change my opinions in conformity with those of the majority. *
17   Speaking up in a work/task group is not a problem for me. *
18   Having a lively imagination is important to me. *
19   Understanding myself is a major goal in my life. *
20   I enjoy being admired for my unique qualities. *
21   I am careful to maintain harmony in my group.
22   When with my group, I watch my words so I won't offend anyone.
23   I would sacrifice my self-interests for the benefit of my group.
24   I try to meet the demands of my group, even if it means controlling my own desires.
25   It is important to consult close friends and get their ideas before making decisions.

26   I should take into consideration my parents' advice when making edu-
     cation and career plans.
27   I act as fellow group members prefer I act.
28   The security of being an accepted member of a group is very important
     to me.
29   If my brother or sister fails, I feel responsible.

Note. Independence items are marked *. The rest are interdependent items.

*Scale provided by the second author. Reprinted with permission.

Self-Construal Scales

Singelis (1994)**

Interdependence Items

1   I have respect for the authority figures with whom I interact.
2   It is important for me to maintain harmony within my group.
3   My happiness depends on the happiness of those around me.
4   I would offer my seat in a bus to my professor.
5   I respect people who are modest about themselves.
6   I will sacrifice my self-interest for the benefit of the group I am in.
7   I often have the feeling that my relationships with others are more
    important then my own accomplishments.
8   I should take into consideration my parents' advice when making
    education/career plans.
9   It is important to me to respect decisions made by the group.
10 If my brother or sister fails, I feel responsible.
11 I will stay in a group if they need me, even when I am not happy with
    the group.
12 Even when I strongly disagree with group members, I avoid an
    argument.

Independence Items

13 I'd rather say "No" directly, than risk being misunderstood.
14 Speaking up during a class is not a problem for me.
15 Having a lively imagination is important to me.
16 I am comfortable with being singled out for praise or rewards.
17 I am the same person at home that I am at school.
18 Being able to take care of myself is a primary concern for me.
19 I feel comfortable using someone's first name soon after I meet them,
    even when they are much older than I am.

20 I prefer to be direct and forthright when dealing with people I've just met.
21 I act the same way no matter who I am with.
22 I enjoy being unique and different from others in many respects.
23 My personal identity, independent of others, is very important to me.
24 I value being in good health above everything.

** © 1995 by Blackwell Publishing. Reprinted by permission.

Self Construal Scales

Gudykunst (1994, 1996) ***

1 I should be judged on my own merit. (ind)
2 Being able to take care of myself is a primary concern for me. (ind)
3 My personal identity is important to me. (ind)*
4 I consult others before making important decisions. (inter)
5 I consult with co-workers on work-related matters. (inter)
6 I prefer to be self-reliant rather than depend on others. (ind)*
7 I will sacrifice my self-interest for the benefit of my group. (inter)*
8 I stick with my group even through difficulties. (inter)*
9 I respect decisions made by my group. (inter)*
10 I will stay in a group if it needs me, even if I am not happy with it. (inter)
11 I maintain harmony in the groups of which I am a member. (inter)*
12 I respect the majority's wishes in groups of which I am a member. (inter)*
13 I remain in the groups of which I am a member if they need me, even though I am dissatisfied with them. (inter)
14 I am a unique person separate from others. (ind)
15 If there is a conflict between my values and values of groups of which I am a member, I follow my values. (ind)
16 I try to abide by customs and conventions at work. (inter)
17 I try not to depend on others. (ind)
18 I take responsibility for my own actions. (ind)*
19 I give special consideration to others' personal situations so I can be efficient at work. (inter)
20 It is better to consult others and get their opinions before doing anything. (inter)
21 It is important to consult close friends and get their ideas before making a decision. (inter)*
22 It is important for me to act as an independent person. (ind)*
23 I should decide my future on my own. (ind)*
24 What happens to me is my own doing. (ind)
25 My relationships with others are more important to me than my accomplishments. (inter)

26   I enjoy being unique and different from others. (ind)*
27   I am comfortable being singled out for praise and rewards. (ind)
28   I help acquaintances, even if it is inconvenient. (ind)**
29   I don't support a group decision when it is wrong. (ind)

Note: ind = independent self construal; inter = interdependent self construal. The items are worded to measure general self construals. We believe that the wording of the items should be modified if behavior in a specific ingroup is studied. Not all items can be modified for ingroup-specific self construals.

* These 12 items all loaded .50 or greater in Gudykunst et al.'s (1994, 1996) study. They can be used to construct short versions of the scales. As would be expected, reliability tends to be a little lower than the full scales, but the short versions are consistently reliable.

**Item no. 28 lacks face validity and we suggest that it be dropped.
(Gudykunst & Lee, 2003, p. 267)

*** © 2003 by Blackwell Publishing.

Sexual Harassment Proclivity Index (SHPI)

Profile by David A. Seibold

Sexual Harassment Proclivity Index (SHPI) authors Shereen Bingham and Brant Burleson (1996) set out to improve upon J. B. Pryor's (1987) Likelihood of Sexually Harassing Scale (LSH). Pryor's scale is a "self-report measure of males' likelihood of engaging in sexual harassment. The scale asks men to imagine themselves in each of ten situations which present opportunities to sexually exploit attractive women without fear of being caught or punished" (Bingham & Burleson, 1996, p. 309). A main goal of SHPI is to establish a coherent structure for assessing sexual harassment proclivity in men, and thus to offer potential redress to a major organizational/workplace problem.

Although the reliability of LSH is relatively and consistently high, there are several potential problems. The first of these problems, according to Bingham and Burleson, is that the content validity is "limited in that it taps only a very narrow range of harassing behaviors" (Bingham & Burleson, 1996, p. 310). Thus, in SHPI, the authors broaden the range of sexually harassing communicative behaviors. Additionally, in instructing respondents to the scale that there would be no negative consequences, Pryor was setting up an unrealistic situation that creates unrealistic test results. Consequently, Bingham and Burleson do not mention in their scale that the men would be "immune to reprisal for their actions" (p. 310). Finally, the SHPI authors felt Pryor's LSH scale is too long and bulky because it asks for responses to ten long situations, making it difficult to administer. Bingham and Burleson reduced their scale to just one scenario.

The SHPI directions ask each respondent to imagine that he is a manager of a large organization and has just hired Donna, an "outgoing and friendly" female employee. Respondents are then asked to read a scenario about Donna, and to respond how likely they would be to use each of a list of "date-getting strategies." Bingham and Burleson (1996) began with 26 such verbal and nonverbal communication behaviors, most of which may be "acceptable of flirtatious in other contexts" (p. 310). However, "each . . . may constitute a form of sexual harassment according to guidelines established by the Equal Employment Opportunity Commission"

(p. 312). Participants indicate their likelihood of using each (potentially harassing) strategy on a 5-point Likert-type scale (1 = *highly unlikely to use*, 5 = *very likely to use*).

The final SHPI retains 16 of the original strategies, all potential forms of harassing behavior. As described in the Validity section below, 9 items represent forms of harassing behavior that comprise what Bingham and Burleson term "Intrusive Harassment" and 7 items represent "Quid Pro Quo Harassment." Both the scenario and the final 16 items (adapted from Table 2 in Bingham and Burleson [1996]) are reprinted at the conclusion of this profile.

Reliability

Factor 1 in the Sexual Harassment Proclivity Index included 9 items that represent Intrusive Harassment. The internal reliability of items comprising this factor was .89 (Cronbach's alpha). The second factor of SHPI included 7 items considered Quid Pro Quo Harassment. The items "loading on Factor II exhibited a high degree of internal consistency; Cronbach's alpha was .87" (Bingham & Burleson, 1996, p. 317). Proclivity to engage in these two forms of harassment were moderately associated (.40 to .44), suggesting "some tendency, then, for individuals with a proclivity to engage in one form of harassment to engage in other forms as well" (p. 317).

Validity

Bingham and Burleson (1996) established the validity of the Sexual Harassment Proclivity Index in several ways. First, face and representational validity of the scenario and the items was demonstrated by showing, in a separate study involving women, that potential victims (females) of harassment viewed SHPI behaviors as objectionable and harassing. Second, the convergent validity of the two SHPI subscales was established through moderate, statistically significant correlations between either or both of the SHPI factors and attitude measures relevant to sexual harassment: adversarial sexual beliefs (.38, .36), attitudes supporting sexual harassment (.45, .32), acceptance of rape myths (.24, .32), tolerance of sexual harassment (.40, .19), sex-role stereotyping (.14), and Pryor's measure of sexual harassment likelihood (.32 to .46). Third, the discriminant validity of the SHPI was evident from the small, negative, non-significant associations between each SHPI factor and the Marlow-Crowne social desirability measure (–.05, –.10): "reports about the likelihood of engaging in harassing behavior are not influenced by the desire to be seen as acting in socially desirable ways" (p. 318).

Comments

Bingham and Burleson have presented a well conceived, well researched, communication-based alternative to Pryor's (1987) Likelihood of Sexually Harassing scale. The authors successfully expanded the types of sexually harassing behaviors included in the SHPI, though theirs is the only study to validate the SHPI. In reducing the number of items, they have made the measure more manageable and easier to administer. At this time, the SHPI measure has not been used in other studies.

Location*

Bingham, S. G., & Burleson, B. R. (1996). The development of a sexual harassment proclivity scale: Construct validation and relationship to communication competence. *Communication Quarterly, 44(3),* 308–325.

References

Pryor, J. B. (1987). Sexual harassment proclivities in men. *Sex Roles 17,* 269–290.

Scale

Sexual Harassment Proclivity Index*
Instructions: Suppose that during the first few weeks Donna worked for you, you invited her out to dinner several times. She turned you down each time. This was really disappointing to you because you think Donna is very pretty and you would like to get to know her better.

Listed below are various strategies that men have said they might use in this situation. If you were in this situation, how likely would you be to use each of the strategies listed?

Highly unlikely to use   1   2   3   4   5   Very likely to use

1   Try to convince Donna that she would enjoy having dinner with you.
2   Ask Donna if she is romantically involved with anyone.
3   Tell Donna you would like to get to know her on a personal level.
4   Make subtle passes at Donna until she change her mind about dating you.
5   Let Donna know nonverbally how attractive she is.
6   Comment on what a good figure Donna has.
7   Ask Donna if dating her boss would bother her.
8   Comment on how pretty Donna is.
9   Ask Donna about her past romantic relationships.
10 Give Donna difficult, boring assignments until she agrees to have dinner with you.

11 Offer Donna a raise or promotion if she will start seeing you socially.
12 Tell Donna that all your other female assistants have dated you.
13 Tell Donna you will fire her if she doesn't start seeing you socially.
14 Give Donna a raise, hoping she will change her mind about dating you.
15 Let Donna go, and hire someone else who is equally qualified for the job.
16 Remind Donna that you can help her advance in the company.

Note. Items 1–9 represent Intrusive Harassment; 10–16 represent Quid Pro Quo Harassment. Items should be arranged randomly prior to administration.

Small Group Relational Satisfaction Scale (RSS)

Profile by David R. Seibold

Anderson, Martin, and Riddle (2001) developed the small group Relational Satisfaction Scale (RSS) to measure members' satisfaction with relationships and relational communication in their group. Relational satisfaction was defined as "the building and maintaining of member relationships during communicative processes and practices throughout the life span of the group" (p. 220).

In order to develop a unique measure of group members' affective orientations to group communication, Anderson et al. (2001) first asked 60 graduate and undergraduate students enrolled in group communication classes to describe satisfying member relationships in groups, based on their own experiences. Content analysis of their descriptions revealed that relational satisfaction in small groups was characterized by feelings of affection, inclusion, liking, trust, friendship, freedom to communicate, involvement, and getting to know each other, among others. Together with concepts from other, related measures as well as theoretical literature on the "relational side" of groups (Keyton, 1999, 2000), the authors used findings from the content analysis to formulate 12 items designed to measure the relational satisfaction construct. Each is assessed on a five-point scale ranging from *Strongly Disagree* (1) to *Strongly Agree* (5).

Reliability

In the first of two studies reported by Anderson et al. (2001), 228 full-time employees completed the RSS. Each participant was requested to "think of their latest work-related group" (p. 221) in responding to each of the 12 items on the Likert-type scales. Principal components factor analysis revealed a one-factor solution, taken as evidence for a unidimensional scale. Cronbach's alpha reliability for the RSS was .89. In a second study reported by Anderson et al. (2001), involving 210 male and female undergraduate students in small group communication classes at two large universities in the mid-western United States, internal reliability for the small group RSS also was .89.

Validity

Concurrent validity for the small group RSS was investigated in Study 2 of Anderson et al. (2001). The RSS and three other scales were administered to the 210 participants in 5–6 member decision-making groups that had met in class and outside for five weeks. Anticipated positive associations between relational satisfaction in these groups and members' reports of cohesion ($r = .56$) and consensus ($r = .64$) were reported as evidence of the validity of the RSS. A predicted negative relationship between group members' responses on the RSS and a measure of loneliness ($r = -.64$) was considered as further evidence for the concurrent validity of the small group RSS. Findings from the 228 full time employees revealed that relational satisfaction was positively correlated with respondents' attitudes about group work, assertiveness, responsiveness, and perceptions of feedback in small groups.

Comment

Researchers interested in the relational side of groups, not simply group performance processes and outcomes, may find the small group RSS useful. The RSS has not yet been used widely, perhaps owing to its recent publication. However, it has been shown to be reliable when utilized. McCarson (2005) reported alpha coefficients of .93 for the RSS in wave one (and .86 for the RSS in wave two) of her study of the relationship between communication apprehension as well as writing apprehension with relational satisfaction in face-to-face groups and computer-mediated groups. The McCarson study with members of ongoing groups also addresses a limitation of the Anderson et al. (2001) development and validation studies, in which respondents in both samples were recalling their most recent workgroup and class project group experiences, respectively.

Location*

Anderson, C. M., Martin, M. M., & Riddle, B. L. (2001). Small group relational satisfaction scale: Development, reliability, and validity. *Communication Studies, 52,* 220–233.

References

Keyton, J. (1999). Relational communication in groups. In L. R. Frey, D. S. Gouran, & M. S. Poole (Eds.), *Handbook of group communication theory and research* (pp. 192–224). Thousand Oaks, CA: Sage.

Keyton, J. (2000). Introduction: The relational side of groups. *Small Group Research, 30,* 491–518.

McCarson, R. L. (2005). Measuring communication apprehension, writing apprehension, and group satisfaction levels in face-to-face and virtual settings. *Chrestomathy, 4,* 1–32.

Scale

Small Group Relational Satisfaction Scale*

Instructions: In this instrument, we are measuring your perceptions of satisfaction in your latest work-related group. Please use the following scale:

Strongly Disagree   1   2   3   4   5   *Strongly Agree*

1 The group members spend time getting to know each other.
2 The members make me feel a part of the group.
3 I look forward to coming to the group meetings.
4 I do not feel part of the group. (R)
5 The members make me feel liked.
6 My absence would not matter to the group. (R)
7 I can trust group members.
8 We can say anything in this group without worrying.
9 I prefer not to spend time with members of the group. (R)
10 The members made me feel involved in the group.
11 Some of the group members could become my friends.
12 The group atmosphere is comfortable.

Note: (R) Reverse score items 4, 6, and 9.

Small Group Socialization Scale (SGSS)

Profile by David R. Seibold

Communication researchers Riddle, Anderson, and Martin (2000) developed the Small Group Socialization Scale (SGSS) to measure "people's perceptions of the communication effectiveness of group communication that includes task and relationship dimensions" (p. 555). The measure flows from two socialization models explicated by Anderson, Riddle, and Martin (1999) that conceptualized how members and groups reciprocally affect each other and group work as well as how communication affects, and is affected by, socialization processes within the group.

In developing this measure—of the ways in which group communication is centrally implicated in member socialization—Riddle et al. (2000) first surveyed literature concerning the interdependence of task and relational dimensions of groups (Keyton, 1999) as well as socialization literature depicting members' adjustments to groups. "Fitting in," feelings of satisfaction with the group and being at ease with its values, as well as ingroup dynamics were central to group socialization. Open-ended questions based upon these themes were then developed and presented to undergraduate students enrolled in small group communication classes in two Midwestern U.S. universities. The questions asked them to reflect on their experiences in groups, especially why and when they felt they fit into the group. Thirty-five items were created from these responses in order to measure small group socialization.

Reliability

In the first of two studies reported by Riddle et al. (2000), 445 undergraduate students enrolled in communication courses at a midwest U.S. university responded to each of the 35 items on a five-point, Likert-type scale ranging from "Strongly Disagree" (1) to "Strongly Agree" (5). (p. 558 of Riddle et al., 2000, incorrectly states that the scale poles are from 1 = *Strongly Agree* to 5 = *Strongly Disagree*, but the actual, correct poles of 1 = *Strongly Disagree* to 5 = *Strongly Agree* are noted on p. 564 and confirmed by the third author, Martin, Personal Correspondence, 5/12/08).

Multiple factor analyses resulted in a one-factor solution with 14 items, reported by the authors as grounds for a unidimensional measure of small group socialization (SGSS). Cronbach's coefficient alpha reliability for the 14-item SGSS was .88. In a second study reported by Riddle et al. (2000), involving 210 male and female undergraduate students in communication classes at two midsized state universities in the mid-western United States, the coefficient alpha for the SGSS was .76.

Validity

Concurrent validity for the Small Group Socialization Scale (SGSS) was examined in the second study reported by Riddle et al. (2000). The SGSS and four other communication measures were administered to the 210 participants in 4–7 member project groups that had met inside and outside the class from six to ten times, with their meetings lasting from 20 to 60 minutes. Predicted positive associations between small group socialization and cohesion ($r = .43$), consensus ($r = .43$), and communication satisfaction ($r = .65$) were considered indicative of the validity of the SGSS. A negative relationship between group members' responses on the SGSS and a measure of loneliness ($r = -.65$) was considered as further evidence for the validity of the SGSS.

Comment

The Small Group Socialization Scale has not been employed widely, given its recent development. However, the SGSS has the potential to be utilized by researchers in many areas of the field. For example, organizational communication researchers Myers and McPhee (2006) utilized selected items from the SGSS in their study of firefighters' assimilation in workgroups in a large municipality. Their study also did not have limitation of the Riddle et al. (2001) studies of the development and validation of the SGSS. Respondents in both Riddle et al. studies were asked to recall their recent project group experiences; memory effects were not a potential validity threat in Myers and McPhee (2006) investigation. Future research should continue to investigate the reliability and validity of the SGSS. In particular, the scale should be validated against organizational socialization measures with known psychometric properties and that assess group-level socialization dynamics (see review in Miller, Hart, Dibble, & Fritz, 2005).

Location*

Riddle, B. L., Anderson, C. M., & Martin, M. M. (2000). Small group socialization scale: Development and validity. *Small Group Research, 31,* 554–572.

References

Anderson, C. M., Riddle, B. L., & Martin, M. M. (1999). Socialization processes in groups. In L. R. Frey, D. S. Gouran, & M. S. Poole (Eds.), *Handbook of group communication theory and research* (pp. 139–166). Thousand Oaks, CA: Sage.

Keyton, J. (1999). Relational communication in groups. In L. R. Frey, D. S. Gouran, & M. S. Poole (Eds.), *Handbook of group communication theory and research* (pp. 192–224). Thousand Oaks, CA: Sage.

Miller, V., Hart, Z., Dibble, J., & Frtiz, J. H. (2005, November). *Organizational socialization and the measurement of process.* Paper presented at the annual meeting of the National Communication Association, Boston, MA.

Myers, K. K., & McPhee, R. D. (2006). Influences on member assimilation in workgroups in high-reliability organizations: A multilevel analysis. *Human Communication Research, 32,* 440–468.

Scale

Small Group Socialization Scale*

Instructions: In this instrument, we are measuring your perceptions of socialization in your last group experience. Please use the following scale:

Strongly Disagree   1   2   3   4   5   *Strongly Agree*

1 I understood what was appropriate dress for group meetings.
2 I understood the authority the group had for doing its work.
3 I did not see myself as an effective group member. (R)
4 I understood the "group talk" the group used to do its work.
5 I found someone in the group who could provide me with emotional support.
6 It was clear what was expected of me in this group.
7 I found someone in the group with whom I could talk about career plans.
8 It was not at all clear what was expected of me in this group. (R)
9 I depended on other group members for support in the group.
10 I found someone in the group who could help me adjust to the group.
11 I found someone in the group on whom I could depend for support.
12 I had no clear idea what this group was to accomplish. (R)
13 I found someone in the group with whom I could discuss personal matters.
14 There was no one in the group on whom I could depend for support. (R)

Note 1: (R) Reverse score items 3, 8, 12 and 14. (The last item is not noted with an (R) in Table 1 of Riddle et al., 2000, but Martin confirmed that Item 14 needs to be reverse coded; personal correspondence 5/12/08.)

Note 2: The scale can be presented in present tense for ongoing groups.

Social Presence Scale

Profile by Elizabeth M. Perse

Short, Williams, and Christie (1976) theorized that people choose communication channels based on the tasks they are performing, and that one of the guiding factors in their decision is the medium's level of social presence. Social presence is defined as "the degree to which a medium is perceived as conveying the actual, physical presence of the communicating participants" (Rice, 1992, p. 476). *Social presence* is differentiated from *telepresence*. Telepresence is the sense of "being there." Social presence is the sense of "being together with another" (Biocca, Burgoon, Harms, & Stoner, 2001). Along with verbal communication, many nonverbal cues, such as facial expression, direction of gaze, posture, attire, and physical distance, influence a channel's level of social presence (Rice, 1992).

Media that are high in social presence convey more communication cues to the participants. For example, face-to-face communication and television are generally rated as high in social presence because they convey both verbal and nonverbal information. These media are considered information rich and are useful for negotiating, developing relationships, generating ideas, resolving conflicts, and exchanging confidential information. In contrast, media, such as email and written letters, have low social presence and are best used for exchanging information, asking questions, and staying in touch. Therefore, social presence is both an objective characteristic of each medium and a product of each person's communication goals.

Short et al.'s (1976) semantic differential scale is the most widely used measure of social presence (Biocca et al., 2001). The scale asks respondents to rate media according to how personal, sensitive, warm, and social they perceived each channel to be. Responses to the surveys are then averaged for each medium and compared to determine how it is rated on social presence. Studies have used both 5-point and 7-point semantic differential scales. The scale has been used with college student, adult, and working adult samples.

Originally, the social presence scale was developed in the 1970s as a way to compare various forms of face-to-face, video, and audio communication. Short and his colleagues originally wrote that social presence was "a quality of the communication medium" (1976, p. 65). Their measure, however, clearly assesses people's perceptions of various communication channels. Another theoretical approach, media richness (Daft & Lengel, 1986), focuses on the objective capacities of different communication media to carry information through different channels (e.g., video, audio). The study of social presence has been applied to "new media" such as email (Perse, Burton, Kovner, Lears, & Sen, 1992) voice mail and fax (Straub & Karahanna, 1998), the Internet (Papacharissi & Rubin, 2000), computers (Perse & Courtright, 1993), and computer bulletin boards (Garramone, Harris, & Anderson, 1986).

Reliability

The four-item social presence scale has been used reliably in prior research. Straub and Karahanna (1998) reported that Cronbach alphas for the social presence of five channels (telephone, face-to-face, email, fax, and voice mail) all exceeded .80. Perse et al. (1992) found that e-mail social presence was more modest, $\alpha = .63$. Garramone et al. (1986) used a three-item version of the scale (sociable, personal, and sensitive) reliably ($\alpha = .77$). Some researchers used a five-item version, adding "active" to the scale. Perse and Courtright reported that the five-item scale was reliable across 12 different communication channels (cable TV, movies, television, VCR, conversation, telephone, magazines, books, newspapers, computer, radio, and recorded music); Cronbach alphas ranged from .72 to .86. Papacharissi and Rubin reported a Cronbach alpha of .62 for their five-item scale assessing Internet social presence.

Social presence should be a fairly stable perception about communication channels. Test-retest reliability, however, has not been reported.

Validity

There are some concerns about the scale's content validity. Short et al. (1976) originally developed their scale by assuming that the appropriate way to assess subjective feelings was Osgood's semantic differential method. Although this has been useful, the proliferation of new media forms has led several writers to question the breadth of the scale. Writers suggest that Short et al.'s scale does not get at the additional dimensions added by newer media (e.g. Biocco et al., 2001; Tu, 2002). Short et al.'s Social Presence Scale should be treated as a general measure of social presence.

As a general measure, the Social Presence Scale appears to measuring what it is designed to measure. There is strong evidence of concurrent validity. Asking respondents to rate media according to the broad qualities of insensitive-sensitive, sociable-unsociable, sensitive-insensitive, and personal-impersonal, seems to produce expected and somewhat consistent results concerning overall social presence rating. The averaged results of two studies by Short et al. (1976) indicated that face-to-face conversations were rated the highest in social presence, followed by television, multi-speaker audio, monaural speakerphone, and a business letter. Later, these consistent results were partially replicated by Perse and Courtright (1993). They found that social presence was highest for interpersonal communication channels and lowest for computers, which were not widely used then for communication.

Short et al. (1976) offer evidence of criterion-related validity for their scale. In some of their original research, respondents completed the social presence scale and several Likert scale statements. Social presence was significantly related to statements such as "People at the other end [of the channel] do not seem 'real'."

Other studies provide evidence of construct validity for the scale. Garramone and her colleagues (1986) found that those who posted to an online political bulletin board reported higher social presence for the medium than those who did not post. Perse and her colleagues (1992) found a positive relationship between social presence and use of email. Papacharissi and Rubin (2000) reported that social presence was a significant predictor of Internet affinity, or beliefs that using the Internet was important. They also found that Internet social presence was related to using the Internet for personal and social reasons.

Comments

The Social Presence Scale was one of the first to be developed to conduct research on newer communication technologies. As our understanding of the different dimensions of social and telepresence has increased (e.g., Biocco et al., 2001), the scale is best conceptualized and used as a measure of general social presence. Various other measures of presence have been developed to allow researchers to focuses on more specific measures of the concept.

Location

Short, J., Williams, E., & Christie, B. (1976). *The social psychology of telecommunications*. New York: Wiley.

References

Biocca, F., Burgoon, J., Harms, C., & Stoner, M. (2001, May). *Criteria and scope conditions for theory and measure of social presence*. Paper presented at the International Workshop on Presence, Philadelphia, PA. Retrieved July 8, 2008, from http://www.temple.edu/ispr/prev_conferences/proceedings/2001/Biocca1.pdf

Daft R. L., & Lengel, R. H. (1986). Organizational information requirements, media richness and structural design. *Management Science, 32*, 554–571.

Garramone, G. M., Harris, A. C., & Anderson, R. (1986). Uses of political computer bulletin boards. *Journal of Broadcasting & Electronic Media, 30*, 325–339.

Papacharissi, Z., & Rubin, A. M. (2000). Predictors of Internet use. *Journal of Broadcasting & Electronic Media, 44*, 175–196.

Perse, E. M., Burton, P. I., Kovner, E. S., Lears, M. E., & Sen, R. J. (1992). Predicting computer-mediated communication in a college class. *Communication Research Reports, 9*, 161–170.

Perse, E. M., & Courtright, J. A. (1993). Normative images of communication media: Mass and interpersonal channels in the new media environment. *Human Communication Research, 19*, 485–503.

Rice, R. E. (1992). Task analyzability, use of new media, and effectiveness: A multi-site exploration of media richness. *Organization Science, 3*, 475–500.

Straub, D., & Karahanna, E. (1998). Knowledge worker communication and recipient availability: Toward a task closure explanation of media choice. *Organization Science, 9*, 160–175.

Tu, C-H. (2002). The measurement of social presence in an online learning environment. *International Journal on E-Learning, 1*(2), 34–45.

Scale

Social Presence Scale*
Instructions: Please place an X between the pair of words that most closely represents your feelings.

Impersonal	____	____	____	____	____ Personal
Insensitive	____	____	____	____	____ Sensitive
Unsociable	____	____	____	____	____ Sociable
Cold	____	____	____	____	____ Warm

Socio-Communicative Style (SCS) Scale

Profile by Rebecca B. Rubin

Socio-communicative style (also referred to as "orientation") is conceived as a teacher's ability to respond to students, adapt to the situation, and initiate communication with students (Thomas et al., 1994). Lately, two dimensions—assertiveness and responsiveness—have become the main elements of the concept (Richmond & Martin, 1998). Bem's (1974) work on assertiveness guided the development of the assertiveness dimension, which refers to an individual's ability to initiate, maintain, and terminate conversations and to stand up for oneself when necessary. Responsiveness is based on McCroskey and Richmond's (1996) concept specifying that responsive individuals are other-oriented, empathic, good listeners, and adaptive. Responsiveness is also a prominent dimension of interaction involvement (Cegala, 1981) and assertiveness is a prime component of interpersonal competence (Rubin & Martin, 1994). McCroskey, Richmond, and Stewart (1986) previously identified assertiveness and responsiveness as two of three components of interpersonal communication competence.

Some researchers have identified four types of style, based on assertiveness and responsiveness (Aylor & Oppliger, 2003). Early on, Merrill and Reid (1981) identified *expressives* as assertive and responsive, *analyticals* as neither assertive nor responsive, *amiables* as responsive but not assertive, and *drivers* as assertive but not responsive. Later research termed these *competents, incompetents, submissives,* and *aggressives,* respectively (Martin, Mottet, & Chesebro, 1997). Respondents are partitioned into the four styles based on median scores on the Socio-communicative Style Measure.

Richmond and McCroskey (1990) developed a 20-item measure with 10 items measuring assertiveness and 10 items measuring responsiveness. A 5-point Likert-type scale asks respondents how strongly they agree or disagree that each characteristic applies to a target person. Items in each subscale are summed. Completion can be accomplished in just a few minutes.

Richmond and McCroskey found two uncorrelated (–.03) factors with split-half reliabilities of .88 for assertiveness and .93 for responsiveness.

Only a few studies have reported overall means and standard deviations for comparative or normative purposes. Campbell et al. (2001) reported an overall mean of 47.58 (*SD* = 12.25) for assertiveness and 43.68 (*SD* = 13.51) for responsiveness, Martin et al. (1997) reported a mean of 47.11 (*SD* = 12.59) for assertiveness and a mean of 45.51 (*SD* = 14.07) for responsiveness, and Wanzer and Frymier (1999) reported a mean of 33.45 (*SD* = 7.11) for assertiveness and 34.81 (*SD* = 7.60) for responsiveness, and Frymier (2005) reported a mean of 32.76 (*SD*=6.15) for assertiveness and 35.07 (*SD* = 7.03) for responsiveness.

Reliability

This scale has been used in many studies, most of which report alpha reliabilities. As displayed in Table 1, alphas for assertiveness have ranged from .81 to .93, and for responsiveness from .87 to .96. In addition, L. L. McCroskey (2003) found alphas of .85 and .94 for foreign instructors and .84 and .90 for domestic instructors. Wooten and McCroskey (1996) asked students to rate themselves (rather than another person) on sociocommunicative orientation, and found .91 alphas for each dimension.

Table 1 Alpha Reliability Coefficients

Assertiveness	Study	Responsiveness
.87	Anderson & Martin, 1995	.89
.86	Aylor & Oppliger, 2003	.93
.84	Anderson, Martin, Zhong, & West, 1997	.68
.91	Campbell, Martin, & Wanzer, 2001	.93
.81	Cole & McCroskey, 2000	.87
.81	Frymier, 2000	.89
.91	Martin, Mottet, & Chesebro, 1997	.96
.90	Myers, 1998	.95
.89	Myers & Avtgis, 1997	.96
.88	Sidelinger & McCroskey, 1997	.94
.83	Teven, 2001, 2005	.94
.90	Thomas, Richmond, & McCroskey, 1994	.91
.93	Wanzer & Frymier, 1999	.88
.87	Wanzer & McCroskey, 1998	.96
.88	Wooten & McCroskey, 1996	.92

Validity

Most of the validity research has been concerned with concurrent validity. Both assertiveness and responsiveness have been found to be significantly related to teacher immediacy, a key component of competent instructional communication (Thomas et al., 1994). Teven (2001) found relatively high, significant correlations between responsiveness and perceived caring, but low (yet significant) correlations between teacher assertiveness and perceived caring. Assertiveness and responsiveness correlated significantly with teacher clarity, oral clarity, and written clarity (Sidelinger & McCroskey, 1997). Also, Wooten and McCroskey (1996) found that teacher responsiveness and, to a lesser degree, assertiveness were related to teacher trust. High assertive students trusted high assertive teachers more than low assertive teachers, whereas low assertiveness students trusted low assertive teachers more than high assertive teachers. Responsiveness was linearly related to teacher trust.

Personality traits have been examined concurrently with SCS. Assertiveness has been found to be correlated with extraversion, and responsiveness was correlated with extraversion, agreeableness, and openness (Cole & McCroskey, 2000). And humor orientation was related to responsiveness, but not to assertiveness, for employee perceptions of their managers (Campbell, Martin, & Wanzer, 2001). Teacher immediacy was significantly correlated with assertiveness and responsiveness (Thomas, Richmond, & McCriskey, 1994), and students trusted teachers whom they thought were more assertive and responsive (Wooten & McCroskey, 1996). Competents were more argumentative and less verbally aggressive (Myers, 1997).

Some research studies have attempted to be predictive, but have collected students' perceptions of their teachers at the same point in time. For instance, assertive teachers have been perceived as misbehaving less often in the classroom (Wanzer & McCroskey, 1998). SCS is also related to affective and cognitive learning, especially the responsiveness dimension (Teven, 2005). And SCS was positively related to four criterion learning measures for both domestic and foreign instructors (L.L. McCroskey, 2003).

Studies dealing with construct validity have attempted to find additional qualities or behaviors related to the teacher's style. For instance, responsiveness, but not assertiveness, was found to be related to informal out-of-class communication (OCC) and satisfaction with OCC (Aylor & Oppliger, 2003).

Some researchers have partitioned instructors into four style groupings, and have predicted differences among these "known groups." Competents were found to be higher than aggressives (high assertiveness, low responsiveness), submissives (responsive but not assertive) and noncompetents (low in both assertiveness and responsiveness) in expertise, character, and caring dimensions of credibility and in situational motivation,

People in the four groups also differ in their communication with others (Anderson & Martin, 1995; Martin & Anderson, 1996a; Martin, Sirimangkala & Anderson, 1996; Myers & Avtgis, 1997; Patterson & Beckett, 1995). Myers (1998) found that competents were rated higher in argumentativeness than submissives, and aggressives were perceived to be higher in argumentativeness than noncompetents and submissives. Also, noncompetents and aggressives were rated higher in verbal aggression than competents and submissives. Myers and Avtgis (1997) also found that competents were higher in the use of nonverbal immediacy behaviors than noncompetents and differed from submissives and aggressives in vocalics, facial expression, body position, and touch.

Comments

The scale is used mainly by students or subordinates to evaluate their teachers or superiors. More often than not, scores on these style traits are compared to other traits or behaviors expected by perceivers. Mean scores might be useful to provide a collective view of superiors or teachers for comparative purposes. Although the scale was created as an alternative to Bem's Sex-Role Inventory, it should be used for the purpose for which it was developed—socio-communicative style—rather than sex-role orientation. However, a Chinese sample provided support that Chinese males were higher on assertiveness than were females (Anderson, Martin, Zhong, & West, 1997).

Some intercultural comparison studies have reported cultural differences for Fins, Japanese, Koreans, and Americans (Thompson & Klopf, 1991). Other researchers have reported lower coefficient alphas when the scale was translated into Russian (Christophel, 1996), Chinese (Anderson et al., 1997), and Japanese (Thompson et al., 1990). The adjectives used in the scale may not translate directly for all cultures. And there might actually be cultural differences on the scale based on cultural characteristics.

Future research should carefully examine the stability of the factor structure of the scale. Confirmatory factor analysis failed to support the two-factor model for a sample of Chinese citizens. A broad sample of American citizens might provide some norms for partitioning into the four groups for interpersonal communication research.

Location

http://www.jamescmccroskey.com/measures/scs.htm
McCroskey, J. C., & Richmond, V. P. (1996). *Fundamentals of human communication: An interpersonal perspective*. Prospect Heights, IL: Waveland Press.*
Richmond, V. P., & McCroskey, J. C. (1990). Reliability and separation of factors on the assertiveness-responsiveness scale. *Psychological Reports, 67*, 449–450.

References

Anderson, C. M., & Martin, M. M. (1995). Communication motives of assertive and responsive communicators. *Communication Research Reports, 12*, 186–191.

Anderson, C. M., Martin, M. M., Zhong, M., & West, D. (1997). Reliability, separation of factors, and sex differences on the assertiveness-responsiveness measure: A Chinese sample. *Communication Research Reports, 14*, 58–64.

Aylor, B., & Oppliger, P. (2003). Out-of-class communication and student perceptions of instructor humor orientation and socio-communicative style. *Communication Education, 52*, 122–135.

Bem, S. L. (1974). The measurement of psychological androgyny. *Journal of Consulting and Clinical* Pyschology, *42*, 155–162.

Campbell, K. L., Martin, M. M., & Wanzer, M. B. (2001). Employee perceptions of manager humor orientation, assertiveness, responsiveness, approach/avoidance strategies, and satisfaction. *Communication Research Reports, 18*, 67–74.

Cegala, D. J. (1981). Interaction involvement: A cognitive dimension of communicative competence. *Communication Education, 30*, 109–121.

Christophel, D. M. (1996). Russian communication orientations: A cross-cultural examination. *Communication Research Reports, 13*, 43–67.

Cole, J. G., & McCroskey, J. C. (2000). Temperament and socio-communicative orientation. *Communication Research Reports, 17*, 105–114.

Frymier, A. B., and Houser, M. L. (2000). The teacher-student relationship as an interpersonal relationship. *Communication Education, 49*, 207–219.

Martin, M. M., Mottet, T. P., & Chesebro, J. L. (1997). Students' perceptions of instructors' socio-communicative style and the influence on instructor credibility and situational motivation. *Communication Research Reports, 14*, 431–440.

Martin, Sirimangkala, P., & Anderson, C. M. (1999). Subordinates' socio-communicative orientation and their use of conflict strategies with superiors. *Communication Research Reports, 16*, 370–376.

McCroskey, J. C., Richmond, V. P. , & Stewart, R. A. (1986). *One on one: The fundamentals of interpersonal communication.* Englewood Cliffs, NJ: Prentice Hall.

McCroskey, L. L. (2003). Relationships of instructional communication styles of domestic and foreign instructors with instructional outcomes. *Journal of Intercultural Communication Research, 32*, 75–96.

Merrill, D. W., & Reid, R. H. (1981). *Personal styles and effective performance.* Bradner, PA: Chilton Book Company.

Myers, S. A. (1998). Instructor socio-communicative style, argumentativeness, and verbal aggressiveness in the college classroom. *Communication Research Reports, 15*, 141–150.

Myers, S. A., & Avtgis, T. A. (1997). The association of socio-communicative style and relational type on perceptions of nonverbal immediacy. *Communication Research Reports, 14*, 339–349.

Patterson, B. R., & Beckett, C. S. (1995). A re-examination of relational repair and reconciliation: Impact of socio-communicative style on strategy selection. *Communication Research Reports, 12*, 235–240.

Richmond, V. P., & Martin, M. M. (1998). Sociocommunicative style and sociocommunicative orientation. In J. C. McCroskey, J. A. Daly, M. M. Martin, & M. J. Beatty (Eds.), *Communication and personality: Trait perspectives* (pp. 133–148). Cresskill, NJ: Hampton Press.

Rubin, R. B., & Martin, M. M. (1994). Development of a measure of interpersonal communication competence. *Communication Research Reports, 11*, 33–44.

Sidelinger, R. J., & McCroskey, J. C. (1997). Communication correlates of teacher clarity in the college classroom. *Communication Research Reports, 14,* 1–10.

Teven, J. J. (2001). The relationship among teacher characteristics and perceived caring. *Communication Education, 50,* 159–170.

Teven, J. J. (2005). Teacher socio-communicator style and tolerance for disagreement and their association with student learning in the college classroom. *Texas Speech Communication Journal, 30,* 23–35.

Thomas, C. E., Richmond, V. P., & McCroskey, J. C. (1994). The association between immediacy and socio-communicative style. *Communication Research Reports, 11,* 107–114.

Thompson, C. A., Ishii, S., & Klopf, D. W. (1990). Japanese and Americans compared on assertiveness/responsiveness. *Psychological Reports, 66,* 829–830.

Thompson, C. A., & Klopf, D. W. (1991). An analysis of social style among disparate cultures. *Communication Research Reports, 8,* 65–72.

Wanzer, M. B., & Frymier, A. B. (1999). The relationship between student perceptions of instructor humor and students' report of learning. *Communication Education, 48,* 48–62.

Wanzer, M. B., & McCroskey, J. C. (1998). Teacher socio-communicative style as a correlate of student affect toward teacher and course material. *Communication Education, 47,* 43–52.

Wooten, A. B., & McCroskey, J. C. (1996). Student trust of teacher as a function of socio-communicative style of teacher and socio-communicative orientation of student. *Communication Research Reports, 13,* 94–100.

Scale

Socio-Communicative Style (SCS) Scale *
Instructions: The questionnaire below lists twenty personality characteristics. Please indicate the degree to which you believe each of these characteristics applies to (**Some Person**) while interacting with others by marking whether you (5) strongly agree that it applies, (4) agree that it applies, (3) are undecided, (2) disagree that it applies, or (1) strongly disagree that it applies. There are no right or wrong answers. Work quickly; record your first impression.

——1   helpful
——2   defends own beliefs
——3   independent
——4   responsive to others
——5   forceful
——6   has strong personality
——7   sympathetic
——8   compassionate
——9   assertive
——10 sensitive to the needs of others
——11 dominant

——12 sincere
——13 gentle
——14 willing to take a stand
——15 warm
——16 tender
——17 friendly
——18 acts as a leader
——19 aggressive
——20 competitive

Scoring:

For the assertiveness score, add responses to items 2, 3, 5, 6, 9, 11, 14, 18, and 20.
For the responsiveness score, add responses to items 1, 4, 7, 8, 10, 12, 13, 15, 16, and 17.

Note: In the instruction, "Some Person" is the target to whom the observer should respond. According to the authors, this can be replaced by either a person's name or by a description of the person (e.g., "your supervisor," "your teacher," "your spouse," "your physician").

Student Motives to Communicate Scale

Profile by Rebecca B. Rubin

Instead of focusing on teachers and their communication in the classroom (a predominant line of research in instructional communication), Martin, Myers and colleagues focused on students to see how their communicative behaviors—and reasons for them—might affect student-instructor relationship development and learning. This research stems from research on interpersonal motives previously studied in dyadic (R. Rubin, Perse, & Barbato, 1988) and group (Anderson & Martin 1995b) interactions. This line of inquiry is partly based on Schutz's (1966) interpersonal needs and the uses and gratifications perspective that has focused on media motives (A. Rubin, 2002).

In developing this scale, Martin and Myers (1999) asked 112 students in an introductory communication course why they talk with their instructors. Content analysis revealed 54 different reasons. These were then reviewed by undergraduates, additional reasons were added, and minor wording changes made for clarity. The list was then given to 302 students who were asked how often they used each for communicating with instructors; they also filled out the Interpersonal Communication Motives scale (Rubin et al., 1988).

Principal components factor analysis with varimax rotation resulted in 5 factors (Martin & Myers, 1999). Items loading higher than .60 were then included in a second analysis with 5 factors accounting for 63.7% of variance: Relate, Functional, Excuse, Participation, and Sycophancy with coefficient alphas of .89, .84, .82, .81, and .78 respectively. The Relate factor described motives aimed at establishing a personal relationship with the instructor, the Functional motives focused on seeking information and clarification of assignments, the Excuse motive challenged grades or provided reasons for late or missing work, the Participation motive aimed at showing interest and understanding, and the Sycophancy motive described communication to seek a favorable impression or accrue brownie points. The Relate and Participation motives were correlated with all the interpersonal motives, whereas the Excuse, Participation, and Sycophantic motives were related to interpersonal control.

The scale, as used since published in 2000 (Martin, Mottet, & Myers), contains 30 items, with 6 items representing each of the five factors. A 5-point response scale ranges from "Exactly Like Me" (5) to "Not at all like me" (1). The scale can be completed in 5 minutes or less.

Reliability

Several studies have shown consistent coefficient alphas for the five motive factors. Myers, Martin, & Mottet (2002a, 2002b) and Mottet, Martin, & Myers (2004) reported alpha ranging from .82 to .89 for the five factors, and Myers, Mottet, and Martin (2000) and Martin, Valencic, and Heisel (2002) reported alphas ranging from .86 to .90.

Validity

Tests of concurrent validity have shown significant relationships between the SMC scale and other student qualities or behaviors. Martin, Myers, and Mottet (1999) reported that students who communicated with instructors more often mainly had relational and participatory motives. Students with these motives report higher affective and cognitive learning (Martin et al., 2000). One reason for relational and participatory motives is to show interest in the class, and Weber et al. (2005) found significant correlations with the impact and meaningfulness dimensions of class interest. One additional study found the students low in communication apprehension have higher scores for relational, participatory, and functional motives; apprehension doesn't seem to affect excuse-making or sycophancy motives.

Also, Myers, Martin, and Mottet (2002b) found that students who communicate with their instructors for sycophantic, relational and participatory motives used indirect and observational information-seeking strategies. Students who communicated for functional motives used overt information-seeking strategies, and not testing strategies.

In addition, Myers, Martin, and Mottet (2002a) classified students into high and low motive groups. Students reporting high relational reasons also reported high assertiveness and responsiveness for both themselves and for their instructors. In addition, students high in functional reasons reported high assertiveness and responsiveness. Students reported communicating for participatory reasons when instructors were responsive and students were assertive. Assertive students also communicated to make excuses and for sycophantic reasons. In addition, female students communicated more for functional motives, and male students communicated more for relational and sycophantic motives. No gender differences were found for participatory and excuse making motives.

Additional research has attempted to look at the impact of teacher qualities on student motives. For instance, Cayanus and Martin (2004) developed an instructor self-disclosure scale and found instructor self-disclosure to be related to student relational, excuse-making, and syco-phancy motives. All correlations were very small, but statistically significant. Another study looked at communicator style qualities of teachers and how these affected students' motives. Myers, Mottet, and Martin (2000) found that friendly and contentious qualities were significantly correlated with all five motives, and students who communicated for relational reasons also found their instructors to be impression leaving. Animated teachers aligned with participatory motives, and attentive styles were aligned with excuse-making motives. These findings provide evidence of construct validity.

Comments

More research is needed for this measure in terms of stability (test-retest reliability) and construct validity. One useful approach might be to see if students high in participatory behavior actually score higher on that dimension than students who rarely participate in class. Identifying additional student motive groups should be fairly easy for teachers; students who ask a lot of questions and check on assignment details should score high on functional motives; relational, excuse-givers, and sycophant students are also easy to identify. The connection between motives and communicative behavior would be highly informative within this instructional context.

Location

Martin, M. M., Myers, S. A., & Mottet, T. P. (1999). Students' motives for communicating with their instructors. *Communication Education, 48*, 155–164.*

References

Anderson, C. M., & Martin, M. M. (1999). The effects of communication motives, interaction involvement, and loneliness on satisfaction: A model of small groups. *Small Group Research, 26*, 118–137.

Cayanus, J. L., & Martin, M. M. (2004). An instructor self-disclosure scale. *Communication Research Reports, 21*, 252–263.

Martin, M.A., & Myers, S. A. (1999). Students' motives for communicating with their instructors. *Communication Education, 48*, 155–164.

Martin, M. M., Mottet, T. P., & Myers, S. A. (2000). Students' motives for communicating with their instructors and affective and cognitive learning. *Psychological Reports, 87*, 830–834.

Martin, M. M., Myers, S. A., & Mottet, T. P. (1999). Students' motives for communicating with their instructors. *Communication Education, 48*, 155–164.

Martin, M. M., Myers, S. A., & Mottet, T. P. (2002). Student motives for communicating in the college classroom. In J. L. Chesebro & J. C. McCroskey (Eds.), *Communication for teachers* (pp. 35–46). Boston: Allyn & Bacon.

Martin, M. M., Valencic, K. M., & Heisel, A. D. (2002). The relationship between students' communication apprehension and their motives for communicating with their instructors. *Communication Research Reports, 19,* 1–7.

Mottet, T. P., Martin, M. M., & Myers, S. A. (2004). Relationships among perceived instructor verbal approach and avoidance relational strategies and students' motives for communicating with their instructors. *Communication Education, 53,* 116–122.

Myers, S. A., Martin, M. M., & Mottet, T. P. (2002a). Students' motives for communicating with their instructors: Considering instructor socio-communicative style, student socio-communicative orientations, and student gender. *Communication Education, 51,* 121–133.

Myers, S. A., Martin, M. M., & Mottet, T. P. (2002b). The relationship between students' communication motives and information seeking. *Communication Research Reports, 19,* 352–361.

Myers, S. A., Mottet, T. P., & Martin, M. M. (2000). Students' motives for communicating with their instructors: The relationship between student communication motives and perceived instructor style. *Communication Research Reports, 17,* 161–170.

Rubin, A. M. (2002). The uses-and-gratifications perspective of media effects. In J. Bryant & D. Zillmann (Eds.), *Media effects: Advances in theory and research* (pp. 525–548). Mahwah, NJ: Erlbaum.

Rubin, R. B., Perse, E. M., & Barbato, C. A. (1988). Conceptualization and measurement of interpersonal communication motives. *Human Communication Research, 14,* 602–628.

Schutz, W. C. (1966). *The interpersonal underworld.* Palo Alto, CA: Science and Behavior Books.

Weber, K. D., Martin, M. M., & Cayanus, J. L. (2005). Why students communicate with their instructors: A multi-study reexamination of student interest. *Communication Quarterly, 53,* 71–86.

Scale

Student Motives to Communicate Scale*
Instructions: Below are reasons people give for why they talk to their instructors. For each statement, please put the appropriate number in the space provided that expresses your reasons for talking to YOUR INSTRUCTOR immediately preceding this class.

Exactly Like Me	A Lot Like Me	Somewhat Like Me	Not Much Like Me	Not at All Like Me
5	4	3	2	1

I talk to my instructor:

1 ____ to learn about him/her personally
2 ____ so we can develop a friendship
3 ____ to build a personal relationship
4 ____ to learn more about the teacher personally
5 ____ because I find the instructor interesting
6 ____ because we share common interests
7 ____ to clarify the material
8 ____ to get assistance on assignments/exams
9 ____ to learn how I can improve in the class
10 ____ to ask questions about the material
11 ____ to get academic advice
12 ____ to get more information on the requirements of the course
13 ____ to explain why my work is late
14 ____ to explain my absences
15 ____ to explain why I do not have my work done
16 ____ to challenge a grade I received
17 ____ to explain why my work does not meet the instructor's expectations
18 ____ to explain the quality of my work
19 ____ to appear involved in class
20 ____ to demonstrate I understand the material
21 ____ to demonstrate my intelligence
22 ____ because my input is vital for class discussion
23 ____ because my classmates value my contribution to class discussions
24 ____ because my instructor values class participation
25 ____ to pretend I'm interested in the course
26 ____ to give the instructor the impression that I like him/her
27 ____ to give the impression that I think the instructor is an effective teacher
28 ____ to give the impression that I'm learning a lot from the instructor
29 ____ to get special permission/privileges not granted to all students

Note. Items 1–6 are Relational, 7–12 are Functional, 13–18 are Excuse-making, 19–24 are Participation, and 25–30 are Sycophancy.

Teacher Misbehaviors Scale

Profile by Rebecca B. Rubin

Research has consistently looked at student misbehaviors in the classroom, but Kearney, Plax, Hays, and Ivey (1991) reasoned that teacher misbehaviors might affect learning, as well. Kearney et al. were interested in finding teacher behaviors that might interfere with instruction and learning. Accordingly, they conducted two studies to develop this scale. Study 1 was designed to solicit college student reports of these misbehaviors, and Study 2 focused on examining the factor structure of the categories. The premise of having students complete the scale is that attributions of misbehavior are just as real as actual misbehaviors and that the best observers are students in the classroom.

In Study 1, 254 students completed an open-ended questionnaire in which students recalled as many descriptions of misbehaviors that they could think of, and 1762 emerged (Kearney et al., 1991). These behaviors were content analyzed, and 28 categories emerged: absent, tardy, keeps students overtime, early dismissal, strays from subject, confusing/unclear lectures, unprepared/disorganized, deviates from syllabus, late returning work, sarcasm and putdowns, verbally abusive, unreasonable and arbitrary rules, sexual harassment, unresponsive to students' questions, apathetic to students, inaccessible to students outside of class, unfair testing, unfair grading, boring lectures, information overload, information underload, negative personality, negative physical appearance, does not know subject matter, shows favoritism or prejudice, foreign or regional accents, inappropriate volume, and bad grammar/spelling.

In study 2, 261 students were asked to focus on a particular teacher and report how frequently that teacher uses the behavior (Kearney et al., 1991). The five most frequently used misbehaviors were: strays from subject, unfair testing, boring lectures, sarcasm/putdowns, and absent from class. Factor analysis resulted in three factors. The first factor, Incompetence, contained: confusing/unclear lectures, apathetic to students, unfair testing, boring lectures, information overload, and bad grammar/spelling. Factor two was Offensiveness: sarcasm/putdowns, verbally abusive, unreasonable/arbitrary rules, sexual harassment, negative personality, and shows favoritism/prejudice. Factor 3 was Indolence: absent, tardy, unprepared/disorganized, deviates from syllabus, late returning work, and information underload. The remaining 7 items failed to meet a liberal 50/30 criterion. The authors used a random split sample and created two sample subsets and forced 3-factor extractions for each. They also used a factor matching procedure and computed concordant coefficients to show factor invariance across paired factor loadings.

The scale contains all of the original 28 misbehaviors. When students are asked to indicate how likely it is for their teacher to engage in each of the misbehaviors, they rely on the following response options: *very unlikely* (1), *somewhat unlikely* (2), *undecided* (3), *somewhat likely* (4), and *very likely* (5) (Kelsey, Kearney, Plax, Allen, & Ritter, 2004). Alternatively, when students are asked to indicate how frequently their teacher engages in each of the representative behaviors, they might use response options ranging from 0 = never to 4 = very often (Wanzer & McCroskey, 1998). Many students would require 8–10 minutes for completing it.

Reliability

The overall scale and subscales appear to be highly reliable. In the initial study, alpha reliabilities for the three factors were: Incompetence, .86 ($M = 5.70$, $SD = -6.31$), Offensiveness, .80 ($M = 2.17$, $SD = 3.51$), and Indolence, .80 ($M = 3.97$, $SD = -4.04$) (Kearney et al., 1991). The authors also used randomized split sample and factor matching procedures to compute concordant coefficients, which ranged from .995 to .999. In addition, Kelsey et al. (2004) reported an alpha of .90 for the overall 28-item scale, and .80 for offensiveness, .67 for indolence, and .83 for incompetence.

Validity

Several studies have provided evidence of concurrent and construct validity. Kelsey et al. (2004) incorporated an attribution theory understanding of how students attribute misbehaviors either to teachers or to the situation. They tested the construct validity of the scale by using qualitative analysis to examine the causes (attributions) for such misbehaviors; they found both internal and external causes.

Wanzer and McCroskey (1998) found that assertiveness and responsiveness were modestly negatively correlated with teacher misbehavior. Also, there were no differences in behaviors between teaching assistants and regular faculty. Students also reported less affect for misbehaving teachers and their course materials. All but one of the misbehaviors significantly distinguished liked from less-liked professors. In order to satisfy the institutional review board at their university who felt that some of items might be actionable, Wanzer and McCroskey (1998) eliminated some of the more "offensive" misbehaviors, resulting in a one-dimensional, 24-item version, with an alpha of .91.

Toale (2001) found, as hypothesized, that teachers high in misbehaviors (all three factors) had students with less positive outcomes: Affect toward content, teacher, enrollment with related content, enrollment with same teacher, and perceptions of teacher competence, caring, and trustworthiness were lower. Teachers high in misbehaviors differed from those low on teacher clarity (especially for high clarity, low misbehavior teachers). In addition, factor analysis of Kearny et al.'s (1991) original items resulted in the same three original factors (Toale, Thweatt, & McCroskey, 2001).

Instead of measuring misbehavior, Banfield, Richmond, and McCroskey (2006) used the categories to create fictional teacher profiles (see also Berkos, Allen, Kearney, & Plax, 2001; Thweatt & McCroskey, 1996) and, again, confirmed that non-misbehaving teachers were liked more and seen as more credible. This provides some construct validity for the scale.

Comments

This scale is used by students to identify behaving or misbehaving teachers. Most often it is used as a correlational or independent variable, one that can affect learning and classroom interaction. The instrument is fairly long and might take about 10 minutes to administer. Graduate assistants and teacher trainees might find the results informative should entire classes of students provide perceptions to their teachers.

Studies of student age, year in school, and culture might produce some interesting results. Also, classrooms of students reporting on their teacher should produce relatively stable collections of perceptions, with low ranges and standard deviations; this would be an ultimate test of reliability and validity.

Researchers should be aware that all the misbehavior statements have an element of negativity to them, so students who do not like (or like very much) their instructors after completing the scale might be in a response mode to provide additional negative (or positive) responses to instruments that follow. A better technique would be to have the dependent variable measures completed first or at another time.

Location

Kearney, P., Plax, T. G., Hays, E. R., & Ivey, M. J. (1991). College teacher misbehaviors: What students don't like about what teachers say and do. *Communication Quarterly, 39*, 309–324.**

McPherson, M. B., Kearney, P., & Plax, T. G. (2006). College teacher misbehaviors. In T. P. Mottet, V. P. Richmond, & J. C. McCroskey (Eds.), *Handbook of Instructional communication: Rhetorical and relational perspectives* (pp. 213–234). Boston: Allyn and Bacon.

References

Banfield, S. R., Richmond, V. P., & McCroskey, J. C. (2006). The effect of teacher misbehaviors on teacher credibility and affect for the teacher. *Communication Education, 55,* 63–72.

Berkos, K. M., Allen, T. H., Kearney, P., & Plax T. G. (2001). When norms are violated: Imagined interactions as processing and coping mechanisms. *Communication* Monographs, *68,* 289–300.

Kelsey, D. M., Kearney, P., Plax, T. G., Allen, T. H., & Ritter, K. J. (2004). College students' attributions of teacher misbehaviors. *Communication Education, 53,* 40–55.

Mottet, T. P., Beebe, S. A., & Fleuriet, C. (2006). Students' influence messages. In T. P. Mottet, V. P. Richmond, & J. C. McCroskey (Eds.), *Handbook of instructional communication: Rhetorical and relational perspectives* (pp. 143–166). Boston: Allyn & Bacon.

Thweatt, K. S., & McCroskey, J. C. (1996). Teacher nonimmediacy and misbehavior: Unintentional negative communication. *Communication Research Reports, 13,* 198–204.

Toale, M. C. (2001). *Teacher clarity and teacher misbehaviors: Relationships with students' affective learning and teacher credibility.* Ed.D. dissertation, West Virginia University, United States—West Virginia. Retrieved February 13, 2008, from ProQuest Digital Dissertations database. (Publication No. AAT 3014964).

Toale, M. C., Thweatt, K. S., & McCroskey, J. C. (2001). *Factor analysis of 114 teacher misbehavior items.* Unpublished manuscript.

Wanzer, M. B., & McCroskey, J. C. (1998). Teacher socio-communicative style as a correlate of student affect toward teacher and course material. *Communication Education, 47,* 43–52.

Scale

Teacher Misbehaviors Scale**

Instructions: Below are a series of behaviors that some teachers have been observed doing. Some teachers have been known to "misbehave" in these ways. For each statement, please indicate how likely it is for your teacher to engage in these or similar kinds of misbehaviors using a scale from *very unlikely* (1), *somewhat unlikely* (2), *undecided* (3), *somewhat likely* (4), *very likely* (5). In other words, how likely would your teacher enact in these, or similar misbehaviors in your class? **Remember: Keep in mind only the teacher from the class that meets *immediately before (or after) this one.**

3____   1   Does not show up for class, cancels class without notification, and/or offers poor excuses for being absent.

3____   2   Is late for class or tardy.

*____   3   Keeps class overtime, talks too long or starts early before all the students are there.

*____   4   Lets class out early, rushes through the material to get done early.

*____   5   Uses the class as a forum for her/his personal opinions, goes off on tangents, talks too much about family and personal life and/or generally wastes class time.

1____   6   Unclear about what is expected, lectures are confusing and vague, contradicts him/herself, jumps from one subject to another and/or the lectures are inconsistent with assigned readings.

3____   7   Is not prepared for class, unorganized, forgets test dates, and/or makes assignments but does not collect them.

3____   8   Changes due dates for assignments, behind schedule, does not follow the syllabus, changes assignments, and/or books but does not use them.

3____   9   Late in returning papers, late in grading and turning back exams, and/or forgets to bring graded papers to class.

2____   10   Is sarcastic and rude, makes fun of and humiliates students, picks on students, and/or insults and embarrasses students.

2____   11   Uses profanity, is angry and mean, yells and screams, interrupts and/or intimidates students.

2____   12   Refuses to accept late work, gives no breaks in 3-hour classes, punishes entire class for one student's misbehavior, and/or is rigid, inflexible and authoritarian.

2____   13   Makes sexual remarks to students, flirts with them, makes sexual innuendos and/or is chauvinistic.

*____   14   Does not encourage students to ask questions, does not answer questions or recognize raised hands, and/or seems "put out" to have to explain or repeat him/herself.

1____   15   Doesn't seem to care about the course or show concern for students, does not know the students' names, rejects students' opinions and/or does not allow for class discussion.

*____   16   Does not show up for appointments or scheduled office hours, is hard to contact, will not meet with students outside of office time and/or doesn't make time for students when they need help.

1____   17   Asks trick questions on tests, exams do not relate to the lectures, tests are too difficult, questions are too ambiguous, and/or teacher does not review for exams.

*____   18   Grades unfairly, changes grading policy during the semester, does not believe in giving A's, makes mistakes when grading and/or does not have a predetermined grading scale.

1____ 19 Is not an enthusiastic lecturer, speaks in monotone and rambles, is boring, uses too much repetition, and/or employs no variety in lectures.

1____ 20 Talks too fast and rushes through the material, talks over the students' heads, uses obscure terms and/or assigns excessive work.

3____ 21 The class is too easy, students feel they have not learned anything, and/or tests are too easy.

2____ 22 Teacher is impatient, self-centered, complains, acts superior and/or is moody.

*____ 23 Teacher dresses sloppy, smells bad; clothes are out of style, and cares little about his/her overall appearances.

1____ 24 Doesn't know the material, unable to answer questions, provides incorrect information, and/or isn't current.

2____ 25 Plays favorites with students or acts prejudiced against others, is narrow-minded or close-minded, and/or makes prejudicial remarks.

1____ 26 Teacher is hard to understand, enunciates poorly, and has a strong accent that makes it difficult to understand.

1___ 27 Doesn't speak loudly enough or speaks too loud.

1____ 28 Uses bad grammar, writes illegibly, misspells words on the exam (or on the board) and/or generally uses poor English.

Note: Incompetence 1, Offensiveness 2, Indolence 3.

Items that do not load on any of the 3 factors are asterisked.

** © 1991 by Taylor & Francis.

Television Addiction Scale

Profile by Elizabeth M. Perse

As television plays a central role in daily lives, discussions of its effects are abundant. However, as Smith (1986) pointed out, most research has focused on the effects of particular types of content. Research exploring the relationship individuals develop with the medium itself has received less attention. One such relationship that has spawned widespread discussion, though considerably less sound empirical evidence, is that of television addiction. McIlwraith, Jacobvitz, Kubey, and Alexander (1991) identified television addiction as a medium-specific effect: "Television addiction does not mean being "hooked" on particular TV content. TV addiction means dependence on the television medium itself, regardless of whatever content happens to be on" (p. 104). McIlwraith (1998) wrote that the term originally appeared in the popular media during the late 1970s, and was "bolstered only by anecdotal evidence" (p. 371). Though the evidence was sparse, the similarities between commonly identified motives for addictive behavior—reduction of pain and awareness, enhanced sense of control and self-esteem, and ritualistic experience (Horvath, 2004)—and motives that have been identified for television-viewing behavior (Rubin, 1981) were striking. With these similarities in mind, scholars have attempted to determine what separates normal television viewing from dysfunctional television viewing and, in doing so, create a useful diagnostic instrument for television addiction.

The largest difficulty communication scholars have faced in their discussions of television addiction seems to lie in the challenge of settling on a definition of addiction itself. First and foremost, if one is to discuss addiction to a mass communication medium like television, it is necessary to accept the notion that addiction is not a purely physiological phenomenon (Smith, 1986). This has been supported by the literature on drug addiction, which indicates that addiction is a complex process that occurs through an individual's psychological and environmental dynamics. Likewise, scholars who study addiction are also quick to point out that although heavy use is associated with addiction, it seems to be a necessary, but not sufficient, condition for addictive behavior (Horvath, 2004;

Smith, 1986). In her attempt to develop the first scale for measuring tele-vision addiction, Smith began by using content analysis to identify com-mon behaviors associated with this hypothesized affliction in the popular literature. This analysis identified 12 categories of anecdotal statements about addiction, which were used to create an 18-item television addiction scale. Through confirmatory factor analysis, Smith identified two factors, the first of which assessed feelings of depression and nervousness when respondents were unable to watch television, as well as behaviors indicat-ing a loss of control. The second factor represented a dimension assessing feelings of guilt, anger, and depression about, during, and after viewing. The single most frequent response to 17 of the 18 questions was "never," which indicated that the behavior designated as characteristic of television addicts in the popular literature was not something the majority of the respondents thought was characteristic of them.

Horvath (2004) questioned the validity of Smith's (1986) anecdotal items, particularly given the fact that very few addicts were identified in Smith's study, or in subsequent uses of the measure (e.g., McIlwraith, 1998). Instead, Horvath looked to the psychiatric definition of addiction, used to diagnose drug dependence. Criteria for diagnosis of dependence or addiction, as outlined by the American Psychiatric Association's (1994) *Diagnostic and Statistical Manual of Mental Disorders* (DSM-IV), includes the following seven symptoms: (1) tolerance, or "a need for more of the substance to achieve the same effect"; (2) withdrawal, which describes "a substance-specific syndrome that results if the substance use is reduced or stopped that is unrelated to another physical illness, or use of the substance or a related one to reduce withdrawal symptoms"; (3) tak-ing the substance in greater amount over a longer-than-intended amount of time; (4) unsuccessful efforts to cut down, despite a persistent desire to do so; (5) a large amount of time committed to the substance, including obtaining it, using it, and recovering from its use; (6) reduction of other activities that were once of importance; and (7) continued use of the sub-stance despite physical and psychological problems (Horvath, p. 379). Although the second symptom seems to pertain to physical withdrawal, Horvath (2004) makes the argument that individuals could also experi-ence psychological withdrawal when the substance at hand is reduced or stopped, consisting of feelings of irritability, anxiety, and fear (p. 380).

In the measure profiled here, Horvath (2004) created five statements to represent each of the seven criteria for dependence/addiction. Respon-dents marked their agreement with each item using 5-point Likert responses (5 = *strongly agree*, 4 = *agree*, 3 = *agree some and disagree some*, 2 = *disagree*, 1 = *strongly disagree*). Principal components analysis with varimax rotation identified four factors explaining 55.45% of the vari-ance. Responses to each item were averaged to indices of four addiction subscales: Problem Viewing, Heavy Viewing, Craving for Viewing, and

Withdrawal. In a second study, Horvath (2004) used a less liberal principal components analysis and identified a two-factor solution (Problem Viewing and Guilty Viewing) that was, interestingly enough, similar to Smith's two factors. Subsequent analysis of the 20 items that fit into this two-factor solution found that the two factors were highly correlated $(r = .78, p < .001)$, and principal components analysis with oblique rotation supported the notion that these two factors were actually unidimensional in nature. Horvath used both the original 35-item scale and this 20-item unidimensional scale in analyses. She does not, in this study, draw a conclusion as to which version of the scale is more valid.

Reliability

Both versions of Horvath's (2004) scale are reliable. All four factors used in the first version of Horvath's scale have fairly high internal consistency as measured by Cronbach's alpha: Problem Viewing ($\alpha = .93$), Heavy Viewing ($\alpha = .89$), Craving for Viewing ($\alpha = .75$), and Withdrawal ($\alpha = .65$). The unidimensional 20-item measure was also extremely reliable ($\alpha = .95$).

No measures of test-retest reliability have been provided for this scale, to date. In order to determine whether this is a construct that changes over time, test-retest reliability should be assessed by future research: "More stringent criteria for establishing the presence of a clinically significant dependence, analogous to substance dependence, must also include a temporal dimension: have these behaviors been present for some time, or are they only fleeting or situational?" (McIlwraith et al., 1991, p. 118).

Validity

Because Horvath's new scale measures television addiction based entirely on the American Psychiatric Association's (1994) list of seven symptoms, it improves upon the face validity of Smith's (1986) scale that was based on content analysis of episodic discussions of addiction. To establish construct validity, Horvath (2004) incorporated an adapted version of the CAGE questionnaire (Ewing, 1984), an alcoholism screening-device, into her study. The acronym CAGE represents four indications physicians use to determine a patient's potential for alcoholism: Cutting down, Annoyance by criticism, Guilty feelings, and Eye openers. According Horvath, this measure has been validated by prior research, with accuracy ratings of more than 90% for predicting alcoholism (Ewing, 1984). Horvath predicted that since high scores on CAGE and her television addiction measure are both expected to predict television addiction, they should be positively correlated. Indeed, CAGE scores were positively related to Heavy Viewing $(r = .44, p < .001)$, Withdrawal $(r = .31, p < .001)$, Problem

Viewing (r = .30, p < .001), and Craving (r = .23, p < .001). The 20-item scale was also correlated with the CAGE instrument (r = .57, p < .001). Though we cannot be certain that the adapted version of CAGE is as valid as the original that was used for alcoholism, these correlations indicate that both scales are most likely speak to the same construct. Horvath also found that, as expected, those who watched more hours of television scored higher on all four factors of the multidimensional television addiction measure and the unidimensional measure, as well as the CAGE scale. This supports the previously discussed notion that heavy viewers are more likely to be addicted to television than light viewers.

In her second study, Horvath (2004) used purposive sampling in order to identify and compare light and heavy television users. This sampling choice was implemented because other studies (e.g., McIlwraith, 1998; Smith, 1986) have found it difficult to find self-reported television addicts. In this case, undergraduate students were offered extra credit for bringing in two participants they characterized as heavy users of television and two identified as light users (using a "yes" response to any one of the four CAGE criteria as a qualification for heavy viewing, and at least one "no" for light viewers). Though this sampling procedure allowed Horvath to look at a larger quantity of potentially addicted individuals, the external validity of this type of sample is clearly lacking. Fortunately, the sample used in his first study is more diverse and resulted in similar findings, providing more support for the external validity. Horvath, however, still has not used a geographically-diverse random sample to test this scale.

When discussing validity, it is also important to note that research in the social sciences has found on numerous occasions that social desirability issues can alter individuals' responses to self-report measures. McIlwraith (1998) found that total scores on Smith's (1986) television addiction scale correlated negatively with the EPQ Lie Scale (r = −.19, p < .005), suggesting that concerns regarding social desirability may lead participants to under-report addictive behaviors. To determine whether social desirability impacted individuals' responses to her scale, Horvath (2004) administered the Marlowe-Crowne Social Desirability Scale Form C (Reynolds, 1982) in her second study. As expected, the 20-item Television Addiction Scale was negatively related to the measure of social desirability (r = −.27, p < .001), suggesting that those who are less concerned about social desirability of their responses are more likely to appear to be addicted to television. This indicates that self-report measures are indeed problematic when looking at the possibility of television addiction. McIlwraith et al. (1991) echoed this sentiment, writing that, "although it is interesting to know what sort of person is willing to diagnose him- or herself as a 'TV addict,' such self-report studies can have little clinical significance" (p. 118). According to Horvath, these concerns are indicative of the possibility that a Type II error occurred in these studies. In this case, more robust effects could exist that were not identified by these analyses.

Comments

Television addiction research has tested hypothesized relationships with psychological variables, and has also explored relationships with demographic variables. Studies using Smith's television addiction scale tested theoretical models from the popular and psychological literature, including relationships with viewers' fantasy lives, arousal level, orality, and uses and gratifications of television viewing (McIlwraith, 1998; McIlwraith et al., 1991). Also, mood management theory has been associated with addiction research; Anderson, Collins, Schmitt, and Jacobvitz (1996) found that stress, as measured by life events, was positively related to scores on Smith's (1986) television addiction scale for women. Researchers have also looked for correlations between demographic variables and television addiction. Smith (1986) found no significant relationships between television addiction and any of the demographic variables, possibly due to the skewed nature of her findings. Analyses using Horvath's (2004) multidimensional measure found that people scoring highest were generally male, older, and less educated than non-addicts. Using the unidimensional measure, Horvath found that gender produced the only significant difference in television addiction scores. An independent t-test indicated that men ($M = 2.07$) scored significantly higher than women ($M = 1.82$) on the television addiction measure, $t(315) = 2.88$, $p < .01$.

Future research should use this measure to answer the following three questions. *First, what is it about television as a medium that induces addiction?* If addiction truly has nothing to do with the content of programs (this in itself should be investigated in relation to this scale), there must be aspects of television as a medium that lead to this type of attachment. *Second, which characteristics of people are associated with TV addiction?* This question is tied closely to the first, as McIlwraith (1998) looked at relationships between individual characteristics, such as neurotic rumination, impoverished imagination, use of interactive versus passive media, and orality, and television addiction scores. *Third, what are the consequences of television addiction?* Horvath's (2004) scale offers a promising tool to explore these questions. If we know *why* people become addicted to television, as opposed to *who* is addicted, we may be able to help these people combat their addiction or prevent these problems in the future.

Finally, it would also be interesting to see if this scale could be adapted to look at addiction to other types of media, especially with recent interest in Internet addiction (Griffiths, 2000). If it is possible to validly use symptoms of drug addiction to identify television addiction, this measure should also be applicable to any other medium. With this possibility, we return to the importance of determining the most useful conceptual definition of addiction. In any case, Horvath (2004) provides strong evidence toward the validity of this measure, but only continued research will tell if this scale is anything more than a promising one.

Location**

Horvath, C. W. (2004). Measuring television addiction. *Journal of Broadcasting & Electronic Media, 48*, 378–398.

References

American Psychiatric Association. (1994). *Diagnostic and statistical manual of mental disorders* (4th ed.).Washington, DC: Author.

Anderson, D. R., Collins, P. A., Schmitt, K. L., & Jacobvitz, R. S. (1996). Stressful life events and television viewing. *Communication Research, 23*, 243–260.

Ewing, J. A. (1984). Detecting alcoholism: The CAGE questionnaire. *Journal of the American Medical Association, 252*, 1905–1907.

Griffiths, M. (2000). Does Internet and computer addiction exist? Some case study evidence. *CyberPsychology & Behavior, 3*, 211–218.

McIlwraith, R.D. (1998). "I'm addicted to television:" The personality, imagination, and TV watching patterns of self identified TV addicts. *Journal of Broadcasting & Electronic Media, 42*, 371–386.

McIlwraith, R., Jacobvitz, R. S., Kubey, R. & Alexander, A. (1991). Television addiction: Theories and data behind the ubiquitous metaphor. *American Behavioral Scientist, 35*, 104–121.

Reynolds, W. M. (1982). Development of reliable and valid short forms of the Marlowe-Crowne Social Desirability Scale. *Journal of Clinical Psychology, 38*, 119–125.

Rubin, A. M. (1981). An examination of television viewing motives. *Communication Research, 8*, 141–165.

Smith, R. (1986). Television addiction. In J. Bryan & D. Anderson (Eds.), *Perspectives on media effects* (pp. 109–128). Hillsdale, NJ: Lawrence Erlbaum.

Scale

Television Addiction Scale*
Instructions. Please read each statement about TV use and indicate whether you **strongly agree** (5), **agree** (4), **agree some and disagree some** (3), **disagree** (2), or **strongly disagree** (1) with each.

Tolerance

*1   I feel like I watch more TV than I used to in order to feel the same.
 2   I've watched the same amount of TV as I always have.
*3   It seems like I watch more and more shows lately for the same amount of enjoyment.

4 I watch about the same amount of TV as I used to but I don't get the same effect from it anymore.

5 I watch more and more shows to try to feel the same as I used to.

Withdrawal

*6 When I am unable to watch television, I miss it so much that you could call it withdrawal.

*7 Sometimes I watch TV just because I missed it a great deal.

8 If I have to miss a favorite show, I feel upset.

9 I can't imagine going without TV.

10 I could easily go without TV with no problem.

Unintended Use

11 I often watch TV for a longer time than I intended.

12 Time really gets away from me when I watch TV.

*13 Sometimes I only plan to watch TV for a few minutes, and wind up spending hours in front of it.

14 I follow a very exact TV-watching schedule.

15 I usually watch TV for exactly as long as I planned to watch.

Cutting Down

*16 I often think that I should cut down on the amount of television that I watch.

17 I've tried to reduce the amount of TV I watch, but it hasn't really worked.

*18 I often feel guilty about watching so much television.

*19 I feel bad that I watch so much television, but I can't seem to stop.

*20 I would be embarrassed to tell people how much TV I actually watch.

Time Spent

*21 Compared to most people, I spend a great deal of time watching television.

22 Much of my time is spent in front of the television.

23 Television viewing takes up almost all of my leisure time.

24 I don't spend that much time watching television.

*25 I spend more time watching TV than just about anything else.

Displacement of Other Activities

26 I sometimes watch television when I should be spending time with friends or family.

*27 I often watch TV when I should be working or going to school.

*28 Sometimes I feel like my whole life revolves around TV, and I never do anything else.

*29 I would be a lot more productive if I didn't watch so much TV.

*30 I would spend more time with hobbies if I didn't watch so much TV.

Continued Use

*31 I keep watching TV even though it is causing serious problems in my life.

*32 My family members get angry and tell me I watch too much TV, but I can't stop.

*33 I sometimes feel like my TV watching is alienating my loved ones.

*34 My TV watching has created real problems for me, but I keep watching.

*35 I keep watching TV even though my loved ones can't stand it.

Note: Items 2, 10, 14, 15, and 24 are reverse-scored. Scale items should be randomly presented and subscale titles removed. Items marked by * are used in the 20-item unidimensional scale.

** © 2004 by Taylor & Francis.

Television Mediation Scale

Profile by Elizabeth M. Perse

As effects studies have uncovered trends that suggest a causal relationship between media use and anti-social behaviors, the idea that parents have the power to intervene, and therefore reduce or counteract negative media effects, has spawned widespread interest in television mediation (Nathanson, 1999). Television mediation refers to parental rule-making and social interaction about television's use, meaning, and effects.

Prior to the development of the instrument profiled here, numerous researchers attempted to classify different types of parental television mediation. Early studies identified three general television mediation: *Restrictive mediation*, also known as rule-making, occurs when parents set rules for viewing or prohibit certain types of content (Bybee, Robinson, & Turow, 1982); *Instructive/Active mediation* refers to discussions of certain aspects of programs with children (Austin, 1993; Bybee et al., 1982); and *Coviewing,* which takes place when adults and children share the television viewing experience (Bybee et al., 1982).

Valkenburg and her colleagues (1999) argued that previous measures of parental television mediation were unreliable and measured mixed types of mediation styles (e.g., Austin, 1993; Bybee et al., 1982). They built on prior research to create reliable scales that identified and measured each of the styles of television mediation. To do this, they compiled 13 items from existing scales (Austin, 1993; Bybee et al., 1982) and created an additional 17 five-point Likert-type items. Their goal was to assess restrictive, instructive, and active mediation styles identified in prior research, as well as explore if there were other dimensions to parental mediation. The initial 30-item scale was administered in a phone survey to a pilot sample of 123 Dutch parents. Principle components analysis identified three factors: Instructive mediation, restrictive mediation, and a new factor, social coviewing. The first two factors replicated those of prior research. The third factor reflects more a companionship function of coviewing, watching television together while sharing common interests. The final 15-item scale is made of up the items that had the highest loadings in each factor.

Research using this scale has explored the variables that predict different television mediation styles. These included demographic variables, such as gender of parents and children, children's age, and parents' education levels (Valkenburg et al., 1999). Other research has considered how parents' concerns about specific negative effects of television, including television-induced aggression, fright, and sexual content are reflected in different types of mediation (Valkenburg et al., 1999; Warren, 2003, 2005; Warren, Gerke, & Kelly, 2002).

Subsequent studies have used this scale to tap into the relationship between television mediation and some social theories. For example, Warren and his colleagues (2002) used Valkenburg et al.'s instrument to look at parental involvement (i.e., accessibility and engagement) as a predictor of mediation strategy. Others have modified the instructive and restrictive subscales to assess the impact of parental mediation of television advertising (Buijzen & Valkenburg, 2005).

The 15-item Television Mediation Scale is reported here. It is completed by parents who are asked to answer the questions with one particular child in mind. When a parent has more than one child, the parent is asked to respond to the questions by thinking about one of the children. In telephone interviews, Valkenburg et al. (1999) asked half of the parents with more than one child to think about the child whose birthday occurred first after the interview, while the other half were asked to choose the child whose birthday occurred most recently. Valkenburg and her colleagues used four response options (*never, rarely, sometimes, often*). Warren (2005) added a midpoint to the response scale: 1 = *never*, 2 = *sometimes*, 3 = *about half the time*, 4 = *most of the time*, and 5 = *almost always*.

Reliability

The five-item subscales of the Television Mediation Scale are reliable. Valkenburg and her colleagues (1999) report the following Cronbach alphas: α = .80 for instructive mediation, α =.79 for restrictive mediation, and: α =.79 for social coviewing. Warren (2003, 2005) and his colleagues (Warren et al., 2002) have used the scale with US samples and found the subscales to be reliable: instructive mediation (alphas range from .88 to .96), restrictive mediation (alphas range from .80 to .84, and social coviewing (alphas range from .79 to .83. Instructive and restrictive subscales modified to reference parental mediation of television advertising were also reliable: instructive α =.80, restrictive = α =.73 (Buijzen & Valkenburg, 2005).

The scale has been used reliably with parents of children ranging in age from 1 to 17. The scale does not appear to be affected by question order; Valkenburg and her colleagues (1999) presented items to their respondents in randomized order.

The factor structure of the subscales appears stable. Warren (2003, 2005) and his colleagues (Warren et al., 2002) has identified a consistent three-factor solution using the 15 items in three separate data collections. Test-retest reliably has not been assessed for this measure. Parents' mediation styles should be consistent over time, changing only with children's age.

This scale has been used reliably with respondents who are parents of children from a variety of age groups, including preschool students (Warren, 2003) and 5- through 12-year-olds (Valkenburg et al., 1999). Samples have come from not only U.S. schools (e.g., Warren et al., 2002), but also Dutch populations (Valkenburg et al., 1999). Warren (2003) also translated the measure for Spanish-speaking participants.

Validity

The derivation of the Television Mediation Scale from prior widely used instruments provides face validity. Nathanson (2001), however, suggested that the active mediation subscale might confuse positive and negative mediation. That is, because it includes items that reference parents' positive and negative comments about television comment, it might not be clearly linked to endorsement or restriction of content.

Valkenburg et al.'s measure improves upon the face validity of previous scales that included the unfocused mediation style (e.g., Bybee et al., 1982). Valkenburg et al. referred to these items as "unrelated conceptually" (p. 54) and believed them to be merely leftover items from a principal components analysis. The social coviewing factor of the Television Mediation Scale includes several of these factors, but is conceptually unified by each item's focus on experiences in which parents and children view television together.

The scale's three subscales appear to have discriminant validity, but they can be differentiated empirically. The moderate correlations show that the indices are not necessarily mutually exclusive: restrictive and instructive mediation ($r = .41$, $p < .001$) restrictive mediation and social coviewing ($r = .15$, $p < .001$), and instructive mediation and social coviewing ($r = .32$, $p < .001$, Valkenburg et al., 1999). Warren (2003), however, found strong correlations among the three subscales: restrictive and instructive mediation ($r = .58$, $p < .001$) restrictive mediation and social coviewing ($r = .38$, $p < .001$), and instructive mediation and social coviewing ($r = .57$, $p < .001$).

There is some evidence of concurrent validity. Because mothers typically spend more time with children than fathers, there is evidence that mothers engage in more instructive mediation (Valkenburg et al., 1999). There is a positive relationship between the amount of time that children watch television and the amount of social coviewing (Valkenburg et al., 1999). And, there is a negative relationship between the amount of time a parent spends watching television and social coviewing (Warren, 2005).

Research has provided strong evidence for the construct validity of the three subscales. One would expect that mediation patterns would change with the age of the children. Researchers have found that parents of younger children use more instructive mediation than parents of older children (Valkenburg et al., 1999; Warren et al., 2002). Buijzen and Valkenburg (2005) found that their modified instructive mediation scale was a significant moderator of advertising effects on Dutch middle-school-age children. The relationship between advertising exposure and materialism and advertising exposure and product requests was significantly stronger for children whose parents did not use instructive/active mediation.

The strongest theoretical support for the validity of the scale comes from Warren's (2005) research program. Warren built on Bronfenbrenner's (1979) explanation that families can be viewed as a micro social system that is influenced by the parents' social roles. Because education affects the type of work that people do, and subsequently access to and amount of time spent on outside activities, parents' education and work should affect their interactions with their children. Warren's research found that education was linked to instructive mediation: More educated parents interact verbally with their children more. He also found that less educated parents spend more time watching television, and engage in more social coviewing. More educated parents work more hours, spend less time watching television, and engage in less social coviewing. Finally, parents who are married have more time for activities with their children, and engage in more social coviewing.

The internal validity of this measure could be improved if its uses were supplemented by more controlled experiments and observation of both parents' mediation behaviors and children's responses. As with any self-report measure, it is questionable whether or not people can accurately describe their own attitudes and behaviors. This is particularly of concern when it comes to measures involving violence and other anti-social behaviors. Nathanson and Cantor (2000), however, supported the use of self-report measures of aggression, explaining that "self-ratings of aggression have been shown to be valid measures, bearing significant relationships with peer nominations and teacher ratings of aggression" (p. 130). Though this may be the case, it seems possible that social desirability could come into play when parents report their mediation behaviors, and even when children report their responses to mediation. With this in mind, it is clear that researchers should remain cognizant of the possible biases involved with such reports.

Comments

Because of the confounding of positive and negative comments in the instructive mediation subscale, researchers should recognize that the quality of the instruction is not uniform. As Nathanson (2001) pointed out, parents with positive attitudes toward content might praise it, while those in opposition of the programming would criticize it. The valence of an instructive mediation message could lead to a different effect on the child who receives it.

Second, Van den Bulck and Van den Bergh (2000) suggested that the study of parental mediation could benefit from expanding focus to other media than television. A child who is not allowed to watch television, for example, might play video games or surf the Web more. Second, they suggest television mediation should gather data about children's perceptions about their parents' efforts and the effects of television mediation on children. Fujioka and Austin (2003) echo this sentiment, writing that "there seems to be a danger that what a child observes and learns from a parent may not necessarily reflect what a parent wants their child to observe and learn" (p. 430). When looking at outcomes of television mediation, Fujioka and Austin found that the children's reports predicted self-reported outcomes more reliably than parents' reports did. Though they acknowledge that it is unclear whether these differences are due to methodological limitations or real differences, it seems important to further investigate these findings.

Finally, the measure in its original form suffers from wording that is somewhat awkward. Rephrasing some of the items (as in Warren et al., 2002) would eliminate any error that could occur due to confusion about question wording.

Location*

Valkenburg, P. M., Krcmar, M., Peeters, A., & Marseille, N. M. (1999). Developing a scale to assess three styles of television mediation: "restrictive mediation," "instructive mediation," and "social coviewing." *Journal of Broadcasting and Electronic Media, 43,* 52–66.

References

Austin, E. W. (1993). Expecting the effects of active parental mediation of television content. J*ournal of Broadcasting & Electronic Media, 37,* 147–158.

Buijzen, M., & Valkenburg, P. M. (2005). Parental mediation of undesired advertising effects. *Journal of Broadcasting & Electronic Media, 49,* 153–165.

Bybee, C., Robinson, D., & Turow, J. (1982). Determinants of parental guidance of children's television viewing for a special subgroup: Mass media scholars. *Journal of Broadcasting, 26,* 697–710.

Fujioka, Y., & Austin, E. W. (2002). The relationship of family communication patterns to parental mediation styles. *Communication Research, 29,* 642–665.

Nathanson, A. (1999). Identifying and explaining the relationship between parental mediation and children's aggression. *Communication Research, 26*, 124–143.

Nathanson, A. (2001). Parent and child perspectives on the presence and meaning of parental television mediation. *Journal of Broadcasting & Electronic Media, 45*, 201–220.

Nathanson, I. A., & Cantor, J. (2000). Reducing the aggression-promoting effect of violent cartoons by increasing children's fictional involvement with the victim: A study of active mediation. *Journal of Broadcasting & Electronic Media, 44*, 125–142.

Van den Bulck, J., & Van den Bergh, B. (2000).The influence of perceived parental guidance patterns on children's media use: Gender differences and media displacement. *Journal of Broadcasting & Electronic Media, 44*, 329–348.

Warren, R. (2003). Parental mediation of preschool children's television viewing. *Journal of Broadcasting & Electronic Media, 47*, 394–417.

Warren, R. (2005). Parental mediation of children's television viewing in low-income families. *Journal of Communication, 55*, 847–863.

Warren, R., Gerke, P., & Kelly, A. K. (2002). Is there enough time on the clock? Parental involvement and mediation of children's television viewing. *Journal of Broadcasting & Electronic Media, 46*, 87–107.

Scale

Television Mediation Scale*

How often do you . . .

1 = Never   2 = Rarely   3 = Sometimes   4 = Often

INSTRUCTIVE MEDIATION

1   try to help the child understand what s/he sees on TV?
2   point out why some things actors do are good?
3   point out why some things actors do are bad?
4   explain what something on TV really means?
5   explain what something on TV really means?

RESTRICTIVE MEDIATION

6   say to your child to turn off TV when s/he is watching an unsuitable program?
7   set specific viewing hours for your child?
8   forbid your child to watch certain programs?
9   restrict the amount of child viewing?
10   specify in advance the programs that may be watched?

SOCIAL COVIEWING

11 watch together because you both like a program?
12 watch together because of a common interest in a program?
13 watch together just for fun?
14 do you watch your favorite program together?
15 do you laugh with your child about the things you see on TV?

Note: Items should be randomly ordered and subscale labels removed prior to administration.

Third-Person Effect

Profile by Elizabeth M. Perse

The third-person effect (TPE) places the power of the media not in direct effects, but rather, in the manner in which individuals perceive others in society will be influenced by the content (Davison, 1983). Ongoing research through this perspective has resulted in a large body of literature in the fields of communication, public opinion and psychology (see Paul, Salwen, & Dupagne, 2000; Perloff, 2002 for reviews). Davison's original hypothesis includes both a perceptual and a behavioral component. The perceptual component predicts that people will tend to overestimate the influence that mass communications have on the attitudes and behaviors of others (Davison, 1983, p. 3). The behavioral component hypothesizes that these perceptions lead people to take action.

In Davison's original conceptualization, the third-person effect was identified solely in the context of persuasive communication (for example, political messages or advertisements); however, more recent studies have explored a wider range of application, including media messages "without explicit persuasive intent" (McLeod, Detenber, & Eveland, 2001, p. 679). Such studies have observed the third-person effect in news viewing, television violence, song lyrics, and pornography (Paul et al., 2000). Within the past decade, many researchers have shifted their focus from merely identifying the third-person perception to looking at the second component of Davison's hypothesis. Through this new generation of studies, many have come to view the significance of the third-person perception as its tendency to lead individuals to advocate socially relevant action in order to protect others from the perceived harmful influence of the media.

The scale profiled here assesses the perceptual component of the TPE, that is, the difference between the perceived effects on self and others. McLeod, Eveland, and Nathanson (1997) developed a three-item scale to explore third-person perceptions about effects of the lyrics of antisocially-themed rap music. Respondents estimated the effects of listening to songs with these types of lyrics on knowledge, attitudes, and behaviors of four referent groups, ranging in degree of social distance from themselves: university students, people their own age in New York and Los Angeles, and the average person. The third-person perceptions are measured on an 11-point scale ranging from 0 (*no effect*) to 10 (*a great deal of effects*). Responses to the three items are summed to create perceived effects scores for each referent group. Third-person perception scores are represented by difference scores—between self and each of the other referent groups.

This scale references the effects of lyrics adapted from violent and misogynic rap. It has been used exclusively with college students enrolled in introductory mass communication classes.

Although there has been no standard measure for assessing TPE percep-tions, this promising scale is highlighted here for several reasons. Much research often relies on single-item measures of third-person perceptions that focus on general influence of media content on self and others (e.g., Price & Tewksbury, 1996). Other researchers have used multiple items to assess third-person perceptions, but did not create summated or averaged scales. Hoffner and Buchanan (2002, for example, consider third-perceptions of three different separate effects of television violence (mean-world percep-tions, approval of aggression, and aggressive behavior). Huh, Delorme, and Reid (2004) used 22 different items to assess perceptions of positive and neg-ative effects of direct to consumer (DTC) pharmaceutical advertising. Those items, however, were quite specific to the DTC advertising.

The three-item scale developed by McLeod and his colleagues (1997) overcomes the limits of using a single-item measure, has been used in two different studies so that we can examine its reliability and validity, and it can be easily adapted to other contexts, as it focuses on general knowledge, attitudes, and behavior. It has also been used in several different, though related contexts: violent rap lyrics, misogynic rap lyrics, rap lyrics that crit-icize violence, and rap lyrics that reject mistreatment of women.

Reliability

The three-item third-perception scale has been used reliably. Cronbach alphas support the internal consistency of the third-person perception indices in McLeod et al. (1997): effects on self (α =.79), effects on Delaware students (α =.82), effects on New York/Los Angeles youth (α =.85), and effects on the average person (α =.85). These indices remained reliable when used for only two referent groups in Eveland and McLeod's (1999) study (effects on self, α =.88 and effects on other university stu-dents, α =.87). Although theory would predict that third-person percep-tions should be stable, test-retest reliability has not been assessed.

Validity

This three-item scale improves on the content validity of single-item meas-ures of third-person perceptions by including effects on general knowledge, attitudes, and behavior. More specificity in the items could increase content validity, but limit the scale's use in other contexts. Two studies offer evidence of construct validity for the scale; it operates as expected. In all situations, effects on self are perceived to be smaller than on different reference others (McLeod & Eveland, 1999; McLeod et al., 1997).

The external validity of this instrument remains in question, however, due to sampling methods used in these, and many other studies of the third-person effect. The use of a convenience sample of college students may not be generalizable across the entire population, especially as meta-analyses have found that college student and nonrandom samples typically yield larger third-person effects than other samples (Paul et al., 2000).

Comments

Despite the modest evidence of validity for this scale, it remains a promising measure to use and adapt to the study of third-person perceptions and behaviors. Scholars recognize the complexity of the phenomenon. Davison (1996) revealed that his original evaluation of the third-person hypothesis was incorrect: The third-person effect was not a manifestation of a single psychological tendency, but was a complex reaction that varied with the type of communication, the characteristics of the individual, and the situation (p. 114). Research has only begun to delve into the myriad factors that impact third-person perceptions. In short, this instrument should be modified for application to a wider range of content and respondents.

Even with these shortcomings, the instrument discussed here vastly improves upon the use of single-item measures, multiple items measures, and highly contextualized measures that cannot be adapted to other contexts. Future studies can add to understanding of the value of this scale by using it with broader samples and modifying it to be used in exploring third-person effects of other media content.

Location*

McLeod, D. M., Eveland, W. P., Jr., & Nathanson, A. I. (1997). Support for censorship of misogynic rap lyrics: An analysis of the third-person effect. *Communication Research, 24*, 153–174.

References

Davison, W. P. (1983). The third-person effect in communication. *Public Opinion Quarterly, 47*, 1–15.

Davison, W. P. (1996). The third-person effect revisited. *International Journal of Public Opinion Research, 8*, 113–119.

Eveland, W. P., & McLeod, D. M. (1999). The effect of social desirability on perceived media impact: Implications for third-person perceptions. *International Journal of Public Opinion Research, 11,* 315–333.

Hoffner, C., & Buchanan, M. (2002). Parents' responses to television violence: The third-person perception, parental media, and support for censorship. *Media Psychology, 4,* 231–252.

Huh, J., Delorme, D. E., & Reid, L. (2004). The third-person effect and its influence on behavioral outcomes in a product advertising context: The case of direct-to-consumer prescription drug advertising. *Communication Research, 31,* 568–599.

McLeod, D. M., Detenber, D. H., & Eveland, W. P., Jr. (2001). Behind the third-person effect: Differentiating perceptual processes for self and other. *Journal of Communication, 51,* 678–695.

Paul, B., Salwen, M. B. & Dupagne, M. (2000). The third-person effect: A meta-analysis of the perceptual hypothesis. *Mass Communication & Society, 3,* 231–252.

Perloff, R. M. (2002). The third-person effect. In J. Bryant & D. Zillmann (Eds.), *Media effects: Advances in theory and research* (2nd ed., pp. 489–506). Mahwah, NJ: Erlbaum.

Price, V. & Tewksbury, D. (1996). Measuring the third-person effect of news: The impact of question order, contrast, and knowledge. *International Journal of Public Opinion Research, 8,* 119–141.

Scale

Perceived Effects of Rap*

Instructions: In answering the following questions, think about other songs that have lyrics similar to those you just read.

a   Overall, how much do you think *you* would learn from listening to songs with these types of lyrics?

| 0 | 1 | 2 | 3 | 4 | 5 | 6 | 7 | 8 | 9 | 10 |

Not at all   A great deal

b   Overall, how much would you say *your* attitudes would be influenced

| 0 | 1 | 2 | 3 | 4 | 5 | 6 | 7 | 8 | 9 | 10 |

Not at all   A great deal

Note: These same questions were asked with "other University of Delaware students," "people your age in New York," "people your age in Los Angeles, and "the average person" as the referent groups.

Topic Avoidance

Profile by Elizabeth E. Graham

Recognizing the important, but unheralded close cousin of self-disclosure, Laura Guerrero and Walid Afifi (1995a) initiated the study of topic avoidance. Topic avoidance is distinct from concealing secrets in that all parties are aware of the information that is being suppressed or avoided whereas secrets are the privileged domain of a few. For example, we might choose not-to talk about the fact that Uncle Horace spent time in prison, but it is not a secret that is kept hidden. Secrets, a specific form of topic avoidance, are subsumed within the broader study of topic avoidance (W. Afifi & Guerrero, 2000). Four relational theories, including uncertainty reduction theory, social penetration, communication boundary management, and dialectic theory inform the study of topic avoidance and each suggests that information is regulated through self-disclosure in concert with shares of restraint. Guerrero and Afifi concluded that what is concealed and revealed in conversation has a profound effect on both the depth and limits to intimacy in personal, and more specifically, family relationships. Indeed, countless studies bear out the need and the function for both disclosure and restraint as keys to healthy satisfying relationships (Caughlin & Petronio, 2004).

With this in mind, Guerrero and Afifi (1995a) developed measures to assess the topics that are avoided as well as the motives responsible for the avoidance. Based on prior research (i.e., Baxter & Wilmot, 1985; Burke, Weir, & Harrison, 1976) they identified eight topics avoided in conversation and they include: (1) relationship norms (relationships rules and expectations), (2) dating experiences (past and current romantic experiences), (3) state of the relationship (feelings about the relationship), (4) negative life-experiences (damaging and emotionally traumatic past experiences), (5) failures (unsuccessful at school or work), (6) sexual experiences (sexual desires), (7) friendships (feelings for and about past and current friends), and (8) negative relational behavior (behaviors that produce relationship strain). These eight topics were subsequently collapsed into five dimensions comprised of eight-items. Extant research has augmented the measure in various ways (see T. Afifi & Schrodt, 2003a,

2003b; Caughlin & T. Afifi, 2004; Caughlin & Golish, 2002 for more details).

The second measure developed by Guerrero and Afifi (1995a) characterizes the motives to engage in topic avoidance, and include: (1) self-protection (desire to avoid vulnerability), (2) relationship protection (avoid doing harm to the relationship), (3) partner unresponsiveness (fear that discussant would be uninvolved), and (4) social inappropriateness (discussion of the topic would be unsuitable). These four motives were cast into a 12-item measure. Subsequent research modified the measure by including additional motives to account for topic avoidance and these include lack of closeness, maintaining privacy, and preventing conflict (see T. Afifi & Schrodt, 2003a, 2003b; Caughlin & T. Afifi, 2004; Caughlin & Golish, 2002; Golish & Caughlin, 2002).

Reliability

Guerrero and Afifi (1995b) reported Cronbach's alpha for two of the five topics avoided in conversation and these include relationship issues/norms $\alpha = .83$ and negative life-experiences $\alpha = .78$. Subsequent research (W. Afifi & Guerrero, 1998; Golish & Caughlin, 2002) produced similar reliability estimates for the same two subscales (i.e., relationship issues and negative life experiences). The remaining topic avoidance items were measured by a single-item and therefore not amenable to reliability analysis. However, Cronbach's interitem alpha measuring an overall reliability estimate reflecting the five topics avoided (i.e., relationship issues, dating experiences, sexual experiences, negative life experiences, and friendships) has been calculated at .93 (Guerrero & Afifi, 1995b).

Guerrero and Afifi (1995a) found that when mothers were the target of conversation, reasons for topic avoidance produced the following reliabilities (Cronbach's alpha): self-protection $\alpha = .73$; relationship protection $\alpha = .80$; and partner unresponsiveness $\alpha = .77$. Reliabilities cannot be computed for the social inappropriateness subscale because it is comprised of a single item. When fathers were the target of conversation, the following Cronbach alphas were reported: self-protection $\alpha = .76$; relationship protection $\alpha = .86$; and partner unresponsiveness $\alpha = .78$. Subsequent research (W. Afifi & Guerrero, 1998; Golish & Caughlin, 2002; Guerrero & Afifi, 1995b) produced equivalent or slightly higher reliability estimates.

Validity

Although Guerrero and Afifi (1995a, 1995b) did not proffer any explicit validity claims in regard to these two typologies, a degree of confirmation of the measures can be culled from the wealth of research employing all or part of the scales. Indeed the construct validity of topic avoidance and

motives for topic avoidance is evidenced in the extensive amount of theoretically generated and supported hypotheses. To date, topic avoidance
has been studied in conjunction with gender, age, family configuration,
and parenting style in the context of families and friendships.

Contrary to a substantial amount of research and conventional wisdom,
results indicate no significant difference for sons and daughters in regard
to avoiding communicating with parents (Guerrero & Afifi, 1995a). However, Caughlin and Golish (2002) report that boyfriends more than girl-
friends engage in topic avoidance. In addition, Guerrero and Afifi (1995b)
revealed that boys and young men avoided discussing relationship issues,
negative life experiences, and dating experiences with family members
more than girls and young women. Consistent with conventional wisdom,
Guerrero and Afifi (1995b) concluded that there is the least amount of
topic avoidance between mothers and daughters, particularly concerning
relationship and friendship issues.

As hypothesized, both sons and daughters revealed that they engaged in
more topic avoidance (i.e., relationships norms, the state of the parent-
child relationship, negative relational behavior, friendships, dating activities, romantic experiences, and dangerous activities they participated in)
with their fathers than with their mothers. Not surprisingly, daughters
indicated that they avoided talking about dating experiences with their
fathers more so than with their mothers. Although the topic of sexual
experiences were avoided by both sons and daughters (also true in stepfamilies, see Golish & Caughlin, 2002) research revealed that children
avoided communicating about sexual experiences more with their opposite-sex parent than with their same-sex parent. Subsequent research
(Guerrero & Afifi, 1995b) also found this to be true and further suggested
that sexual experiences were also more likely to be shared with same-sex
rather than opposite-sex siblings. Guerrero and Afifi concluded that it is
not so much the gender of the child but rather it is the gender of the target
of the communication (i.e., parent, sibling) that best predicts which topics
will be avoided.

The study of gender and topic avoidance has been extended into the
realm of friendship studies as well. W. Afifi and Guerrero (1998) found
that both men and women avoided talking about negative life experiences
and relationship issues with male friends more than female friends. Furthermore, opposite sex-friends tended to avoid discussion of dating and
sexual experiences more than same-sex friends did. Although W. Afifi and
Burgoon (1998) reported little difference between cross-sex and romantic
relationship pairs in regard to overall topic avoidance, they too found that
cross-sex friends avoided talking about relationship issues more so than
romantic partners.

Guerrero and Afifi (1995a) revealed that age is a salient variable in the
parent-child relationship supporting the hypothesis that teenagers engage

in more topic avoidance (except for the topics of failures and state of the relationship) with their parents than either preteens or young adults. These results, when viewed through a dialectical lens, are consistent with teenagers' search for autonomy and are evidenced in avoidance behaviors. And last, preteen females avoided the topic of friendships (i.e., feelings for and about past and current friends), more than preteen males; however young adult males avoided the same topic more than young adult females. Interestingly, parents report less topic avoidance than their children (Caughlin & Golish, 2002). Further research conducted by Guerrero and Afifi (1995b) concluded that young people avoided communicating more with parents than siblings about such topics as negative life experiences and dating experiences. These findings, according to the authors, lend credence to the "value of applying a developmental perspective to family communication . . ." (p. 243).

Extending the study of information regulation into the domain of various family configurations, Golish and Caughlin (2002) found that adolescents and young adults were more likely to practice topic avoidance with their stepparents than with either their father or mother. Interested in the relationship between uncertainty and topic avoidance, in post-divorce, single-parent, step, and first-marriage families, T. Afifi and Schrodt (2003b) concluded that children from stepfamilies and post-divorce single-parent families reported similar levels of uncertainty and avoidance whereas children from first-marriage families reported less uncertainty and avoidance compared to children from post-divorce single-parent and stepfamilies. Further support for these findings was offered by T. Afifi and Schrodt (2003a) as they revealed that children from divorced families reported engaging in more topic avoidance with their parents than children from non-divorced households.

These avoidance patterns make sense in view of prior research (i.e., W. Afifi & Burgoon, 1998; Golish & Caughlin, 2002) which suggest that topic avoidance might serve as a useful function if it protects one from negative and perhaps hurtful information. Equally true however, are the results that contend that the more satisfied stepfamily members are with one another and the more that parents exhibit a permissive or authoritative parenting style (as compared to an authoritarian style), the less likely they will be to engage in topic avoidance (Golish, 2000). These inconsistent findings prompted Caughlin and T. Afifi (2004) to search for moderating factors that might better explain the relationship between topic avoidance and relationship satisfaction. Operating from a privacy management perspective, Caughlin and Afifi concluded that moderating variables such as relationship protection, perceived competence, and closeness account for the connection between topic avoidance and dissatisfaction. Simply put, information regulation, in the form of topic avoidance, can contribute to relational harmony and goodwill lending credence to the old adage "ignorance is bliss" (at least under certain circumstances and relationships). This adage might also explain why avoiding relationship concerns is associated with satisfaction and closeness across relationship types (i.e., significant others, mother-young adult, father-young adult relationships) (Dailey & Palomares, 2004). Additional support for the value of ambiguity and ignorance might explain why siblings engage in topic avoidance, particularly in regard to romantic/sexual experiences (Bevan, Stetzenbach, Batson, & Bullo, 2006).

Findings concerning the motivations to engage in topic avoidance are equally compelling. For example, a series of studies (Golish & Caughlin, 2002; Guerrero & Afifi, 1995a; Guerrero & Afifi, 1995b) revealed that the desire to protect oneself was a primary motive for topic avoidance for all family relationships (including stepfamilies) other than the sister to sister relationship in which case, fear of unresponsiveness and inappropriateness accounted for topic avoidance. Consistent with these findings, W. Afifi and Guerrero (1998) also found self-protection to be a primary predictor of topic avoidance for male/female same-sex and cross-sex friendships.

An additional motive for the children to avoid disclosure with parents rests with their fear that their father will be unresponsiveness (Guerrero & W. Afifi, 1995a). Also, social inappropriateness norms were noted as the reason that children chose to communicate more with same-sex rather than with opposite-sex parents. Self-protection (desire to avoid vulnerability) and relationship protection (avoid doing harm to the relationship) were unrelated to gender and target gender. However, subsequent research (W. Afifi & Guerrero, 1998) revealed that males were more likely than females to engage in topic avoidance (with male targets rather than female targets) for relationship protection purposes. In addition, Guerrero and W. Afifi (1995a) concluded that children were motivated to engage in relationship protection as they avoided disclosing to parents.

Comments

The strength of these two measures (topic avoidance and reasons for topic avoidance) rests on their theoretical conceptualization which features the paradoxical nature and utility of concealing and revealing information. The study of topic avoidance, and the practice of information regulation, is rich with theoretical applications for the study of strategic communication. The construct validity of the measures is evidenced by the wealth of hypotheses generated and supported. These measures offer a particularly useful mechanism in which to address the multiplicity of ways that communication operates in relationships.

The content validity of both avoidance measures is perhaps its most obvious shortcoming. In the initial operationalization of the measures, items were drawn solely from prior research which contributed to a narrow and perhaps incomplete collection of items that do not completely capture the constellation of topics avoided as well as motives that account for avoidance in conversation. To remedy this problem, subsequent research efforts have modified the measures by the addition of items over the years. For more information on specific items contact Tamara Afifi.

In the early stages of these instruments' existence, the extensive use of an undergraduate student population as the primary participant pool was problematic. However, recent research has attended to this concern (see Afifi & Schrodt, 2003a, 2003b; Caughlin & T. Afifi, 2004; Caughlin & Golish, 2002).

Location

Guerrero, L. K., & Afifi, W. A. (1995a). What parents don't know: Topic avoidance in parent-child relationships. In T. J. Socha & G. H. Stamp (Eds.), *Parents, children, and communication: Frontiers of theory and research* (pp.219–245). Mahwah, NJ: Erlbaum.

References

Afifi, T. D., & Schrodt, P. (2003a). "Feeling caught" as a mediator of adolescents' and young adults' avoidance and satisfaction with their parents in divorced and non-divorced households. *Communication Monographs, 70,* 142–176.

Afifi, T. D., & Schrodt, P. (2003b). Uncertainty and the avoidance of the state of one's family in stepfamilies, postdivorce single-parent families, and first marriage families. *Human Communication Research, 29,* 516–532.

Afifi, W. A., & Burgoon, J. K. (1998). "We never talk about that": A comparison of cross-sex friendships and dating relationships on uncertainty and topic avoidance. *Personal Relationships, 5,* 255–272.

Afifi, W. A., & Guerrero, L. K. (1998). Some things are better left unsaid II: Topic avoidance in friendships. *Communication Quarterly, 46,* 231–249.

Afifi, W. A., & Guerrero, L. K. (2000). Motivations underlying topic avoidance in close relationships. In S. Petronio (Ed.), *Balancing the secrets of private disclosures* (pp. 165–179). Mahwah, NJ: Erlbaum.

Baxter, L. A., & Wilmot, W. W. (1985). Taboo topics in close relationships. *Journal of Personal and Social Relationships, 2,* 253–269.

Bevan, J. L., Stetzenbach, K. A., Batson, E., & Bullo, K. (2006). Factors associated with general partner and relational uncertainty within early adulthood sibling relationships. *Communication Quarterly, 54,* 367–381.

Burke, R. J., Weir, T., & Harrison, D. (1976). Disclosure of problems and tensions experienced by marital partners. *Psychological Reports, 38,* 531–542.

Caughlin, J. P., & Afifi, T. D. (2004). When is topic avoidance unsatisfying? Examining moderators of the association between avoidance and dissatisfaction. *Human Communication Research, 30,* 479–513.

Caughlin, J. P., & Golish, T. D. (2002). An analysis of the association between topic avoidance and dissatisfaction: Comparing perceptual and interpersonal explanations. *Communication Monographs, 69,* 275–295.

Caughlin, J. P., & Petronio, S. (2004). Privacy in families. In A. L. Vangelisti (Ed.), *Handbook of Family Communication* (pp. 379–412.). Mahwah, NJ: Erlbaum.

Dailey, R. M., & Palomares, N. A. (2004). Strategic topic avoidance: An investigation of topic avoidance frequency, strategies used, and relational correlates. *Communication Monographs, 71,* 471–496.

Golish, T. D. (2000). Is openness always better? Exploring the role of topic avoidance, satisfaction, and parenting styles of stepparents. *Communication Quarterly, 48,* 137–158.

Golish, T. D., & Caughlin, J. P. (2002). "I'd rather not talk about it": Adolescents' and young adults' use of topic avoidance in stepfamilies. *Journal of Applied Communication Research, 30,* 78–106.

Guerrero, L. K. Afifi, W. A. (1995b). Some things are better left unsaid: Topic avoidance in family relationships. *Communication Quarterly, 43,* 276–296.

Scale

Topic Avoidance*
Instructions: Please rate the degree to which you avoid discussing these topics with the referenced partner using a 7-point interval scale (1 = never avoid, 4 = occasionally avoid, 7 = always avoid).

Relationship Issues/Norms

1   Relationship norms, rules, roles, expectations, and acceptable behavior.
2   State of the relationship, discussion of feelings toward one another and how the relationship is going.
3   Negative relational behavior, defined as discussing past behavior that caused strain on the relationship.

Dating Experiences

4   Discussing past/present romantic relationships and dates.

Negative Life Experiences

5   Discussing past negative personal experiences, including traumatic events and face-threatening behaviors.
6   Discussing failures, such as doing poorly in a class or being fired from a job.

Sexual Experiences

7   Discussing past/present sexual behavior and preferences.
Friendships

8   Discussing current friendships with others, as well as feelings about friends.

Reasons for Topic Avoidance
Instructions: Please rate whether you agree or disagree with the reasons for topic avoidance using a 7-point interval scale (1 = strong disagreement and 7 = strong agreement

Self-Protection

1   It would leave me too vulnerable.
2   I would be embarrassed to disclose.
3   This person may judge me.
4   I prefer not to replay negative experiences.

Relationship Protection

5   Disclosure could lead to conflict.
6   It might ruin our relationship.
7   It might make this person angry.

Partner Unresponsiveness

8   This person will probably be unresponsive.
9   This person lacks knowledge relevant to my problem.
10   This person would view the issue as trivial.
11   It would be futile to talk about it with this person.

Social Inappropriateness

12   It would be socially inappropriate to discuss this topic.

Note: Items should be presented randomly and subscale labels should be eliminated when preparing the scale for presentation.

Willingness to Censor Survey

Profile by Elizabeth M. Perse

Serving as a testament to the importance of free expression in American society and throughout the democratic world, attitudes toward censorship have been studied in a variety of fields, including communication, social psychology, and political science. Lambe (2002) wrote that "the varied efforts to understand censorship attitudes reflect a normative desire to predict and modify opinions believed to be detrimental to freedom of expression" (p. 188). The goal of censorship research, then, is to identify predictor variables for pro-censorship attitudes. Though its interdisciplinary relevance has led to countless studies reflecting the specific concerns of the fields at hand, Lambe (2002) argued that censorship research would benefit from a unified conceptual framework.

Lambe (2002) discussed different types of censorship studies that utilize different conceptual definitions of censorship. One type views censorship as opinions about a range of free expression situations. Studies of this type generally use large nationwide samples and include questions about a wide range of censorship issues including abstract support for free speech and press and attitudes about specific First Amendment situations. The questions in these studies often change over time in order to reflect topics of current interest, and therefore, they only provide "snapshots" or status reports of censorship attitudes at a specific point in time. This approach is useful to track changes in general public attitudes toward First Amendment freedoms over time, but do little to help uncover the predictor of the attitudes.

A second type of censorship research regards censorship attitudes as part of the larger construct of political tolerance, or the degree to which individuals are willing to extend the protection of civil liberties to various. These studies, however, rarely consider the type of speech or medium of expression and "does not provide the specificity necessary for predicting censorship attitudes across a variety of expressive situations" (Lambe, 2002, p. 191).

Another group of censorship studies focuses on censorship attitudes as reactions to specific controversies. This approach has been frequently used in communication research (e.g., third-person effects research) and looks at a wide array of mediated content including pornography, violence, misogynic content, hate speech, political communication, and advertising for controversial products. Often the focus of this literature is not on developing a valid and reliable censorship measure, but rather on explaining when situation-specific censorship is endorsed. Censorship is measured with varied quality, including single-item indicators. The specificity of the measures and the results of these tend to be limited and shed little light on a unified conceptual framework.

Lambe's (2002) Willingness to Censor (WTC) Survey profiled here fits within a fourth category of censorship studies that consider censorship attitudes as an individual attribute. These studies use a social-psychological perspective and are comprised of a set of declarative statements to which respondents indicate their level of agreement. Lambe's scale shows promise, despite its relative youth, by improving upon many of the shortcomings of earlier studies. The scale includes items that are all based on real cases from First Amendment law and deal with publication and distribution of expressive materials. In other words, Lambe operationalized censorship by its legal definition—occurring only when the government restrains expression through legislation. By examining Supreme Court decisions and media law textbooks, Lambe identified seven categories of expression that have been afforded different levels of First Amendment protection by the United States Supreme Court: pornography, speech that raises privacy issues, political speech, abortion speech, defamatory speech, and commercial speech. Because the Supreme Court has also used a medium-specific approach in some of its litigation, seven types of media were also incorporated into the WTC survey items in addition to the categorical system: "pure" speech, demonstrations (defined by the inclusion of a behavior such as picketing, in addition to speech), newspaper, magazine, television, cable, and the Internet. One item was created representing each possible combination of medium and category. Combined, these 49 items generate a "willingness to censor score" along with subscores for each category and medium.

Lambe sought to offer subjects a fuller spectrum of options for government reactions to potential censorship situations. Respondents choose from five possible government reactions to expressive behavior: (a) Prior restraint—the "classic form of censorship" that stops the undesirable communication before it occurs (b) Subsequent punishment—imposing penalties such as fines after the communication has happened (c) Time, place, and other manner restrictions—regulating content-neutral aspects of expression (d) Allowing expression, and (e) Protecting expression—actively ensuring that expression can take place.

Reliability

The 49-item global measure of willingness to censor seems to be internally consistent, with a Cronbach alpha of .91 (Lambe, 2002). This establishes the empirical unidimensionality of attitudes about free expression. Alpha scores for the seven-item subscales were less impressive in some cases: hate speech = .81, pornography = .80, political speech = .68, abortion speech = .67, commercial speech = .62, defamation = .58, and privacy = .56 (Lambe, 2002, 2004). As Lambe points out, this could merely be a result of the Cronbach alpha's sensitivity to the number of scale items. The alpha scores for the medium subscales are lower, ranging from .44 to .64. Lambe suggests that this may indicate that people view free expression issues more consistently in terms of content categories rather than by medium of expression. However, because low reliability scores in both category and medium could also be due to problems with the measure, Lambe (2002) used only subscales with a reliability of .65 or greater for analysis. Additionally, item analyses found that removal of the privacy-Internet item improved the overall alpha and the alphas for its category and medium subscale simultaneously. For this reason, the item was deleted from further analyses.

Because Lambe (2002) defines the WTC survey as a genotypic measure, it should provide an indication of an individual's tendency toward censorship, rather than predicting with certainty an individual's response to any particular censorship issue. Thus, it seems that this measure should be stable over time, and test-retest reliability should be assessed make sure this is the case.

Validity

Lambe improves upon the content validity of other censorship scales by operationalizing the WTC through theory and case law of First Amendment jurisprudence. This improvement speaks to Lambe's concerns about other social-psychological censorship studies and their lack of an underlying rationale for which scenarios were excluded from the scales, as well as problems with the mixing of abstract and concrete items about free expression. This allows Lambe to combine facets of censorship attitudes into a global measure of censorship, and examine variable relationships with the global construct and subfacets of public willingness to censor (Lambe, 2002, p. 198).

The construct validity of this measure is demonstrated by the relationships between censorship support and certain predictor variables. For example, one would expect that a politically conservative individual would be more likely to support censorship than someone who is more liberal. This hypothesis was supported by the significant Pearson correlations with liberal-conservative self-ranking for the WTC survey as a whole, and all of the categories except for abortion speech. Lambe (2002) found that, consistent with her hypothesis, educational level was negatively related to willingness to censor. Later research supported the construct validity of several of the subscales. Women are more likely to endorse censorship of pornography (Lambe, 2004). Authoritarianism and need for cognition were both positively linked to willingness to censor both pornography and hate speech (Lambe, 2004). And, commitment to democratic principles was strongly and negatively correlated with willingness to censor pornography and hate speech.

The sample for Lambe's initial study was selected in order to provide variance on the independent measures so several hypothesized relationships could be tested with the global measure and subscales. The sample consisted of 10 groups of individuals, including University of Minnesota students, their relatives, members of a church reform group, elementary school teachers, members of an Army reserve unit, and members of several community groups. All of these individuals were from Minnesota, Nebraska, Nevada, Wisconsin, and Texas. Despite the fact that this sample is an improvement over the convenience samples of college students commonly used in academic research, the generalizability and external validity remains limited due to the lack of randomization.

Comments

Lambe discussed the low reliabilities of this measure's subscales and pointed out the dangers of revising the scale in order to improve the reliability of these facets of censorship attitudes: "It is important to balance the desire for higher reliability scores with the need to maintain content validity—if key aspects of complicated areas of the law such as privacy and defamation are not included, the resulting measures may be reliable but not valid" (p. 219). In other words, the low reliability scores for certain subscales may not be an issue of the measure's design as much as it is a question about the consistency of people's attitudes toward free expression. Perhaps, as Lambe points out, people truly do not hold consistent attitudes about certain types of free expression.

Several questions arise regarding Lambe's inclusion of only legal government censorship behaviors in her instrument. Lambe justifies this operationalization of censorship, writing that "although other efforts or desires to restrict expression may be of interest, most of the consequences of public opinion about free expression of concern flow through the legal system" (Lambe, 2002, p. 200). Is this a fair statement to make? Hoffner and Buchanan (2002) looked at both support for censorship and parental mediation in relationship to third-person perceptions and found that both were related to perceived negative effects of television violence. Future research using this instrument should include variables looking at private mediation behaviors and their relationships with support for larger-scale government censorship actions.

The five possible government actions from which respondents can choose for each item of the scale may also be cause for concern. Do people really rate these government actions in the hypothesized order of severity? For example, it seems that some people may view a subsequent punishment for expression as a less serious restrictive behavior than "time, place, and other manner restrictions." Lambe suggests that qualitative interviews could help us understand the schemas people use to organize their feelings about censorship issues and whether these feelings are actually compatible with the law.

Lambe's scale is a bit long. But, its comprehensive nature means that researchers should consider using subscales to explore censorship about specific issues and media (see Lambe, 2004). Research should also explore the scale's utility in third person effects research (e.g., McLeod, Eveland, & Nathanson, 1997). Future research should continue to refine the operationalization of willingness to censor. Lambe's WTC survey, however, is a promising and solid starting point in our quest for unified conceptual framework in censorship research.

Location*

Lambe, J. L. (2002). Dimensions of censorship: Reconceptualizing public willingness to censor. *Communication Law & Policy, 7*, 187–235.

References

Hoffner, C., & Buchanan, M. (2002). Parents' responses to television violence: The third-person perception, parental mediation, and support for censorship. *Media Psychology, 4*, 231–252.

Lambe, J. L. (2004). Who wants to censor pornography and hate speech? *Mass Communication & Society, 7*, 279–299.

McLeod, D. M., Eveland, W. P., Jr., & Nathanson, A. I. (1997). Support for censorship of violent and misogynic rap lyrics: An analysis of the third-person effect. *Communication Research, 24*, 153–174.

Scale

Willingness to Censor Survey*
Instructions: In this section, you will be presented with situations in which freedom of speech comes into conflict with other important social and individual goals. You are asked to indicate what you think would be the best response in each situation.

There are no right or wrong answers. You are being asked for your opinion.

There are five possible responses listed for each situation. *Please mark the **one** answer which you feel to be **most** appropriate.*

1 A company promoting a rock musical, which contains scenes where the actors are naked, wants to lease a municipal auditorium to present their production.
   I think city officials should:
   — refuse to allow them to lease the auditorium for this production, because it violates a city ordinance against public nudity
   — grant the lease for the production, but sue the producers if they leave the scenes with nudity in the show
   — grant the lease for the production, but require that audience members be 18 or older, or accompanied by an adult
   — grant the lease with no conditions
   — grant the lease, and provide police officers to insure the security of the performers

2 The Aryan Nation, a white-supremacist group, is publishing and distributing a newspaper in your state.
   I think state officials should:
   — close down the newspaper
   — levy a tax on special interest newspapers, like this one
   — not allow the publisher to send the newspaper through the mail
   — allow the newspaper to be distributed
   — protect the publisher's right to print and distribute the newspaper

3 A television news photographer takes video of a famous person entering a house of prostitution. The celebrity seeks a court order to stop the TV station from using the footage.
   I think the judge should:
   — order the TV station not to air the video
   — fine the TV station to compensate the celebrity
   — order the TV station to alter the video so the celebrity can't be identified
   — take no action against the TV station
   — issue a ruling protecting the right of the TV station to use the video

4 An anti-government militia group maintains a page on the World Wide Web that includes step-by-step instructions for making bombs.
   I think the government should:
   — confiscate their computer equipment so they can't have a presence on the WWW
   — bring criminal charges against the militia's members
   — require them to take the bomb information off their page
   — do nothing
   — protect their right to publish on the WWW

5 A group of protesters is picketing outside an abortion clinic, sometimes obstructing the paths of patients who are entering the clinic.
   I think city officials should:
   — forbid the protesters from picketing outside the clinic
   — arrest the protesters for disturbing the peace
   — require the protesters to stay at least 15 feet away from the clinic
   — take no action against the protesters
   — protect the right of the protesters to express their beliefs
6 During a campaign, the current mayor was speaking at a civic group's
   meeting. Discussing his opponent, he commented that she had the
   same name as a missing Nazi war criminal and asked "Is this the same
   Ilse Koch? Who knows?" Koch sued the mayor for trying to destroy
   her reputation.
   I think the judge hearing the case should:
   — order the mayor not to talk about his opponent in public
   — fine the mayor to compensate Koch
   — require the mayor to make a public apology
   — not take any action against the mayor
   — issue a ruling upholding the mayor's right to speak
7 A local pharmacist places an ad, which includes price information for
   prescription medication, in a magazine targeted at the elderly.
   I think the government should:
   — forbid the pharmacist from advertising prices for   prescription
     medication
   — fine the pharmacist for advertising price information
   — require the pharmacist to list the price information in small print
   — take no action against the pharmacist
   — protect the right of the pharmacist to advertise price information
8 As you are surfing the World Wide Web, you accidentally come across
   a site that contains graphic sexual images.
   I think the U.S. government should:
   — confiscate the computer equipment of the site's producers
   — fine the producers of the site
   — require the site's producers to install a blocking mechanism so
     that it can't be accessed accidentally
   — let the site's producers decide what to do
   — protect the right of the producers to choose what to include in
     their site
9 A newspaper publishes a story that reveals that a certain community
   member is gay. He had not wanted to reveal this fact publicly, and he
   sues the newspaper for invading his privacy.
   I think the judge hearing the case should:
   — order the newspaper not to publish such information again
   — fine the newspaper to compensate the man

— require the newspaper to issue a public apology
— take no action against the newspaper
— issue a ruling supporting the right of the newspaper to publish true information

10 A group protesting the U.S. government's foreign policy in Iran burns the flag on a street corner
I think the government should:
— make it illegal to burn the flag
— arrest the protesters for disturbing the peace
— require the protesters to hold their demonstration in a less populated area
— do nothing
— protect the protesters right to demonstrate

11 The first of a three part TV mini-series just aired on your local NBC affiliate. It included two characters who frequently makes racist remarks against African-Americans and Mexicans.
I think the Federal Communications Commission, which grants the station's license, should:
— forbid the station from airing the last two parts of the mini-series
— revoke the station's license to broadcast if it airs the last to parts of the mini-series
— require that the last two parts of the mini-series be aired after 9:00 p.m.
— let the local station decide whether or not to air the last two parts of the series
— make sure that the last two parts of the series air as scheduled

12 A newspaper editor publishes an editorial on election day endorsing a particular candidate.
I think state officials should:
— make it illegal to solicit votes on election day
— fine the editor for his partisanship
— require the editor to issue a special edition with a statement supporting the other candidate
— do nothing
— protect the editor's right to express his views on the election

13 An arts and entertainment program on your cable system included a negative review of a local restaurant. The critic said that the restaurant owners "are rude and vulgar people" and are "pigs." The owners sued the critic for ruining their reputations.
I think the judge hearing the case should:
— forbid the critic from doing any more negative reviews
— fine the critic to compensate the restaurant owners
— require the critic to issue a public apology
— not take any action against the critic

— issue a ruling defending the critic's right to express his opinion

14 The chamber of commerce issues a yearly magazine that profiles the various civic organizations in your community. A chamber staff member, who is the head of a local pro-life group, plans to include a feature on his group in the next issue.

I think the city officials who oversee the chamber of commerce should:
— refuse to allow an article on the group to be included in the magazine
— fire the staff member if he insists on publishing the article about his group
— require the staff member to include an article about pro-choice groups, also
— let the staff member decide what to do
— protect the right of the staff member to include the article in the magazine

15 A site on the World Wide Web includes nude photographs of a woman who is a fashion model. She has sued the site's producers for invasion of privacy.

I think the judge hearing the case should:
— issue an injunction prohibiting further publication of the photographs
— fine the site's producers to compensate the woman
— require the site's producers to include a caption explaining that the photos are included without the model's consent
— take no action against the site's producers
— issue a ruling protecting the right of the site's producers to include the photographs

16 A new certified public accountant (CPA) is going door-to-door soliciting business.

I think the government should:
— not allow CPA's to solicit clients in this way
— fine the CPA for violating people's privacy
— only allow the CPA to solicit to people who have expressed an interest in receiving such information
— take no action against the CPA
— protect the right of the CPA to solicit clients door-to-door

17 A cable channel is promoting an upcoming series about the assassination of President John F. Kennedy. The promotion names several authors that it claims are "guilty of misleading the American public" about the assassination. One of the authors sues the cable channel for portraying him in a false light.

I think the judge who is hearing the case should:
— order the cable channel not to air the series
— fine the cable channel to compensate the author

— require the cable channel to include an interview with this author in their series, so he can state his point of view
— take no action against the cable channel
— issue a ruling protecting the right of the cable channel to air the series

18 An alternative newspaper in your community runs a singles column each week which sometimes includes graphic descriptions of sexual encounters.
I think city officials should:
— force the paper to stop running that column
— fine the paper each time the column includes graphic descriptions of sex
— require the paper to run a warning on the front page of any issue that contains graphic sexual descriptions
— let the paper decide what to do
— protect the paper's right to publish the column

19 A magazine article about on-duty drunkenness by certain police officers mistakenly included a picture of an officer who was not involved. The officer sued the magazine for damaging his reputation:
I think the judge hearing the case should:
— not allow the magazine to publish any more articles about police behavior
— fine the magazine to compensate the officer
— require the magazine to make a public apology
— not take any action against the magazine
— issue a ruling protecting the magazine's right to publish, even when they've made a mistake

20 The names and home phone numbers of an abortion clinic's medical staff and board of directors are provided by an anti-abortion activist on the Internet.
I think the government should:
— confiscate the activist's computer equipment so she can't publish such information on the Internet
— press charges against the activist for endangering the lives of the clinic's staff and directors
— order the activist to remove the phone numbers from her Internet site
— take no action against the activist
— protect the right of the activist to provide the information on the Internet

21 In a meeting at a public hall, a speaker is preaching hatred against gays and lesbians.
I think the police officers on the scene should:
— arrest the speaker to stop him from finishing the presentation

— fine the speaker for disturbing the peace
— require the speaker to apologize for the offensive language
— do nothing
— protect the speaker's right to say whatever he thinks

22 A television station which broadcasts into two states accepts advertising for a lottery in one of the states. The other state prohibits lotteries. I think the Federal Communications Commission, which grants the station's license, should:
— forbid the TV station from broadcasting any lottery advertising
— fine the TV station for accepting the lottery advertising
— require the TV station also to run public service announcements about the dangers of gambling
— take no action against the TV station
— protect the right of the TV station to accept the lottery advertising

23 A pro-life corporation published a special edition of its quarterly newspaper the week before national elections, urging people to vote for anti-abortion candidates.
I think the Federal Election Commission should:
— make it illegal for corporations to spend money in support of particular candidates
— fine the corporation for publishing a special "election edition" of its newspaper
— require the organization to provide space in its newspaper for candidates to respond
— take no action against the organization
— protect the right of the organization to express its views concerning political candidates

24 The local news programs on a TV station in your city always favors one political party over the other.
I think the Federal Communications Commission, which grants the station's license, should:
— not allow the station to cover political stories
— fine the station to compensate the other political party
— require the station to give an equal amount of favorable coverage to the other political party
— do nothing
— issue a ruling supporting the right of the TV station to choose what to include on its news programs

25 A magazine is planning to publish an in-depth article about a 20-year old murder case, involving a son convicted for murdering his parents. The piece discusses family relationships while raising issues of child abuse and rehabilitation. The murderer's brother sues the publisher for invading his privacy.
I think the judge hearing the case should:

— order the magazine not to publish the article
— fine the magazine to compensate the brother
— order the magazine to change the names in the article so that the brother won't be identified
— take no action against the magazine
— issue an order protecting the magazine's right to publish the article

26 College students are holding a rally to protest the University's decision not to allow condoms to be distributed in residence halls. They are carrying signs and banners with sexual language and pictures.
I think University officials should:
— break up the rally
— put the students who participate in the rally on probation
— take the signs and banners from the rally
— do nothing
— supply campus police to provide security for the rally

27 A group of neo-Nazis produces a weekly call-in program on the public access channel of your cable system.
I think the city officials who granted the cable company its franchise should:
— demand that the group's program not appear on your cable system
— fine the group and the cable company each time the program appears
— require that the program only be shown after 9:00 p.m.
— allow the cable company to handle the situation
— protect the right of the group to produce the program on public access

28 An on-line service provides a forum for information about and discussion of current events. In the forum, allegations were made about the illegal actions of an investment company. The investment company sued the on-line service for damaging its reputation.
I think the judge hearing the case should:
— force the on-line service to close down its forum for discussion of current events
— fine the on-line service to compensate the investment company
— require the on-line service to make a public apology
— take no action against the on-line service
— issue a ruling protecting the right of the on-line service to provide a forum for discussion

29 A personal injury lawyer is running an ad on your cable system, soliciting business from people who had suffered injuries as a result of using a certain product.
I think the government should:

—   forbid the lawyer from soliciting clients through advertising
—   fine the lawyer for soliciting business in this manner
—   require the lawyer to mention his fees for service in his ad
—   not take any action against the lawyer
—   protect the lawyer's right to solicit clients through advertising

30 A newspaper ran editorials and cartoons stating that anti-nuclear pro-
    testers are "bums," "deluded," and "insane," and that signs they have
    been carrying are "gibberish," "un-American," and "trash." The pro-
    testers have sued the newspaper for attacking their reputations.
    I think the judge hearing the case should:
—   stop the paper from printing any more editorial commentary on
    the protesters
—   levy a fine against the newspaper to compensate the protesters
—   require the newspaper to run guest editorials from the protesters'
    point-of-view
—   not take any action against the newspaper
—   issue a ruling protecting the newspaper's right to express its edi-
    torial position

31 One of the new prime-time television series this year on the ABC affil-
    iate in your city regularly includes explicit nudity.
    I think the Federal Communications Commission, which grants the
    station's license, should:
—   require the station to stop airing any episode with explicit nudity
—   fine the station each time an episode with explicit nudity airs
—   require the station to air the series after 9:00 p.m.
—   let the station decide the appropriate action to take
—   protect the right of the station to air the series

32 A magazine for U.S. members of the socialist party regularly publishes
    articles in support of foreign governments and against the U.S. gov-
    ernment.
    I think the government should:
—   close down the magazine
—   fine the magazine's publishers
—   make the publishers include articles explaining the U.S. govern-
    ment point of view
—   take no action
—   protect the right of the magazine's publishers to express their
    opinions

33 The Ku Klux Klan has filed for a permit to hold a march through your
    town.
    I think the city permit office should:
—   refuse to give them a permit
—   hold them responsible for any physical or personal damage that
    occurs as a result of the march

    — require them to hold the march in a sparsely populated area of town

    — issue a permit for the march

    — issue a permit, and provide police escorts to make sure their right to march is protected

34 An individual who is opposed to abortion is shouting his beliefs in front of a doctor's office where abortions are performed. The office is in a residential neighborhood.

I think city officials should:

    — forbid him from protesting there in the future

    — arrest him for disturbing the peace

    — require him to protest with signs instead of by shouting

    — allow him to continue to protest

    — protect his right to protest

35 A group advocating welfare reform publishes a leaflet which includes photos and stories about women who are "shamelessly and brazenly violating the law by having children out of wedlock and receiving welfare to support them." One of the women whose photo is included sues the group for portraying her in a false light.

I think the judge hearing the case should:

    — order the group to stop distributing the leaflet

    — fine the group to compensate the woman

    — order the group to take the woman's photo out of the leaflet

    — take no action against the group

    — issue a ruling protecting the right of the group to publish their leaflet

36 A bookstore in your city sells magazines featuring pictures of nude and partially-clothed adults in various sexual positions.

I think city officials should:

    — force the bookstore to stop selling the magazines

    — file charges against the bookstore's owner for distributing pornographic material

    — require the store to place the magazines behind the counter, so customers have to ask for them

    — let the store's owner decide what to do

    — protect the right of the bookstore to sell the magazines

37 A radical Jewish organization which advocates violence against Muslims has a home-page on the World Wide Web.

I think the government should:

    — confiscate the group's computer equipment so they can't have a home-page

    — arrest the group's leaders for advocating violence

    — require the organization to place a warning about the content that appears before their page is accessed

— do nothing
— protect the organization's right to express its beliefs

38 An anti-abortion organization produces a monthly program on the public access channel on your cable system. During the program, they show pictures of local physicians who perform abortions, and label them as "murderers" and "killers."
I think the city officials who run the public access channel should:
— not allow the organization to air their program on the public access channel
— fine the organization for improper use of a public facility
— require the organization to refrain from identifying any particular physician
— take no action against the organization or its program
— protect the right of the organization to air its program

39 Several students at a public university were protesting the University's contracts with two businesses known to be anti-union. They were speaking on the library lawn in the center of campus, using bullhorns to amplify their voices.
I think University officials should:
— have campus police remove the protesters
— put the students involved in the protest on probation
— require the students to stop using bullhorns
— do nothing
— protect the students' right to speak their opinions

40 A liquor store includes price information in their newspaper ads for alcoholic beverages.
I think the government should:
— issue on a ban on price advertising for alcohol
— fine the liquor store for advertising alcohol prices
— require the liquor store to advertise prices in very small print
— take no action against the liquor store
— issue a ruling supporting the right of the liquor store to advertise price information

41 A TV news program showed a picture of a local doctor while the voice-over indicated that some health practitioners use "quack machines, fraudulent tests, and illegal drugs to treat cancer." The doctor has sued the television station for damaging his reputation.
I think the judge hearing the case should:
— not allow the TV station to run these kinds of stories in the future
— fine the TV station to compensate the doctor
— require the TV station to broadcast a story correcting their mistake
— take no action against the TV station
— issue a ruling supporting the TV station's right to air these kinds of stories

42 A black separatist organization in your city is publishing a "humor" magazine which makes fun of whites, especially Jewish people and Catholics.
I think city officials should:
— close down the magazine
— levy a tax on special interest magazines, like this one
— revoke the special mailing rates for their magazine
— allow the group to continue to publish and distribute the magazine
— protect the right of the group to publish and distribute the magazine

43 In a public speech criticizing the practice of placing mentally ill people in boarding homes, the speaker reveals that Ed Samuels, one of the boarding home operators, had been convicted of certain criminal sexual acts 30 years ago. Samuels sues the speaker for disclosing private facts.
I think the judge hearing the case should:
— forbid the speaker from commenting publicly on the boarding home issue again
— fine the speaker to compensate Samuels
— require the speaker to make a public apology
— take no action against the speaker
— issue a ruling protecting the right of the speaker to criticize the boarding home operators

44 Volunteers for a political advocacy group set up a table outside of the post office to solicit contributions and sell subscriptions to their newspaper.
I think the post office should:
— order the group to leave the premises
— fine the group's members for soliciting on government property
— make the group move so they are not blocking the path of post office customers
— not take any action against the group
— protect the group's right to solicit contributions and subscriptions

45 A locally produced, sexually explicit program has begun to air on a public access channel on your cable system.
I think the city officials who granted the cable company its franchise should:
— require the cable company to stop airing the program
— fine the cable company each time the program airs
— require that the program be aired after 9:00 p.m.
— let the cable company decide what to do
— protect the right of the local producers to show their program

46 A pro-life organization has bought time on an independent television

station in your city. They want to air a 15 minute program which includes graphic pictures of aborted fetuses.

I think the Federal Communications Commission, which grants the station's license, should:

— forbid the station to air the program with the graphic footage included
— fine the station if it airs the program as is
— allow the station to show the program with the graphic footage, as long as it is shown after 10:00 p.m.
— leave the decision of whether or not to air the program up to the station
— require the station to let the program air as scheduled

47 An on-line promotion company is sending unsolicited e-mail to people who have Internet access through a state University.

I think University officials should:

— block all messages the promotion company tries to send to University e-mail accounts
— sue the promotion company for improper use of state resources
— require the promotion company to stop sending messages to individuals who make such a request
— not take any action against the promotion company
— protect the right of the promotion company to send their messages

48 On a picket line during a strike, one of the union banners says "#1 Scab Jacobsen Sucks." Jacobsen has sued the union leader, saying that his character was called into question.

I think that the judge hearing the case should:

— forbid the union leader from having any signs directed at individual workers
— fine the union leader to compensate Jacobsen
— require the union leader to make a public apology
— not take any action against the union leader
— issue a ruling protecting the union leader's right to speak

49 A cable channel is planning to air films produced outside of the U.S. that explore global political issues like acid rain and nuclear power.

I think the U.S. government should:

— not allow the cable channel to air the programs
— fine the cable channel for airing these programs
— require the cable company to label the films as "political propaganda"
— do nothing
— protect the cable channel's right to air the films

Note. The responses for each situation move from most restrictive (greater willingness to censor) to least restrictive (protection of free expression). Context scales include the following items: Pornography (1, 8, 18, 26, 31, 36, 45), Hate speech (2, 11, 21, 27, 33, 37, 42), Speech that raises privacy issues (3, 9, 15, 17, 25, 35, 43), Political speech (4, 10, 12, 24, 32, 39, 49), Abortion speech (5, 14, 20, 23, 34, 38, 46), Defamatory speech (6, 13, 19, 28, 30, 41, 48), and Commercial speech (7, 16, 22, 29, 40, 44, 47).

Medium scales include the following items: Pure speech (1, 6, 16, 21, 34, 39, 43), Demonstrations (5, 10, 26, 33, 35, 44, 48), Newspapers (2, 9, 12, 18, 23, 30, 40), Magazines (7, 14, 19, 25, 32, 36, 42), Television (3, 11, 22, 24, 31, 41, 46), Cable (13, 17, 27, 29, 38, 45, 49), and Internet (4, 8, 15, 20, 28, 37, 47).

Part III

Imported Measures

Measures Imported from Related Disciplines

Alan M. Rubin

Communication researchers, especially those interested in the role of personality and individual differences in explaining communication processes and effects, have imported various measures, over the years, from related fields such as psychology. Investigators have applied these measures to operationalize a multitude of antecedent, intervening, and, even, consequent variables defined in questions and predictions about communication attitudes and behavior. Such variables include anxiety, aggression, locus of control, and need for cognition. Some of these measures of hostility, self-esteem, locus of control, and social desirability, for example, date back 40 years or more. Rosenberg's (1965) SELF-ESTEEM Scale and Crowne and Marlowe's (1960) SOCIAL DESIRABILITY Scale, for instance, have been the most widely used measures of those constructs in the social sciences. Some measures have been refined over time. Other measures of anxiety, loneliness, personality, and sensation seeking, for example, have been developed, revised, and adapted since that time.

Measures

In this section, we have selected more than 15 measures to highlight and discuss in 10 profiles. With established records of application, validity, and reliability, communication researchers have often used these measures. For example, using the Buss and Durkee (1957) HOSTILITY Inventory or the Buss and Perry (1992) AGGRESSION Questionnaire, researchers have examined hostility and aggression as antecedents, mediators, and consequents of media use. Using the LOCUS OF CONTROL Scale (Rotter, 1966) or the Health LOCUS OF CONTROL Scale (Wallston, Wallston, Kaplan, & Maides, 1976), researchers have considered how internal control and external control influence cultivation effects from television viewing or patients' compliance in health-care situations. Using Russell, Peplau, and Cutrona's (1980) UCLA LONELINESS Scale, investigators have examined how the absence of interpersonal connection affects relationship satisfaction and communication in a variety of contexts including computer-mediated communication. Using Cacioppo, Petty, and Kao's (1984) NEED FOR COGNITION Scale, researchers have examined how variations in the felt need for information influence communication motivation, message processing, and attitude change. Using Zuckerman and Lubin's (1985) SENSATION-SEEKING Scale, investigators have found positive links between disinhibition and media exposure to fright and violence.

We could have selected many other measures in addition to the ones included. For example, Moe and Zeiss's (1982) Self-efficacy Questionnaire for Social Skills (SEQSS) is grounded in Bandura's (1977) self-efficacy construct. Bandura expected self-efficacy to be fundamental to initiating and sustaining behavior needed for competent or successful performance, which can be achieved through participatory modeling. Moe and Zeiss developed the SEQSS, which had internal consistency (via coefficient alpha), stability (via test-retest reliability), and predictive validity. Using the SEQSS, R. B. Rubin, Martin, Bruning, and Powers (1993) found self-efficacy mediated the effect of past experience and situation difficulty on interpersonal communication outcomes. In addition, Snyder's (1974) Self-monitoring Scale assesses how sensitive people to how they express themselves in social situations. The 25-item measure contains extraversion, other-directedness, and acting dimensions, and includes such items as "when I am uncertain how to act in a social situation, I look for the behavior of others for cues" and "in different situations and with different people, I often act like very different people." Self-monitors can monitor and adjust their actions to create an appropriate appearance in interactions with others.

Besides the personality measures included in the PERSONALITY TRAITS profile, Hendricks, Hofstee, and de Raad (1999) developed a 100-item Five-factor Personality Inventory (FFPI), and asked participants how descriptive each statement was of their personality. The FFPI exhibited internal consistency within its five dimensions: agreeableness, conscientiousness, extraversion, autonomy, and emotional stability. There are two early personality measures, Adorno, Levinson, Frenkel-Brunswik, Levinson, and Sanford's (1950) F Scale and Rokeach's (1954) Dogmatism Scale that are particularly applicable to political, public, and organizational communication. The 78-item F Scale (there are shorter versions) measures nine aspects of the authoritarian personality, such as authoritarian aggression, authoritarian submission, conventionalism, and destructiveness and cynicism. Items include "human nature being what it is, there will always be war and conflict" and "obedience and respect for authority are the most important virtues children should learn." The 40-item Dogmatism Scale (there are shorter versions) measures open versus closed belief systems. It includes such items "there are two kinds of people in this world: those who are for the truth and those who are against the truth" and "even though freedom of speech for all groups is a worthwhile goal, it is unfortunately necessary to restrict the freedom of certain political groups."

There are also several measures of aging and generational communication. For example, researchers have argued that measures of aging need to consider more than chronological or biological age. Referring to A. M. Rubin and Rubin's (1986) construct of contextual age, Beutler, Brown, Crothers, Booker, and Seabrook (1996) observed that contextual age is a more valid indicator of one's psychological state than is chronological age. Contextual age, they noted, is a more accurate descriptor of the variations in biological, psychological, cultural, social, and communication experiences an individual brings to measurement. The Contextual Age Scale includes items representing six lifestyle dimensions: physical health, mobility, life satisfaction, interpersonal interaction, social activity, and economic security. It has been used in contexts ranging from interpersonal to mass communication. For example, working on the assumption that one's identity is formed by communication interaction, Kundrat and Nussbaum (2003) examined the effect of invisible illness on identity, as represented by contextual age, throughout the life span. They used the Contextual Age Scale to assess self-perceived and other-perceived contextual age. In both self-report and other-report instances, Kundrat and Nussbaum reported invisibly ill people had significantly higher contextual age scores than did the same chronologically aged-matched non-ill people.

Kaplan, Bally, Brandt, Busacco, and Pray (1997) developed the Communication Scale for Older Adults (CSOA), comprised of a 31-item communication attitudes scale (e.g., "I become angry when people do not speak clearly enough for me to understand"), and a 41-item communication strategies scale (e.g., "you are talking with one person but are not understanding; you interrupt the person before he finishes to say what you think") for dealing with communication problems. The measures are aimed at perceived attitudes and strategies for coping with hearing loss. Kaplan et al. presented normative data, changes in clients' attitudes and strategies after completing an aural rehabilitation program for hearing loss over two periods, and internal consistency and test-retest reliability data.

In addition, based on consumer socialization theory, Viswanathan, Childers, and Moore (2000) developed and assessed the reliability and validity of an intergenerational communication measure about whether parents play a crucial role in the consumer socialization of children. They developed multi-item scales across three dimensions: consumer skills, preferences, and attitudes about information supplied by marketers. They also included a cross-cultural analysis in the U.S. and Thailand.

Issues

There are several overriding issues surrounding such imported measures. These issues include utility, adaptability and sustainability, validity and reliability, including stability and generalizability, cultural sensitivity, and accessibility. In light of the latter issue, and given the proprietary nature of several measures developed in fields such as psychology, we treat this section differently from the other profiles in this book. In most instances, we present portions or samples and examples of items comprising the measure. In addition, some profiles such as "AGGRESSION, HOSTILITY, AND ANGER," "PERSONALITY TRAITS," and "SHYNESS AND SOCIABILITY" highlight or mention more than a single measure. Others present earlier and revised, adapted, or shortened measures in the profiles such as "LOCUS OF CONTROL," "SENSATION SEEKING," and "SOCIAL DESIRABILITY."

These measures have been developed for a specific purpose, typically in another field, and applied in communication. For example, psychological approaches have guided communication interests in examining how personality traits (including extraversion, neuroticism, openness, agreeableness, and conscientiousness) affect such communication facets as group behavior, public speaking, media preferences, and information seeking in organizations. It is important for researchers to keep focused on the conceptual rationale for examining such relationships, rather than focusing on the variable analytic similarities and differences.

The measures also highlight issues within communication. For example, the STATE-TRAIT Inventory (STAI; Spielberger, 1983) includes components of situational perceptions of fear, apprehension, and avoidance in a certain context (e.g., public speaking) versus relatively stable individual differences that transcend any individual situation (e.g., anxiety leading to differences in communication needs and motives).

In many cases, especially with the scales selected for inclusion in this volume, researchers have addressed measurement validity. This is particularly important, as social desirability is a potential hazard with these self-report measures. Assessments of validity have included construct and concurrent validity. There are many examples of these assessments: (a) supporting theoretical distinctions between state and trait anxiety; (b) finding chronically lonely people score higher on a self-report loneliness measure; (c) finding scores from the self-report measure of anxiety correspond to physiological measurements of anxiety arousal or heart rate; and (d) observing positive links between shyness and both communication apprehension and loneliness, and negative links between shyness and both social assertiveness and interaction involvement. Few assessments, though, have addressed external validity, that is, issues of generalizability based on sample selection when using the self-report measures.

This is especially apparent in questions surrounding the cultural sensitivity and fit of various measures in different cultures. Measurement plays out differently in different cultures. Meanings and values differ, as do cultural norms. Researchers must be sensitive to this. Western-based measurement validity and reliability assessments, for example, may not apply to different cultural settings. Cultural bias is another issue affecting measurement in this context, as evidenced by issues surrounding accurate and discernible measurements of social desirability. Some cultures might foster a norm of agreement with questionnaire statement.

Typical assessments of reliability for the measures include internal consistency or homogeneity of scale items, and occasional considerations of test-retest stability across time (e.g., 1 week, 1 month). Trait-like measures such as self-esteem and sensation seeking should be stable across time. Internal consistencies of these imported measures are typically quite good, although some have used dimensions in multidimensional scales with low reliability coefficients, even in the .5s.

The proprietary nature of some imported measures limits their accessibility and utility. For example, although there are versions of the manual and measures in over 25 languages, the entire STATE-TRAIT ANXIETY Inventory (Spielberger, 1983) is available for purchase from the Consulting Psychologists Press. There is also a tendency to reduce lengthier measures to shorter measures so that a variant of the original measure can fit within the parameters of a study. This sometimes results in fewer items being used (e.g., sample items that have been referenced in the scholarly literature) or alternative measures being developed. It is not rare to read about the use of shortened 5-item versions of the 20-item scale. There are two-, four-, and eight-item brief versions of Zuckerman and Lubin's (1985) SENSATION-SEEKING Scale. There are several shorter versions of Crowne and Marlowe's (1960) SOCIAL DESIRABILITY Scale. It is difficult to assess how the adapted or shortened instrument captures the full essence of the theoretical construct being measured.

Researchers have often altered the original measuring instrument in some manner (e.g., adapting items to a particular context), have changed response options or the scale of responses, or have shifted a multidimensional measure to a unidimensional index or vice versa, as in suggesting multiple dimensions of locus of control or need for cognition. It is sometimes difficult to determine how such changes alter the meaning or construct validity of the measure and affect whether earlier reports of concurrent or criterion-related validity or measurement stability still apply. Investigators have applied the outcome of the measurement differently, for example, using the interval-level continuous scale or using a median split to dichotomize responses into high and low groups, for instance, those high and low in need for cognition or sensation seeking. Various formats also exist for the measures of personality, which have included three- and five-factor models, and 100 and 135 adjective and 35 and 40 bipolar scales.

Time is another bias affecting measurement in several ways. Revisions or adaptations of measures over time change the measure. Sometimes, wording in the original measures needs to be updated. Sometimes, the measure needs to be shortened to fit the research circumstances. Sometimes, it needs to be adapted to a different context or stimulus (e.g., to the Internet instead of the newspaper). Sometimes, the measure needs to reflect the currency of new knowledge about the construct or about the manner of measurement or analysis. Still, we need to be cautious about the tendency to treat the altered or abbreviated measure as if it possesses the validity and reliability track record of the original measure. In addition, older, yet important, writings and research studies are simply less accessible via electronic databases. An important history that has led to the development and transitions of research and measurement across our fields of study needs to be re-gained.

References

Adorno, T. W., Levinson, D. J., Frenkel-Brunswik, E., & Sanford, R. N. (1950). *The authoritarian personality.* New York: Harper.

Bandura, A. (1977). Self-efficacy: Toward a unifying theory of behavioral change. *Psychological Review, 84,* 191–215.

Beutler, L. E., Brown, M. T., Crothers, L., Booker, K., & Seabrook, M. K. (1996). The dilemma of factitious demographic distinctions in psychological research. *Journal of Consulting and Clinical Psychology, 64,* 892–902.

Buss, A. H., & Durkee, A. (1957). An inventory for assessing different kinds of hostility. *Journal of Consulting Psychology, 21,* 343–349.

Buss, A. H., & Perry, M. (1992). The Aggression Questionnaire. *Journal of Personality and Social Psychology, 63,* 452–459.

Cacioppo, J. T., Petty, K. E., & Kao, C. F. (1984). The efficient assessment of need for cognition. *Journal of Personality Assessment, 48,* 306–307.

Crowne, D. P., & Marlowe, D. (1960). A new scale of social desirability independent of psychopathology. *Journal of Consulting Psychology, 24,* 349–354.

Hendricks, A. A. J., Hofstee, W. K. B., & de Raad, B. (1999). The Five-factor Personality Inventory (FFPI). *Personality and Individual Differences, 27,* 307–325.

Kaplan, H., Bally, S., Brandt, F., Busacco, D., & Pray, J. (1997). Communication Scale for Older Adults (CSOA). *Journal of the American Academy of Audiology, 8,* 203–217.

Kundrat, A. L., & Nussbaum, J. F. (2003). The impact of invisible illness on identity and contextual age across the life span. *Health Communication, 15,* 331–347.

Moe, K. O., & Zeiss, A. M. (1982). Measuring self-efficacy expectations for social skills: A methodological inquiry. *Cognitive Therapy and Research, 6,* 191–205.

Rokeach, M. (1956). Political and religious dogmatism: An alternative to the authoritarian personality. *Psychological Monographs, 70.*

Rosenberg, M. (1965). *Society and adolescent self-image.* Princeton, NJ: Princeton University Press.

Rotter, J. B. (1966). Generalized expectations for internal versus external control of reinforcement. *Psychological Monographs, 80,* 1–28.

Rubin, A. M., & Rubin, R. B. (1986). Contextual age as a life-position index. *International Journal of Aging and Human Development, 23,* 27–44.

Rubin, R. B., Martin, M. M., Bruning, S. S., & Powers, D. E. (1993). Test of a self-efficacy model of interpersonal communication competence. *Communication Quarterly, 41,* 210–220.

Russell, D., Peplau, L. A., & Cutrona, C. E. (1980). The revised UCLA Loneliness Scale: Concurrent and discriminant validity evidence. *Journal of Personality and Social Psychology, 39,* 472–480.

Snyder, M. (1974). The self-monitoring of expressive behavior. *Journal of Personality and Social Psychology, 30,* 526–537.

Spielberger, C. D. (1983). *Manual for the State-Trait Anxiety Inventory: STAI (Form Y).* Palo Alto, CA: Consulting Psychologists Press.

Viswanathan, M., Childers, T. L., & Moore, E. S. (2000). The measurement of intergenerational communication and influence on consumption: Development, validation, and cross-cultural comparison of the IGEN scale. *Journal of the Academy of Marketing Science, 28,* 406–424.

Wallston, B. S., Wallston, K. A., Kaplan, G. D., & Maides, S. A. (1976). Development and validation of the Health Locus of Control (HLC) Scale. *Journal of Consulting and Clinical Psychology, 44,* 580–585.

Zuckerman, M., & Lubin, B. (1985). *Manual for the Revised Multiple Affect Adjective Check List.* San Diego: Educational & Industrial Testing Service.

Aggression, Hostility, and Anger

Profile by Alan M. Rubin

Aggressive predispositions and tendencies have been at the center of much social science research over the years. Aggression, hostility, and anger have been studied as potentially influential mediators of communication processes and effects. Anger, for example, has been described as an emotional state or disposition "made up of feelings ranging from intensity to minor irritation to fury and rage" (Williams, Barefoot, & Shekille, 1985, p. 173). Investigators have found that aggressive tendencies predicted antisocial behavior in adults, especially as their tendencies interacted with situational factors (e.g., Huesmann & Eron, 1986). They have also have observed links between aggressive attitudes and behavior and exposure to various media and arousing genres (Paik & Comstock, 1994).

The Buss-Durkee Hostility Inventory (BDIH) is an often-cited measure of aggression, as is the subsequent version of the Buss and Perry (1992) Aggression Questionnaire. The 10-item Assault subscale of the BDIH, for instance, assesses the disposition to resort to physical violence against other people (Buss & Durkee, 1957). For example:

> Once in a while I cannot control my urge to harm others.
> If I have to resort to physical violence to defend my rights, I will.
> I have known people who have pushed me so far that we came to blows.
> I can't think of a good reason for hitting anyone. (Buss & Durkee, 1957, p. 346)

Participants indicate whether they feel each statement is *true* or *false*; higher scores reflect greater hostility and aggression.

Haridakis (2002) measured aggression with the 29-item Buss and Perry (1992) Aggression Questionnaire (AQ), which contains physical aggression, verbal aggression, anger, and hostility scales. Researchers have argued the AQ is a well-suited aggression measure, which addresses instrumental (e.g., propensity or readiness to hurt or harm others), affective (e.g., preparation for aggression), and cognitive (feelings of ill will or injustice) areas. The AQ assesses specific behavior, not just dispositions. Haridakis used it to measure aggression as an outcome of media use. He noted that scores on the measure have correlated with peer nominations of aggression, suggesting convergent validity, and that the measure may be less affected by social desirability than other measures. Also supporting validity, Haridakis found higher disinhibition sensation-seeking scores predicted physical aggression, verbal aggression, anger, and total aggression.

Typical of the measure's use, Haridakis (2002) had participants rate their agreement with each of the 29 items on a 5-point scale (1 = *extremely uncharacteristic of me*, 5 = *extremely characteristic of me*) with higher summated scores suggesting higher levels of aggression. Haridakis reported .83, .85, .81, and .81 Cronbach alphas, respectively, for the physical, verbal, anger, and hostility subscales of the AQ, with a .90 Cronbach α for the entire 29-item measure. Similarly, Rubin, Haridakis, and Eyal (2003) reported a .88 Cronbach α for the 10-item BDHI scale, when examining preferences for different television talk programs. Rubin, West, and Mitchell (2001) reported a .75 Cronbach α for the BDHI scale when examining links to popular-music preferences.

Other measures of hostility and anger have also been employed in communication research. For example, Finn (1992) used Cook and Medley's (1954) 50-item, true-false hostility index, which was initially designed to assess how teachers get along with others, but was extended to hostile attitudes toward co-workers, customers, patients, and employees. Sample items include:

> I would certainly enjoy beating a crook at his own game.
> When someone does me a wrong I feel I should pay him back if I can, just for the principle of the thing.
> I have often met people who were supposed to be expert who were no better than I. (Cook & Medley, 1954, p. 417)

According to Cook and Medley, a teacher scoring low on the scale would feel students are dishonest, insincere, untrustworthy, and lazy. Each true response counts one point in the summated measure.

The Multidimensional Anger Inventory is a 12-item measure of anger as a disposition to being irritated or annoyed (Siegel, 1985). For example:

> I tend to get angry more frequently than most people.
> It is easy to make me angry.
> Something makes me angry almost every day.
> I often feel angrier than I should.
> At times I feel angry for no specific reason. (Siegel, 1985, p. 73)

Participants respond on a 5-point scale indicative how descriptive each statement is of them (*completely descriptive* to *completely undescriptive*). Rubin, West, and Mitchell (2001) reported a .89 Cronbach α for the 12 items, and found anger was a significant indicator of the likelihood of being more aggressive, distrusting, and having less respect for women.

Measures of aggression, anger, and hostility have been widely employed in social and behavioral research. Communication researchers have considered aggression, hostility, and anger as they relate to various types of communication behavior, especially concerning relationships with others and preferences for and outcomes of exposure to various media.

Locations

Buss, A. H., & Durkee, A. (1957). An inventory for assessing different kinds of hostility. *Journal of Consulting Psychology, 21,* 343–349.

Buss, A. H., & Perry, M. (1992). The Aggression Questionnaire. *Journal of Personality and Social Psychology, 63,* 452–459.

Cook, W. W., & Medley, D. M. (1954). Proposed hostility and pharisaic-virtue scales for the MMPI. *Journal of Applied Psychology, 38,* 414–418.

Siegel, J. (1985). The measurement of anger as a multidimensional construct. In M. A. Chesney & R. H. Rosenman (Eds.), *Anger and hostility in cardiovascular and behavioral disorders* (pp. 59–82). Washington, DC: Hemisphere.

References

Finn, S. (1992). Television "addiction?" An evaluation of four competing media-use models. *Journalism Quarterly, 69,* 422–435.

Haridakis, P. M. (2002). Viewer characteristics, exposure to television violence, and aggression. *Media Psychology, 4,* 325–353.

Huesmann, L. R., & Eron, L. D. (1986). The development of aggression in children of different cultures: Psychological processes and exposure to violence. In L. R. Huesmann & L. D. Eron (Eds.), *Television and the aggressive child: A cross-national comparison* (pp. 1–27). Hillsdale, NJ: Erlbaum.

Paik, H., & Comstock, G. (1994). The effects of television violence on antisocial behavior: A meta-analysis. *Communication Research, 21,* 516–546.

Rubin, A. M., Haridakis, P. M., & Eyal, K. (2003). Viewer aggression and attraction to television talk shows. *Media Psychology, 5,* 331–362.

Rubin, A. M., West. D. V., & Mitchell, W. S. (2001). Differences in aggression, attitudes toward women, and distrust as reflected in popular music preferences. *Media Psychology, 3,* 25–42.

Williams, R. G., Barefoot, J. C., & Shekille, R. B. (1985). The health consequences of hostility. In M. A. Chesney & R. H. Rosenman (Eds.), *Anger and hostility in cardiovascular and behavioral disorders* (pp. 173–185). Washington, DC: Hemisphere.

Anxiety: State-Trait Inventory

Profile by Alan M. Rubin

Anxiety is a form of stress or tension, which people seek to reduce or avoid. It is a complex reaction involving fear, apprehension, tension, and nervousness (Levitt, 1980; Spielberger, 1972). People experience pain from increased tension or anxiety and pleasure from the release of tension (McGuire, 1985).

Researchers have distinguished between trait and state components of anxiety (Cattell & Scheier, 1961; Spielberger, 1966, 1975). State anxiety (A-State) is situational and transitory; people perceive a specific situation as threatening at a point in time. Trait anxiety (A-Trait) is dispositional and enduring. It is a personality trait that transcends a specific situation; people perceive a wide array of situations as threatening. "A-States vary in intensity and fluctuate over time as a function of the amount of stress that impinges upon an individual. Trait anxiety (A-Trait) refers to relatively stable individual differences in anxiety proneness" (Gaudry, Vagg, & Spielberger, 1975, p. 331). Whereby trait anxiety is more enduring and predispositional, state anxiety is more fleeting and is induced by the event or situation. A low A-Trait person can experience state anxiety if he or she perceives a situation to be stressful or tense (Fluck, Harrigan, & Brindley, 2001).

Spielberger, Gorsuch, and Lushene (1970) developed the State-Trait Anxiety Inventory (STAI) to measure self-reported trait (i.e., dispositional) and state (i.e., situational) anxiety (see, Spielberger, 1983). Social and behavioral researchers, including those in communication, have widely used the STAI. Researchers have found the STAI to have good concurrent validity and reliability in a range of psychological and communication settings (see, e.g., Blood & Blood, 1994; Witt & Behnke, 2006).

The STAI A-Trait component focuses on stable predispositions. It "requires people to describe how they generally feel in terms of the frequency with which they have experienced specific symptoms of anxiety" (Gaudry et al., p. 332). The A-Trait scale contains 20 statements and asks participants to select the appropriate response to indicate how they *generally feel*, that is, typically feel across situations. For example:

- I am "calm, cool, and collected."
- I feel pleasant.
- I feel satisfied with myself.
- I feel inadequate.
- I feel secure.
- I lack self-confidence.
- I wish I could be as happy as others seem to be. (Blood & Blood, 1994; Miller & Watson, 1992, Appendix A; Spielberger, 1983).

The STAI's A-State component focuses on transitory emotional states and situational introspection. The A-State scale "requires respondents to indicate the intensity of their feelings of anxiety at a particular moment in time" (Gaudry et al., 1975, p. 332). It contains 20 statements and asks participants to select an appropriate response to indicate how they feel *right now, at this moment,* that is, in a certain situation (e.g., public speech). For example:

- I feel secure.
- I feel calm.
- I am tense.
- I feel at ease.
- I feel upset.
- I feel nervous.
- I feel satisfied. (Blood & Blood, 1994; Miller & Watson, 1992, Appendix A; Spielberger, 1983).

For both A-Trait and A-State STAI scales, four response options follow the items: (1) *not at all,* (2) *somewhat,* (3) *moderately so,* and (4) *very much so.* Reverse-direction items are recoded so that higher scores indicate more anxiety, and a greater likelihood of responding to threatening situations by being tense, fearful, or nervous.

Some investigators have used modifications of the STAI. For example, on a scale of 1 (*not at all*) to 9 (*very*), Fluck et al. (2001) had coders use three adjective scales—uncomfortable, nervous, and apprehensive—to rate the anxiety levels of participants facing an anxiety-inducing event and a happy event. They chose the adjectives from the A-State scale of the STAI. Witt and Behnke (2006) used a 5-item trait scale suggesting "manifestations of calmness or anxiety": "I feel tense, I feel calm, I feel relaxed, I feel at ease, and I feel jittery" (p. 171). Participants indicated their agreement (1 = *strongly disagree* to 5 = *strongly agree*) with each item. The researchers recoded items, as necessary, so that higher scores indicate greater anxiety. Ayres et al. (1995) used a 5-item state version in a public speaking situation: "I felt tense; I felt calm; I felt relaxed; I felt at ease; and I felt jittery" (p. 187).

Researchers studying anxiety and public speaking have often used the STAI. Some have grounded their research in psychological anxiety theory (Spielberger, 1966), examining psychological and physiological indicators of speech anxiety in college communication classes (e.g., Behnke & Beatty, 1981). In one form of that research, narrowband research, investigators assess anxiety levels in participants who focus on certain milestones surrounding public speaking assignments (e.g., Behnke & Sawyer, 2000). Witt and Behnke (2006) found different types of public speaking assignments create narrowband trait public speaking anxiety in students. Sawyer and Behnke (2002) found state anxiety across anticipatory, confrontation, adaptation, and release milestones or stages of public speaking. Clay, Fisher, Xie, Sawyer, and Behnke (2005) examined state anxiety at anticipation (before the speech) and confrontation (first minute of the speech) milestones. McCullough, Russell, Behnke, Sawyer, and Witt (2006) found a negative relationship between a speaker's state of mind and anticipatory public speaking anxiety.

Others studying nonverbal assessments of anxiety and anxiety related to broadcasting and media use have also used the STAI in research. As noted above, Fluck et al. (2001) used adjectives from the STAI to examine coders' recognition of anxiety in participants facing anxious or happy events. Adams, Behnke, Carlile, and Platts (1975) used the A-State scale of the STAI in their experiment, and found experience diminished radio news announcers' levels of anxiety. Conway and Rubin (1991) used the STAI's A-Trait scale, and found high levels of trait anxiety predicted pass-time and escape motives for watching television.

Speech and language investigators, especially those assessing anxiety levels in stutterers, have also used the STAI (e.g., Blood & Blood, 1994). For example, Craig (1990) found, before treatment, those who stutter have higher chronic fear in demanding speech situations than those who do not stutter. Miller and Watson (1992), though, found anxiety to be "speech specific" and that those who stutter do not differ significantly from those who do not stutter on the STAI A-Trait scale. Craig and Kearns (1995) found acupuncture treatment did not reduce anxiety levels for those who stutter.

The STAI has demonstrated concurrent and construct validity in anxiety studies. Researchers have found self-report anxiety measures correspond with physiological measures of anxiety arousal (e.g., Menasco & Hawkins, 1978; O'Neil, Spielberger, & Hansen, 1969). In his study of anxiety arousal and heart rate, Porter (1974) noted the STAI A-Trait scale compares favorably with other generalized measures. Roberts, Finn, Harris, Sawyer, and Behnke (2005) noted the A-Trait and A-State STAI scales consistently perform as theoretically expected. Supporting such construct differences between state and trait anxiety measures, Johnson and Spielberger (1968) found A-State measures declined in response to the relaxation training, but A-Trait measures did not. Ferreira and Murray (1983) concluded the STAI is an appropriate measure of state and trait anxiety in motor-performance studies. Beatty, Dobos, Balfantz, and Kuwabara (1991) selected five items from the STAI A-State scale for their state anxiety measure. Supporting concurrent validity, they found state anxiety predicts communication apprehension.

Supporting construct validity, Rule and Traver (1983) noted, whereas state anxiety fluctuates with the stress of a situation, trait anxiety is a relatively stable "proneness to anxiety" (p. 276). The results of their study supported the theoretical expectation that state anxiety increases under a stressful situation, but trait anxiety remains the same. In addition, Greene, Rucker, Zauss, and Harris (1998) expected state anxiety to interfere with acquiring communication skills because it diverted attention from the task. Supporting construct validity of their adapted 6-item state anxiety measure, they found highly anxious people had low rates of skill acquisition and more variability in the quality of task performance.

Barnes, Harp, and Jung (2002) found only 6% of the 816 research studies they identified using the STAI actually computed reliability for their own data. Those that did, though, presented acceptable internal consistency and test-retest reliability. For studies reporting such data, the STAI has shown consistent measurement homogeneity. For example, Roberts et al. (2005) found a .69 ($p < .05$) Pearson r between public speaking trait and state anxiety, and reported .94 and .92 α reliabilities for the A-Trait and A-State scales, respectively. Witt and Behnke (2006) reported α reliabilities of .91 to .92 for the A-Trait scale for manuscript reading, extemporaneous speaking, and impromptu speaking. Sawyer and Behnke (2002) reported α reliabilities of .87 to .93 for a portion of the modified A-State scale across different stages of public speaking anxiety. Clay et al. (2005) reported .92 and .90 α reliabilities for the A-State STAI at the anticipation and confrontation milestones of public speaking. McCullough et al. (2006) reported .92 α reliability for their version of the A-State scale to assess situational anxiety experienced in public speaking. Booth-Butterfield (1988) used a shortened version of the STAI as revised by Leherissey, O'Neil, and Hansen (1971), and reported a .85 reliability coefficient for the 5-item measure. In their study of performance visualization, Ayres et al. (1995) reported .81 pretest reliability and .85 posttest reliability for the 5-item version of the A-State scale. Beatty et al. (1991) reported .80 and .81 α reliabilities for two administrations of the 5-item measure adapted from the STAI A-State scale. Greene et al. (1998) reported .86 and .87 Cronbach alphas for two administrations of their 6-item state measure: "I feel tense, I feel self-confident, I feel anxious, I feel poised and in control, I feel calm and relaxed, I feel nervous" (p. 345). In a study of anxiety and television use, Conway and Rubin (1991) reported a .91 Cronbach α for the 20-item STAI A-Trait scale.

Researchers have also provided mixed evidence of measurement sta
bility. For example, Spielberger et al. (1970) reported values of .54 (state)
and .86 (trait) test-retest correlation for a 20-day period. Rule and Traver
(1983) found similar test-retest values of .40 (state) and .86 (trait). Porter
(1974) also reported considerable test-retest stability (*r* = .82).

The STAI is a widely used measure to assess state and trait anxiety
across cultures and disciplines, including psychology, communication,
marketing, and communication disorders. The manual and measure are
available in over 25 languages, even though the proprietary nature of the
scale makes it less accessible than desired. In general, the STAI A-Trait and
A-State scales have impressive records of research application and established validity and reliability.

Location

Spielberger, C. D. (1983). *Manual for the State-Trait Anxiety Inventory: STAI
    (Form Y)*. Palo Alto, CA: Consulting Psychologists Press.
Spielberger, C. D., Gorsuch, R. L., & Lushene, R. E. (1970). *STAI: Manual for the
    State-Trait Anxiety Inventory*. Palo Alto, CA: Consulting Psychologists Press.

References

Adams, W. C., Behnke, R. R., Carlile, L. W., & Platts, D. E. (1975). Effects of radio
    announcing experience on self-perceived anxiety. *Western Speech
    Communication, 39,* 120–122.
Ayres, J., Ayres, D. M., Grudzinskas, G., Hope, T., Kelly, E., & Wilcox, A. K.
    (1995). A component analysis of performance visualization. *Communication
    Research Reports, 8*(2), 186–192.
Barnes, L. B., Harp, D., & Jung, W. S. (2002). Reliability generalization of scores
    on the Spielberger State-Trait Anxiety Inventory. *Educational and
    Psychological Measurement, 62,* 603–618.
Beatty, M. J., Dobos, J. A., Balfantz, G. L., & Kuwabara, A. Y. (1991).
    Communication apprehension, state anxiety and behavioral disruption: A
    causal analysis. *Communication Quarterly, 39*(1), 48–57.
Behnke, R. R., & Beatty, M. J. (1981). A cognitive physiological model of speech
    anxiety. *Communication Monographs, 48,* 158–163.
Behnke, R. R., & Sawyer, C. R. (2000). Anticipatory anxiety patterns for male and
    female public speakers. *Communication Education, 49,* 187–195.
Blood, G. W., & Blood, I. M. (1994). Subjective anxiety measures and cortisol
    responses in adults who stutter. *Journal of Speech & Hearing Research, 37,*
    760–768.
Booth-Butterfield, S. (1988). Inhibition and student recall of instructional mes-
    sages. *Communication Education, 37,* 312–324.
Cattell, R. B. & Scheier, H. I. (1961). *The meaning and measurement of neuroti-
    cism and anxiety*. New York: Ronald Press.
Clay, E., Fisher, R. L., Xie, S., Sawyer, C. R., & Behnke, R. R. (2005). Affect

intensity and sensitivity to punishment as predictors of sensitization (arousal) during public speaking. *Communication Reports, 18*(2), 95–103.

Conway, J. C., & Rubin, A. M. (1991). Psychological predictors of television viewing motivation. *Communication Research, 18,* 443–463.

Craig, A. (1990). An investigation into the relationship between anxiety and stuttering. *Journal of Speech and Hearing Disorders, 55,* 290–294.

Craig, A. R., & Kearns, M. (1995). Results of a traditional acupuncture intervention for stuttering. *Journal of Speech & Hearing Research, 38,* 572–578.

Ferreira, R., & Murray, J. (1983). Spielberger's State-Trait Anxiety Inventory: Measuring anxiety with and without an audience during performance on a stabilometer. *Perceptual and Motor Skills, 57*(1), 15–18.

Fluck, S. A., Harrigan, J. A., & Brindley, J. (2001). Children and young adults' recognition of anxiety. *Journal of Nonverbal Behavior, 25*(2), 127–146.

Gaudry, E., Vagg, P., & Spielberger, C. D. (1975). Validation of the state-trait distinction in anxiety research. *Multivariate Behavioral Research, 10,* 331–341.

Greene, J. O., Rucker, M. P., Zauss, E. S., & Harris, A. A. (1998). Communication anxiety and the acquisition of message-production skills. *Communication Education, 47,* 337–345.

Johnson, D. T., & Spielberger, C. D. (1968). The effects of relaxation training and the passage of time on measures of state- and trait-anxiety. *Journal of Clinical Psychology, 24*(1), 20–23.

Leherissey, B., O'Neil, H., & Hansen, D. (1971). Effects of memory support upon anxiety and performance in computer-assisted learning. *Journal of Educational Psychology, 62,* 412–420.

Levitt, E. (1980). *The psychology of anxiety.* Hillsdale, NJ: Erlbaum.

McCullough, S. C., Russell, S. G., Behnke, R. R., Sawyer, C. R., & Witt, P. L. (2006). Anticipatory public speaking state anxiety as a function of body sensations and state of mind. *Communication Quarterly, 54*(1), 101–109.

McGuire, W. J. (1985). Attitudes and attitude change. In G. Lindzey & E. Aronson (Eds.), *The handbook of social psychology* (3rd ed., Vol. 2, pp. 233–346). New York: Random House.

Menasco, M. B., & Hawkins, D. I. (1978). A field test of the relationship between cognitive dissonance and state anxiety. *Journal of Marketing Research, 15,* 650–655.

Miller, S., & Watson, B. C. (1992). The relationship between communication attitude, anxiety and depression in stutterers and nonstutterers. *Journal of Speech and Hearing Research, 35,* 789–798.

O'Neil, H. F., Jr., Spielberger, C. D., & Hansen, D. N. (1969). The effects of state anxiety and task difficulty on computer-assisted learning. *Journal of Educational Psychology, 60,* 343–350.

Porter, D. T. (1974). Self-report scales of communication apprehension and autonomic arousal (heart rate): A test of construct validity. *Speech Monographs, 41,* 267–276.

Roberts, J. B., Finn, A. N., Harris, K. B., Sawyer, C. R., & Behnke, R. R. (2005). Public speaking state anxiety as a function of trait anxiety and reactivity mechanisms. *Southern Communication Journal, 70*(2), 161–167.

Rule, W. R., & Traver, M. D. (1983). Test-retest reliabilities of State-Trait Anxiety

Inventory in a stressful social analogue situation. *Journal of Personality Assessment, 47*, 276–277.

Sawyer, C. R., & Behnke, R. R. (2002). Reduction in public speaking state anxiety during performance as a function of sensitization processes. *Communication Quarterly, 50*(1), 110–121.

Spielberger, C. D. (1966). Theory and research on anxiety. In C. D. Spielberger (Ed.), *Anxiety and behavior* (pp. 3–20). New York: Academic Press.

Spielberger, C. D. (1972). Anxiety as an emotional state. In C. D. Spielberger (Ed.), Anxiety: *Current trends in theory and research* (Vol. 1, pp. 23–49). New York: Academic Press.

Spielberger, C. D. (1975). Anxiety: State-trait-process. In C. D. Spielberger & I. G. Sarason (Eds.), *Stress and anxiety* (Vol. 1, pp. 115–143). New York: Wiley.

Witt, P. L., & Behnke, R. R. (2006). Anticipatory speech anxiety as a function of public speaking assignment type. *Communication Education, 55*(2), 167–177.

Locus of Control

Profile by Alan M. Rubin

Social learning theory provides the framework for the concept of *locus of control*. As Rotter (1966) explained, "the effects of reward or reinforcement on preceding behavior depend in part on whether the person perceives the reward to be contingent on his own behavior or independent of it" (p. 1). Locus of control indicates how much people feel in control of their own lives. Lefcourt (1982) traced related locus of control to *learned helplessness*; those who saw themselves as responsible for their own actions and interactions attended to and had the tendency to use the information.

Mostly, locus of control is an expectancy of whether one believes his or own skill, ability, or behavior vis-à-vis luck, chance, fate, or powerful others produces the outcome. A belief in the efficacy of one's own skill, ability, or behavior (i.e., internal causes) producing the outcome denotes internal control, suggesting one's own effort can alter outcomes. A belief in luck, chance, fate, or powerful others (i.e., external causes) producing the outome denotes external control, suggesting the world is random, unordered, and unpredictable. According to Brenders (1987), over 1,000 studies "confirm that one's belief in personal control profoundly influences his or her attitude toward the self and the environment" (p. 92).

Rotter (1966) summarized 10 years of early research by him and his students. He noted that Phares (1957) first attempted to measure "individual differences in a generalized expectancy or belief in external control as a psychological variable" (Rotter, 1966, p. 9). Phares developed a Likert-type scale with 13 statements of internal attitudes and 13 statements of external attitudes. This was followed by research revising and extending Phares' work.

Subsequently, Rotter (1966) described the development of a personality measure of internal versus external control. He reported work on a 60-item scale, reducing items receiving sizable socially desirable responses and considering item validity, producing a 29-item forced-choice test, which included 6 filler items. This I-E Scale was considered to be an assessment of a generalized expectancy. The items in that scale focused on "subjects' beliefs about the nature of the world" (Rotter, 1966, p. 10). Across several samples, Rotter reported reliability data of the 29-item scale, including "reasonable" internal consistency estimates (split half, Spearman-Brown, and Kuder-Richardson) and test-retest consistency, 1 and 2 months after administration. He also observed that weak relationships with measures of social desirability, intelligence, and political liberalness indicate discriminant validity for the scale, and that multimethod comparisons with other assessments (e.g., resisting attempts to be influenced) supported construct validity by predicting behavior of those above and below the median of the I-E Scale.

For each of 29 pairs of statements (23 test items and 6 filler items), the questionnaire has participants read each pair of alternative statements and select the one they "more strongly believe to be the case as far as you're concerned" (Rotter, 1966, p. 26). The measure concerns one's beliefs about the world and requires participants to select either an internal or external response (contrasted by "a" and "b" pairs below). For example:

a   Without the right breaks one cannot be an effective leader.
b   Capable people who fail to become leaders have not taken advantage of their opportunities.
a   Becoming a success is a matter of hard work, luck has little or nothing to do with it.
b   Getting a good job depends mainly on being in the right place at the right time.
a   As far as world affairs are concerned, most of us are the victims of forces we can neither understand nor control.
b   By taking an active part in political and social affairs, the people can control world events.
a   Most people don't realize the extent to which their lives are controlled by accidental happenings.
b   There really is no such thing as "luck."
a   With enough effort we can wipe out political corruption.
b   It is difficult for people to have much control over the things politicians do in office.
a   Many times I feel that I have little influence over the things that happen to me.
b   It is impossible for me to believe that chance or luck plays an important role in my life.
a   What happens to me is my own doing.
b   Sometimes I feel that I don't have enough control over the direction my life is taking. (Rotter, 1966, pp. 11–12)

External statements are paired with internal ones. One point is given for each external statement chosen. The summated score ranges from 0 (most internal) to 23 (most external).

Despite the forced choice between alternative statements, Rotter (1966) suggested the need to interpret locus of control on a continuum of internal to external control, rather than an either/or typology. *Internals* tend to attribute outcomes of events to their own efforts (e.g., hard work produces achievement). *Externals* attribute outcomes of events to external circumstances (e.g., bad luck or poor assessment produces subpar results). Consequently, externals are less likely to expend the needed effort to achieve better outcomes. Lefcourt (1983) argued locus of control could be a moderator when predicting affective and behavioral outcomes such as stress. For example, locus of control would modify how stress is experienced. The same could be said for other outcomes such as locus of control's effect on mood, anxiety, performance, and life satisfaction. Similarly, Nowicki and Duke (1983) suggested internals are more attractive because they are less anxious and better liked; their tendency toward competent and prosocial behavior fosters achievement and social relationships through effective behavior.

Locus of control has been found to mediate processes and effects in communication. For example, Wheeless, Erickson, and Behrens (1986) found locus of control helps explain cultural differences in interpersonal disclosiveness. Wheeless, Stewart, Kearney, and Plax (1987) observed that externals perceived greater teacher use of behavioral alteration techniques (e.g., immediate and deferred reward) than did internals. Burgoon et al. (1990) found locus of control of patients to interact with the severity of illness and physicians' compliance-gaining strategies to predict patients' compliance. In addition, when examining possible cultivation effects of television exposure, Wober and Gunter (1982) reported that externals watched more television and had more fearful beliefs about their surrounding world than did internals. Haridakis (2006) found external locus of control predicted greater viewer aggression among women. And, Haridakis and Rubin (2005) found internals felt others would be more affected by media portrayals than they would be.

Some have criticized Rotter's (1966) I-E Scale because of its forced-choice format, questionable social desirability bias, and whether it was assessing a homogeneous concept (e.g., Duttweiler, 1984). In their study of intercultural differences in disclosiveness, Wheeless et al. (1986) reported a split-half reliability of .65 for the 23-item I-E Scale. In her study of perceptions of sexually harassing communication, Booth-Butterfield (1989) reported Cronbach alphas of .66 and .67 for student and adult samples, respectively. Conway and Rubin (1991) reported a .77 Cronbach α for the measure. Sprott, Brumbaugh, and Miyazaki (2001) used a 4-point version of the I-E Scale, seeking improved reliability and reporting a standardized α of .79. In addition, Brenders (1987) noted that, subsequent to Rotter, research has supported distinctions between the sources of external control and research participants "vary their behavior based on the perceived source of external control" (p. 96).

Others, such as Levenson (1974), challenged the I-E Scale's unidimensionality, arguing that, besides internal control, *chance* and *powerful others* represent different dimensions of external control. Levenson developed a Likert-type measure assessing those three dimensions of locus of control: internal, chance, and powerful others' control. Levenson's measure included the following sample items:

Internal Scale:

Whether or not I get to be a leader depends mostly on my ability.
When I make plans, I am almost certain to make them work.
I can pretty much determine what will happen in my life.

Powerful Others Scale:

I feel like what happens in my life is mostly determined by powerful people.
My life is chiefly controlled by powerful others.
Getting what I want requires pleasing those people above me.

Chance Scale:

To a great extent my life is controlled by accidental happenings.
I have found that what is going to happen will happen.
Whether or not I get into a car accident is mostly a matter of luck.
(Levenson, 1974, pp. 381–382)

Levenson (1981) reported modest split-half and Kuder Richardson reliabilities of .51 to .79 across several studies for the three dimensions, and convergent and discriminant validity with other psychometric tests. Walkey (1979) used factor analysis and supported Levenson's 3-factor structure. Rubin and Rubin (1989) reported Cronbach alphas of .64, .66, and .70, respectively, for fewer items in Levenson's three dimensions. However, Wheeless et al. (1987) found Levenson's 24 items performed better as a unidimensional indicator of internality-externality, consistent with Rotter's (1966) original formulation, and reported a .74 α across all items. Haridakis (2006) reported a .74 Cronbach α for a shortened, 12-item unidimensional scale combining Levenson's three dimensions, noting the overall α was more substantial than the reliabilities for the separate dimensions. This supported the unidimensional treatment of locus of control, similar to Rubin's (1993) finding when he used a shortened version of Levenson's measure. Rubin and Haridakis (2005) reported a .71 Cronbach α for the 12-item unidimensional version of the scale.

Locus of control has been examined in specific contexts, including the study of health communication (e.g., Burgoon et al., 1990). This has resulted in the development and application of context-specific and population (e.g., children) measures such as the Health Locus of Control

Scale (HLCS: Wallston, Wallston, Kaplan, & Maides, 1976). Sample items of the HLCS include:

Internal Scale:

If I get sick, it is my own behavior which determines how soon I get well again.
I am in control of my health.

Powerful Others Scale:

Having regular contact with my physician is the best way for me to avoid illness.
Whenever I don't feel well, I should consult a medically trained professional.

Chance Scale:

No matter what I do, if I am going to get sick, I will get sick.
Most things that affect my health happen to me by accident. (Wallston et al., 1976, p. 581)

Empirical data on various and specific health locus of control were reviewed by Norman and Bennett (1995).

Locus of control has shown to be a significant predictor of human behavior throughout the social and behavioral sciences. Measurement of locus of control has been adapted in a myriad of contexts in the field of communication, including health, instructional, media, and newer communication technologies. With different degrees of succes, variations of the locus of control measures, as unidimensional or multidimensional indices, have achieved support for validity and reliabilty.

Locations

Levenson, H. (1974). Activism and powerful others: Distinctions within the concept of internal-external control. *Journal of Personality Assessment, 38,* 377–383.

Rotter, J. B. (1966). Generalized expectations for internal versus external control of reinforcement. *Psychological Monographs, 80,* 1–28.

Wallston, B. S., Wallston, K. A., Kaplan, G. D., & Maides, S. A. (1976). Development and validation of the Health Locus of Control (HLC) Scale. *Journal of Consulting and Clinical Psychology, 44,* 580–585.

References

Booth-Butterfield, M. (1989). Perception of harassing communication as a function of locus of control, work force participation, and gender. *Communication Quarterly, 37,* 262–275.

Brenders, D. A. (1987). Perceived control: Foundations and directions for communication research. *Communication Yearbook, 10,* 86–116.

Burgoon, M., Parrott, R., Burgoon, J. K., Coker, R., Pfau, M., & Birk, T. (1990). Patients' severity of illness, noncompliance, and locus of control and physicians' compliance-gaining messages. *Health Communication, 2*(1), 29–46.

Conway, J. C., & Rubin, A. M. (1991). Psychological predictors of television viewing motivation. *Communication Research, 18,* 443–463.

Duttweiler, P. C. (1984). The internal control index: A newly developed measure of locus of control. *Educational and Psychological Measurement, 44,* 209–221.

Haridakis, P. M. (2006). Men, women, and televised violence: Predicting viewer aggression in male and female television viewers. *Communication Quarterly, 54,* 227–255.

Haridakis, P. M., & Rubin, A. M. (2005). Third-person effects in the aftermath of terrorism. *Mass Communication & Society, 8*(1), 39–59.

Lefcourt, H. M. (1982). *Locus of control: Current trends in theory and research.* Hillsdale, NJ: Erlbaum.

Lefcourt, H. M. (1983). The locus of control as a moderator variable: Stress. In H. M. Lefcourt (Ed.), *Research with the locus of control construct: Volume 2. Developments and social problems* (pp. 253–270). New York: Academic Press.

Levenson, H. (1981). Differentiating among internality, powerful others, and chance. In H. M. Lefcourt (Ed.), *Research with the locus of control construct: Volume 1. Assessment methods* (pp. 15–63). New York: Academic Press.

Norman, P., & Bennett, P. (1995). Health locus of control. In M. Conner & P. Norman (Eds), *Predicting health behaviour* (pp. 62–94). Buckingham, England: Open University Press.

Nowicki, S., Jr., & Duke, M. P. (1983). The Nowicki-Strickland life-span locus of control scales: Construct validation. In H. M. Lefcourt (Ed.), *Research with the locus of control construct: Volume 2. Developments and social problems* (pp. 9–51). New York: Academic Press.

Phares, E. J. (1957). Expectancy changes in skill and chance situations. *Journal of Abnormal and Social Psychology, 54,* 339–342.

Rubin, A. M. (1993). The effect of locus of control on communication motivation, anxiety, and satisfaction. *Communication Quarterly, 41,* 161–171.

Rubin, A. M., & Rubin, R. B. (1989). Social and psychological antecedents of VCR use. In M. R. Levy (Ed.), *The VCR age: Home video and mass communication* (pp. 92–111). Newbury Park, CA: Sage.

Sprott, D. E., Brumbaugh, A. M., & Miyazaki, A. D. (2001). Predictors of play behavior in state- sponsored lotteries: An empirical assessment of psychological control. *Psychology & Marketing, 18,* 973–983.

Walkey, F. H. (1979). Internal control, powerful others, and chance: A confirmation of Levenson's factor structure. *Journal of Personality Assessment, 43,* 532–535.

Wheeless, L. R., Erickson, K. V., & Behrens, J. S. (1986). Cultural differences in disclosiveness as a function of locus of control. *Communication Monographs, 53,* 36–46.

Wheeless, L. R., Stewart, R. A., Kearney, P., & Plax. T. G. (1987). Locus of control and personal constructs in students' reactions to teacher compliance attempts: A reassessment. *Communication Education, 36,* 250–258.

Wober, M., & Gunter, B. (1982). Television and personal threat: Fact or artifact? A British survey. *British Journal of Social Psychology, 21,* 239–247.

Loneliness

Profile by Alan M. Rubin

Loneliness has been examined in the social sciences as an internal psychological state, suggesting a lack of desired relationships. It refers to "the unpleasant experience that occurs when a person's network of social relations is deficient in some important way" (Perlman & Peplau, 1981, p. 31). It is often accompanied by less self-esteem and more anxiety. Russell, Peplau, and Ferguson (1979) found lonely people to be unhappy, to feel less attractive, to feel depressed, and to be less satisfied with their relationships with others. In the communication literature, Zakahi and Duran (1985) found loneliness related negatively to communicative competence (i.e., social experience and social confirmation). Bell and Daly (1985) found loneliness related to difficulty in communicating and feeling anxious and apprehensive.

The original UCLA Loneliness Scale appeared in 1978 (Russell, 1978). The Revised UCLA Loneliness Scale (and its subsequent revisions, including version 3, see Russell, 1996) has been the most widely used measure of loneliness in the social science literature. Cramer and Barry (1999) discussed the substantial contribution of the measure to the study of social loneliness. The scale contains 20 items, 10 indicating satisfaction and 10 indicating dissatisfaction with social relationships (Russell, Peplau, & Cutrona, 1980). Participants are asked to express how they feel about each statement on a 4-point scale: (1) *never*, (2) *rarely*, (3) *sometimes*, or (4) *always* "feel the way described" in the statement. Higher scores indicate a greater degree of loneliness. Sample items include:

> How often do you feel you are "in tune" with the people around you? (reversed item)
> How often do you feel that you lack companionship?
> How often do you feel there is no one you can turn to?
> How often do you feel alone?
> How often do you feel part of a group of friends? (reversed item)
> How often do you feel you have a lot in common with the people around you? (reversed item)

How often do you feel that you are no longer close to anyone? (Russell, 1996, p. 23)

Russell et al. (1980) reported a .94 alpha reliability and construct validity evidence for the revised measure, including a correlation between loneliness and negative affect. Using data from earlier studies across several populations (e.g., nurses, teachers, students, the elderly), Russell (1996) reported extensive reliability and validity data for the UCLA Loneliness Scale, Version 3. He reported coefficient alphas ranged from .89 to .94, and 1-year test-retest reliability was $r = .73$. Significant correlations with other loneliness measures supported convergent validity. Links with assessments of interpersonal relationships and of health and well-being supported construct validity. Confirmatory factor analysis supported a global bipolar loneliness factor.

Zakahi and Duran (1982) reported a .92 Cronbach alpha for the 20-item UCLA Loneliness Scale. Chory-Assad and Yanen (2005) reported a .86 standardized α on 15 of the 20 Russell et al. (1980) items identified in a confirmatory factor analysis. Finding loneliness and socially anxious adolescents value the controllability of Internet communication, Peter and Valkenburg reported a .84 Cronbach α for a loneliness scale of the eight items with the highest item-total correlation from Russell et al. (1996). In addition, noting that some researchers have found two factors on the loneliness measure, based on positive and negative wording of items, Valkenburg and Jochen (2007) reported a Cronbach α of .84 for a scale composed of five of Russell's negative items. They found that the effects on well-being of both Internet communication and Internet communication with strangers were most adverse for lonely adolescents. Supporting construct validity, they found loneliness was negatively related to life satisfaction and to closeness with friends.

Supporting validity of the measure, Hojat (1983) found chronically lonely people scored high on the scale, and Spitzberg and Canary (1985) reported moderate correlations between responses to the UCLA Scale and measures of chronic loneliness. Perse and Rubin (1990) found the chronically lonely group scored significantly higher on the scale than the non-lonely group in their distribution. Rubin, Perse, and Powell (1985) used a 5-point agreement scale and reported a .88 Cronbach α for the measure. They also found loneliness related negatively to using interpersonal alternatives to loneliness (e.g., friends, family), but positively to reliance on television. Perse and Rubin (1990) found lonely viewers watched television news and soap operas to fill time when compared with nonlonely viewers.

Loneliness suggests the lack of or difficulty with achieving satisfactory interpersonal relationships. It relates to feelings of anxiety and apprehension, and a lack of life satisfaction and communication competence. The UCLA Revised Loneliness Scale has been the dominant measure used to assess loneliness throughout the social and behavioral sciences, including interpersonal and mass communication. The measure has consistently demonstrated a good degree of validity and reliability.

Locations

Russell, D., Peplau, L. A., & Ferguson, M. L. (1978). Developing a measure of loneliness. *Journal of Personality Assessment, 42*, 290–294.

Russell, D., Peplau, L. A., & Cutrona, C. E. (1980). The revised UCLA Loneliness Scale: Concurrent and discriminant validity evidence. *Journal of Personality and Social Psychology, 39*, 472–480.

Russell, D. W. (1996). UCLA Loneliness Scale (version 3): Reliability, validity, and factor structure. *Journal of Personality Assessment, 66*(1), 20–40.

References

Bell, R. A., & Daly, J. A. (1985). Some communicator correlates of loneliness. *Southern Speech Communication Journal, 50*, 121–142.

Chory-Assad, R. M., & Yanen, A. (2005). Hopelessness and loneliness as predictors of older adults' involvement with favorite television performers. *Journal of Broadcasting & Electronic Media, 49*, 182–201.

Cramer, K. M., & Barry, J. E. (1999). Conceptualizations and measures of loneliness: A comparison of subscales. *Personality and Individual Differences, 27*, 491–502.

Hojat, M. (1983). Comparison of transitory and chronic loners on selected personality variables. *British Journal of Psychology, 74*, 199–202.

Perlman, D., & Peplau, L. A. (1981). Towards a social psychology of loneliness. In S. Duck & R. Gilmour (Eds.), *Personal relationships in disorder* (pp. 31–56). London: Academic Press.

Perse, E. M., & Rubin, A. M. (1990). Chronic loneliness and television use. *Journal of Broadcasting & Electronic Media, 34*, 37–53.

Peter, J., & Valkenburg, P. M. (2006). Research note: Individual differences in perceptions of Internet communication. *European Journal of Communication, 21*, 213–226.

Rubin, A. M., Perse, E. M., & Powell, R. A. (1985). Loneliness, parasocial interaction, and local television news viewing. *Human Communication Research, 12*, 155–180.

Russell, D., Peplau, L. A., & Ferguson, M. L. (1979). Developing a measure of loneliness. *Journal of Personality Assessment, 42*, 290–294.

Spitzberg, B. H., & Canary, D. J. (1985). Loneliness and relationally competent communication. *Journal of Social and Personal Relationships, 2*, 387–402.

Valkenburg, P. M., & Jochen, P. (2007). Internet communication and its relation to well-being: Identifying some underlying mechanisms. *Media Psychology, 9*, 43–58.

Zakahi, W. R., & Duran, R. L. (1985). Loneliness, communicative competence, and communication apprehension: Extension and replication. *Communication Quarterly, 33*, 50–60.

Need for Cognition

Profile by Alan M. Rubin

The need for cognition (NFC) is an individual characteristic or personality trait expected to influence motivation, processing, and effects of messages, especially persuasive messages. The NFC is "an individual's tendency to engage in and enjoy effortful cognitive activity" (Cacioppo & Petty, 1982, p. 116). Based on the Elaboration Likelihood Model (ELM; Petty & Cacioppo, 1986), NFC is expected to influence motivation to process messages centrally, making changes in attitude and behavior more likely to occur (Harrington, Lane, Donohew, & Zimmerman, 2006). High NFC individuals enjoy challenging cognitive tasks, have increased motivation to engage in such tasks, and exhibit increased cognitive effort to process messages than low NFC individuals (see, e.g., Cacioppo & Petty, 1982; Cacioppo, Petty, Kao, & Rodriguez, 1986; Cacioppo, Petty, & Morris, 1983; Harrington et al., 2006; Thompson, Chaiken, & Hazelwood, 1993).

The NFC is a crucial motivational variable, which affects central route processing in the ELM's framework. As a dual-process model of processing persuasive messages (i.e., via central and peripheral routes), the ELM aims at explaining how individual, contextual, and message characteristics influence information processing. These characteristics affect the likelihood of message elaboration, which indicates whether people critically examine messages and "add something of their own to the specific information provided in the communication" (Petty & Wegener, 1999, p. 46). Messages processed based on the central route require greater cognitive effort and result in greater elaboration and attitude change than messages processed based on the peripheral route.

The original Need for Cognition Scale (Cacioppo & Petty, 1982, pp. 120–121) includes 34 items and the shortened NFC Scale (Cacioppo, Petty, & Kao, 1984, p. 307) contains 18 items. The Scale measures NFC as a continuous variable, "ranging from cognitive misers to cognizers in terms of level of intrinsic motivation to engage in effortful cognitive activities" (Liu & Eveland, 2005, p. 913). High scores on the NFC Scale suggest an appreciation for engaging in effortful thought, such as thinking abstractly, deliberating, and problem solving. Items from the scales include:

1   I would prefer complex to simple problems.
2   I like to have the responsibility of handling a situation that requires a lot of thinking.
3   Thinking is not my idea of fun. (R)
4   I would rather do something that requires little thought than something that is sure to challenge my thinking abilities. (R)
5   I try to anticipate and avoid situations where there is a likely chance I'll have to think in depth about something. (R)
6   I find satisfaction in deliberating hard and for long hours.
7   I only think as hard as I have to. (R)
8   I prefer to think about small daily projects to long-term ones. (R)
9   I like tasks that require little thought once I've learned them. (R)
10 The idea of relying on thought to get my way to the top appeals to me. (R)
11 I really enjoy a task that involves coming up with new solutions to problems.
12 Learning new ways to think doesn't excite me very much. (R)
13 I prefer life to be filled with puzzles that I must solve.
14 The notion of thinking abstractly is appealing to me.
15 I would prefer a task that is intellectual, difficult, and important to one that is somewhat important but does not require much thought.
16 I feel relief rather than satisfaction after completing a task that required a lot of mental effort. (R)
17 It's enough for me that something gets the job done; I don't care how or why it works. (R)
18 I usually end up deliberating about issues even when they do not affect me personally. (Cacioppo et al., 1984, p. 307)*

Note. (R) Reverse-coded item.

Perse (1992) measured NFC with a shortened 10-item version of the NFC Scale, using the 10 items, which did not discriminate among males and females, with the highest inter-item correlations from Cacioppo and Petty's (1982) NFC Scale. Typical of NFC measurement, she asked participants to indicate their agreement with each statement, ranging from (1) *strongly disagree* to (5) *strongly agree*, and reported a .82 Cronbach α. Unlike many other studies of NFC (e.g., Sicilia Ruiz, & Munuera, 2005; Thompson, 1995; Williams-Piehota, Schneider, Pizarro, Mowad, & Salovey, 2003), she used the resultant score as a continuous measure of NFC, rather than dichotomizing the measure into high and low NFC groups via a median split. Similarly, Hawkins et al. (2001) used a 5-item index of the highest loading items from Cacioppo and Petty's NFC Scale. They also asked participants to indicate their agreement with each item, ranging from (1) *strongly disagree* to (5) *strongly agree*, and reported a .79 α for their summative index. In addition, Tsfati and Cappella (2005) used a shortened 9-item version of the NFC Scale in their study of skepticism and news consumption. They asked participants to rate how well each statement described them, ranging from (1) *not at all like me* to (5) *a lot like me*, and reported a .76 reliability coefficient. They also used the resultant score as a continuous measurement of NFC.

Cacioppo et al. (1984) found a .95 Pearson *r* between participants' scores on the 18-item and 34-item NFC Scales. They performed a principal-component factor analysis and found a single dominant factor for the 34-item and the 18-item versions of the NFC Scale. They also reported theta coefficients (i.e., maximized Cronbach α coefficients) of .90 and .91 for the 18- and 34-item versions, respectively. They concluded little is sacrificed in terms of reliability by using the shorter NFC Scale, and the shorter version is more efficient than the longer version.

Several studies have supported the validity of the NFC construct and measurement. For example, researchers have found NFC predicts verbal ability and knowledge (Tidwell, Sadowski, & Pate, 2000), study skills and academic achievement (Guelgoez, 2001), and problem-solving performance (Nair & Ramnarayan, 2000). Cacioppo et al. (1984) found low NFC participants thought less about a persuasive message than did high NFC participants. In addition, Liu and Eveland (2005) gathered data on the 18-item NFC Scale (Cacioppo et al., 1984) from a sample of college students to help validate a 2-item NFC index in their study using data from the 2000 and 2004 American National Election Studies (ANES). They reported a Pearson *r* of .64 between the 18-item NFC Scale and the 2-item ANES measure, and found significant positive correlations between the 2-item NFC measure and education level, political campaign interest, and newspaper use. In addition, when studying an interactive website, Sicilia et al. (2005) used a median split of responses to the 18-item NFC Scale to segregate participants into high and low NFC groups. They found those exposed to the interactive website processed information more thoroughly than those exposed to a noninteractive website did. Similarly, Tuten and Bosnjak (2001) found NFC "significantly and positively correlated with all Web activities involving cognitive thought" (p. 391).

Also supporting construct validity, Perse (1992) found NFC had "a positive influence on watching local (television) news for utilitarian reasons, and a negative influence on watching for pass time reasons" (p. 48). Tsfati and Cappella (2005) also found NFC to affect news exposure, finding that "people consume news they do not trust when their media skepticism is irrelevant to their motivation for news exposure" (p. 251). They observed that NFC moderates the link between media skepticism and news consumption. To the contrary, though, Hawkins et al. (2001) failed to find support for their expectation of NFC predicting selective viewing of, attention to, and thinking about television genres.

As noted above, researchers have found support for the reliability of the NFC Scales. Martin, Sherrard, and Wentzel (2005) measured NFC with the 18-item Cacioppo, Petty, and Kao (1984) scale, and reported a .86 Cronbach α. They found high NFC participants evaluated websites containing high verbal and low visual complexity more favorably than did low NFC participants. Knobloch-Westerwick and Keplinger (2006) used a 16-item German version (Bless, Waenke, Bohner, Fellhauer, & Schwarz, 1994) of the NFC Scale (Cacioppo & Petty, 1982). They reported an α of .85 for the measure. They found that enjoyment of reading mysteries decreased with higher NFC levels. Thompson (1995) reported a .82 α for a 10-item NFC Scale in a study of thinking about free speech issues. In addition, in their field experiment examining the interaction of message type and NFC, Williams-Piehota, Pizarro, Silvera, Mowad, and Salovey (2006) selected three items with high factor loadings from the short-form of the NFC Scale (Cacioppo, Petty, & Kao, 1984), and reported a .77 Cronbach α. They found complex telephone and brochure messages were more effective than simple messages in motivating fruit and vegetable consumption 1 and 4 months later. Harrington et al. (2003) reported a .86 Cronbach alpha for the 18-item NFC Scale they used in their study of persuasive strategies for effective anti-drug messages.

Some researchers have raised issues about the NFC Scale. Although the NFC Scale is usually treated as a unidimensional measure, some have argued the construct and scale are multidimensional. For example, using maximum-likelihood factor analysis, Lord and Putrevu (2006) found four dimensions in the longer and shorter versions of the NFC Scale, which they labeled enjoyment of cognitive stimulation, preference for complexity, commitment of cognitive effort, and desire for understanding. In addition, as mentioned above, some have questioned the dichotomous application of the NFC Scale, when investigators recode continuous NFC scores and segregate participants into high and low NFC groups via a median split, reducing the level of measurement (cf., Tsfati & Cappella, 2005).

The Need for Cognition Scale has been widely used in the social and behavioral sciences, including communication, to examine the role of cognitive thought and thoughtful effort as a personality variable to explain attitudes and behaviors. In communication, researchers have employed the NFC construct and measure in the context of persuasive messages, health communication, advertising, political messages, and media content and genres. Investigators have used shorter versions of the NFC Scale to operationalize the construct in a more efficient, yet valid and reliable, manner than the original scale.

Location

Cacioppo, J. T., & Petty, R. E. (1982). The need for cognition. *Journal of Personality and Social Psychology, 42,* 116–181.

Cacioppo. J. T., Petty, K. E., & Kao, C. F. (1984). The efficient assessment of need for cognition. *Journal of Personality Assessment, 48,* 306–307. © 1984 Taylor & Francis.

References

Bless, H., Waenke, M., Bohner, G., Fellhauer, R. F., & Schwarz, N. (1994). Need for cognition: Eine Skala zur Erfassung von Engagement und Freude bei Denkaufgaben [Need for cognition: A scale measuring engagement and happiness in cognitive tasks]. *Zeitschrift für Sozialpsychologie, 25*(2), 147–154.

Cacioppo, J. T., Petty, R. E., Kao, C. F., & Rodriguez, R. (1986). Central and peripheral routes to persuasion: An individual difference perspective. *Journal of Personality and Social Psychology, 51,* 1032–1043.

Cacioppo, J. R., Petty, R. E., & Morris, K. J. (1983). Effects of need for cognition on message evaluation, recall, and persuasion. *Journal of Personality and Social Psychology, 45,* 805–818.

Guelgoez, S. (2001). Need for cognition and cognitive performance from a cross-cultural perspective: Examples of academic success and solving anagrams. *Journal of Psychology, 135,* 100–112.

Harrington, N. G., Lane, D. R., Donohew, L., & Zimmerman, R. S. (2006). An extension of the activation model of information exposure: The addition of a cognitive variable to a model of attention. *Media Psychology, 8,* 139–164.

Harrington, N. G., Lane, D. R., Donohew, L., Zimmerman, R. S., Norling, G. R., An, J., Cheah, W. H., McClure, L., Buckingham, T., Garofalo, E., & Bevins, C. C. (2003). Persuasive strategies for effective anti-drug messages. *Communication Monographs, 70,* 16–38.

Hawkins, R. P., Pingree, S., Hitchon, J., Gorham, B. W., Kannaovakun, P., Gilligan, E., Radler, B., Gudbjorg, H., Kolbeins, G. H., & Schmidt, T. (2001). Predicting selection and activity in television genre viewing. *Media Psychology, 3,* 237–263.

Knobloch-Westerwick, S., & Keplinger, C. (2006) Mystery appeal: Effects of uncertainty and resolution on the enjoyment of mystery. *Media Psychology, 8,* 193–212.

Liu, Y., & Eveland, W. P., Jr. (2005). Education, need for cognition, and campaign interest as moderators of news effects on political knowledge: An analysis of the knowledge gap. *Journalism & Mass Communication Quarterly, 82,* 910–929.

Lord, K. R., & Putrevu, S. (2006). Exploring the dimensionality of the Need for Cognition Scale. *Psychology & Marketing, 23*(1), 11–34.

Martin, B. A., Sherrard, M. J., & Wentzel, D. (2005). The role of sensation seeking and need for cognition on web-site evaluations: A resource matching perspective. *Psychology & Marketing, 22*(2), 109–126.

Nair, K., & Ramnarayan, S. (2000). Individual differences in need for cognition and complex problem solving. *Journal of Research in Personality, 34,* 305–328.

Perse, E. M. (1992). Predicting attention to local television news: Need for cognition and motives for viewing. *Communication Reports, 5*(1), 41–49.

Petty, R. E., & Cacioppo, J. T. (1986). *Communication and persuasion: Central and peripheral routes to attitude change.* New York: Springer-Verlag.

Petty, R. E., & Wegener, D. T. (1999). The Elaboration Likelihood Model: Current status and controversies. In S. Chaiken & Y. Trope (Eds.), *Dual process theories in social psychology* (pp. 41–72). New York: Guilford.

Sicilia, M., Ruiz, S., & Munuera, J. L. (2005). Effects of interactivity in a web site: The moderating effect of need for cognition. *Journal of Advertising, 54*(3), 31–43.

Thompson, E. P., Chaiken, S., & Hazelwood, J. D. (1993). Need for cognition and desire for control as moderators of extrinsic reward effects: A person x situation approach to the study of intrinsic motivation. *Journal of Personality and Social Psychology, 64,* 987–999.

Thompson, M. E. (1995). The impact of need for cognition on thinking about free speech issues. *Journalism & Mass Communication Quarterly, 72,* 934–947.

Tidwell, P. S., Sadowski, C. J., & Pate, L. M. (2000). Relationships between need for cognition, knowledge, and verbal ability. *Journal of Psychology, 134,* 634–644.

Tsfati, Y., & Cappella, J. N. (2005). Why do people watch news they do not trust? The need for cognition as a moderator in the association between news media skepticism and exposure. *Media Psychology, 7,* 251–271.

Tuten, T. L., & Bosnjak, M. (2001). Understanding differences in web usage: The role of need for cognition and the five factor model of personality. *Social Behavior & Personality, 29,* 391–398.

Williams-Piehota, P., Pizarro, J., Silvera, S. A. N., Mowad, L., & Salovey, P. (2006). Need for cognition and message complexity in motivating fruit and vegetable intake among callers to the cancer information service. *Health Communication, 19*(1), 75–84.

Williams-Piehota, P., Schneider, T. R., Pizarro, J., Mowad, L., & Salovey, P. (2003). Matching health messages to information-processing styles: Need for cognition and mammography utilization. *Health Communication, 15,* 375–392.

Personality Traits

Profile by Alan M. Rubin

Various factor models have evolved as frameworks to understand personality. Several psychological approaches have guided communication interests in examining personality traits as dispositions that can affect communication behavior. Psychologists have proposed three-factor (see H. J. Eysenck & Eysenck, 1985; S. B. Eysenck, Eysenck, & Barrett, 1985) and five-factor (see Costa & McCrae, 1992; Goldberg, 1992) models.

The measures for the five-factor or big five model (Costa & McCrae, 1992; McCrae & John, 1992) and the three-factor model (S. B. Eysenck et al., 1985) have been used regularly in social and behavioral research, including communication research. The measure for Goldberg's (1992) five-factor model contains 100 adjectives, 20 items for each of five factors, to which participants respond on a 9-point scale (*extremely accurate* to *extremely inaccurate*) as to how these "common human traits describe yourself as accurately as possible." The responses factored into five dimensions: extraversion (surgency), agreeableness, conscientiousness (dependability), emotional stability (neuroticism), and intellect (culture, intellect, or openness).

> Extraversion refers to sociability or an orientation toward interacting with others, agreeableness refers to pleasantness and friendliness, conscientiousness refers to being trustworthy and well-organized, emotional stability refers to a calm, even-tempered person with a general absence of nervousness, and intellect refers to sophistication or openness to new experiences. (MacIntyre & Thivierge, 1995, p. 126)

Goldberg (1992) suggested that 35 bipolar scales could provide a briefer inventory of the five-factor model, but found them less robust than the 100 adjectives. Saucier (1994) selected the most robust of Goldberg's adjectives and created a mini-marker scale with 40 adjectives. Those loading highest on the five factors comprise Saucier's mini-marker version:

Extraversion: talkative, extroverted, bold, energetic; and shy, quiet, bashful, withdrawn (the latter three are reverse coded)

Agreeableness: sympathetic, warm, kind, cooperative; and cold, unsympathetic, rude, harsh (the latter four are reverse coded)

Conscientiousness: organized, efficient, systematic, practical; and disorganized, sloppy, inefficient, careless (the latter four are reverse coded)

Emotional Stability: unenvious, relaxed; and moody, jealous, tempermental, envious, touchy, fretful (the latter six are reverse coded)

Intellect (Openness): creative, imaginative, philosophical, intellectual, complex, deep; and uncreative, unintellectual (the latter two are reverse coded). (Saucier, 1994, p. 512)

MacIntyre and Thivierge (1995) used seven of Goldberg's (1992) items on a 9-point semantic differential scale, contrasting: extraversion and introversion, agreeableness and disagreeableness, conscientiousness and negligence, emotional stability and neuroticism, and intellect and unsophisticated.

The five-factor model includes the following dimensions of personality: extraversion, neuroticism, openness to experience, agreeableness, and conscientiousness (Costa & McCrae, 1992; McCrae & John, 1992). McCrae and John provide a discussion of the conceptualization and evolution of the five-factor models. The short form NEO Personality Inventory Revised (NEO-PI-R) is a 60-item measure using 5-point Likert scales within the five dimensions (Costa & McRae, 1992; McCrae & John, 1992). The more recent revised NEO uses five items for each of 30 facets included in the five dimensions (Piedmont, 1998). Krcmar and Kean (2005) used Costa and McCrae's short form to examine antecedents to media use. Booth-Butterfield and Booth-Butterfield (2002) used Costa and McRae's NEO-FFI, Form S, with 12 5-point items for each of the five personality dimensions, with higher scores suggesting greater presence of the trait. Sample items included:

I rarely feel lonely or blue. (neuroticism)
I like to have a lot of other people around me. (extraversion)
I have a lot of intellectual curiosity. (openness)
I would rather cooperate with others than compete with them. (agreeableness)
I have a clear set of goals and work toward them in an orderly fashion. (conscientiousness). (Booth-Butterfield & Booth-Butterfield, 2002, p. 306)

Earlier, Weaver (1991) considered links between media preferences and personality, as assessed in the Eysenck Personality Questionnaire. The short form of the Eysenck Personality Questionnaire (EPQ) assesses the PEN model of temperament (S. B. Eysenck et al., 1985), which suggests personality is comprised of the three dimensions: psychoticism, extraversion, neuroticism. The measure contains 12 items to assess each of the three dimensions. Participants answer *yes* or *no* to each of 12 items across each of the three dimensions.

Other communication studies also employed these personality scales. For example, in group deliberation research (Sager & Gastil, 2002), personality factors led to more confirming interaction. MacIntyre and Thivierge (1995), using parts of Goldberg's (1992) measure, focused on how personality affects public speaking. Cole and McCroskey (2000) found extraversion, in both the Eysenck Personality Inventory and the McCrae and John (1992) Five-Factor Model was linked to perceptions of responsiveness and assertiveness in sociocommunicative orientation. Booth-Butterfield and Booth-Butterfield (2002) found that only two factors of the five-factor model—extraversion and neuroticism—related to affective orientation to process emotional information.

Other studies demonstrate the diversity of applications when examining how personality traits might affect communication. For example, Krcmar and Kean (2005) examined how personality leads to liking and viewing violent media. Tidwell and Sias (2005) looked at the effect of personality dimensions on information seeking in organizational communication. Eaton and Tinsley (1999) considered how maternal personality factors affect health communication. In addition, Shim and Paul (2007) studied attention to television program genre from a uses and gratifications perspective, which expects personality to filter message response. Using the short form of the Eysenck Personality Questionnaire, they found psychoticism related negatively to attention to news and reality programs. Extraversion related positively to attention to reality programs, and neuroticism related positively to attention to the five television genres studied: news, reality, soap operas, talk, and crime drama.

Overall, the personality measures have demonstrated mostly good reliability, and factor analysis (including confirmatory factor analysis) has supported their dimensions. For example, when considering temperament and sociocommunicative orientation, Cole and McCroskey (2000) reported .69, .78, .77 Cronbach alphas, respectively, for the psychoticism, extraversion, and neuroticism dimensions of the EPQ (H. J. Eysenck, & Eysenck, 1985; S. B. Eysenck et al., 1985). Shim and Paul (2007) reported alphas of .49, .82, and .77 for the psychoticism, extraversion, and neuroticism dimensions of the EPQ, respectively.

Saucier (1994) reported Cronbach alphas comparable to those of Goldberg (1992) for "self" measurement: extraversion (.83), agreeableness

(.81), conscientiousness (.83), emotional stability (.78), and intellect (.78), although Saucier's 40 bipolar mini-markers were slightly less robust than Goldberg's 100 unipolar adjectives. Goldberg had reported alphas of .82 to .97 for the 20-item Big-Five factors. Goldberg (1993) noted the consistency in reported structure and replication across cultures and samples for the five-factor model. Test-retest reliability over 3 years, 6 years, and 7 years has ranged from .51 to .83 (Costa & McCrae, 1992). Costa and McCrae also reported reliabilities of .71 for the five-factor scales. Booth-Butterfield and Booth-Butterfield (2002) reported internal reliabilities ranging from .58 to .76 for the five dimensions. Eaton and Tinsley (1999) reported internal consistency coefficients for the five NEO-PI-R factors, ranging from .68 to .87. Shim and Paul (2007) reported α coefficients ranging from .69 to .85 for the measures of the five-factor model (McCrae & John, 1992). In addition, the NEO-PI-R has been extensively validated (Eaton & Tinsley, 1999).

Focused on "affective traits," an additional measure (in both state and trait forms) cuts across personality, hostility, depression, anxiety, and sensation-seeking dimensions (Zuckerman & Lubin, 1965, 1985). The Revised Multiple Affect Adjective Check List (MAACL-R) contains 132 adjectives for participants to check to describe how they feel *today* (for the state form) or how they *generally* feel (for the trait form). The adjectives cluster into five subscales: anxiety (A), depression (D), hostility (H), positive affect (PA), and sensation seeking (SS). The adjectives for each subscale include:

> A scale: nervous, tense, afraid, worrying, panicky.
> D scale: lost, tormented, sad, forlorn, rejected.
> H scale: disagreeable, disgusted, cross, irritated, cruel.
> PA scale: pleased, good, happy, joyful, warm.
> SS scale: enthusiastic, energetic, adventurous, merry, active, daring, and (reverse scored) mild, quiet, tame. (Lubin et al., 1988, p. 133)

The subscales also cluster into two higher order affects: dysphoria (summated A, D, and H responses) and well-being (summated PA and SS responses). In a national probability looking at links between the MAACL-R and self-ratings of health, Lubin et al. (1988) found positive affect related directly to health self-ratings, and dysphoric affect related negatively to health self-ratings. They reported α reliability coefficients of .79, .81, .84, .74, and .09 for the A, D, H, PA, and SS subscales, respectively. The reliability of the SS measure was highly suspect, especially on the trait measure. The measure has had considerably less application in communication research than the three- and five-factor personality measures. Zuckerman and Lubin (1985) indicate support for discriminant and convergent validity of the scales.

Existing in several formats and lengths, measures of personality have proven to be important antecedent, mediating, moderating variables in the social and behavioral sciences, including communication research. These measures of personality, including the three and five-dimensional scales, have evolved over the years and have been applied in many contexts of communication research, including organization and group, health, public, and media studies.

Locations

Costa, P. T., & McCrae, R. R. (1992). *The NEO Personality Inventory—Revised manual.* Odessa, FL: Psychological Assessment Resources.

Eysenck, S. B., & Eysenck, H. J., & Barrett, P. (1985). A revised version of the psychoticism scale. *Personality and Individual Differences, 6,* 21–29.

Goldberg, L. R. (1992). The development of markers for the big-five factor structure. *Psychological Assessment, 4,* 26–42.

Saucier, G. (1994). Mini-markers: A brief version of Goldberg's unipolar big-five markers. *Journal of Personality Assessment, 63,* 506–516.

Zuckerman, M., & Lubin, B. (1965). *Manual for the Multiple Affect Adjective Check List.* San Diego: Educational & Industrial Testing Service.

Zuckerman, M., & Lubin, B. (1985). *Manual for the Revised Multiple Affect Adjective Check List.* San Diego: Educational & Industrial Testing Service.

References

Booth-Butterfield, M., & Booth-Butterfield, S. (2002). The role of affective orientation in the five factor personality structure. *Communication Research Reports, 19,* 301–313.

Cole, J. G., & McCroskey, J. C. (2000). Temperament and socio-communicative orientation. *Communication Research Reports, 17,* 105–114.

Eaton, L. G., & Tinsley, B. J. (1999). Maternal personality and health communication in the pediatric context. *Health Communication, 11*(1), 75–96.

Eysenck, H. J., & Eysenck, M. W. (1985). *Personality and individual differences.* New York: Plenum.

Goldberg, L. R. (1993). The structure of phenotypic personality traits. *American Psychologist, 48,* 26–34.

Krcmar, M., & Kean, L. G. (2005). Uses and gratifications of media violence: Personality correlates of viewing and liking violent genres. *Media Psychology, 7,* 399–420.

Lubin, B., Zuckerman, M., Breytspraak, L. M., Bull, N. C., Oumbhir, A. K., & Rinck, C. M. (1988). Affects, demographic variables, and health. *Journal of Clinical Psychology, 44*(2), 131–141.

McCrae, R. R., & John, O. P. (1992). An introduction to the five-factor model and its applications. *Journal of Personality, 60,* 175–215.

McIntyre, P. D., & Thivierge, K. A. (1995). The effects of speaker personality on anticipated reactions to public speaking. *Communication Research Reports, 12,* 125–133.

Piedmont, R. L. (1998). *The revised NEO personality inventory*. New York: Plenum Press.

Sager, K. L., & Gastil, J. (2002). Exploring the psychological foundations of democratic group deliberation: Personality factors, confirming interaction, and democratic decision making. *Communication Research Reports, 19,* 56–65.

Shim, J. W., & Paul, B. (2007). Effects of personality types on the use of television genres. *Journal of Broadcasting & Electronic Media, 51,* 287–304.

Tidwell, M., & Sias, P. (2005). Personality and information seeking. *Journal of Business Communication, 42*(1), 51–77.

Weaver, J. B. (1991). Exploring the links between personality and media references. *Personality and Individual Differences, 12,* 1293–1299.

Self-Esteem

Profile by Alan M. Rubin

How one feels about himself or herself has been an important factor in explaining human behavior. Self-esteem represents an affective evaluation of one's worth. It suggests how a person values his or her own importance and place in the surrounding environment. Self-esteem is presumed to possess trait properties of self-evaluation, transcending individual situations. Rosenberg, Schooler, Schoenbach, and Rosenberg (1995), though, have differentiated between global self-esteem and specific self-esteem, the latter being more situational and fleeting (e.g., academic self-esteem). They noted that global self-esteem would be more relevant to psychological well-being than specific self-esteem. Self-esteem has typically been employed as an antecedent, mediating, or moderating factor in research studies.

Negative or diminished self-esteem can affect behavior, information strategies, and attitudes. Miller and Jablin (1991) argued those "low in self-esteem are less likely to search for information and engage in risk-taking behavior than persons with high self-esteem" (p. 100). Teboul (1995) found self-esteem related negatively to covert information-seeking, suggesting those low in self-esteem were more likely to rely on indirect observation and surveillance in organizations than overt information strategies in organizations. Pfau, Van Bockern, and Kang (1992) found that inoculation efforts fostered resistance to smoking initiation only among adolescents of low self-esteem. Among eighth-grade students, Daly, Kreiser, and Roghaar (1994) found a positive relationship between self-esteem and question-asking comfort.

The literature contains many studies that include the self-esteem construct. For example, addictive behavior has been linked to low self-esteem, as low self-esteem tends to reflect negative evaluation of one's self (Barrera, Chassin, & Rogosch, 1993). Rangarajan and Kelly (2006), however, observed no significant relationship between alcoholism of parents and their adult children's level of self-esteem. Mesch (2006) did observe that self-esteem was negatively linked to family cohesiveness, and Kalbfleisch and Davies (1993) found self-esteem plays an indirect role in mentoring relationships via perceived risk in intimacy. In addition, students with low to moderate self-esteem rated their instructors higher in verbal aggressiveness than those with high self-esteem (Schrodt, 2003). Similarly, Rancer, Kosberg, and Silvestri (1992) reported significant negative relationships between self-esteem and verbal aggressiveness. Vangelisti, Maguire, Alexander, and Clark (2007) also found that verbal hostility and self-esteem affected people's views of their family environment being aggressive. In the intercultural context, Cai, Giles, and Noels (1998) examined elderly Chinese people's perceptions of intergenerational communication in China and found communication with older adults was a better predictor of self-esteem than was communication with younger adults.

There are a host of studies of self-esteem in the media context. For example, Kubic and Chory (2007) found self-esteem related negatively to the frequency of viewing television makeover programs. When examining links between television viewing motivation and social isolation and social support, Finn and Gorr (1988) found that self-esteem correlated positively with the mood-management viewing motive and negatively with the social-compensation viewing motive. Besides television, researchers have also looked at self-esteem and reading preferences. In an experiment, Knobloch-Westerwick, Bruck, and Hastall (2006) found self-esteem and gender role orientation influenced the preferences of German readers of an online news magazine. Knobloch-Westerwick and Keplinger (2006) found high self-esteem readers disliked a resolution of a mystery short story that was consistent with their expectations, whereas low self-esteem readers disliked an unexpected resolution.

Rosenberg's (1989) Self-Esteem Scale has been the most widely used measure of self-esteem in communication and social sciences. Rosenberg defined self-esteem as a favorable or unfavorable attitude toward oneself. His unidimensional scale contains 10 Likert-type items, asking participants to report responses to statements about themselves on a 4-point scale: *strongly agree, agree, disagree*, or *strongly disagree*. The items include:

1. I feel that I am a person of worth, at least on an equal basis with others.
2. I feel that I have a number of good qualities.
3. All in all, I am inclined to feel that I am a failure. (reversed item)
4. I am able to do things as well as most other people.
5. I feel I do not have much to be proud of. (reversed item)
6. I take a positive attitude toward myself.
7. On the whole, I am satisfied with myself.
8. I wish I could have more respect for myself. (reversed item)
9. I certainly feel useless at times. (reversed item)

10 At times I think I am no good at all. (reversed item). (Rosenberg, 1989)

Rosenberg's (1989) Self-Esteem Scale has consistently shown to be a valid and reliable measure. Because the construct deals with an evaluation of one's self, social desirability is a potential problem in measurement, so are positively skewed scores, making it difficult to get a true low self-esteem group for comparison. Demo (1985), however, compared responses to Rosenberg's (1989) and Coopersmith's (1967) self-esteem measures with peer and trained observer assessments and found convergence between the self-report and other-report measures, supporting validity of the measures. Bachman and O'Malley (1984) observed that self-esteem scores have a degree of stability over time.

Internal reliability has been very consistent. For example, when finding no significant relationship between parental alcoholism and self-esteem, Menees (1997) reported a .85 coefficient α for the Self-Esteem Scale. Rubin, West, and Mitchell (2001) reported a .85 Cronbach α in their study of aggression and popular music preferences. Others have reported α coefficients ranging from .79 to .88 (Daly et al., 1994; Kalbfleisch & Davies, 1993; Knobloch-Westerwick et al., 2006; Knobloch-Westerwick & Keplinger, 2006; Rangarajan & Kelly, 2006; Schrodt, 2003; Schrodt, Ledbetter, & Ohrt, 2007; Teboul, 1995).

Researchers have also reported favorable reliability data for abbreviated versions of Rosenberg's (1989) measure. For example, Cai et al. reported a .89 Cronbach α using four items. Mesch (2006) reported a .79 Cronbach α for five items. Aubrey (2007) reported a .84 Cronbach α for nine of Rosenberg's items.

As it relates to one's outlook across a variety of situations, self-esteem has been an often studied construct in social and behavioral research, including studies in various communication contexts such as intergenerational and intercultural communication, interpersonal and family communication, mass media, and instructional communication. For over 40 years, Rosenberg's (1989) Self-Esteem Scale has proven to be a simple, widely used, valid, and reliable measure of the construct.

Location

Rosenberg, M. (1989). *Society and adolescent self-image.* (Rev. ed.) Middletown, CT: Wesleyan University Press. http://www.bsos.umd.edu/socy/Research/rosenberg.htm

References

Aubrey, J. S. (2007). The impact of sexually objectifying media exposure on negative body emotions and sexual self-perceptions: Investigating the mediating role of body self-consciousness. *Mass Communication & Society, 10*(1), 1–23.

Bachman, J. G., & O'Malley, P. M. (1984). Yea-saying, nay-saying, and going to extremes: Black-white differences in response styles. *Public Opinion Quarterly, 48,* 491–509.

Barrera, M., Chassin, L., & Rogosch, F. (1993). Effects of social support and conflict on adolescent children of alcoholic and nonalcoholic fathers. *Journal of Personality and Social Psychology, 64,* 602–612.

Cai, D., Giles, H., & Noels, K. (1998). Elderly perceptions of communication with older and younger adults in China: Implications for mental health. *Journal of Applied Communication Research, 26,* 32–51.

Coopersmith, S. (1967) *The antecedents of self-esteem.* San Francisco: W. H. Freeman.

Daly, J. A., Kreiser, P. O., & Roghaar, L. A. (1994). Question-asking comfort: Explorations of the demography of communication in the eighth grade classroom. *Communication Education, 43,* 27–41.

Demo, D. H. (1985). The measurement of self-esteem: Refining our methods. *Journal of Personality and Social Psychology, 48,* 1490–1502.

Finn, S., & Gorr, M. (1988). Social isolation and social support as correlates of television viewing motivations. *Communication Research, 15,* 135–158.

Kalbfleisch, P. J., & Davies, A. B. (1993). An interpersonal model for participation in mentoring relationships. *Western Journal of Communication, 57,* 399–415.

Knobloch-Westerwick, S., Bruck, J., & Hastall, M. R. (2006). The gender news use divide: Impacts of sex, gender, self-esteem, achievement, and affiliation motive on German newsreaders' exposure to news topics. *Communications, 31,* 329–345.

Knobloch-Westerwick, S., & Keplinger, C. (2006). Mystery appeal: Effects of uncertainty and resolution on the enjoyment of mystery. *Media Psychology, 8,* 193–212.

Kubic, K., & Chory, R. (2007). Exposure to television makeover programs and perceptions of self. *Communication Research Reports, 24,* 283–291.

Menees, M. M. (1997). The role of coping, social support, and family communication in explaining the self-esteem of adult children of alcoholics. *Communication Reports, 10,* 9–19.

Mesch, G. S. (2006). Family relations and the Internet: Exploring a family boundaries approach. *Journal of Family Communication, 6*(2), 119–138.

Miller, V. D., & Jablin, F. M. (1991). Information seeking during organizational entry: Influences, tactics, and a model of the process. *Academy of Management Review, 16,* 92–120.

Pfau, M., Van Bockern, S., & Kang, J. G. (1992). Use of inoculation to promote resistance to smoking initiation among adolescents. *Communication Monographs, 59,* 213–230.

Rancer, A. S., Kosberg, R. L., & Silvestri, V. N. (1992). The relationship between self-esteem and aggressive communication predispositions. *Communication Research Reports, 9,* 23–32.

Rangarajan, S., & Kelly, L. (2006). Family communication patterns, family environment, and the impact of parental alcoholism on offspring self-esteem. *Journal of Social & Personal Relationships, 23,* 655–671.

Rosenberg, M., Schooler, C., Schoenbach, C., & Rosenberg, F. (1995). Global self-esteem and specific self-esteem: Different concepts, different outcomes. *American Sociological Review*, 141–156.

Rubin, A. M., West, D., & Mitchell, W. (2001). Differences in aggression, attitudes toward women, and distrust as reflected in popular music preferences. *Media Psychology, 3*, 25–42.

Schrodt, P. (2003). Student perceptions of instructor verbal aggressiveness: The influence of student verbal aggressiveness and self-esteem. *Communication Research Reports, 20*, 240–250.

Schrodt, P., Ledbetter, A. M., & Ohrt, J. K. (2007). Parental confirmation and affection as mediators of family communication patterns and children's mental well-being. *Journal of Family Communication, 7*(1), 23–46.

Teboul, J. (1995). Determinants of new hire information-seeking during organization encounter. *Western Journal of Communication, 59*, 305–325.

Vangelisti, A., Maguire, K., Alexander, A., & Clark, G. (2007). Hurtful family environments: Links with individual, relationship, and perceptual variables. *Communication Monographs, 74*, 357–385.

Sensation Seeking

Profile by Alan M. Rubin

Sensation seeking is a biologically based personality trait "defined by the need for varied, novel and complex sensations and experiences, and the willingness to take physical and social risks (Zuckerman, 1979, p. 10). It is conceptually rooted in theories of arousal (Finn, 1992). People approach or avoid experiences felt to have high arousal potential (Zuckerman, 1979). Sensation seeking is characterized by wanting novelty and risk taking. It correlates with participating in risky behaviors. Sensation seekers aim to fulfill their needs for sensation, and seek arousing behaviors and activities to reach optimal levels of arousal. In distinguishing between high and low sensation seekers, Zuckerman (1988) observed, "The high sensation seeker is receptive to novel stimuli; the low tends to reject them, preferring the more familiar and less complex" (pp. 181–182).

Sensation seeking has been linked to communication and media behavior. For example, high sensation seekers watch less television than do low sensation seekers (Finn, 1992; Lorch et al., 1994). When they do watch television, they prefer anti-social humor and action-adventure and sexual violent programming (Aluja-Fabregat, 2000; Perse, 1996; Schierman & Rowland, 1985; Slater, 2003). Donohew, Palmgreen, and Duncan (1980) found under-stimulated people sought stimulation from news stories, but over-stimulated people sought less arousing information. Zillmann and Bryant (1984) found that bored participants preferred to watch exciting programs and to avoid watching relaxing programs. Perse found that high sensation seekers watch television more ritualistically while engaging in concurrent activities; they also change channels more often than low sensation seekers. Zuckerman (1996) noted that research has shown a strong association between the disinhibition dimension of sensation seeking and interest in and exposure to fright and violence.

Donohew, Lorch, and Palmgreen (1991) also used sensation seeking to design televised public service announcements (PSAs) for preventing drug abuse. They found high stimulus PSAs were more effective for high sensation seekers, and low stimulus messages were more effective for low sensation seekers. Sensation seeking also has been positively related to rock music preferences, and negatively related to slow music preferences (Litle & Zuckerman, 1986). In intercultural communication, when examining social initiative in intercultural interactions, Morgan and Arasaratnam (2003) found higher sensation seekers more likely to indicate they would pursue intercultural friendships. Arasaratnam (2004) found sensation seeking to be positively correlated with social initiative and with motivation to communicate with culturally different others.

Besides biological measures of sensation seeking (e.g., Lang, Chung, Lee, Schwartz, & Shin, 2005), the Sensation-Seeking Scale evolved from an early version containing a single scale to Form V, a 40-item scale developed by Zuckerman (1979) and Zuckerman, Eysenck, and Eysenck (1978). Besides the combined SSS-V, that measure includes 10 items within four dimensions:

a   *Thrill and Adventure Seeking (TAS)*, or engaging in socially acceptable physical and risky activities, which entail speed and danger and provide unusual and novel experiences (e.g., desire to parachute, mountain climb, ride motorcycles).

b   *Experiences (ES)*, or seeking novel experiences through the mind and senses of nonconformity (e.g., art, music, travel, drugs, unconventional friends).

c   *Disinhibition (Dis)*, or engaging in experiences for excitement and variety through social stimulation (e.g., parties, drinking, sexual variety).

d   *Boredom Susceptibility (BS)*, or lacking the tolerance for unexciting people and repetitious experiences and work.

Zuckerman et al. (1978) reported positive correlations between the SSS-V and the psychoticism and extraversion scales of the Eysenck Personality Questionnaire (Eysenck & Eysenck, 1975), supporting the construct validity of the SSS-V as a trait measure of sensation seeking being an "uninhibited, nonconforming, impulsive, dominant type of extraversion" (Eysenck & Zuckerman, 1978, p. 485).

The scales present a forced choice between possible high and low sensation-seeking behaviors (contrasted in "a" and "b" pairs below). For example:

a   I like "wild" uninhibited parties.
b   I prefer quiet parties with good conversation. (Dis)
a   I get bored seeing the same old faces.
b   I like the comfortable familiarity of everyday friends. (BS)
a   A sensible person avoids activities that are dangerous.
b   I sometimes like to do things that are a little frightening. (TAS)
a   I find that stimulants make me feel uncomfortable.
b   I often like to get high (drinking liquor or smoking marijuana). (Dis)

a   I would like to try parachute jumping.
b   I would never want to try jumping out of a plane with or without a parachute. (TAS)
a   I prefer friends who are excitingly unpredictable.
b   I prefer friends who are reliable and predictable. (BS)
a   There is altogether too much portrayal of sex in the movies.
b   I enjoy watching many of the "sexy" scenes in movies. (ES)
a   People should dress according to some standards of taste, neatness, and style.
b   People should dress in individual ways even if the effects are sometimes strange. (ES). (Zuckerman, 1979, pp. 107–109; Zuckerman, Eysenck, & Eysenck, 1978, pp. 144–145)

Participants are asked to choose between two possible behaviors, with scores computed by summing a point for each appropriate sensation-seeking choice within each category (0 to 10 range of scores) or across all four categories (0 to 40 range; see, e.g., Finn, 1992). The scales have also been used in a Likert-type format, where respondents state their agreement about participating in the sensation-seeking activities on a 5- or 7-point scale (*strongly agree* to *strongly agree*) for 10 items in each dimension. Typically, those scoring above the median of the summated scale are classified as high sensation seekers, and those scoring below the median are classified as low sensation seekers (see, e.g., Perse, 1996).

The SSS-V has been a widely used measure over recent decades, with demonstrated validity and reliability (Zuckerman, 1994). For example, D' Silva & Palmgreen (2007) used the 40-item SSS-V, and reported a .82 Cronbach α. To avoid part-whole correlation concerns, they had removed three drug use items. They found high sensation seekers recalled more anti-drug PSAs than did low sensation seekers. Perse (1996) averaged responses to the 40-item SSS-V and reported a .94 Cronbach α. She used a median split to classify respondents as high or low sensation seekers. Finn (1992), though, summed and averaged sensation-seeking behaviors, using a continuous measure, and reported a .80 Cronbach α. Haridakis (2002) reported a .91 Cronbach α for the disinhibition dimension. Conway and Rubin (1991) reported .91 and .92 Cronbach alphas for the thrill and disinhibition dimensions, respectively, when finding disinhibition predicted pass-time and escape television viewing motives. They also supported expectations that the over-stimulated would seek less arousing information. Also supporting the construct validity of the measure, disinhibition has predicted delinquent behavior (see Krcmar & Greene, 1999) and has positively correlated with sociopathy and social nonconformity of prison inmates (Zuckerman, 1979).

Others have sought to use or to develop alternative or briefer sensation-seeking measures. For example, Hunsaker, Kelly, and Duran (1999) used a 7-point Likert scale and randomly selected 20 high and 20 low sensation-seeking items from the SSS-V. They reported a .77 Cronbach α, and failed to find significant linear links between sensation seeking and communication apprehension. Kwak, Fox, and Zinkhan (2002) also used a 7-point Likert scale and randomly selected 13 of the 40 items from the SSS-V to gauge consumers' risk taking for products on the Internet. They reported a .89 Cronbach α.

Hoyle et al. (2002) developed a Brief Sensation-Seeking Scale (BSSS) measure to correspond to the original scale based on a subset of 8 of the 40 SSS-V, items, and reported a .76 internal consistency coefficient. Hoyle et al. asked participants to respond on a 5-point *strongly agree* to *strongly disagree* scale to the items.

> I would like to explore strange places.
> I like to do frightening things.
> I like new and exciting experiences, even if I have to break the rules.
> I prefer friends who are exciting and unpredictable. (Hoyle et al., 2002, p. 405)

Arasaratnam (2004) and Morgan and Arasaratnam (2003) reported a coefficient α of .81 for the 8-item BSSS.

Stephenson, Hoyle, Palmgreen, and Slater (2003) argued there was a need to develop shorter valid and reliable sensation-seeking measures. They tested a 2-item SS-2 measure on risk-taking elements and a 4-item BSSS-4 measure, which retained the conceptual framework of the 40-item SSS-V. They tested the measures against longer measures including a 19-item impulsive sensation-seeking scale (Zuckerman, Kuhlman, Joireman, Teta, & Kraft, 1993) and the 8-item BSSS (Hoyle et al., 2002).

The 4-item BSSS-4 measure ($\alpha = .66$) retained four of eight BSSS items (one from each original SSS-V dimension; see the items above). Participants responded on 5-point scales (*strongly agree* to *strongly disagree*) to those BSSS-4 items. Participants responded on 5-point scales (*not at all* to *often*) to the 2-item SS-2 measure ($\alpha = .81$): "How often do you do dangerous things for fun?" "How often do you do exciting things, even if they are dangerous?" (Stephenson et al., 2003, p. 282).

Stephenson et al. (2003) found the brief measures were internally consistent across age and gender groups, correlated well with risk and protective factors such as smoking and alcohol use, and performed similarly to longer measures. They argued the 2-item and 4-item measures "are psychometrically sound and, when necessary, can be substituted for their longer counterparts without significant loss of predictive power" (p. 285). Because it retains the four content dimensions of the SSS-V, the BSSS-4 may be preferred over the SS-2.

Given its application in multiple communication research studies, especially those related to media behavior, including film, television, and music, researchers have sought to refine the measures of sensation seeking over the years. Researchers have also sought to apply sensation-seeking measures in health and comparative intercultural contexts. Investigators have sought to achieve briefer measures that capture the essence of Zuckerman's (1994) longer scale, with acceptable validity and reliability. To some degree, they have achieved this, although it is important to ensure the very brief versions capture the scope of intended meanings of the original measure.

Locations

Hoyle, R. H., Stephenson, M. T., Palmgreen, P., Lorch, E. P., & Donohew, L. R. (2002). Reliability and validity of a brief measure of sensation seeking. *Personality and Individual Differences, 32,* 401–414.

Stephenson, M. T., Hoyle, R. H., Palmgreen, P., & Slater, M. D. (2003). Brief measures of sensation seeking for screening and large-scale surveys. *Drug and Alcohol Dependence, 72,* 279–286.

Zuckerman, M. (1979). *Sensation-seeking: Beyond the optimal level of arousal.* Hillsdale, NJ: Erlbaum.

Zuckerman, M. (1994). *Behavioral expressions and biosocial bases of sensation seeking.* New York: Cambridge University Press.

Zuckerman, M., Eysenck, S. B., & Eysenck, H. J. (1978). Sensation seeking in England and America: Cross-cultural, age, and sex comparisons. *Journal of Consulting and Clinical Psychology, 46*(1), 139–149.

References

Aluja-Fabregat, A. (2000). Personality and curiosity about TV and film violence in adolescents. *Personality and Individual Differences, 29,* 379–392.

Arasaratnam, L. A. (2004). Sensation seeking as a predictor of social initiative in intercultural interactions. *Journal of Intercultural Communication Research, 33*(4), 215–222.

Bryant, J., & Zillmann, D. (1984). Using television to alleviate boredom and stress: Selective exposure as a function of induced excitational states. *Journal of Broadcasting, 28,* 1–20.

Conway, J. C., & Rubin, A. M. (1991). Psychological predictors of television viewing motivation. *Communication Research, 18,* 443–463.

Donohew, L., Lorch, E., & Palmgreen, P. (1991). Sensation seeking and targeting televised anti-drug PSAs. In L. Donohew, H. E. Sypher, & W. Bullenski (Eds.), *Persuasive communication and drug abuse prevention* (pp. 209–226). Hillsdale, NJ: Erlbaum.

Donohew, L., Palmgreen, P., & Duncan, J. (1980). An activation model of information exposure. *Communication Monographs, 47,* 295–303.

D' Silva, M. U., & Palmgreen, P. (2007). Individual differences and context: Factors mediating recall of anti-drug public service announcements. *Health Communication, 21*(1), 65–71.

Eysenck, H. J., & Eysenck, S. B. (1975). *Manual of the Eysenck Personality Questionnaire (junior and adult)*. London: Hodder & Stoughton.

Eysenck, S., & Zuckerman, M. (1978). The relationship between sensation-seeking and Eysenck's dimensions of personality. *British Journal of Psychology, 69,* 483–487.

Finn, S. (1992). Television "addiction?" An evaluation of four competing media-use models. *Journalism Quarterly, 69,* 422–435.

Haridakis, P. M. (2002). Viewer characteristics, exposure to television violence, and aggression. *Media Psychology, 4,* 325–353.

Hunsaker, F. G., Kelly, L., & Duran, R. L. (1999). Sensation seeking and communication apprehension: Biological and genetic correlates of approaching or avoiding communication events. *Communication Research Reports, 16*(2), 121–130.

Krcmar, M., & Greene, K. (1999). Predicting exposure to and uses of television violence. *Journal of Communication, 49*(3), 24–45.

Kwak, H., Fox, R. J., & Zinkhan, G. M. (2002). What products can be successfully promoted and sold via the Internet? *Journal of Advertising Research, 42*(1), 23–38.

Lang, A., Chung, Y., Lee, S., Schwartz, N., & Shin, M. (2005). It's an arousing, fast-paced kind of world: The effects of age and sensation seeking on the information processing of substance-abuse PSAs. *Media Psychology, 7,* 421–454.

Litle, K., & Zuckerman, M. (1986). Sensation seeking and music preferences. *Personality and Individual Differences, 4,* 575–578.

Lorch, E. P., Palmgreen, P., Donohew, L., Helm, D., Baer, S., & D'Silva, M. U. (1994). Program context, sensation seeking, and attention to televised anti-drug public service announcements. *Human Communication Research, 20,* 390–412.

Morgan, S. E., & Arasaratnam, L. A. (2003). Intercultural friendship as a social excitation: Sensation seeking as a predictor of intercultural friendship seeking behavior. *Journal of Intercultural Research, 31,* 175–186.

Perse, E. M. (1996). Sensation seeking and the use of television for arousal. *Communication Reports, 9,* 37–49.

Schierman, M. J., & Rowland, G. L. (1985). Sensation seeking and selection of entertainment. *Personality and Individual Differences, 5,* 599–603.

Slater, M. D. (2003). Alienation, aggression, and sensation-seeking as predictors of adolescent use of violent film, computer and website content. *Journal of Communication, 53,* 105–121.

Zuckerman, M. (1988). Behavior and biology: Research on sensation seeking and reactions to the media. In L. Donohew, H. E. Sypher, & E. T. Higgins (Eds.), *Communication, social cognition and affect* (pp. 173–194). Hillsdale, NJ: Erlbaum.

Zuckerman, M. (1996). Sensation seeking and the taste for vicarious horror. In J. B. Weaver & R. Tamborini (Eds.), *Horror films: Current research on audience preferences and reactions* (pp. 147–160). Mahwah, NJ: Erlbaum.

Zuckerman, M., Kuhlman, D. M., Joireman, J., Teta, P., & Kraft, M. (1993). A comparison of three structural models for personality: The big three, the big five, and the alternative five. *Journal of Personality and Social Psychology, 65,* 757–768.

Shyness and Sociability

Profile by Alan M. Rubin

Shyness is a sense of apprehension or lack of confidence felt about social interaction with others. Shy individuals are apprehensive about and tend to avoid uncomfortable or unfamiliar situations. Shyness suggests avoidance tendencies, whereas sociability suggests approach tendencies. Cheek and Buss (1981) defined shyness as "one's reaction to being with strangers or casual acquaintances: tension, concern, feelings of awkwardness and discomfort, and both gaze aversion and inhibition of normally expected social behavior" (p. 330); they defined sociability as "a tendency to affiliate with others and to prefer being with others to remaining alone" (p. 330). Zimbardo (1977) observed that shyness is a problem evidenced by low self-esteem, anxiety, inadequate social skills, and self-consciousness. According to Kelly, Duran, and Stewart (1990), "the shy person may experience fear, self-consciousness, and worry, and may behave awkwardly in social situations" (p. 209).

Shyness has been the object of research in communication and social sciences. Duran and Kelly (1989), for example, found shy participants in their study of communication adaptability reported having more articulation problems, being less relaxed socially, and having fewer social experiences than non-shy participants (p. 30). In a different context, Stritzke, Nguyen, and Durkin (2004) addressed the effect of computer mediated communication on shyness. They used the Revised Cheek and Buss Shyness Scale (RCBSS; Cheek, 1983) to compare shy and non-shy Internet users in online and offline contexts. They found that, offline, shy and non-shy participants differed on rejection sensitivity, initiating relationships, and self-disclosure, but they did not differ in the online context. In addition, Hammermeister, Brock, Winterstein, & Page (2005) found that those who watched more television scored higher on the Shyness Scale than those in the moderate and low television viewing groups.

Based on a factor analysis, Cheek and Buss (1981) concluded that shyness and sociability are distinct personality traits. They noted that shyness was not just unsociability, and found shy-sociable participants talked less, averted their gaze more, and engaged in more self-manipulation than did the other participants. They argued it was important to recognize this distinction between the traits. Other researchers have supported the distinction between shyness and sociability (e.g., Schmidt & Fox, 1995).

Cheek and Buss (1981) developed a 9-item Shyness Scale focusing on experiences or behaviors during social interaction:

1   I am socially somewhat awkward.
2   I don't find it hard to talk to strangers. (reverse item)
3   I feel tense when I'm with people I don't know well.
4   When conversing I worry about saying something dumb.
5   I feel nervous when speaking to someone in authority.
6   I am often uncomfortable at parties and other social functions.
7   I feel inhibited in social situations.
8   I have trouble looking someone right in the eye.
9   I am more shy with members of the opposite sex. (Cheek & Buss, 1981, p. 332)*

They adapted past measures to create a 5-item Sociability Scale focusing on people's desire to be with others:

1   I like to be with people.
2   I welcome the opportunity to mix socially with people.
3   I prefer working with others rather than alone.
4   I find people more stimulating then anything else.
5   I'd be unhappy if I were prevented from making many social contacts. (Cheek & Buss, 1981, p. 332)*

Participants responded to the items of the Shyness and Sociability Scales on a 5-point scale as being *extremely uncharacteristic* (coded, 0) or *extremely characteristic* (coded, 4). Responses to the 7-item Shyness Scale correlated .88 with a measure they created based on Rosenberg's Self-Esteem Scale (1965), suggesting similarity between shyness and global self-esteem. The α reliability coefficients for the 9-item Shyness Scale and the 5-item Sociability Scale were .79 and .70, respectively. Cheek and Buss (1981) reported a 90-day test retest correlation of .74 for the Shyness Scale, and correlations of .67 to .81 with other shyness measures, supporting concurrent validity. The correlation between the Shyness and Sociability Scales was –.30, suggesting the measures are tapping different traits. In a follow-up assessment, Cheek and Buss concluded, "shyness and sociability independently affected how subjects behaved in a social situation" (p. 336).

Supporting the validity and reliability of the Cheek and Buss (1981) Shyness Scale, Hopko, Stowell, Jones, Armento, and Cheek (2005) reported strong support for expected relationships with measures of shyness and social anxiety, stability of normative data over time, and reliability. Bell, Tremblay, and Buerkel-Rothfuss (1987) supported the convergent and discriminant validity of the Cheek and Buss (1981) Shyness Scale by finding significant positive correlations between shyness and communication apprehension and loneliness, and significant negative correlations between shyness and social assertiveness, interaction involvement, self-monitoring, affinity-seeking competence, and strategic performance. Schroeder (1995) found positive correlations between shyness and measures of test anxiety. In a study of television cultivation and psychosocial health, Hammermeister et al. reported a .85 coefficient α, and Bell et al. reported a .76 α for the Shyness Scale. Duran and Kelly (1989) eliminated the three reverse items from the Shyness and Sociability Scales and reported a .84 Cronbach α for the remaining 11-item unidimensional measure.

Shyness and sociability have been studied as distinct personality traits. Shyness suggests a lack of confidence and sense of apprehension in social interaction. Sociability suggests a desire to be with others. Both constructs affect how people interact and communicate in a variety of situations, including interpersonal, media, and newer communication technology contexts. Researchers have used the Shyness Scale more often than the Sociability Scale. It has achieved a good degree of support for measurement validity and reliability.

Location

Cheek, J. M. (1983). The revised Cheek and Buss Shyness Scale. Unpublished manuscript, Wellesley College, Wellesley, MA.

*Cheek, J. M., & Buss, A. H. (1981). Shyness and sociability. *Journal of Personality and Social Psychology, 41,* 330–339. Copyright © by the American Psychological Association. Adapted with permission.

References

Bell, R. A., Tremblay, S. W., & Buerkel-Rothfuss, N. L. (1987). Interpersonal attraction as a communication accomplishment: Development of a measure of affinity-seeking competence. *Western Journal of Speech Communication, 51,* 1–18.

Cheek, J. M., & Briggs, S. R. (1990). Shyness as a personality trait. In W. R. Crozier (Ed.), *Shyness and embarrassment* (pp. 315–337). Cambridge: Cambridge University Press.

Duran, R. L., & Kelly, L. (1989). The cycle of shyness: A study of self-perceptions of communication performance. *Communication Reports, 2,* 30–38.

Hammermeister, J., Brock, B., Winterstein, D., & Page, R. (2005). Life without TV? Cultivation theory and psychosocial health characteristics of television-free individuals and their television-viewing counterparts. *Health Communication, 17,* 253–264.

Hopko, D. R., Stowell, J., Jones, W. H., Armento, M. E., & Cheek, J. M. (2005). Psychometric properties of the Revised Cheek and Buss Shyness Scale. *Journal of Personality Assessment, 84,* 185–192.

Kelly, L., Duran, R. L., & Stewart, J. (1990). Rhetoritherapy revisited: A test of its effectiveness as a treatment for communication problems. *Communication Education, 39,* 207–226.

Rosenberg, M. (1965). *Society and adolescent self-image.* Princeton, NJ: Princeton University Press.

Schmidt, L. A., & Fox, N. A. (1995). Individual differences in young adults' shyness and sociability: Personality and health correlates. *Personality and Individual Differences, 19,* 455–462.

Schroeder, J. E. (1995). Self-concept, social anxiety, and interpersonal perception skills. *Personality and Individual Differences, 19,* 955–958.

Stritzke, W. G., Nguyen, A., & Durkin, K. (2004). Shyness and computer-mediated communication: A self-presentational theory perspective. *Media Psychology, 6,* 1–22.

Zimbardo, P. G. (1977). *Shyness: What it is, what to do about it.* Reading, MA: Addison-Wesley.

Social Desirability

Profile by Alan M. Rubin

Social desirability is the most often studied response bias in social and behavioral science questionnaires, suggesting that, when participants complete questionnaires, they provide answers that make them "look good" (Paulhus, 1991, p. 17). Social desirability (SD) bias is the tendency of research participants "to respond to test items in such a way as to present themselves in socially acceptable terms in order to gain the approval of others" (King & Bruner, 2000, p. 81). Because of SD bias, participants often over-report socially desirably behaviors and under-report socially undesirable behaviors (Raghubir & Menon, 1996). Besides self-reported behaviors, SD also affects measurement of attitudes and personality traits. Social desirability distorts measurement in susceptible people (Crowne & Marlowe, 1960; Edwards, 1953; Furnham, 1986; Linehan & Nielsen, 1981; Nevid, 1983). It can "attenuate, inflate, or moderate variable relationships" (Fisher & Katz, 2000, p. 105).

In actuality, there have been two schools of thought about the effect of social desirability in measuring instruments. First, some argue SD is a response set, which confounds the results of measuring instruments (e.g., Linehan & Nielsen, 1981). As a form of measurement bias stemming from the nature of the question, measurement, or motivation to respond, SD would be treated as an intervening variable, as one's response would not reflect an actual attitude or behavioral tendency (Furnham, 1986; Nicotera, 1996). Second, others argue SD is a personality trait, which motivates and predisposes people to respond and act in socially desirable ways (e.g., Nevid, 1983). As such, SD would be "one's tendency to perform socially and culturally acceptable and approved behaviors" (Chen, 1994, p. 434).

Researchers often have neglected to examine the impact of SD bias in their research. For example, in reviewing 20 years of marketing research, King and Bruner (2000) noted a growth in multi-item measurement and attention to scale reliability, but limited attention to measurement validity and especially to SD bias "in scale construction, evaluation, and implementation" (p. 79).

Including response bias produced by both actual test items and participants' test behavior, Edwards (1953, 1957) conceptualized SD as measurement bias, and developed an early measure of social desirability. Edwards asked participants to rate items on a 5-point Likert-type scale (1 = *generally unacceptable by others in society*, 5 = *generally acceptable by others in society*). Nicotera (1996) used this method in her analysis of Infante and Rancer's (1982) Argumentativeness Scale, concluding gender differences were partly due to SD bias. Vanlear used Edmonds' (1967) 15-item social desirability measure and found SD inflated correlations between reported marital satisfaction and Fitzpatrick's (1977) types of couples. Wheeless and Berryman-Fink (1985) used the 33-item, true-false Marlowe-Crowne Social Desirability Scale (M-C SDS; Crowne & Marlowe, 1960), noting researchers have suggested social desirability might be a contaminant when studying employees in organizations. They found SD did not significantly correlate with measures of gender and equal-employment issues in organizations.

Researchers use SD scales to help establish discriminant validity of a study's primary instruments, as a low correlation between the SD scale and the other measures suggests SD bias does not confound the other measures. If investigators find significant relationships, correlation and regression analyses can determine the percentage of variance attributable to the SD measure. For example, because variables in their study of relational communication and sexual encounters were associated with SD, Theiss and Solomon (2007) included SD as a covariate and analyzed it as a moderator in regression analyses. Horvath (2004) controlled for the influence of SD, and reported a significant positive partial correlation between television addiction and level of television exposure. Donavan, Brown, and Mowen (2004) tested SD's moderation effects in their structural equation model aimed at explaining how customer orientation affects job satisfaction, organizational commitment, and organizational citizen behaviors. Agne, Thompson, and Cusella (2000) found SD to be the weakest contributor to a discriminant function in their analysis of face influences on disclosing HIV status to health providers. And, Pawlowski and Hollwitz (2000) used regression analysis to explain the percentage of variance explained by "outguessing" the interviewer in a structured pre-employment interview, beyond that explained by SD.

Originally designed to be a measure of self-report SD (i.e., the Personal Reaction Inventory), the Marlowe-Crowne Social Desirability Scale (M-C SDS) is the measure of social desirability bias that has achieved the widest acceptance (Crowne & Marlowe, 1960). Crowne and Marlowe (1964) suggested the measure actually taps a more general motive or need for approval. The M-C SDS is a 33-item true-false summated rating scale. Research participants are presented with 33 statements about their personal attitudes and traits, and asked to decide whether each statement is true or false. Potential scores range from 0 (very low SD) to 33 (very high SD). Sample M-C SDS items, which also comprise Strahan and Gerbasi's 10-item M-C Form X1, include:

1 I'm always willing to admit it when I make a mistake.
2 I always try to practice what I preach.
3 I never resent being asked to return a favor.
4 I have never been irked when people expressed ideas very different from my own.
5 I have never deliberately said something that hurt someone's feelings.
6 I like to gossip at times. (R)
7 There have been occasions when I took advantage of someone. (R)
8 I sometimes try to get even rather than forgive and forget. (R)
9 At times I have really insisted on having things my own way. (R)
10 There have been occasions when I felt like smashing things. (R)
    (R) reverse-coded item (Crowne & Marlowe, 1960; Strahan & Gerbasi, 1972, p. 192) Copyright © Wiley Periodicals, Inc., A Wiley Company.

Supporting construct and convergent validity of the M-C SDS, Crowne and Marlowe (1964) found SD positively linked to seeking social reinforcement, conforming to norms, being sensitive to social influence, being cautious about revealing oneself, and trying not to endanger one's self-esteem. The evaluation of others influences one's performance on tasks. Lynn and Harris (1997) reported no correlation between the M-C SDS and a scale they developed reflecting a desire for unique consumer products. Pawlowski and Hollwitz (2000) found that those scoring highest on the M-C SDS scored highest on structured pre-employment interviews, that is, the interview reflected SD motivation.

Researchers also have supported the reliability of the M-C SDS. For example, Crowne and Marlowe (1960) reported .88 reliability for the measure. Strahan and Gerbasi (1972) reported KR-20 reliability coefficients for the M-C SDS ranging from .73 to .87 for four sample groups, higher than for 10- and 20-item shortened versions of the measure. Reynolds (1982) reported KR-20 coefficients of .82 and .76 for the M-C SDS and for the Reynolds' 13-item M-C Form C, respectively; Reynolds' 13-item M-C Form C correlated .93 with the M-C SDS and .85 with Strahan and Gerbasi's 10-item M-C Form X1. Wheeless and Wheeless (1982) reported .71 reliability, and Wheeless and Berryman-Fink (1985) reported .72 split-half reliability for the scale. Lynn and Harris (1997) and Pawlowski and Hollwitz (2000) reported .95 and .89 Cronbach alphas, respectively, for the M-C SDS.

Given the length of the M-C SDS, some have used or proposed shorter versions (see, e.g., Ballard, 1992). Fisher and Katz (2000) studied how SD reflects the importance of human values in a culture. They used Reynolds'

(1982) 13-item M-C Form C. Sample items included "no matter who I'm talking to, I'm always a good listener" and "I sometimes feel resentful when I don't get my way" (Fisher & Katz, 2000, p. 111). Horvath (2004) also used Reynolds' 13-item M-C Form C measure, but eliminated one item to increase its Cronbach α from .59 to .74. She found SD correlated negatively and significantly with television addiction. When studying disclosure of HIV status to health providers, Agne et al. (2000) used four items with the highest item-total correlation from the M-C SDS (Cronbach α = .74) for their measure: "there have been times when I felt like rebelling against people in authority even though I knew they were right," "there have been occasions when I took advantage of someone," "I sometimes try to get even, rather than forgive and forget," and "I am always courteous, even to people who are disagreeable" (p. 246).

In addition, Donavan et al. (2004) sought to explain the effect of customer orientation on organizational satisfaction, commitment, and behavior. They used a 6-item SD measure based on Strahan and Gerbasi's (1972) shorter version of the M-C SDS. Sample items included "there have been occasions when I took advantage of someone," "I sometimes try to get even rather than forgive and forget," and "at times I have really insisted on having things my own way" (Donavan et al., 2004, p. 144). In their study of communication and relational consequences of sexual encounters, Theiss and Solomon (2007) also used Strahan and Gerbasi's Form X1, which is a subset of 10 summated true-false M-C SDS items. Sample items included "I have never deliberately said something that hurt someone's feelings," "I like to gossip at times," and "I'm always willing to admit it when I make a mistake" (Theiss & Solomon, 2007, p. 189). Fischer and Fick (1993) did a confirmatory factory analysis of several short versions of the M-C SDS, and their results supported Strahan and Gerbasi's Form X1, which had high internal reliability and correlated substantially with the original M-C SDS.

Besides the length of the instrument, some have questioned whether the M-C SDS contains multiple dimensions (e.g., Ballard, Crino, & Rubenfeld, 1988; Paulhus, 1984). Zerbe and Paulhaus (1987), for example, reported self-deception and impression-management dimensions. Others have noted cultural differences in SD response bias across Eastern and Western research participants, raising some concerns about the generalizability of the M-C SDC across different cultures (e.g., Middleton & Jones, 2000). When examining power distances and facework strategies in six Eastern and Western countries, however, Merkin (2006) found no significant M-C SDS differences among participants from the different cultures.

Social desirability is an important construct affecting measurement and the interpretation of relationships between variables in social and behavioral research, including communication. SD influences responses to questionnaire items and performance on research tasks. As Crowne and Marlowe (1964) argued, SD is more than a self-report behavior; it reflects a more generalized motive or need for approval. SD has influenced face-saving in organizational, cultural, health, and other settings. Researchers also have been concerned about the length of the M-C SDS, and the potential dimensionality and cultural biases in the theoretical construct and resulting measure. The shortened versions by Strahan and Gerbasi (1972) and Reynolds (1982), in particular, have had utilitarian appeal. It is somewhat surprising, given the potential contamination by SD of research findings, how infrequently an SD measure has been included in communication research studies.

Location

Crowne, D. P., & Marlowe, D. (1960). A new scale of social desirability independent of psychopathology. *Journal of Consulting Psychology, 24,* 349–354.

Reynolds, W. M. (1982). Development of reliable and valid short forms of the Marlowe-Crowne Social Desirability Scale. *Journal of Clinical Psychology, 38,* 119–125.

Strahan, R., & Gerbasi, K. C. (1972). Short, homogeneous versions of the Marlowe-Crowne Social Desirability Scale. *Journal of Clinical Psychology, 28,* 191–193.

References

Agne, R. R., Thompson, T. L., & Cusella, L. P. (2000). Stigma in the line of face: Self-disclosure of patients' HIV status to health care providers. *Journal of Applied Communication Research, 28,* 235–261.

Ballard, R. (1992). Short forms of the Marlowe-Crowne Social Desirability Scale. *Psychological Reports, 71,* 1155–1160.

Ballard, R., Crino, M. D., & Rubenfeld, S. (1988). Social desirability response bias and the Marlowe-Crowne Social Desirability Scale. *Psychological Reports, 63,* 227–237.

Chen, G. (1994). Social desirability as a predictor of argumentativeness and communication apprehension. *Journal of Psychology, 128,* 433–438.

Crowne, D. P., & Marlowe, D. (1964). *The approval motive.* New York: Wiley.

Donavan, D. T., Brown, T. J., & Mowen, J. C. (2004). Internal benefits of service-worker customer orientation: Job satisfaction, commitment, and organizational citizenship behaviors. *Journal of Marketing, 68,* 128–146.

Edmonds, V. H. (1967). Marital conventionalization: Definition and measurement. *Journal of Marriage and the Family, 29,* 681–688.

Edwards, A. L. (1953). The relationship between the judged desirability of a trait and the probability that the trait will be endorsed, *Journal of Applied Psychology, 2,* 90–93.

Edwards, A. L. (1957). *The social desirability variable in personality assessment and research.* New York: Dryden Press.

Fischer, D. G., & Fick, C. (1993). Measuring social desirability: Short forms of the Marlowe-Crowne Social Desirability Scale. *Educational and Psychological Measurement, 53,* 417–424.

Fisher, R. J., & Katz, J. E. (2000). Social-desirability bias and the validity of self-reported values. *Psychology & Marketing, 17*(2), 105–120.

Fitzpatrick, M. A. (1977). A typological approach to communication in relationships. *Communication Yearbook, 1,* 263–274.

Furnham, A. (1986). Response bias, social desirability and dissimulation. *Personality and Individual Difference, 7,* 385–400.

Horvath, C. W. (2004). Measuring television addiction. *Journal of Broadcasting & Electronic Media, 48,* 378–398.

Infante, D. A., & Rancer, A. S. (1982). A conceptualization and measure of argumentativeness. *Journal of Personality Assessment, 46,* 72–80.

King, M. F., & Bruner, G. C. (2000). Social desirability bias: A neglected aspect of validity testing. *Psychology & Marketing, 17*(2), 79–103.

Linehan, M., & Nielsen, S. (1981). Assessment of suicide ideation and parasuicide: Hopelessness and social desirability. *Journal of Consulting and Clinical Psychology, 49,* 773–775.

Lynn, M., & Harris, J. (1997). The desire for unique consumer products: A new individual differences scale. *Psychology & Marketing Vol. 14,* 601–616.

Merkin, R. S. (2006). Power distance and facework strategies. *Journal of Intercultural Communication Research, 35*(2) 139–160.

Middleton, K. L., & Jones, J. L. (2000). Socially desirable response sets: The impact of country culture. *Psychology & Marketing, 17*(2), 149–163.

Nevid, J. (1983). Hopelessness, social desirability and construct validity. *Journal of Consulting and Clinical Psychology, 51,* 139–140.

Nicotera, A. M. (1996). An assessment of the Argumentativeness Scale for social desirability bias. *Communication Reports, 9*(1), 23–35.

Paulhus, D. L. (1984). Two-component models of socially desirability responding. *Journal of Personality and Social Psychology, 46,* 598–609.

Paulhus, D. L. (1991). Measurement and control of response bias. In J. P. Robinson, P. R. Shaver, & L. S. Wrightsman (Eds.), *Measures of personality and social psychological attitudes* (pp. 17–59). San Diego: Academic Press.

Pawlowski, D. R., & Hollwitz, J. (2000). Work values, cognitive strategies, and applicant reactions in a structured pre-employment interview for ethical integrity. *Journal of Business Communication, 37*(1), 58–76.

Raghubir, P., & Menon, G. (1996). Asking sensitive questions: The effects of type of referent and frequency wording in counterbiasing methods. *Psychology & Marketing, 13,* 633–652.

Theiss, J. A., & Solomon, D. H. (2007). Communication and the emotional, cognitive, and relational consequences of first sexual encounters between partners. *Communication Quarterly, 55*(2), 179–206.

Vanlear, C. A. (1990). Communication and marital satisfaction: Social desirability and nonlinearity. *Communication Research Reports, 7*(1), 38–44.

Wheeless, L. R., & Wheeless, V. E. (1982). Attribution, gender orientation, and adaptability: Reconceptualization, measurement, and research results. *Communication Quarterly, 30,* 56–66.

Wheeless, V. E., & Berryman-Fink, C. (1985). Perceptions of women managers and their communicator competencies. *Communication Quarterly, 33,* 137–148.

Zerbe, W. J., & Paulhus, D. L. (1987). Socially desirable responding in organizational behavior: A reconception. *Academy of Management Review, 12,* 250–264.

Scale Author Index

Subject Index

Statistical Methods for Communication Science
Andrew Hayes, Ohio State University

Statistical Methods for Communication Science is the only statistical methods volume currently available that focuses exclusively on statistics in communication research. Writing in a straightforward, personal style, author Andrew F. Hayes offers this accessible and thorough introduction to statistical methods, starting with the fundamentals of measurement and moving on to discuss such key topics as sampling procedures, probability, reliability, hypothesis testing, simple correlation and regression, and analyses of variance and covariance. Hayes takes readers through each topic with clear explanations and illustrations. He provides a multitude of examples, all set in the context of communication research, thus engaging readers directly and helping them to see the relevance and importance of statistics to the field of communication.

Highlights of this text include:

- thorough and balanced coverage of topics;
- integration of classical methods with modern "resampling" approaches to inference;
- consideration of practical, "real world" issues;
- numerous examples and applications, all drawn from communication research;
- up-to-date information, with examples justifying use of various techniques; and
- a CD with macros, data sets, figures, and additional materials.

This unique book can be used as a stand-alone classroom text, a supplement to traditional research methods texts, or a useful reference manual. It will be invaluable to students, faculty, researchers, and practitioners in communication, and it will serve to advance the understanding and use of statistical methods throughout the discipline.

ISBN 13 hbk 978–0–8058–5487–9

For ordering and further information please visit:
www.routledge.com

Visual Communication Research Designs
Keith Kenney

Visual Communication Research Designs offers detailed guidance for using a variety of research methods to investigate visual communications. This book embeds each method—interview, draw-and-write, diary, Photovoice, case study, visual ethnography, focus group, discourse analysis, and content analysis—within a research design. Chapters begin with a brief, engaging story, such as:

- Why people really include visuals on Facebook.
- Why Picasso could draw but barely pass elementary school.
- How camera phones can be used for intimate communication.

They then address key research components for each method, such as theoretical perspective, units of analysis, sampling, data analysis, data display, quality control, advantages/disadvantages, ethical issues, and the resources needed to complete the research.

Author Keith Kenney provides both a consistent voice as well as a variety of perspectives from eleven contributors, each describing his/her work on a particular research project. With this book, Kenney moves visual communication away from a medium-centered approach (such as television or film) to a communication-centered approach (including intrapersonal, interpersonal, group, organization, public and mass communication).

Providing explicit, practical guidance in an accessible, understandable format, this book will facilitate more and better research about visual communication.

Keith Kenney (Ph.D. Michigan State University) is an associate professor in the School of Journalism and Mass Communications at the University of South Carolina. He is the founding editor of *Visual Communication Quarterly*, and he served as an editor of the *Handbook of Visual Communication*.

ISBN 13 hbk 978–0–415–98869–8
ISBN 13 pbk 978–0–415–98870–4

For ordering and further information please visit:
www.routledge.com